T0235180

Lecture Notes in Computer Science 10338

More information about this series at http://www.springer.com/series/7407

José Manuel Ferrández Vicente
José Ramón Álvarez-Sánchez
Félix de la Paz López · Javier Toledo Moreo
Hojjat Adeli (Eds.)

Biomedical Applications Based on Natural and Artificial Computing

International Work-Conference on the Interplay Between Natural and Artificial Computation, IWINAC 2017
Corunna, Spain, June 19–23, 2017
Proceedings, Part II

Editors
José Manuel Ferrández Vicente
Departamento de Electrónica, Tecnología de Computadoras y Proyectos
Universidad Politécnica de Cartagena
Cartagena
Spain

José Ramón Álvarez-Sánchez
Departamento de Inteligencia Artificial
Universidad Nacional de Educación a Distancia
Madrid
Spain

Félix de la Paz López
Departamento de Inteligencia Artificial
Universidad Nacional de Educación a Distancia
Madrid
Spain

Javier Toledo Moreo
Departamento de Electrónica, Tecnología de Computadoras y Proyectos
Universidad Politécnica de Cartagena
Cartagena
Spain

Hojjat Adeli
The Ohio State University
Columbus, OH
USA

ISSN 0302-9743 ISSN 1611-3349 (electronic)
Lecture Notes in Computer Science
ISBN 978-3-319-59772-0 ISBN 978-3-319-59773-7 (eBook)
DOI 10.1007/978-3-319-59773-7

Library of Congress Control Number: 2017942995

LNCS Sublibrary: SL1 – Theoretical Computer Science and General Issues

Printed on acid-free paper

This Springer imprint is published by Springer Nature
The registered company is Springer International Publishing AG
The registered company address is: Gewerbestrasse 11, 6330 Cham, Switzerland

Preface

The hybridization between social sciences and social behaviors with robotics, neurobiology and computing, ethics and neuroprosthetics, cognitive sciences and neurocomputing, neurophysiology and marketing will give rise to new concepts and tools that can be applied to information and communication technology (ICT) systems, as well as to natural science fields. Through IWINAC we provide a forum in which research in different fields can converge to create new computational paradigms that are on the frontier between neural sciences and information technologies.

As a multidisciplinary forum, IWINAC is open to any established institutions and research laboratories actively working in the field of this interplay. But beyond achieving cooperation between different research realms, we wish to actively encourage cooperation with the private sector, particularly small and medium-sized enterprises (SMEs), as a way of bridging the gap between frontier science and societal impact, and young researchers in order to promote this scientific field.

In this edition, there were four main themes highlighting the conference topics: affective computing, signal processing and machine learning applied to biomedical and neuroscience applications, deep learning and big data, and biomedical applications.

Traditionally, when ICT research has been performed in relation to the human brain, the focus has been on the cognitive brain. Primary research in computer science, engineering, psychology, and neuroscience has been aimed at developing devices that recognize human affects and emotions. In computer science, affective computing is a branch of the study and development of artificial intelligence that deals with the design of systems and devices that can recognize, interpret, and process human emotions. It is an interdisciplinary field spanning computer sciences, psychology, and cognitive science.

Emotion recognition refers to the problem of inferring the significance of human expressions of different emotions. This inference is natural for human observers but is a non-trivial problem for machines. The data gathered on the cues humans use to perceive emotions in others may be used in machine-learning techniques. Emotional speech processing recognizes the user's emotional state by analyzing speech patterns. EEG analysis may also detect human emotions by studying the positive and negative peaks located in specific areas around 450 ms after stimulus induction. Another area within affective computing is the design of computational devices proposed to exhibit either innate emotional capabilities or that are capable of convincingly simulating emotions. Robots may be used for embodying personality traits that induce desired emotions in humans and behave in an appropriate manner when recognizing human emotional state. Neuroprosthetics may be used for treating emotional disorders by electrical stimulation of certain specific areas in the thalamus or other neural centers.

The increasing spread of in vivo imaging technologies, such as magnetic resonance imaging (MRI), diffusion tensor imaging (DTI), functional MRI (fMRI), single photon emission computed tomography (SPECT), positron emission tomography (PET) and other non-invasive techniques such as electroencephalography (EEG) or magnetoencephalography (MEG), have meant a breakthrough in the diagnosis of several pathologies, such as Alzheimer's disease, Parkinson's disease, etc. Today, signal processing and machine learning methods are crucial as supporting tools for a better understanding of diseases. In this way, signal processing and machine learning applied to biomedical and neuroscience applications became an emergent and disruptive field of research.

Deep learning has presented a breakthrough in the artificial intelligence community. The best performances attained so far in many fields, such as computer vision or natural language processing, have been overtaken by these novel paradigms to a point that only ten years ago was pure science fiction. In addition, this technology has been open sourced by the main artificial intelligence (AI) companies, thereby and hence making it quite straightforward to design, train, and integrate deep-learning based systems. Moreover, the amount of data available every day is not only enormous, but, growing at an exponential rate over the past few years, there has been an increasing interest in using machine-learning methods to analyze and visualize massive data generated from very different sources and with many different features: social networks, surveillance systems, smart cities, medical diagnosis, business, cyberphysical systems, or media digital data. This special session is designed to serve researchers and developers to publish original, innovative, and state-of-the art machine-learning algorithms and architectures to analyze and visualize large amounts of data.

Finally, biomedical applications are essential in IWINAC meetings. For instance, brain–computer interfaces (BCI) implement a new paradigm in communication networks, namely, brain area networks. In this paradigm, our brain inputs data (external stimuli), performs multiple media-access control by means of cognitive tasks (selective attention), processes the information (perception), makes a decision (cognition) and, eventually, transmits data back to the source (by means of a BCI), thus closing the communication loop. Image understanding is a research area involving both feature extraction and object identification within images from a scene, and a posterior treatment of this information in order to establish relationships between these objects with a specific goal. In biomedical and industrial scenarios, the main purpose of this discipline is, given a visual problem, to manage all aspects of prior knowledge, from study start-up and initiation through data collection, quality control, expert independent interpretation, to design and development of systems involving image processing capable of tackling these tasks. These areas are clear examples of innovative applications in biology or medicine.

The wider view of the computational paradigm gives us more elbow room to accommodate the results of the interplay between nature and computation. The IWINAC forum thus becomes a methodological approximation (set of intentions, questions, experiments, models, algorithms, mechanisms, explanation procedures, and engineering and computational methods) to the natural and artificial perspectives of the mind embodiment problem, both in humans and in artifacts. This is the philosophy that prevails at IWINAC meetings, the "interplay" movement between the natural and the artificial, facing this same problem every two years. This synergistic approach will permit us not only to build new computational systems based on the natural measurable phenomena, but also to understand many of the observable behaviors inherent to natural systems.

The difficulty of building bridges between natural and artificial computation was one of the main motivations for the organization of IWINAC 2017. The IWINAC 2017 proceedings contain the works selected by the Scientific Committee from nearly 200 submissions, after the review process. The first volume, entitled *Natural and Artificial Computation for Biomedicine and Neuroscience*, includes all the contributions mainly related to the methodological, conceptual, formal, and experimental developments in the fields of neural sciences and health. The second volume, entitled *Biomedical Applications Based on Natural and Artificial Computing*, contains the papers related to bioinspired programming strategies and all the contributions related to computational solutions to engineering problems in different application domains.

An event of the nature of IWINAC 2017 could not be organized without the collaboration of a group of institutions and people whom we would like to thank, starting with UNED and Universidad Politécnica de Cartagena. The collaboration of the Universidade da Coruña was crucial, as was the efficient work of the local Organizing Committee, chair by Richard Duro with the close collaboration of José Santos and their colleagues José Antonio Becerra Permuy, Francisco Bellas Bouza, Abraham Prieto, Fernando López Peña, Álvaro Deibe Díaz, and Blanca Priego. In addition to our universities, we received financial support from the Spanish CYTED, Red Nacional en Computación Natural y Artificial, Programa de Grupos de Excelencia de la Fundación Séneca and from Apliquem Microones 21 s.l.

We want to express our gratitude to our invited speakers Prof. Hojjat Adeli (Ohio State University, USA), Prof. Manuel Graña (Universidad del País Vasco, Spain), Prof. Martin Greschner (Carl von Ossietzky Universit of Oldenburg, Germany), and Prof. Gusz Eiben (Vrije Universiteit Amsterdam, The Netherlands) for accepting our invitation and for their magnificent plenary talks.

We would also like to thank the authors for their interest in our call for papers and their effort in preparing the papers, condition sine qua non for these proceedings. We thank the Scientific and Organizing Committees, in particular the members of these committees who acted as effective and efficient referees and as promoters and managers of pre-organized sessions and workshops on autonomous and relevant topics under the IWINAC global scope.

Our sincere gratitude also goes to Springer and especially to Alfred Hofmann and his team, Anna Kramer, Elke Werner, and Christine Reiss, for the continuous receptivity, help, and collaboration in all our joint editorial ventures on the interplay between neuroscience and computation.

Finally, we want to express our special thanks to Viajes Hispania, our technical secretariat, and to Chari García and Beatriz Baeza, for making this meeting possible and for arranging all the details that comprise the organization of this kind of event.

We would like to dedicate these two volumes of the IWINAC proceedings to Professor Mira. In 2018, it will have been 10 years without him, without his inquiring spirit. We miss him greatly.

June 2017

José Manuel Ferrández Vicente
José Ramón Álvarez-Sánchez
Félix de la Paz López
Javier Toledo Moreo
Hojjat Adeli

Organization

General Chairman

José Manuel Ferrández Vicente, Spain

Organizing Committee

José Ramón Álvarez-Sánchez, Spain
Félix de la Paz López, Spain
Javier Toledo Moreo, Spain

Honorary Chairs

Hojjat Adeli, USA
Rodolfo Llinás, USA
Zhou Changjiu, Singapore

Local Organizing Committee

Richard Duro Fernández, Spain
José Santos Reyes, Spain
José Antonio Becerra Permuy, Spain
Francisco Bellas Bouza, Spain
Abraham Prieto, Spain
Fernando López Peña, Spain
Álvaro Deibe Díaz, Spain
Blanca Priego, Spain

Invited Speakers

Hojjat Adeli, USA
Manuel Graña, Spain
Martin Greschner, Germany
Gusz Eiben, The Netherlands

Field Editors

Juan Carlos Burguillo Rial, Spain
Alfredo Cuesta Infante, Spain
Adriana Dapena, Spain
Antonio Fernández-Caballero, Spain
Jose García-Rodríguez, Spain
Juan Manuel Górriz, Spain
Javier de Lope Asiain, Spain
Miguel Angel López Gordo, Spain
Dario Maravall Gomez-Allende, Spain
Arturo Martínez-Rodrigo, Spain
Jesus Minguillón, Spain
Juan José Pantrigo, Spain
Blanca Priego, Spain
Javier Ramirez, Spain
Jose Santos Reyes, Spain

International Scientific Committee

Antonio R. Anaya, Spain
Diego Andina, Spain
Manuel Arias Calleja, Spain
José M. Azorín, Spain
Margarita Bachiller Mayoral, Spain
Emilia I. Barakova, Netherlands
Francisco Bellas, Spain
Guido Bologna, Italy
Enrique J. Carmona Suarez, Spain
José Carlos Castillo, Spain
Sung-Bae Cho, Korea
Carlos Colodro Conde, Spain
Ricardo Contreras, Chile
Luis Correia, Portugal
Jose Manuel Cuadra Troncoso, Spain
Richard J. Duro, Spain
Paulo Félix Lamas, Spain
Miguel A. Fernandez-Graciani, Spain
Francisco J. Garrigos Guerrero, Spain
Elena Gaudioso, Spain
Pedro Gomez Vilda, Spain
Manuel Graña, Spain
Roberto Iglesias, Spain
Joost N. Kok, Netherlands
Markus Lappe, Germany
Emilio Leton Molina, Spain
Maria Teresa Lopez Bonal, Spain
Manuel Luque, Spain
Francisco Martínez Álvarez, Spain
Jose Javier Martinez-Alvarez, Spain
Oscar Martinez Mozos, Spain
Rafael Martinez Tomas, Spain
Sergio Miguel-Tomé, Spain
Jose Manuel Molina Lopez, Spain
Miguel Angel Patricio Guisado, Spain
Francisco Peláez, Brazil
Francisco Pelayo, Spain
David Pérez Lizán, Spain
Maria Pinninghoff, Chile
Alberto de Ramón Fernández, Spain
Mariano Rincon Zamorano, Spain
José C. Riquelme, Spain
Camino Rodriguez Vela, Spain
Daniel Ruiz Fernández, Spain
Ramon Ruiz Merino, Spain
Jose M Sabater-Navarro, Spain
Diego Salas-Gonzalez, Spain
Angel Sanchez, Spain
Eduardo Sánchez Vila, Spain
Luis M Sarro, Spain
Andreas Schierwagen, Germany
Antonio J. Tallón-Ballesteros, Spain
Rafael Toledo-Moreo, Spain
Jan Treur, Netherlands
Ramiro Varela Arias, Spain
Carlos Vazquez Regueiro, Spain
Hujun Yin, UK

Contents – Part II

Computational Intelligence in Data Coding and Transmission

Applications

Contents – Part I

Natural Computing in Bioinformatics

Physiological Computing in Affective Smart Environments

Biomedical Applications

Automatic Detection of Blood Vessels in Retinal OCT Images

Joaquim de Moura(✉), Jorge Novo, José Rouco, M.G. Penedo, and Marcos Ortega

Department of Computing, University of A Coruña, A Coruña, Spain
{joaquim.demoura,jnovo,jrouco,mgpenedo,mortega}@udc.es

Abstract. The eye is a non-invasive window where clinicians can observe and study in vivo the retinal vasculature, allowing the early detection of different relevant pathologies. In this paper, we present a complete methodology for the automatic vascular detection in retinal OCT images. To achieve this, we analyse the intensity profiles between representative layers of the retina, layers that are previously segmented. Then, we propose the use of two threshold-based strategies for vessel detection, a fixed and an adaptive approach. Both methods have been tested and validated with 128 OCT images, that include 560 vessels that were labelled by an ophthalmologist. The approaches provided satisfactory results, facilitating the doctors' work and allowing better analysis and treatment of vascular diseases.

Keywords: Computer-aided diagnosis · Retinal imaging · Optical coherence tomography · Vessel detection

1 Introduction

Retinal vascular morphology can represent an important biomarker for diseases like diabetes [1], hypertension [2] or arteriosclerosis [3], among others. In recent years, the introduction and popularization of Optical Coherence Tomography (OCT) as a non-invasive exploratory technique for the analysis of the eye fundus became a reality. This image modality allows the doctors to obtain images of the retinal tissues, including the presence and location of the retinal vascular structure [4]. These images enable the experts to make a clinical evaluation of the retinal vascular tree morphology, permitting the identification and analysis of different types of diseases.

In OCT imaging, the retinal vessels are visualized as structures that block the transmission of light and leave a shadow. In the literature, we can find many different approaches that solve this problem in classical retinographies. As reference, the method in [5] is based on the use of a Hessian multiscale enhancement filter to detect the vessels. [6] uses an approach based on Gaussian and Kalman filters. Other approach include the use of neural networks [7]. A similar aim was proposed in [8] where authors use a deformable contour model

J.M. Ferrández Vicente et al. (Eds.): IWINAC 2017, Part II, LNCS 10338, pp. 3–10, 2017.
DOI: 10.1007/978-3-319-59773-7_1

to identify the vasculature. However, few studies were proposed in OCT images, as the works in [9–11], but using as support the corresponding near-infrared reflectance retinography for the vascular detection process.

We propose a complete methodology for the automatic detection of retinal vessels using, only, the histological sections of the OCT images. The method segments the retinal layers and detects the vessel structures by the analysis of statistical features of the intensity profile obtained between these layers. Two approaches are considered for this purpose: one using a fixed threshold and a second using an adaptive threshold.

2 Methodology

The proposed methodology, represented in Fig. 1, is divided into four main steps: a first step, where the retinal layers are segmented using the input image; a second step, applying a preprocessing to enhance the characteristics of the vascular structures; a third step, where a set of statistical features is extracted; and a fourth step, where the vessels are finally detected. Each one of these steps is going to be discussed next.

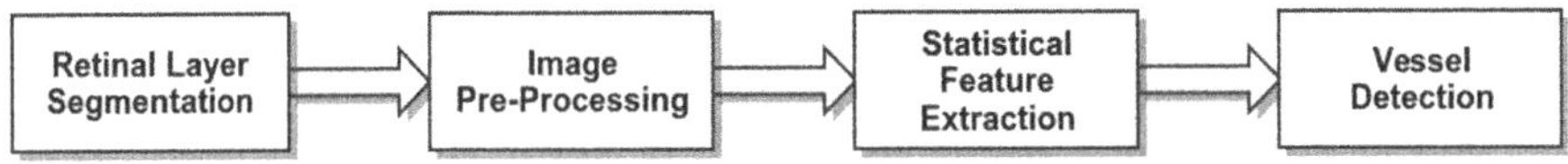

Fig. 1. Main steps of the proposed methodology.

2.1 Retinal Layer Segmentation

The proposed method receives, as input, an OCT image. This image corresponds to a histological section representing the morphology of the retinal layers. Using these images, the retinal layers are identified and segmented, delimiting the region where the vessels are placed. For this purpose, we follow the methodology proposed in [12], where the retinal layers are segmented using an active contour-based technique. In particular, two layers are considered in this work: the Pigment Epithelium Bruch's Complex with the Choroid (RPE/C) and top boundaries of the Ellipsoid (M/E). Between these layers, a higher contrast is perceived in the areas where vascular shadows are present (Fig. 2).

2.2 Image Pre-processing

Speckle noise is a common distortion that is frequently present in OCT images. For that reason we applied a pre-processing step, removing the noise and increasing the contrast of the vascular shadows in the region between the previously detected layers. Firstly, we apply a Gaussian Blur Filter to reduce noise in the image. Then, a top-hat transform is used vertically to increase the contrast of vascular shadows. Figure 3 illustrates the results obtained in this stage.

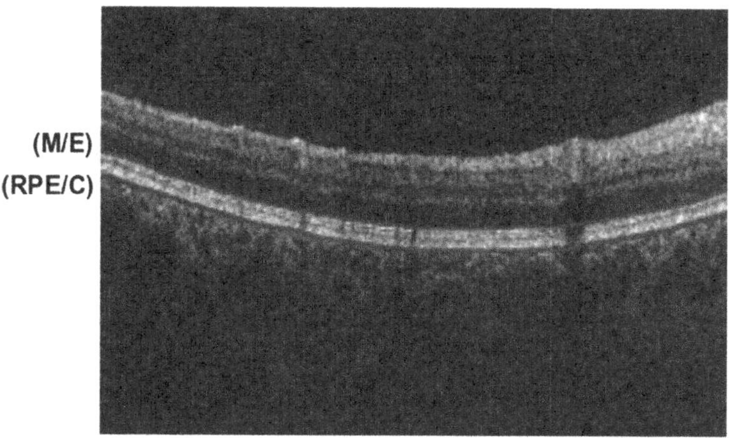

Fig. 2. Input OCT image marked with the retinal layers considered in this work: (RPE/C) and (M/E).

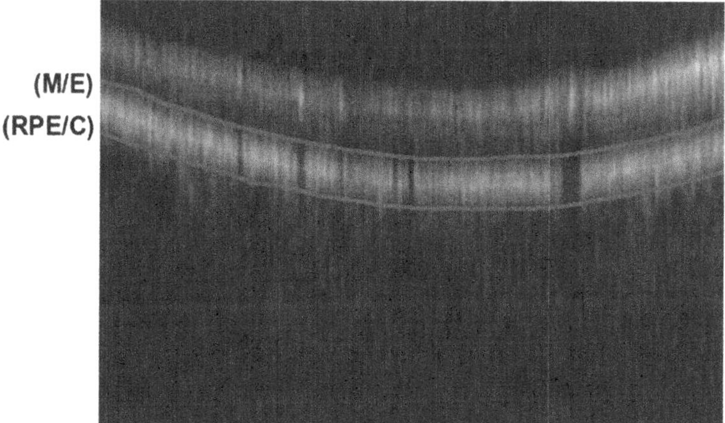

Fig. 3. Pre-processed image after noise removal and contrast enhancement.

2.3 Statistical Feature Extraction

In this phase, we detect the vessel structures by the analysis of the intensity profiles between the layers of the retina. To achieve this, we calculate a signal where each point represents the mean μ_i of the intensity I_j in each column c_i within the region of interest (ROI), as indicated in the Eq. 1, where n represents the number of elements in the column c_i.

$$\mu_i = \frac{\sum_{j=0}^{n} I_j}{n} \tag{1}$$

We calculate these values on the pre-processed image and within the ROI that is delimited by the layers (RPE/C) and (M/E). Figure 4 shows the graphic representing the mean intensity profile from the OCT images. Global mean μ and standard deviation σ are also calculated using all the column means μ_i.

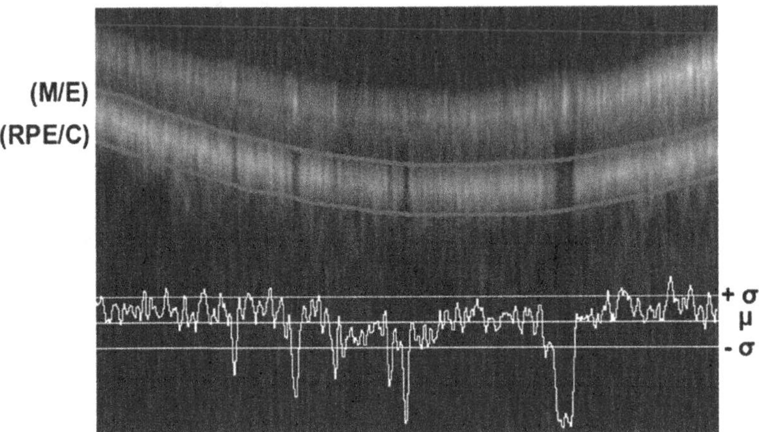

Fig. 4. Graphic representing the statistical features: μ_i, μ and σ.

2.4 Vessel Detection

In this phase, we detect the vascular structures in the slices using the information of the column means μ_i. For that purpose, we use two strategies, fixed and adaptive threshold approaches, that will be detailed below.

Fixed Threshold. In this first approach, we consider that the values obtained for the means μ_i of each column c_i approximate a Normal distribution. Therefore, we can consider that the atypical values (outlayers) of the left tail of the distribution identify the vascular shadows. Consequently, we elaborate a model that uses a fixed threshold th_{fix}, as shown in Eq. 2, where Q_1 represent the 1st quartile and Q_3 and the represent the 3rd quartile. This value allows us to detect the outlayers that represent the vascular structures.

$$th_{fix} = \frac{3}{2}(Q_3 - Q_1) + Q_3 \tag{2}$$

The results of this approach can be observed in Fig. 6(a), (c), where the values that are below the fixed threshold th_{fix} represent the vascular detections in the OCT image.

Adaptive Threshold. The fixed threshold approach presents, as main limitation, that the column means μ_i do not always oscillate around the global mean μ. Instead of that, many times the column means tendency is deviated to bright and dark values due to local intensity alterations. These deformations can make that a global fixed threshold miss-detects vessels (when the tendency moves brighter) or produce many false positives (when the tendency moves darker). This motivated the second approach. Based on the principle that the vessel presence produces a significant intensity depression, this second approach uses the mathematical concepts of local maxima (peak) and minima (valley) to determine the presence of vascular structures in the graphic of means μ_i. Generally, between two consecutive peaks multiples valleys can appear. In this work, we select a unique valley v between two consecutive peaks to represent a unique candidate for a vessel. Then, we obtain the set V_{cand} with all valleys v_i. Finally, we process the set V_{cand} by selecting the candidates that represent the vascular structures. For this, we will use as selection criterion the force of fall f of the valley v_i with respect to its two nearest peaks (see Fig. 5). The results of this approach can be observed in Fig. 6(b), (d).

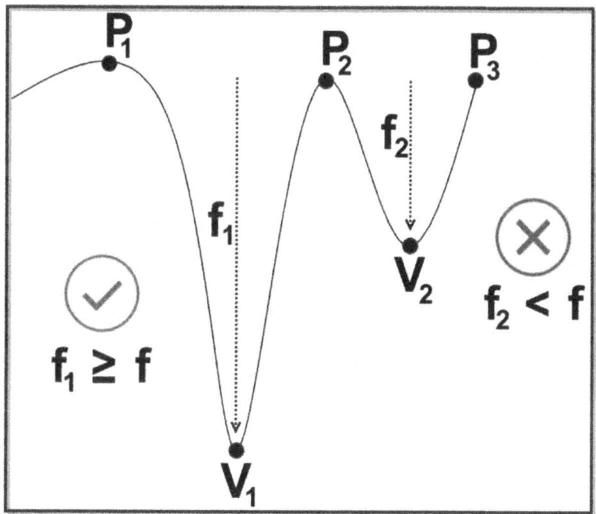

Fig. 5. Adaptive threshold approach, where v_i represents an valley and p_i represents an peak. The valleys with force $f_i \geq f$ are marked as vessels.

3 Experimental Results

The proposed method was tested with 128 OCT histological sections, where 560 vascular structures have been manually labelled by an expert clinician. The images were taken with a confocal scanning laser ophthalmoscope, CIRRUS^{TM} HD-OCT Zeiss, with Spectral Domain Technology, at a resolution of 490×500 pixels. Regarding the adaptive threshold approach, a force of fall, f, has been empirically established to a value of 50. We evaluated the accuracy of the proposed method using two metrics: precision and recall. Table 1 summarizes the results obtained by each approach. As we can see, the adaptive threshold approach offers a better and more complete performance.

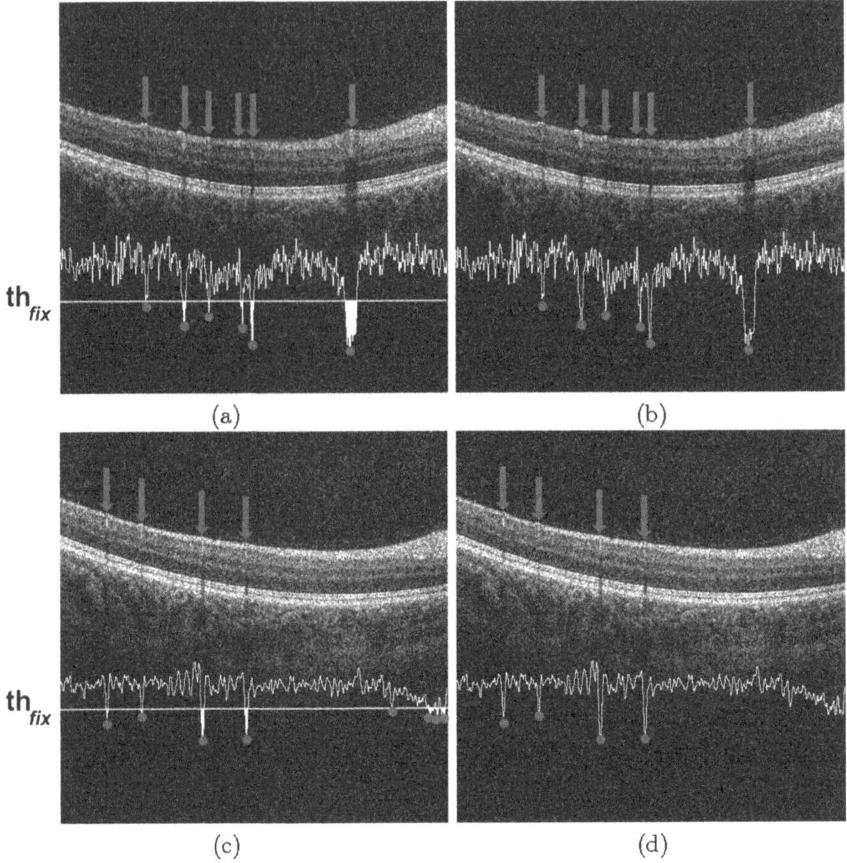

Fig. 6. Results of the approaches. Red arrows, the vascular segments annotated by the experts. Red circles, the results of the different approaches. (a), (c) Fixed threshold approach. (b), (d) Adaptive threshold approach. (Color figure online)

4 Discussion and Conclusions

In this paper, new strategies for the automatic detection of retinal blood vessels in OCT images are presented. The proposed methodology exploits two approaches, a fixed and an adaptive threshold, over the mean intensity of all the columns between the retinal layers (RPE/C) and (M/E), to detect vascular structures. We used OCT images labelled by an expert clinician to evaluate the robustness and accuracy of the proposals, obtaining promising results. Analysing the results of the experiments (see Table 1), we can conclude that the adaptive threshold approach offers a more robust and coherent behaviour than the method with the fixed threshold. This is because the adaptive method is more robust to deviations in the global tendency of the column means, as explained before. An example of this situation is illustrated in Fig. 6(c), (d), where we can observe

Table 1. Precision and recall results in the vessel detection process.

Method	Precision	Recall
Fixed threshold	68.42%	90.37%
Adaptive threshold	96.55%	80.02%

that the mean tendency moves darker at the right columns of the image, making that the fixed threshold approach produce several false positives in this region. However, the adaptive threshold approach, as there is no significant dropping profiles with respect to their surroundings, is capable to overcome this situation. Both proposals offer an automatic vessel identification, facilitating the work of the ophthalmologists in diagnostic processes of many vascular pathologies that are present in the retina facilitating, therefore, therapeutic processes.

Acknowledgments. This work is supported by the Instituto de Salud Carlos III of the Spanish Government and FEDER funds of the European Union through the PI14/02161 and the DTS15/00153 research projects.

References

1. Nguyen, T., Wong, T.Y.: Retinal vascular changes and diabetic retinopathy. Curr. Diab. Rep. **113**(9), 277–283 (2009)
2. Won, T.Y., Mitchell, P.: Retinal vascular changes and diabetic retinopathy. N. Engl. J. Med. **351**, 2310–2317 (2004)
3. Klein, R., Sharrett, A.R., Klein, B.E., Chambless, L.E., Cooper, L.S., Hubbard, L.D., Evans, G.: Are retinal arteriolar abnormalities related to atherosclerosis? The atherosclerosis risk in communities study. Arterioscler. Thromb. Vasc. Biol. **20**, 1644–1650 (2000)
4. Huang, D., Swanson, E., Lin, C., Schuman, J., Stinson, W., Chang, W., Hee, M., Flotte, T., Gregory, K., Puliafito, C.: Optical coherence tomography. Science **254**, 1178 (1991)
5. Elbalaoui, A., Fakir, M., Taifi, K., Merbouha, A.: Automatic detection of blood vessel in retinal images. In: 13th International Conference on Computer Graphics, pp. 324–332 (2016)
6. Chutatape, O., Zheng, L., Krishnan, S.: Retinal blood vessel detection and tracking by matched Gaussian and Kalman filters. In: Engineering in Medicine and Biology Society, pp. 3144–3149 (1998)
7. Nekovei, R., Sun, Y.: Back-propagation network and its configuration for blood vessel detection in angiograms. IEEE Trans. Neural Netw. **6**, 64–72 (1995)
8. Espona, L., Carreira, M., Penedo, M., Ortega, M.: Retinal vessel tree segmentation using a deformable contour model. IEEE Trans. Neural Netw. 1–4 (2008)
9. Niemeijer, M., Garvin, M., Ginneken, B., Sonka, M., Abramoff, M.: Vessel segmentation in 3D spectral OCT scans of the retina. In: Medical Imaging, p. 69141 (2008)
10. Guimarães, P., Rodrigues, P., Lobo, C., Leal, S., Figueira, J., Serranho, P., Bernardes, R.: Ocular fundus reference images from optical coherence tomography. Comput. Med. Imaging Graph. **38**, 381–389 (2014)

11. Moura, J., Novo, J., Ortega, M., Barreira, N., Penedo, M.G.: Vessel tree extraction and depth estimation with OCT images. In: Luaces, O., Gámez, J.A., Barrenechea, E., Troncoso, A., Galar, M., Quintián, H., Corchado, E. (eds.) CAEPIA 2016. LNCS, vol. 9868, pp. 23–33. Springer, Cham (2016). doi:10.1007/978-3-319-44636-3_3
12. Ortega, M., López, A.G., Penedo, M.G., Cardeñoso, P.C.: Implementation and optimization of a method for retinal layer extraction and reconstruction in optical coherence tomography images. Med. Appl. Artif. Intell. **12**, 175–191 (2013)

Emergency Department Readmission Risk Prediction: A Case Study in Chile

Arkaitz Artetxe[1,2], Manuel Graña[2(✉)], Andoni Beristain[1], and Sebastián Ríos[3]

[1] Vicomtech-IK4 Research Centre, Mikeletegi Pasealekua 57, 20009 San Sebastian, Spain
aartetxe@vicomtech.org

[2] Computation Intelligence Group, Basque University (UPV/EHU), P. Manuel Lardizabal 1, 20018 San Sebastian, Spain
manuel.grana@ehu.es

[3] Business Intelligence Research Center (CEINE), Industrial Engineering Department, University of Chile, Beauche 851, 8370456 Santiago, Chile

Abstract. Short time readmission prediction in Emergency Departments (ED) is a valuable tool to improve both the ED management and the healthcare quality. It helps identifying patients requiring further post-discharge attention as well as reducing healthcare costs. As in many other medical domains, patient readmission data is heavily imbalanced, i.e. the minority class is very infrequent, which is a challenge for the construction of accurate predictors using machine learning tools. We have carried computational experiments on a dataset composed of ED admission records spanning more than 100000 patients in 3 years, with a highly imbalanced distribution. We employed various approaches for dealing with this highly imbalanced dataset in combination with different classification algorithms and compared their predictive power for the estimation of the ED readmission probability within 72 h after discharge. Results show that random undersampling and Bagging (RUSBagging) in combination with Random Forest achieves the best results in terms of Area Under ROC Curve (AUC).

Keywords: Readmission risk · Imbalanced data · Classification · Bagging

1 Introduction

In hospitals inside public and private healthcare systems, there is a growing concern on the quality and sustainability of the service. The readmission events, defined as the recurrent visits of a patient in a time span smaller that a given threshold, has become one of the quality measures, both regarding patient attention and economical factors. In some countries, insurance companies have set a time threshold below which they decline to answer for the cost of the patient care, and the hospital must assume it. Therefore, the prediction and prevention

J.M. Ferrández Vicente et al. (Eds.): IWINAC 2017, Part II, LNCS 10338, pp. 11–20, 2017.
DOI: 10.1007/978-3-319-59773-7_2

of these events is becoming economically critical for some institutions. In other countries, healthcare quality is the primary concern, so that preventing readmissions is a measure of improved patient attention. Readmission predictors are built by machine learning techniques, as specific two-class classifiers. A specific issue building these predictors from data is that the readmission events are much less frequent than normal admissions, i.e. the datasets are class imbalanced.

In supervised classification, data imbalance occurs when the a priori probabilities of the classes are significantly different, i.e. there exists a minority (positive) class that is underrepresented in the dataset in contrast to the majority (negative) class. In healthcare, as well as in other fields (e.g. fraud detection or fault diagnosis), instances of the minority class are outnumbered by the negative instances. Also, the minority class is the target class to be predicted because it is related to the highest cost/reward events. Most classification algorithms assume equal a priori probability for all the classes, so when this premise is violated the resulting classifier is biased towards the majority class. The resulting classifier has a higher predictive accuracy over the majority class, but poorer predictive accuracy over the minority class.

The degree of class imbalance is given by the imbalance ratio (IR), defined as the ratio of the number of instances in the majority class and the number of those in the minority class. Some studies have shown that classifier performance deteriorates even with modest class imbalance in the training data [11].

Although imbalanced data classes have been recognized as one of the key problems in the field of data mining [14], it is not usually taken into account in the literature of readmission risk prediction, despite some authors [2] have encountered class imbalance problems when building their predictive models. Some works such as [1,12,15] point out the existence of the class imbalance problem and propose methods to circumvent it. Nevertheless, only simple preprocessing approaches such as oversampling and under sampling are considered. Recent works [8,10] in the field of disease risk prediction have attacked the problem of class imbalance using different preprocesing and ensemble techniques such as SMOTE or RUSBoost among others.

The main contributions of this paper are:

- A methodology proposal for overcoming the class imbalance problem based on RUSBagging
- An experimental study using real-world data where we compare the performance of different methods

The paper is organized as follows. In Sect. 2 we present our dataset as well as the methodological approach followed in order to build our models. Next, we describe the evaluation methodology and the experimental results. In Sect. 4 we discuss the conclusions and future work.

2 Materials and Methods

2.1 Experimental Dataset

We used a pseudonymised dataset composed of 99858 admission records recorded between January 2013 and April 2016 in the Hospital José Joaquín Aguirre of the Universidad de Chile, which is part of the public health system of Chile. The variables recorded in the dataset are divided into three main groups: (i) Sociodemographic and administrative data, (ii) Health status (iii) Reasons for consultation or diagnoses made at admission. Records with missing values are discarded for this study. Table 1 shows the characteristics of the dataset and the distribution of 72-hour readmissions among different variables[1].

2.2 Data Pre-processing

Data was provided in a large ASCII text file containing 156120 admission records corresponding to 102534 different patient identities. After parsing the data, we built a dataset combining admission and patient-related data. Next, we cleaned the data by removing inconsistent and missing samples. Missing values where imputed using the arithmetic mean for continuous variables and the mode for categorical variables.

For each admission of a patient to the ED we calculated the number of days elapsed since his last visit. In order to build our model following a binary classification approach, the target variable meaning was set to readmitted/not readmitted. Those patients returning to the ED within 72 h after being discharged where considered readmitted, otherwise they were considered not readmitted.

Notice that a patient returning the very first day after discharge and another one returning the third day are both considered as readmitted. On the other hand, a patient returning the 73rd hour from discharge is considered as not readmitted.

2.3 Evaluation Metrics

The evaluation metrics that we have used are: sensitivity, specificity, accuracy and Area Under ROC Curve (AUC), defined as follows:

- Accuracy. In binary classification, accuracy is defined as the proportion of true results among the total population:

$$Accuracy = \frac{\Sigma TN + \Sigma TP}{\Sigma TN + \Sigma TP + \Sigma FN + \Sigma FP}, \tag{1}$$

  where TN is a true negative, TP a true positive, FN is a false negative and FP a false positive. In heavily umbalanced datasets it is not very meaningful because a simple strategy such as assigining each test sample to the majority class provides high accuracy.
- Sensitivity. Sensitivity is a classification performance measure defined as the proportion of correctly classified positives:

$$Sensitivity = \frac{TP}{TP + FN}, \tag{2}$$

  Sensitivity provides more informative about the success on the target class.

[1] Most common categorical values are only shown.

Table 1. Characteristics of the dataset

Variable	All patients n=99858	Readmitted n=3425	Not readmitted n=96433	p-value
age, mean (SD)	41.0 (22.4)	36.1 (22.9)	41.2 (22.4)	<0.001
male sex (%)	44956 (45.0)	1624 (1.6)	43332 (43.4)	0.004
daytime (%)	69321 (69.4)	2171 (2.2)	67150 (67.2)	<0.001
evaluation, mean (SD)	5.0 (3.3)	4.8 (3.5)	5.0 (3.3)	0.040
fragility idx, mean (SD)	0.0 (2.5)	0.0 (2.3)	0.0 (2.5)	0.991
triage (%)				<0.001
I	182 (0.2)	2 (0.0)	180 (0.2)	
II	12694 (12.7)	317 (0.3)	12377 (12.4)	
III	77813 (77.9)	2718 (2.7)	75095 (75.2)	
IV	9131 (9.1)	387 (0.4)	8744 (8.8)	
V	38 (0.0)	1 (0.0)	37 (0.0)	
pathology (%)				<0.001
Gineco-obstetrics	236 (0.2)	6 (0.0)	230 (0.2)	
General medicine	77192 (77.3)	2458 (2.5)	74734 (74.8)	
Pedaitrics	7094 (7.1)	563 (0.6)	6531 (6.5)	
Traumatology	15336 (15.4)	398 (0.4)	14938 (15.0)	
destination (%)				<0.001
External center	3372 (3.4)	116 (0.1)	3256 (3.3)	
Home	71999 (72.1)	2703 (2.7)	69296 (69.4)	
Hospital	14700 (14.7)	61 (0.1)	14639 (14.7)	
Left without being seen	9787 (9.8)	545 (0.5)	9242 (9.3)	
reason for consultation (%)				<0.001
Cephalea	6421 (6.4)	192 (0.2)	6229 (6.2)	
Pain - abdomen gen.	9861 (9.9)	404 (0.4)	9457 (9.5)	
Pain - epigastrium	3177 (3.2)	143 (0.1)	3034 (3.0)	
Pain - lumbar	2964 (3.0)	107 (0.1)	2857 (2.9)	
Pain - foot	2909 (2.9)	92 (0.1)	2817 (2.8)	
General malaise	3027 (3.0)	78 (0.1)	2949 (3.0)	
Other	10867 (10.9)	374 (0.4)	10493 (10.5)	
...				
saturation, mean (SD)	96.6 (9.6)	96.2 (12.1)	96.6 (9.5)	<0.001
tad, mean (SD)	74.1 (22.3)	67.6 (29.4)	74.3 (21.9)	<0.001
tas, mean (SD)	125.8 (35.9)	114.5 (48.8)	126.2 (35.3)	<0.001
temperature, mean (SD)	35.9 (4.5)	35.5 (5.9)	35.9 (4.4)	<0.001
heart rate, mean (SD)	87.2 (22.3)	92.7 (29.1)	87.0 (22.0)	<0.001
breath rate, mean (SD)	17.0 (5.6)	15.1 (7.6)	17.0 (5.5)	<0.001
Prevision (%)				0.408
2	5943 (6.0)	180 (0.2)	5763 (5.8)	
5	3641 (3.6)	108 (0.1)	3533 (3.5)	
6	27903 (27.9)	1022 (1.0)	26881 (26.9)	
9	11060 (11.1)	432 (0.4)	10628 (10.6)	
18	44464 (44.5)	1468 (1.5)	42996 (43.1)	
35	1011 (1.0)	30 (0.0)	981 (1.0)	
37	1103 (1.1)	33 (0.0)	1070 (1.1)	
48	2074 (2.1)	70 (0.1)	2004 (2.0)	
...				

- Specificity. Specificity is defined as the proportion of negatives that are correctly identified as such:

$$Specificity = \frac{TN}{TN + FP}, \tag{3}$$

- AUC. The Area Under ROC Curve (AUC) shows the trade-off between the sensitivity or TP_{rate} and FP_{rate} (1 - specificity):

$$AUC = \frac{1 + TP_{rate} - FP_{rate}}{2} \tag{4}$$

where the True Positive rate is equal to the Sensitivity and the False Positive rate is defined as $FP_{rate} = \frac{\Sigma FP}{\Sigma FP + \Sigma TN}$.

Table 2. Confusion matrix for a binary classifier

Actual	Predicted	
	Positive	Negative
Positive	True positive (TP)	False negative (FN)
Negative	False positive (FP)	True negative (TN)

2.4 Learning from Imbalanced Data

The main issue of learning from imbalanced datasets is that classification learning algorithms are often biased towards the majority class and hence, there is a higher misclassification rate of the minority class instances (which is usually the most interesting ones from the practical point of view). Figure 1 depicts a taxonomy of methods developed to deal with class imbalance [9] where three main techniques are identified, namely *preprocessing*, *cost-sensitive learning* and *ensemble* techniques. We give a quick overview of the different strategies.

Preprocessing. Methods following this strategy carry out resampling of the original dataset in order to change the class distribution. Resampling techniques can be divided into three groups: (i) *Undersampling techniques*, consisting on deleting instances of the majority class, (ii) *Oversampling techniques*, that replicate or create new instances of the minority class, such as the Synthetic Minority Over-sampling Technique (SMOTE) [4], and (iii) *Hybrid techniques*, those that combine both resampling techniques.

Cost-Sensitive Learning. The strategy followed by cost-sensitive learning methods is to assign different cost values to each class misclassifications, so that the bias towards the majority class is balanced by the lower cost of misclassifications. A cost matrix is build assigning cost values to the entries of the confussion matrix giving (see Table 2). The usual approach is to heavily penalize misclassifications of the minority class. They are categorized into the following groups:

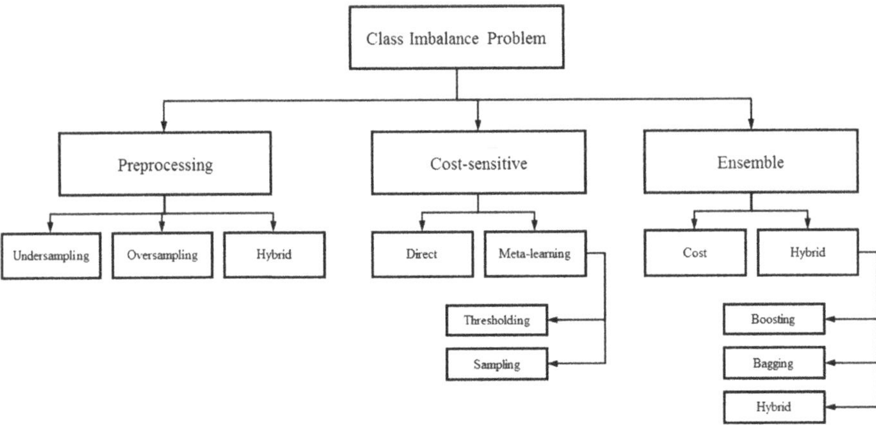

Fig. 1. Taxonomy of Class imbalance problem addressing techniques as proposed in [9]

- Direct methods, that introduce the misclassification cost within the classification algorithm.
- Meta-learning, where the algorithm itself is not modified. Instead, a preprocessing (or postprocessing) mechanism is introduced to handle the costs. Meta-learning methodologies can be divided into two categories, namely *thresholding* and *sampling*.

Ensemble Classifiers. Ensemble methods rely on the idea that the combination of many "weak" classifiers can improve the performance of a single classifier [6]. They are divided in two groups, namely *cost-sensitive* ensembles and *data and algorithmic* approaches.

- Cost-sensitive ensemble techniques, are analogous to cost-sensitive methods mentioned earlier, although in this case, the cost minimization is undertaken by the boosting algorithm.
- Data and algorithmic approaches, which embed a data preprocessing technique in an ensemble algorithm. Depending on the ensemble algorithm they use, three groups are identified: (i) Boosting, (ii) Bagging and (iii) Hybrid.

Bagging [3] consists in creating bootstrapped replicas of the original dataset with replacement (i.e. different copies of the same instance can be found in the same bag), so that different classifiers are trained on each replica. Originally each new data-set or bag mantained the size of the original data-set. Nevertheless, UnderBagging and OverBagging strategies embed a resampling process, so that bags are balanced by means of undersampling or oversampling techniques. To classify an unseen instance, the output predictions of the weak classifiers are collected performing a majority vote in order to produce the joint ensemble prediction. In this group we find, among others, algorithms like SMOTEBoost [5] or UnderBagging [13] which embed undersampling within the ensemble algorithm.

We propose RUSBagging which carries out a random undersampling for each bag generated in the ensemble creation. An individual weak classifier is trained from the data in each bag.

3 Experimental Results

In this section we present the results obtained when trying to predict the readmission risk before 72 h over the dataset presented in the previous section. We have tested two data balancing methods: random undersampling (RUS) and random undersampling embedded in a bagging approach. We used the following well-known classification algorithms, implemented in the open source machine learning library scikit-learn[2]:

1. Decision Tree (DT), setting Gini impurity as splitting criterion
2. Random Forest (RF), setting Gini impurity as splitting criterion and number of estimators = 10

The models were evaluated using 10-fold cross-validation, performing 10 independent executions. Accuracy, specificity, sensitivity and AUC were calculated for each execution, so average and standard deviation were computed. In order to statistically compare results we employed an Analysis of Variance (ANOVA) approach.

The following data balancing approaches were compared: (i) Original dataset with its imbalanced class distribution, (ii) Undersampling with random undersampling and (iii) RUSBagging. Table 3 shows the average accuracy, sensitivity, specificity and AUC along with its respective standard deviation, for each method and classifier.

3.1 Comparison of Classifiers

According to the results shown in Table 3, both classification algorithms, Random Forest achieve significantly better results ($p < 0.001$) than Decision Trees looking at the AUC. Though DT performs better in the original dataset (anyhow both classifiers perform poorly), when preprocessing and ensemble approaches are utilized RF performs much better. As shown in Fig. 3, the AUC is significatively greater for RF when RUSBagging is used, however, sensitivity is sacrificed if compared with DT. Overall, results are poor, however they compare well with the state of the art in readmission prediction. In a recent review [7], most studies reported performances measured by AUC near 0.5, with some outliers achieving a maximum of 0.7 (Fig. 2).

[2] http://scikit-learn.org/.

Table 3. Mean (±standard deviation) of performance metrics for each data balance method and classifier model configuration

Method	Classifier	Accuracy	Specificity	Sensitivity	AUC
None	DT	.9293 ± .0006	.9599 ± .0006	.0673 ± .0030	.5136 ± .0017
	RF	.9655 ± .0001	.9997 ± .0001	.0012 ± .0003	.5005 ± .0002
RUS	DT	.5578 ± .002	.5574 ± .002	.5674 ± .012	.5624 ± .005
	RF	.6622 ± .0016	.6676 ± .0018	.5086 ± .0096	.5881 ± .0043
RUSBagging	DT	.6530 ± .0011	.6576 ± .0012	.5244 ± .0079	.5910 ± .0037
	RF	.7679 ± .0014	.7796 ± .0015	.4359 ± .0041	.6078 ± .0020

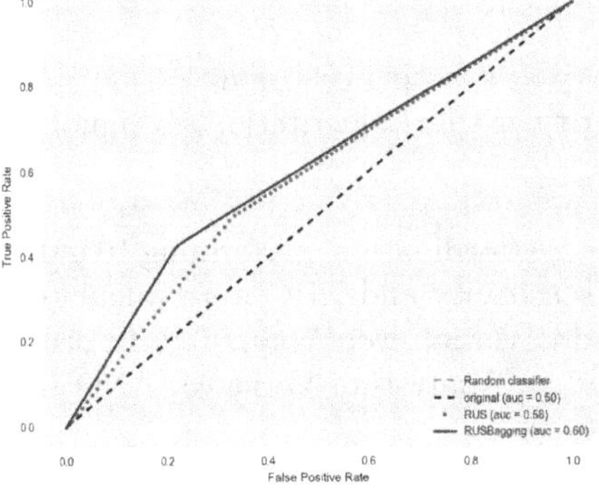

Fig. 2. ROC curve for DT using undersampling, RUSBagging and original

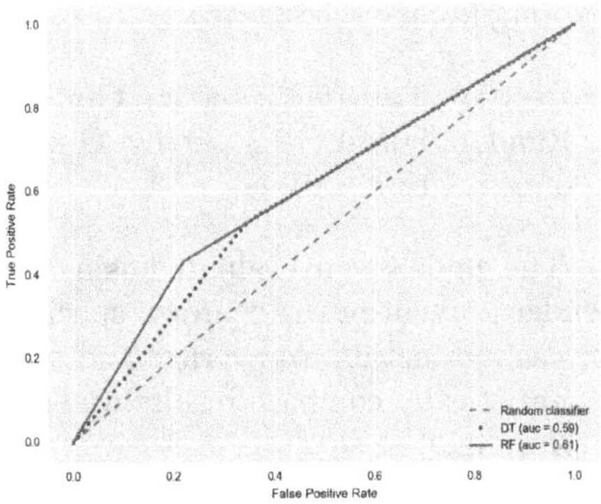

Fig. 3. ROC curve for DT and RF algorithms using RUSBagging method

3.2 The Effect of Preprocessing and Ensemble Methods

Several conclusions can be extracted from the results shown in Table 3.

- The models trained without modifying the original class distribution were clearly biased towards the majority class. Although accuracy scores were high (>90%), specificity was close 100% while sensitivity tended to zero. Thus, according to the AUC scores, models performed similar or just slightly better than a random classifier.
- Using random undersampling for class balancing had a direct effect in the performance of the resulting model. Results show that both DT and RF get better AUC scores, 0.56 and 0.58 respectively, and sensitivity increases considerably. However, as could be expected, both accuracy and specificity tend to decrease.
- RUSBagging, which embeds random undersampling within a bootstrap aggregating algorithm, outperforms both previous methodologies. According to the AUC scores, the combination of RUSBagging and Random Forest shows the best performance with a mean of 0.60.

– The performance of the models considering the AUC metric, suggests poor discrimination ability. Nevertheless, a systematic review on risk prediction models for hospital readmission documented similar AUC scores (ranging from 0.50 to 0.70) in most of the studies [7].

4 Conclusions and Future Work

In this paper we have presented the results of readmission prediction based on a real dataset from a hospital in Santiago, Chile. To overcome the class imbalance problem we propose an approach called RUSBagging, that carries out random undersampling for each bag in a bagging ensemble training.

Results show that RUSBagging in combination with Random Forest significantly improves predictive performance in the context of a highly imbalanced dataset. Nevertheless, our model has shown limited predictive ability for clinical purposes, what seems to be related with the inherent dfficulties and limitations of the readmission risk prediction problem. We have attacked one major issue (data imbalance) but others such as the appriate selection and measurement of varaibles remain untouched in this paper. In order to validate the usefulness of our presented approach, we plan to gather and include additional baseline status and administrative data, to perform a prospective study. Future work will also include an extension of our comparative study including new methodologies and classifiers.

References

1. Artetxe, A., Beristain, A., Graña, M., Besga, A.: Predicting 30-day emergency readmission risk. In: Graña, M., López-Guede, J.M., Etxaniz, O., Herrero, Á., Quintián, H., Corchado, E. (eds.) ICEUTE/SOCO/CISIS -2016. AISC, vol. 527, pp. 3–12. Springer, Cham (2017). doi:10.1007/978-3-319-47364-2_1
2. Billings, J., Blunt, I., Steventon, A., Georghiou, T., Lewis, G., Bardsley, M.: Development of a predictive model to identify inpatients at risk of re-admission within 30 days of discharge (parr-30). BMJ Open **2**(4), e001667 (2012)
3. Breiman, L.: Bagging predictors. Mach. Learn. **24**(2), 123–140 (1996)
4. Chawla, N.V., Bowyer, K.W., Hall, L.O., Kegelmeyer, W.P.: SMOTE: synthetic minority over-sampling technique. J. Artif. Intell. Res. **16**, 321–357 (2002)
5. Chawla, N.V., Lazarevic, A., Hall, L.O., Bowyer, K.W.: SMOTEBoost: improving prediction of the minority class in boosting. In: Lavrač, N., Gamberger, D., Todorovski, L., Blockeel, H. (eds.) PKDD 2003. LNCS, vol. 2838, pp. 107–119. Springer, Heidelberg (2003). doi:10.1007/978-3-540-39804-2_12
6. Galar, M., Fernandez, A., Barrenechea, E., Bustince, H., Herrera, F.: A review on ensembles for the class imbalance problem: bagging-, boosting-, and hybrid-based approaches. IEEE Trans. Syst. Man Cybern. Part C (Appl. Rev.) **42**(4), 463–484 (2012)
7. Kansagara, D., Englander, H., Salanitro, A., Kagen, D., Theobald, C., Freeman, M., Kripalani, S.: Risk prediction models for hospital readmission: a systematic review. JAMA **306**(15), 1688–1698 (2011)

8. Khalilia, M., Chakraborty, S., Popescu, M.: Predicting disease risks from highly imbalanced data using random forest. BMC Med. Inform. Decis. Mak. **11**(1), 1 (2011)
9. López, V., Fernández, A., García, S., Palade, V., Herrera, F.: An insight into classification with imbalanced data: empirical results and current trends on using data intrinsic characteristics. Inf. Sci. **250**, 113–141 (2013)
10. Mateo, F., Soria-Olivas, E., Martınez-Sober, M., Téllez-Plaza, M., Gómez-Sanchis, J., Redón, J.: Multi-step strategy for mortality assessment in cardiovascular risk patients with imbalanced data. In: European Symposium on Artificial Neural Networks, Computational Intelligence and Machine Learning (2016)
11. Mazurowski, M.A., Habas, P.A., Zurada, J.M., Lo, J.Y., Baker, J.A., Tourassi, G.D.: Training neural network classifiers for medical decision making: the effects of imbalanced datasets on classification performance. Neural Netw. **21**(2), 427–436 (2008)
12. Meadem, N., Verbiest, N., Zolfaghar, K., Agarwal, J., Chin, S.C., Roy, S.B.: Exploring preprocessing techniques for prediction of risk of readmission for congestive heart failure patients. In: International Conference on Knowledge Discovery and Data Mining (KDD), Data Mining and Healthcare (DMH) (2013)
13. Wang, S., Yao, X.: Diversity analysis on imbalanced data sets by using ensemble models. In: IEEE Symposium on Computational Intelligence and Data Mining, CIDM 2009, pp. 324–331. IEEE (2009)
14. Yang, Q., Wu, X.: 10 challenging problems in data mining research. Int. J. Inf. Technol. Decis. Mak. **5**(04), 597–604 (2006)
15. Zheng, B., Zhang, J., Yoon, S.W., Lam, S.S., Khasawneh, M., Poranki, S.: Predictive modeling of hospital readmissions using metaheuristics and data mining. Expert Syst. Appl. **42**(20), 7110–7120 (2015)

Vowel Articulation Distortion in Parkinson's Disease

P. Gómez-Vilda[1(✉)], J.M. Ferrández-Vicente[2], D. Palacios-Alonso[1], A. Gómez-Rodellar[1], V. Rodellar-Biarge[1], J. Mekyska[3], Z. Smekal[3], I. Rektorova[4,6], I. Eliasova[4,6], and M. Kostalova[5,6]

[1] Neuromorphic Speech Processing Lab, Center for Biomedical Technology, Universidad Politécnica de Madrid, Campus de Montegancedo, 28223 Pozuelo de Alarcón, Madrid, Spain
pedro@fi.upm.es, pedrogvilda@telefonica.net
[2] Universidad Politécnica de Cartagena, Campus Universitario Muralla del Mar Pza. Hospital 1, 30202 Cartagena, Spain
[3] Department of Telecommunications, Brno University of Technology, Technicka 10, 61600 Brno, Czech Republic
[4] First Department of Neurology, Faculty of Medicine, St. Anne's University Hospital, Masaryk University, Pekarska 53, 656 91 Brno, Czech Republic
[5] Department of Neurology, Faculty Hospital, Masaryk University, Jihlavska 20, 63900 Brno, Czech Republic
[6] Applied Neuroscience Research Group, Central European Institute of Technology, CEITEC, Masaryk University, Kamenice 753/5, 625 00 Brno, Czech Republic

Abstract. Neurodegenerative pathologies produce important distortions in speech. Parkinson's Disease (PD) leaves marks in fluency, prosody, articulation and phonation. Certain measurements based in configurations of the articulation organs inferred from formant positions, as the Vocal Space Area (VSA) or the Formant Centralization Ratio (FCR) have been classically used in this sense, but these markers represent mainly the static positions of sustained vowels on the vowel triangle. The present study proposes a measurement based on the mutual information contents of kinematic correlates derived from formant dynamics. An absolute kinematic velocity associated to the position of the articulation organs, involving the jaw and tongue is estimated and modelled statistically. The distribution of this feature is rather different in PD patients than in normative speakers when sustained vowels are considered. Therefore, articulation failures may be detected even in single sustained vowels. The study has processed a limited database of 40 female and 54 male PD patients, contrasted to a very selected and stable set of normative speakers. Distances based on Kullback-Leibler's Divergence have shown to be sensitive to PD articulation instability. Correlation measurements show that the distance proposed shows statistically relevant relationship with certain motor and non-motor behavioral observations, as freezing of gait, or sleep disorders. These results point out to the need of defining scoring scales specifically designed for speech-based diagnose and monitoring methodologies in degenerative diseases of neuromotor origin.

J.M. Ferrández Vicente et al. (Eds.): IWINAC 2017, Part II, LNCS 10338, pp. 21–31, 2017.
DOI: 10.1007/978-3-319-59773-7_3

Keywords: Neurologic disease · Parkinson's disease · Speech neuromotor activity · Aging voice · Hypokinetic dysarthria

1 Introduction

Parkinson's Disease (PD) is an illness produced by neurotransmitter decay in basal ganglia, which mainly produces motor symptoms in early stages, to derive in cognitive impairments at latter stages. Its effects in speech and phonation are well documented and have been described and treated in different publications. The interested reader can check [10] for a comprehensive review. These effects may be summarized as rough and asthenic phonation, monotonicity, monoloudness, phonation blocking, velo-pharyngeal hypernasality, low tone, and others similar collected under the general name of hypokinetic dysarthria. Traditionally, its effects in phonation have been studied using mainly distortion features as jitter, shimmer, noise-harmonic ratio, and tremor on emissions of sustained vowels. Articulation has been less studied, and in such case, static measurements as Vowel Space Area (VSA) or Formant Centralization Ratio (FCR) have been used mainly [13]. The deterioration of the patient as illness progresses is evaluated using general scales as Hoehn and Yahr [9] or UPDRS [5], which have not been specifically designed to take speech or phonation into account. On the one hand, to study the influence of disease progress, neurologists have resourced to other indices, as freezing of gait test (FOG), non-motor symptoms (NMSS), REM sleep behaviour disorder (RBDSQ), levodopa equivalent dose in mg. (LED), faciokinesis (FK), phonorespiratory competence (PRC), or phonetic competence (PC) to evaluate the state of the patient under different points of view [4,11,14,17]. On the other hand, having into account that PD is an illness characterized by the failure of the peripheral neuromotor activity, it could be possible that a description of the neuromotor activity, supported by features estimated from speech, could serve as a possible semantic descriptor of patient's conditions. A possible description of the neuromotor activity from speech can be given in terms of the dynamic changes experimented by the resonant frequencies of the vocal tract, which are known classically as formants. The aim of the present study is to evaluate if features derived from the dynamic behaviour of formants in sustained vowels are related with some of these indices, and to establish to which extent dynamic measures can be used in the multimodal study of PD speech production. Initially, dynamic measurements on formant activity, as the absolute kinematic velocity (AKV), which will be defined in the sequel, seeming to be highly correlated with the superficial myoelectric activity of certain facial muscles (see a related paper in this same issue [7], seem to be the adequate candidates for such study). The structure of the present paper is as follows: the biomechanical foundations explaining distortion of vowel articulation by means of formant dynamics is explained in Sect. 2. Section 3 is devoted to explain the Information Theory fundamentals behind the distance measurements used in distinguishing healthy and control utterances. Section 4 presents the data and experimental methods used in the study. The results derived from the present work are shown and discussed in Sect. 5. Conclusions are given in Sect. 6.

2 Biomechanical Model of Formant Dynamics

Speech production is planned and instantiated in the linguistic neuromotor cortex [2]. The activity of cortical neurons (primary) is encoded as neuromotor actions in the basal ganglia, where secondary neurons connected to the muscles of the pharynx, tongue, larynx, chest and diaphragm through sub-thalamic secondary pathways produce sequences of motor actions which activate the respiratory, phonatory and articulatory systems responsible of speech production. Regarding articulation, the principal structures to consider are the jaw, tongue and lip muscles. For the purposes of the present study, only the Jaw-Tongue Biomechanical System (JTBS), as depicted in Fig. 1 will be considered.

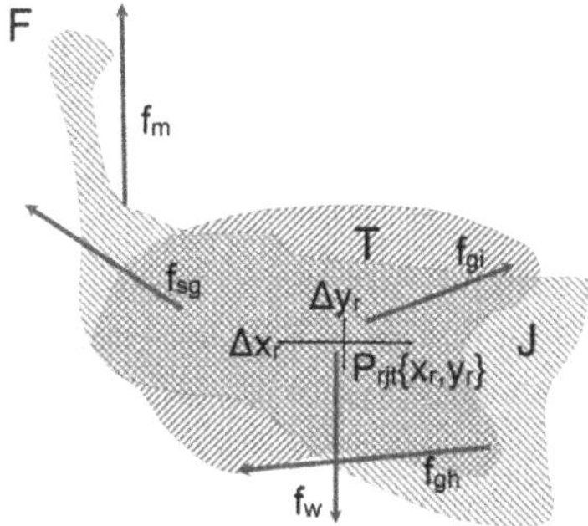

Fig. 1. Jaw-Tongue biomechanical system. The jaw (J: \-dash) is fixed against the skull bone at fulcrum (F) as in a third-class lever system. The tongue (T: /-dash) is supported by jaw and the hyoid bone. A reference point of the jaw-tongue system is defined at P_{rjt}, where forces acting on the system induce movements in the sagital plane (x: horizonal, y: vertical). See the text for a detailed explanation.

The dynamics of the JTBS [8,12] can be approximated by a third-order lever fixed at the skull in (F), allowing movements mainly in the sagital plane (x, y). For the purposes of articulation, it can be considered in a first approach as a joint lumped mass system subject to different forces actuating on the Jaw-Tongue Reference Point P_{rjt} (x_r, y_r). The main forces considered are the masseter uplift (f_m), the stylo-glossus pull-up-back (f_{sg}), the genio-hyoglossus pull-down-back (f_{gh}) and the gravity (f_w). Besides, due to the action of genio-glossus and glosso-intrinsic muscles (f_{gi}), the tongue blade and appex may be projected forwards. As a result, P_{rht} will experience changes in both directions $(\Delta x_r, \Delta y_r)$. To associate these movements with formants (resonances of the oro-naso-pharyngeal tract) is not a simple task, as the system acoustic properties are rather complex. Nevetheless, a first-approach relationship could be expressed for the first two formants F_1 and F_2 as:

$$\begin{bmatrix} F_1(t) \\ F_2(t) \end{bmatrix} = \begin{bmatrix} a_{11} & a_{12} \\ a_{21} & a_{22} \end{bmatrix} \begin{bmatrix} x_r(t) \\ y_r(t) \end{bmatrix}; \ \mathbf{A} = \begin{bmatrix} a_{11} & a_{12} \\ a_{21} & a_{22} \end{bmatrix} \tag{1}$$

where a_{ij} are the transformation functions associating P_{rjt} to formants, and t is the time. The functional $\mathbf{A}$ expressing the relationship is known to be non-linear, time-variant and multi-valued, i.e.: the relation between P_{rjt} and formant values do not follow a linear rule (superposition could not be applied), the relationship would be time-dependent, $\mathbf{A} = \mathbf{A}(\mathrm{t})$, and different articulation positions may produce identical formant pairs. Therefore, to facilitate a first-order approach to study the system, the following assumptions had to be taken into account:

- A linear functional $\mathbf{A}$ could be considered provided that movement amplitude ranges are not large (small-signal approach).
- Time invariance could be granted if only low-frequency movements are considered (i.e.: if dynamic variables are low-pass filtered during measurement and estimation) with respect to estimation windows (quasi-stationary approach).
- The one-to-many association of formant positions could be handled provided that the joint probability between formant pairs and articulatory positions is carefully modelled for the utterances of interest [3].
- Assuming that functional $\mathbf{A}$ is invertible, i.e., that an inverse matrix exists: $\mathbf{W} = \mathbf{A}^T$.
- The first formant and second formant drifts could be associated with the vertical and horizontal kinematics of P_{rjt} one to one (no cross-talk between drifts and kinematic cross-varables, or in other words, the main diagonal of $\mathbf{W}$ will be null).

Once these premises have been granted, it will be possible to associate the drifts of the first formants with a hypothetical absolute kinematic velocity AKV of the reference point P_{rjt} as:

$$|v_r(t)| = \sqrt{\left(w_{21}\frac{dF_1(t)}{dt}^2 + w_{12}\frac{dF_2(t)}{dt}^2\right)} \tag{2}$$

where w_{12} and w_{21} are the corresponding weights of $\mathbf{W}$ associating the first and second formants with the vertical and horizontal drifts of P_{rjt}, respectively.

3 Distance Based on Mutual Information

The AKV of the reference point is a very semantic correlate, as it can be associated to streams of neuromotor actions in precedent studies using phonation [1]. Its histogram-derived probability density function is especially relevant, as it has been shown to contain information related to phonated intervals and pauses, syllable nuclei, vowel onsets and trails, and other dynamic features present in speech articulation [6]. Among other applications, it may be used in estimating mutual information contents in sustained vowel stability production by healthy controls and PD patients. In Fig. 3 an examples of $p(v_r)$ from a PD patient contrasted against the same distribution form a healthy controls is shown. The control file is the one with highest divergence (worst case). The PD file is the one with the lowest one (best case). Having into account what has been said in

Sect. 2 about formant dynamics in relation to neuromotor activity, it may be seen that the PD patient distribution is spread over the span of low and high speeds, up to 40 cm.s^{-1}, with little activity above this value, whereas the distribution of the healthy control is limited to 20 cm.s^{-1}, confirming the differential behaviour of both types of speakers. Measuring how different both dynamic behaviours could be is based on the Mutual Information contents of these two pdf's, which is provided by Kullback-Leibler's Divergence [15], defined as:

$$D_{KLij}\left\{p_{Ti}\left(v_r\right), p_{Mj}\left(v_r\right)\right\} = -\int_{\zeta=0}^{\infty} p_{Ti}(\zeta) log\left[\frac{p_{Ti}(\zeta)}{p_{Mj}(\zeta)}\right] d\zeta \tag{3}$$

where $p_{Mj}(v_r)$ and $p_{Ti}(v_r)$ are the pdf's of the *j-th* model and *i-th* target subjects (control and patient) respectively, and $v_r \in \mathbf{R}_{\geq 0}$ as per (2). In what follows, a study on PD vowel formant stability will be conducted to compare the results from two population cohorts with their corresponding health controls by gender (Fig. 2).

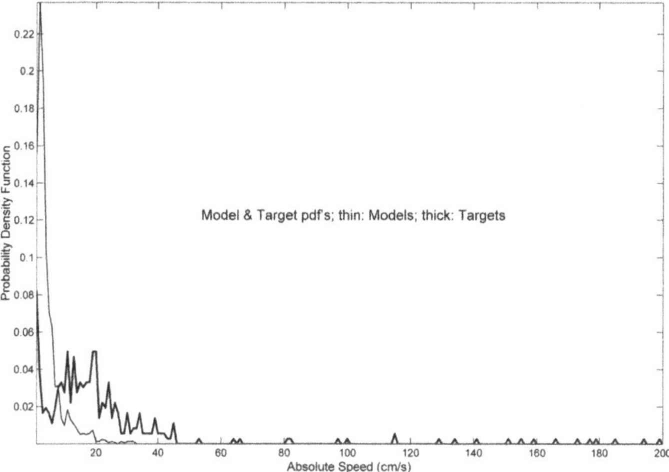

Fig. 2. Probability density functions of the absolute kinematic velocity v_J from a female healthy control (thin line) and a PD patient (thick lines). The AKV is given in $cm.s^{-1}$.

4 Materials and Methods

The present study has a marked exploratory nature, as to our knowledge, vowel formant kinematics has not been used before in PD detection, grading or monitoring. The intention of the study is to show the performance of this methodology in population grading studies of PD patients. A database of recordings from a set of 50 male and 50 female normative subjects free from organic or neurologic pathology selected by the ENT services of Hospital Gregorio Marañón of Madrid has been used to supply the normative models. Long sustained vowels (/a/) were recorded at a 44,000 Hz sampling frequency and 16 bits from each subject. Fragments of 500 ms long of /a/ recordings were analyzed the probability density of

AKV was obtained from each normative subject. The accumulated D_{KL} with respect to the whole set of fifty speakers per gender is defined as:

$$D_{KLj}\left(M_{f,m}\right) = \sum_{i \in M_{f,m}} D_{KLij};\ j \in M_{f,m} \tag{4}$$

where $M_{f,m}$ refers to the sets of normative male and female subjects mentioned before. A subset of eight subjects from each gender were selected on the condition of showing the lowest accumulated $D_{KLj}(M_{f,m})$ to become the normative model set. These model sets were used to estimate the accumulated D_{KL} of PD patients of both genders against their respective model set, as:

$$D_{KLj}\left(T_{f,m}, M_{f,m}\right) = \sum_{i \in T_{f,m}} D_{KLij};\ j \in M_{f,m} \tag{5}$$

The pathological database used is a part of the Parkinsonian Speech Database (PARCZ) recorded at St. Anne's University Hospital in the Czech Republic and consisted in four sets of 5 Czech vowels (/a, e, i, o, u/) pronounced in 4 different ways: short vowels uttered in a natural way; long vowels uttered in a natural way; long vowels uttered with maximum loudness, long vowels pronounced with minimum loudness, but not whispering. The subset selected corresponded to utterances by 54 male and 40 female PD patients, respectively. Recordings of long vowel /a/ at maximum loudness were selected and processed to obtain the first two formants during the utterance, and the respective pdf's of their AKV were estimated as referred before. The distributions for the female set of 40 PD patients plus 8 normative ones is depicted in Fig. 3 as an example.

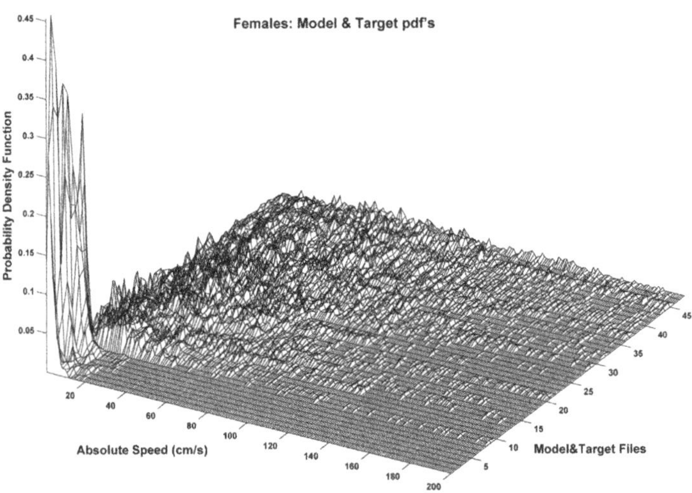

Fig. 3. Probability density functions of the AKV v_J from female healthy controls (files 1–8) and PD patients (files 9–48). The AKV is given in $cm.s^{-1}$.

It may be seen that healthy controls show activity mainly below 20 cm.s^{-1}, whereas PD patient distributions show activity spread over higher frequencies, ranging from 0–80 cm.s^{-1} for subjects 8–25, to 0–160 cm.s^{-1} and beyond for subjects 26–48.

5 Results and Discussion

An important issue in monitoring pathology is that of grading, as short-term timely monitoring of PD may be highly relevant for patient treatment and rehabilitation [16]. One of the intentions of the study was to relate D_{KL} (objective grading) with different clinic evaluation scales currently in use (subjective grading). When the D_{KL} as given in (3) for each patient in the female target set $\{T_f\}$ is estimated with respect to the corresponding model set $\{M_f\}$ a matrix of distances is produced, which is depicted in Fig. 4.

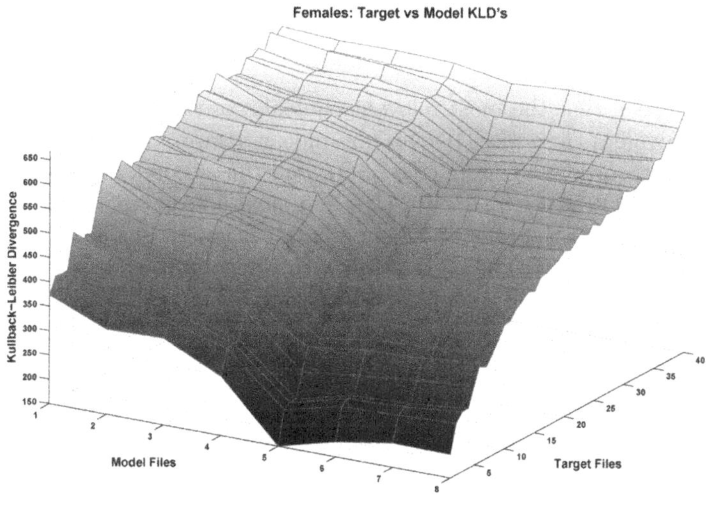

Fig. 4. KL Divergence between eight female healthy controls (models) and forty female PD patients (targets).

The model set has been ordered accordingly to its inner accumulated D_{KL} as given in (4), whereas the target set has been ordered accordingly to (5). Therefore, the first target file is supposed to be the less divergent with respect to the model set, whereas the 40th target file should be the most divergent. It may be seen that the less divergent pair is the 1st target file with respect to the 5th model file. In this way, an ordered set of files by divergence to the model set is produced. The question now is to find out to which extent D_{KL} is related to subjective evaluation scales. For such, Pearson's correlation has been evaluated between D_{KL} and each of the available scores in the set S = {Age, UPDRSIII, UPDRSIV, FOG, NMSS, RBDSQ, LED, FK, PRC, PC, OC, PRN}, OC being the average of FK, PRC and PC, whereas PRN is the z-scored correlate of PRC. Besides, a global composite score (CS) has been produced to represent the set of objective scores in a single value as:

$$CS = \sum_{i \in \Omega} \omega_{ci} S_i \tag{6}$$

where $\mathbf{\Omega} = \{\omega_{ci}\}$ is the set of weights associated with the set of neurological evaluation scores in **S**. The results of the comparisons for the female set are given in Table 1.

Table 1. Pearson's correlation coefficient with KLD (females)

Age	UIII	UIV	FOG	NMSS	RBDSQ	LED	FK	PRC	PC	OC	PRN	CS	p-value
−0.03	−0.06	−0.12	−0.09	−0.26	−0.25	−0.37	−0.02	0.07	0.11	0.07	0.22	−0.45	0.0065

It may be seen that the most relevant clinical scores related to D_{KL} are the levodopa equivalent dose (LED), the non-motor symptom score (NMSS), the sleep behavior disorder screening (RBDSQ), and the z-scored phono-respiratory competence (PRN). General UPDRS (III) is almost no relevant, UPDRS (IV) is testimonial, as well as the phonetic competence (although it is unclear how this last score was estimated). The correlation with the composite score is moderate and negative (the lower the score, the higher the divergence), with a significant p-value to reject null correlation. The same comparison for the male set is given in Table 2.

Table 2. Pearson's correlation coefficient with KLD (males)

Age	UIII	UIV	FOG	NMSS	RBDSQ	LED	FK	PRC	PC	OC	PRN	CS	p-value
−0.04	0.13	−0.12	−0.25	−0.21	−0.34	0.15	−0.16	−0.09	−0.25	−0.22	−0.27	−0.57	0.0000

In this case, as similar situation may be observed with slight variations. The sleep behavior disorder is the most relevant clinical score, followed by the normalized phono-respiratory competence, the freezing of gait, the phonetic competence, the average facial-respiratory-phonetic competence, and the non-motor symptom score. Again, the correlation to both UPDRS scales is testimonial. The correlation to the composite score is a bit larger for the male subset than for the female one, and also negative, with a significant p-value to reject null correlation. The score plots of the D_{KL} and CS for each set are given in Fig. 5.

The first observation from the results presented is that the male set presents better correlation between D_{KL} and CS that the female one. This is not an uncommon situation in this kind of studies, as generally models and analysis

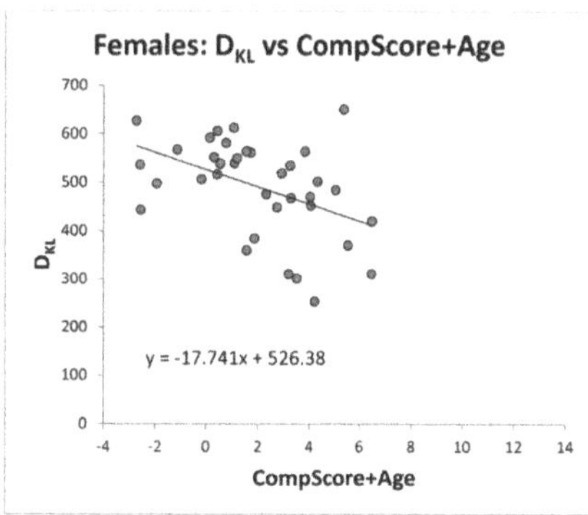

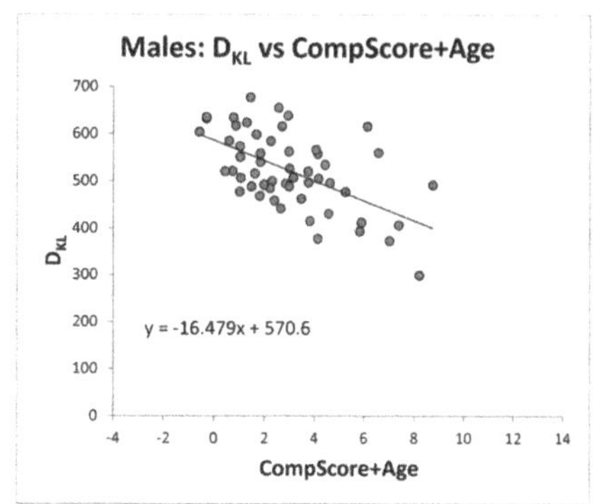

Fig. 5. Scatter plots of D_{KL} vs CS. Left: female subset. Right: male subset. Linear regression lines have been drawn and formulated for comparison purposes.

protocols were initially modelled on a male population, and only latter on, were they adapted to a female population, This fact may result in an underlying gender skew. Besides, the larger number of male cases available in the version of the PARZ database currently used could also have an influence in the results. Another factor to consider would be the wider spread of formant frequencies in female voice, which would introduce more dispersion in the results. Another factor of dispersion to be taken into account is the variability and low reliability of subjective scoring scales. No matter how well designed they may be or well-trained raters are involved, a human subjective factor is implicit and difficult to be removed. This fact stresses the need of developing objective scoring methods even more. But in general, it may be concluded that a certain degree of correlation between formant dynamics and a wide set of motor and non-motor scoring scales exist in PD, and could be conveniently exploited if fused with other articulation static features as VSA or FCR.

6 Conclusions

The main conclusion from the study is that formant kinematics may be a good candidate for PD stage detection, which has to be further exploited. Some other conclusions from the present study are the following:

- Formant dynamics can be transformed to speech kinematics in a robust way.
- Mutual-information-based distance measures may be defined on this basis.
- Patient sets may be graded and ordered using AKV probability densities, for easy database building. This is especially so in building normative sets.
- Structured and ordered data sets can be used in comparative studies.
- PD patients have to be graded accordingly to different motor and non-motor behavioural features.
- A specific speech-oriented scoring scale is a real need in PD studies.
- Composite scores should take these features into account.

- Databases oriented to the validation of speech-based methodologies should include a wide set of motor and non-motor evaluations for a richer comprehension of neuromotor pathologies under speech production bases.

As a final reflection, the accurate scoring of PD symptoms is a very urging need, both for diagnose as well as for monitoring PD patient stage and progression in a daily basis. Speech is a very convenient reference, as it is ubiquitous, easy to record, and feasible for feature estimation using not very sophisticated or expensive resources. The problem to validate this methodology is the lack of good rating scales adapted to speech. Definitively UPDRS, no matter how well has been fitted using brute force methods, is not a good candidate for these studies, as it lacks important speech-related motor and non-motor items, totally different from those involved in other motor tasks. In this sense, the biomechanics of limbs, in which many of the UPDRS items are based, is completely different from those of phonation and articulation systems, and this fact will induce false estimations and apparent correlates not funded on solid grounds. Therefore, new methods and correlates have to be sought based on phenomena which are truly related to speech and phonation. The current study is to be extended to larger databases with a stronger insight in speech technologies.

Acknowledgements. This work is being funded by grants TEC2012-38630-C04-01, TEC2012-38630-C04-04 and TEC2016-77791-C4-4-R from the Ministry of Economic Affairs and Competitiveness of Spain, and by grants 16-30805A, SIX (CZ.1.05/2.1.00/03.0072), and LO1401 from the Czech Republic Government.

References

1. Carmona-Duarte, C., Plamondon, R., Gómez-Vilda, P., Ferrer, M.A., Alonso, J.B., Londral, A.R.M.: Application of the lognormal model to the vocal tract movement to detect neurological diseases in voice. In: Chen, Y.-W., Tanaka, S., Howlett, R.J., Jain, L.C. (eds.) Innovation in Medicine and Healthcare 2016. SIST, vol. 60, pp. 25–35. Springer, Cham (2016). doi:10.1007/978-3-319-39687-3_3
2. Démonet, J.F., Thierry, G., Cardebat, D.: Renewal of the neurophysiology of language: functional neuroimaging. Physiol. Rev. **85**(1), 49–95 (2005)
3. Dromey, C., Jang, G.O., Hollis, K.: Assessing correlations between lingual movements and formants. Speech Commun. **55**(2), 315–328 (2013)
4. Fénelon, G., Mahieux, F., Huon, R., Ziégler, M.: Hallucinations in Parkinson's disease: prevalence, phenomenology and risk factors. Brain **123**, 733–745 (2000)
5. Goetz, C.G., Fahn, S., Martinez-Martin, P., Poewe, W., Sampaio, C., Stebbins, G.T., Stern, M.B., Tilley, B.C., Dodel, R., Dubois, B., et al.: Movement disorder society-sponsored revision of the unified Parkinson's disease rating scale (MDS-UPDRS): process, format, and clinimetric testing plan. Mov. Disord. **22**(1), 41–47 (2007)
6. Gómez-Vilda, P., López de Ipiña, M.K., Rodellar-Biarge, V., Palacios-Alonso, D., Ecay-Torres, M.: Articulation characterization in AD speech production. In: Ibáñez, J., González-Vargas, J., Azorín, J., Akay, M., Pons, J. (eds.) Converging Clinical and Engineering Research on Neurorehabilitation II. Biosystems & Biorobotics, vol. 15, pp. 861–866. Springer, Cham (2016). doi:10.1007/978-3-319-46669-9_140

7. Gómez-Vilda, P., Palacios-Alonso, D., Gómez-Rodellar, A., Ferrández-Vicente, J., Álvarez-Marquina, A., Martínez-Olalla, R., Nieto-Lluis, V.: Relating facial myoelectric activity to speech formants. In: Ferrández Vicente, J.M., et al. (eds.) IWINAC 2017, Part II. LNCS, vol. 10338, pp. 520–530. Springer, Cham (2017)
8. Hannam, A.G., Stavness, I., Lloyd, J.E., Fels, S.: A dynamic model of jaw and hyoid biomechanics during chewing. J. Biomech. **41**(5), 1069–1076 (2008)
9. Hoehn, M.M., Yahr, M.D., et al.: Parkinsonism: onset, progression, and mortality. Neurology **50**(2), 318–318 (1998)
10. Mekyska, J., Janousova, E., Gomez-Vilda, P., Smekal, Z., Rektorova, I., Eliasova, I., Kostalova, M., Mrackova, M., Alonso-Hernandez, J.B., Faundez-Zanuy, M., et al.: Robust and complex approach of pathological speech signal analysis. Neurocomputing **167**, 94–111 (2015)
11. Pérez-Lloret, S., Negre-Pages, L., Damier, P., Delval, A., Derkinderen, P., Destée, A., Meissner, W.G., Schelosky, L., Tison, F., Rascol, O.: Prevalence, determinants, and effect on quality of life of freezing of gait in Parkinson disease. JAMA Neurol. **71**(7), 884–890 (2014)
12. Sanguineti, V., Laboissiere, R., Payan, Y.: A control model of human tongue movements in speech. Biol. Cybern. **77**(1), 11–22 (1997)
13. Sapir, S., Ramig, L.O., Spielman, J.L., Fox, C.: Formant centralization ratio: a proposal for a new acoustic measure of dysarthric speech. J. Speech Lang. Hear. Res. **53**(1), 114–125 (2010)
14. Stiasny-Kolster, K., Sixel-Döring, F., Trenkwalder, C., Heinzel-Gutenbrunner, M., Seppi, K., Poewe, W., Högl, B., Frauscher, B.: Diagnostic value of the rem sleep behavior disorder screening questionnaire in Parkinson's disease. Sleep Med. **16**(1), 186–189 (2015)
15. Thomas, J.A., Cover, T.M.: Elements of Information Theory. Wiley, Hoboken (2006)
16. Tsanas, A., Little, M.A., McSharry, P.E., Spielman, J., Ramig, L.O.: Novel speech signal processing algorithms for high-accuracy classification of Parkinson's disease. IEEE Trans. Biomed. Eng. **59**(5), 1264–1271 (2012)
17. Ziemssen, T., Reichmann, H.: Non-motor dysfunction in Parkinson's disease. Parkinsonism Relat. Disord. **13**(6), 323–332 (2007)

Koniocortex-Like Network Unsupervised Learning Surpasses Supervised Results on WBCD Breast Cancer Database

J. Fombellida[1(✉)], F.J. Ropero-Peláez[2], and D. Andina[1]

[1] Group for Automation in Signals and Communications, Universidad Politécnica de Madrid, 28040 Madrid, Spain
jfv@alumnos.upm.es, d.andina@upm.es

[2] Center of Mathematics, Computation and Cognition, Universidade Federal do ABC, Santo André, Brazil
francisco.pelaez@ufabc.edu.br

Abstract. Koniocortex-Like Network is a novel category of Bio-Inspired Neural Networks whose architecture and properties are inspired in the biological koniocortex, the first layer of the cortex that receives information from the thalamus. In the Koniocortex-Like Network competition and pattern classification emerges naturally due to the interplay of inhibitory interneurons, metaplasticity and intrinsic plasticity. Recently proposed, it has shown a big potential for complex tasks with unsupervised learning. Now for the first time, its competitive results are proved in a relevant standard real application that is the objective of state-of-the-art research: the diagnosis of breast cancer data from the Wisconsin Breast Cancer Database.

Keywords: Metaplasticity · Koniocortex · Plasticity · KLN · WBCD · Feature extraction · Competition

1 Introduction

The koniocortex is a common denomination for all regions of the cerebral cortex containing a granular layer (layer IV). The granular (grainy) texture of this layer is due the abundance of spiny stellate neurons that directly receive neural projections from the thalamus. The thalamus, at the center of the brain, is the main relay station from the senses to the cortex. The Koniocortex-like networks (KLN) are neural models that possess at least two layers: the first layer containing neurons that are similar to the thalamo-cortical neurons of the thalamus, and the second layer whose neurons resemble the spiny and the inhibitory interneurons of the fourth layer of the koniocortex. As demonstrated with living brain tissues in which only the fourth layer of the cortex was active (remaining layers were reset through freezing [8]), these two layers constitute a network in which competition and auto-organization are found. For example, the biological

J.M. Ferrández Vicente et al. (Eds.): IWINAC 2017, Part II, LNCS 10338, pp. 32–41, 2017.
DOI: 10.1007/978-3-319-59773-7_4

koniocortex network exhibits competition [13] because only a very small number of spiny stellate neurons are active in the presence of sensory stimuli. This behavior resembles the Winner-Take-All (WTA) process of competitive artificial networks. In WTA, the most active neuron remains active while the other neurons are set to zero. The difference between conventional competitive networks and the biologically inspired KLN is that, while conventional competitive neurons find the most active neuro through calculation, in the case of the KLNs, the winning neuron emerges naturally from the interaction between the neurons. At the same time, non-winning neurons become silent due to the dynamics of the neurons in the network, not because they are algorithmically reset. Previous seminal works also studied the neural dynamics leading to emergent competition in terms of the different properties potentially involved in the process, like the strength and range of lateral inhibition [9–11], the value of the firing threshold [10,18] and the steepness of the activation function [18].

Regarding the KLN, the main properties involved in competitive learning are synaptic metaplasticity and intrinsic plasticity. Intrinsic plasticity adjusts the global excitability of the neuron so that highly excited neurons will be less excitable in the future, and vice versa. In this paper, we continue the research started in previous works [3,4,14–17]. Here we use KLN networks to classify the patterns in the Wisconsin Breast Cancer Database (WBCD) [19]. For assessing the classification accuracy of this algorithm, we used the most common performance measures: specifity, sensitivity and accuracy. The results obtained were validated using the 10-fold cross-validation method. The paper is organized as follows. Section 2 presents a detailed description of the database and the algorithms. In Sect. 3 the experimental results obtained are shown. A brief discussion of these results is showed in Sect. 4 and, finally, Sect. 5 summarizes the main conclusions.

2 Materials and Methods

2.1 WBCD Dataset

Breast cancer is a malignant tumor that develops from breast cells. Although research has identified some of the risk factors that increase a woman's chance of developing breast cancer, the inherent cause of most breast cancers remains unknown.

The correct pattern classification of breast cancer is an important worldwide medical problem. Cancer is one of the major causes of mortality around the world and research into cancer diagnosis and treatment has become an important issue for the scientific community. If the cancerous cells are detected before they spread to other organs, the survival rate is greater than 97%. For this reason, the use of classifier systems in medical diagnosis is increasing. Artificial intelligence classification techniques can enhance current research.

This study analyzed the Wisconsin Breast Cancer Database (WBCD). This data base has been used several times in the literature and many high impact studies has used these inputs for classification including systems based in Artificial Neural Networks (ANNs), Support Vector Machines (SVMs) and Neuro-Fuzzy techniques, among others. This situation makes this database very useful in order to compare the performances of the results obtained with the state of the art.

2.2 Data Preparation

The WBCD contains 699 patterns, each of this pattern is composed by 9 numerical attributes that corresponds to different physical characteristics that can be considered as markers of the possible presence of cancer in the sample. Numerically the attributes have been evaluated manually by an expert with values between 1 and 10, being value 1 the closest to an indicator of a benign nature of the sample and value 10 the closest to an indicator of a malicious nature of the sample. The database contains a field that indicates the final diagnosis of the nature of the sample.

In the original data base there are 16 samples whose attributes are not completely filled. In order to work with a homogeneous set of patterns with all the numerical attributes filled, incomplete elements have been eliminated from the experiment. Finally we will use 683 patterns that are divided in 444 benign samples (65%) and 239 malicious samples (35%).

It has empirically been proved that the classifiers based on neural networks produce better results if the training sets are equilibrated presenting the same number of patterns belonging to each one of the possible classes. In order to achieve this situation in the creation of the sets used to train and to evaluate the system some malicious patterns will be repeated instead of eliminating some benign patterns to get these equilibrated sets. It has been considered better to duplicate a small number of malicious elements as inputs for the networks instead of losing the potential information present in some of the benign elements.

Depending on the concrete inputs used for training and for performance evaluation it is possible to have a numerical influence on the results. To obtain results statistically independent of the distribution of the patterns a *10 fold cross validation* evaluation method has been considered. Using this method the possible dependence of the results with the distribution of the samples in the training or performance evaluation sets is eliminated: all the samples are used to train the networks and all the samples are used to evaluate the performance of the results in different executions of the experiment for the same initial neural networks, mean values are calculated to establish the final performance results.

For this experiment we have created ten data sets from the WBCD with the following distribution of patterns:

- G1: 90 total patterns: 45 benign and 45 malign
- G2: 90 total patterns: 45 benign and 45 malign
- G3: 90 total patterns: 45 benign and 45 malign
- G4: 88 total patterns: 44 benign and 44 malign
- G5: 88 total patterns: 44 benign and 44 malign

- G6: 88 total patterns: 44 benign and 44 malign
- G7: 88 total patterns: 44 benign and 44 malign
- G8: 88 total patterns: 44 benign and 44 malign
- G9: 88 total patterns: 44 benign and 44 malign
- G10: 90 total patterns: 45 benign and 45 malign

Using these 10 initial sets we will create 10 different data groups. In each one of the training sets that will be used as inputs to the networks for training the system and evaluating the evolution of the error will consist in 9 of the previous 10 groups. The final evaluation that calculates the performance of the performance of the network will use the other initial set. The 10 folders will be created with the variation of the initial set that is used for evaluation and not for training.

The networks are trained from the same initial aleatory weights presenting the data corresponding to each of the 10 final sets created from the initial ones. Finally the mean values of the results will be calculated to eliminate the possible statistical influence in the results due to the concrete fixed selection of some patterns to train the system and the fixed selection of other patterns to evaluate the results.

2.3 Koniocortex-Like Network Model

The KLN network is based in a mathematical model formed by rate code neurons whose outputs O_j are limited between the values 0 and 1. These values represent the probability of occurrence of an action potential. Considering in one side the normalized input pattern $\overrightarrow{i} = \overrightarrow{I} / || \overrightarrow{I} ||$ (lower case notation meaning vector normalization) yields the net-input of neuron j. Normalization is performed with the l_1-norm in which:

$$|| \overrightarrow{I} || = \sum_{i=1}^{n} |I_i| \quad (1)$$

And in the other side the neuron's j weights as the components of a vector prototype $\overrightarrow{T^j}$, so that $\overrightarrow{T^j}=\overrightarrow{W^j}= [W_{j1}, W_{j2}, ..., W_{jn}]$. The inner product of weights and the pattern to be classified, the net-input of neuron j is calculated as $net_j = || \overrightarrow{W^j} \cdot \overrightarrow{i} || = || \overrightarrow{T^j} \cdot \overrightarrow{i} || = || \overrightarrow{T^j_{\overrightarrow{I}}} ||$, the modulus of the projection of prototype $\overrightarrow{T^j}$ over input pattern $\overrightarrow{I}$.

During the training the weights are modified using the incremental version of the presynaptic rule:

$$\triangle \omega = \xi I(O - \omega) \quad (2)$$

where O and I are the postsynaptic and presynaptic action potential probabilities, respectively, and ξ, a learning factor.

The presynaptic rule is based in the empirical plasticity curve [5] that shows a relation between postsynaptic voltage and the modification of the synaptic weight. This rule is also influenced by metaplasticity [1,2], a homeostatic property which elongates the plasticity curves rightwards for higher initial synaptic weights.

For relating the net-input of neuron O^j to its firing probability, O_j a conventional sigmoidal activation function was used.

$$O_j = \frac{1}{1 + e^{-k(net_j + 0.5 - 2s^j)}} \tag{3}$$

where k is a curve-compressing factor and s^j the horizontal shift of the activation function ranging from zero to one, $0 < s^j < 1$. In our experiment the adjustment of the shifting is completely shifted leftwards with $s^j = 0$ and when it is completely shifted rightwards with $s^j = 1$.

Real neuron exhibits intrinsic plasticity [6,7] as shown in Fig. 1, the homeostatic property that makes very active neurons to be moderated and inactive neurons to increment its firing rate. According to this property [7], the activation function gradually shifts leftwards or rightwards regulating the activation of scarcely or highly activated neurons, respectively.

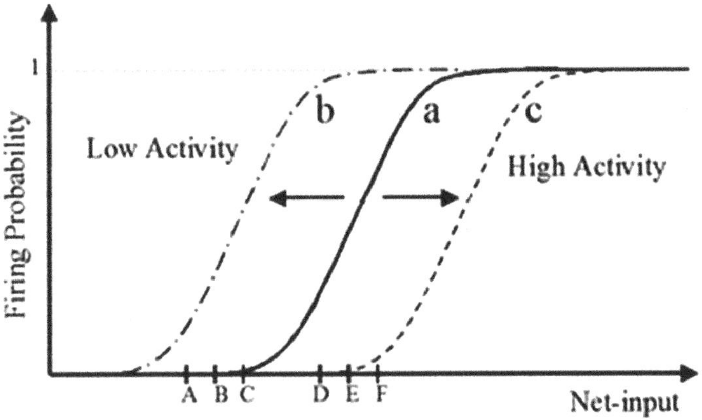

Fig. 1. Intrinsic plasticity allows the neurons' activation function to shift horizontally so that the activation function "follows" the average net-input of the neuron. (a) Initial position of the sigmoidal activation function. (b) In the case of a low regime of net-input values (as in A, B and C), intrinsic plasticity shifts the sigmoid leftwards. (c) In the case of a high regime of net-input values (as in D, E and F), intrinsic plasticity shifts the sigmoid rightwards increasing the sensitivity of the neuron.

In the experiment, parameter s^j is mathematically incorporated to the simulations in the neuron's activation function $f()$ relating the net-input of the neuron to its spiking probability O_j:

$$O^j = f(|| \overrightarrow{T^j_{\vec{I}}} ||, s^j) \tag{4}$$

The following equation calculates the shift of the activation function, s at time t in terms of the shift and output probability of the neuron at time $t-1$.

$$s_t^j = \frac{\upsilon.O_{t-1} + s_{t-1}^j}{\upsilon + 1} \tag{5}$$

where υ is the shifting velocity parameter. It is a small arbitrary factor for adjusting the shifting rate of the activation function. Notice that when both the shift and the output at time $t-1$ are equal, the shift at time t continues having the same value of the shift at time $t-1$.

Figure 2 is the complete version of the KLN model used in the experiment. In the KLN, "B" labeled neurons are inhibitory neurons endowed with intrinsic plasticity. "S" labeled neurons are the main neurons engaged in competition and also present intrinsic plasticity. Since each S contacts a single B, intrinsic plasticity is concomitantly regulated in both types of neurons. So if S is highly activated it is the same for associated B. This implies that S reduces its excitability and B, the inhibitory field surrounding S, affecting the final activated neuron in future classification performances. TC neurons can use intrinsic plasticity to remove the mean of a series of input values. When removing the average, patterns become more uncorrelated and easier to classify.

Figure 2 shows that each S neuron has a recurrent connection on itself that was initially intended for allowing a sustained activation over time in simple rate-code neurons. Recurrent connections are extremely rare in real neurons. Despite of this, this kind of recurrent connection was indeed present in the koniocortex.

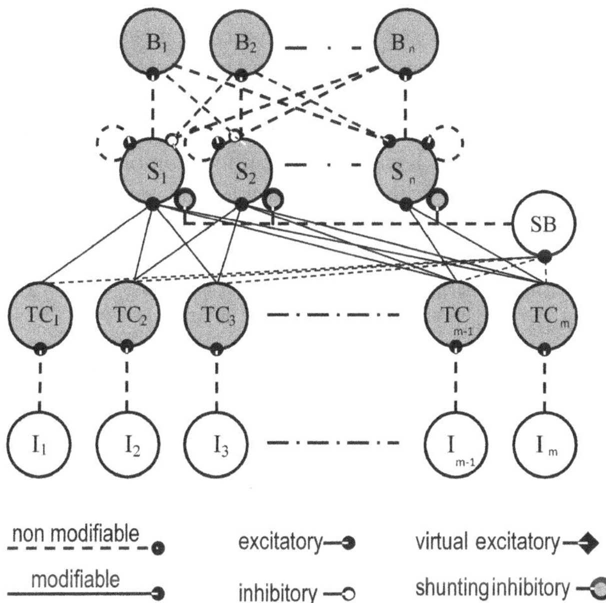

Fig. 2. Architecture of KLN applied to the classification of WBCD.

Finally SB neuron is incorporated to the model to be used in pattern normalization. Similarly to real shunting/dividing inter-neurons, SB neurons perform the arithmetical summation of its inputs (TC outputs), dividing the activation of its target neurons (the Sneurons) by this quantity.

3 Results

3.1 Network Characteristics

In this section we present the results obtained in this research. All the models used in this study were trained and tested with the same data and validated using 10-fold cross-validation.

This KLN has 9 neurons in its input layer corresponding to the number of elements that form each input pattern, 9 neurons in its TC layer (similar number as input layer to be coherent with the KLN structure), 2 neurons in the S layer as two classes are considered in the experiment, and 2 neurons in the upper B layer. Once the input is fed to the network, its activation is "propagated" until all layers are activated. At the end of the process one of the neurons presents a higher output than the other one, so it is possible to classify the patterns taking into account which output is activated and which one is inhibited. The WTA process occurs naturally as an emergent consequence of the individual computation of each neuron without the need of externally monitoring the network.

It is very important to remark that this first prototype of the network applied to the WBCD classification has demonstrated to be extremely sensitive to the concrete values of the training mathematical parameters. Even minimal deviations from the values used in this experiment can cause a non convergence of the learning algorithm, so we cannot consider this prototype as a robust implementation of the mathematical theory. In this case the values obtained for the parameters have been obtained using a Montecarlo approach with many simulations until adequate results have been obtained demonstrating that for very concrete values the network is able to learn without external supervision. The final values used in this simulation are υ set to 0.025 and ξ to 0.001, the initial sigmoid shift was 0.5, initial weights from TC to S neurons were negligible and random, and non-modifiable weights were set to $W_{S_S} = 0.85$, $W_{S_B} = 0.98$, $W_{I_{TC}} = 1.0$ and $W_{B_S} = 0.5$.

3.2 Evaluation Method

In each one of the experiments 50 networks have been trained. Using the 10 fold cross validation method the results are not dependent of the concrete patterns used for training and for performance evaluation. Using 50 different initial networks and calculating mean values we assure that the results are independent of the initial random values in the creation of the networks. From the results obtained for the same network with each one of the folders the mean confusion matrix is obtained for each network. Once we have these 50 mean values an additional calculation is made and the final mean value is obtained as the final result of the experiment.

The following hypothesis are defined and used to define the confusion matrix:

- $H\,(1/1)$: The pattern is malicious and has been classified as malicious.
- $H\,(1/0)$: The pattern is benign and has been classified as malicious.
- $H\,(0/1)$: The pattern is malicious and has been classified as benign.
- $H\,(0/0)$: The pattern is benign and has been classified as benign (Table 1).

Table 1. Confussion matrix model

True positive $H\,(1/1)$	False positive $H\,(1/0)$
False negative $H\,(0/1)$	True negative $H\,(0/0)$

The most important figure in these experiments in the sensitivity (considered as true positive percentage), these is due to the intrinsic nature of the experiment (it is much more important to detect all the malicious patterns than classifying as malicious a benign input).

3.3 Classification Results

We have performed different experiments with different number of epochs in each experiment (considering one epoch like presenting the full set of input patterns once to the network). The output of the network is integrated by two neurons, depending on which one presents the higher level at the output we have considered that one of the classes (benign or malign sample) is selected by the network. Table 2 presents the results obtained:

Table 2. Sensitivity and accuracy evolution depending on the number of epochs

Epochs	Sensitivity%	Accuracy%
1	61.92%	58.33%
5	73.76%	61.36%
10	76.04%	64.77%
50	85.79%	77.97%
100	89.97%	83.69%
250	96.70%	92.51%
500	98.72%	95.57%
1000	99.94%	96.91%

The best results obtained correspond to 1000 epochs where almost all the malign patterns are correctly recognized. Confusion matrix for this experiment is shown in Table 3.

Table 3. Confusion matrix 1000 epochs

99.94%	6.12%
0.06%	93.88%

4 Discussion

- The first point to be considered is the concrete application of the network as a cancer pattern classifier. In this concrete application the most important figure is sensitivity because we want to detect all the malign patterns above all. The objective of the network as a classifier is to reduce to the minimal the false negative results although this can cause a worsening in the figure corresponding to false positive classifications.
- The best sensitivity is obtained with the higher number of epochs in the training. Almost all the patters corresponding the malign inputs are correctly classified. On the contrary several benign patterns are misclassified, in this particular application is not considered a problem as the sensitivity and not accuracy is the driver figure.
- The evolution of the sensitivity shows that even one epoch is sufficient to start learning, the results improve highly when repeating the inputs.
- Comparing the KLN unsupervised results, they improve the results of advanced supervised methods as those presented in [12], so KLN performs a Deeper Learning of the information in the Data Set, without the need of a Deep Network.

5 Conclusions

In this paper we have applied the theoretical basis of the Koniocortex-Like Network to a real complex Data Set as is the classification of real breast cancer input patterns. The simulations show that the unsupervised learning that emerges from individual neurons properties surpasses results even of several advanced state-of-the-art supervised learning algorithms. Nevertheless KLN is still a very novel model and the results presented are just from a non optimized prototype, this bio-inspired model seems to be able to compete in deeper learning and better performance than many state-of-the-art Artificial Neural Network models.

References

1. Abraham, W.C., Bear, M.F.: Metaplasticity: the plasticity of synaptic plasticity. Trends Neurosci. **19**, 126–130 (1996)
2. Abraham, W.C., Tate, W.P.: Metaplasticity: a new vista across the field of synaptic plasticity. Prog. Neurobiol. **52**, 303–323 (1997)
3. Andina, D., Alvarez-Vellisco, A., Jevtic, A., Fombellida, J.: Artificial metaplasticity can improve artificial neural network learning. Intell. Autom. Soft Comput. Spec. Issue Sig. Process. Soft Comput. **15**(4), 681–694 (2009)

4. Andina, D., Ropero-Pelaez, J.: On the biological plausibility of artificial metaplasticity learning algorithm. Neurocomputing (2012). http://dx.doi.org/10.1016/j.neucom.2012.09.028
5. Artola, A., Brocher, S., Singer, W.: Different voltage-dependent threshold for inducing long-term depression and long-term potentiation in slices of rat visual córtex. Nature **347**, 69–72 (1990)
6. Desai, N.S.: Homeostatic plasticity in the CNS: synaptic and intrinsic forms. J. Physiol. **97**(4–6), 391–402 (2003)
7. Desai, N.S., Rutherford, L.C., Turrigiano, G.G.: Plasticity in the intrinsic excitability of cortical pyramidal neurons. Nat. Neurosci. **2**, 515–520 (1999)
8. Ferster, D., Chung, S., Wheat, H.: Orientation selectivity of thalamic input to simple cells of cat visual cortex. Nature **380**(6571), 249–252 (1996)
9. Fukai, T., Tanaka, S.: A simple neural network exhibiting selective activation of neuronal ensembles: from winner-take-all to winners-share-all. Neural Comput. **9**(1), 77–97 (1997)
10. Kaski, S., Kohonen, T.: Winner-take-all networks for physiological models of competitive learning. Neural Netw. **7**(6/7), 973–984 (1994)
11. Mao, Z.H., Massaquoi, S.G.: Dynamics of Winner-Take-All competition in recurrent neural networks with lateral inhibition. IEEE Trans. Neural Netw. **18**, 55–69 (2007)
12. Marcano-Cedeño, A., Quintanilla-Dominguez, J., Andina, D.: Breast cancer classification applying artificial metaplasticity algorithm. Neurocomputing **74**(8), 1243–1250 (2011)
13. Miller, K.D.: Synaptic economics: competition and cooperation in synaptic plasticity. Neuron **17**, 371–374 (1996)
14. Quintanilla-Dominguez, J., Cortina-Januchs, M.G., Ojeda-Magaa, B., Jevtic, A., Vega-Corona, A., Andina, D.: Microcalcification detection applying artificial neural networks and mathematical morphology in digital mammograms. In: World Automation Congress (WAC) (2010)
15. Ropero-Peláez, F.J., Andina, D.: Do biological synapses perform probabilistic computations? Neurocomputing (2012). http://dx.doi.org/10.1016/j.neucom.2012.08.042
16. Ropero-Peláez, F.J., Andina, D.: The Koniocortex-like network: a new biologically plausible unsupervised neural network. In: Ferrández Vicente, J.M., Álvarez-Sánchez, J.R., de la Paz López, F., Toledo-Moreo, F.J., Adeli, H. (eds.) IWINAC 2015. LNCS, vol. 9107, pp. 163–174. Springer, Cham (2015). doi:10.1007/978-3-319-18914-7_17
17. Ropero-Peláez, F.J., Aguiar-Furucho, M.A., Andina, D.: Intrinsic plasticity for natural competition in Koniocortex-like neural networks. Int. J. Neural Syst. **26**(5), 1650040 (2016). http://www.worldscientific.com/doi/abs/10.1142/S0129065716500404
18. Yang, J.F., Chen, C.M.: Winner-Take-All neural network using the highest threshold. IEEE Trans. Neural Netw. **11**, 194–199 (2000)
19. http://archive.ics.uci.edu/ml/datasets.html

Ongoing Work on Deep Learning for Lung Cancer Prediction

Oier Echaniz and Manuel Graña(✉)

Grupo de Inteligencia Computacional (GIC),
Universidad Del País Vasco (UPV/EHU), San Sebastián, Spain
manuel.grana@ehu.es

Abstract. Deep learning is one of the breakthrough technologies that have emergent in the last few years. It has been applied to a wide variety of problems, most of them related with image processing. It is also being considered for 3D data in medical image processing. This paper is a report of ongoing work about the development of deep learning architectures for lung cancer prediction. Data has been extracted from an ongoing Kaggel challenge, involving multi-center CTA data. First we have normalized in intensity the images. Then we have devised an auto encoder architecture with convolutional layers to obtain a compressed representation of the lung images. These representations are fed as features to a random forest classifier.

1 Introduction

In the United States, lung cancer strikes 225,000 people every year, and accounts for $12 billion in health care costs. Early detection is critical to give patients the best chance at recovery and survival. Realization of this urgent need has sparkled initiatives of the american institutions directed to improve the availability of data to researchers in order to advance on the detection and prediction issues, the so called Cancer Moonshot initiative[1].

As part of the activities under this initiative, a large dataset of CTA chest images from many hospitals and health institutions has been released and a computational challenge has been proposed in the Kaggle Data Science Bowl convening the data science and medical communities to develop lung cancer detection algorithms. The dataset offers thousands of high-resolution lung scans provided by the National Cancer Institute. The goal is set to develop algorithms that accurately determine when lesions in the lungs are cancerous. The aim is to reduce the false positive rate, which is very high for the current detection technology. Therefore, patients may get earlier access to life-saving interventions, while radiologists have more time to improve attention to their patients.

Deep learning is everywhere. Several articles [4] and works had already probe that deep learning is working really well in image based problems. In the last years, Convolutional Neural Networks (CNNs) [2,3] have achieved excellent

[1] https://www.cancer.gov/research/key-initiatives/moonshot-cancer-initiative.

J.M. Ferrández Vicente et al. (Eds.): IWINAC 2017, Part II, LNCS 10338, pp. 42–48, 2017.
DOI: 10.1007/978-3-319-59773-7_5

performance in many computer vision tasks. Several advances have solved convergence issues, and the advent of easy to exploit powerful Graphics Processing Units (GPUs) has speed up the training times by several orders of magnitude [1]. A CNN is a shared-weight neural network: all the neurons in a hidden layer share the same weights and bias. In fact, each layer implements a linear convolution filter whose kernel is learnt by gradient descent. Therefore, the output of the successive layers is a series of filtered/subsampled images which are interpreted as progressively higher level abstract features. Most CNN are applied to 2D signals, i.e. images, however in the medical image domain they are increasingly applied to 3D signals, i.e. volumetric imaging information. Autoencoders [6] are deep architectures that can be trained unsupervisedly, because their training error is the reconstruction error of the input after being processed by the entire auto encoder. The typical architecture has a middle hidden layer of small dimension, which is supposed to provide the features for further processing. Autoencoders have been used for soft organ segmentation [5].

The main objective of this work was to develop and compare existing deep learning methods capable of determining whether or not the patient will be diagnosed with lung cancer within one year of the date the scan was taken. When making this predictions we need to take in account that giving a wrong diagnosis is never equal, diagnosis as a non cancer patient into a cancer patient has less live cost than predicting a cancer patient to a non cancer patient, since no having treatment because of a wrong diagnosis will lead to death easily. Prediction method has to be accurate, reproducible and, above all, comparable to pathologists diagnosis.

2 Materials and Methods

Data. The dataset comes from a kaggle competition[2]. The dataset, provides over a thousand low-dose CT images from high-risk patients in DICOM format, coming from several institutions across the states. Each DICOM image sequence contains a series with multiple axial slices of the chest cavity which put together provide a 3D image of the chest of the patient. The number of 2D slices may vary between patients due to differences in the machines taking the scan. The ground truth labels (i.e. developing cancer or not) were confirmed by pathology diagnosis and were provided in the challenge dataset.

Server. We are using for this work a server with 2 connected nvidia 1080 GPU cards. The deep architectures have been implemented in Python using Keras[3] with Tensorflow as backend. For the explained methods the time considered for preprocessing is for about 10 h and to train the network for less than a day.

[2] https://www.kaggle.com/c/data-science-bowl-2017.
[3] https://keras.io.

Data Preprocessing. The image data were provided in Digital Imaging and Communication in Medicine (DICOM) format. For easier processing, we transform the images to a unique HDF file using Python scientific libraries. The individual image data had wide differences in intensity range, and resolution. Therefore, we need to carry out several preprocessing steps:

1. We have to correct the geometry of the image to a standard square capture layout. Some of the CAT systems have a circular filed of view.
2. We have to resample the images to obtain the same voxel size for all the images.
3. We have to correct the intensity in order to have the same correspondence of signal values to materials (air, fat, muscle, etc.).
4. We reduce the image size to 50 x 50 x 20 by subsampling in order to be able to process the entire volume.

Figure 1 shows an example of a slice before and after preprocessing, the top row shows the histograms of the images in the bottom row, so that it is possible to appreciate the change in distribution made by the intensity correction. After preprocessing we have volumetric images of the same size. Figure 2 shows two example input volumes after preprocessing.

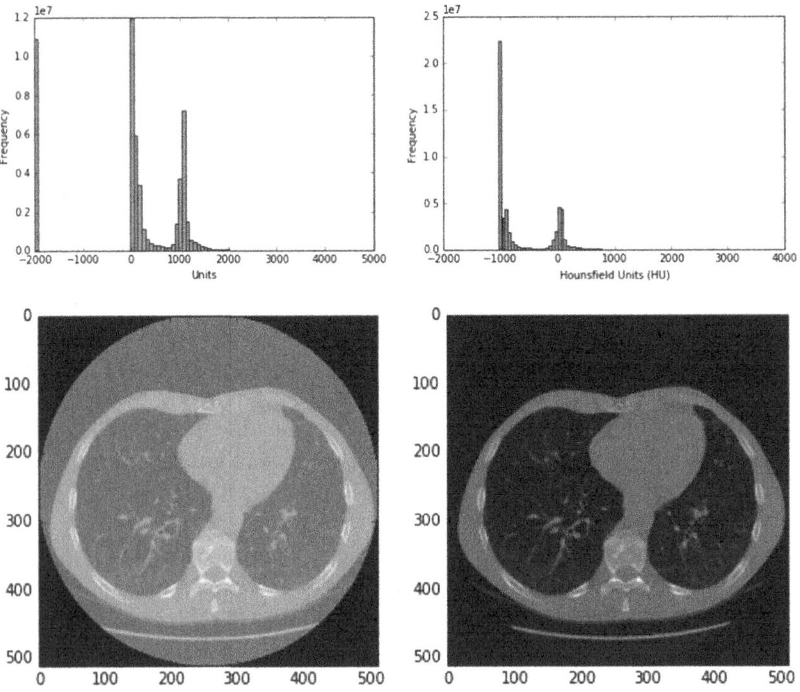

Fig. 1. Example of raw data (left) and preprocessed data (right). Top row: histograms of the images. Bottom row: visualization of the central slice.

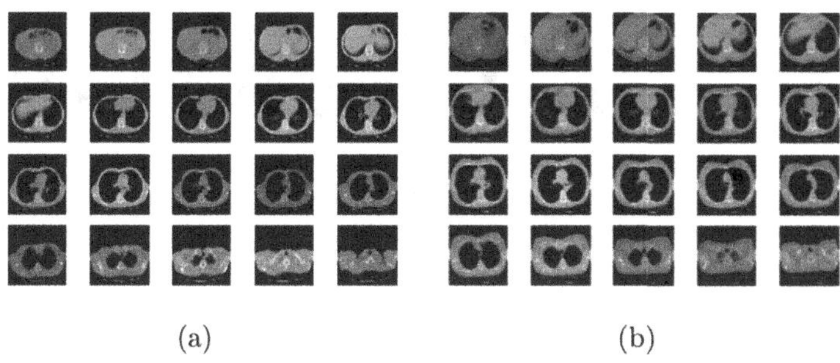

(a) (b)

Fig. 2. An example of a input volume to the networks, showing the 20 axial slices. (a) cancer patient (b) no cancer patient.

Table 1. Autoencoder architecture layout

Layer	Output shapes	Params
Input	(None, 1, 50, 50, 20)	
Convolution3D	(None, 32, 50, 50, 20)	896
MaxPooling3D	(None, 32, 10, 10, 4)	
Dropout	(None, 32, 10, 10, 4)	
Convolution3D	(None, 64, 10, 10, 4)	55360
MaxPooling3D	(None, 64, 3, 3, 1)	
Dropout	(None, 64, 3, 3, 1)	
Convolution3D	(None, 64, 3, 3, 1)	110656
(**Code**) Dropout	(None, 64, 3, 3, 1)	
UpSampling3D	(None, 64, 9, 9, 3)	
ZeroPadding3D	(None, 64, 11, 11, 5)	
Convolution3D	(None, 32, 11, 11, 5)	55328
UpSampling3D	(None, 32, 55, 55, 25	
Convolution3D	(None, 1, 53, 53, 23)	865
(Decoded) Cropping3D	(None, 1, 50, 50, 20)	
Total params: 223,105		
Trainable params: 223,105		
Non-trainable params: 0		

Architectures. We have trained two architectures:

1. 3D Convolutional Neural Network (CNN). It is a conventional architecture with 3D input volume corresponding to the CAT volume, the output is the decision units, and we have two 3D convolution layers interspersed by three maxpooling layers that produce the dimension reduction.
2. Autoencoder + classifier: We build an auto encoder whose hidden layers are convolutional networks as specified in Table 1. The middle layer, denoted Code

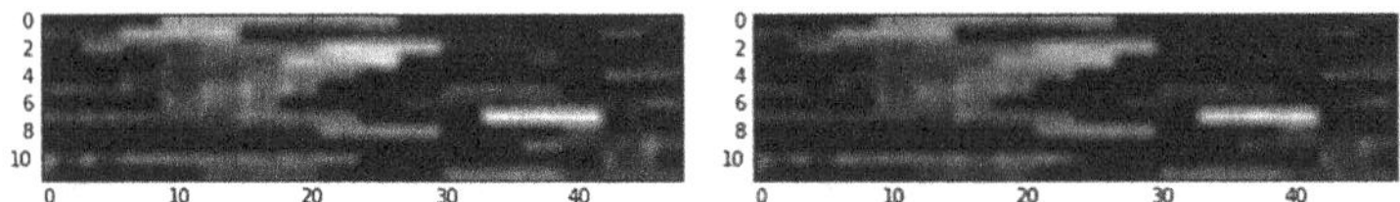

Fig. 3. The code achieved by the auto encoder after training for the input volumes in Fig. 2. Left cancer patient, right no cancer patient. The code has been reshaped into a matrix for visualization.

in the table, provides the features for classification carried out by conventional machine learning classifiers. Figure 3 shows the representation of the code for example cancer and non-cancer subjects, in fact it is not apparent the existence of discriminant features. We have tested Random Forest (RF) and Support Vector Machines (SVM), and k-NN with k = 5. The architecture has three convolution layers interspersed by maxpooling and dropout layers, all in 3D, to reduce the input to the Code dimensions. The reconstruction by up-sampling and zero padding interspersed by 3D convolutions.

We have benefitted from the great flexibility of Keras and easy specification of the architecture, as well as its easy interface to the GPUs for training speedup.

3 Results

One of the characteristics of the dataset is its class imbalance, there are much more non-cancer subjects than cancer patients. We have carried out training of the CNN with a small sample of 200 non cancer subjects and 100 cancer subjects, training it for 10 epochs. Results are shown in Fig. 4. The maximum accuracy is low, and there is a clear overfitting effect in the last epochs. The auto encoder architecture has been trained with three different training sets featuring diverse imbalance ratios, and they have been tested with 100 randomly selected subjects, 28 cancer and 72 non-cancer. Table 2 gives the results of our experiments so far. We provide the confusion matrices, whose rows correspond to the actual class,

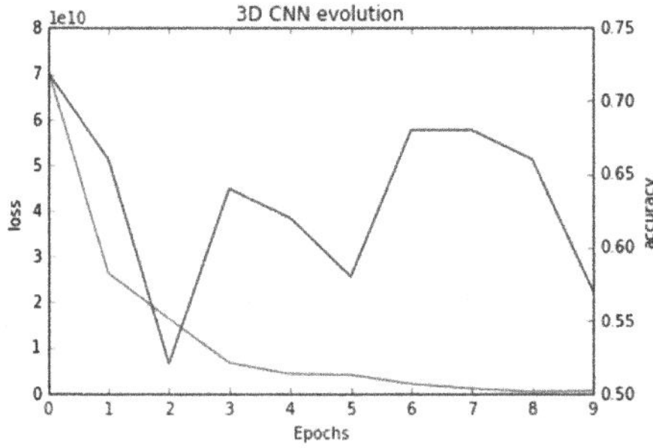

Fig. 4. The evolution of the error function (blue plot) and accuracy (red) of 3D CNN training. (Color figure online)

Table 2. Results given by the confussion matrices of the classifiers obtained with different distributions of imbalance of the test data for the auto encoder

training imbalance	RF			SVM			5-NN		
50 cancer 100 non cancer		nc	c		nc	c		nc	c
	nc	68	4	nc	48	24	nc	50	22
	c	26	2	c	16	12	c	16	12
100 cancer 50 non cancer		nc	c		nc	c		nc	c
	nc	19	53	nc	20	52	nc	12	60
	c	5	23	c	7	21	c	6	22
75 cancer 75 non cancer		nc	c		nc	c		nc	c
	nc	42	30	nc	32	40	nc	29	43
	c	14	14	c	11	17	c	11	17

and columns to the predicted class. Highest specificity (correct classification of cancer) is obtained when training with the imbalanced dataset containing more cancer subjects. These experiments are not according to the orthodox treatment of imbalanced datasets, which consist on one of the following strategies:

- manipulating the dataset adding new instances of the minority class by random interpolation between minority class samples, i.e. the SMOTE algorithm. Obviously, in the case at hand this amounts to generating new images of cancer prone patients, which is not feasible.
- manipulating the dataset removing instances of the majority class. This corresponds to the experiments with balanced datasets, which are not very successful.
- changing the error function to weight more the minority class errors. We are working on that solution as the most promising, but having to deal with technical problems.

The conclusion from Table 2 is that the auto encoder is still very sensitive to the class distribution of the training set, biasing towards the majority class in the training set.

4 Conclusions

Lung cancer is a very dramatic and urgent problem in many countries, specifically the initiative in the USA has brought this kind of cancer to the forefront of the search for innovative technical solutions to its diagnosis. The recent ongoing Kaggle challenge provides thousands of chest images from many medical institutions, which is a very hard testing ground for image based diagnosis tools. We are working with this data applying deep learning architectures. So far we have achieved the normalization of the images, and testing preliminary architectures with modest success. We have found that deep architectures are not immune to problems raised by imbalanced datasets, which are specially difficult to attack when the input data are complex images where subtle features may induce dramatic change of the output. We are working in the near future to submit some competitive solution to the Kaggle competition.

References

1. Ciresan, D.C., Giusti, A., Gambardella, L.M., Schmidhuber, J.: Deep neural networks segment neuronal membranes in electron microscopy images. In: Advances in neural information processing systems, pp. 2843–2851 (2012)
2. Donahue, J., Jia, Y., Vinyals, O., Hoffman, J., Zhang, N., Tzeng, E., Darrell, T.: Decaf: a deep convolutional activation feature for generic visual recognition. CoRR, abs/1310.1531 (2013)
3. Lecun, Y., Bottou, L., Bengio, Y., Haffner, P.: Gradient-based learning applied to document recognition. Proc. IEEE **86**(11), 2278–2324 (1998)
4. Oquab, M., Bottou, L., Laptev, I., Sivic, J.: Learning and transferring mid-level image representations using convolutional neural networks. In: Proceedings of the IEEE Conference on Computer Vision and Pattern Recognition, CVPR 2014, pp. 1717–1724. IEEE Computer Society Washington, DC, USA (2014)
5. Shin, H.C., Orton, M.R., Collins, D.J., Doran, S.J., Leach, M.O.: Stacked autoencoders for unsupervised feature learning and multiple organ detection in a pilot study using 4D patient data. IEEE Trans. Pattern Anal. Mach. Intell. **35**(8), 1930–1943 (2013)
6. Vincent, P., Larochelle, H., Bengio, Y., Manzagol, P.-A.: Extracting and composing robust features with denoising autoencoders. In: Proceedings of the 25th International Conference on Machine Learning, ICML 2008, pp. 1096–1103, New York, NY, USA, ACM (2008)

Identification of the Semantic Disconnection in Alzheimer's Patients Conducted by Bayesian Algorithms

Susana Arias Tapia[1], Rafael Martínez Tomás[2], Margarita Narváez Ríos[1(✉)], Hector F. Gómez[1], Cristina Páez Quinde[1], Verónica E. Chicaiza R.[1], and Judith Núnez Ramirez[1]

[1] Facultad de Ciencias Humanas y de la Educación, Universidad Técnica de Ambato, Ambato- Ecuador, Ecuador
{sa.arias,mm.narvaez,hf.gomez,mc.paez,ve.chicaiza, judithnunezr}@uta.edu.ec

[2] Dpto. Inteligencia Artificial, Universidad Nacional de Educación a Distancia, Juan Del Rosal 16, 28040 Madrid, Spain
rmtomas@dia.uned.es

Abstract. In recent years efforts to find mechanisms that allow early identification of neurodegenerative disease with an impact on Alzheimer's cognitive abilities or progress have been a concern of the scientific community and caregivers. For this, we start from the hypothesis, supported by the bibliography of the subject, which states that people with early Alzheimer's present semantic disconnections between the emotions that is showed in the face and feeling, they are shown by an oral or textual phrase. The key point here is that the caregivers can't be awaiting all the time to find the number of disconnections, but these can be recorded in video and audio as well as be analyzed automatically. Our proposal is to develop a methodology that is based on a software that detects emotions in the face of the participants developed in our study group and in some Bayesian rhythms that allow to classify the sentimental polarity of the conversational phrases. This methodology allows the comparison of results and obtain the moments of semantic disconnection when there is no coincidence between the emotions and the polarity. The experimental results show that it has been possible to identify the disconnections with an 82% success. Our study is an initial proposal, although following previous work that qualifies this line of work....

Keywords: Analysis of feelings · Human emotions · Labels · Alzheimer's

1 Introduction

Human emotions' study has been of great interest to Psychology and Sociology, which is why researchers disagree on the number of basic emotions, but there is consensus to include among them, joy, anger, fear, sadness, surprise

J.M. Ferrández Vicente et al. (Eds.): IWINAC 2017, Part II, LNCS 10338, pp. 49–58, 2017.
DOI: 10.1007/978-3-319-59773-7_6

and disgust. The results of emotional analysis contribute in a great deal to the treatment of mental illness to try to identify mechanisms of cure or slow the progression of the disease [1]. We focused our study on the hypothesis that finding patients with early Alzheimer have few disconnections between the emotions that are reflected in their face and feeling that can be expressed in a sentence. The proposal of this particular work is based on the idea that words alone have a certain orientation of feeling, especially adjectives and adverbs, so that one way to determine that orientation of the input text is based on its probability of occurrence with positive and negative terms. Section three details each phase of the methodology proposed for the analysis and recognition of human emotions in people with Alzheimer, as well as the techniques that we use for the detection of emotions in both text and video and as the final phase of the methodology performed for text mining using Naive Bayes algorithms and Bayesian Multinomial Network. To collect the conversations, the methodology proposed in [2] was used and for the transcripts of videos the data files of the UK were used as format (http://www.data-archive.ac.uk/) create Bayesian algorithms used in other invasive diagnostic investigations [3] and [4] are trained with manual labeling done by experts. The labeling belongs to the semantic polarity of each of the sentences said by the patients in video. To verify validity labels were used applying Kappa index. This process shows that there are connectors that do not contribute to the classification, and therefore it was necessary to repeat the experiments until finding the combination - pattern - of adjectives, connectors and articles suitable to achieve a classification with the smallest possible error. Hence a single word and phrase may have a positive, negative, or neutral percent-age charge of polarity depending on the context in which it is found. The results of Bayesian algorithms are compared with the analysis of emotions obtained with the software DetectionEmotion (HER) developed in our work team and validated in [5] and [1], this allows to determine whether or not there is a dissociation between what the patient says -text- and his facial expression, in order to conclude a possible advance of the disease-alert. The next section shows the experimentation phase. The sample for our study is in an age range between patients ranging from 60 to 90 years. This age range is important in a disease such as Alzheimer's dementia because it is progressive and usually has more involvement in the range chosen. In this investigation, it was necessary to formalize the record of videos of patients with Alzheimer of the Adult Hospital and Foundation Perpetuo Socorro (Quito), and the Center for the Elderly Adult (Catamayo), by signing a document between the parties in which the relatives authorized the procedure respecting the patient's identity. Here the multimodal Bayesian network showed a better result with an F1Score of 0.8. Finally some conclusions and recommendations were obtained. The ones that are used as basis for further research.

2 State of the Art

According to [6] and [1] there is a direct relationship between text polarity and the emotion of the person, for example if the person recorded in the video mainly positive emotions, then the polarity of the text should be positive as well, if given this case would be considered a normal person, but in case there is no coincidence between the polarity of the text and the emotions identified in the facial expression of the person to be analyzed, this one presents an alert. An advantage of this semantic disconnection hypothesis is taken in order to develop our proposal and present an alternative for patients' caregivers, which may indicate a possible advance of Alzheimer when there is no relationship between the variables. This proposal fits within the group's general line of work to apply artificial intelligence techniques to advance the early diagnosis of mild cognitive impairment, proposed by [7] in which it tries to identify by means of neuropsychological tests the cognitive decline, which allows them to obtain new characteristics of quantitative description of the advance of the decline. In the research of [4] a decision model based on a Bayesian network is proposed to support the diagnosis of dementia and cognitive decline. The proposed Bayesian network was modeled using a combination of expert knowledge oriented to get data. The structure of the network was built on the basis of current diagnostic criteria contributed by experts in this field. The decision model was evaluated using quantitative methods and a sensitivity analysis. [3] proposed the Multifold Bayesian Kernelization algorithm which is a synthesis analysis of multimodal biomarkers, which builts a nucleus for each biomarker that maximizes the local affinity of the block, and also evaluates the contribution of each biomarker based on a Bayesian frame achieving significant improvements in all diagnostic groups as compared to the methods used in the technique. In [8]. It uses a Bayesian model to automatically identify distinct latent factors of overlapping atrophy patterns from structural magnetic resonance imaging in patients with late-onset Alzheimer's disease (AD). The results show that different patterns of atrophy influence the decline of different cognitive domains [8]. The lexical-semantic-conceptual deficit (LSCD) in the oral definitions of the semantic categories of the basic objects is an important early indicator in the evaluation of the cognitive state of the patients. Bayesian networks have been applied for the diagnosis of mild and moderate Alzheimer by analyzing the oral production of semantic characteristics. The performance of BN classification is remarkable compared to other methods of mechanical learning, achieving 91% accuracy and 94% accuracy in patients with mild and moderate AD. Aside from this, the BN model facilitates the explanation of the reasoning process and the validation of the conclusions and allows the study of the rare declarative semantic memory deficiencies [9]. In this study it is intend to use the multimodal bayesian network to classify the conversations of the patients into positive, negative or neutral. It is required to make an analysis phrase by phrase. This result will be compared to the emotion that prevails in the patient's face, all of this in order to identify the semantic disconnection. The details of the classification and comparison are described in the following section.

3 Methodology

Conversations in which people with Alzheimer participated were recorded on video and transcribed as reference to the orientations of [2] for the analysis of conversations in special populations and with that a corpus was constructed. The expert performs a manual labeling of the polarity of each phrase of the conversation. To proved the manual labeling, the Kappa index is run to obtain the correctness of the label (Fig. 1).

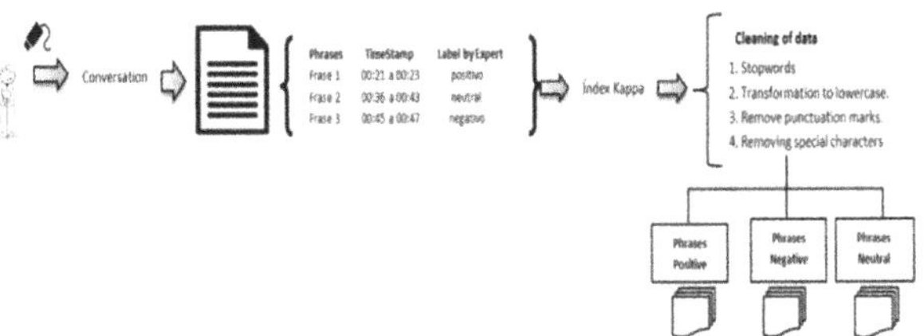

Fig. 1. Sentiment analysis process

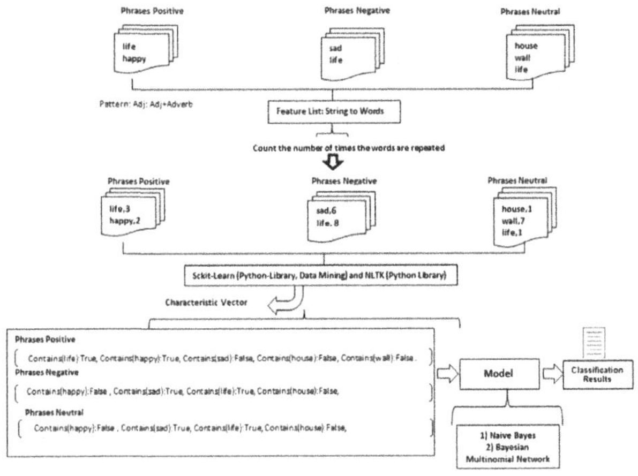

Fig. 2. Architecture system classification

Figure 2 Shows the set of steps for the classification by means of the application of the probabilistic algorithms of Naïve Bayes and Multinomial Bayesian Networks: 1. Probabilistic weights of Multinomial Bayesian Network links are automatically learned from the linguistic corpus, NB estimates the conditional probability of a word or phrases given to a type as the relative frequency of the term (t) in files Belonging to type (c). 2. Variables considered as text or input factors are deterministic. 3. To find conditional probabilities a priori is calculated directly as the proportion of cases in the corpus. 4. The Multinomial Bayesian network takes into account the number of times a word appears on the files of class c. This model captures the frequency information of words in the file fragments, so the file is an ordered sequence of phrase events, extracted from the same vocabulary. Then, to find the variables of interest, Eq. 1 is calculated by simplifying Bayesian Multinomial Networks using the following phrases of a file.

Table 1. Example of a multinomial Bayesian network of training data set

	File	Text	Label
Training	F1	"Life Happy"	Positive
		"Life"	
		"Life"	
		"House wall"	Neutral
		"Sad"	Negative

As seen in Table 1. There are instances that are previously classified (Positive, + Negative and Neutral) these files are used as training to determine the class of a new file.

Equation 1:

Formula for positive phrases file (Frequency of the word in file pos +1)/(No. input words + Positive words).

Formula for positive phrases file (Frequency of the word in the file neg + 1)/(No. input words + Negative words).

Formula for positive phrases file (Frequency of the word in the file neu + 1)/(No. input words + Neutral words) Vocabulary = life, happy, sad, house, wall Number of input words is taken into account Features List = 28 Where: CPOS: Positive Characteristics CNEG: Negative Characteristics CNEU: Neutral Characteristics.

The Eq. 1 that is used to perform the calculation and find the probabilities of the training phrases using the algorithm of the Multinomial Bayesian Networks in the programming language Python we can see the following form of the generated file:

To model a Multinomial Bayesian Network is described below: 1. It starts from the transcripts of the conversations obtaining thus the corpus of training. 2. The assignment of each class of phrases of the conversations is done subjectively for their previous classification. 3. A phrase is obtained for each probability of each polarity, using the algorithm of Multinomial Bayesian Network trained with the conversations. 4. Identify the polarity that has the highest percentage, to assign the most representative class (Table 2).

Table 2. File generated with the training phrases and their probabilities using the algorithm of the Multinomial Bayesian Network.

Phrases	Probability positive	Probability negative	Probability neutral	Class (High percentage)
Life	0.12	0.21	0.054	Negative
Happy	0.090	0.024	0.02	Positive
Sad	0.030	0.17	0.027	Negative
House	0.030	0.023	0.054	Neutral
Wall	0.030	0.023	0.22	Neutral

3.1 Structure of Multinomial Bayesian Networks

In the structure of Multinomial Bayesian Networks the following can be found:

1. Standardized files are used, from which the phrases are extracted that will be sent to the model who will be in charge of assigning a polarity to each phrase of the corpus.

2. After obtaining the normalized files, the frequency of characteristics of the phrases is obtained.

3. Natural language processing techniques are used for classifying texts consisting mainly of finding patterns and characteristics of the language that allow assigning a class to a document. For the case of the classification of short texts, the task of preprocessing is also performed, in order to standardize the texts, to obtain documents with words or characteristics that can be understood by the system, which in Summary is the conversion of the document into a structure of boolean variables (True: present and False: absent), when the phrase is not in the positive file it is false (absent) and if it is in the file of negative sentences it will be true (present), based on the dictionary of words or slogans created from the training corpus.

4. The objective variable of this research is to find that early or healthy dementia values that can be taken in patients. Keep in mind that our model only takes into account the classes included in the corpus; However, it could easily be extended to the diagnosis of other problems that is cause by the cognitive decline.

5. The variable that refers to the three types of polarities (positive, negative and neutral) are those that evaluate the result of the highest probability percentage of the phrases. Implementation Output of the Multinomial Bayesian Network Algorithm.

The system generates outputs throughout its execution, which are useful in different processes. These outputs are flat txt files that are listed below:

1. Dictionary of features.
2. Classified documents.
3. Evaluation of results and performance.

The purpose of the dictionary is to serve as a resource for future implementations, it means to avoid create a new dictionary each time it is run.

In order to determine the class of a new phrase of a file the following is done:

1. Enter a new phrase
2. Perform data cleaning (data preprocessing)
3. Converting Documents to a Feature Vector
4. Modifying vocabulary with the new phrases
5. Checking the number of input words
6. Applying with the framework nltk and scikit-learn the algorithm as a new phrase, the probability for the new words are multiplied by an estimate value of 0.5 since this phrase had no previous labeling, nor was it in training.

The sample was taken of F1 as training and F2 as we do not know which polarity has performed, calculations were done with the positive, negative and neutral words and the phrase is classified according the majority probability obtained (Fig. 3).

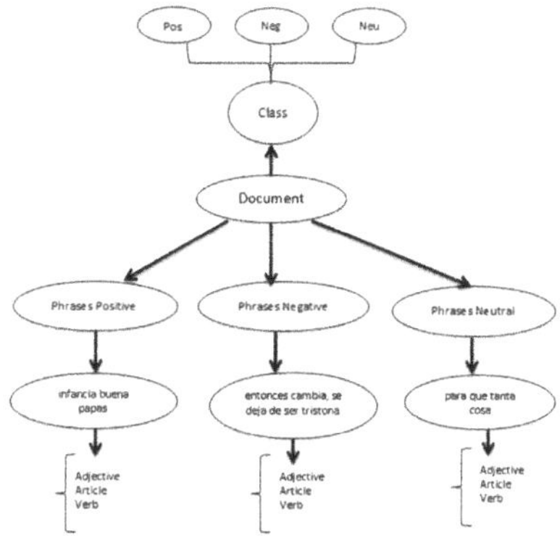

Fig. 3. Structure of Multinomial Bayesian Networks

4 Evaluation of Results and Performance

The dictionary of characteristics has the purpose of serving as a resource for future implementations, that is to say, to avoid the system creating a dictionary each time it is executed.

In order to determine the class of a new phrase of a file the following is done:

1. There is input a new phrase.
2. Perform the data cleansing (preprocessing of data).
3. Conversion of documents to characteristics Vector.
4. Modifying vocabulary with new phrases.

5. Applying the algorithm with the nltk and scikit-learn framework and as the phrase is new, the probability for the new words is multiplied by the value of estimation of 0.5 as this phrase didn't have previous label, nor was it in the training.

Comparing the Bayesian Network model with the publication of [9], the main advantage of the model is that it has the ability to extend new categories to predict. In our model the same way has the ability to predict new phrases, otherwise with the resulting methodology new patterns can be applied for the Cognitive impairment. With our Bayesian model, and the [9] model, it is possible to expand a structure that can be used in clinical tests to detect Alzheimer in its early stages.

5 Experimentation

This section describes the tests and results obtained with the implemented system. It was necessary to have a corpus on which the experiments were performed, with 100 conversations of patients with early Alzheimer's disease. The phases of the experiment were:

Training Phase: The training structure contained 3 files, having positive, negative and neutral sentences, previously classified by an expert. Later, we applied the comparison of the labeling by the expert and HER.

Table 3. Example of the Naive Bayes classifier and Multinomial NB of the conversations.

Conversation	Number of analyzed lines	Naive Bayes			Class
		Positive	Negative	Neutral	
Conversation 1	34	11.76	32.35	55.88	Neutral
Conversation 2	62	22.58	27.42	50.00	Neutral
Conversation 3	107	14.02	11.21	74.77	Neutral
Conversation 4	94	30.85	22.34	46.81	Neutral
Conversation 5	70	27.14	7.14	65.71	Neutral
Conversation	Number of analyzed lines	Bayesian Multinomial			Class
		Positive	Negative	Neutral	
Conversation 1	34	8.82	50.00	41.18	Negative
Conversation 2	62	20.97	51.61	27.4	Negative
Conversation 3	107	14.94	41.12	43.93	Neutral
Conversation 4	94	30.85	35.11	34.04	Negative
Conversation 5	70	30.00	24.29	45.71	Neutral

In Table 3 the results obtained from the Bayesian classifier and Bayesian Multinomial Network are shown in each of the conversations as can be seen in conversation 2, 3, 5 in two classifiers point to the same class. Which in this case is Neutral, but in conversation 1 and 4, point to a different class in both classifiers, which is expected with the analysis given that the expert was asked to analyze each class (positive, negative, neutral) of the conversations of the dataset and thus verify if what has obtained Naive of Bayes and Bayesian Multinomial Network is correct. In Table 4 proved with the analysis in each conversation and the classification of both classifiers by the expert and the classification obtained by the Bayesian Multinomial Network have the same similarity in the conversation 2, 3 and 5. In Tables 3 and 4 the alert generating semantic disconnection rows are shown for the caregiver. We proceeded to apply the methodology and to obtain the accuracy and recall.

Table 4. Results of analysis with the expert Human and HER.

Conversation	Subjective classification of the human expert	Classification on of the expert HER
Conversation 1	Neutral	Fear
Conversation 2	Negative	Surprise
Conversation 3	Neutral	Sadness
Conversation 4	Neutral	Fear
Conversation 5	Neutral	Surprise

Table 5. Sensitivity and specificity analysis using the results of polarity in text and emotions in video by the software Detection Emotion (HER).

Emotions in video and text polarity	Precision	Recall	F1 Score
Test 1	0.68	0.75	0.71
Test 2	0.74	0.85	0.79
Test 3	0.76	0.91	0.82

Table 5 shows the results of the use of the software Detection Emotion (HER) and the use of the feeling analysis in the tests. It can be observed that the results of precision and recall are good because the F1-Score index is close to 1.

6 Conclusions

The interest of this type of research allows to contribute valuable information of the advance of Alzheimer's disease to the expert. Our proposal allows us to identify the semantic disconnections between the emotions in the patient's face and what he says, while the same is recorded on video. The HER software was used to obtain the facial emotions, while Bayesian, Naive Bayes and

Bayesian Multinomial Network algorithms were used to obtain the classification of the conversation. This last one obtained improvements in relation to the first reaching an F1Score of 0.82 in one of the applied tests. This value is close to other Alzheimer's classifiers in which Bayesian networks were also used as in [9]. Bayesian networks are probabilistic and act closely to the human behavior therefore they allow to work with probabilistic errors in order to detect the progress of the disease, in fact the results are comparable between HER, Multinomial Naive Bayes and Expert as shown in Tables 3, 4 and 5. Our work is undergoing experimentation, therefore, our next step is to compare our results with the application of Bayesian methodologies applied in cerebral images for Alzheimer's detection [3], to identify more clearly the difference between invasive and non-invasive methods for the detection of the disease.

References

1. Arias, T.S.A., Martínez-Tomás, R., Gómez, A.H.F., Hernández del Salto, V., Sánchez Guerrero, J., Mocha-Bonilla, J.A., et al.: The dissociation between polarity, semantic orientation, and emotional tone as an early indicator of cognitive impairment. Front. Comput. Neurosci. **10**, 1–9 (2016)
2. Pietrosemoli, L.: Análisis del discurso en poblaciones especiales: la conversación con afásicos. Caracas: Los Libros de El Nacional (2007)
3. Liu, S., Song, Y., Cai, W., Pujol, S., Kikinis, R., Wang, X., Feng, D.: Multifold Bayesian Kernelization in Alzheimer's Diagnosis. In: Mori, K., Sakuma, I., Sato, Y., Barillot, C., Navab, N. (eds.) MICCAI 2013. LNCS, vol. 8150, pp. 303–310. Springer, Heidelberg (2013). doi:10.1007/978-3-642-40763-5_38
4. Seixas, F.L., Zadrozny, B., Laks, J., Conci, A., Muchaluat Saade, D.C.: A Bayesian network decision model for supporting the diagnosis of dementia. Alzheimer's disease and mild cognitive impairment. Comput. Biol. Med. **51**, 140–158 (2014)
5. Torres-Carrión, P., González-González, C., Mora Carreño, A.: Facial emotion analysis in down's syndrome children in classroom. In: Proceedings of the XVI International Conference on Human Computer Interaction. Vilanova i a la Geltrú: ResearchGate (2015)
6. Mohammad, S., Turney, P.: Crowdsourcing a word-emotion association lexicon. Comput. Intell. **29**, 436–465 (2013)
7. Rincón, M., García-Herranz, S., Díaz-Mardomingo, M.C., Martínez-Tomás, R., Peraita, H.: Automatic drawing analysis of figures included in neuropsychological tests for the assessment and diagnosis of mild cognitive impairment. In: Ferrández Vicente, J.M., Álvarez-Sánchez, J.R., de la Paz López, F., Toledo-Moreo, F.J., Adeli, H. (eds.) IWINAC 2015. LNCS, vol. 9107, pp. 508–515. Springer, Cham (2015). doi:10.1007/978-3-319-18914-7_53
8. Zhang, X., Mormino, E., Sun, N., Sperling, R., Sabuncu, M., Thomas Yeo, B.: Bayesian model reveals latent atrophy factors with dissociable cognitive trajectories in Alzheimer's disease. Alzheimer Disease Neuroimaging Initiative, 6535–6544 (2016)
9. Guerrero, J., Martínez-Tomás, R., Rincón, M., Peraita, H.: Diagnosis of cognitive impairment compatible with early diagnosis of Alzheimer's Disease. A Bayesian network model basaed on the analysis of oral definitions of semantic categories. Methods Inf. Med. **55**, 42–49 (2016)

Mobile Brain Computer Interaction

Classification of Gait Motor Imagery While Standing Based on Electroencephalographic Bandpower

I.N. Angulo-Sherman[1], M. Rodríguez-Ugarte[2], E. Iáñez[2(✉)], and J.M. Azorín[2]

[1] CINVESTAV, Monterrey's Unit, Vía del Conocimiento 201, PIIT, Km 9.5 de la Autopista Nueva al Aeropuerto, 66600 Apodaca, Nuevo León, Mexico
iangulo@cinvestav.mx

[2] Brain-Machine Interface Systems Lab, Systems Engineering and Automation Department, Miguel Hernández University of Elche, Avda. de la Universidad s/n. Ed. Innova, 03202 Elche (Alicante), Spain
{maria.rodriguezu,eianez,jm.azorin}@umh.es
http://www.monterrey.cinvestav.mx/
http://bmi.umh.es/

Abstract. Brain-computer interfaces (BCIs) translate brain signals into commands for a device. BCIs are a complementary option in therapy during gait rehabilitation. This paper presents a strategy based on electroencephalographic (EEG) bandpower for detecting gait motor imagery (MI) while being standing. In particular, μ (8–13 Hz) and 20–35 Hz bands were used. Preliminary results show that two out of three users could achieve an accuracy above 70% of correct classifications. The proposed strategy could be used in a MI-based BCI to enhance brain activity associated to the gait process.

Keywords: Sensorimotor · μ rhythm · Motor imagery · BCI · EEG

1 Introduction

A brain-computer interface (BCI) is a system that is capable of translating user's intentions from only brain activity, usually electroencephalographic (EEG) signals, into commands for an external device [1]. These systems have been studied as a complementary option during rehabilitation therapy in patients that have suffered a stroke [2].

Motor imagery (MI) and actual movement share part of their neural substrate [3]. Hence, there is interest on using MI-based BCIs for inducing brain plasticity and enhancing motor rehabilitation by allowing the repetitive practice of brain motor activity. In particular, efforts have been focused on gait recovery as it represents a major improvement on life-quality [4] for people with motor impairment at the lower limb level.

J.M. Ferrández Vicente et al. (Eds.): IWINAC 2017, Part II, LNCS 10338, pp. 61–67, 2017.
DOI: 10.1007/978-3-319-59773-7_7

Motor imagery and real movement are related to the attenuation of EEG power, known as event-related desynchronization or ERD, in μ (8–13 Hz) and β (14–26 Hz) bands [5]. Such motor activity is expected to occur in premotor and supplementary motor (SMA) areas, since they are key structures for motor imagery [5]. Also, there is a high amplitude in the γ band within 60–80 Hz during gait compared to being standing, while there is also modulation in 70–90 Hz relative to the gait cycle and inversely coupled to 24–40 Hz [6]. These changes are expected mostly over the standardized position of Cz, near the feet motor area and relatively close to the SMA.

In the present study, we evaluated the spectral changes of gait MI while being standing. Then, the frequency bands where changes were found were used to train a naïve Bayesian classifier and its percentage of correct classifications was evaluated. This work was performed as part of the Associate project, which is aimed to validate the effectiveness of a new neurorehabilitation intervention for promoting gait motor relearning that integrates a BCI system, brain electrical stimulation and a lower limb exoskeleton. Therefore, one of the goals within the framework of this project is to develop an algorithm that allows gait motor imagery detection from EEG signals in order to control an exoskeleton.

2 Experiments

This section explains the process of EEG recording for different mental conditions and the analysis of the data. The main purpose of these experiments was to determine the most evident EEG differences in terms of frequency that are associated to gait MI and to use them to train a classifier that detects gait MI. Hence, three subjects participated in one experimental session in which the accuracy of gait MI detection is evaluated.

2.1 EEG Recording

The Starstim 32 system (Neuroelectrics®) was used to acquire EEG data at a sample rate of 500 Hz, using a right-earlobe reference. EEG signals from the 10/10 international system positions Cz, Pz, Fz, FC1, FC2, CP1, CP2, C3, and C4 were obtained. In terms of software, Neuroelectrics Instrument Controller (NIC) and a Matlab® platform were used to record data, while the Matlab routines were also used to control the visual cue system in this study.

2.2 Recording Session

Users stood in front of a computer screen and they were instructed to either imagine they were walking or to remain standing but relaxed in response to visual cues, as shown in Fig. 1. If the word "Go" appeared on the screen (7 s), then the user had to imagine to walk at approximately one gait cycle per second that simulated a continuous and comfortable walking rate. On the other hand, if the screen was cleared out (6–8 s), the user stopped motor imagery. Participants were encouraged not to anticipate the "Go" cue but to wait until it appeared to prepare their MI. In this case, MI condition was compared while standing because future evaluations of a gait MI-BCI would require the user to be at that position.

The session consisted of three runs of 30 attempts or trials of MI with a corresponding lapse of relaxing state. The temporal sequence of a run is presented in Fig. 2.

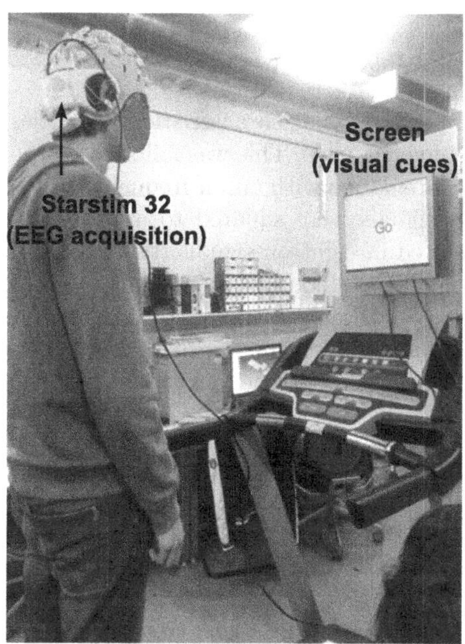

Fig. 1. Subject performing the experimental session.

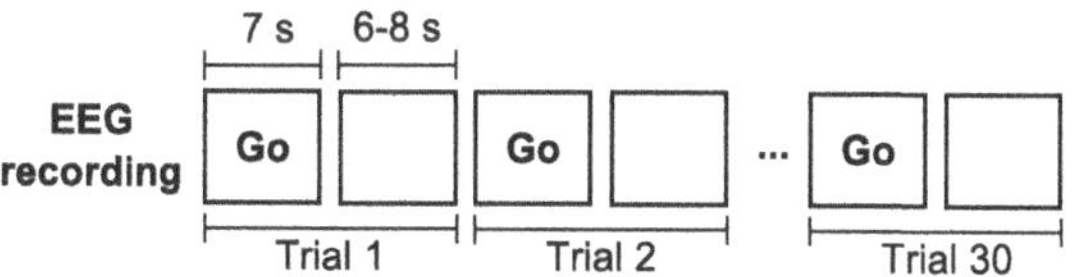

Fig. 2. Temporal sequence of one run.

2.3 EEG Analysis

After EEG was obtained, the mean ERD from the first run was estimated to determine the most evident spectral changes. First, a Laplacian filter and a 1–100 Hz bandpass filter was applied on Cz. The resulting signal was divided in MI and rest (just standing) epochs. Spectra from each epoch was calculated with fast Fourier transform using non-overlapping windows of 100 samples (0.2 s). Then, the mean spectrum of the windows of each rest epoch was subtracted to the spectra of the corresponding MI epoch, which represents the varying ERD per MI trial across time. Finally, mean ERD of all trials was computed and inspected visually to determine the frequency features that would be used for classifying MI for all subjects: 8–13 Hz (μ-rhythm) and 20–35 Hz bands. This decision is detailed in Sect. 3.1.

Once characteristic features were selected, EEG data was processed to obtain two signals from each channel that represented the two chosen bandwidths. The following procedure was performed in windows of 0.5 s (i.e., 250 samples) to simulate an online processing:

1. Obtaining spectral power at the characteristic frequencies: A Laplacian filter was applied to the nine channels. This was followed by the parallel processing with two bandpass filters, one with cutoff frequencies of 8–13 Hz and another of 20–35 Hz. Then, signals were squared to approximate EEG bandpower. This procedure resulted in eighteen signals (twice per EEG channel).
2. Smoothing: Each signal was smoothed by assigning to the current signal value the mean of the last 4 s of the spectral power. Such smoothing introduced slow variations on the signal. In consequence, further detrending was required.
3. Detrending: Each signal was detrended by removing the straight-line fit of the last 8 s of the smoothed signal.
4. Obtaining a representative value of the window: The mean of the last window of detrended signal was obtained. This value was the one introduced in the classifier.

Processed signals from the first run were used to train a naïve Bayesian classifier [7] to identify MI from rest. The remaining runs were used to test the accuracy of classification, which is evaluated as the percentage of correct classifications in the run. Note that classification into rest or MI is performed every 0.5 s, due to the selected window size for signal processing.

3 Results

This section presents the mean ERD results that were used to select frequency bands as features for the classifier. Then, accuracy results are described for the second and third runs.

3.1 ERD Results

Figure 3 shows the mean ERD associated to gait MI for all subjects. As can be seen, Subject 3 presents the most evident bandpower attenuation on the μ rhythm and on the range of approximately 20–40 Hz, which seems to correspond to the reported modulation on 24–40 Hz [6] that is coupled to the gait cycle. However, the attenuation band seems shifted a couple of Hz lower respect to results from [6]. A similar behavior is observed for Subject 1, but with a less evident ERD for the higher band. In the case of Subject 2 there too much variability in the mean ERD across time to find a spectral trend. Based on these results, the characteristic frequencies were chosen as 8–13 Hz (μ-rhythm) and 20–35 Hz bands.

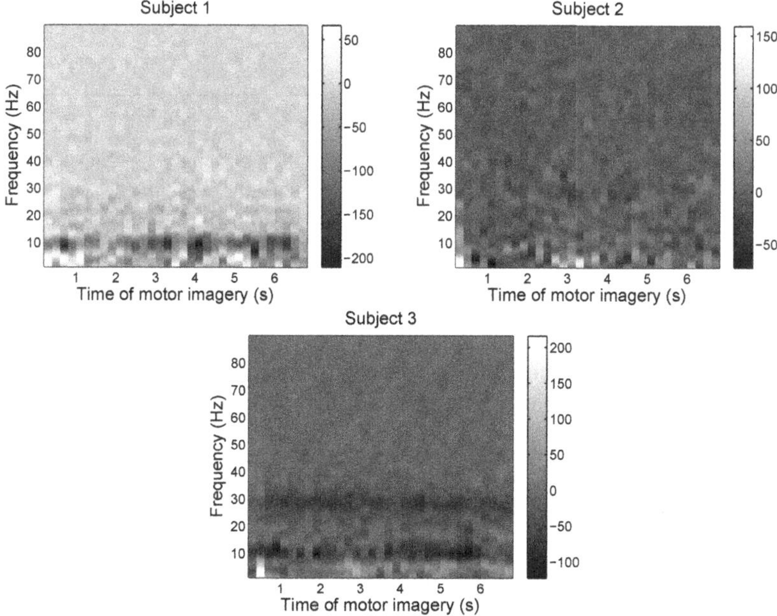

Fig. 3. Mean ERD on Cz associated to gait MI across time.

3.2 Accuracy Results

Table 1 shows the accuracy for the three subjects and the two runs in which classification performance was evaluated. In the table, it can be observed that two of the subjects could achieve in at least one of the runs an accuracy above 70%. This accuracy level is commonly used as a threshold to define if there is enough control of the system to allow communication [8]. To illustrate the kind of errors in classification that occurred in one of the best classifications, a fragment from the second run of Subject 3 is presented in Fig. 4. There it can be seen that the classified state is similar than the real one. However, there are cases where the intention may be misclassified, as in the period from 225–250 s. Also, the detection of the Standing+MI condition, which shown as a pulse with variable width, can be narrower or broader than the pulse of the actual condition. Note that sometimes the MI state is detected before the cue is presented, this could be either due to the non-specificity of the classifier or to the possible preparation of the subject to perform MI, despite of the instruction of trying not to anticipate to the cue presentation. However, as MI or the lack of it are the only tasks the user is performing, it is not surprising that the user suspects when the next cue is appearing soon.

Table 1. Accuracy for each subject and run

Subject	Run 2	Run 3
1	63.47	71.00
2	58.22	62.63
3	78.98	79.10

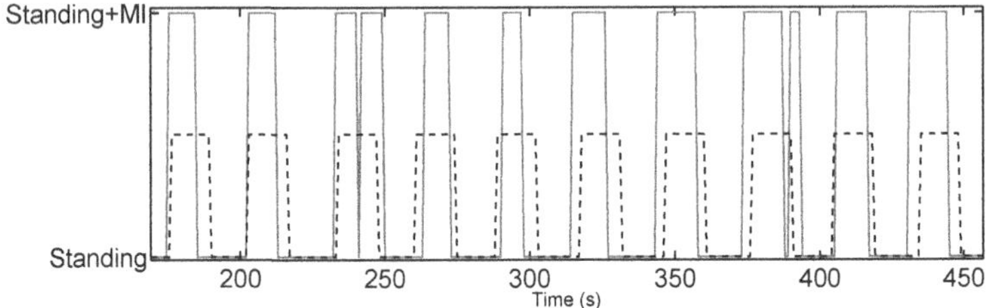

Fig. 4. Classification fragment from the second run of Subject 3. The decision of the classifier (*continuous*) is shown with respect to the real condition (*dashed*) according to cue presentation.

4 Discussion

Based on the previous results, it seems that the output from the classifier is similar to the real condition, according to the visual cue presentation in the best cases of classification, even if the accuracy is still far from 100%. It is important to note that accuracy can vary depending on the velocity of the user to change from one cognitive state to another and on the ability of sustaining the mental state. In addition, it must be considered that the user might move during EEG recording to sustain body balance, which for the purpose of framework in which the study is developed, is a required condition. In this case, the protocol is not adequate for evaluating the potential of classifier, but just observing the time relation between cue apparition and the spectral changes. However, note that this kind of classification strategy is not expected to give satisfactory results for all subjects since the beginning, since it is oriented to a learning process of brain activity modulation.

It should be noted that the number of features that are used for classification is high. This may be reduced or optimized depending on the subject to reduce computational cost. Nevertheless, it would be recommended to cover with electrodes a broader spatial area than just around Cz in the case of an application for people with motor impairments, since their brain activity is more heterogeneous compared to healthy people.

As future work, it is planned to evaluate the strategy on more subjects. If results suggest the strategy is suitable for motor relearning in terms of brain activity, the protocol could be implemented in a BCI system that provides feedback, so improvements in brain activity modulation can be evaluated.

5 Concluding Remarks

The proposed protocol allowed two out of three subjects to obtain an accuracy level above 70%, which is related to a reasonably control level. Nevertheless, the strategy is oriented to the improvement of brain activity modulation, so it could not work in all subjects since the first session. Note that this protocol implements as classifiable features the most evident EEG spectral changes that were observed during gait and that are also reported in the literature. However, improvements in reducing the number of the features that are used for classification could be performed. Future work involves further evaluation of the strategy with more subjects.

Acknowledgments. This research has been carried out in the framework of the project Associate - Decoding and stimulation of motor and sensory brain activity to support long term potentiation through Hebbian and paired associative stimulation during rehabilitation of gait (DPI2014-58431-C4-2-R), funded by the Spanish Ministry of Economy and Competitiveness and by the European Union through the European Regional Development Fund (ERDF) "A way to build Europe". Also, the Mexican Council of Science and Technology (CONACyT) provided I.N. Angulo-Sherman her scholarship.

References

1. Alamdari, N., Haider, A., Arefin, R., Verma, A., Tavakolian, K., Fazel-Rezai, R.: A review of methods and applications of brain computer interface systems. In: 2016 IEEE International Conference on Electro Information Technology (EIT), pp. 0345–0350. IEEE Press, North Dakota (2016)
2. Teo, W.P., Chew, E.: Is motor-imagery brain-computer interface feasible in stroke rehabilitation? J. PM&R. **6**, 723–728 (2014)
3. Decety, J.: Do imagined and executed actions share the same neural substrate? Cogn. Brain. Res. **3**, 87–93 (1996)
4. Belda-Lois, J.M., Mena-del Horno, S., Bermejo-Bosch, I., Moreno, J.C., Pons, J.L., Farina, D., Iosa, M., Molinari, M., Tamburella, F., Ramos, A., Caria, A., Solis-Escalante, T., Brunner, C., Massimiliano, R.: Rehabilitation of gait after stroke: a review towards a top-down approach. J. Neuroeng. Rehabil. **8**, 1–19 (2011). Article no. 66
5. Hanawaka, T.: Organizing motor imageries. Neurosci. Res. **104**, 56–63 (2016)
6. Seeber, M., Scherer, R., Wagner, J., Solis-Escalante, T., Müller-Putz, G.R.: High and low gamma EEG oscillations in central sensorimotor areas are conversely modulated during the human gait cycle. Neuroimage **112**, 318–326 (2015)
7. Naït-Ali, A., Fournier, R.: Signal and Image Processing for Biometrics. John Wiley & Sons, London (2012)
8. Kübler, A., Neumann, N., Wilhelm, B., Hinterberger, T., Birbaumer, N.: Predictability of brain-computer communication. J. Psychophysiol. **18**, 121–129 (2004)

A Mobile Brain-Computer Interface for Clinical Applications: From the Lab to the Ubiquity

Jesus Minguillon[1(✉)], Miguel Angel Lopez-Gordo[2], Christian Morillas[1], and Francisco Pelayo[1]

[1] Department of Computer Architecture and Technology - CITIC, University of Granada,Granada, Spain
{minguillon,cmg,fpelayo}@ugr.es

[2] Department of Signal Theory, Telematics and Communications - CITIC, University of Granada, Granada, Spain
malg@ugr.es

Abstract. Technological advances during the last years have contributed to the development of wireless and low-cost electroencephalography (EEG) acquisition systems and mobile brain-computer interface (mBCI) applications. The most popular applications are general-purpose (e.g., games, sports, daily-life, etc.). However, clinical usefulness of mBCIs is still an open question. In this paper we present a low-cost mobile BCI application and demonstrate its potential utility in clinical practice. In particular, we conducted a study in which visual evoked potentials (VEP) of two subjects were analyzed using our mBCI application, under different conditions: inside a laboratory, walking and traveling in a car. The results show that the features of our system (level of synchronization, robustness and signal quality) are acceptable for the demanding standard required for the electrophysiological evaluation of vision. In addition, the mobile recording and cloud computing of VEPs offers a number of advantages over traditional in-lab systems. The presented mobile application could be used for visual impairment screening, for ubiquitous, massive and low-cost evaluation of vision, and as ambulatory diagnostic tool in rural or undeveloped areas.

Keywords: EEG · VEP · mHealth · mBCI · Mobile brain-computer interface · Cloud-computing · Clinical · Ubiquity

1 Introduction

Mobile technology has become an essential part in people's lives. Numerous technological advances have contributed to the development of this technology during the last years, with application in diverse fields. Apart from general-purpose applications such as telephone, mobile and low-cost clinical applications are increasingly becoming more and more frequent. For example, some smartphone-based approaches have been proposed for disease diagnosis [1,2] and

J.M. Ferrández Vicente et al. (Eds.): IWINAC 2017, Part II, LNCS 10338, pp. 68–76, 2017.
DOI: 10.1007/978-3-319-59773-7_8

attention detection [3]. All this has led to introduce new technological concepts such as telemedicine [4], eHealth [5] and mHealth [6].

In the context of brain-computer interface (BCI) applications, the development of wireless and low-cost electroencephalography (EEG) acquisition systems, together with the advances in processing and classification algorithms, has favored the release of mobile BCI (mBCI) [7]. The most popular mBCI applications proposed to date are general-purpose, including mBCIs as part of body area networks (WBAN) [8,9], games [10], sports [11], daily-life [12–15] and others [16]. However, the usefulness of wireless EEG acquisition systems and mBCIs in clinical practice is still an open question [17].

In this paper we present a low-cost mBCI application for clinical practice (see Fig. 1). In particular, the fully functional system (hardware and software) is able to perform the visual evoked potentials (VEP) test following the standard of the International Society for Clinical Evaluation of Vision (ISCEV) for stimulation and recording [18]. Visual evoked potentials are electrophysiological responses caused by visual stimuli. These responses are present in the EEG and can be recorded by placing one or more electrodes in the occipital area of the brain cortex. They are used in clinical practice to diagnose and monitor a broad list of diseases such as optic chiasm [19], Parkinson's disease [20], multiple sclerosis [21], cataract [22], retinopathy [23], glaucoma [24], optic neuropathy [25] and stroke [26]. The proposed system consists of the RABio w8 low-cost device (developed by the University of Granada) for wireless EEG acquisition and a mobile device (e.g., smartphone, tablet, etc.) to perform the stimulation. After RABio w8 records the event-related responses (i.e., EEG data), they are sent to the cloud (i.e., a remote server) in charge of computing the VEPs in real-time. Once the VEPs have been extracted, the remote server sends the results to both the mobile device used for stimulation and the email addressed specified by the user. A comprehensive description of the mBCI application is reported in Sect. 2.3.

We conducted a study in order to prove the potential usefulness of our mBCI application for clinical practice. Those essential features in the VEP test such as level of synchronization, robustness and quality of VEPs (based on the amplitude, latency and morphology, that is, the quantifiable parameters of VEPs [27,28]) were analyzed. The results show that they are acceptable for the standard requirements for the electrophysiological evaluation of vision, even under unfavorable environmental conditions (presence of severe artifacts).

Low-cost mobile applications have positive impact on society. The cost of many clinical test could be significantly reduced by using low-cost mobile technology. In addition, many clinical test could move from the lab (i.e., laboratories and hospitals) to everywhere and be performed at whenever time. In case of our mBCI application, it could be used as screening tool, as well as for massive studies in schools, local health centers, etc. by combining the mBCI application with big data in the cloud.

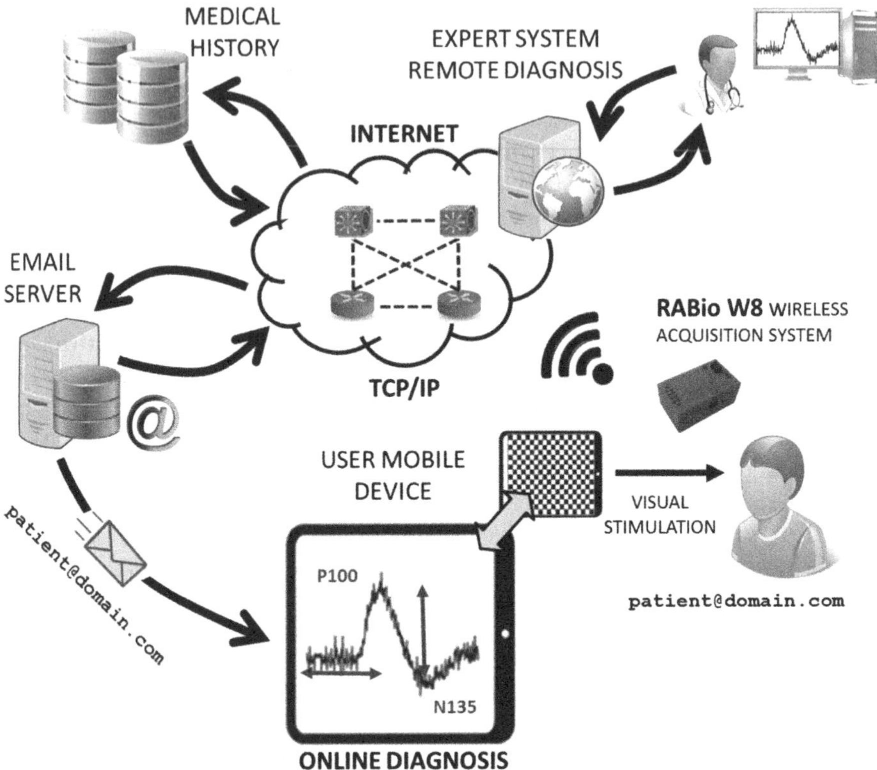

Fig. 1. Graphical description of the mBCI application for real-time and cloud-computing of VEPs. When VEPs are computed, they are sent to the email addresses specified by the user, e.g., the email address of a doctor for clinical evaluation of vision.

2 Methods

The aim of the conducted study was to test the performance of our mBCI application in the VEP clinical test, under different daily-life conditions, some of them with severe artifacts. The ISCEV standard for stimulation and recording of VEPs was followed. The details about the methodology are reported in this section.

2.1 Subjects and EEG Setup

Two healthy male volunteers participated in the study. They were not paid for their participation. All the subjects declared no visual pathologies or they used glasses to correct their vision during the experiment. They were informed about the experimental procedure and signed the informed consent prior to the beginning of the experiment.

One EEG electrode was placed at Oz position of the 10–20 International System. The reference and the ground were placed at Fz and the left ear lobe, respectively. The impedance of the electrodes was below 5 KΩ.

2.2 Materials

Stimulation was performed by using a mobile device with 13.3-inch screen and Matlab software (The Mathworks, MA, USA). EEG signals were recorded at 500 Hz with the RABio w8 device. This device is a wireless 8-channel EEG acquisition system based on a 24-bit analog/digital converter with programmable amplifiers, a microcontroller and a Bluetooth module. Server used for cloud-computing of VEPs was a desktop PC with Matlab software.

2.3 Generation, Mobile Recording and Cloud-Computing of VEPs

Visual evoked potentials were elicited by pattern-reversal stimuli with checkerboard. Square size was 1 degree of visual field with the subject placed at 50 cm from the screen. Stimulation rate was 2 stimuli per second. The VEP test consisted in 4 trials of 80 stimuli (i.e., a total of 320 stimuli) with an inter-trial rest time of 10 s.

The subjects performed the VEP test in three different conditions with an inter-condition rest time of 5 min (see Fig. 2): sitting in a chair within a laboratory (condition I), walking along a corridor (condition II) and sitting in the passenger seat of a moving car (condition III). Condition I is considered as the gold standard since it is the closest implementation of the ISCEV standard. Although lighting conditions were stable, severe motion artifacts are expected in condition II due to the walking movement. In condition III, severe artifacts caused by environmental lighting changes are expected. For the sake of simplicity, in this paper subjects and conditions are denoted as (subject, condition). For instance (S2, III) denotes subject 2, condition III.

During the VEP test, as mentioned before, RABio w8 device is in charge of recording the EEG. Stimulus onset information is also recorded by RABio w8. It sends the EEG data (including stimulus onset information), sample by sample, to the mobile stimulation device via Bluetooth (IEEE 802.15.1 standard). This device collects the EEG data corresponding to one trial and sends them to the cloud by using TCP/IP communication through a wireless access point and router. In condition III, a smartphone was used as gateway to connect to the 4G network. Once the one-trial EEG data have been received by the server, a bandpass filtering (1–100 Hz) is performed. Afterwards, the epoch corresponding to every stimulus is extracted by using the stimulus onset information. No epoch was discarded. All the epochs are averaged to obtain the mean. This mean is the stimulus response. Negative (N1) and positive (P1) VEPs are automatically identified and marked in the resulting plot (see Fig. 3). Finally, this plot, raw and processed EEG data are sent, through a simple mail transfer protocol (SMTP)

Fig. 2. Pictures of conditions during the experiment. From left to right, conditions I, II and III.

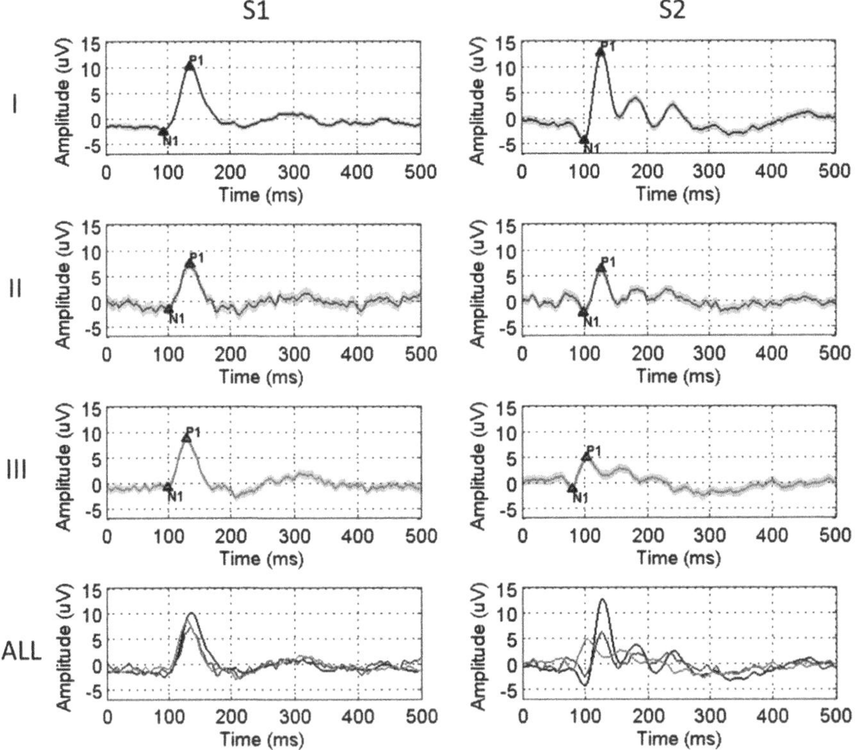

Fig. 3. Visual evoked potentials (mean) for all cases. N1 and P1 VEPs are marked in plots. Shadow behind the plots represents twice the standard error of the mean (for a better visualization).

server, to both the stimulation device and the email addresses specified by the user. All this is performed in real-time. The whole system is displayed in Fig. 1.

3 Results

The results of the study are reported in this section (see Fig. 3, Tables 1 and 2).

Table 1. Maximum cross-correlation of conditions I and II with condition I (gold standard). The delay needed to achieve the maximum cross-correlation is also reported.

Comparison	Cross-corr. (%)	Delay (ms)
(S1, I), (S1, II)	90.38	2
(S1, I), (S1, III)	93.00	6
(S2, I), (S2, II)	90.57	2
(S2, I), (S2, III)	82.21	24

Table 2. Amplitude and latency of N1 and P1 VEPs for all cases. P1-N1 differences in amplitude and latency are also reported.

Case	N1 (μV)	P1 (μV)	P1-N1 (μV)	N1 (ms)	P1 (ms)	P1-N1 (ms)
(S1, I)	−2.49	10.11	12.60	92	134	42
(S1, II)	−1.71	7.32	9.03	100	134	34
(S1, III)	−0.88	8.61	9.49	98	128	30
(S2, I)	−4.28	12.64	16.92	100	126	26
(S2, II)	−2.36	6.26	8.62	98	126	28
(S2, III)	−1.24	4.87	6.11	80	102	22

4 Discussion

In this paper we have proposed a low-cost mBCI for clinical applications. Our implementation is based on a RABio w8 device and the performance was validated by means of a clinical test. The results have shown that the level of synchronization, robustness and signal quality (amplitude, latency and morphology) are sound enough for the demanding standard required for the electrophysiological evaluation of vision. Moreover, the mobile recording and cloud computing of VEPs offers a number of advantages over traditional in-lab systems. Our low-cost mBCI application can be accommodated for ubiquitous and massive evaluation of vision, for visual impairment screening, and used as ambulatory diagnostic tool in rural or undeveloped areas.

Figure 3 shows the VEP of two subjects under the three conditions of the experiment. VEPs under condition I correspond to the closest implementation of the ISCEV standard and we considered it in this experiment as the gold standard for conditions II and III. For both subject we observe that under conditions II and III, VEPs are contaminated with noise (i.e., it is not as smooth as the condition I). This was expected since the ISCEV standard describe simply filters for EEG signals recorded in an isolated room and with small number of artifacts. The noise could be easily mitigated with standard procedures for artifacts reduction (e.g., by reducing the bandwidth low-band filter or by eliminating trials with disparate amplitudes). Despite that, VEPs under conditions II and III exhibits and high correlation level with condition I (90.38%, 93.00%, 90.57% and 82.21% in cases (S1, II), (S1, III), (S2, II) and (S2, III) respectively, see Table 1) and the error latency is just small except for (S2, III) (2 ms, 6 ms, 2 ms and 24 ms in cases (S1 ,II), (S1 ,III), (S2, II) and (S2, III) respectively, see Table 1). The last row of Fig. 3 shows the three conditions overlapping. From visual inspection we can conclude that there is not relevant difference between the three VEPs and our mBCI implementation could be used with some limitations for the rapid and low-cost implementation of this clinical protocol. The only exception (S2, III).

Table 2 shows the amplitudes and latencies of negative (N1) and positive (P1) visual potentials. The amplitude and latency of these potentials help for the diagnosis of optic nerve impairment (WEB). Specifically, the N70 and P100 peak latencies and N70-P100 amplitude difference have been reported as sensitive measures of resolved optic neuritis [29]. For instance, people with resolved optic neuritis (ON) may have of 24 ms of mean delay of P1 in comparison with normal people [29]. Absolute and relative N1-P1 differences in amplitude and latency (compared with condition I), with the sole exception of (S2, III), are small (see Table 2). Therefore, it seems unlikely that the use of our mBCI system could give rise to a false positive of ON.

In conclusion, only (S2, III) shows amplitudes and latencies significantly different from those of the gold standard. This was expected because of the environmental lighting changes that could affect the vision of the subject. Our study needs to be extended in order to achieve reliable and comprehensive conclusions.

Acknowledgments. This work was supported by Nicolo Association for the R+D in Neurotechnologies for disability, the Ministry of Economy and Competitiveness DPI2015-69098-REDT, the research project P11-TIC-7983 of Junta of Andalucia (Spain), and the Spanish National Grant TIN2015-67020-P, co-financed by the European Regional Development Fund (ERDF).

References

1. Woods, A.M., Nowostawski, M., Franz, E.A., Purvis, M.: Parkinson's disease and essential tremor classification on mobile device. Pervasive Mob. Comput. **13**, 1–12 (2014)
2. Maxhuni, A., Munoz-Melendez, A., Osmani, V., Perez, H., Mayora, O., Morales, E.F.: Classification of bipolar disorder episodes based on analysis of voice and motor activity of patients. Pervasive Mob. Comput. **31**, 50–66 (2016)
3. Okoshi, T., Nozaki, H., Nakazawa, J., Tokuda, H., Ramos, J., Dey, A.K.: Towards attention-aware adaptive notification on smart phones. Pervasive Mob. Comput. **26**, 17–34 (2016)
4. Ubeyli, E.D., Güler, N.F.: Theory and applications of telemedicine. J. Med. Syst. **26**(3), 199–220 (2002)
5. Black, A.D., Car, J., Pagliari, C., Anandan, C., Cresswell, K., Bokun, T., McKinstry, B., Procter, R., Majeed, A., Sheikh, A.: The impact of ehealth on the quality and safety of health care: a systematic overview. PLoS Med. **8**(1), 1–16 (2011)
6. Lorenz, A., Oppermann, R.: Mobile health monitoring for the elderly: designing for diversity. Pervasive Mob. Comput. **5**(5), 478–495 (2009)

7. Minguillon, J., Lopez-Gordo, M.A., Pelayo, F.: Trends in EEG-BCI for daily-life: requirements for artifact removal. Biomed. Sig. Process. Control **31**, 407–418 (2017)
8. Valenzuela-valdés, J.F., López, M.A., Padilla, P., Padilla, J.L., Minguillon, J.: Human neuro-activity for securing body area networks: application of brain-computer interfaces to people-centric internet of things. IEEE Commun. Mag. **55**(2), 62–67 (2017)
9. Lopez-Gordo, M.A., Pelayo Valle, F.: Brain-computer interface as networking entity in body area networks. In: Aguayo-Torres, M.C., Gómez, G., Poncela, J. (eds.) WWIC 2015. LNCS, vol. 9071, pp. 274–285. Springer, Cham (2015). doi:10.1007/978-3-319-22572-2_20
10. Liao, L., Chen, C., Wang, I.: Gaming control using a wearable and wireless EEG-based brain-computer interface device with novel dry foam-based sensors. J. NeuroEng. Rehabil. **9**(5) (2012)
11. Park, J.L., Fairweather, M.M., Donaldson, D.I.: Making the case for mobile cognition: EEG and sports performance. Neurosci. Biobehav. Rev. **52**, 117–130 (2015)
12. Wang, Y., Wang, Y., Jung, T.: A cell-phone-based braincomputer interface for communication in daily life. J. Neural Eng. (2011)
13. Brennan, C., McCullagh, P., Lightbody, G., Galway, L., Feuser, D., González, J.L., Martin, S.: Accessing tele-services using a hybrid BCI approach. In: Rojas, I., Joya, G., Catala, A. (eds.) IWANN 2015. LNCS, vol. 9094, pp. 110–123. Springer, Cham (2015). doi:10.1007/978-3-319-19258-1_10
14. Mihajlovi, V., Grundlehner, B., Vullers, R., Penders, J.: Wearable, wireless EEG solutions in daily life applications: what are we missing? IEEE J. Biomed. Health Inf. **19**(1), 6–21 (2015)
15. Lin, C., Lin, F., Chen, S.: EEG-based brain-computer interface for smart living environmental auto-adjustment. J. Med. Biol. Eng. **30**(4), 237–245 (2010)
16. Lin, C., Chang, C., Lin, B.: A real-time wireless braincomputer interface system for drowsiness detection. Biomed. Circ. Syst. IEEE Trans. **4**(4), 214–222 (2010)
17. Duvinage, M., Castermans, T., Petieau, M., Hoellinger, T., Cheron, G., Dutoit, T.: Performance of the Emotiv Epoc headset for P300-based applications. Biomed. Eng. Online **12**(1), 56 (2013)
18. Odom, J.V., Bach, M., Brigell, M., Holder, G.E., McCulloch, D.L., Mizota, A., Tormene, A.P.: ISCEV standard for clinical visual evoked potentials: (2016 update). Doc. Ophthalmol. **133**(1), 1–9 (2016)
19. Brecelj, J.: A VEP study of the visual pathway function in compressive lesions of the optic chiasm. Full-field versus half-field stimulation. Electroencephalogr. Clin. Neurophysiol./Evoked Potentials **84**(3), 209–218 (1992)
20. Nightingale, S., Mitchell, K.W., Howe, J.W.: Visual evoked cortical potentials and pattern electroretinograms in Parkinson's disease and control subjects. J. Neurol. Neurosurg. Psychiatry **49**, 1280–1287 (1986)
21. Frederiksen, J.L., Larsson, H.B.W., OlesenI, J., Stigsby, B.: MRI, VEP, SEP and biothesiometry suggest monosymptomatic acute optic neuritis to be a first manifestation of multiple sclerosis. Acta Neurol. Scand. **83**, 343–350 (1991)
22. McCulloch, D.L., Skarf, B.: Pattern reversal visual evoked potentials following early treatment of unilateral, congenital cataract. Arch. Ophthalmol. **112**, 510 (1994)
23. Folk, J.C., Thompson, H.S., Han, D.P., Brown, C.K.: Visual function abnormalities in central serous retinopathy. Arch. Ophthalmol. **102**, 1299–1302 (1984)
24. Hood, D.C., Greenstein, V.C.: Multifocal VEP and ganglion cell damage: applications and limitations for the study of glaucoma. Prog. Retinal Eye Res. **22**(2), 201–251 (2003)

25. Carroll, W.M., Mastaglia, F.L.: Leber's optic neuropathy: a clinical and visual evoked potential study of affected and asymptomatic members of a six generation family. Brain: J. Neurol. **102**, 559–580 (1979)
26. Julkunen, L., Tenovuo, O., Vorobyev, V., Hiltunen, J., Teräs, M., Jääskeläinen, S.K., Hämäläinen, H.: Functional brain imaging, clinical and neurophysiological outcome of visual rehabilitation in a chronic stroke patient. Restorative Neurol. Neurosci. **24**(2), 123–132 (2006)
27. Van den Bruel, A., Gailly, J., Hulstaert, F., Devriese, S., Eyssen, M.: The value of EEG, evoked potentials in clinical practice, Good Clinical Practice (GCP). Brussel: Belgian Health Care Knowledge Centre (KCE), KCE report 109C, pp. 1–138 (2009)
28. Evans, A.B.: Clinical utility of evoked potentials. Medscape, 1–28 (2014)
29. Brigell, M., Kaufman, D.I., Bobak, P., Beydoun, A.: The pattern visual evoked potential. A multicenter study using standardized techniques. Ophthalmic Lit. **48**(4), 308 (1995)

Spatial Resolution of EEG Source Reconstruction in Assessing Brain Connectivity Analysis

Jorge Ivan Padilla-Buriticá[1,2(✉)], J.D. Martínez-Vargas[1], A. Suárez-Ruiz[1], J.M. Ferrandez[2], and G. Castellanos-Dominguez[1]

[1] Universidad Nacional de Colombia,Manizales, Colombia
jipadilla@unal.edu.co
[2] Universidad Politécnica de Cartagena,Cartagena, Spain

Abstract. Brain connectivity analysis has emerged as a tool to associate activity generated in diverse brain areas, making possible the integration of functionally specialized brain regions in networks. However, estimation of the areas with relevant activity is well influenced by the applied brain mapping methods. This paper carries out the comparison of three reconstruction principles that differ in the way the prior covariance is adjusted, including its generalization through multiple and sparse spatial priors. To cluster the locations with significant brain activity (regions of interest), we select the most powerful areas, for which the functional connectivity is measured by the coherence and Kullback-Liebler divergence. From the obtained results on simulated and real-world EEG data, both measures show that the mapping method that includes Multiple Sparse Priors allows improving the connectivity accuracy regardless the used measure for all tested values of added noise.

1 Introduction

In the last years, connectivity analysis has gained considerable importance to study the behavior of the brain during different tasks and cognitive processes, as well as in the detection of some pathological conditions. In this regard, several approaches have discussed whether the connectivity analysis should be performed on EEG channel space or source space. As a result, it has been shown that due to the effects of field spread, it is difficult to carry out a connectivity analysis in the measured recordings on the scalp [15]. Moreover, it is difficult to associate an anatomical meaning with the connections, as the measured signals do not locate in direct spatial proximity to the underlying sources. On the other hand, EEG reconstruction methods each time achieve better performance on space and time domains), because they take into account the propagation of cortical activity towards the scalp. Furthermore, when the connectivity analysis is performed at the source level, it might yield a better interpretation of calculated interactions, which can be easily associated with the brain processes of integration and segregation [14].

J.M. Ferrández Vicente et al. (Eds.): IWINAC 2017, Part II, LNCS 10338, pp. 77–86, 2017.
DOI: 10.1007/978-3-319-59773-7_9

Unfortunately, despite the latest advances in source connectivity analysis, several problems that directly influence the accurateness of this analysis have not been solved. These problems can be summarized as: (i) developing a realistic conductivity model of the head, (ii) selection of the brain mapping method, (iii) selection of a proper connectivity measure and (iv) validation of the obtained results. In this work, we focus in how the chosen brain mapping method influences the performance of the source connectivity analysis.

In this regard, to select the brain mapping method, it must be considered that there exist several models to estimate the source activity, which can be classified into two groups: (i) dipole-fitting models that represent brain activity as a small number of dipoles with unknown positions and, (ii) the distributed-source models that represent the brain activity as a large number of dipoles in fixed positions [5]. Distributed source models present a highly ill-posed inverse problem, with no unique solution in the most general unconstrained case. Consequently, a unique solution can only be obtained by making additional assumptions (spatial and temporal) about the neural activity. For example, these assumptions can be made by introducing prior beliefs on the structure of possible source configurations in Bayesian inference framework [11] or based on geometric or physiological properties of the brain. In this regard, the more realistic the considered assumptions, the more accurate the reconstructed source space, and consequently, the connectivity analysis. However, to the best of our knowledge, there are no studies that systematically consider the influence of estimated source activity over the source connectivity analysis, in spite of the fact that brain mapping errors are known to have a significant effect on the accuracy of connectivity [4].

In this work, we compare three methods solving the inverse problem due to they have a common mathematical framework differing only in the prior assumptions of the estimation of the source covariance matrix. This prior covariance adjusts the primary differences between often used regularization schemes in the source estimation and is generalized by the use of multiple and sparse spatial priors. The comparison approach comprises three stages: (i) brain activity is estimated through Empirical Bayesian Beamformer (BMF) [1], Low-resolution brain electromagnetic tomography (LORETA) [13] and Multiple sparse priors (MSP) [6] approaches. (ii) Some regions of interest are selected based on the recovered sources with the highest energy. (iii) A connectivity brain measure is employed to quantify the changes in the information flow over the selected regions of interest. Obtained results show that the performance of brain connectivity depends strongly on the employed mapping method because different regions of interest (ROI) are obtained and, in the lower degree, on the used measure of similarity between the estimated regions of interest.

2 Methods

2.1 Estimation of Brain Source Activity

With the aim of estimating brain activity from measured EGG recordings, We will consider the following distributed inverse solution $\boldsymbol{Y} = \boldsymbol{L}\boldsymbol{J} + \boldsymbol{\Xi}$, so that

$\boldsymbol{Y} \in \mathbb{R}^{C \times T}$ is the EEG data measured by $C \in \mathbb{N}$ sensors at $T \in \mathbb{N}$ time samples, $\boldsymbol{J} \in \mathbb{R}^{D \times T}$ is the amplitude of the $D \in \mathbb{N}$ current dipoles, which placed in each three-dimensional dimension and distributed through cortical surface, and the lead field matrix $\boldsymbol{L} \in \mathbb{R}^{C \times D}$ is the relationship between sources and EEG data. Besides, the EEG measurements are assumed to be corrupted by zero mean Gaussian noise $\boldsymbol{\Xi} \in \mathbb{R}^{C \times T}$, having matrix covariance $\boldsymbol{Q}_{\Xi} = \sigma_{\Xi}^2 \boldsymbol{I}_C$, where $\boldsymbol{I}_C \in \mathbb{R}^{C \times C}$ is an identity matrix, and σ_{Ξ}^2 is the noise variance. Under these constraints, brain source activity can be estimated as:

$$\widehat{\boldsymbol{J}} = \boldsymbol{Q}\boldsymbol{L}^{\top}(\boldsymbol{Q}_{\Xi} + \boldsymbol{L}\boldsymbol{Q}\boldsymbol{L}^{\top})^{-1}\boldsymbol{Y}, \tag{1}$$

being $\boldsymbol{Q} \in \mathbb{R}^{D \times D}$ the source covariance matrix. For EEG brain mapping, the used approaches differ in the imposed prior assumptions upon $\boldsymbol{Q}$ as follows:

- *Low-Resolution Brain Electromagnetic Tomography* (LORETA) or maximally smoothed solution, $\boldsymbol{Q} = \boldsymbol{I}_D$.
- *Empirical Bayesian Beamformer* (BMF) that imposes spatial priors to include multiple modalities and subjects. In practice, the global prior assumes a covariance with the following q_{dd} element of the main diagonal:

  $$q_{dd} = (\boldsymbol{l}_d^{\top}(\boldsymbol{Y}\boldsymbol{Y}^{\top})\boldsymbol{l}_d)^{-1}/\delta_d, \quad \forall d = 1, \ldots, D,$$

  where $\boldsymbol{l}_d \in \mathbb{R}^{C \times 1}$ stands for the d–th column of $\boldsymbol{L}$, and $\delta_d = 1/\boldsymbol{l}_d^{\top}\boldsymbol{l}_d$ is the normalization parameter. So, the source covariance is $\lambda_p \boldsymbol{Q}$.
- *Multiple Sparse Priors* (MSP) that constructs the source covariance as a weighted sum of P possible patches $\{\boldsymbol{Q}_p : p \in P\}$ so that each one regards a single potentially activated cortex region and is weighted by its respective hyperparameter, $\lambda_p \in \mathbb{R}^+$, as follows:

  $$\boldsymbol{Q} = \sum\nolimits_{p \in P} \exp(\lambda_p)\boldsymbol{Q}_p.$$

2.2 Measurement of Brain Connectivity

To assess the brain connectivity analysis, we calculate, within the distributed brain networks, a set of relevant regions of interest (ROI) that make evident the existence of meaningful brain neural activity for the task at hand. Therefore, we must localize a set of reproducible and accurate cortical ROIs that should be consistent for all tested subjects. From EEG data, each brain is parcelled into a set of ROI by selecting those areas encircling the recovered sources with the highest energy. Each ROI area of the cortical surface has a 10 mm radius, covering approximately 300 dipoles, as suggested in [3]. However, the close active dipoles are gathered so that each one belongs to just one ROI, avoiding spurious connectivity. Further, the averaged time series over each ROI is extracted to analyze the functional connectivity among all obtained regions. Thus, we estimate the functional connectivity for the computed ROI sets, using the following measures:

- *Coherence*: This real-valued bivariate measure of the correlation between signals $u(t)$ and $v(t)$ is defined trough their spectral representations, $S_{u,v}(t,f)$ [8]:

$$\rho_{uv}(t,f) = \frac{\langle S_u(t,f)S_v^*(t,f)\rangle}{\langle|S_u(t,f)|\rangle \cdot \langle|S_v(t,f)|\rangle} \tag{2}$$

- *Kullback-Liebler (K-L) divergence* that is computed for the random processes $\boldsymbol{u}$ and $\boldsymbol{v}$ with finite states u_i and v_i, respectively, as follows:

$$\varrho(\boldsymbol{u},\boldsymbol{v}) = H(\boldsymbol{u},\boldsymbol{v}) - H(\boldsymbol{u}),\ \varrho(\boldsymbol{u},\boldsymbol{v}) \in \mathbb{R}^+ \tag{3}$$

where $H(\boldsymbol{u}) = -\sum_{n\in N} p(u_n)\log p(u_n)$ is the entropy of $\boldsymbol{u}$ and $H(\boldsymbol{u},\boldsymbol{v}) = -\sum_{n\in N} p(u_n,v_n)\log p(u_n,v_n)$ is the cross entropy between $\boldsymbol{u}$ and $\boldsymbol{v}$.

3 Experimental Set-Up and Results

For the purpose of validation, we investigate the influence of neural reconstruction on the brain connectivity analysis calculated from the assessed ROI sets. Due to the shared mathematical framework, we compare three inverse problem solutions (LORETA, BMF, MSP), differing only in the prior assumptions made upon the estimation of source covariance.

Simulated EEG Data. Initially, we simulate the EEG data that reproduce different brain activities. To this end, two active dipoles are assumed, where each one is a nonstationary source. All non-stationary time series are generated using the real Morlet wavelet, encouraging a behavior similar to an evoked response potential. Each recording lasts 1.5 s length and is sampled at 200 Hz. The random central frequency of the Morlet wavelet is sampled from a Gaussian distribution with a mean 9 Hz and standard deviation 2 Hz. The produced stimulus starts at $t = 0$ and the activity is propagated from simulated active dipole #1 to #2 at $t = 0.1$ s. Besides, the background noise of the dipole signals is set to have a $1/f$ spectral behavior. Then, each simulated EEG is calculated by multiplying the simulated brain activity to the lead field matrix. For source space modeling, a tessellated surface of the gray-white matter interface is used that has 8196 vertices (possible source localizations) with source orientations fixed orthogonally to the surface. Also, the lead fields are computed by the BEM volume conductor with a mean distance between neighboring vertices adjusted to 5 mm. As a result, we obtain synthetic EEG data for 128-channels. Three experimental configurations, carrying out 100 simulations each one, are performed to test sensibility to the noise of the proposed connectivity-based approach. To this, measurement noise is added to obtain SNR levels, ranging from −6 till 6 dB. Location of active dipoles is randomly selected for each simulation.

Real-World EEG Database. We also carry out the experimental testing using an EEG database provided by the *Wellcome Trust Centre for Neuroimaging*, holding faces and scrambled faces. This data were collected from a single subjects at the time he made symmetry judgements on faces and scrambled faces as described in [10]. All EEG recordings were acquired on a 128-channel ActiveTwo system, sampled at 2048 Hz, plus electrodes on left earlobe, right earlobe, and two bipolar channels. The epochs (168 faces and 168 scrambled faces) were baseline-corrected from 200 to 0 ms. Also, data were down-sampled at 200 Hz and averaged for each condition. For modeling the source space, we used a tessellated surface of the gray-white matter interface with 8196 vertices (possible source localizations) with source orientations fixed and being orthogonal to the surface. Finally, the head model was computed using a boundary element method (BEM) to estimate the forward operator $\boldsymbol{L}$.

Validation Results of Simulated EEG Data. Figure 1 shows the values of connectivity computed between each couple of the simulated sources depending on the employed estimator of neural activity. The connectivity values of a couple of sources are estimated after carrying 100 runs, allocating randomly over the head surface either source for each trial. As expected, the coherence measure (plotted by dashed lines) rises as the SNR level grows higher. By contrast, the K-L divergence (plotted in continued lines) reduces as the noise level decreases. At the same time, the assessed connectivity measures are differently influenced by the used mapping approach. Thus, the use of MSP makes either connectivity measure to be more accurately estimated regardless of the SNR added.

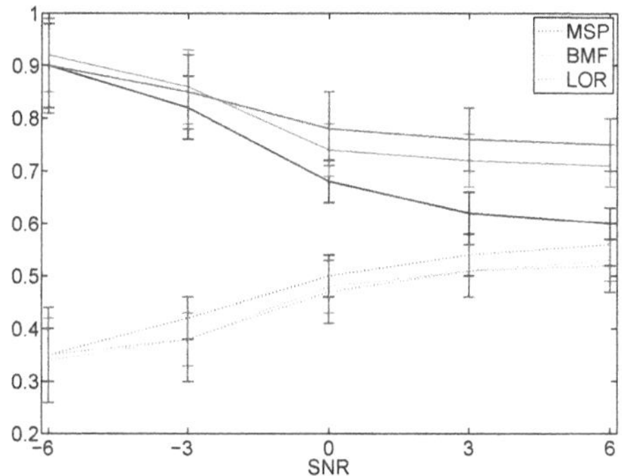

Fig. 1. Assessed values of connectivity after using different mapping approaches: coherence (dashed lines), KL divergence (continuous lines)

It is worth noting that either used estimator of connectivity shows very close standard deviation (KL-divergence provides 0.054 while coherence −0.058), making both measures similar in terms of confidence.

Validation Results of ERP Data. Figure 2 shows the estimated ROIS after mapping as well as the obtained values of connectivity (matrix of coherence). For either testing paradigm (termed *faces* or *scrambled faces*), the top row

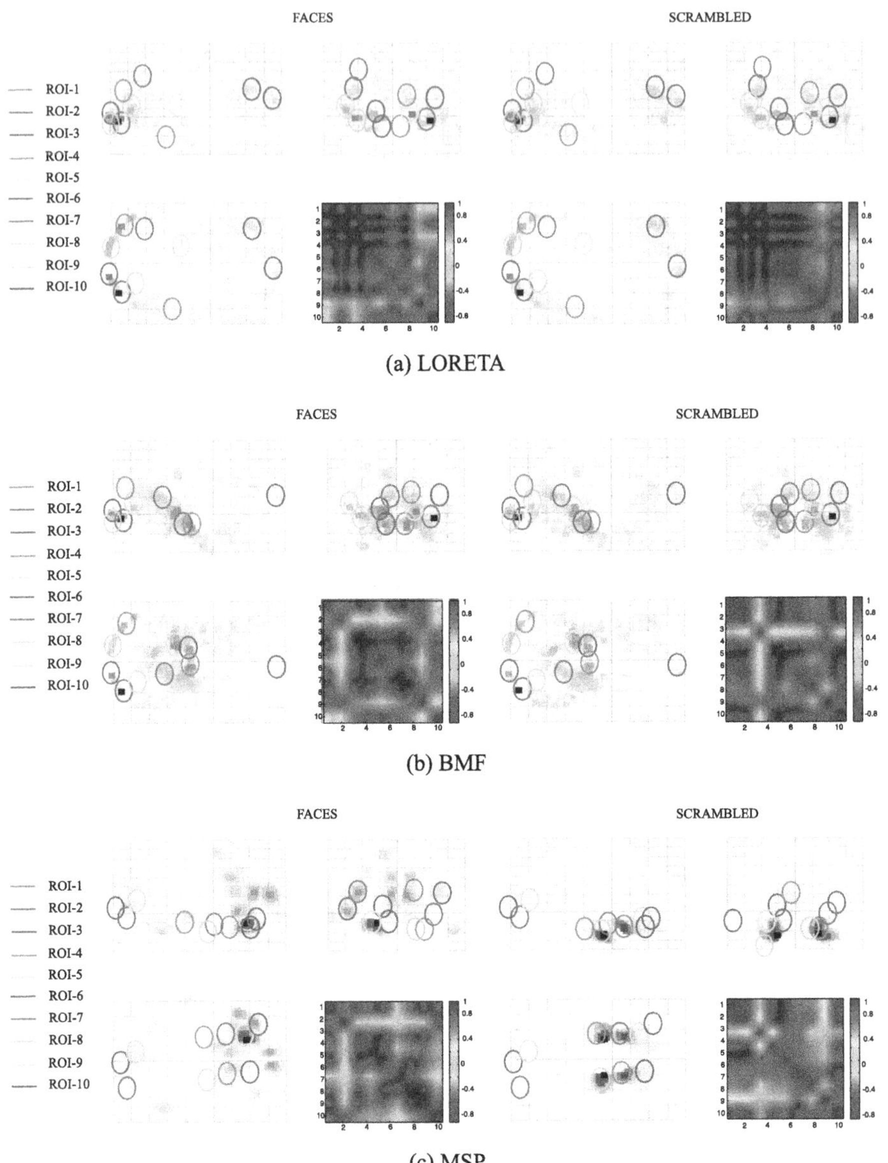

Fig. 2. EEG brain activity estimated by each considered brain mapping approach for a concrete task with the paradigm *faces* and *scrambled faces*. (Color figure online)

(see Fig. 2a) shows the lateral, superior, and sagittal views of the performed LORETA mapping, where the estimated ROIs are marked by circles with a different color. Likewise, Fig. 2b and c display performed results for the BMF and MSP methods, respectively. Visual inspection allows concluding that every tested mapping registers activity in the visual cortex (Occipital Lobe) and somatosensory area. So far, this finding totally agrees the commonly accepted physiological interpretation about visual stimulation. However, each mapping approach produces different amounts of spurious activity that is identified as ROI, but without any reported clinical meaning. Thus, LORETA provides the highest number of meaningless connections as can be corroborated in the coherence matrix, yielding an activity in areas where it is assumed not to be at all, namely, ROI 3 (Broca's area), ROI 5 (Motor function), ROI 7 (Wernicke's area). This result may be explained because of its widely-known poor spatial resolution. Further, BMF performs fewer ROIs with spurious, having even the less power. So, Broca's and Wernicke's (rather related to speech) areas, Motor function and auditory areas are wrongly labeled as salient ROIs for face recognition. Lastly, MSP produces lower values of coherence for ROIs not belonging to the occipital lobe. As a result, MSP yields the lowest number of the wrong ROIs, and thus, it promotes the most accurate connectivity estimation since it focuses most of the estimated ROIS on the Occipital lobe (ROI 4), linking correctly to the visual area.

For either paradigm *faces* (Top row) and *scrambled faces* (bottom row), Fig. 3 displays the values of connectivity computed by the K-L divergence upon the same ROI set as in the case of the coherence measure. Although every mapping method produces the same groups of associated activity, the MSP method makes more evident the relation among ROIs (see Fig. 3c and f).

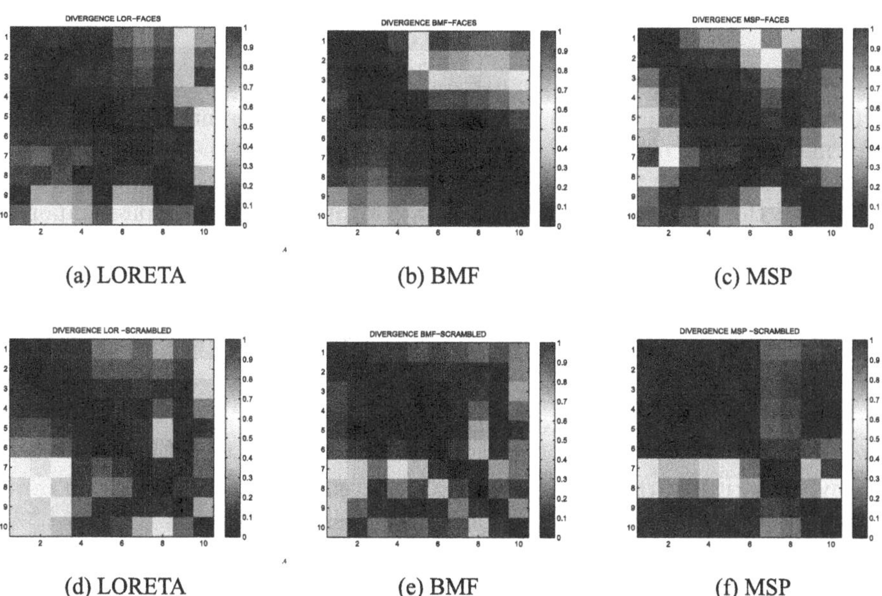

Fig. 3. Estimated matrices of connectivity using the K-L divergence for either paradigm *faces* (Top row) and *scrambled faces* (bottom row).

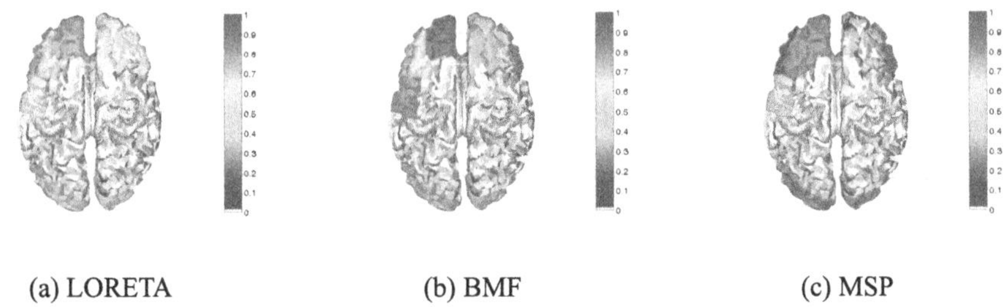

(a) LORETA (b) BMF (c) MSP

Fig. 4. Results of the paired t-test for the estimated sets of ROI by each mapping method with K-L divergence.

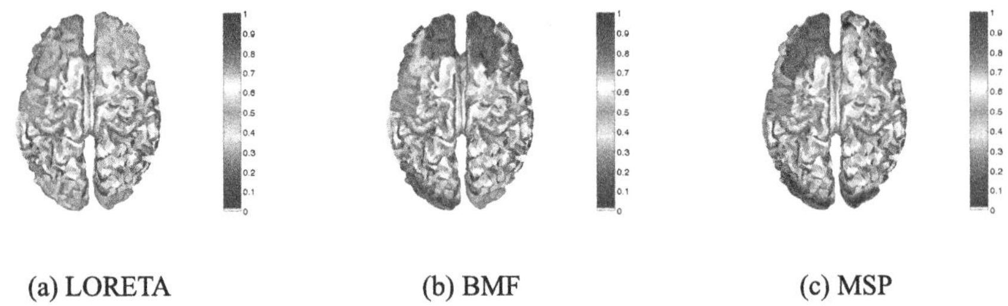

(a) LORETA (b) BMF (c) MSP

Fig. 5. Results of the paired t-test for the estimated sets of ROI by each mapping method with Coherence.

On the other hand, we carry out the paired t-test over the set of estimated ROIs to make clear which areas contribute the most to differentiate between the different conditions, namely, faces and scrambled faces. For the sake of generalization, we also merge the obtained sets of ROI for both considered paradigms. As a result, the most discriminating areas are identified in the occipitotemporal brain (see Figs. 4 and 5). Meanwhile, this area has been reported to be related to the structural encoding of faces [12]. In this regard, MSP is the mapping technique that shows the most powerful and localized activity in the occipitotemporal area, favoring the interpretation of the assessed connectivity measures.

4 Discussion and Concluding Remarks

We have investigated the influence of EEG source reconstruction for brain connectivity analysis, according to the following steps:

1. Selection of brain mapping method, contrasting LORETA, BMF and MSP
2. ROI selection based on the estimated maps of neural activity
3. We apply two connectivity measures: Kullback-Leibler divergence and Coherence

The main aspect concerns the selected brain mapping method for imaging EEG activity. The first tested method of brain mapping was LORETA has a relatively low spatial resolution because the localization is preserved with a certain amount of dispersion [13].Therefore, the estimated brain activity is more blurred, producing broad zones of neural activity. On the other hand, the use of BMF improves identification of the source signals from electroencephalographic measurements [1], nevertheless, BMF tends to estimate several spurious activated areas, misleading the connectivity analysis. This effect appears to be directly related to the estimation complexity of the source covariance matrix [12].

On the other hand, MSP allows to perform source activity reconstruction so that we obtain more precise regions of activation. Furthermore, due to the low spatial resolution, LORETA algorithm often locates erroneous regions with activity, where powerful common sources should not be present. Therefore, although LORETA has been widely used in the last years to reconstruct brain activity, its confidence of estimated areas of activation may be not enough [7]. From obtained results validating on simulated and real-world recordings, MSP-based estimation of ROI time courses allows improving the connectivity accuracy regardless the used measure for all tested values of SNR. Furthermore, MSP allows estimating ROIs centered at locations related to the experimental task at hand (i.e., face perception). Thus, the estimated energy has greater activity in the visual cortex (Occipital Lobe) and the somatosensory area for either testing paradigm (faces or scrambled faces). This result totally matches the accepted physiological interpretation about visual stimulation.

Generally speaking, a challenging issue relating to brain connectivity analysis is how to identify ROI sets (obtained from the brain mapping method) precisely, at very short temporal scales; this dilemma remains common for all cognitive tasks [9] and for the study of the brain pathologies [2,16]. We have used an approach to select regions of interest ROI similar to [12], in order to ensure that the selected regions of interest have been the ones that have had the most energy and best describe the behavior of brain states. As a result, the introduced ROI sets enhance the performed detection accuracy. Another aspect of consideration is the involved measure of connectivity analysis. Here, we compare both Kullback-Liebler divergence and Coherence measures that provide similar behaviors as already had been reported in the literature [8]. Nevertheless, the used EEG source estimation method clearly influences the assessed connectivity. For instance, a poor source reconstruction may lead the incorrect selection of ROIs for separating responses to different stimulus. As a result, the source estimation method must be chosen carefully in all studies conducted in brain connectivity. As future work, authors plan to test the introduced approach over diverse paradigms, clustering, and connectivity measures. Furthermore, an online extension of the brain connectivity analysis can be proposed to include the temporal variations of the inter-channel relationships directly.

Acknowledgments. This work was supported by the research project 11974454838 founded by COLCIENCIAS. J.I. Padilla-Buriticá is founded by Programa nacional de becas de doctorado, convocatoria 647 (2014).

References

1. Belardinelli, P., Ortiz, E., Barnes, G., Noppeney, U., Preissl, H.: Source reconstruction accuracy of MEG and EEG Bayesian inversion approaches. PLoS ONE **7**(12), 51985 (2012)
2. Brier, M.R., Thomas, J.B., Fagan, A.M., Hassenstab, J., Holtzman, D.M., Benzinger, T.L., Morris, J.C., Ances, B.M.: Functional connectivity and graph theory in preclinical Alzheimer's disease. Neurobiol. Aging **35**(4), 757–768 (2014)
3. Brookes, M.J., O'neill, G.C., Hall, E.L., Woolrich, M.W., Baker, A., Palazzo Corner, S., Robson, S.E., Morris, P.G., Barnes, G.R.: Measuring temporal, spectral and spatial changes in electrophysiological brain network connectivity. NeuroImage **91**, 282–299 (2014)
4. Cho, J.-H., Vorwerk, J., Wolters, C.H., Knösche, T.R.: Influence of the head model on EEG and MEG source connectivity analyses. Neuroimage **110**, 60–77 (2015)
5. Costa, F., Batatia, H., Oberlin, T., D'Giano, C., Tourneret, J.-Y.: Bayesian EEG source localization using a structured sparsity prior. NeuroImage **144**, 142–152 (2017)
6. Friston, K., Harrison, L., Daunizeau, J., Kiebel, S., Phillips, C., Trujillo-Barreto, N., Henson, R., Flandin, G., Mattout, J.: Multiple sparse priors for the M/EEG inverse problem. NeuroImage **39**(3), 1104–1120 (2008)
7. Grech, R., Cassar, T., Muscat, J., Camilleri, K.P., Fabri, S.G., Zervakis, M., Xanthopoulos, P., Sakkalis, V., Vanrumste, B.: Review on solving the inverse problem in EEG source analysis. J. Neuroeng. Rehabil. **5**(1), 25 (2008)
8. Greenblatt, R.E., Pflieger, M.E., Ossadtchi, A.E.: Connectivity measures applied to human brain electrophysiological data. J. Neurosci. Methods **207**(1), 1–16 (2012)
9. Hassan, M., Dufor, O., Merlet, I., Berrou, C., Wendling, F.: EEG source connectivity analysis: from dense array recordings to brain networks. PLoS One **9**(8), 105041 (2014)
10. Henson, R.N., Wakeman, D.G., Litvak, V., Friston, K.J.: A parametric empirical Bayesian framework for the EEG/MEG inverse problem: generative models for multi-subject and multi-modal integration. Front. Hum. Neurosci. **5**, 76 (2011)
11. Nummenmaa, A., Auranen, T., Hämäläinen, M.S., Jääskeläinen, I.P., Lampinen, J., Sams, M., Vehtari, A.: Hierarchical Bayesian estimates of distributed MEG sources: theoretical aspects and comparison of variational and MCMC methods. NeuroImage **35**(2), 669–685 (2007)
12. Padilla-Buritica, J.I., Martinez-Vargas, J.D., Castellanos-Dominguez, G.: Emotion discrimination using spatially compact regions of interest extracted from imaging EEG activity. Front. Comput. Neurosci. **10** (2016)
13. Pascual-Marqui, R.D., Esslen, M., Kochi, K., Lehmann, D., et al.: Functional imaging with low-resolution brain electromagnetic tomography (LORETA): a review. Methods Find. Exp. Clin. Pharmacol. **24**(Suppl C), 91–95 (2002)
14. Rubinov, M., Sporns, O.: Complex network measures of brain connectivity: uses and interpretations. Neuroimage **52**(3), 1059–1069 (2010)
15. Schoffelen, J.-M., Gross, J.: Source connectivity analysis with MEG and EEG. Hum. Brain Mapp. **30**(6), 1857–1865 (2009)
16. Sheline, Y.I., Raichle, M.E.: Resting state functional connectivity in preclinical Alzheimer's disease. Biol. Psychiatry **74**(5), 340–347 (2013)

Securing Passwords Beyond Human Capabilities with a Wearable Neuro-Device

Miguel Angel Lopez-Gordo[1], Jesus Minguillon[2(✉)], Juan Francisco Valenzuela-Valdes[1], Pablo Padilla[1], Jose Luis Padilla[3], and Francisco Pelayo[1]

[1] Department of Signal Theory, Communications and Networking - CITIC, University of Granada, Granada, Spain
{malg,juanvalenzuela,pablopadilla,fpelayo}@ugr.es

[2] Department of Computer Architecture and Technology - CITIC, University of Granada, Granada, Spain
minguillon@ugr.es

[3] Department of Electronics and Computers Technology, University of Granada, Granada, Spain
jluispt@ugr.es

Abstract. The election of strong passwords is a challenging task for humans that could undermine the secure online subscription to services in mobile applications. Composition rules and dictionaries help to choose stronger passwords, although at the cost of the easiness to memorize them. When high-performance computers are not available, such as in mobile scenarios, the problem is even worse because mobile devices typically lack good enough entropy sources. Then, the goal is to obtain strong passwords with the best efficiency in terms of level of entropy per character unit. In this study, we propose the use neuro-activity as source of entropy for the efficient generation of strong passwords. In our experiment we used the NIST test suite to compare binary random sequences extracted from neuro-activity by means of a mobile brain-computer interface with (i) strong passwords manually generated with restrictions based on dictionary and composition rules and (ii) passwords generated automatically by a mathematical software running on a work station. The results showed that random sequences based on neuro-activity were much more suitable for the generation of strong passwords than those generated by humans and were as strong as those generated by a computer. Also, the rate at which random bits were generated by neuro-activity (4 Kbps) was much faster than the passwords manually generated. Thus, just a very small fraction of the time and cognitive workload caused to manually generate a password has enough entropy for the generation of stronger, shorter and easier to remember passwords. We conclude that in either mobile scenarios or when good enough entropy sources are not available the use of neuro-activity is an efficient option for the generation of strong passwords.

Keywords: Wearable brain-computer interfaces · Neuro-activity · Secure passwords

J.M. Ferrández Vicente et al. (Eds.): IWINAC 2017, Part II, LNCS 10338, pp. 87–95, 2017.
DOI: 10.1007/978-3-319-59773-7_10

1 Introduction

Currently, humans enjoy on-line services and applications such as social networks, web browsing, email, e-commerce, e-Government services, etc. Wireless technologies contribute to the mobility by enabling access to internet working abroad, such as in the tube, in the bus stop or in the canteen while having lunch. Although people typically use passwords as a simply and straight-forward way to gain access to on-line services, it becomes challenging for humans not only to generate a relatively high number of strong passwords, but at the same time to memorize them.

Passwords strength is related to the probability of guessing it by a repetitive at-tack. It depends on both the entropy of the password and the way the server limits the number of unsuccessful attempts. For a giving number of unsuccessful attempts, the entropy of the password determines the assurance level during on-line authentication.

The entropy of a password determines how difficult it is to discover. It is typically measured in terms of bits (H) and in the case of a password of length n, generated by a set with m equally likely characters; it can be easily measured as formulated in (1).

$$H(bit) = log_2(m^n) \tag{1}$$

Computers can also be used to generate passwords based on pseudorandom binary sequences originated from a seed. One inconvenient of this approach is that the generation of the password is determinist. That is, for a given cryptographic algorithm, any password can be reproduced with the only knowledge of the seed, thus being a vulnerability in the password generation.

In mobile context, generation of strong passwords presents an even a more complicated scenario. On the one hand, mobile devices are typically low-cost electronics with very limited hardware resources unable to support high computational loads and storage capabilities. Then, they have not good enough entropy sources such as those from a PC [1] and this justifies the analysis of other physical sources of entropy such as bio-signals. The latter could be a problem when the user is required for an on-line subscription that requires the strongest possible password. On the other hand, the election and memorization of strong passwords is challenging for humans. A strong password typically requires a large number of characters that, in turn, are difficult to remember. Again, the use of a good entropy source guarantees a high efficiency in the quantity of entropy per character.

In this preliminary study, we propose the use of a wearable brain-computer interface (wBCI) as a source of entropy for the generation of strong passwords. In our experiment we used the NIST test suite to compare strong passwords (i) manually generated by a participant with restrictions based on dictionary and composition rules with (ii) the participants neuro-activity while he was manually generating the passwords and with (iii) passwords generated automatically by a mathematical software running on a work station. The promising results suggest that in mobile scenarios the use of neuro-activity is an efficient option for the generation of strong passwords.

2 Related Works

In our days, a large number of the people live connected to networks. They freely commute from home to work, visit leisure spaces and spend their time connected to social networks, or corporative and private services and applications. Every day, we install apparently-free-of-charge applications in our smartphones. Typically we are only required an email account, an username and a password. In occasions we may not need a strong password when we subscribe for a trivial temporal service, but sometimes we would like to provide a strong password, as secure as possible. When a computer is not available, such as in the context of Wireless Body Area Networks (WBANs), bio-signals from wearable devices and bio-inspired solutions can be used to generate cryptographic keys [2,3]. For instance, pulse oximetry, pulse interval, heart rate variability (HRV) or electrocardiography (ECG) [3–6] have been employed as physical sources of entropy in WBANs.

Computers can be used to generate pseudo random seeds for passwords. This is a deterministic process that solely depends on the seed and the generation algorithm. Then, the predictability of the seed is the main vulnerability. Standards of the industry such as the RFC4086 [7] proposes hardware-based random sources to produce unpredictable seeds (e.g. ring oscillators, disk drive timing, system clock, mouse motion, CPU interruptions, etc.). However, under some circumstances, some of these methods (e.g., vectors based in date or time) are very predictable [8]. Sensors integrated in smartphones have been used when a computer was not available. Authors in [9] show that one of the best entropy source could be the microphone. However, it could be hacked or force the random number by means of a simple auditory attack.

Humans can also produce strong passwords. The mayor inconvenient is our inability to memorize them, especially when we need to access or subscribe to many services. When we are asked for a password in an on-line registration, we typically produce a very weak one. Authors in [10] performed a large-scale study about users habits in web password. The study confirmed (i) the poor quality of user passwords; (ii) users reuse them and (iii) they often forget them. Restrictions imposed by services (e.g., composition rules and dictionaries) typically improve the entropy, although still far from being a random password. Another recent study [11] concludes that people habits have changed in different ways from previous studies and surveys. Figure 1 shows an estimation of the bits of entropy in a password when users select it without restrictions, with dictionary and composition rules and completely random [12]. From visual inspection of manually generated passwords (curves with triangles, circles and asterisk), we conclude that (i) a minimum of 8–10 characters is recommended to obtain a substantial benefit using dictionaries and composition rules with respects to no checks; (ii) a completely random password of just 6 characters conveys as much entropy as a manually generated password without checks or either with dictionary of 24 characters length, or with dictionary and composition rules of 18 characters length. In summary, the use of a good source of entropy can help the user to choose an efficient number of characters for a strong password not difficult to remember.

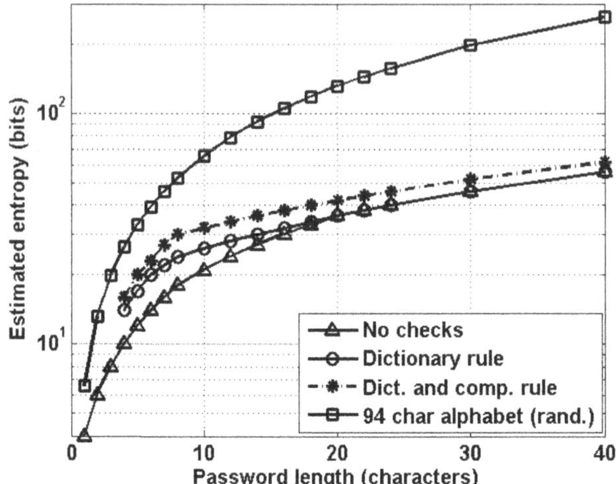

Fig. 1. Estimation of the passwords entropy. The curve with rectangles (upper one) represents the maximum theoretical limit of entropy with 94 equally likely printable characters. The curve with triangles (bottom one) represents a typical password manually generated without any restrictions (i.e., easy to remember). The curves in between represent the entropy when restrictions based on dictionary (curve with circles) and dictionary together with composition rules (curve with asterisks) are imposed. Adapted from [12]

Recent advances in technology have given rise to the development of wearable and mobile BCI that can be part of a wearable WBAN ecosystem [13] (see [14] for a review). Currently, they are wearable and low-cost devices capable to ubiquitously monitor our cognitive and electro-physiological activity. Other WBAN devices such as ECG measurers have been reported as good entropy sources for the generation of cryptographic keys [15]. In comparison with ECG, electroencephalography (EEG) theoretically presents better characteristics for the generation of random binary sequences. For instance, EEG is the result of both endogenous and exogenous cognitive and physiological processes sustained by billions of interconnected neurons. The additive sum of field potentials generated by each of them gives rise to the EEG signals. They depend on the location of the electrode over the scalp and they also need physical contact for their acquisition. In summary, it is very unlikely to hack, reproduce or guess spontaneous EEG activity. EEG is an estimable physical source of entropy that requires a minimum preprocessing and hardware resources usage. Another advantage is the bit rate. ECG can generate circa 16 random bps [3], whereas EEG which is typically acquired at 1000 samples/s with 24 bits of resolution per sample, could offer a maximum of 24 Kbps per EEG channel. Even after a severe process of bit discarding, EEG could be used to generate large data sets of random numbers. For instance, for some NIST tests, a sequence of circa 2Mb is recommended. In this case, ECG and EEG would take more than one day and just a few minutes respectively.

Finally, in [16] the authors proposed the use of a wBCI for the generation of a data set with secure keys to encrypt communication of WBAN devices. This was presented as a contribution to the people-centric Internet of Things. From the best of our knowledge this was the first study in which EEG was evaluated as source of entropy to generate passwords.

3 Experimental Design

The objective of this study was to compare the randomness of binary sequences generated by neuro-activity with the derived from manually generated passwords with severe restrictions and with the automatically generated by a computer. We defined three data sets:

Data Set I: Passwords generated by the neuro-activity exerted by one participant when he was manually generating passwords. An EEG electrode was placed on Cz position of the 10–20 International System [17]. This position (top of the head, see Fig. 2) was chosen because it matches reports of successful studies of random number generation [16]. The channel was referenced and grounded to the left ear lobe. The impedance of the electrodes was much lower than the input impedance of the acquisition system. EEG signals were recorded at 500 Hz and 24 bits per sample with a RABIO w8 developed by the University of Granada.

No preprocessing technique or whitening pre-processing was performed on the EEG data. Even the use of a notch filter to remove power-line coupling was discard-ed. Only raw EEG data was used. Only the eight least significant bits of

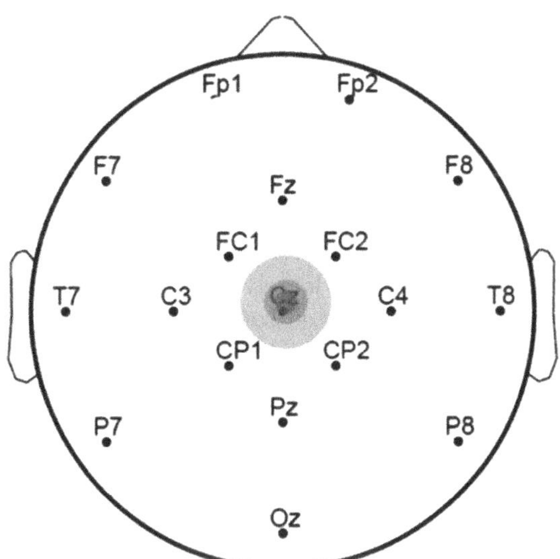

Fig. 2. Top view of the electrical montage. One active EEG channel was located on the top of the head.

each 24-bit data were extracted to generate the random sequence of bits. This generated a random binary sequence at a rate of 4 Kbps. For the comparison with the manually generated passwords (Data set II), only the first 26 Kb were used. For the comparison with the computer (Data set III), the total EEG data were used. The EEG was recorded during the manual generation of passwords. It took approximately 46 min for 40 manual passwords. Then the binary sequence obtained was approximately 11 Mb.

Data Set II: It contains passwords manually generated by a participant with restrictions. The participant (a male) was told to complete 40 independent passwords each one of 12-character length. It took approximately 46 min. He was told to use keys from the 94-character set to produce somehow easy-to-remember passwords. To ensure a high level of randomness, first he had to choose a password classified as strong and without deductions by a password meter available in Internet (http://www.passwordmeter.com/). These passwords were 10-character length. Af-terwards, two more characters were added to complete 12 characters. These two additional characters were chosen to obtain the maximum number of random bits as measured by a tool available in Internet (http://rumkin.com/tools/password/passchk.php). This slow methodology was able to produce only 12-character-length passwords at a rate slower than 1 password per minute. The rest of the passwords of the data set were generated by another participant. He was told to generate passwords, as random as possible. No restrictions about the easiness to memorize were imposed. The whole data set included passwords with a total of 4480 characters. The six least significant bits were extracted to generate the random binary sequence of the same length as Data set I (circa 26 Kb).

Data Set III: Passwords generated by a computer. A PC (Windows 7, Core i7, Matlab 2013b) was used to generate random binary sequence of the same length as Data set I (circa 11 Mb).

4 Statistical Analysis

We used the NIST Test Suite [13] for the assessment of the randomness of the generated sequences. NIST is a tool largely used for validation of secure keys [9–18]. In this experiment we submitted random binary sequences to compare Data set I with Data set II and III. NIST performed 15 tests. For the sake of simplicity, only the most relevant tests are reported in this article. See [14] for comprehensive information about NIST.

5 Results

The randomness of Data set I (based on EEG) versus Data set III (based on a computer) is presented in Table 1. The corresponding to Data set I versus Data set II (manually generated passwords) are presented in Table 2.

Table 1. Randomness evaluation performed by NIST. The sample size was 112 binary sequences of 0.1 million bits each sequence. * stands for p-values $< \alpha$ or under the minimun pass rate (107). In bold: test values in which Data set I performed equal or better.

Data set I (EEG)		Data set II (computer)		
p-value	**Pass rate**	**p-value**	**Pass rate**	**Test name**
7.2E−01	110/112	6.1E−01	112/112	Frequency
8.4E−01	**112/112**	8.9E−01	109/112	BlockFrequency
1.8E−01	110/112	6.5E−01	112/112	CumulativeSums
4.0E−01	110/112	2.3E−02	112/112	CumulativeSums
4.3E−01	109/112	7.9E−02	110/112	Runs
5.2E−01	**112/112**	2.1E−01	110/112	LongestRun
7.4E−01	**112/112**	1.8E−01	112/112	Rank
6.7E−01	**111/112**	4.5E−01	110/112	FFT
0.0E+00*	**112/112**	0.0E+00*	112/112	Universal
2.5E−01	**112/112**	8.8E−02	110/112	ApproximateEntropy
2.7E−01	**111/112**	7.6E−01	110/112	Serial
5.5E−01	110/112	5.5E−01	111/112	Serial
1.6E−01	**112/112**	6.1E−01	112/112	LinearComplexity

Table 2. Randomness evaluation performed by NIST. The sample size was 12 binary sequences of 2240 bits each sequence. * stands for p-values $< \alpha$ or at the minimum pass rate (10). In bold: test values in which Data set I performed better or the same.

Data set I (EEG)		Data set II (computer)		
p-value	Pass rate	p-value	Pass rate	Test name
8.9E−03	**12/12**	3.0E−06*	10/12*	Frequency
3.5E−01	**12/12**	8.9E−03	10/12	BlockFrequency
1.8E−02	**12/12**	3.0E−06*	10/12*	CumulativeSums
3.5E−01	**12/12**	3.0E−06*	11/12	CumulativeSums
5.3E−01	**12/12**	0.0E+00*	2/12*	Runs
3.5E−02	**12/12**	5.3E−01	11/12	LongestRun
8.9E−05*	11/12	1.0E−06*	12/12	Rank
2.1E−01	**12/12**	4.3E−03	11/12	FFT
0.0E+00*	**12/12**	0.0E+00*	12/12	Universal
0.0E+00*	**0/12***	0.0E+00*	0/12*	ApproximateEntropy
6.7E−02	**12/12**	4.4E−04	8/12*	Serial
3.5E−01	**12/12**	6.7E−02	8/12*	Serial
3.5E−01	**12/12**	2.0E−03	11/12	LinearComplexity

6 Discussion and Conclusion

In this preliminary study we have evaluated the use or neuro-activity as a physical source of entropy that can be useful for the generation of strong password in mobile applications. Passwords generated by means of a wearable brain-computer interface were much more random and complex that those manually generated by the human (see Table 2), even when they were generated with restrictions based on dictionaries and composition rules or even generated as random as possible without restrictions about the easiness to memorize. The required cognitive workload and time was just a small fraction of those required for the manually generated passwords. In this study, only 6 s of neuro-activity contained more randomness than 46 min of manual generation of passwords. Efficiency in terms of entropy per character unit, gives rise to shorter (and easier to remember) random passwords. When we compared the randomness in neuro-activity with the one generated by a computer, the test yielded similar or inconclusive results. Then it is difficult to evaluate which data set performed better. We conclude that in mobile scenarios without good enough entropy sources, the use of neuro-activity is an efficient option for the generation of strong passwords. The current development in wireless brain-computer interfaces makes it a feasible solution.

In future, we plan to extend this study to larger data sets. In addition, a comparison with other available sources of entropy in low-cost wearable devices such as smartphones will be included.

Acknowledgments. This work was supported by Nicolo Association for the R+D in Neurotechnologies for disability, the research project P11-TIC-7983 of Junta of Andalucia (Spain), the Spanish National Grant TIN2015-67020-P, co-financed by the European Regional Development Fund (ERDF) and the Spanish National Grant TIN2016-75097-P (AEI/FEDER, UE).

References

1. Chang, C.-C., Wu, H.-L., Sun, C.-Y.: Notes on secure authentication scheme for IoT and cloud servers. Pervasive Mob. Comput. **24**, 210–223 (2016)
2. Altop, D.K., Levi, A., Tuzcu, V.: Deriving cryptographic keys from physiological signals. Pervasive and Mobile Computing (2016)
3. Zheng, G., Fang, G., Shankaran, R., Orgun, M., Zhou, J., Qiao, L., Saleem, K.: Multiple ECG fiducial points based random binary sequence generation for securing wireless body area networks. IEEE J. Biomed. Health Inf. 1–9 (2016)
4. Venkatasubramanian, K.K., Banerjee, A., Gupta, S.K.S.: PSKA: usable and secure key agreement scheme for body area networks. IEEE Trans. Inf. Technol. Biomed.: a publication of the IEEE Eng. Med. Biol. Soc. **14**, 60–68 (2010)
5. Israel, S.A., Irvine, J.M., Cheng, A., Wiederhold, M.D., Wiederhold, B.K.: ECG to identify individuals. Pattern Recogn. **38**, 133–142 (2005)
6. Poon, C., Zhang, Y.-T., Bao, S.-D.: A novel biometrics method to secure wireless body area sensor networks for telemedicine and m-health. IEEE Commun. Mag. **44**, 73–81 (2006)

7. Eastlake, D., Schiller, J., Crocker, S.: Randomness requirements for security (2005)
8. Rukhin, A., Soto, J., Nechvatal, J., Smid, M., Barker, E.: A statistical test suite for random and pseudorandom number generators for cryptographic applications. Technical report NIST Special Publication 800–22 Revision 1a. National Institute of Standards and Technology (2010)
9. Wallace, K., Moran, K., Novak, E., Zhou, G., Sun, K.: Toward sensor-based random number generation for mobile and IoT devices. IEEE Internet Things J. **3**, 1189–1201 (2016)
10. Florencio, D. Herley, C.: A large-scale study of web password habits, pp. 657. ACM Press (2007)
11. Shen, C., Yu, T., Xu, H., Yang, G., Guan, X.: User practice in password security: an empirical study of real-life passwords in the wild. Comput. Secur. **61**, 130–141 (2016)
12. Burr, W.E., Dodson, D.F., Newton, E.M., Perlner, R.A., Polk, W.T., Gupta, S., Nabbus, E.A.: Electronic authentication guideline. Technical report NIST SP 800–63-1. National Institute of Standards, Technology, Gaithersburg, MD (2011). 10.6028/NIST.SP.800-63-1
13. Lopez-Gordo, M.A., Pelayo Valle, F.: Brain-Computer interface as networking entity in body area networks. In: Aguayo-Torres, M.C., Gómez, G., Poncela, J. (eds.) WWIC 2015. LNCS, vol. 9071, pp. 274–285. Springer, Cham (2015). doi:10.1007/978-3-319-22572-2_20
14. Wu, F.-J., Kao, Y.-F., Tseng, Y.-C.: From wireless sensor networks towards cyber physical systems. Pervasive Mob. Comput. **7**, 397–413 (2011)
15. Zhang, Z., Wang, H., Vasilakos, A.V., Fang, H.: ECG-cryptography and authentication in body area networks. IEEE Trans. Inf. Technol. Biomed. **16**, 1070–1078 (2012)
16. Valenzuela-Valdes, J.F., Lopez, M.A., Padilla, P., Padilla, J.L., Minguillon, J.: Human neuro-activity for securing body area networks: application of brain-computer interfaces to people-centric internet of things. IEEE Commun. Mag. **55**, 62–67 (2017)
17. Jasper, H.: Report of the committee on methods of clinical examination in electroencephalography. Electroencephalogr. Clin. Neurophysiol. **10**, 370–375 (1958)
18. Hong, S.L., Liu, C.: Sensor-based random number generator seeding. IEEE Access **3**, 562–568 (2015)

Delta-Theta Intertrial Phase Coherence Increases During Task Switching in a BCI Paradigm

Juan A. Barios[1(✉)], Santiago Ezquerro[1], Arturo Bertomeu-Motos[1], Eduardo Fernandez[1], Marius Nann[2], Surjo R. Soekadar[2], and Nicolas Garcia-Aracil[1]

[1] Biomedical Neuroengineering Research Group (nBio), Systems Engineering and Automation Department of Miguel Hernandez University, Avda. de la Universidad s/n, 03202 Elche, Spain
jbarios@umh.es

[2] Applied Neurotechnology Lab, Department of Psychiatry and Psychotherapy, Institute of Medical Psychology and Behavioral Neurobiology, University Hospital of Tuebingen, Calwerstr. 14, 72076 Tuebingen, Germany
http://nbio.umh.es/
http://www.medizin.uni-tuebingen.de

Abstract. A broad variety of perceptual, sensorimotor and cognitive operations have shown to be linked to electroencephalographic (EEG) oscillatory activity. For instance, movement preparation or cognitive processing were linked to delta band (1–5 Hz) oscillations. Such link could be exploited in brain-computer interface (BCI) paradigms translating modulations of brain activity into control signals of external devices or computers. However, current BCIs are often driven by fast rhythmic brain activity, e.g. in the alpha (9–15 Hz) or beta band (15–30 Hz). Introducing slower oscillations, such as delta or theta (4–8 Hz) band activity, might extent the spectrum of BCI applications, particularly in the context of BCI-related restoration of movements. To detect voluntary modulations of motor cortical activity in such paradign, an active interval during which users are instructed to e.g. imagine hand movements becomes compared to a task-free interval during which users are instructed to relax. We report that cortical oscillations of EEG in delta and theta frequencies clearly synchronize at the onset and at the end of a BCI task, what might be a physiological marker for task switching that could be useful for improving BCI control. We also found that inter-trial-phase coherence (ITPC) significantly increased at the end of reference intervals during which participants were instructed to relax. This may indicate that during initial phases of BCI learning, users are actively relaxing, a finding with important implications for monitoring BCI learning and control.

Keywords: Slow rhythms · EEG · Coherence · BCI

J.M. Ferrández Vicente et al. (Eds.): IWINAC 2017, Part II, LNCS 10338, pp. 96–108, 2017.
DOI: 10.1007/978-3-319-59773-7_11

1 Introduction

Delta oscillatory responses are defined as EEG oscillatory responses in the 1–5 Hz frequency range. Delta-band cortical oscillations are classically associated with slow-wave sleep, but evidence also support the view that delta responses during wakefulness are involved in cognitive processes, mainly in decision-making and attentional processes, both in animal [1,2] and humans [3], as recent reviews have shown [4,5].

Slow rhythms are classically involved in premotor changes of EEG, and were described in early descriptions of EEG activity during volitional movements [6,7]. Movement-related cortical potentials (MRCP) related to task-switching and to general preparation processes have different spatial activation and time course [8]. Increase of coherence in slow rhythms between different cortical areas have been reported in decision making tasks [9], and in a task-switching context [10].

Studies in the BCI field have recently developed increased interest in slow rhythms, and showed that delta band contains relevant movement-related information [11–13], and that information related to phase of slow rhythms might be useful even for decoding hand or arm kinematics (position and velocity) [14]. In summary, the phase of slow rhythms might contain information relevant for the field of BCI.

Event-related phase consistency across trials is an important method allowing researchers to see how phase information varies between trials. Kolev et al. [15] used single-sweep wave identification histograms to analyze phase-locking. Tallon-Baudry et al. [16] defined a method called phase-locking factor, and Delorme and Makeig [17] called this method inter-trial phase coherence (ITPC).

Recently, movement-related phase locking has been described in the delta-theta frequency band [18]. We argue that classical paradigms in BCI usually include several tasks that BCI-users must sequentially complete, so that task switching, besides movement onset, is a relevant point to explore in the analysis of BCI experiments. We hypothesized that described changes in ITPC coherence of low frequencies of EEG in the context of a classical BCI paradigm might be explained by task switching, a potentially relevant finding for physiological interpretation of slow rhythms phase changes in BCI paradigms.

2 Material and Methods

2.1 Participants

Ten healthy volunteers were invited to participate in a 1-hour experimental session. All participants gave written informed consent before the session. All participants were comfortably seated at a desk while EEG was recorded from 4 conventional EEG recording sites (F3, T3, C3, and P3 according to the international 10/20 system) using an EEG neoprene cap (Enobio, Neuroelectrics, Barcelona, Spain) with a reference electrode placed at Fz and ground electrode at Cz. EEG was recorded at a sampling rate of 200 Hz, bandpass filtered at 0.4–70 Hz and pre-processed using a small Laplacian filter. Electroculography (EOG) was recorded in accordance to the standard EOG placement at the left outer canthus. Biosignals recorded by EEG and EOG were used to control a hand-exoskeleton allowing for grasping motions. Skin/electrode resistance was kept below 12 kΩ.

2.2 Experimental Design

A custom version of BCI2000, a multipurpose standard BCI platform [19], was used for calibration and online BCI control. Calibration of the BCI system was performed once at the beginning of the session and kept unvaried for the rest of the session, and comprised two parts: in the first part, participants were instructed to either rest (RELAX task) or imagine hand grasping motions (CLOSE task) following a visual cue (a text label on screen, saying RELAX or CLOSE, respectively) displayed on a computer screen. Visual indications were separated by inter-trial-intervals (ITIs) of 4–6 s.

Before starting the task, all participants were familiarized with the BCI system and performed calibration sequence. For the EEG calibration, the subject had to imagine hand-close motions. As an aid to modulate brain activity, a visual feedback was shown. When the participant thought the grasping movement, a "Pac-Man" (*visual feedback*) started to close. However, if the "Pac-Man" started to close without motor-instruction, the subject could abort the movement looking left. With this calibration task, subject's individual motor imaginery detection threshold was calculated.

For detection of motor-imagery related desynchronization of sensorimotor rhythms (SMR, 8–15 Hz) of each participant, a power spectrum estimation (autoregressive model of order 16 using the Yule Walker algorithm) was performed for each incoming sample, detecting even-related desynchronization (ERD) during motor imagery recorded from C3. Based on the maximum values for ERD, a discrimination threshold was set at two-standard deviations above average SMR-ERD variance at rest, and used for later online BCI control.

2.3 Processing of Recorded Data

For preprocessing and analysis of the EEG data, we used the EEGLAB toolbox [17] and scripts in Matlab R2014a (MathWorks Inc.).

A number of pre-processing steps were performed on the data. First, the data were band-passed in the frequency band 0.5–48 Hz, and then downsampled from 500 to 128 Hz. Next, the raw EEG data were visually inspected for paroxysmal and muscular artifacts not related to eye blinks. Then, the noisy portions of the EEG signal were excluded from further analysis. In the next step, the EEG recordings were epoched to single trials, i.e., they were subdivided into intervals of 11 s, from 3 s before the visual cue marking the onset of task to 8 s after, three seconds after second visual stimulus marking the end of the task. The length of the EEG epochs (−3 to 8 s) encompassed time points beyond the period of interest in order to include signal enough before and after the edges of the period of interest (0 and 5 s related to the onset of the task). The reference point (time zero) was assigned to the start of the visual stimulus (text label on screen).

In this way, both conditions (RELAX and CLOSE) could be compared. The length of the intervals before and after the reference point was chosen such as to take the length (approx. 2 s) of the MRCP. After subdividing the data into single trials, they were further corrected for artifacts. All trials with an amplitude larger than 100 mV in any of the recorded channels or showing a drift that exceeded 75 uV over the whole interval (abnormal drift) were rejected. Trials with other artifacts (blinks, eye movements, muscle activity, and infrequent single-channel noise) were identified by means of a semi-automated procedure based on independent components analysis (ICA). ICA was used with the Info-Max ICA algorithm implemented in EEGLAB. Signals containing blink/oculomotor artifacts or other artifacts that were clearly no brain signals were subtracted from the data by using the procedure *adjust* from EEGLAB. Finally, the trials were baseline-corrected taking the first 500 ms of each interval as baseline. In order to improve the spatial resolution and to eliminate the influence of distortions due to the reference electrode, we used the *common average* montage.

We applied a complex Morlet wavelet analysis to the EEG epochs to examine the electrical activity during BCI experiment, and we obtained the instantaneous phase and amplitude (power) for each frequency. We extracted the phase angles from the complex data to estimate the inter-trial phase coherence for all frequencies and time points in our time-frequency matrix. An important indicator of the phase dynamics between trials is the inter-trial phase coherence, calculated from Phase Locking Index (PLI). We calculated the average value of PLI over the frequency bands. PLI is a measure of similarity of the phases of a signal over many repetitions. PLI ranges from 0 to 1. PLI = 1 means identical phase of the signal across trials. Low values of PLI suggest temporal heterogeneity of the phases between individual trials. Thus, PLI measures the degree of inter-trial variation in phase between the responses to stimuli and thereby quantifies phase locking of the oscillatory activity irrespective of its amplitude. For ITPC and Morlet analysis, EEGLAB toolbox was used. Amplitude and PLI were computed for all recorded channels (electrodes) in the frequency range from 2 to 48 Hz. The frequency range thus included all main frequency bands of the EEG: δ (1–5 Hz), θ (5–7 Hz), α (8–12 Hz), β (13–30 Hz), and low γ (30–48 Hz). For statistical analysis, methods included in EEGLAB were used.

3 Results

3.1 Amplitude Dynamics

First, we investigated the amplitudes (power) of the wavelet transforms near the onset of the task. Our results replicate the well-known event-related desynchronization (ERD) during the movement. Hence, these findings provide evidence for the validity of our data. They are shown in Fig. 1, where ERD or EEG sensorimotor rhythm activity (SMR, 8–15 Hz) related to motor imagery of hand closing motions is observed. EEG changes are significant only in alpha band. Interestingly, slow frequencies did not show significant changes in power. In the right part of the figure, statistical significance of differences between both situations is presented, using montecarlo methods of EEGLAB.

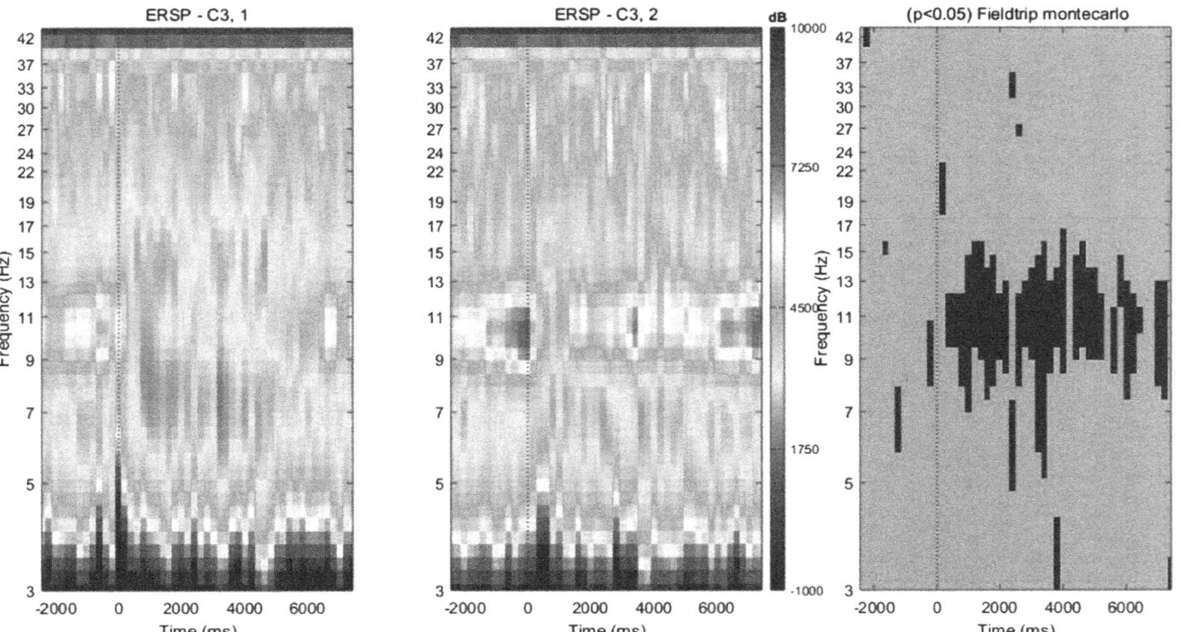

Fig. 1. ERD during BCI task. Illustration of event-related desynchronization (ERD) of electroencephalographic (EEG) sensorimotor rhythm activity (SMR, 8–15 Hz) related to motor imagery of hand closing motions. Left, CLOSE task. Middle, RELAX task. Right, statistical significance (green means $p > 0.05$). Averaging of 10 subjects, C3 derivation is shown (Color figure online)

3.2 Phase Dynamics

In Fig. 2, the group average of the ITPC over all the participants (n = 10) are displayed for the CLOSE (left) and RELAX (right) tasks. The analysis indicates that ITPC increases during switching of BCI task. Notice that the changes are present both at the onset and at the end of the task, and that the magnitude of the changes is similar in RELAX and CLOSE tasks.

In Fig. 3, same analysis were applied but, for comparation, we present the results of different derivations (C3, Cz, P3, T7). It is shown that ITPC increases simultaneously occur in several brain regions, meaning that ITPC increase during task switching is a global brain phenomena.

In Fig. 4, ITPC increases show different frequencies patterns in RELAX and CLOSE tasks (ITPC increase in θ band is more marked in RELAX task, suggesting that physiological meaning of coherence changes in theta and delta bands might be different.

4 Discussion

The main finding of this is sudy is that cortical oscillations in delta and theta band synchronize at the onset and at the end of a BCI task, independent of the actual task (i.e. motor imaginery vs relaxing).

BCI aims to provide a non-muscular communication and control channel for severely disabled patients [20], using EEG suitable signals for monitoring and guiding brain plasticity for motor restoration. Several types of oscillatory activity in the brain can be used: spontaneous EEG oscillations, recorded without any external physical stimulation; evoked oscillations, after application of a pure sensory stimulation, and event-related oscillations, elicited by application of a stimulation containing a task or strategy, i.e. oddball P300 response.

Although successful BCI paradigms have been mainly focused on fast rhythms (alpha and beta bands), the interest of slow rhythms in motor control is not new. Kornhuber and Deecke [6] made the first report of EEG activity preceding volitional movement in humans. They successfully identified two components, one before and one after the EMG onset, called Bereitschaftspotential (BP) or readiness potential, and reafferent Potential (RP). Since then, a number of studies on the MRCP have been reported both in terms of physiological findings and clinical application, but the physiological significance of each identifiable component, among others that of BP, has not been fully clarified yet [6,21].

Between the mixture of frequencies contained in EEG responses, importance of slow rhythms is increasing in the study of cognitive mechanisms. Research has shown several generators of cortical delta oscillations in human brain, mainly pyramidal neurons through long-lasting hyperpolarizations [22], but glial cells have also been reported [23]. Delta oscillations have also been recorded in sub-cortical regions, ventral pallidum and brain stem [4].

Delta-band cortical oscillations are typically associated with slow-wave sleep [22], but recent findings also relate them to attention phenomena, both in animal [1] and humans [3], and their study has an increasing role in neuroscience [4]. Slow rhythms of EEG are neural correlates of decision making [24], and

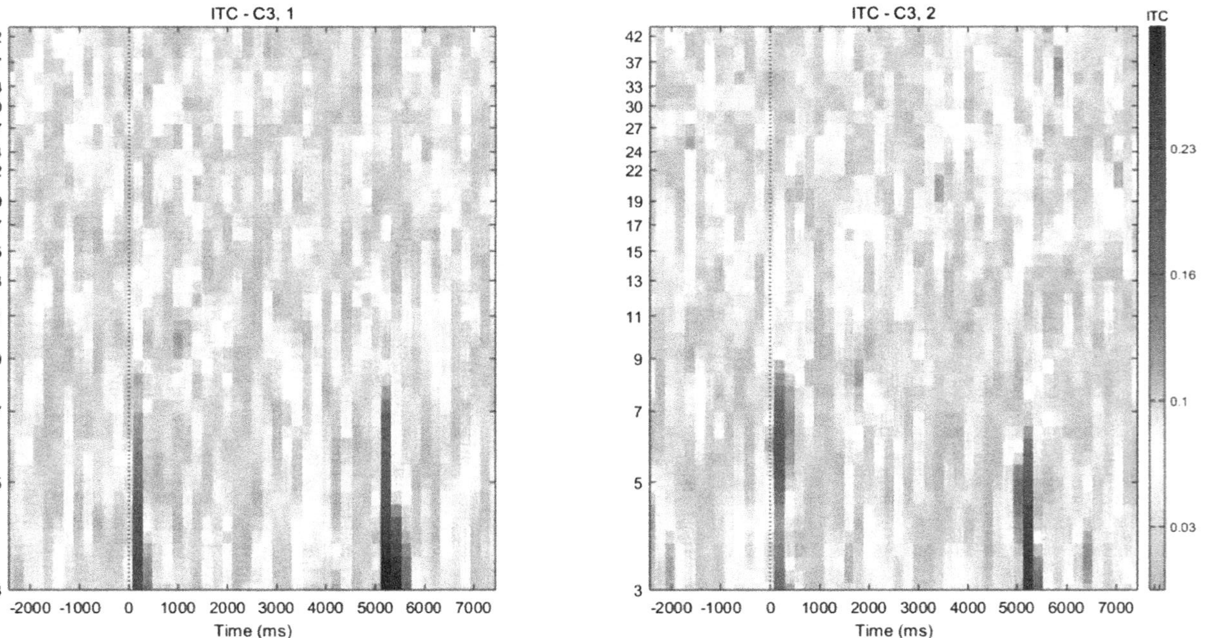

Fig. 2. ITPC changes related to onset of BCI task. Notice that ITPC increases during switching of BCI task, that the magnitude of the changes is similar en RELAX and CLOSE task, and that they are present both at the onset and at the end of the task. Averaging of 10 subjects; Left: CLOSE task, Right: RELAX task; C3 derivation is shown

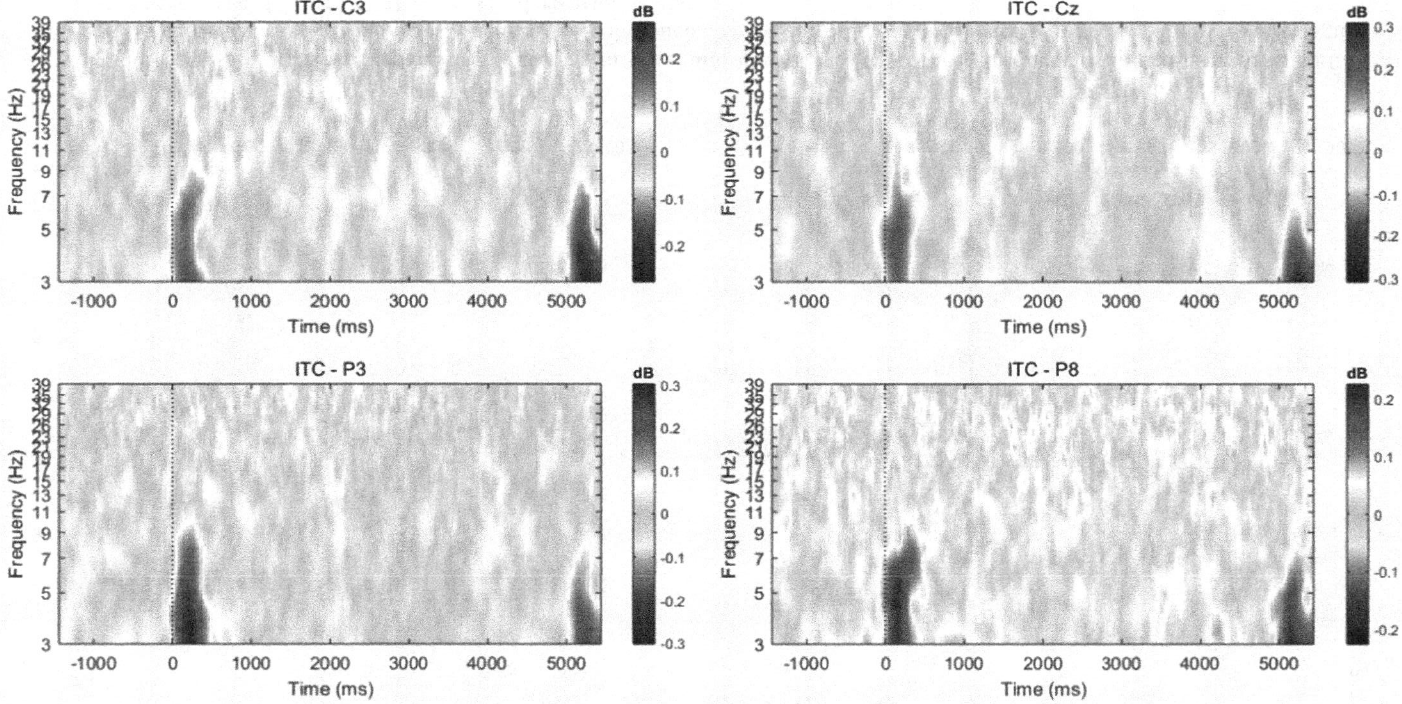

Fig. 3. ITPC increases occur in several brain regions, meaning that it is a global brain phenomena. Averaging of 10 subjects, C3, Cz, P3, T7 derivations are shown.

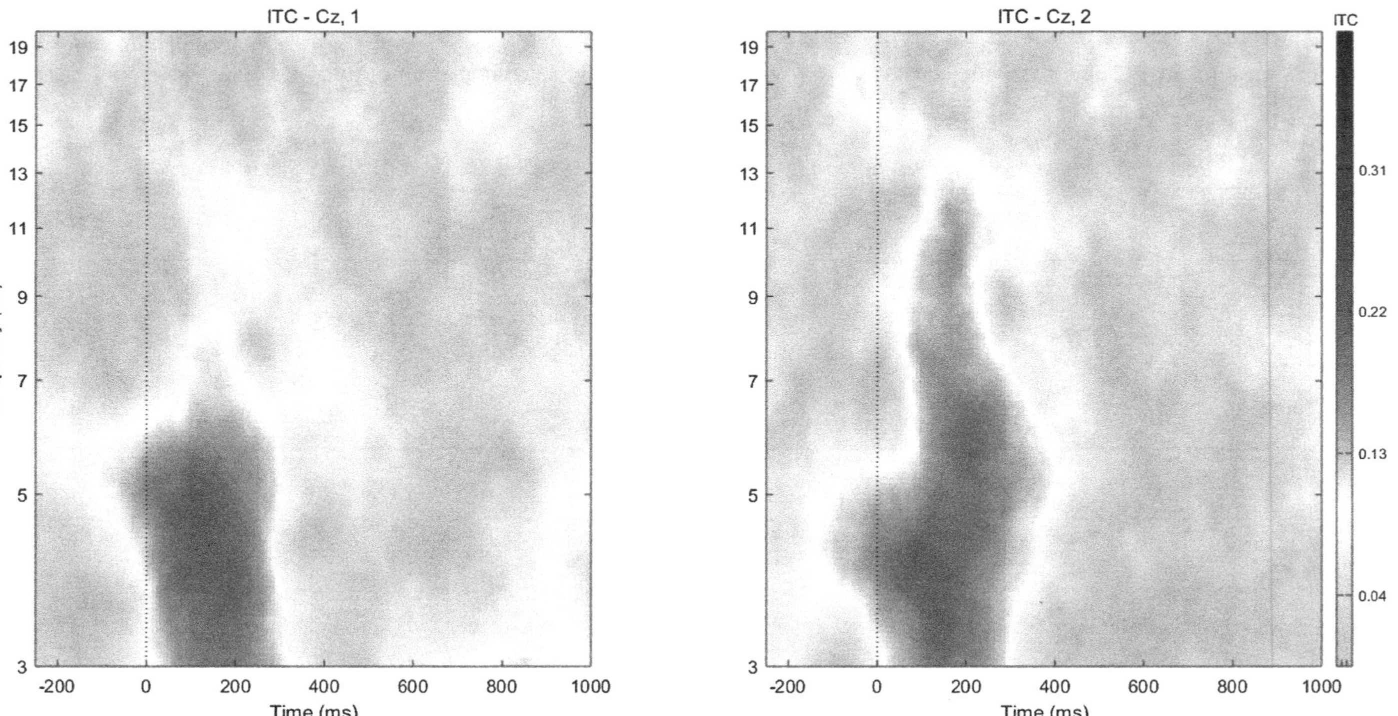

Fig. 4. ITPC increases show different frequencies patterns in relax and close task (ITPC theta frequencies increase more en RELAX than in CLOSE task), suggesting that physiological meaning of coherence changes in different frequencies might be different. Averaging of 10 subjects; Left: CLOSE task, Right: RELAX task; CZ derivation is shown

research in monkeys also support this view [9]. Delta oscillation phase changes have been reported in task-switching context [10]. Delta oscillatory responses are now involved in attention, perception, signal detection, and decision-making [4], and recently in movement preparation [18].

The role of delta oscillations during cognitive processes is also supported by several studies analyzing event-related delta oscillations of different cognitively impaired patient groups during cognitive stimulations, that support the idea that delta responses are involved in cognitive processes, and that could be a general electrophysiological marker for cognitive dysfunction. In several studies, cognitively impaired subject groups (mild cognitive impairment, Alzheimer's disease, schizophrenia, bipolar disorder) showed reduced amplitudes of delta oscillatory responses during cognitive paradigms (for a review, see [4]). Reduction of delta responses during aging upon presentation of cognitive stimulation was also reported during visual oddball paradigms [25] and during go/no-go tasks [26]. On the other hand, elderly subjects showed higher delta coherence upon presentation of auditory oddball paradigm [27].

Phase-reordering by visual and auditory stimulation is an important mechanism in attention processes in the monkey brain [2], which could also be called phase entrainment [28]. Delta phase entrainment also predicts behavioral performance [29,30]. The role of phase synchronization in motor control is also a well-known issue [31,32].

Recently, ITPC increase in wakefulness during a volitional movement has been described [18], a similar finding to the results that we are presenting. Our experiment confirms and extends those results. First, and in the same line of their reported results, we did not find an increase of power in delta-theta frequencies (see Fig. 1), suggesting that the ITPC increase might be related to a task related phase alignment of theta and delta frequency bands. Second, we noticed an increase of ITPC at the onset of BCI task, but also at the end of the task, what suggests an alternative explanation: ITPC might be not only related to movement planning, but to a more general mechanism related to task-switching. In fact, in our experiment, the subject had to decide between imagining or not a movement, a clear example of a GO/NO GO task, where increase of coherence in delta band between different cortical regions has already been clearly described [9,10,31,33].

It must be taken into account that, in both experiments, only one modality of stimulation (visual) was used, so that it cannot be discarded whether ITPC increase is related to visual presentation of stimulus. We can argue that the spatial distribution of the findings, which are not restricted to posterior (visual) areas suggest that this is not the case. Future experiments, including alternative stimulus modalities (i.e. acoustic or haptic), might clarify this point.

From a practical point of view, the presence of significant ITPC changes also *at the end* of the relax task suggests that subjects, at least in initial phases of BCI training, are not "simply relaxing" but "actively relaxing". Although more studies are needed, we suggest that during initial phases of BCI training, an emphasis shoud be done on learning to relax, what should be taken in account in the design of BCI paradigms.

5 Conclusion

We report that cortical oscillations of EEG in delta and theta frequencies clearly synchronize at the onset and at the end of a BCI task, what might be a physiological marker for task switching that could be useful for improving BCI control. We also found that ITPC significantly increased at the end of reference intervals during which participants were instructed to relax. This may indicate that during initial phases of BCI learning, users are actively relaxing, a finding with important implications for monitoring BCI learning and control.

Acknowledgments. This work has been supported by the European Commission through the project AIDE: "Adaptive Multimodal Interfaces to Assist Disabled People in Daily Activities" (Grant agreement no: 645322), through the project HOMEREHAB: "Development of Development of Robotic Technology for Post-Stroke Home Tele-Rehabilitation—Echord++" (Grant agreement no: 601116) and by the Ministry of Economy and Competitiveness through the project DPI2015-70415-C2-2-R.

References

1. Fries, P., Womelsdorf, T., Oostenveld, R., Desimone, R.: The effects of visual stimulation and selective visual attention on rhythmic neuronal synchronization in macaque area v4. J. Neurosci.: Off. J. Soc. Neurosci. **28**, 4823–4835 (2008)
2. Lakatos, P., Karmos, G., Mehta, A.D., Ulbert, I., Schroeder, C.E.: Entrainment of neuronal oscillations as a mechanism of attentional selection. Science **320**, 110–113 (2008)
3. Saleh, M., Reimer, J., Penn, R., Ojakangas, C.L., Hatsopoulos, N.G.: Fast and slow oscillations in human primary motor cortex predict oncoming behaviorally relevant cues. Neuron **65**, 461–471 (2010)
4. Gntekin, B., Baar, E.: Review of evoked and event-related delta responses in the human brain. Int. J. Psychophysiol.: Off. J. Int. Organ. Psychophysiol. **103**, 43–52 (2016)
5. Harmony, T.: The functional significance of delta oscillations in cognitive processing. Front. Integr. Neurosci. **7**, 83 (2013)
6. Kornhuber, H.H., Deecke, L.: Hirnpotentialanderungen beim menschen vor und nach willkurbewegungen dargestellt mit magnetbandspeicherung und ruckwartsanalyse. Pflug. Arch.-Eur. J. Physiol. **281**, 52 (1964). Springer Verlag 175 Fifth Ave., New York, NY 10010
7. Nagamine, T., Kajola, M., Salmelin, R., Shibasaki, H., Hari, R.: Movement-related slow cortical magnetic fields and changes of spontaneous MEG-and EEG-brain rhythms. Electroencephalogr. Clin. Neurophysiol. **99**, 274–286 (1996)
8. Mansfield, E.L., Karayanidis, F., Cohen, M.X.: Switch-related and general preparation processes in task-switching: evidence from multivariate pattern classification of EEG data. J. Neurosci. **32**, 18253–18258 (2012)
9. Nácher, V., Ledberg, A., Deco, G., Romo, R.: Coherent delta-band oscillations between cortical areas correlate with decision making. Proc. Nat. Acad. Sci. **110**, 15085–15090 (2013)
10. Prada, L., Barcel, F., Herrmann, C.S., Escera, C.: EEG delta oscillations index inhibitory control of contextual novelty to both irrelevant distracters and relevant task-switch cues. Psychophysiology **51**, 658–672 (2014)

11. Waldert, S., Preissl, H., Demandt, E., Braun, C., Birbaumer, N., Aertsen, A., Mehring, C.: Hand movement direction decoded from MEG and EEG. J. Neurosci. **28**, 1000–1008 (2008)
12. Presacco, A., Goodman, R., Forrester, L., Contreras-Vidal, J.L.: Neural decoding of treadmill walking from noninvasive electroencephalographic signals. J. Neurophysiol. **106**, 1875–1887 (2011)
13. Garipelli, G., Chavarriaga, R., del R Millán, J.: Single trial analysis of slow cortical potentials: a study on anticipation related potentials. J. Neural Eng. **10**, 036014 (2013)
14. Bradberry, T.J., Gentili, R.J., Contreras-Vidal, J.L.: Reconstructing three-dimensional hand movements from noninvasive electroencephalographic signals. J. Neurosci. **30**, 3432–3437 (2010)
15. Kolev, V., Yordanova, Y., Başar, E.: Phase locking of oscillatory responses an informative approach for studying evoked brain activity. In: Kolev, V., Yordanova, Y., Başar, E. (eds.) Brain Function and Oscillations, pp. 123–128. Springer, Heidelberg (1998)
16. Tallon-Baudry, C., Bertrand, O., Delpuech, C., Pernier, J.: Stimulus specificity of phase-locked and non-phase-locked 40 Hz visual responses in human. J. Neurosci. **16**, 4240–4249 (1996)
17. Delorme, A., Makeig, S.: EEGLAB: an open source toolbox for analysis of single-trial EEG dynamics including independent component analysis. J. Neurosci. Methods **134**, 9–21 (2004)
18. Popovych, S., Rosjat, N., Toth, T., Wang, B., Liu, L., Abdollahi, R., Viswanathan, S., Grefkes, C., Fink, G., Daun, S.: Movement-related phase locking in the delta-theta frequency band. NeuroImage **139**, 439–449 (2016)
19. Schalk, G., McFarland, D.J., Hinterberger, T., Birbaumer, N., Wolpaw, J.R.: Bci2000: a general-purpose brain-computer interface (BCI) system. IEEE Trans. Biomed. Eng. **51**, 1034–1043 (2004)
20. Birbaumer, N., Ghanayim, N., Hinterberger, T., Iversen, I., Kotchoubey, B., Kübler, A., Perelmouter, J., Taub, E., Flor, H.: A spelling device for the paralysed. Nature **398**, 297–298 (1999)
21. Shibasaki, H., Hallett, M.: What is the Bereitschaftspotential? Clin. Neurophysiol. **117**, 2341–2356 (2006)
22. Steriade, M., Contreras, D., Dossi, R.C., Nunez, A.: The slow (<1 Hz) oscillation in reticular thalamic and thalamocortical neurons: scenario of sleep rhythm generation in interacting thalamic and neocortical networks. J. Neurosci. **13**, 3284–3299 (1993)
23. Amzica, F., Steriade, M.: Neuronal and glial membrane potentials during sleep and paroxysmal oscillations in the neocortex. J. Neurosci. **20**, 6648–6665 (2000)
24. Schall, J.D.: Neural basis of deciding, choosing and acting. Nat. Rev. Neurosci. **2**, 33–42 (2001)
25. Emek-Savaş, D.D., Güntekin, B., Yener, G.G., Başar, E.: Decrease of delta oscillatory responses is associated with increased age in healthy elderly. Int. J. Psychophysiol. **103**, 103–109 (2016)
26. Schmiedt-Fehr, C., Basar-Eroglu, C.: Event-related delta and theta brain oscillations reflect age-related changes in both a general and a specific neuronal inhibitory mechanism. Clin. Neurophysiol. **122**, 1156–1167 (2011)
27. Maurits, N.M., Scheeringa, R., van der Hoeven, J.H., de Jong, R.: EEG coherence obtained from an auditory oddball task increases with age. J. Clin. Neurophysiol. **23**, 395–403 (2006)

28. Başar, E., Başar-Eroglu, C., Rosen, B., Schütt, A.: A new approach to endogenous event-related potentials in man relation between EEG and p300-wave. Int. J. Neurosc. **24**, 1–21 (1984)
29. Stefanics, G., Hangya, B., Hernádi, I., Winkler, I., Lakatos, P., Ulbert, I.: Phase entrainment of human delta oscillations can mediate the effects of expectation on reaction speed. J. Neurosci. **30**, 13578–13585 (2010)
30. Kösem, A., Gramfort, A., van Wassenhove, V.: Encoding of event timing in the phase of neural oscillations. NeuroImage **92**, 274–284 (2014)
31. Baker, S., Olivier, E., Lemon, R.: Coherent oscillations in monkey motor cortex and hand muscle EMG show task-dependent modulation. J. Physiol. **501**, 225–241 (1997)
32. Antelis, J.M., Montesano, L., Ramos-Murguialday, A., Birbaumer, N., Minguez, J.: On the usage of linear regression models to reconstruct limb kinematics from low frequency EEG signals. PLoS ONE **8**, e61976 (2013)
33. Cravo, A.M., Rohenkohl, G., Wyart, V., Nobre, A.C.: Endogenous modulation of low frequency oscillations by temporal expectations. J. Neurophysiol. **106**, 2964–2972 (2011)

Using EEG Signals to Detect Different Surfaces While Walking

Raúl Chapero, Eduardo Iáñez(✉), Marisol Rodríguez-Ugarte, Mario Ortiz, and José M. Azorín

Brain-Machine Interface Systems Lab, Systems Engineering and Automation Department, Miguel Hernández University of Elche, Avda. de la Universidad s/n. Ed. Innova, 03202 Elche (Alicante), Spain
raul.chapero@gmail.com,
{eianez,maria.rodriguezu,mortiz,jm.azorin}@umh.es
http://bmi.umh.es/

Abstract. Brain-Computer Interfaces are one of the most interesting ways to work in rehabilitation and assistance programs to people who have problems in their lower limb to march. This paper presents evidence by means of statistical analysis sets that there are specific frequencies ranges on EEG signals while walking on four different surfaces: hard floor, soft floor, ramp and stairs, finding proportional differences in predictions between each pair of tasks for every user through the employ of Matlab classifiers. In that way, our results are statistical sets of successful percentages in classification of signals between two tasks. We worked with five different volunteers and we found an average of 76.5% of success in predictions between soft floor and stairs surfaces. Lower results, around 60%, were obtained when differentiating between hard floor/stairs and ramp/stairs. We can notice that magnitude of these percentages fits with a common sense about real physical differences between four kinds of surfaces. This study means a starting point to go deeper in signal morphology analyzing the specific mathematical characteristics of EEG signals while walking on those surfaces and other ones.

Keywords: Surface detection · EEG Signals · BCI Systems · Walking

1 Introduction

Nowadays computing technologies are increasing fast and strongly due to global spreading of demand in almost every way of human management tasks [1]. One of those fields of study is the design and development of brain-computer interface (BCI) in order to support people who have dysfunctional problems to walk, because of physical injuries in their lower limb, through fit mechanical exoskeletons able to lead movements of muscles to make them strong and functional in the fastest, effective and cheapest programs of rehabilitation [2–7].

J.M. Ferrández Vicente et al. (Eds.): IWINAC 2017, Part II, LNCS 10338, pp. 109–114, 2017.
DOI: 10.1007/978-3-319-59773-7_12

In relation with rehabilitation, several studies have been performed in order to get patients more implicated into their therapies. For example, detection the intention of starting or stopping gait [8,9] or detection the attention paid to walk [10], so rehabilitation therapy can be modified to help more the patient. Moreover, detecting unexpected obstacles can improve safety while working with exoskeletons [11].

This study line works to endue these exoskeletons capability to adapt their mechanical configuration to any kind of surface which user had intention to walk through before he/she steps in by just reading his/her EEG signals, anticipating changes to get the system ready to new walking conditions in the softest way. This objective implies two great development phases: identifying states and tendencies of EEG signal morphology as a function of surface characteristics and implementing that knowledge in exoskeletons controlled by BCI systems with correct responses in every way and an appropriate real time working. This paper presents the most primitive work in which we simply show by statistical analysis that EEG signals walking on a certain surface may high probably have a core morphology related with that surface characteristics in order to be this study the green light to approach EEG signals morphology and the development of the project in general.

2 System Architecture

Experimental tasks consisted in a series of EEG signals registered while walking in different surfaces. There were four different ones: a hard floor, a soft floor, a ramp and stairs. One register file from a user contains data of four tasks, each one corresponding to a different surface.

2.1 Acquisition and Users

Five users with ages between 14 and 25 years old perform the experiments. EEG signals were recorded with the actiCHamp equipment from Brain-Products Company. It allows registering 31 electrodes placed on the scalp following the 10/10 International System. The frequency sample was 500 Hz. They were placed in next positions: FZ, FC5, FC1, FCZ, FC2, FC6, C3, CZ, C4, CP5, CP1, CP2, CP6, P3, PZ, P4, PO7, PO3, PO4, PO8, FC3, FC4, C5, C1, C2, C6, CP3, CPZ, CP4 and P1. The reference was placed on right ear lobe. The equipment allows sending the information to the computer by a wireless connection through the MOVE module. This was an important issue to allow the user climbing stairs.

2.2 Experimental Procedure

After placing the cap to register EEG signals, the users are asked to walk through the four different surfaces. First the hard floor, then the soft floor, next the ramp, and finally the stairs. User last around 7 s walking through each different surface. Users repeat the same process 20 times. Figure 1 shows the environment where the user performs the experiments.

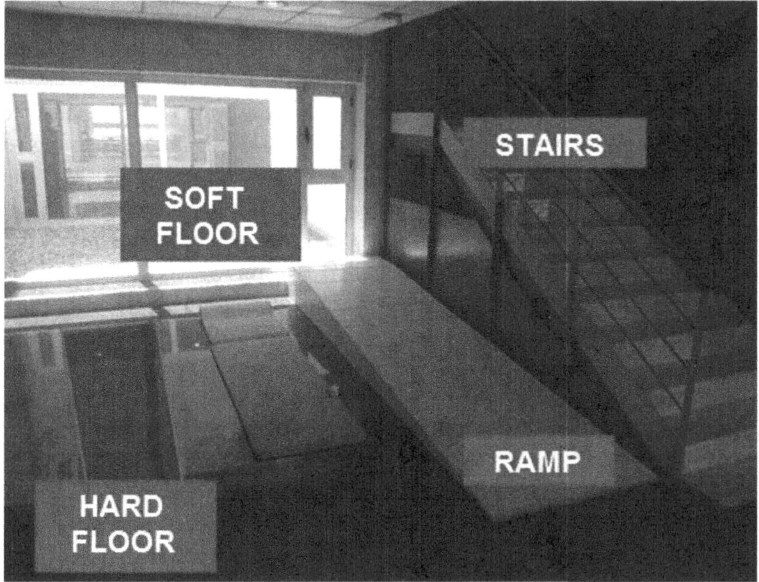

Fig. 1. Environment where users perform the experiments. The four different surfaces are shown: hard floor, soft floor, ramp and stairs.

2.3 Processing

The software was developed in Matlab. EEG registered signals had segments of invalid data due to failures of communication between emitter and receiver in wireless acquisition device during registering. Thus, an initial procedure was performed to clean registers by means of cutting off those parts of invalid data. Secondly, once registers are ready, they are processed in order to extract proper features to run the classification phase. For each clean user register, the program divides the total length into small segments overlapped. Then, a Fourier transform is calculated for each segment to get a simple feature for each task: a geometric mean of power spectrum amplitude in a specific frequencies range for all 31 electrode data arrays and an arithmetic mean of those 31 values. In this point, once processed and consequently to this study, for each register its built a matrix with 4 columns: first one with features for theta rhythm (3 to 7 hz), second one for alpha rhythm (8 to 14 Hz), third one for beta rhythm (14 to 31 Hz) and the last one contains the task number 1 to 4 associated to the row. The number of rows was different for each register depending on the number of overlapped segments, which in turn depends directly on the time length of registering which is slightly variable between registers and users.

2.4 Classification

A classification stage has been developed to determine which field of data a new set belongs to. One features matrix has the processed information of one register.

Classification employs all the registers of one user, just one user once, so what we give to it to be worked for each user is a matrices array as long as number of registers he/she has processed. For most part of user feature data, this number of processed registers is 20, so we introduced an array of 20 features matrices to classify in all cases excepting one in which we just used 19 because one of the registers was corrupt.

The algorithm of classification is based on creating models using all features matrices except one which is later employed to test the model, that is a cross-validation. Creating models is a process called training.

Classification, both for training and for testing, is run by classifiers, which are more or less complex mathematical algorithms implemented on computing program that are able to train and test data. We employed 5 different classifiers to get a large map of results where to observe the best ones and select more successful classifiers to analyze its inner logic in order to study the morphology of surface walking EEG signals in later studies. Best results were provided by classifier Nearest Neighbor. The rest of classifiers employed were Support Vector Machine, Naive-Bayes, Regression Trees and Lineal Discriminant Analysis.

So as to get best quality and accuracy in our results, due to statistic nature of this study, we did a cross validation, that means testing all the 20 feature matrices individually on 20 different models built every time with all the rest of matrices. In such a way, we got a wide number of predictions so our general result values as success likelihoods got consistence.

As we said before, the program process and classify all the registers of one user. Furthermore, classification was always run in pairs, which means that data sets to test are sort in one class between two options. Thus, as there are four tasks submitted to study there are six possible pairs, so the program simultaneously generates six different training models to test six times every testing register. In this way, the program obtains six large columns with all its predictions between two different tasks, so finally results are calculated just comparing done predictions with real corresponding task numbers.

3 Results

Several analysis were performed with the registered data. Theta, alpha and beta rhythms were calculated independently. Also, 3 different overlaps and 4 sizes segments were analyzed. All possible combination of parameters was processed. Table 1 summarizes the best average results for each user indicating the classifier applied, and the size segment, overlap and rhythm used. For each user 960 values were computed.

Its observed that most successful classifier, as we already said, is Nearest Neighbor. Once best average results are showed, we proceed to present the parts that compose those average values, it is mean, the likelihood values of success in classification in each of six specific pair of tasks. Results are shown in Table 2.

We can observe that for all users those results show maximum values for predictions in which walking upstairs is one of the two compared tasks. In three cases R/S has the higher value, followed closely by both Hard and Soft Floor tasks. The other two cases present high similar value in these three predictions. We can also notice that predictions between two Floor tasks and the Ramp one are quite lower than stairs predictions. However for most part of users these values are close to 60%, which is a higher value than predictions between Hard and Soft Floor that have no auspicious percentages.

Table 1. Best results obtained for each user. NN: Nearest Neighbor.

	Success rate (%)	Classifier	Size	Overlap	Rhythm
User 1	62.5	NN	2000	250	Alpha
User 2	64.7	NN	2000	400	Multirr.
User 3	74.3	NN	2000	250	Theta
User 4	62.4	NN	2000	250	Beta
User 5	66.9	NN	2000	400	Alpha

Table 2. Specific results for each pair of tasks (%). HF: Hard Floor; SF: Soft Floor; R: Ramp; S: Stairs.

	Success rate (%)	HF/SF	HF/R	HF/S	SF/R	SF/S	R/S
User 1	62.5	46.8	50.1	72.2	53.7	73.4	72.0
User 2	64.7	43.1	61.2	78.2	58.7	75.7	69.1
User 3	74.3	54.3	68.8	80.5	64.2	80.5	86.2
User 4	62.4	47.4	48.7	77.5	52.8	77.6	79.5
User 5	66.9	54.7	57.1	79.2	62.1	72.3	81.8

4 Conclusions

In this work the EEG signals of user that walks through different surfaces has been analyzed. Most significative point to highlight in results of this study are that values of six predictions have proportional relation for all user: HF/SF are in all cases the lowest value, HF/R and SF/R the medium value and HF/S, SF/S and R/S the highest values. We also consider meaningful the fact that these magnitudes differentiating two tasks by processing EEG signals employing classifiers fit with the difference grade that we could appreciate between tasks with a naked eye.

The results of this study evidence that walking on a specific surface reflects specific EEG signals univocally associated with that task, so in future studies we could go deeper analyzing those signals mathematically to find characteristic EEG signal morphologies relative to type and characteristics of different surfaces. Moreover, the procedure will be improved to be able to differentiate between the four different surfaces simultaneously and online experiments will be performed. These findings will contribute to adapt quickly the mechanics of lower limb exoskeletons for rehabilitation just reading EEG signals.

Acknowledgments. This research has been carried out in the framework of the project Associate - Decoding and stimulation of motor and sensory brain activity to support long term potentiation through Hebbian and paired associative stimulation during rehabilitation of gait (DPI2014-58431-C4-2-R), funded by the Spanish Ministry of Economy and Competitiveness and by the European Union through the European Regional Development Fund (ERDF) A way to build Europe.

The acquisition wireless system of EEG signals with 32 channels from Brain Products has been partially financed by funds from the European Union (P.O. FEDER 2007/2013), with the management of Generalitat Valenciana (Spain).

References

1. World Health Organization: Global health and ageing, Geneva (Switzerland), World Health Organization (2011)
2. Mann, W.C., Hurren, D., Tomita, M.: Comparison of assistive device use and needs of home-based older persons with different impairments. Am. J. Occup. Ther. **47**(11), 980–987 (1993)
3. Akdogan, E., Adli, M.A.: The design and control of a therapeutic exercise robot for lower limb rehabilitation: physiotherabot. Mechatronics **21**(3), 509–522 (2011)
4. Espregueira-Mendes, J., Pereira, R.B., Monteiro, A.: Lower limb rehabilitation. In: Margheritini, F., Rossi, R. (eds.) Orthopedic Sports Medicine, pp. 485–495. Springer, Heidelberg (2011)
5. Kong, K., Jeon, D.: Design and control of an exoskeleton for the elderly and patients. IEEE/ASME Trans. Mechatron. **11**(4), 428–432 (2006)
6. Miskelly, F.G.: Assistive technology in elderly care. Age Ageing **30**(6), 455–458 (2001)
7. Pohl, M., Werner, C., Holzgraefe, M., Kroczek, G., Wingendorf, I., Holig, G., Koch, R., Hesse, S.: A single-blind, randomized multicentre trial, degas. Clin. Rehabil. **21**(1), 17–27 (2007)
8. Hortal, E., Mrquez-Snchez, E., Costa., Piuela-Martn, E., Salazar, R., del-Ama, A.J., Gil-Agudo, A., Azorn, J.M.: Starting and finishing gait detection using a BMI for spinal cord injury rehabilitation. In: IEEE/RSJ International Conference on Intelligent Robots and Systems (IROS 2015), Innovative Session on Wearable Robotics for Motion Assistance and Rehabilitation, pp. 6184-6189, Hamburg, Germany (2015)
9. Hanawaka, T.: Organizing motor imageries. Neurosci. Res. **104**, 56–63 (2016)
10. Costa, Á., Iáñez, E., Úbeda, A., Del-Ama, A.J., et al.: Decoding the attentional demands of gait through EEG gamma band features. PLoS ONE **11**(4), e0154136 (2016)
11. Salazar-Varas, R., Costa, Á., Iáñez, E., Úbeda, A., Hortal, E., Azorín, J.M.: Analyzing EEG signals to detect unexpected obstacles during walking. J. NeuroEng. Rehabil. **12**(101), 1–15 (2015)

Human Robot Interaction

Improved Control of DLO Transportation by a Team of Quadrotors

Julian Estevez and Manuel Graña(✉)

Computational Intelligence Group, University of the Basque Country, UPV/EHU, San Sebastian, Spain
{julian.estevez,manuel.grana}@ehu.es

Abstract. Quasi-stationary sections of a deformable linear object (DLO) hanging freely from two extreme points can be modeled either by catenaries or parabolic curves, depending on the conditions of the UAVs. DLO transportation is an instance of a leader-follower platoon team strategy, in which the local quadrotor control must cope with the dynamic perturbations due to the DLO linking the quadrotors. The quadrotor team control has two phases, one achieving a spatial configuration with equal energy consumption, the other is to manage the horizontal motion which is the transportation process *per se*. We propose a *Model Reference Adaptive Control* (MRAC) for the quadrotors team, which uses fuzzy modeling of the error in order to modulate the activation of the adaptation rules applied to proportional-derivative (PD) controller parameters, which are derived as error gradient descent rules. In this paper, we contribute the parabolic representation of the DLO and improved follow the leader control, testing the MRAC stability and robustness under a series of experiments.

1 Introduction

Cheap and reliable quadrotors are making feasible innovative applications [9] such as the team transportation of deformable linear objects (DLO) by a team of quadrotors [6], which can be extremely useful in emergency situations, such as fires or rescue operations in very unstructured environments. Transporting a hose on the ground by a team of mobile robots [3] is a special case of linked multicomponent robotic systems [2], and its control has been achieved by reinforcement learning [8,12,13]. In our application, the DLO is hanging from the aerial robots in a quasi-stationary state, hence its geometry can be modeled by a closed form expression such as catenary or parabolic curves. Specifically, in this paper we consider the parabolic approximation which remains valid when the distance between drones is small. Parabole simplification of the catenary is widely referenced and used in scientific bibliography [10,18,19].

Transportation of the DLO by a team of quadrotors has two phases. Firstly, a spatial configuration of the DLO and the quadrotors must be reached such that all of them have the same workload and are consuming the same quantity of energy, so that there will not be some member of the team failing to function

J.M. Ferrández Vicente et al. (Eds.): IWINAC 2017, Part II, LNCS 10338, pp. 117–126, 2017.
DOI: 10.1007/978-3-319-59773-7_13

before the others [4,6,7]. Secondly, the quadrotors must move in the XY plane to achieve the transportation of the DLO. For this task, the global team strategy is "follow the leader" strategy, where the quadrotor carrying the tip of the DLO has some predefined trajectory. Each control phase can be achieved by optimized Proportional Integral Derivative (PID) controllers, structured into a *Model Reference Adaptive Control* (MRAC): the outer loop controls forward motion, and the inner loop for attitude control. Offline PID parameter optimization can be achieved by metaheuristics such as Particle Swarm Optimization (PSO) [5], however they can not cope with operational perturbations, such as wind shear. In order to cope with this, adaptive control was implemented based on gradient descent rules for the minimization of the error, which are activated by the fuzzy membership quantification of the relative error in a follow-the-leader navigation strategy [7]. However, when performing demanding paths with the quadrotors system, such as zig-zag trajectories, limitations were observed, and too different torque demands of each robot in the system so as to hold the formation. Thus, in this article, we propose an improved leader-follower strategy based on platoon formation, and check the convergence conditions of the adaptive control algorithm. We demonstrate the efficiency of the system through computational experiments involving an accurate simulation of the system.

The article is structured as follows: Sect. 2 recalls description of the system already presented in previous works and the improvements introduced in this paper. Section 2.3 recalls the fuzzy logic based online parameter adaptation algorithms, and discusses its stability. Section 3 gives the experimental design, reporting results on the robustness and efficiency of our enhanced DLO transportation with the team of quadrotors physical model. Finally, Sect. 4 gives some conclusions about the present work.

2 System Description and Control

As first approximation, the DLO is modeled as a collection of catenary curve sections hanging from the quadrotors [6], restricting the study to quasi-stationary regimes of the system. The motion of quadrotors for transportation produces changes in DLO geometry that can be modeled by transformations between catenary curves, allowing low computational cost simulation, and close form computation of the vertical and horizontal forces at the quadrotors. If the horizontal distance among UAVs is too short or too long enough the conditions for the existence of hyperbolic function of the catenary are overcome. Then, a new geometric model becomes necessary, so that we substitute catenaries by paraboles in the current paper to cope with situations where the sagging of the cable is small enough [14]. Some robotics research articles consider the approximation of the catenary as a parabole [11,21]. The vertical load of the quadrotor when hanging a parabole shaped DLO is computed by interpolation from catenaries according to the horizontal distance.

A reasonable requirement for the operation of the entire systems is that all quadrotors support the same vertical load, so that battery usage is similar for each robot of the system, avoiding early energy depletion by some quadrotor, which would result in failure of the collaborative task. Workload balance is achieved by setting the extreme points of the DLO sections at different height. Previous works [6] achieved robust control parameters to drive the system spatial configuration to the desired equi-workload configuration.

2.1 Quadrotor Control System

Our approach proceeds by adaptively tuning Proportional Integral Derivative (PID) controllers in a Model Reference Adaptive Control (MRAC) configuration, because they provide robust control with lower computational and tuning effort [1]. We use them both for attitude [6] and position control of the individual quadrotors in our collaborative system.

Tuning the PDI parameters to reach the vertical equilibrium equi-workload state illustrated was reported in [4–6]. The control system is scalable and can work with a multiple combination of drones. Moreover, our approach does not need the Integral term in the control, hence we work with PD controllers. Horizontal displacement of quadrotors is obtained by an increase in the corresponding Euler angles. Simply stated, setting ψ angle to 0, while θ and φ are positive, produces a motion in the X, Y axes, respectively.

2.2 Quadrotor Team Control

Quadrotors move in a platoon formation. A *platoon* is a formation where a group of robots lines up one behind the other. It is a very simple and effective formation that is used when a group of vehicles must travel on a path, or through a tight space. The platoon is a direct application of the Leader-Follower formation, with one *Leader*, and multiple *Followers* that follow the *Leader's* motion. The algorithm for calculating the follower's UAV desired position in relation to the Leader is based on [15,16]. This *Leader* following strategy is summarized in Fig. 1.

Most of the calculations for the leader-follower formation are carried out in polar coordinates. The first step in the methodology is to convert Cartesian (x, y, ψ) coordinates to polar (ρ, α, φ) coordinates.

$$\rho = \sqrt{(x_L - x_F)^2 + (y_L - y_F)^2}, \tag{1}$$

$$\alpha = \tan^{-1}(\frac{y_L - y_F}{x_L - x_F}) - \psi_F, \tag{2}$$

where L and F subindices denote the *Leader* and *Follower* parameters, respectively. φ, is the angle that relates the orientation of the *Leader* with respect to the *Follower* UAV. It can be defined as:

$$\varphi = \alpha + \psi_F - \psi_L. \tag{3}$$

Angle ψ is the orientation in the XY plane at each moment of the quadrotor produced by its pitch and roll angles.

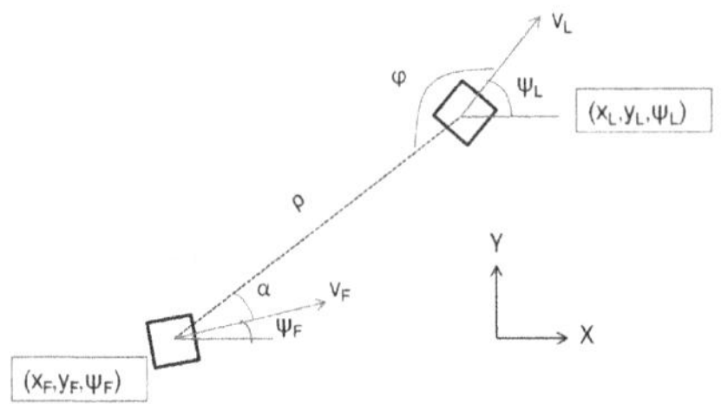

Fig. 1. Leader-following model

After the conversion from Cartesian (x, y, ψ) to polar coordinates (ρ, α, φ), the kinematic model is shown next:

$$\begin{bmatrix} \dot{\rho} \\ \dot{\alpha} \\ \dot{\varphi} \end{bmatrix} = \begin{bmatrix} -\cos\alpha & 0 \\ \frac{\sin\alpha}{\rho} & -1 \\ \frac{\sin\alpha}{\rho} & 0 \end{bmatrix} \begin{bmatrix} v_F \\ \omega_F \end{bmatrix} + \begin{bmatrix} -\cos\varphi & 0 \\ \frac{\sin\varphi}{\rho} & 0 \\ \frac{\sin\varphi}{\rho} & -1 \end{bmatrix} \begin{bmatrix} v_L \\ \omega_L \end{bmatrix}, \tag{4}$$

where $\dot{\rho}, \dot{\alpha}, \dot{\varphi}$ represent the kinematics model for the system of the controller design. The aim of this controller is to calculate the v_F and ω_F of the *Follower* robot, so that it can follow the *Leader* and maintain a constant relative distance. Let ρ_d be the desired distance between the two drones, and α_d the desired angle between the *Follower's* direction of motion and ρ. In order the get the difference among desired and real values to 0 as time increases, the following control is applied:

$$\begin{bmatrix} v_F \\ \omega_F \end{bmatrix} = \begin{bmatrix} k & 0 \\ 0 & k \end{bmatrix} \begin{bmatrix} \rho_d - \rho \\ \alpha_d - \alpha \end{bmatrix}. \tag{5}$$

The value of the k is set so that the system becomes stable. Final step is to calculate the v_F and ω_F of the quadrotor.

$$\begin{bmatrix} v_F \\ \omega_F \end{bmatrix} = \begin{bmatrix} -\frac{1}{\cos\alpha} & 0 \\ -\frac{\tan\alpha}{\rho} & -1 \end{bmatrix} \left(\begin{bmatrix} \dot{\rho} \\ \dot{\alpha} \end{bmatrix} - \begin{bmatrix} -\cos\varphi & 0 \\ \frac{\sin\varphi}{\rho} & 0 \end{bmatrix} \begin{bmatrix} v_L \\ \omega_L \end{bmatrix} \right).$$

The block-diagram of the algorithm is shown in Fig. 2.

The key to achieving this formation is to implement controller variables ρ_d as a desired euclidean distance between drones m and $\alpha_d = 0$. The position of a *Follower* robot related to the *Leader* is given by Eq. 6, maintaining a constant distance.

$$\begin{cases} x_F = x_L - \rho\cos(\alpha + \psi_F) \\ y_F = y_L + \rho\sin(\alpha + \psi_F) \\ \psi_F = \varphi + \psi_L - \pi \end{cases}. \tag{6}$$

Thus, x_F and y_F are the desired x_d and y_d for the *Follower* drone(s), while the desired x and y values are the path equation points for the *Leader* drone.

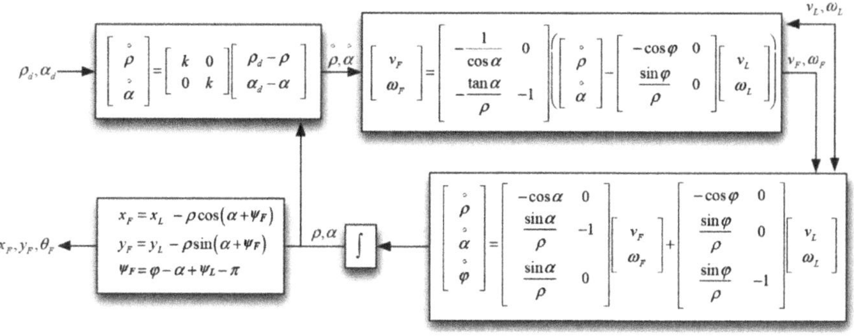

Fig. 2. Platoon formation diagram block control

2.3 Online Fuzzy Adaptation of PD Controllers

As discussed in the introduction, offline tuning of the PD controllers does not allow adaptation to unexpected events and conditions which actually happen when performing the DLO transportation. Therefore, we proposed an online (i.e. on the fly) adaptive tuning. i.e. Adaptive Fuzzy Modulation (AFM) approach [7]. Initial PD values in the experiment are obtained through Ziegler-Nichols algorithm, which is the standard in PID control. The inner-loop PD controllers of each and all the quadrotors in the team is an online adaptive algorithm which combines fuzzy membership function activation and error gradient descent like adaptation rule, achieving an online fuzzy controller as in [20, 22]. The online parameter adaptation equations [7] read as follows:

$$K_p\left(t+1\right) = K_p\left(t\right) + \alpha e(t)\left(\mu_1\left(Pe\left(t\right)\right) + \mu_4\left(Pe\left(t\right)\right)\right) \tag{7}$$

$$K_d(t+1) = K_d\left(t\right) + \alpha e(t)\left(\mu_2\left(Pe\left(t\right)\right) + \mu_3\left(Pe\left(t\right)\right)\right) \tag{8}$$

where α is the adaptation gain, $e(t)$ is the navigation error at each t moment, and $\mu_k\left(Pe\left(t\right)\right)$ is the k-th membership value function, which provides the activation strength of the adaptation function. The adaption factor α is initialized with a value between 0 and 1 and remains constant until the end of the process. The online control will allow the system to adapt to different trajectories, dynamically changing parameters of the quadrotors (such as varying servomotor performances), and unknown DLO weight *per* length.

Convergence of the Fuzzy Modulation Approach. Tuning the controller is not dependent on the physical parameters of the UAV. Thus various payloads do not compel us to retune the controller. The stability proof of the adaptive control law is based on the improved Lyapunov-based Model Reference Adaptive Control

(MRAC) technique [17]. Certainly, the rules presented in Eqs. (7) and (8) follow the general adaptive expression based on the error between desired and real values, $e(t)$:

$$K_{ij}(t+1) = K_{ij}(t) + \alpha_{ij} \int r_i(t) e_i^{(j)}(t) dt + \beta_{ij} r_i(t) e_i^{(j)}(t) \quad j = 0, 1, \tag{9}$$

where α and β are zero or any positive proportional adaptation gains in $e_i^{(j)}(t)$ the superscript "(j)" denotes the jth derivative. $r_i(t)$ is equal to next expression:

$$r_i(t) = W_{pi} e_i(t) + W_{vi} \dot{e}_i(t), \tag{10}$$

where W_{pi} and W_{vi} are positive or zero scalar weighting factors which reflect the relative significance of the position and velocity errors $e_i(t)$ and $\dot{e}_i(t)$ in forming the weighted error $r_i(t)$. Estability of adaptation rules in the form of Eq. (9) is proven in [17].

3 Experiments

The simulation experiment was carried out using a discretization of the time variable and all the simulations cover a time of 60 s, including the transient state of the experiment. Time increment used to compute simulation steps is $0.1s$. Experiments have been coded in house in Scilab 5.4. No other public or private software solutions have been used. The experiment has been carried out with a system of 3 quadrotors following a zig-zag type path shown in Fig. 3. Such kind of path was not feasible for the previous version of the system control [7]. The experiment is carried out twice: with and without wind disturbance. The model for wind disturbance is given by the expression: $d(t) = 5 + 5\sin(\frac{\pi}{2}t)$ $[N]$.

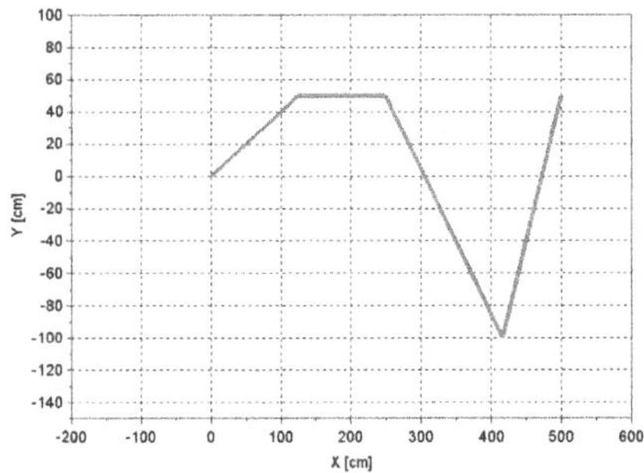

Fig. 3. Path followed by the quadrotors in the *Experiment*

The initial horizontal distance between quadrotors is assumed to be equal for each pair of drones, indeed it is proportional to the total length of the DLO. We assume that the system is in an initial configuration where balanced energy consumption has been achieved. During the experiments, though the horizontal distance between drones may change during task completion, no further correction of altitude is applied. Specific values of system parameters in the experiment are as follows: catenaries with a length of $L_0 = 240\,\text{cm}$; the weight parameter of the hose is $w = 0,005\,[\text{kg/cm}]$. Adaption factor $\alpha = 0.5$ for fuzzy PD tuning. Mass and inertia moments of the quadrotors are assumed as in Table 1. Initial angles of three drones are all set to 0. Outer-loop PD parameters are as computed in [4], which for experiments in this paper are $K_p = 140.66$ and $K_d = 41.36$. $\rho_d = 70\,\text{cm}$ was decided as desired distance in the platoon formation. Thrust of drones is limited by hardware to 20[N]. Initial PD parameter values for X and Y axes in all the drones are $K_{px} = K_{py} = 0.22$; $K_{dx} = K_{dy} = 0.76$, respectively. Drone starting position is in a line along the X axis with a separation of 40 cm. The leader drone flights along the planned reference, followed by the rest of the drones. Conditions and parameter values are stated previously.

Table 1. Dynamic parameters of the quadrotor

Parameter	Value
Mass, m	0.5 kg
Arm length, l	25 cm
Inertia moments, $I_{xx} = I_{yy}$	$5 \cdot 10^{-3}[\text{Nms}^2]$
inertia moment, I_{zz}	$1 \cdot 10^{-2}[\text{Nms}^2]$
Propeller thrust coefficient, b	$3 \cdot 10^{-6}[\text{Ns}^2]$
Drag, d	$1 \cdot 10^{-7}[\text{Nms}^2]$

3.1 Results

In Fig. 4, the trajectory of the three quadrotors is shown, which is equal up to the plotting resolutions for the experiments under wind and no wind conditions. To achieve this response, the thrust of $D1$ presents a slightly different behaviour for

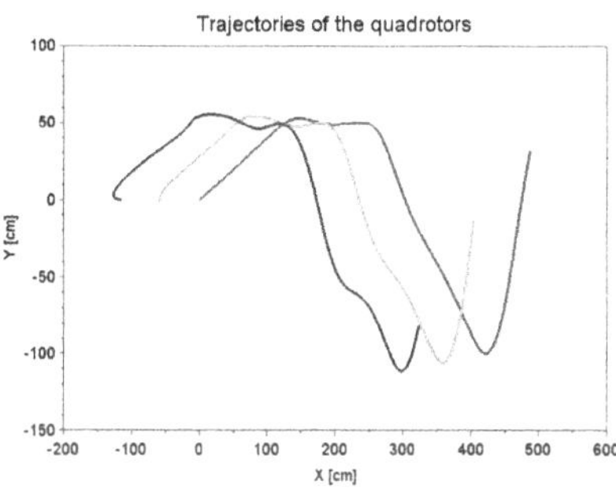

Fig. 4. Trajectory of the quadrotors in *Experiment*, under wind and no wind conditions

two situations, as can be seen in Fig. 5 ($D1$, $D2$ and $D3$ represent the UAVs that go first, second and third in the formation respectively). That is, our approach allows to adapt the system to quite energetic wind perturbations. Next figures correspond to non-windy conditions. Euclidean distances among drones remain quite stable, as can be seen in Fig. 6. Figure 7 presents the evolution in time of the PD parameters tuned by fuzzy logic in X and Y directions. The adaptive control achieves quite sudden changes of the control parameters to estabilize the system around the nominal trajectory.

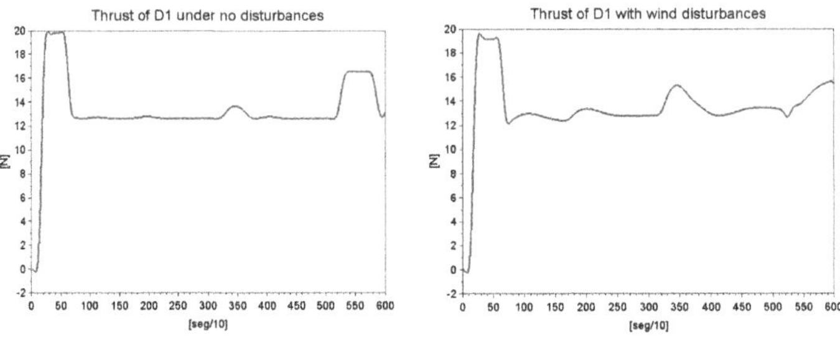

Fig. 5. Thrust of $D1$ comparison between windy and non-windy conditions

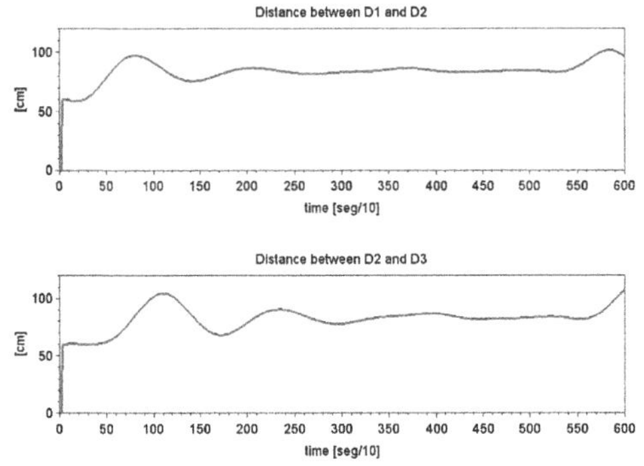

Fig. 6. Distance between drones in *Experiment*

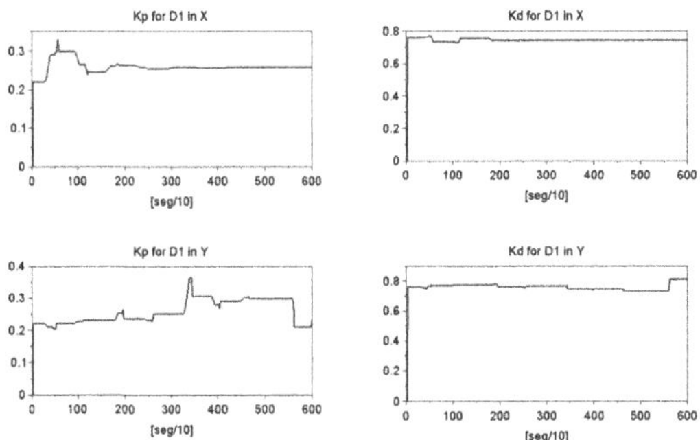

Fig. 7. PD values of $D1$ in *Experiment*

4 Conclusions

We checked the stability and feasibility of the new physical model for the DLO transportation with a team of 3 quadrotors. Parabolic shaped DLO help representing a wider range of situation, and this kind of solutions lead to the opportunity to model the complete system in the dynamic state, taking into consideration non stationary regimes such as take-off and landing of the robots, and contact of the DLO with other surfaces. Moreover, our new platoon formation proved to be able to cope with agressive changes of direction, such as the ones in Fig. 3 helped by an adaptive fuzzy tuned controller, which resulted to be stable.

Future efforts should point to the implementation of a machine learning control strategy and obtaining a real platform to contrast the simulation results.

References

1. Argentim, L.M., Rezende, W.C., Santos, P.E., Aguiar, R.A.: PID, LQR and LQR-PID on a quadcopter platform. In: 2013 International Conference on Informatics, Electronics Vision (ICIEV), pp. 1–6, May 2013
2. Duro, R.J., Graña, M., Lope, J.: On the potential contributions of hybrid intelligent approaches to multicomponent robotic system development. Inf. Sci. **180**(14), 2635–2648 (2010)
3. Echegoyen, Z., Villaverde, I., Moreno, R., Graña, M., d'Anjou, A.: Linked multicomponent mobile robots: modeling, simulation and control. Robot. Auton. Syst. **58**(12), 1292–1305 (2010)
4. Estevez, J., Graña, M.: Robust control tuning by PSO of aerial robots hose transportation. In: Ferrández Vicente, J.M., Álvarez-Sánchez, J.R., de la Paz López, F., Toledo-Moreo, F.J., Adeli, H. (eds.) IWINAC 2015. LNCS, vol. 9108, pp. 291–300. Springer, Cham (2015). doi:10.1007/978-3-319-18833-1_31
5. Estevez, J., Lopez-Guede, J.M., Graña, M.: Particle swarm optimization quadrotor control for cooperative aerial transportation of deformable linear objects. Cybern. Syst. **47**(1–2), 4–16 (2016)
6. Estevez, J., Lopez-Guede, J.M., Graña, M.: Quasi-stationary state transportation of a hose with quadrotors. Robot. Auton. Syst. **63**(2), 187–194 (2015). Cognition-oriented advanced robotic systems
7. Lopez-Guede, J.M., Estevez, J., Graña, M.: Online fuzzy modulated adaptive PD control for cooperative aerial transportation of deformable linear objects. Integr. Comput.-Aided Eng. Preprint(Preprint), 1–15 (2016)
8. Fernandez-Gauna, B., Lopez-Guede, J.M., Graña, M.: Transfer learning with partially constrained models: application to reinforcement learning of linked multicomponent robot system control. Robot. Auton. Syst. **61**(7), 694–703 (2013)
9. Floreano, D., Wood, R.J.: Science, technology and the future of small autonomous drones. Nature **521**(7553), 460–466 (2015)
10. Hsu, Y., Pan, C.: The static WKB solution to catenary problems with large sag and bending stiffness. Math. Probl. Eng. **2014** (2014)
11. Larsen, L., Pham, V.L., Kim, J., Kupke, M.: Collision-free path planning of industrial cooperating robots for aircraft fuselage production. In: 2015 IEEE International Conference on Robotics and Automation (ICRA), pp. 2042–2047, May 2015

12. Lopez-Guede, J.M., Fernandez-Gauna, B., Graña, M.: State-action value modeled by ELM in reinforcement learning for hose control problems. Int. J. Uncertain. Fuzziness Knowl.-Based Syst. **21**(supp02), 99–116 (2013)
13. Lopez-Guede, J.M., Graña, M., Ramos-Hernanz, J.A., Oterino, F.: A neural network approximation of L-MCRS Dynamics for reinforcement learning experiments. In: Ferrández Vicente, J.M., Álvarez Sánchez, J.R., Paz López, F., Toledo Moreo, F.J. (eds.) IWINAC 2013. LNCS, vol. 7931, pp. 317–325. Springer, Heidelberg (2013). doi:10.1007/978-3-642-38622-0_33
14. Nguyen, D.Q., Gouttefarde, M., Company, O., Pierrot, F.: On the simplifications of cable model in static analysis of large-dimension cable-driven parallel robots. In: 2013 IEEE/RSJ International Conference on Intelligent Robots and Systems, pp. 928–934, November 2013
15. Pruner, E., Necsulescu, D., Sasiadek, J., Kim, B.: Control of decentralized geometric formations of mobile robots. In: 2012 17th International Conference on Methods Models in Automation Robotics (MMAR), pp. 627–632, August 2012
16. Pruner,E.: Control of self-organizing and geometric formations. Ph.D. thesis. Université d'Ottawa/University of Ottawa (2014)
17. Seraji, H.: Decentralized adaptive control of manipulators: theory, simulation, and experimentation. IEEE Trans. Robot. Autom. **5**(2), 183–201 (1989)
18. Su, Y., Qiu, Y., Liu, P.: Optimal cable tension distribution of the high-speed redundant driven camera robots considering cable sag and inertia effects. Adv. Mech. Eng. **6** (2014)
19. Wei, K., Zhang, L.X., Ren, A.D.: The analysis method of highline cable of alongside replenishment system based on suspended cable theory. In: Advanced Materials Research, vol. 490, pp. 633–637. Trans Tech Publications (2012)
20. Wen, N., Zhao, L., Xiaohong, S., Ma, P.: Uav online path planning algorithm in a low altitude dangerous environment. IEEE/CAA J. Autom. Sin. **2**(2), 173–185 (2015)
21. Yao, R., Tang, X., Wang, J., Huang, P.: Dimensional optimization design of the four-cable-driven parallel manipulator in fast. IEEE/ASME Trans. Mechatron. **15**(6), 932–941 (2010)
22. Yeh, F.-K.: Attitude controller design of mini-unmanned aerial vehicles using fuzzy sliding-mode control degraded by white noise interference. Control Theory Applications **6**(9), 1205–1212 (2012). IET

Robust Joint Visual Attention for HRI Using a Laser Pointer for Perspective Alignment and Deictic Referring

Darío Maravall[1,2], Javier de Lope[1,2], and Juan Pablo Fuentes[1,2(✉)]

[1] Department of Artificial Intelligence, Faculty of Computer Science, Universidad Politécnica de Madrid, Madrid, Spain
dmaravall@fi.upm.es, javier.delope@upm.es, jpablofuentes@sol.dia.fi.upm.es, juanpablo.fuentes.brea@alumnos.upm.es
[2] Centro de Automática y Robótica (UPM-CSIC), Universidad Politécnica de Madrid, Madrid, Spain

Abstract. In Human Robot Interaction (HRI), it is a basic prerequisite to guarantee joint attention, also known as shared attention, to get a proper coordination of the involved agents. A particular and important case of joint attention is joint visual attention, also referred to as perspective taking alignment, in which both the human agent and the robot must align their corresponding visual perspectives to look at the same scene or object of mutual interest. In this paper we present experimental work on the alignment of the visual perspectives of a humanoid-like robot and a human agent by means of a laser pointer used as a deictic or pointing device by both agents. We have developed experimental work to validate our proposed method using a scenario based on "I spy" game. After a brief discussion of joint visual attention, we introduce the humanoid-like robot specifically built for our experiments and afterwards we discuss the results obtained in the above-mentioned scenario. We would like to emphasize that for this scenario the human agents and the robot use limited linguistic words to facilitate coordination. These verbal exchanges are based on a common language (a lexicon plus grammar rules) for both humans and robots.

Keywords: Human Robot Interaction · Joint visual attention · Deictic · Humanoids

1 Introduction

Joint attention, also known as shared attention, is a basic human cognitive ability allowing social cognitive and emotional development, which is essential in the human species as humans are prematurely born creatures with a high neural plasticity, almost helpless at birth, and who attain their complete cognitive and emotional development after a long period of supervised interactive social learning: Jerome Bruner has emphasized this unique human trait by theorizing about

J.M. Ferrández Vicente et al. (Eds.): IWINAC 2017, Part II, LNCS 10338, pp. 127–136, 2017.
DOI: 10.1007/978-3-319-59773-7_14

the importance of inmaturity in the growth of knowledge and in the acquisition of language in the human child [1].

In synthesis, joint attention means that two agents share the same referential background making it possible for both agents communication and coordination for performing joint activity [2].

A particular and interesting case of joint attention is joint visual attention in which the agents' joint attention is based on visual perception. In this case the robot must align its perspective with the human's visual perspective. For this Human-Robot visual alignment problem two additional and complex support tools are necessary: verbal exchanges and pointing gestures. So that they must coordinate their corresponding visual perspectives in order to look at the same scene. According to George Butterworth and colleagues there can be distinguished the following sequential stages in the development of joint visual attention in the human child [3]: ecological, geometrical and finally representational or symbolic. In the first and most basic stage, the *ecological*, the child just focuses its attention on the most salient regions of his field of vision. Sensu stricto, at this stage, which is purely individual and non social, we cannot speak of joint attention as the child guides his visual attention by exclusively intrinsic motivations driven only by the saliency of the perceived environment without the intervention of his caregivers. However, at the next cognitive development stage, the *geometric* stage, the child is already able to engage on social interactions to coordinate his attention with the visual perspective of the adult by estimating the adult's perspective by means of gaze following (what Butterworth and colleagues call geometric mechanisms for joint visual attention). This is the first and most primitive stage of true joint visual attention in the human species. At a posterior and more advanced cognitive development stage the child is able to get joint visual attention by means of linguistic and verbal propositions: the referential or *symbolic* stage of joint visual attention. Obviously, this advanced referential joint visual attention stage is only possible when the human child has acquired linguistic competence by means of which he can transcend his direct sensory perception and then he can use language for imagination-based planning and goal-oriented imaginary activity thanks to the language's capability of being a tool for the symbolic representation of the state of affairs of the world and for thought expression. In this paper we focus our interest on human-robot joint visual attention in which the robot must align its visual perspective with the visual perspective of an interacting human agent. This shared perspective taking is a basic prerequisite for human-robot cooperative interaction [4,5].

The remaining of the paper is organized as follows. First, we present the humanoid robotic platform specifically developed for our experiments, including the crucial idea of using a pointer laser as a deictic tool by the robot and the human user. Afterwards we describe the experimental scenario used to test our proposed solution for visual deictic alignment based on the "I spy" game. For this experimental scenario we distinguish two basic stages: visually grounded lexicon acquisition and dynamic deictic interactions (for search and recognition of objects in the I spy game). The paper ends with the discussion of the experimental results.

2 Joint Visual Attention Based on a Pointer Laser as a Deictic Device

As an alternative to verbal and gestural scaffolding for human-robot joint visual attention, we introduce a solution based on a pointer laser, used as a deictic or pointing device by both the human and the robot (Fig. 1). Apart from being a simpler solution to cooperative referring, this laser-based method also gives a more precise and robust localization of the referential objects.

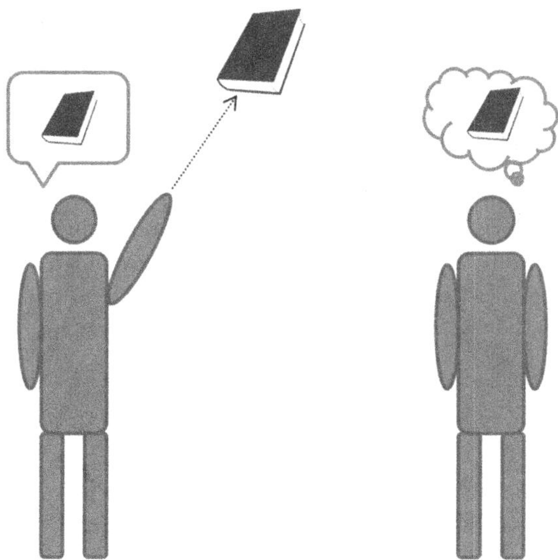

Fig. 1. Joint Visual Attention and deictic interactions based on a laser pointer.

For the visuomotor coordination and control of the humanoid vision-based pointing gestures, we distinguish two main stages: visual search of objects and factual pointing to the object as explained below.

2.1 Visual Search of the Object

In this first stage, the robot after receiving the name of the object of interest, starts the search of the object by means of its motorized camera, by using the difference between the current image captured by the robot camera and a dataset previously defined of labeled objetcs as signal error. For this objects recognition we have implemented a K-NN classifier [6], using the 3 RGB channels as discriminant variables. As a result of this classifier are obtained: the name of the recognized object, the (x, y) coordinates of its location within the current image and the corresponding ε error.

Let us suppose a pan-tilt camera with θ pan angle and φ tilt angle; then we can apply a conventional PD control algorithm [7] to each control angle of the camera for searching the object of interest. The parameters of the control algorithm$(K_{p_\theta}, K_{d_\theta}, K_{p_\varphi}, K_{d_\varphi})$ are set experimentally:

$$\theta = K_{p_\theta} \cdot \varepsilon + K_{d_\theta} \cdot \dot{\varepsilon} \tag{1}$$

$$\varphi = K_{p_\varphi} \cdot \varepsilon + K_{d_\varphi} \cdot \dot{\varepsilon} \tag{2}$$

When the object is finally recognized, the camera is centered to achieve a visual alignment with it, setting the θ pan angle and φ tilt angle using the (x_o, y_o) coordinates obtained from the classifier. These coordinates correspond to the center of the object within the current image.

2.2 Pointing Gesture Control

After having found the object of interest, in this second stage, the robot must point at the object with the laser pointer. Let's suppose that the robot arm has two degrees of freedom: α shoulder angle and β elbow angle then we can also apply a conventional PD algorithm [7] for pointing at the object of interest. As in the previous stage, the parameters of the control algorithm$(K_{p_\alpha}, K_{d_\alpha}, K_{p_\beta}, K_{d_\beta})$ are set experimentally:

$$\alpha = K_{p_\alpha} \cdot \varepsilon_y + K_{d_\alpha} \cdot \dot{\varepsilon}_y \tag{3}$$

$$\beta = K_{p_\beta} \cdot \varepsilon_x + K_{d_\beta} \cdot \dot{\varepsilon}_x \tag{4}$$

where ε_x and ε_y stand for the error or distance between the projected laser point with (x_{laser}, y_{laser}) coordenates, and the object's mass center in the image plane with the (x_o, y_o) coordinates:

$$\varepsilon_x = (x_o - x_{laser}) \tag{5}$$

$$\varepsilon_y = (y_o - y_{laser}) \tag{6}$$

$$\varepsilon_t = \varepsilon_x + \varepsilon_y \tag{7}$$

The projected laser point (x_{laser}, y_{laser}) coordinates are obtained using a mathematical morphological method. This method is based on a set of morphological and smoothing operators (sequentially: dilation, median blur and erosion), which are applied to the image resulting from performing a logical AND operation between the R channel (from RGB space) and V channel (from HSV space). The R channel is used because of the laser pointer is red. Within the resulting image, the projected laser point is detected by executing the Canny algorithm [8], and their coordinates within the humanoid visual field are finally obtained.

When the laser pointer is aligned with the recognized object the ε_t error converges to zero, and the humanoid indicates the name of the object of interest to the human.

3 The Humanoid-Like Robotic Platform

As robotic platform for the execution of experimental work, we have built a humanoid-like robotic based on aluminum profiles design from scratch (Fig. 2). The different components that allow a correct interaction with humans are mounted on the aluminum chassis.

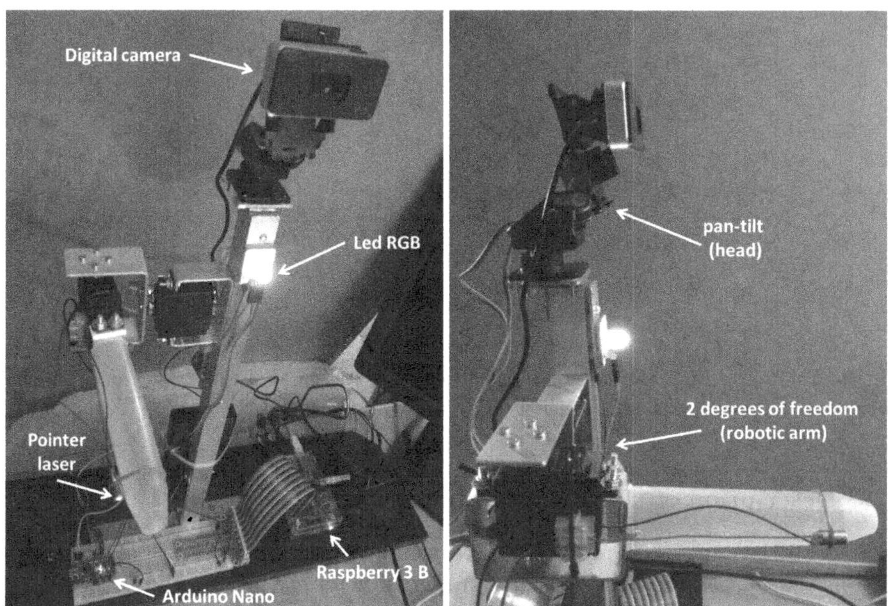

Fig. 2. The images show the humanoid-like robotic platform.

3.1 Description of the Morphology of the Humanoid

The humanoid is composed of a head with capacity to acquire sensory information of the environment, besides a robotic arm to execute a deictic process:

- The head is composed of a digital camera actuated by means of a pan-tilt unit built with 2 mini-servomotors located perpendicularly (Fig. 3). The robotic head with the digital camera can be used as a visual sensor for the recognition of objects within the environment, as well as actuator for alignment with the object detected during interaction with the human.
- For the robotic arm of two degrees of freedom 2 servomotors of 11 kg-cm of torque are used (Fig. 3), as well as a laser pointer connected in the end of the arm. Thus, the humanoid can use the laser pointer as a deictic facility during the joint visual attention process.

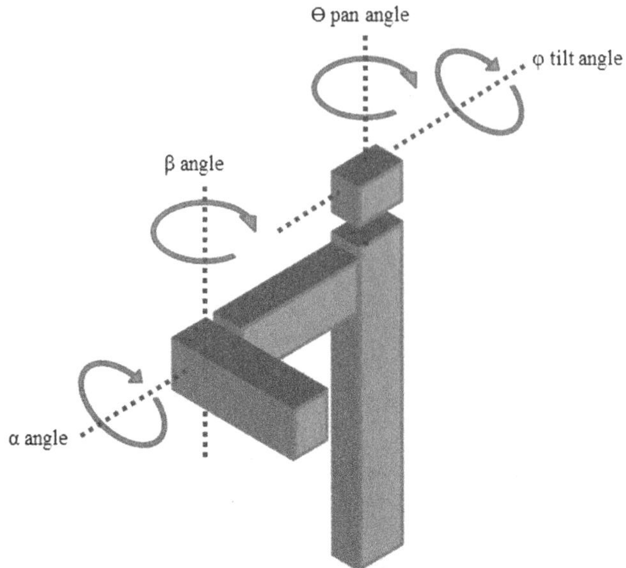

Fig. 3. The figure depicts the pan-tilt head (θ pan angle and φ tilt angle), in addition to the two degrees of freedom on the robotic arm (α shoulder angle and β elbow angle).

3.2 Description of the Humanoid Modules

The control system consists of two interconnected modules. The master main module (based on Raspberry PI [9]) is responsible of executing the main control loop, collecting all sensory information and recognizing the objects. This module sends the appropriate control signals to the actuators connected to a second slave control module (based on Arduino Nano), which controls the mini-servos in the head and servomotors of the robotic arm. The technical characteristics of both modules are following:

- Main module: Raspberry Pi 3 B with linux-based operating system. This module is connected with a HD digital camera (Real 720P HD resolution, 16:9 wide screen output) for the visual recognition of objects, in addition a multimedia system of speakers and microphone for interaction with the human. The I2C protocol is used to send the control signals to the actuators.
- Slave module: Arduino Nano motor controller. It is an event-based micro-controller for the management of all control signals received through the I2C protocol. This module is connected with the actuators (mini-servomotors, servomotors and laser). In addition, a led RGB is connected for showing the state of the humanoid.

The power supply has two independent sources (5 V for the main module Raspberry Pi and 6 V for the rest of elements including the servomotors).

4 Description of the Experimental Scenario and Discussion of the Results

We have defined an experimental scenario for the experimentation on joint visual attention (Fig. 4), where we distinguish two basic stages: (1) visually grounded lexicon acquisition and (2) dynamic deictic interactions between the humanoid and human, using the pointer laser as a deictic device. The scenario is based on the well-known "I spy" children game, in which both the robot and the human agents play and compete in searching specific objects.

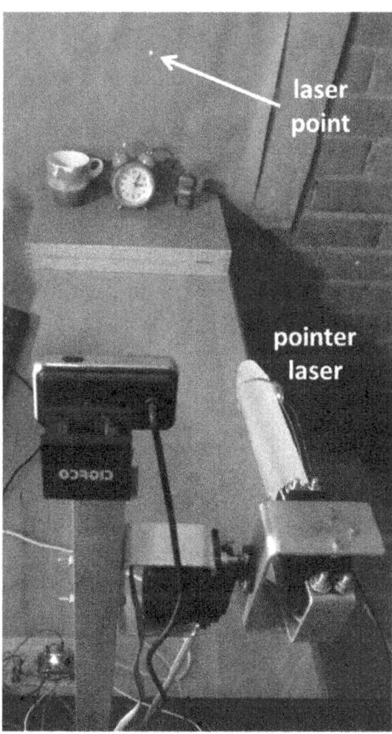

Fig. 4. This picture shows the experimental scenario used during the "I spy" game. The humanoid uses the pointer laser as deictic device.

The humanoid needs to learn the objects within the environment for playing. Thus, the human have to show each object to the robot for visual processing and gives the name of the object as lexicon acquisition. As a result it is generated a dataset that associates each labeled object with the information from the RGB channels of the object image. In this paper we have used as objects an alarm clock, an eraser rubber and a cup of coffee.

The game begins when the human asks to the humanoid by the name of a specific object. It initiates in the humanoid a process of visual search of this object within the environment. The control loop generates the control signals for the pan-tilt angles of the digital camera, by using the error resulting from the K-NN classifier.

When the humanoid finds visually the object, the deictic process is started using the laser pointer anchored at the end of its robotic arm. In order to project the laser point on the object for the joint attention between the robot and human, the control loop generates the control signals for the two degrees of freedom on the robotic arm. Then, the humanoid says the name of the object to the human; if it is correct, the humanoid wins the game and its led RGB is green, else the led is red.

Figure 5 shows three "I spy" games (one for each object) between the humanoid and the human: the α and β angles used for the robotic arm, and the reduction of the ε_t error along the k trials computed during each game.

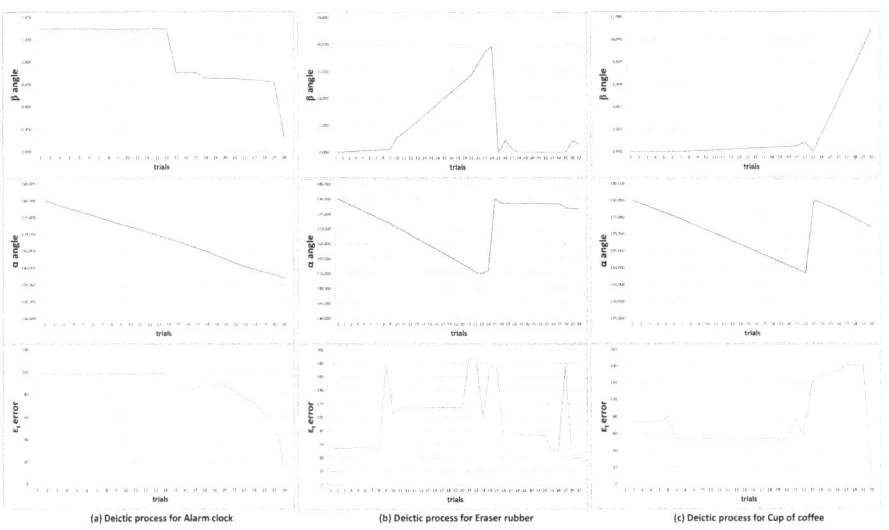

(a) Deictic process for Alarm clock (b) Deictic process for Eraser rubber (c) Deictic process for Cup of coffee

Fig. 5. The α and β angles generated at each k trial during the test "I spy" games: (a) Deictic process for Alarm clock, (b) Deictic process for Eraser rubber and (c) Deictic process for Cup of coffee.

As a result of these test games, the humanoid indicates the object of interest for the human by the laser pointer. Figure 6 shows the first person view of the humanoid when projects the laser point on the objects during the deictic process.

The values used for the parameters of the control algorithm PD have been obtained experimentally. The Fig. 7 shows the settings of values used during the "I spy" game.

During the game the ε_t error is calculated between the projected laser point and the object's mass center in the captured image at each iteration or trial of the control loop. This ε_t error converges to zero for all objects defined in this experimental scenario.

From the experimental results obtained in our laboratory and previously shown, we can conclude that the present solution complies with the requirements

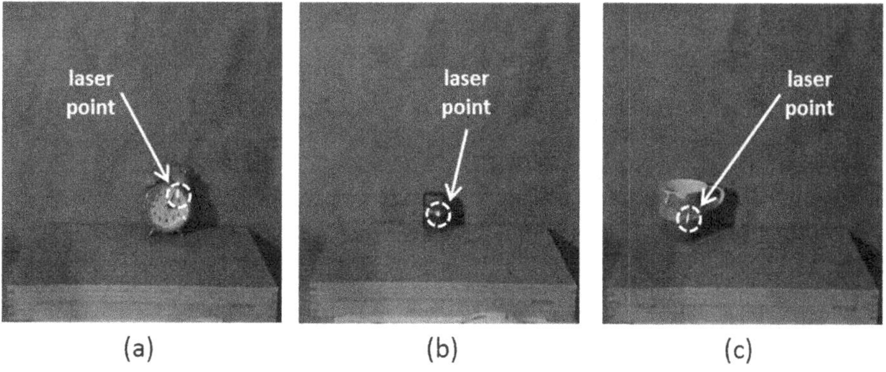

Fig. 6. First Person View of the humanoid when: (a) laser point on alarm clock, (b) laser point on eraser rubber and (c) laser point on cup of coffee.

visual search of the object		Pointing gesture control	
$K_{p_\theta} = 0.001$	$K_{d_\theta} = 0.05$	$K_{p_\beta} = 0.01$	$K_{d_\beta} = 0.5$
$K_{p_\varphi} = 0.001$	$K_{d_\varphi} = 0.05$	$K_{p_\alpha} = -0.01$	$K_{d_\alpha} = -0.5$

Fig. 7. Parameters of the PD control algorithm for the "I spy" game.

to guarantee joint visual attention between a humanoid and a human through a game of mutual interaction.

The humanoid is able to successfully play the "I spy" game with a human, sharing attention through the developed deictic process in this work.

5 Conclusions and Future Work

The proposed solution for joint visual attention between a humanoid and a human allows the knowledge sharing between both through the execution of a deictic process on a defined dataset of objects within a given environment.

The humanoid is able to achieve the visual alignment of the objects with the human through an adequate positioning of the robotic head, in addition to the use of a laser device for the projection of a laser point over the shared object. Through the experimental work performed to verify this joint visual attention solution, satisfactory results have been obtained. The experiments have been based on the "I spy" game between the humanoid-like robotic platform and the human, where the robot has been able to reach the object established in a reduced number of iterations of the control loop. In conclusion, we can afirm that this solution can be used in other similar HRI scenarios.

Future work is planned to expand the actual humanoid-like robotic platform with new joints and degrees of freedom in robotic arms, and the implementation of new touch and multimedia sensors. Currently, a hyper-realistic model is being developed for implementation on the chassis of humanoid, to achieve a higher level of empathy between the robot and the human.

References

1. Bruner, J.: Nature and uses of immaturity. In: Conolly, K., Bruner, J. (eds.) The Growth of Competence, pp. 11–45. Academic Press, Cambridge (1974)
2. Bratman, M.E.: Shared Agency: A Planning Theory of Acting Together. Oxford University Press, Oxford (2014)
3. Butterworth, G.: The ontogeny and phylogeny of joint visual attention. In: Whiten, A. (ed.) Natural Theories of Mind, pp. 233–251. Blackwell, Oxford (1991)
4. Liu, C., Fang, R., Chai, J.Y.: Shared gaze in situated referential grounding: an empirical study. In: Nakano, Y.I., Conati, C., Bader, T. (eds.) Eye Gaze in Intelligent User Interfaces, pp. 23–37. Springer, Heidelberg (2013)
5. Perzanowski, D., et al.: Integrating natural language and gesture in robotics domain. In: Proceedings of the IEEE International Symposium Intelligent Control, Piscataway, NJ, pp. 144–149 (1998)
6. Maravall, D., de Lope, J., Fuentes Brea, J.P.: Vision-based anticipatory controller for the autonomous navigation of an UAV using artificial neural networks. Neurocomputing **151**, 101–107 (2015)
7. Fuentes Brea, J.P., Maravall, D., de Lope, J.: Entropy-based search combined with a dual feedforward-feedback controller for landmark search and detection for the navigation of a UAV using visual topological maps. In: Armada, M.A., Sanfeliu, A., Ferre, M. (eds.) ROBOT 2013. AISC, vol. 253, pp. 65–76. Springer, Cham (2014). doi:10.1007/978-3-319-03653-3_6
8. Canny, J.: A computational approach to edge detection. IEEE Trans. Pattern Anal. Mach. Intell. **6**, 679–698 (1986)
9. Maravall, D., Lope, J., Fuentes, J.P.: Visual bug algorithm for simultaneous robot homing and obstacle avoidance using visual topological maps in an unmanned ground vehicle. In: Ferrández Vicente, J.M., Álvarez-Sánchez, J.R., de la Paz López, F., Toledo-Moreo, F.J., Adeli, H. (eds.) IWINAC 2015. LNCS, vol. 9108, pp. 301–310. Springer, Cham (2015). doi:10.1007/978-3-319-18833-1_32

Agent-Based Spatial Dynamics Explaining Sustained Opinion Survival

Leire Ozaeta and Manuel Graña(✉)

Computational Intelligence Group, Department of CCIA,
University of the Basque Country, Lejona, Spain
manuel.grana@ehu.es

Abstract. Opinion is the aggregate of many thinking processes that lead to decision and action in humans. Therefore, the diffussion of opinion in social networks is of great relevance in many fields. Influence is the mechanism by which a human can drive a change in opinion in other human mind. Most current computational models of influence spread are motivated by the need to identify which social actors have maximal influence. An example application aims to achieve high penetration in the market with minimal effort. However, we are interested in the propagation of the opinions per se, and specifically in the mechanisms that allow some minority opinions to survive against the mainstream pressure. We assume that the agents are moving in space, so that spatial relations are modulating friendship and influence relations. We propose a model that shows opinion survival properties, and explore the effect of spatial perception parameters in the opinion difussion and survival process.

1 Introduction

How some minorities can maintain their characteristics against the pressure of the mainstream, sometimes even produce a change of the majority towards accepting their specificities, has been an intriguing question in sociology and cognitive science [12], with few attempts to produce computational models which can be used to assess the value of the diverse mechanisms and hypothesis proposed. Multi-agent and dynamic-network models have already established themselves as suitable methods for analyzing "complex social systems" and to formalize models of real-world systems [11], even if they are hard to validate against real data. Therefore, they are one of the most popular techniques to study the social dynamics [1,5,9,13], even if other approaches as sociophysics [2], threshold models [8], and dynamic models [3] has been widely considered.

We focus in the spreading and survival of opinions in a population of agents. Contrary to [9] which poses the problem in a static spatial scenario, we endow the agents with the ability to move in a virtual space, so that their spatial relations allow their opinions to interact. Moreover we consider the existence of influence relations among agents, and some kind of charisma property that gives weight to the influence when forcing the change of opinions of other agents. The analysis of influence propagation through social media started from the consideration

J.M. Ferrández Vicente et al. (Eds.): IWINAC 2017, Part II, LNCS 10338, pp. 137–146, 2017.
DOI: 10.1007/978-3-319-59773-7_15

of phenomena such as mobs, riots or strikes [7] as pure physical phenomena, stripped out of psychological considerations. The same model applies to propagation of opinions, including advertising [6], where the research question was to determine the appropriate balance between marketing efforts and word-of-mouth propagation through personal social networks defined by strong and weak links. The two basic spread models of influence propagation over graphs are the Independent Cascade model (ICM) [6], and the Linear Threshold model (LTM) [7]. It must be noted that we do not deal with Influence Maximization (IM) [4,10], which is the problem of finding the minimal subset of influential nodes (IM-seed nodes) with maximal influence, i.e. that affect the largest number of nodes in the network, where influence is computed by propagation in the network according to a spread model. Instead, we let the friendship graph to be dynamic, according to the actual agent perception of their surroundings. Our model is like an ICM with moving agents, and changing graph topology.

Intended Contribution. The aim of the work in this article is to develop a multi-agent system model to explore the effect of spatial relations in the diffusion of opinions over a population of agents with ability to move in a virtual space. Specifically, we define the influence relations and charisma of the agents as constant features, and the friendship relations as dynamic ones, mediated by the changing spatial distribution of the agents. Influence is defined in terms of spatial relations at the simulation initialization time. Moreover, the agent can be aware of other agents only if they are located inside its circle of perception. Awareness implies that influence can be exerted. Besides, agent motion is determined by the strategy of moving towards the friends and avoiding not friends. Changing the radius of this circle we can influence the dynamics of opinion in the community of agents.

The paper contents are as follows: Sect. 2 describes the model we consider for the search of best conditions to maximize opinion entropy. Section 3 comments the experimental designs of our simulations. Section 4 provides results of ongoing analysis. Section 5 gives some conclusions.

2 Model

We have a collection of N agents $A = \{a_i\}_{i=1}^{N}$. At time t, each agent a_i is characterized by spatial position in a virtual discrete space $P_i(t) \in \mathbb{N}^2$, and an opinion $o_i(t) \in O$ from a given opinion set $\Omega = \{\omega_k\}_{k=1}^{M}$. Friendship graph $G(t) = (A_t, E_t, W_t)$ determines the attraction/repulsion forces that move the agents spatially. Edges are defined between friends. Edge weights determine the strength of friendship, so that the edge disappears when its weight becomes zero. Agents will try to join friends and evade not-friends, but after a period of spatial closeness agents can change their friendship relations accepting new people, or friendship can be lost after a period being out of touch. Each agent recognizes the following relevant subsets of the collective of agents:

- Local neighbors, $\{L_i(t) \subseteq A\}_{i=1}^{N}$, which are agents that are perceived by the agent at time t because they lie in a position inside a spatial circle of radius θ^L around the agent: $L_i(t) = \{a_j \,|\, \|P_i(t) - P_j(t)\| < \theta^L\}$. The agent determines its motion in space according to the attraction/repulse felt to the agents perceived spatially in this collective, moving away from the unfriendly and towards the friendly ones.
- The set of friends $\{F_i(t) \subseteq A\}_{i=1}^{N}$, which is the set of agents linked with a_i through the friendship graph. That is: $F_i(t) = \{a_j \,|\exists\, (a_i, a_j) \in E_t\}$.
- Influential neighbors, $\{I_i \subseteq A\}_{i=1}^{N}$, which are that agents that may induce a change of agents' opinion. This is a static set created at the beginning of the simulation, it can be a subset or a superset of the initial set of friends.

These sets are defined at the start of the simulation, according to the spatial distribution of the agents, as will be explained below. Besides, each agent a_i has the following attributes:

- Charisma c_i, defined as agent ability agent to influence neighboring agents. The charisma value is bounded $c \in (-1, 1)$, considering 0.9 the highest level of charisma and -0.9 the lowest level. Agent's charisma is set initially in the simulation at the time of agent creation, and does not change along the simulation.
- Resistance r_i, defined as agent reluctance to change opinion (i.e. stubbornness), it is set in the range $r_i \in [0, 1)$ at the simulation initialization. At each iteration of the simulation, the stubbornness of the agent is decreased if it changes opinion at this step, otherwise it is increased according to the rule $r_i(t+1) = r_i(t) + 0.1$. Thus, the agents have a conservative policy regarding opinion changes, with a strong tendency to conserve an opinion once they reached it. Therefore, habit increases stubbornness, while frequent opinion change reduces it.

The system simulation is as follows:

1. Initially, the agents are randomly placed in the virtual arena at positions $P_i(0)$, their opinion o_i, charisma c_i, and stubbornness r_i are generated by random sampling from a uniform distribution. Moreover, at time 0:
   (a) We create the group of local neighbors, $L_i(0)$, as the nearest neighbors of each agent inside the perception radius in this initial spatial configuration.
   (b) We create the initial friendship graph as the local neighbors at time 0, something like defining the families of agents at birth,

$$E_0 = \{(a_i, a_j) \,|\, \|P_i(0) - P_j(0)\| < \theta^L\},$$

   Each created edge has initial weight $w_{ij}(0) = 0.5$.
   (c) The group of influential neighbors, I_i, is composed of all the agents lying inside a circle of radius θ^I around the influenced agent, i.e. $I_i = \{a_j \in I_i \Leftrightarrow \|P_i(t) - P_j(t)\| < \theta^I\}$.

2. Simulation is carried out in discrete time steps. At each time instant t the agent attributes, i.e. position, opinion, influencers, stubbornness, friends and are recomputed according to the following rules:
   (a) The agent considers changing its opinion with probability $(1-r_i)$. The new opinion is a random sample from a discrete distribution $\{p_k\}_{k=1}^{M}$, which can be built up in three different ways depending of the influenced agent's own attitude. Let us define the set of the agents that are influencers of our agent, are inside the local neighborhood, and have opinion ω_k, formally: $\Psi_k^i = \{a_j \in I_i \cap L_i(t) \,|o_j = \omega_k\}$. The first way to construct the distribution is by considering the charisma of the influencers with the same opinion, that is:

$$p'_k(a_i) = \sum_{a_j \in \Psi_k^i} c_j, \tag{1}$$

   the second way considers the charisma relative to the whole amount of charisma in the influencers regardless of opinion, formally:

$$p'_k(a_i) = \left\{ \frac{\sum_{j \in \Psi_k^i} c_j}{\sum_{j \in I_i} c_j} \right\}, \tag{2}$$

   the third way is the number of influencers supporting the opinion, regardless of charisma

$$p'_k(a_i) = \left|\Psi_k^i\right|. \tag{3}$$

   The new opinion o_i is obtained by sampling the discrete distribution obtained after normalization of the above values, that is

$$p_k = \frac{p'_k(a_i)}{\sum_{k=1}^{M} p'_k(a_i)}.$$

   Opinion changes can be evaluated with a frequency lower than the actual simulation time steps, that is, the agent can perform several motion steps in between opinion changes.
   (b) The agent motion equation is as follows:

$$P_i(t+1) = P_i(t) + \triangle(P_i(t), L_i(t), F_i(t)), \tag{4}$$

   where

$$\triangle_t(P_i, L_i, F_i) = d^*(L_i \cap F_i)\left(P_i - \frac{\sum_{k \in L_i \cap F_i} P_k}{n}\right) - d^*\left(L_i \cap \overline{F}_i\right)\left(P_i - \frac{\sum_{k \in L_i \cap \overline{F}_i} P_k}{n}\right) + \eta, \tag{5}$$

   where $d^*(L_i \cap F_i)$ denotes the minimum distance from agent a_i position to the position of any agent in the set $L_i \cap F_i$, and η is a random perturbation. The first term of Eq. 5 represents the attraction to the friends, and the second the evasion from not-friend agents.

(c) The weights in the friendship graph are updated as follows: for existing friendship links $w_{ij}(t) > 0$, we have $w_{ij}(t+1) = w_{ij}(t) - 0.1$ if $a_j \notin L_i(t)$, otherwise $w_{ij}(t+1) = w_{ij}(t) + 0.1$.

(d) If $w_{ij}(t+1) < 0$ then the link disappears from the friendship graph and the agent from the set of friends, i.e. $E_{t+1} = E_t - \{(a_i, a_j)\}$ and $F_i(t+1) = F_i(t) - \{a_j\}$.

(e) If an agent is close to a not friend agent, then friendship is started with a small weight value. Formally, if $a_j \notin F_i(t) \,\&\, a_j \in L_i(t)$ then $w_{ij}(t+1) = 0.1$, $E_{t+1} = E_t \cup \{(a_i, a_j)\}$ and $F_i(t+1) = F_i(t) \cup \{a_j\}$.

3. Simulation stops when the time limit is reached.

3 Experimental Design

The aim of the experimental work in this paper is to assess the effect of the spatial perception parameters θ^I and θ^L in the preservation of opinion entropy. The hypothesis is that under certain values of these parameters the small communities may retain their opinions, thus spatial perception influences opinion entropy. Therefore, one important measure of the system evolution is the number of different opinions at the end of the simulation. The number of simulation steps before convergence to a single opinion is an additional measure of the speed of system evolution. We have implemented the model in Netlogo[1]. We repeat all simulations seven times in order to get some average value. The size of agent population is 200 in all simulations. Size of the set of opinions was selected in the set $\{2, 3, 4\}$, and influence and local neighbors radii were selected in the set $\{1, 5, 10, 15, 20, 25, 30\}$ measured in patches, which the discrete unit of space in Netlogo. We considered a maximum path deviation degree of 45° to both sides. Also we added an opinion delay so the more complex spatial behavior of the agents had a real impact in the opinion spread, this supposed that an agent moved 10 times in between opinion reconsideration steps. The simulation time was set to 6,000 ticks. We observed that the system always reached steady states before this time limit. The meaning of steady state is that opinion distribution remained constant for a long period of time.

4 Results

The research question "do spatial perception parameters determine the survival of opinions?" is answered by the results in Fig. 1 where we show the percentage of the simulations that end in a state where more than one opinion is sustained by the agents in the population as a function of the radius of influence (Fig. 1a) and the radius of the local neighborhood (Fig. 1b). Increasing both radii produces a decrease in the number of simulations that end with two or more opinions alive. The effect of the local neighborhood radius is stronger than the influence radius. In Fig. 1b the percentage decreases from 100% when $\theta^L < 10$ down to 65% when

[1] http://ccl.northwestern.edu/netlogo/.

$\theta^L = 25$, while in Fig. 1b if goes from 85% when $\theta^I = 5$ down to 75% when $\theta^I = 15$. The salient fact is that the spatial perception has a strong effect on the preservation of alternative opinions, we have better preservation when the radius is small so that spatial disconnection leads to more compact communities which may preserve minority opinions.

Regarding the delay in the disappearance of the opinion diversity we can observe in Fig. 2 that both plots, when considering the values from 10 to 30, reflect a invert behavior with peaks in the values 15 and 10 regarding the neighborhood radius whereas a drop is shown in the same values when the influence radius is considered. It is significant also that there are no fast convergence towards opinion homogeneity in any case, with all the situations considered showing a number of steps slightly above 3000. Regarding the deviation, we can observe that it is wider and more stable during changes in neighborhood radius, in comparison with the values associated to changes in the influence radius, specially when considering 10 and 15 patches.

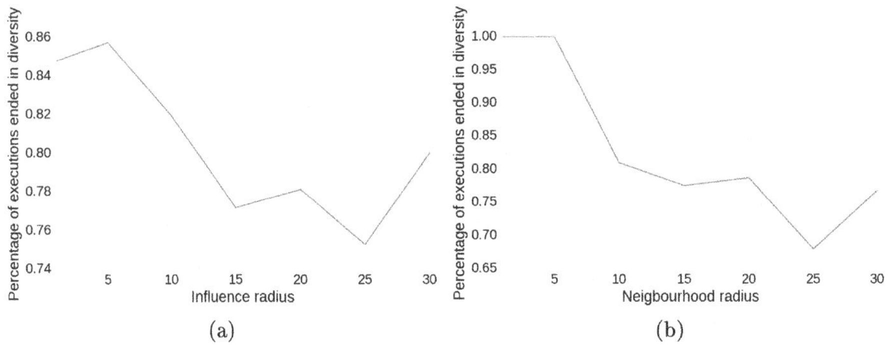

Fig. 1. The effect of increasing influential (a) and neighborhood (b) radius measured by the percentage of simulation runs ending with more than one opinion alive.

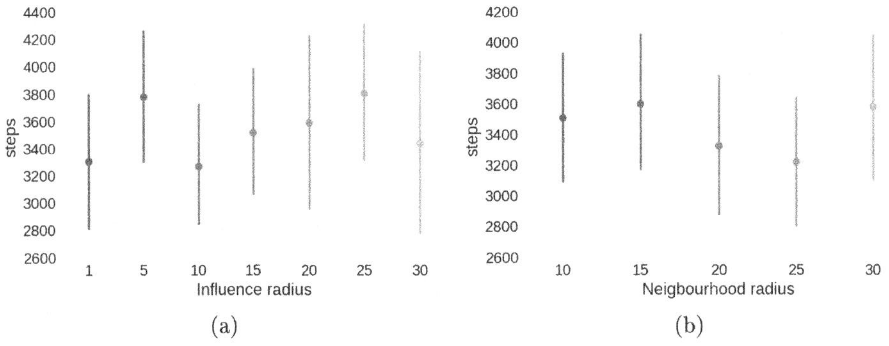

Fig. 2. The effect of increasing influential (a) and neighborhood (b) radius measured in number of steps needed to the disappearance of opinion diversity, i.e. convergence to a single opinion.

To further assess the speed of convergence, we recorded the number of opinion changes in each step and get the mean to observe the evolution of said number during the simulations. In Fig. 3 the two plots shows a big drop in the first steps to then stabilize in a fairly low number of opinion changes, a tiny percentage of the 200 agents in the population. However is interesting to notice that while when considering changes in influence radius all the cases converge to similar values. When considering changes in neighborhood radius (Fig. 3b) there are two clearly separated groups: the first, formed by the cases where the neighborhood radius is 1 or 5, that shows a number of opinion changes around 2.5, and the second, formed by all the other cases, that shows a similar trend to the first group although with a number of opinion changes around 3.5.

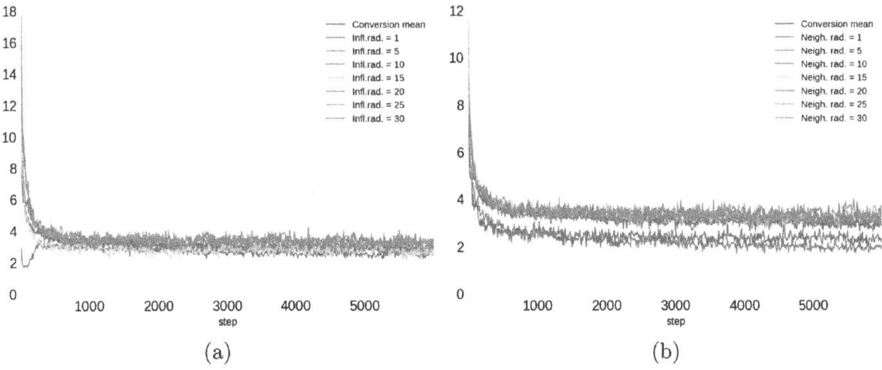

Fig. 3. Evolution of number of opinion changes in groups as a response to the increasing influential (a) and neighborhood (b) radius.

Focusing in the drop of number of opinion changes that occurs in the first steps in Fig. 4 we can observe that, regarding the plot of changes in influence radius, the number of changes in the very first steps seems linked to the size of the radius, which can be expected. However is interesting to notice the gap between the evolution of radius 1 and 5 in the first 250, and 15 and 20 in the first 200 steps to then converge in similar values. It is specially notorious the evolution of the case where the influence radius considers a unique patch as is the only case when the number of opinion changes rises during the first steps to the same values as the other cases. When focused in the plot regarding changes in neighborhood radius we can observe a gap between the two smallest radius and the rest of the cases. However, unlike the previous plot, the two groups maintain a constant gap between them with a similar stabilization point near step 150.

In order to find significant relationships between the two radius we considered the data grouped by said differences in contrast to changes in one or other of the radius. As we observe in Fig. 5 the cases where the influence radius and the neighborhood radius are equal converge to a lower number of opinion changes, even if it starts with a number similar to the total mean of opinion changes.

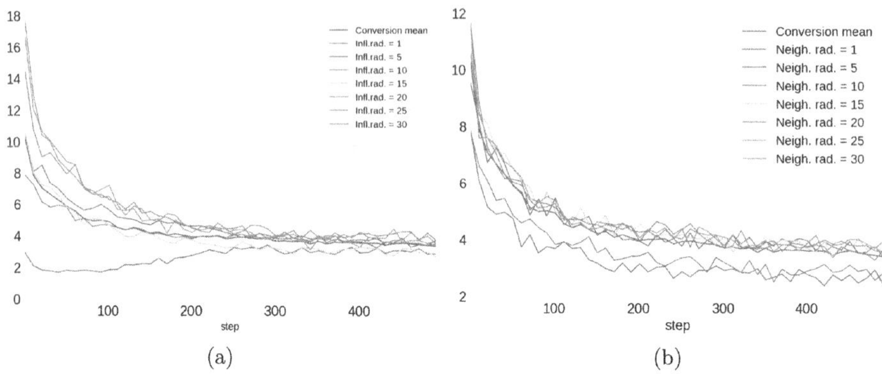

Fig. 4. Evolution of number of opinion changes in groups regarding influential (a) and neighborhood (b) radius in the first 500 steps.

Following with the first steps of each case, the data shows that when the influence radius is smaller then the neighborhood radius it converges faster than any other case, which seems to go along the lines that the wider neighborhood radius helps a faster opinion group creation.

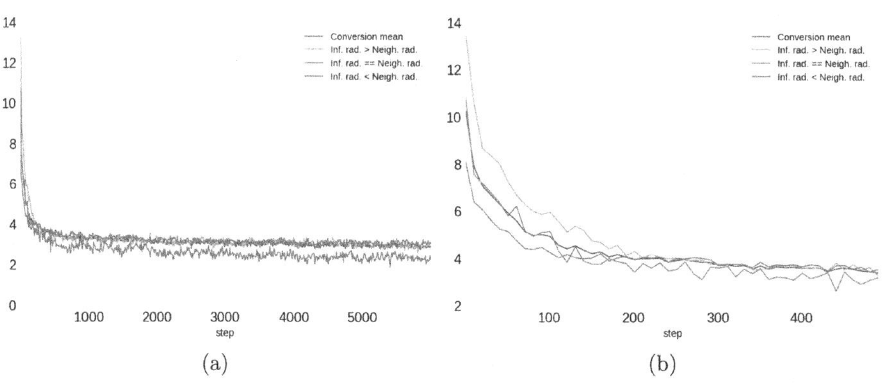

Fig. 5. Evolution of number of opinion changes in groups regarding relationships between influential and neighborhood radius (a). (b) shows a close up to the first 500 steps.

5 Discussion and Conclusions

We are interested in the dynamics of opinion in human communities, which is a topic of research in many areas, such as recommender systems, security, and in general social system analysis. Resistance to homogeneous opinion spreading processes and maximization of opinion entropy in favor to opinion variety in a system with no equilibrium point is a complex and interesting phenomena with a high number of details. The construction of sufficient detailed agent-based models it is yet to be done and the phenomena itself is far from being understood. Most conventional approaches consider some kind of graph representation of the community, and model opinion spreading as some kind of epidemic diffusion over the graph. Our approach is to consider the dynamics of the agents moving in a space where they can establish new relations that affect the dynamics of opinion spreading. More precisely, we are very interested in the survival of opinions despite the pressure exerted by mainstream opinions. This phenomena is pervasive in human social societies. In this paper we provide some results that show that smaller perception radius both when considering influence and neighborhood result in higher percentage of runs preserving opinion diversity at the end. Also, local neighborhood radius, linked both to agent movement and opinion spreading, have a significant influence in opinion variety preservation. Therefore, spatial perception can help explain the survival of minority opinions. We plan to improve the detail of the models, and to extend the computational experiments and their detailed analysis in order to improve our understanding of the mechanisms of opinion survival. Finally, we will try to fit the model to some actual social systems showing this kind of behavior using public macro-scale data.

Acknowledgments. Leire Ozaeta has been supported by a Predoctoral grant from the Basque Government.

References

1. Banisch, S., Lima, R., Araujo, T.: Agent based model and opinion dynamics as Markov chains. Soc. Netw. **34**, 549–561 (2012)
2. Crokidakis, N.: Effects of mass media on opinion spreading in the Sznajd sociophysics model. Phys. A: Stat. Mech. Appl. **391**, 1729–1734 (2012)
3. Deffuant, G., Amblard, F., Weisbuch, G., Faure, T.: How can extremism prevail? A study based on the relative agreement interaction model. J. Artif. Soc. Soc. Simul. **5**(2) (2002)
4. Domingos, P., Richardson, M.: Mining the network value of customers. In: Seventh International Conference on Knowledge Discovery and Data Mining (2001)
5. Gil, S., Zanette, D.H.: Coevolution of agent and networks: opinion spreading and community disconnection. Phys. Lett. A **356**, 89–94 (2006)
6. Goldenberg, J.: Talk of the network: a complex systems look at the underlying process of word-of-mouth. Mark. Lett. **12**, 211–223 (2001)
7. Granovetter, M.: Threshold models of collective behavior. Am. J. Sociol. **83**(6), 1420–1443 (1978)
8. Dreyer Jr., P.A., Roberts, F.S.: Irreversible k-threshold processes: graph-theorical threshold models of the spread of disease and of opinion. Discret. Appl. Math. **157**, 1615–1627 (2008)
9. Jung, J., Bramson, A.: An agent - based model of indirect minority influence on social change. In: ALIFE 14 (2014)
10. Kempe, D., Kleinberg, J., Tardos, E.: Maximizing the spread of influence through a social network. In: Proceedings of the Ninth ACM SIGKDD International Conference on Knowledge Discovery and Data Mining, KDD 2003, pp. 137–146. ACM, New York (2003)

11. Louie, M.A., Carley, K.M.: The role of dynamic-network multi-agent models of socio-political systems in policy. Technical report, CASOS (2007)
12. Mucchi-Faina, A., Paclilli, M.G., Pagliaro, S.: Minority influence, social change and social stability. Soc. Pers. Psychol. Compass **4**, 1111–1123 (2010)
13. Rouly, O.C.: At the root of sociality: working towards emergent, permanent, social affines. In: Proceedings of The European Conference on Artificial Life, pp. 82–89 (2015)

Enhancing Neuropsychological Testing with Gamification and Tangible Interfaces: The Baking Tray Task

Antonio Cerrato(✉) and Michela Ponticorvo

Department of Humanistic Studies,
University of Naples "Federico II", Naples, Italy
antonio.cerrato@unina.it

Abstract. Neuropsychological tests are performance-based tasks to evaluate cognitive functions, but often they are particularly long and boring during their execution; these issues can interfere with performance provided by patients or healthy participants. In this paper, we present our gamified and virtually enhanced version of a specific neuropsychological test: The Baking Tray Task (BTT), aimed to assess unilateral spatial neglect (USN), a visuospatial processing disorder. This enhanced BTT version has been developed through STELT (Smart Technologies to Enhance Learning and Teaching) software, a platform which allows implementation of augmented reality systems based on RFID/NFC technology. These materials permit to link together smart technologies and physical materials, uniting the manipulative approach and digitalized technologies.

Keywords: Adaptive learning · Artificial Intelligence · Gamification · Technology enhanced assessment · Unilateral spatial neglect

1 Introduction

Neuropsychological testing and assessment consists into performance-based assessments of various cognitive skills. Normally, neuropsychological assessment is performed with a battery approach, implicating tests of different cognitive skills, with several proofs for each considered skill. This procedure provides assessment of abilities such as memory, attention, reasoning, judgment, problem-solving, visuospatial, and language functions. The battery of tests can be standardized or targeted to the individual participant in the assessment. Successively, the tests scoring may be collected either directly by a neuropsychologist, a psychologist or by a trained examiner.

Neuropsychological tests are intrinsically performance-based. They are structured to require individuals to exercise their skills in the presence of an examiner/observer. Other important information are registered by self-reports of functioning, as well as observations of behavior during testing; these tests have been

J.M. Ferrández Vicente et al. (Eds.): IWINAC 2017, Part II, LNCS 10338, pp. 147–156, 2017.
DOI: 10.1007/978-3-319-59773-7_16

validated for the administration of reliable tests able to pinpoint a potential deficit involving a specific cognitive ability, or to discriminate among impairments in different cognitive domains. However, neuropsychological evaluation can also provide information concerning normal brain functioning and allows monitoring the cognitive status of an individual, especially during older age. Tests are helpful also to determine possible changes in cognition.

The majority of neuropsychological tests are carried out in traditional paper-and-pencil way that requires a long time administration and for this reason this kind of tests are time-consuming for examiners and participants; another disadvantage of traditional tests is that they are tiresome for many participants and patients, who, sometimes, don't complete o perform incorrectly the assessment for tiredness [2]. These problems could be overcome with digitalization and gamification of tests, an approach that will be described in the next sections.

1.1 Gamification of Neuropsychological Tests

Gamification consists in assigning game characteristics to a non-game situation [12] or in implementing design concepts from games, in order to keep involved participants [36]. Gamification also presupposes the concept of flow, represented by the fact that the person who performs the gamified activity is completely absorbed and immersed in it.

In general, each process using games and game-like phenomena in non-leisure settings can be linked with Gamification [22]. A wide variety of contexts has experimented Gamification, including tests. Psychologist, for example, has adopted some gamified tests, utilizing game features in the real assessment situation. The common phrase '*Imagine of*' is easy to find in some tests and participants, unconsciously, accept to play imaging themselves in a fictional dimension to perform task. Also in the field of Education, some learning tools are structured in reference to gamification strategies. In this regard, a large contribution has come from Serious Games [24] applied to assessment [11]: in this case the assessing situation is completely translated in a game. Serious Game have the advantage to be easily carried out on laptop or other electronic devices, substituting traditional tests assessing cognitive abilities, personality traits etc. [32,34].

An example of Serious Game applied to assessment is provided by the evaluation of cognitive abilities or future work trajectories; they can also be fruitfully used with children, evaluating their skills and their preferences for school-related activities [9,16]. This method gives some remarkable benefits, such as a more accurate data recording process; moreover, individuals performing a Serious Game are more involved in the session itself, due to the greater participation promoted by gamification [30]. Using game mechanics and characteristics to motivate and engage people, participation become more implicit and individuals feel themselves completely involved in the performing activity.

1.2 The Birth of Computer-Based and Digitalized Assessment

Modern and digital technologies have opened new opportunities for neuropsychological testing, allowing new computerized testing tools to be developed and paper-and-pencil testing tools to be translated into new computerized devices. Computerized tests have been used in research since 1970s; this digitalization presents some issues, mainly linked to the fact that, although many different test batteries have been developed and new batteries are introduced every year for clinical screening, there are not sufficient normative data and standardized psychometric measures. Conversely, paper and pencil tests are widely approved and adopted due to their high validity and reliability. Paper-and-pencil neuropsychological tests require the presence of a neuropsychologist, essential for the assessment of cognitive abilities, especially for the administration, evaluation and interpretation of scores. One of the important advantages of the conventional paper and pencil neuropsychological tests is their ecological validity (that is the degree to which test performance corresponds to real-world performance).

Despite these numerous advantages, traditional paper and pencil tools show some limitations, for instance, the most commonly administered tests usually do not provide alternative administration forms, this implicates the impossibility to repeat testing over short intervals. Other specific limitations concern the intrinsic nature of tests (time-consuming procedures) including the greater costs, the impossibility to provide accurate reaction times, potential bias related to different examiners etc. All of these limitations could be overcome by a digitalized assessment, on condition that efficacies and ecological measurements are respected. About these issues, the American Psychological Association [1] has recognized the importance of computerized psychological testing and has suggested how to implement and interpret computerized test results in its guidelines.

Furthermore, computerized assessment of cognitive functions can be self administered and can have a shorter duration (e.g., by reducing dead times in stimuli presentation). They may have great validity and reliability due to their great objectivity, precision, and standardization. Computerized performance can also minimize the so called floor and ceiling effects, occurring when differences among participant performance are not fully captured; thus, they can provide more standardized measures of subject performance, crucial for an accurate and early detection of specific pathological disease (e.g., dementia).

It appears clearly that computerized testing will represent an essential part of the clinical setting in the nearest future, above all, in screening procedures, providing an automatized diagnosis, on condition that these new instruments and their results are governed by experts. Feasible, efficacious, and ecological computerized testing could be carried out also at home, with patients and their caregivers, without the specialized clinician support. This is not a no-issue translation: one of the issue represented by automatic assessment could be the fact that clinical sensitivity, allowing neuropsychologists to capture potential shades in a specific domain and to trace a specific cognitive profile, may result difficult to be translated in a computer-based assessment.

In recent times, several tests have been used in clinical field with new technologies support, adopting digitalized and computer enhanced assessment tools. Neuropsychology is the main subject that takes advantage of computer bases diagnostics, as showed by instruments such as Cantab, NeuroTrax and Cabpad. *Cantab* (Cambridge Neuropsychological Test Automated Battery) [28] is focused on three cognitive domains: attention, visuospatial memory and working memory/planning skills. Two main characteristics regarding Cantab are that the battery is quite independent of verbal instruction and responses are provided by touch screen; moreover, is one of the most used computerized battery.

NeuroTrax [14] is designed to assess brain wellness across an array of several cognitive domains: memory, executive function, visual spatial perception, verbal function, attention, information processing speed, and motor skills. In particular, with NeuroTrax it is possible to detect the presence of *Mild Cognitive Impairment* in elderly people. Several tasks are reported as a digitalized version of *old-fashioned* paper and pencil tests. One of the advantages of this software regards some psychometric properties like the accuracy of reaction times.

CABPad (Cognitive Assessment at Bedside for iPad) [35] is a digitalized neuropsychological test battery for bedside screening for cognitive dysfunctions after stroke, in particular the software has the purpose to measure the most common and significant neuropsychological symptoms caused by stroke. The battery is aimed to assess several disorders: anosognosia, aphasia, spatial neglect, depression, episodic memory, attention span, working memory, mental speed, manual motor speed, and executive function (response inhibition). This specific suite adopts a digital version of *Baking Tray Task* (BTT), a particular test that is one of the main interests of the present work and which it will be described later. BTT is a sensitive instrument to assess unilateral neglect, a particular disease be-longing to the group of visuospatial disorders, which will be briefly described in the following section.

2 The Case of Visuospatial Disorders

Visuospatial disorders are, prevalently but not uniquely, caused by posterior right hemispheric lesions and they includes sensory perception disorders, spatial attention disorders, spatial awareness disorders, spatial elaboration disorders, apraxic disorders, sensory ataxia and topographical agnosia.

Humans get information about their body position and other objects through different sensory modalities, keeping in mind, when they move, the starting position of their own body and other surrounding objects. These abilities comprehend the perceptual elaboration of signals coming by senses and the execution of motor actions such as pointing or grasping objects and simple body movements. Sensorimotor information gives internal representation of the body position and other nearby objects. The integration of different sensory signals with information regarding body and objects position permits two type of spatial representation [21] consisting in two principal spatial reference system [26]:

- *Egocentric spatial representations* (also called egocentric frames of reference), with which the position of the objects is codified in relation to the body axis or his parts
- *Allocentric spatial representations* (also called allocentric frames of reference), with which the position of the objects is encoded referring to the location of one object (or its parts) with respect to other objects

Egocentric spatial representations are useful to organize finalized movements such as reaching a target or avoiding an object; conversely allocentric spatial representations are useful to identify objects and to body movements in a space full of objects. Spatial orientation is based on the perception of the surrounding objects from several and mutable prospective, with a strong integration of the two spatial reference systems above described.

2.1 Unilateral Spatial Neglect (USN)

When the ability of analyze and being aware of stimuli and events occurring in a hemispace is compromised and actions towards that part of the space are not possible, we are in presence of the unilateral spatial neglect (USN). USN is usually caused by cortical or subcortical hemispheric lesions and regards the incapacity of elaboration of the part of the space controlateral to the brain lesion [7,10,33].

Nevertheless right USN has been identified following left hemisphere damage (resulting in the neglect of the right hemispace), in the vast majority of cases, the brain lesion responsible of USN is settled in the right brain hemisphere and the neglect regards the left hemispace. Right hemisphere of the brain is usually associated with spatial perception and memory, whereas the left hemisphere is specialized for language plus a compresence of the elaboration of visual information of right side space in both brain hemispheres. Hence the right hemisphere is able to compensate for the loss of left hemisphere function (Fig. 1), but not vice versa [19].

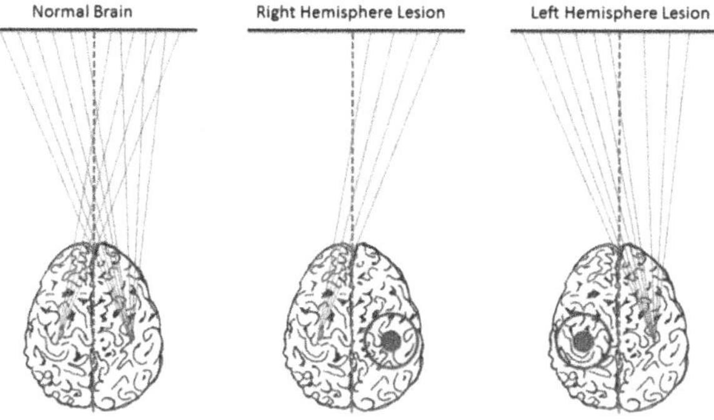

Fig. 1. A model representing the spatial perception processing of the brain

This hemispheric asymmetry supports the hypothesis according to which USN represents a deep cognitive disorder rather a sensorimotor deficits related disorder. Patients suffering of USN can maintain eye direction and head towards the right side of the space and they ignore each stimulus coming from the neglected side; also if the doctors, located in the left side of the room, ask them questions, they can search the origin of the voice in the right side.

These patients, in case of right-brain damage, can also sometimes experiment confabulation about the neglected part of images presented in their peripersonal space, or believe to be in another place [3]. Sometimes they can also avoid having food in the left side of the plate and can ignore also the left side of their own body (experiencing difficulty in dressing and in the care of their personal hygiene) and this compromises seriously the daily-life routine of these people. In neuropsychological field, there are several test adopted by clinicians to diagnose and assess USN and some of them are described in the next paragraph.

2.2 Tools and Instruments Assessing USN

There are many tests adopted by clinicians to assess USN, and different reviews [8,23] describes deeply several USN assessment tool. For example the *Comb and Razor Test* [6] and the *Semi-Structured Scale for the Functional Evaluation of Hemi-inattention in Personal Space* [37] are tests adopted to evaluate USN symptoms through the exploration of personal space in functional activities, such as using a comb or applying makeup.

USN can regard also extrapersonal space, and related assessment tools are usually easy to administer by the bedside once the patient is sufficiently alert. For example, the *Line Bisection Test* [29] is a simple administered test through which the patient is asked to found the middle point, tracing a sign on a paper, of a series of 18 horizontal lines.

Another example is provided by the *Single Letter Cancellation Test* [13] requires the individual to found and delete all '*H letter*' presented on a paper among 52 typed letters. Other two widely used tests have been developed by Arthur Benton and colleague: the *Facial Recognition Test* [4] and *Judgment of Line Orientation test* [5]. These tests present some administration difficulties and their methods of administration could beneficiate of a digitalized/computerized version.

In order to detect USN, there are also several tests requiring the patient to draw; however, these tools have to be used with caution because the presence of apraxia, aphasia, motor deficits, and other visual perception deficits can influence the performance.

An example of these type of test is provided by the famous *Draw-A-Man Test* [15] and *Rey Complex Figure Test* [17], well-known assessment drawing task, especially in Psychology, that are reliable in evaluating perceptual organization, visual memory, and visual motor skills post stroke. Finally, another drawing task assessing USN is represented by the *Clock Drawing Test* [20], where the patient has to write numbers clock inside of an empty circle (usually patients with USN draw all numbers on the right side of the circle). All the presented instruments are validated tools to assess USN but both patients and doctors can benefit from a computer based version of them, as the task described in the next paragraph.

3 The Baking Tray Task (BTT)

Another choice for assessment of USN is represented by the Baking Tray Task (BTT) [31], a recent neglect test, where patients are asked to dispose 16 cubes as neatly as possible over a 75 × 100 cm board with an edge of 3.5 cm height, as if they were buns on a baking tray to put in the oven. The 16 cubes have a dimension of 3.5 cm and they are placed in a box directly in front of the subject. For the administration of BTT there is no time limit and all the cubes have to be disposed. As regards the scoring of the test, each cube is counted with an accuracy position of 0.5 cm. The cut-off score was based on the worst performance of a normal subject. The baking tray task proved to be a quick and yet sensitive test, suitable for screening purposes and longitudinal studies. Despite standard USN tests, such as cancellation and line bisection tests BTT appears to pick up all cases of at least moderately severe neglect, while standard tests missed a few patients [18]. Moreover, BTT seems requiring low-effort attentional resources in contrast to other neglect task like Cancellation Task [27] and it results to be insensitive to practice and set effects.

3.1 E-BTT: A New Technology-Enhanced Version of BTT

We reproduced BTT in a virtual environment by *STELT (Smart Technologies to Enhance Learning and Teaching)* that allows to create prototypes based on a well-known Artificial Intelligence methodology (Agents Based Modelling) and tangible interfaces (usually concrete objects equipped with RFID/NFC sensors) as tools to support user-computer interactions [25]. It mainly consists in three parts/modules: Storyboarding (aimed to create personalized scenarios), Recording (to track users data) and Adaptive Tutoring (that consists in on-time intelligent feedbacks). In particular, in our idea of gamified BTT, the user has to help a cartoon baker in its work, trying to place 16 toy buns on the baking tray (actually, it is a tablet surface detector) as evenly as possible.

The object of the research is mainly to test the possibility to develop a virtual *Enhanced Baking Tray Task* (E-BTT) able to detect USN (like traditional BTT) and to provide a clear diagnosis of cognitive disorders related to visuospatial abilities. The storyboarding consist, mainly in the presentation of personalized scenarios (the cartoon baker, Fig. 2) useful to provide the test instructions to participants. We expect that the E-BTT will have comparable psychometric properties and will be more engaging for patients. Moreover, with the use of augmented reality systems and adaptive tutoring systems, we aim to add at the assessment procedure another module thought with the purpose of starting a training and rehabilitation program for people affected by USN. Finally, we decided to integrate during E-BTT administration an Artificial Vision module, supported by a camera, able to scan and recognize the cubes pattern arranged

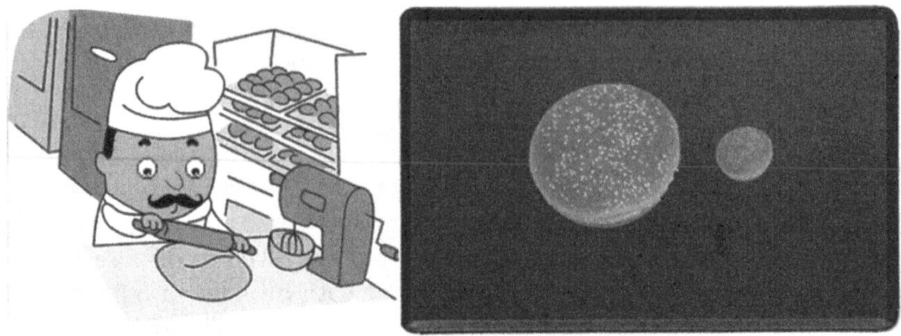

Fig. 2. The starting image of E-BTT: individual is aimed to help Louis (on the left), a famous baker of Paris. The goal is to dispose on the baking tray (on the right), as evenly as possible, 16 small buns, that are a petit version of the traditional one

on the tablet surface simulating the baking tray. In this manner, we aim to reach a clear and accurate performance scoring, and, potentially, it could be recorded also the motor program strategy adopted by subjects in the cubes disposition.

4 Future Directions

The aims of this study will be to evaluate the efficacy of E-BTT adopting not only a computerized modality but also the use of tangible interfaces. More specifically, through STELT software, beyond making the users interaction less boring and tiresome but more participated and involved, we aim to reach an automated diagnosis of performances users, able to retrace the same one made by a clinician, with the advantage to be no more necessary his supervision. It is also important respect the ecological validity criteria of the test, replaying the same reliability of the traditional version in the digital one.

Additionally, STELT enables also the possibility to administrate the task with an adaptive tutoring system, able to give recurring feedback about participants performance and able to adapt test requests on the users specific requirements, keeping trace of their improvements; starting from this point, it would be possible integrate a training and rehabilitation program for patient suffering of USN, enriching the potentialities of the assessment tool.

Once collected E-BTT data, it will be possible include also a learning analytics module; with recorded statistics will be possible deduce more information about the data: the single user performance, the comparison of more sessions in different times, the trend of the whole population etc.

Acknowledgements. This project has been supported by INF@NZIA DIGI.tales, funded by Italian Ministry for Education, University and Research under PON-Smart Cities for Social Inclusion programme.

References

1. American Psychological Association: Committee on Professional Standards, American Psychological Association, Board of Scientific Affairs, and Committee on Psychological Tests and Assessment. Guidelines for Computer-Based Tests and Interpretations. The Association (1986)
2. Appelros, P., Karlsson, G.M., Thorwalls, A., Tham, K., Nydevik, I.: Unilateral neglect: further validation of the baking tray task. J. Rehabil. Med. **36**(6), 258–261 (2004)
3. Bartolomeo, P., de Vito, S., Malkinson, T.S.: Space-related confabulations after right hemisphere damage. Cortex **87**, 166–173 (2016)
4. Benton, A.L., Van Allen, M.W.: Impairment in facial recognition in patients with cerebral disease. Cortex **4**, 344–358 (1968)
5. Benton, A.L., Varney, N.R., Hamsher, K.D.: Visuospatial judgment: a clinical test. Arch. Neurol. **35**, 364–367 (1978)
6. Beschin, N., Robertson, I.H.: Personal versus extrapersonal neglect: a group study of their dissociation using a reliable clinical test. Cortex **33**(2), 379–384 (1997)
7. Bisiach, E., Vallar, G.: Unilateral neglect in humans (2000)
8. Canini, M., Battista, P., Della Rosa, P., Catrical, E., Salvatore, C., Gilardi, M., Castiglioni, I.: Computerized neuropsychological assessment in aging: testing efficacy and clinical ecology of different interfaces. Comput. Math. Methods Med. (2014)
9. Cerrato, A., Ferrara, F., Ponticorvo, M., Sica, L.S., Di Ferdinando, A., Miglino, O.: DILIGO assessment tool: a smart and gamified approach for preschool children assessment (in press)
10. Chokron, S., Bartolomeo, P.: Patterns of dissociation between left hemineglect and deviation of the egocentric reference. Neuropsychologia **35**(11), 1503–1508 (1997)
11. Dell'Aquila, E., Marocco, D., Ponticorvo, M., Di Ferdinando, A., Schembri, M., Miglino, O.: ENACT: virtual experiences of negotiation. Educational Games for Soft-Skills Training in Digital Environments. AGL, pp. 89–103. Springer, Cham (2017). doi:10.1007/978-3-319-06311-9_5
12. Deterding, S., Khaled, R., Nacke, L., Dixon, D.: Gamification: toward a definition. In: Proceedings of CHI Workshop on Gamification, Vancouver, BC, pp. 12–15 (2011)
13. Diller, L., Weinberg, J., Gordon, W., Goodkin, R., Gerstman, L.J., Ben-Yishay, Y.: Studies in cognition and rehabilitation in hemiplegia (1974)
14. Doniger, G.M.: NeuroTrax computerized cognitive tests: test descriptions. NeuroTrax Brain Funct. Made Clear (2013)
15. Ferber, S., Karnath, H.O.: How to assess spatial neglect-line bisection or cancellation tasks? J. Clin. Exp. Neuropsychol. **23**(5), 599–607 (2001)
16. Ferrara, F., Ponticorvo, M., Di Ferdinando, A., Miglino, O.: Tangible interfaces for cognitive assessment and training in children: LogicART. In: Uskov, V.L., Howlett, R.J., Jain, L.C. (eds.) Smart Education and e-Learning 2016. SIST, vol. 59, pp. 329–338. Springer, Cham (2016). doi:10.1007/978-3-319-39690-3_29
17. Goodenough, F.L.: Measurement of intelligence by drawings (1926)
18. Halligan, P.W., Marshall, J.C.: Left visuo-spatial neglect: a meaningless entity? Cortex **28**, 525–535 (1992)
19. Iachini, T., Ruggiero, G., Conson, M., Trojano, L.: Lateralization of egocentric and allocentric spatial processing after parietal brain lesions. Brain Cogn. **69**(3), 514–520 (2009)

20. Ishiai, S., Sugishita, M., Ichikawa, T., Gono, S., Watabiki, S.: Clock-drawing test and unilateral spatial neglect. Neurology **43**(1 Part 1), 106 (1993)
21. Klatzky, R.L.: Allocentric and egocentric spatial representations: definitions, distinctions, and interconnections. In: Freksa, C., Habel, C., Wender, K.F. (eds.) Spatial Cognition. LNCS, vol. 1404, pp. 1–17. Springer, Heidelberg (1998). doi:10.1007/3-540-69342-4_1
22. Lieberoth, A., Mrin, A.C., Mller, M.: Deep and shallow gamification - shaky evidence and the forgotten power of good games. In: Engaging Consumers Through Branded Entertainment and Convergent Media. IGI-Global, Hershey (2014)
23. Menon, A., Korner-Bitensky, N.: Evaluating unilateral spatial neglect post stroke: working your way through the maze of assessment choices. Top. Stroke Rehabil. **11**(3), 41–66 (2004)
24. Michael, D.R., Chen, S.L.: Serious Games: Games That Educate, Train, and Inform. Muska and Lipman/Premier-Trade (2005)
25. Miglino, O., Di Ferdinando, A., Di Fuccio, R., Rega, A., Ricci, C.: Bridging digital and physical educational games using RFID/NFC technologies. J. e-Learn. Knowl. Soc. **10**, 89–106 (2014)
26. Paillard, J.: Motor and representational framing of space. In: Brain and Space, pp. 163–182 (1991)
27. Rapcsak, S.Z., Verfaellie, M., Fleet, W.S., Heilman, K.M.: Selective attention in hemispatial neglect. Arch. Neurol. **46**, 178–182 (1989)
28. Sahakian, B.J., Owen, A.M.: Computerized assessment in neuropsychiatry using CANTAB: discussion paper. J. R. Soc. Med. **85**(7), 399 (1992)
29. Schenkenberg, T., Bradford, D.C., Ajax, E.T.: Line bisection and unilateral visual neglect in patients with neurologic impairment. Neurology **30**(5), 509 (1980)
30. Skalski, P., Dalisay, F., Kushin, M., Liu, Y.I.: Need for presence and other motivations for video game play across genres. In: Proceedings of the Presence Live (2012)
31. Tham, K., Tegner, R.: The baking tray task: a test of spatial neglect. Neuropsychol. Rehabil. **6**, 19–25 (1996)
32. Tong, T., Chignell, M., Tierney, M.C., Lee, J.: A serious game for clinical assessment of cognitive status: validation study. JMIR Serious Games **4**(1), e7 (2016)
33. Urbanski, M., Angeli, V., Bourlon, C., Cristinzio, C., Ponticorvo, M., Rastelli, F., Thiebaut de Schotten, M., Bartolomeo, P.: Ngligence spatiale unilatrale: une consquence dramatique mais souvent nglige des lsions de lhmisphre droit. Revue Neurologique **163**(3), 305–322 (2007)
34. van Nimwegen, C., van Oostendorp, H., Modderman, J., Bas, M.: A test case for GameDNA: conceptualizing a serious game to measure personality traits. In: 2011 16th International Conference on Computer Games (CGAMES), pp. 217–222. IEEE (2011)
35. Willer, L., Pedersen, P.M., Gullach, A., Forchhammer, H.B., Christensen, H.K.: Abstract T P415: Assessment of cognitive symptoms in sub-acute stroke with an iPad test-battery (2015)
36. Zichermann, G., Linder, J.: The Gamification Revolution: How Leaders Leverage Game Mechanics to Crush the Competition. McGraw-Hill Education, New York (2013)
37. Zoccolotti, P., Antonucci, G., Judica, A.: Psychometric characteristics of two semi-structured scales for the functional evaluation of hemi-inattention in extrapersonal and personal space. Neuropsychol. Rehabil. **2**(3), 179–191 (1992)

Hierarchical-Architecture Oriented to Multi-task Planning for Prosthetic Hands Controlling

César Quinayás[1(✉)], Andrés Ruiz[1], Leonardo Torres[1], and Carlos Gaviria[2]

[1] Antonio Nariño University, Popayán, Colombia
{cquinayas,andresru,leotorres}@uan.edu.co
[2] University of Cauca, 190001 Popayán, Colombia
cgaviria@unicauca.edu.co
http://www.uan.edu.co
http://www.unicauca.edu.co

Abstract. In this paper, a hierarchical hardware/software architecture for controlling hand prostheses is presented. It is based on both the task planning paradigm and the central nervous system (CNS) so it can be considered as a smart tool which helps people to develop tasks. A hand prostheses prototype, with force and position sensors, controlled by myoelectric commands is used for the validation of the hierarchical control between the user and the prosthesis. The proposed hierarchical control has been validated by people without disability through grasp tasks used in daily life.

Keywords: Hand prosthesis · Hierarchical architecture · Task planning

1 Introduction

The human hand is a versatile instrument, with a large number of degrees of freedom (DoFs), sensory units, actuators and a complex hierarchical control that allows interaction with the environment [1]. Despite the fact that in the last few decades there have been great advances in the development of novel prosthetic hands, dexterous hands such as the DLR hand [2], Vanderbilt hand [3] and Smarthand [4], there is still a great gap in the achievement of a hand replacement that allows the acceptable combination of highly functionality, durability, cosmetic, comfort in its operation, and reasonable cost.

Studies carried out by Santello and Soechting [5], showed that the central nervous system (CNS) coordinates multiple effectors when performing grasping tasks, this often requires the CNS to govern more effectors than are minimally necessary. This problem has been known as motor redundancy/abundance [6]. The redundant motor system of the hand leads to an infinite number of solutions for the same grasping task. This approach allows for introducing an operational definition of synergies as neural organizations of elemental variables that stabilize particular performance variables in a task-specific manner. In the case of prehensile actions, elemental variables can be associated with forces and moments of

J.M. Ferrández Vicente et al. (Eds.): IWINAC 2017, Part II, LNCS 10338, pp. 157–166, 2017.
DOI: 10.1007/978-3-319-59773-7_17

force produced by individual fingers, while performance variables may be associated with the total force and total moment of force applied to the hand-held object.

Nowadays, myolectric control is the most extend approach for electrically-powered upper limb prostheses. The basic myoelectric controllers use as inputs electromyographic signals (EMG) acquired from a pair of antagonistic muscles [7]. A disadvantage of myoelectric control is being able to control different DoFs with a reduced number of EMG signals that can be acquired from the upper limb amputee, this approach generates in the patients a great mental effort for the control of the prosthesis, especially during the first months after fitting. Reason why the patients abandon the device and the desire of a prosthesis that requires a less effort for its control. This is still reflected in the current design of prosthetic hand, such as the Ottobock hands [8] which only have one or two DoFs, to provide basic functionality, grip reliability and elemental manipulation. Early commercial prosthesis such as I-Limb Ultra [9] and Bebionic [10] can perform different prehensile patterns, but their control strategy continues using the two-channel myoelectric control for opening and closing of the hand. The classification of EMG signals using pattern recognition algorithms has allowed greater success in controlling hand prosthesis. Hence many classification algorithms based on pattern-recognition were proposed in recent years [11].

Different approaches have been proposed for controlling of artificial limb using peripheral information (Surface EMG [12], Implantable EMG [13], Target muscle reinnervation [14] and Implantable muscle interfaces [15]), but currently dexterous prosthesis hand have not yet acceptance in clinical trials due to the lack of adequate user interfaces. Hierarchical control approaches are adopted by the hands: Manus Hand [16], RTR II [17] and Smarthand [18] which are based on a two-level control. The high level responsible for supervising the global control of the hand, and the decoding EMG signals and the low level where control strategies are implemented for each joint. The previous examples of prosthesis hand controlled through EMG signals, even when the manipulation system is radically different, they are based on the same paradigm, where the user is not included in the control loop through the feedback and therefore the hand prosthesis is considered as an actuator or end effector that allows executing the task of grasping objects through the motor control system of the hand.

This paper presents the proposal of a hierarchical control hardware/software architecture based on the hierarchical control of the central nervous system (CNS) of the human being and the task planning approach [19]. With this control approach it is possible to consider the prosthesis as an intelligent tool to solve tasks that cooperate with the amputee. In this way, it would be possible to compensate the deficiency of not having a large number the amputee intentions extracted from EMG signal recorded in a noninvasive and invasive ways, to control multiple DoFs. This control strategy is implemented in the experimental prototype of UC2 hand prosthesis.

2 Hierarchical Control Architecture

A hierarchical architecture inspired by the human motor control system is been proposed for the control of an intelligent robotic hand. The cognitive architecture supports fast perception, control and task execution on a low level, coordination of the task on a middle level, and interpretation of the intentions of the users and planning of the task on a high level. The building blocks of the architecture are depicted in Fig. 1.

Returning functionality to the amputee requires that through the development of an adequate control strategy, the prosthesis becomes a smart tool that cooperates with the amputee. For this reason, this architecture allows solving tasks with little intervention of the patient, through of a set of motor programs [20], which can recognize different human-machine interfaces and allows the implementation of control strategies with a reduced design effort.

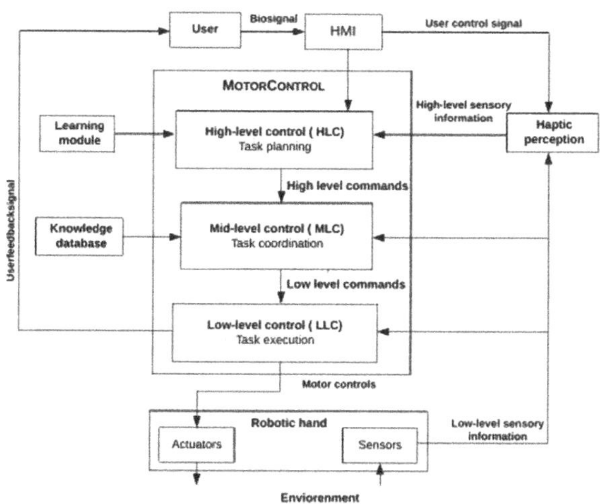

Fig. 1. Hierarchical architecture of the UC2 hand.

In daily life, an amputee develops tasks involving a pre-set prehensile grips to keep the object partially or totally enclosed without slipping, and tasks involving non-prehensile grips such as touching or pressing an object, where it is not necessary to enclose the object but manipulate it by the whole hand or with the individual fingers.

In this approach of hierarchical architecture, tasks are described by means of the Petri net formalism, where a place represents a motor program and the transitions represent an action or event that leads to the execution of a motor program. A Petri net description of the grasping an object and touching object are shown in Fig. 2. In Petri nets the painted places correspond to the actions developed by the human, unpainted places correspond to the actions that the prosthesis develops and the transitions are events coming from sensor data.

2.1 Human-Machine Interface (HMI)

The HMI is a collection of sensors and signal processing algorithms that measure and interpret biosignals from the human and transform them into machine control electrical signals. In the HMI two system were implemented: a movement intention detection system through a K-NN classifier and temporary features such as the variance (VAR), the mean of the absolute value (MAV) and root mean square (RMS), allowing to identify four types of grip postures (rest, open hand, power grip and tripod grip) [21]; and a system of receiving commands via Bluetooth from a mobile application, which allows the user to select predefined grip postures.

2.2 Haptic Perception (HP)

Haptic perception comprises fast interpretation algorithms of sensor data. The haptic perception module receives information from the proprioceptive and exteroceptive sensors of the robotic hand and information from the user through the HMI. It generates high-level sensory information (contact and slip), information that is relevant to high-level control (HLC) decision-making. This module also allows the communication of the hand prosthesis with a graphical user interface (GUI) for the monitoring of the sensory systems.

Contact between the prosthetic hand and the object is characterized by a positive increase in the sensor output. A minimum threshold is set to differentiate between signal noise and object contact; this threshold is chosen as 0.15 N above the resting state of the sensor once it is mounted on the prosthetic finger. To determine the contact condition it is necessary to know the type of grip that the user wishes to perform. If it is a power grip or a tripod grip three points of contact are necessary, if it is a precision grip two points of contact are necessary and if it is a configuration in finger point or lateral grip only a point of contact is needed.

Slip is determined by a first-order time derivative of the force sensor signal, which is calculated using a moving average filter for fifty values of the force applied at each point of contact. For this experiment, object contact initialization and slip are defined as occurring when the force derivative signal is above 0.1 N/ms or below −0.1 N/ms, respectively. These values were chosen in an effort to reduce the number of false positives from the sensor output signal.

2.3 High-Level Control (HLC)

High-level control plans the task using task knowledge. The planning process is started when the desired task has been successfully interpreted of the amputee's intention from HMI module. The task planning is done through a task interpreter and a task flow generator. The task interpreter selects the task that the user has planned and is represented through the hierarchical Petri net of Fig. 2. The task flow generator coordinates the order of execution of the motor programs for the development of the given task (subnets: grasp task and touch task). This module receives high-level sensory information from the haptic perception module and movement intention from the HMI module and sends the high-level commands to the mid-level control.

High-level control also shares information with the learning module that has the function of acquiring new behaviors and storing recently learned information.

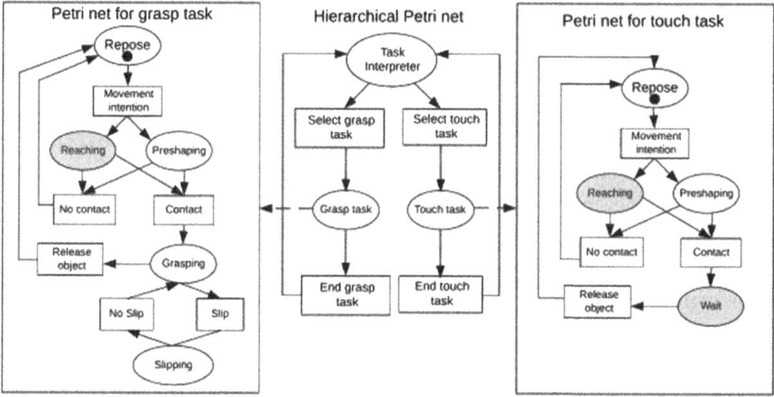

Fig. 2. Hierarchical Petri net that represents the interpreter of tasks. Subnet: grasp task and touch task.

2.4 Mid-Level Control (MLC)

Mid-level control performs the execution of motor programs that have been coordinated by the HLC for the development of a specific task, receives sensory information from the hand prosthesis and generates low- level commands. The MLC shares information with the knowledge database as joint positions, motor primitives and sends newly learned facts to be stored in a memory cache.

The motor programs necessary for the execution of different tasks are the following:

Repose: default state of the hand. Preshaping: the hand is configured on a grip primitive following a path to prepare to grasp the object. Grasping: Executes a force control strategy to keep the object gripped without slipping. Slip: Proportionally increases the force on the fingertips to prevent the object from slipping. Release: open the hand, release any type of grip. Point Finger: the posture of the hand where the index finger is extended. Reaching: movement of the forearm running parallel to the prosthesis to reach the object. Wait: standby state while an action is executed.

Preshaping Motor Program. The preshaping phase is carried out through the kinematic analysis of the fingers and the constraints between their joints [22]. For the implementation of the preshaping motor program in the embedded system, an algorithm was developed that initially determines the current position of each finger joint and when detecting an intention of movement (repose, open hand, close hand and tripod grip) on-line in the DSP are generated the positions that the joints must follow be maintaining the restrictions between them. In such a way that a joint path similar to that of the human fingers is generated, and finally reaching the desired value and configure the hand to the grip posture. Joint values of the grip postures for a natural movement are extracted from the literature [23]. For this work, we have used the restriction between the MCP and PIP joints that is given by $Qpip = 3/4 * Qmcp$.

Grasping Motor Program. This motor program is executed when the HLC detects the contact condition between the fingertip and the object. For the development of grip tasks involving two or three points of contact, the average of 100 data acquired from the current signal of the force sensors was selected as set-points of the PI force control. In the presence of sliding in some of the contact points, the sliding motor program is executed. In tasks such as touching or sliding an object, the grasping and sliding motor programs are not executed, the task is performed according to the Petri net shown in Fig. 2.

Slipping Motor Program. The motor sliding program is executed when the HLC detects the sliding condition. Based on the superposition principle that establishes the decoupling of the gripping force and the resulting torque [24], it is possible to control actions such as grasp an object and rotating the object independently. Therefore, it is established as an anti-slip strategy by increasing the force proportionally in the finger where the slip occurs. Experimentally, a 10 percent increase in the force applied at the moment of slip has been selected, thus imitating the reflex action of the human being.

2.5 Low-Level Control (LLC)

Module responsible for running control loops according to the motor program being developed by the MLC. This module receives sensory information from the hand prosthesis and generates motor commands for the prosthesis actuator system and for the patient sensory feedback system. The low-level control strategy is performed through a PID position control that allows tracking of trajectories in the preshaping phase and a PI control that allows maintaining the desired force at the fingertips in the grasping phase.

2.6 Robotic Hand

The prototype of UC2 hand prosthesis consists of a three-finger structure and 9 DoFs. The fingers are composed of three phalanges (proximal, intermediate and distal) and three DoFs (phalangeal metacarpal joint (MCP), proximal interphalangeal joint (PIP) actuated by motors and distal interphalangeal joint (DIP) passive). The fingers allow flexion/extension movements and the thumb also allows for opposing/repositioning movements. The kinematic and dynamic models are described in [25]. The prosthesis actuation system consists of DC motors and a tactile system at the fingertip conformed by an FSR force sensor and a silicone cover.

3 Hardware/Software Architecture

The hardware architecture has been designed to maximize the flexibility between the interfaces and control strategies of a hand prosthesis so that it can be easily adapted to patients with trans-radial amputation. The hardware architecture is shown in Fig. 3, and is based primarily on a hierarchy of three levels: HLC is described in a hierarchical Petri network that runs in real time on a FPGA Spartan 3E, MLC and LLC running on a Digital signal processor DsPIC30f6012. The LLC is associated with the prosthesis actuator module through TB6612FNG (H-bridge) and a patient sensory feedback system by means of vibrotactile actuators (C2-tactor). Two different power suppliers, one for the motors (5 V) and one for the controller (3.3 V) are needed. The HLC, in master configuration, communicates through a standard RS232 bus with the MLC. A Bluetooth-serial protocol has been implemented between the App and the HMI for the user control. The software is based on a multiprocessor FPA-DSP architecture. The software component of the HLC is described through hierarchical Petri net and interpreted subnets. For representation of the Petri net, the Snoopy IOP software was used, which allows the Petri net to be exported to PNML format and generate VHDL code. Using Xilinx Ise Foundation software, the VHDL code was embedded in the FPGA Spartan 3E. The software component of the LLC has the function of executing control strategies. These control strategies are first implemented and tested in the Simulink MathWorks development environment, later the Real-Time Workshop and Embedded Coder tools are used to generate high-efficiency source code in ANSI C language, this optimized code is embedded in a dsPIC30f6012.

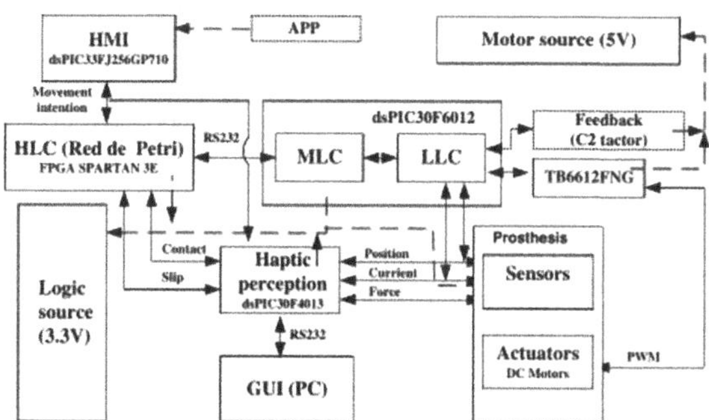

Fig. 3. Hardware architecture of UC2 hand

4 Experimental Validation

With the aim of experimentally evaluating the effective of the proposed control architecture, a person without amputation is asked to perform the object grasp task to monitor in real time the performance of the different modules of the

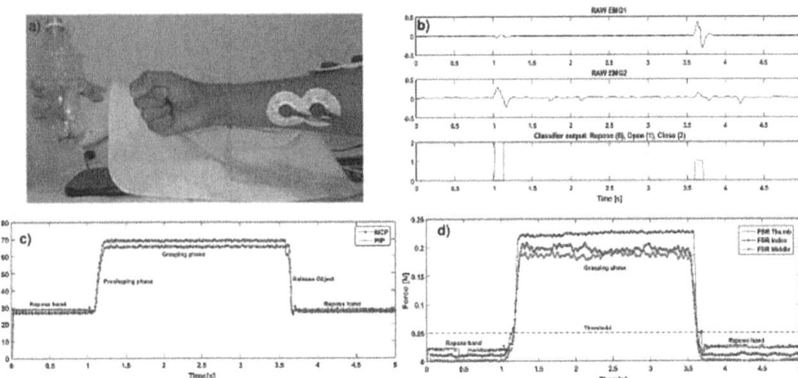

Fig. 4. Experimental trial. (a) Prosthetic hand grasping a bottle, (b) movement intention, (c) preshaping phase and (d) grasping phase.

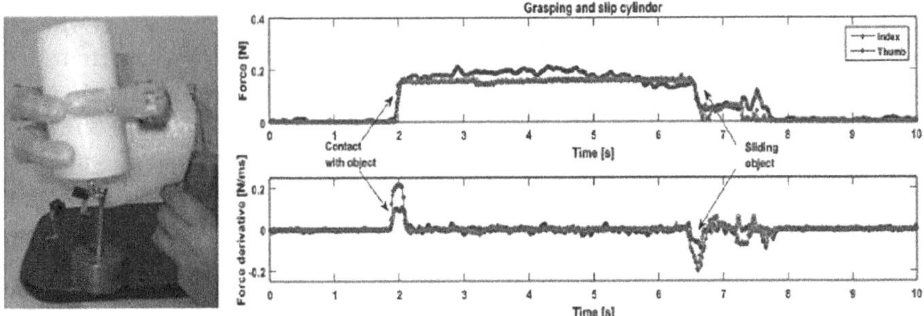

Fig. 5. Results from the cylinder grasping task. The bottom chart shows the time derivative of the force signal. Large positive spikes and negative spikes indicate object contact and slip, respectively.

architecture (see Fig. 4a). A Labview application was written to run on a PC, able to communicate with the hand controller by means of the communication protocol. This application allows continuous monitoring of the sensors of the MCP and PIP joints of the fingers and the force sensors located in the fingertips. The intention of opening and closing of the hand was determined from the K-NN classifier implemented in the HMI and is shown in Fig. 4b, where 0 corresponds to rest, 1 open and 2 close. The measurement of the index finger joint angles during the preshaping, grasping and release object phases are plotted in Fig. 4c. The response of the fingertip forces sensors to when the object is grasped and released are shown in Fig. 4d.

In another experimental trial, a person without amputation is asked to grasp a cylindrical object of 190 g. Weights were added to generate the sliding condition. The result of the trial is shown in Fig. 5. The top chart of the figure is the normal force signal from the thumb and index fingers of the prosthetic hand while the bottom chart shows the force derivative of those signals. The initial contact between the fingers and the object is made around of 2 s, which can be easily detected by applying a threshold on the time derivative of the force signal. The onset of object slip is realized with the synchronous decrease in applied grip force the thumb and index fingers. The abrupt reduction of the force is translated into negative spikes in the force derivative signal. The object slides but the anti-slip strategy increases the applied force to keep the object gripped.

5 Conclusion

In this work, a hierarchical control architecture has been proposed, which is constituted of general modules allow conceiving a hand prosthesis as a smart tool able to solve the execution of tasks of medium complexity, instead of the conventional approach that considers a prosthesis of Hand as a tool that runs low-level motor commands. This approach aims to provide intelligence with the motor control of the prosthesis allowing to compensate the sensorial limitations that can present the hand prosthesis such as the hand UC2 Hand, which only has position sensors and force sensors.

References

1. Kapandji, I.A.: Physiology of the Joints. The Upper Limb. Churchill Livingstone, New York (1982)
2. Butterfass, J., Grebenstein, M., Liu, H., Hirzinger, G.: DLR-Hand II: next generation of a dextrous robot hand. In: IEEE International Conference on Robotics and Automation, Seoul, pp. 109–114 (2001)
3. Dalley, S.A., Wiste, T.E., Withrow, T.J., Goldfarb, M.: Design of a multifunctional anthropomorphic prosthetic hand with extrinsic actuation. IEEE/ASME Trans. Mechatron. **14**, 699–706 (2009)
4. Capriani, C., Controzzi, M., Carrozza, M.C.: Mechanical design of a transradial cybernetic hand. In: IEEE/RSJ International Conference on Intelligent Robots and Systems, Nice, pp. 576–581 (2008)
5. Santello, M., Soechting, J.F.: Force synergies for multifingered grasping. Exp. Brain Res. **133**, 457–467 (2000)
6. Bernstein, N.A.: The problem of interrelaton between coordination and localization. Arch. Biol. Sci. **38**, 1–35 (1935)
7. Zecca, M., Micera, S., Carrozza, M.C., Dario, P.: Control of multifunctional prosthetic hands by processing the electromyographic signal. Crit. Rev. Biomed. Eng. **30**, 459–485 (2002)
8. Sensor Hand Speed w/Flex. https://professionals.ottobockus.com/c/Sensor-Hand-Speed-w-Flex/p/8E41 58-R7%201 24-F
9. Touch bionics. http://www.touchbionics.com/products/active-prostheses/i-limb-ultra
10. Steeper. http://es.bebionic.com/the_hand
11. Kim, K., Choi, H., Moon, C., Mun, C.: Comparison of k-nearest neighbor, quadratic discriminant and linear discriminant analysis in classification of electromyogram signals based on the wrist-motion directions. Curr. Appl. Phys. **11**, 740–745 (2011)

12. Oskoei, M., Hu, H.: Myoelectric control systems—A survey. Biomed. Signal Process. Control **2**, 275–294 (2007)
13. Farina, D., Yoshida, K., Stieglitz, T., Koch, K.P.: Multichannel thin-film electrode for intramuscular electromyographic recordings. J. Appl. Physiol. **104**, 821–827 (2008)
14. Kuiken, T.A., Dumanian, G.A., Lipschutz, R.D., Miller, L.A., Stubblefield, K.A.: The use of targeted muscle reinnervation for improved myoelectric prosthesis control in a bilateral shoulder disarticulation amputee. Prosthet. Orthot. Int. **28**, 245–253 (2004)
15. Dhillon, G.S., Horch, K.W.: Direct neural sensory feedback and control of a prosthetic arm. IEEE Trans. Neural Syst. Rehabil. Eng. **13**, 468–472 (2005)
16. Pons, J.L., Rocon, E., Ceres, R., Saro, B., Levin, S., Van Moorleghem, W.: The MANUS-HAND dextrous robotics upper limb prosthesis: mechanical and manipulation aspects. Auton. Robots **16**, 143–163 (2004)
17. Cipriani, C., Zaccone, F., Stellin, G., Beccai, L., Cappiello, G., Carrozza, M.C., Dario, P.: Closed-loop controller for a bio-inspired multi-fingered underactuated prosthesis. In: Proceedings of the IEEE International Conference on Robotics and Automation, pp. 2111–2116 (2006)
18. Cipriani, C., Controzzi, M., Carrozza, M.C.: The SmartHand transradial prosthesis. J. NeuroEng. Rehabil. **8**, 1–13 (2011)
19. Burghart, C., Mikut, R., Stiefelhagen, R., Asfour, T.: A cognitive architecture for a humanoid robot: a first approach. In: International Conference on Humanoid Robots, pp. 357–362 (2005)
20. Schaal, S., Ijspeert, A., Billard, A.: Computational approaches to motor learning by imitation. Philos. Trans. R. Soc. Lond. B: Biol. Sci. **358**, 537–547 (2003)
21. Quinayás, C., Gaviria, C.: Sistema de identificación de intención de movimiento para el control mioelctrico de una prótesis de mano robótica. Ing. Univ. **19**, 27–50 (2015)
22. Rijpkema, H., Girard, M.: Computer animation of knowledge- based human grasping. In: 18th Annual Conference on Computer Graphics and Interactive Techniques, pp. 339–348 (1991)
23. Cobos, S., Ferre, M., Sanchez-Uran, M.A., Ortego, J., Pena, C.: Efficient human hand kinematics for manipulation tasks. In: IEEE/RSJ International Conference on Intelligent Robots and Systems, pp. 2246–2251 (2008)
24. Arimoto, S., Tahara, K., Yamaguchi, M., Nguyen, P.T.A., Han, H.Y.: Principles of superposition for controlling pinch motions by means of robot fingers with soft tips. Robotica **19**, 21–28 (2001)
25. Quinayás, C., Anãsco, M., Vivas, O., Gaviria, C.: Disenõ y construcción de la prótesis robótica de mano UC-1. Ing. Univ. **14**, 223–237 (2010)

Smart Gesture Selection with Word Embeddings Applied to NAO Robot

Mario Almagro-Cádiz[1], Víctor Fresno[1], and Félix de la Paz López[2(✉)]

[1] Departamento de Lenguajes y Sistemas Informáticos, Universidad Nacional de Educación a Distancia (UNED), Madrid, Spain
{malmagro,vfresno}@lsi.uned.es

[2] Departamento de Inteligencia Artificial, Universidad Nacional de Educación a Distancia (UNED), Madrid, Spain
delapaz@dia.uned.es

Abstract. Nowadays, Human-Robot Interaction (HRI) field is growing by the day, a fact which is evidenced by the increasing number of existing projects as well as the application of increasingly advanced techniques from different areas of knowledge and multi-disciplinary approaches. In a future where technology automatically controls services such as health care, pedagogy or construction, social interfaces would be one of the necessary pillars of HRI field. In this context, gesture plays an important role in the transmission of information and is one of fundamental mechanisms relevant to human-robot interaction. This work proposes a new methodology for gestural annotation in free text through a semantic similarity analysis using distributed representations based on word embeddings. The intention with this is to endow NAO robot with an intelligent mechanism for gesture allocation.

Keywords: Word embeddings · Co-verbal gesture · HRI · NAO robot

1 Introduction

Over the last several decades, service automation scope has been the focus of most technological advances. Robotics presents itself as one of the future main pillars of society for guaranteeing the quality of life in all areas. Lines of robotic research are tackling many varied fields such as medicine, rehabilitation, cleaning, refuelling, agriculture, construction or teaching [38]. Among these researches, one of the most promising lines is therapeutic robotics [15], and specifically psycho-pedagogic interventions for people with cognitive difficulties, both in childhood and elderly [31].

Coexistence of robots and humans in the same space inevitably leads to the development of social interfaces for mutual interaction through natural language and physical expressions. Thus, gesture as a linguistic complement for improving communication and interaction's naturalness assume special significance in *HRI* field. With the future role of robotics in society, affinity for robotic prototypes take on a new significance, with degree of humanity being a decisive factor [21].

J.M. Ferrández Vicente et al. (Eds.): IWINAC 2017, Part II, LNCS 10338, pp. 167–179, 2017.
DOI: 10.1007/978-3-319-59773-7_18

In the context of gestures in robotics, different gestural taxonomies have been defined [19,24], which can be grouped into two main typologies: gestures of interaction with the environment and co-verbal gestures [13,25]. Whereas deictic or object-manipulation gestures have been the most studied [11,30,36], a shortage of studies on rhetorical gestures for accompanying speech, or symbolic gestures related to meaning, doesn't necessarily imply less importance. Whilst important progress in integrating co-verbal gesture has been achieved in the digital environment with avatars, the synchronization of gestures with speech has been a largely unexplored area in robotics [33]. The idea behind this synchronization is the gesture association with specific and fixed keywords applying rule-based and statistical model-based approaches, so new methods are needed in order to extend synchronization coverage. Some systems are based on analysis of speech-based video fragments to develop measures for establishing rules [17]. It is also common to use systems requiring text annotated with gestures in order to generate *Hidden Markov Models* (*HMMs*), as Chiu et al. show [6].

Considering the lack and limitations of interfaces that integrate co-verbal gestures, this paper proposes a new methodology for a intelligent association between symbolic gestures and speech words. These symbolic gestures are used to extend or reiterate verbal meaning, so its use has an enormous impact on human-robot communication.

Given that the techniques in association of terms with gestures have traditionally been limited to the fact that animations are activated when detects certain keywords, this paper outlines an approach based on semantic similarities that intends to associate both in a more flexible way. In this manner a gesture will be activated from any word having a similar semantic meaning. This new methodology for integrating co-verbal gestures employs Natural Language Processing (*NLP*) techniques and semantic analysis through word embeddings. To do this, it applies semantic similarity measures between gestures and words by determining which gestural expression is more in line with verbal meaning.

2 Related Work

Due to the success of gesture recognition researches, there are a large number of studies on robots that can react to human gestures, as a result of which projects such as *ALBERT* [32] and *BIRON* [9] robots have emerged.

Murthy and Jadon make a review of gesture recognition systems based on hand movements [22], noting that most of researches employ *HMMs* to identify static positions.

Recently scientific community have focused on gesture synthesis and integration, which remain largely unexplored, particularly in the robotic scope. Even though most of synthesis works use predefined gestures [34], there exists some projects generating real-time gestural expression such as *Fritz* robot [2]. Traditionally projects in this area focused on deictic [11] or collaborative [30] gesture integration. Also, significant progress has been achieved on the other typologies; for example, *WE-4RII* robot has been implemented for emotional expressions [12].

As regards co-verbal gestures, nearly any type of work derives from rule-based or grammatical model-based approaches for activating them according to fixed words. Our proposal aims precisely to expand that set of already-defined words in accordance with a semantic similarity criterion. Co-verbal gesture generation has been a line of research more recurrent in virtual interfaces, with access to lexicons being the most common method. A number of more complex systems have emerged by using visual information such as *Greta* system [27] or *Max* agent [14].

Co-verbal gestures are semantically, temporarily and pragmatically synchronised with speech in an unconscious way according to McNeil [18]. Bergmann et al. bring together the main complexities of gestural synchronization in two issues, information distribution and packaging [3]. As distribution indicates how verbal concepts and gestural ideas provide different aspects of the meaning, packaging relates to amount of information contained in those aspects.

For the purpose of determining the information packaging, video fragments containing hand motions have been analysed [35]. Similarly, Levine et al. extract measures from gestural movements in various different videos to generate motions in real time [17]. However, measures are useful for quantifying emphasis and emotional degree but says nothing about semantic. Thereby different systems assume text entry annotated with types of gestures and parameters [10,14]. Neff et al. employ manually annotated semantic tags to create gestures through a probabilistic trained model [23]. Likewise, Endrass et al. use techniques aimed at gestural corpus [8]. Other systems apply dialogue managements to planning puntual gestures from communicative targets [37]. There are also teleoperated gestural systems and based on *Wizard of Oz* methods [7].

Some systems based on *NLP* have emerged like *REA* architecture, which lexicalizes gestures to manage them as words in a language generator [4], or *BEAT*, a system that suggests a more advanced approach for synchronising gestures and speech [5]. The last one applies a rule set to determine what types of gesture must be activated, selecting rhetorical gestures by default. Finally, Ng-Thow-Hing et al. proposes an improved system with the integration of all types of gestures implemented in a *Honda* robot [26]. For that, one Part-Of-Speech (*POS*) tagging process [39] and five grammatical models are used. These are attached to each type of gesture defined by McNeill to determine to which it belongs and hence what rule system based on the identification of keywords should be applied. Grammatical models consist of gestural lexicons created by the annotation of video conferences under the following assumptions: there are simpler gestures to model than others, those are usually associated with certain words, rhetorical gestures become accentuated in topic changes and a word can be combined with several gestures due to the context.

3 A New Methodology for Selecting NAO Robot's Gestures from Free Text

Nowadays, the most consolidated tools for co-verbal gesture integration are built on the idea of relating relevant words with gestures, so that they are activated when detects one of those speech words. To improve this basic approach, our proposal consists of a new speech pre-processing methodology based on the use of semantic similarities through word embeddings. The main idea is to increase the coverage of terms with which a gesture will be activated through that semantic search. This methodology analyses incoming speech and a series of gestural representations, and associate it with significant words depending on its semantic similarity.

In order to develop the proposal, it is necessary to prepare a gestural representation set, each consisting of an identifying tag and a set of related terms for constituting a semantic space representation. Those vector representations are used in quantifying the similarity of gestures with word meanings by comparing every term through similarity measures.

Once the gestural representation list is made up, this new methodology implies a speech segmentation into sentences first, and a text tokenization after. Assuming that some grammatical categories provide most of the meaning to every speech sentence, a *POS* tagging process is subsequently established to determine those grammatical categories and identify the most significant words in the message. From a pre-trained vector-based model of word embeddings, it is pretended to quantify the similarity between sentences and related terms to finally select gestures in accordance with a semantic similarity criteria. The entire process is shown in Fig. 1.

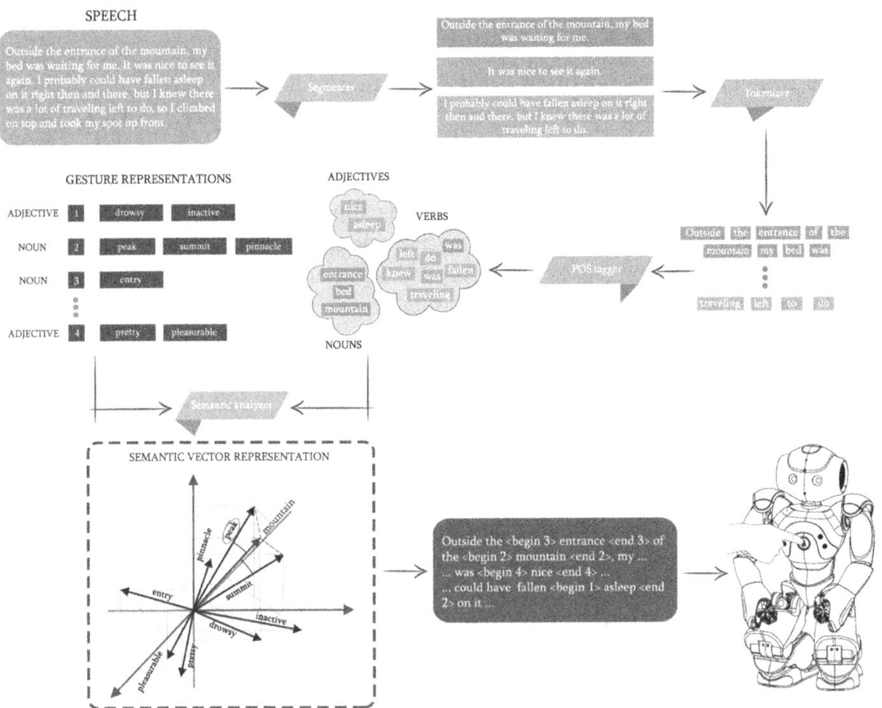

Fig. 1. Proposed methodology for applying to systems such as *NAO* robot.

Word embeddings are word vector representations obtained from its contexts through transformations into reduced semantic spaces; for that, neuronal network training process and other mathematical techniques are applied to reduce the initial dimension of word representations into a reduced semantic space [16]. As each word is represented by a parameter vector, the similarity between two words results in a vector comparison; in this way, the semantic similarity between the gesture meaning, defined by its related terms, and the word meaninig can be established.

In order to evaluate the proposal, an experimentation has been carried out by determining under what conditions of semantic comparison and what association criteria optimize the gesture selection.

4 Experimental Design

Experimentation consists of the behavior analysis of word embeddings in a context of gesture association issues from its semantic spaces, as defined by related terms. Different semantic similarities have been studied applying two measures to 1200 words and 60 gesture representation with two different pre-trained word embeddings models: *word2vec*[1] model of Mikolov et al. [20], trained from *Google News*[2], and *GloVe*[3] model [29], an Stanford implementation generated from *Wikipedia*[4] and *Gigaword*[5] texts. Although both cases are partially based on a news repository resulting in a global scope, *Wikipedia* data strictly belongs to an academic scope; for this reason, *word2vec* model is estimated to offer a better word semantic representation in a general context.

In regarding to measures, euclidean distance and cosine similarity are employed. In the semantic space word embeddings are located, euclidean distance represents relations between concepts, whereas cosine similarity means semantic proximity between concepts. Therefore, a more efficient approach is a priori expected to be achieved with this last measure.

The 60 gesture representations employed in experimentation have been objectively generated from most common terms in language, provided by *Word frequency data*[6] corpus, with the purpose of assuring the coverage of used concepts. Words have been selected from the words related to these terms; for that, related vocabulary search pages have been used in addition to an subsequent review by an expert for choosing those with a similar meaning among the recommended words. Knowing what gesture belongs to each bag of words, semantic similarities between all terms and words have been calculated through the described measures.

[1] http://code.google.com/archive/p/word2vec.
[2] http://news.google.com.
[3] http://nlp.stanford.edu/projects/glove.
[4] http://wikipedia.org.
[5] http://catalog.ldc.upenn.edu/ldc2011t07.
[6] http://www.wordfrequency.info.

The comparative analysis of contextual constraints and assignment methods about those similarities intends to determine which method is most effective in associating gestures with words in accordance with similarity measures, allowing the presented methodology to be configured.

5 Experimental Results and Discussion

Experimentation has been planned in three phases by evaluating different features to be considered for the methodology at each stage.

First analysis covers the similarity of all semantic relations by comparing two alternative systems for assigning gestures to words: a system that enables multiple assignments against another one which limits assignments to an unique gesture.

Multiple assignment system establish a lower minimum membership threshold in such a way as to associate every terms above this value with the respective word. The location of this threshold will be determined by representing Precision and Recall for each measures and model, shown in Figs. 2 and 3. In these graphs

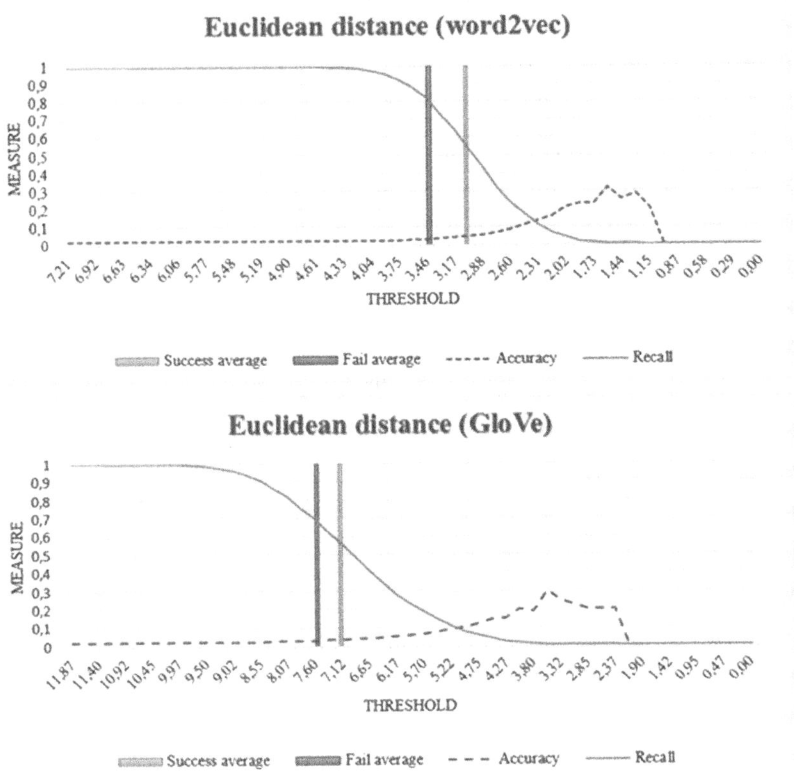

Fig. 2. Precision and Recall curves as a function of the threshold. Euclidean distance.

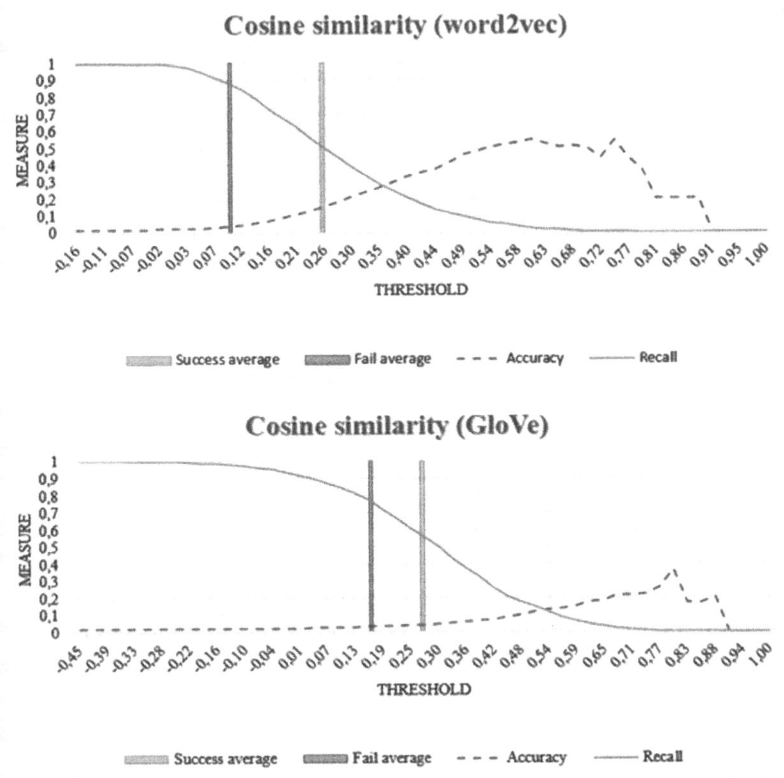

Fig. 3. Precision and Recall curves as a function of the threshold. Cosine similarity.

the average value of similarities assessed as correct as well as the average value of wrong similarities are drawn in order to stimate a range of possible locations. In this way, an intermediate threshold would exclude most of faulty relations and would allow a large number of right relations.

In this context, Precision curve represents successful gestures rate on the whole performed gestures, whereas Recall curve expresses successful gestures rate on the gestures which should have been activated. Whether a threshold is located in the right side, a high Precision and a near-zero Recall are obtained what means only a small number of gestures are performed, with half being successful. However, a threshold on the left side of graph results in a large number of executed gestures with a near-zero Precision. Therefore, the most interesting region is the middle area in which a Precision value no higher than 0.3 without compromising Recall is achieved.

Concerning unique assignment, system is limited to the closest gesture, linking simply each word to gesture containing the most similar term. Even though a minimum threshold is fixed, Precision is significantly increased in all values.

For measuring system performance, the minimum Precision value has been calculated from null threshold for each measure, shown in Table 1. Precision reaches 0.4 for cosine similarity with *word2vec* model.

Table 1. Unique assignment making no distinction between grammatical categories.

Similarity measure	Precision
Cosine similarity (word2vec)	**0.42**
Euclidean distance (word2vec)	0.31
Cosine similarity (GloVe)	0.29
Euclidean distance (GloVe)	0.21

Faced with the impossibility of locating a satisfactory threshold and reaching promising Precision, unique assignment method has been considered as the best option by establishing it during the whole experimentation.

Starting from the idea that the context surrounding a word depends on its grammatical category, one could think our system should consider grammatical information. For that reason, we have raised the need of applying a grammatical restriction for the semantic comparison with the goal of improving rates. Thus a second phase based on a category-by-category analysis is considered, in which each term is only evaluated against words in the same category.

The results shown in Table 2 support that division into categories by obtaining better Precision values when limits the comparison of similar context. The fact that cosine similarity measure get the highest rates for all categories confirms the initial suspicions about a better quantification of similarity based on proximity between context. High Precision over nouns is appreciated in these results divided by categories. This could be explained by the fact that nouns and verbs better reflect semantics in sentences than adjectives or adverbs; whilst adjectives qualify nouns, adverbs often describe circunstancial aspects of sentences.

On the other hand, the fact that not all grammatical categories appear with the same frequency in language must be also considered. For example, adverbs tends to be rarer and have fewer synonyms than nouns. One could then think that the poor results of the adverbs arise partly because until now we have forced experimentation to have the same related term proportion in each category;

Table 2. Unique assignment separated into grammatical categories.

Similarity measure	Precision				
	Global	Noun	Verb	Adjective	Adverb
Cosine similarity (word2vec)	**0.51**	**0.70**	**0.45**	**0.50**	**0.36**
Cosine similarity (GloVe)	0.44	0.64	0.38	0.48	0.27
Euclidean distance (word2vec)	0.43	0.55	0.41	0.47	0.28
Euclidean distance (GloVe)	0.36	0.47	0.32	0.37	0.26

this means that there is a possibility of considering non-existent similarities by demanding a large number of adverbs related to gestures. Thereby, a last phase has been taken into account by presenting a modification of data distribution in each grammatical category to analyse it. More specifically, less strongly relationships have been removed, giving rise to an decrease of adverbs and a lesser verb number. This has provided slightly greater Precision values, displayed in Table 3, which show an meaningful increase in adverb Precision but not sufficient to ignore the quantitative step between categories.

Given the preceding results, we can conclude that nouns should be prioritized against other categories when selecting a gesture from free text.

Table 3. Redistribution of data in each grammatical category.

Similarity measure	Precision				
	Global	Noun	Verb	Adjective	Adverb
Cosine similarity (word2vec)	**0.53**	**0.70**	**0.46**	**0.50**	**0.40**
Cosine similarity (GloVe)	0.48	0.64	0.39	**0.50**	0.32

6 Final Algorithm Proposal

Once the results have been analysed in every experiment phase, the following key conclusions can be drawn:

- A membership threshold for gestures is not feasible because of the overlap between successful and wrong similarities; association based on the closest gesture has better results.
- Cosine similarity measure is most successful at capturing semantic similarity with word embeddings. In turn, pre-trained embeddings by Mikolov have proved to be the most appropriate in a general context.
- Semantic comparison between words and terms into the same grammatical category is more effective due to the shared features of context.
- A better semantic capture by nouns is observed, what makes us consider an order of priority to narrow the search of related gestures to each category by analysing nouns first, followed by adjectives if no relationships are found, verbs and finally adverbs.

In view of all this, the final proposal for gestural assignment from free text in a NAO robot will should consider the comparison between a word meaning and each term meaning composing the semantic space of the gesture. Unique assignment based on the closest gestures will should be included, adding a minimum similarity threshold; in this way, the gesture containing the term with a greater degree of semantic similarity with respect to the speech word in the same grammatical category will be assigned, provided that exceeds minimum threshold for subsequent activation.

Our final proposed methodology is based on detecting the most significant words in speech through segmentation, tokenization and POS tagging processes.

Fig. 4. Preview image of a video showing a *NAO* robot movements in accordance with the final algorithm proposal.

Starting with nouns, semantic similarity will should be analysed from the comparison of word embedding vectors with the goal of determining gesture assignment. For that, the word shall be compared to all terms belonging to the same category; if one or more gestures exceed a minimum cosine similarity value, the one most closest will be assigned.

To validate the methodology, we have implemented an algorithm including the *FreeLing* package [28] for segmentation and POS tagging processes and the pre-trained word embeddings by Mikolov. A story has been annotated with gestures of *Animations* library and applied to a Nao robot. Results have been recorded for a future distribution and can be visualized in a video (Fig. 4)[7].

7 Conclusions and Future Work

Robotics aims to draw a future marked by a high quality of life, encompassing both social and physical capabilities. Disposition of social interfaces for an interaction between people and machines more akin to interactions between human beings will be of central importance in this future. To this end the gesture integration into speech will be essential.

The importance of symbolic co-verbal gestures lies in the semantic transmission of the oral message. The suggested methodology is intended to integrate

[7] http://www.ia.uned.es/personal/delapaz/tfm_NAONLP_en.html.

them to provide a smart gestural annotation tool for gestural synchronization with language. In this sense, the use of naturalness improvement-oriented word embeddings involves a step forward compared to the techniques employed at the time in *HRI* scope.

Those semantic vector-based model also have a low computing cost after training, since that is estimated by calculating similarity through a simple vector operation such as cosine. Moreover, the proposed methodology is directly applicable to other languages whether the respective models are available.

Experimentation confirms that the inherent semantic in word embeddings contains information about the role of words in language, what penalizes the comparison between categories. Nouns are showing greater semantic characterization, partly due to an enormous amount of synonymous and a better conceptual reflection, whilst adverb meaning representation is considerably worse. Hence, the viability of word embeddings in the *HRI* field is confirmed through a tiered semantic approach from nouns to the rest of categories, leaving open other unexplored avenues for improving adverb captures.

The proposed methodology has been developed as first approximation of semantic-based gesture integration. Nevertheless, this proposal leaves open other lines of research and future improvements. Among these stand out the rule-based heuristic layer development to improve fluency, introduction of negation detectors, gestures memorisation for increasing variability or establishment of a confidence interval for toggling between gestures with similarity semantic values. Another confluent line of research would be *sentiment analysis* with which effusivity may be qualified based on the study of emotional issues in sentences through polarity classifiers. Finally, a point of view from a discourse analysis has arisen by using *Rhetorical Structure Theory* or *RST* [1]. It is intended to detect causal, contrast, justify, condition or concession relationships to activate animations for transition between concepts.

Acknowledgements. This research was partially supported by the Spanish Ministry of Science and Innovation (VoxPopuli Project, TIN2013-47090-C3-1-P).

References

1. Bateman, J., Delin, J.: Rhetorical structure theory. In: Encyclopedia of Language and Linguistics, 2nd edn. Elsevier, Oxford (2005)
2. Bennewitz, M., Faber, F., Joho, D., Behnke, S.: Fritz-a humanoid communication robot. In: The 16th IEEE International Symposium on Robot and Human Interactive Communication, RO-MAN 2007, pp. 1072–1077. IEEE (2007)
3. Bergmann, K., Kahl, S., Kopp, S.: Modeling the semantic coordination of speech and gesture under cognitive and linguistic constraints. In: Aylett, R., Krenn, B., Pelachaud, C., Shimodaira, H. (eds.) IVA 2013. LNCS, vol. 8108, pp. 203–216. Springer, Heidelberg (2013). doi:10.1007/978-3-642-40415-3_18
4. Cassell, J., Bickmore, T., Campbell, L., Vilhjalmsson, H.: Human conversation as a system framework: designing embodied conversational agents. In: Cassell, J., Sullivan, J., Prevost, S., Churchill, E. (eds.) Embodied Conversational Agents, pp. 29–63. MIT Press, Cambridge (2000)

5. Cassell, J., Vilhjálmsson, H.H., Bickmore, T.: BEAT: the behavior expression animation toolkit. In: Prendinger, H., Ishizuka, M. (eds.) Life-Like Characters, pp. 163–185. Springer, Heidelberg (2004)
6. Chiu, C.-C., Morency, L.-P., Marsella, S.: Predicting co-verbal gestures: a deep and temporal modeling approach. In: Brinkman, W.-P., Broekens, J., Heylen, D. (eds.) IVA 2015. LNCS, vol. 9238, pp. 152–166. Springer, Cham (2015). doi:10.1007/978-3-319-21996-7_17
7. Dahlbäck, N., Jönsson, A., Ahrenberg, L.: Wizard of Oz studies-why and how. Knowl.-Based Syst. **6**(4), 258–266 (1993)
8. Endrass, B., Damian, I., Huber, P., Rehm, M., André, E.: Generating culture-specific gestures for virtual agent dialogs. In: Allbeck, J., Badler, N., Bickmore, T., Pelachaud, C., Safonova, A. (eds.) IVA 2010. LNCS, vol. 6356, pp. 329–335. Springer, Heidelberg (2010). doi:10.1007/978-3-642-15892-6_34
9. Haasch, A., Hohenner, S., Hüwel, S., Kleinehagenbrock, M., Lang, S., Toptsis, I., Fink, G.A., Fritsch, J., Wrede, B., Sagerer, G.: BIRON-the bielefeld robot companion. In: Proceedings of the International Workshop on Advances in Service Robotics, pp. 27–32. Stuttgart, Germany (2004)
10. Hartmann, B., Mancini, M., Pelachaud, C.: Implementing expressive gesture synthesis for embodied conversational agents. In: Gibet, S., Courty, N., Kamp, J.-F. (eds.) GW 2005. LNCS, vol. 3881, pp. 188–199. Springer, Heidelberg (2006). doi:10.1007/11678816_22
11. Hato, Y., Satake, S., Kanda, T., Imai, M., Hagita, N.: Pointing to space: modeling of deictic interaction referring to regions. In: 2010 5th ACM/IEEE International Conference on Human-Robot Interaction (HRI), pp. 301–308. IEEE (2010)
12. Itoh, K., Miwa, H., Matsumoto, M., Zecca, M., Takanobu, H., Roccella, S., Carrozza, M.C., Dario, P., Takanishi, A.: Various emotional expressions with emotion expression humanoid robot we-4RII. In: First IEEE Technical Exhibition Based Conference on Robotics and Automation, TExCRA 2004, pp. 35–36. IEEE (2004)
13. Kendon, A.: Current issues in the study of gesture. Biol. Found. Gestures: Motor Semiot. Asp. **1**, 23–47 (1986)
14. Kopp, S., Wachsmuth, I.: Synthesizing multimodal utterances for conversational agents. Comput. Animat. Virtual Worlds **15**(1), 39–52 (2004)
15. Krebs, H.I., Hogan, N.: Therapeutic robotics: a technology push. Proc. IEEE **94**(9), 1727–1738 (2006)
16. Lebret, R., Legrand, J., Collobert, R.: Is deep learning really necessary for word embeddings? Technical report, Idiap (2013)
17. Levine, S., Theobalt, C., Koltun, V.: Real-time prosody-driven synthesis of body language. ACM Trans. Graph. (TOG) **28**, 172 (2009). ACM
18. McNeill, D.: Hand and Mind: What Gestures Reveal About Thought. University of Chicago Press, Chicago (1992)
19. McNeill, D., Levy, E.: Conceptual Representations in Language Activity and Gesture. ERIC Clearinghouse, Columbus (1980)
20. Mikolov, T., Sutskever, I., Chen, K., Corrado, G.S., Dean, J.: Distributed representations of words and phrases and their compositionality. In: Advances in Neural Information Processing Systems, pp. 3111–3119 (2013)
21. Minato, T., Shimada, M., Ishiguro, H., Itakura, S.: Development of an Android robot for studying human-robot interaction. In: Orchard, B., Yang, C., Ali, M. (eds.) IEA/AIE 2004. LNCS, vol. 3029, pp. 424–434. Springer, Heidelberg (2004). doi:10.1007/978-3-540-24677-0_44
22. Murthy, G., Jadon, R.: A review of vision based hand gestures recognition. Int. J. Inf. Technol. Knowl. Manag. **2**(2), 405–410 (2009)

23. Neff, M., Kipp, M., Albrecht, I., Seidel, H.P.: Gesture modeling and animation based on a probabilistic re-creation of speaker style. ACM Trans. Graph. (TOG) **27**(1), 5 (2008)
24. Nehaniv, C.L., Dautenhahn, K., Kubacki, J., Haegele, M., Parlitz, C., Alami, R.: A methodological approach relating the classification of gesture to identification of human intent in the context of human-robot interaction. In: IEEE International Workshop on Robot and Human Interactive Communication, ROMAN 2005, pp. 371–377. IEEE (2005)
25. Nespoulous, J.L., Lecours, A.R.: Gestures: nature and function. Biol. Found. Gestures: Motor Semiot. Asp., 49–62 (1986)
26. Ng-Thow-Hing, V., Luo, P., Okita, S.: Synchronized gesture and speech production for humanoid robots. In: 2010 IEEE/RSJ International Conference on Intelligent Robots and Systems (IROS), pp. 4617–4624. IEEE (2010)
27. Niewiadomski, R., Bevacqua, E., Mancini, M., Pelachaud, C.: Greta: an interactive expressive ECA system. In: Proceedings of the 8th International Conference on Autonomous Agents and Multiagent Systems, vol. 2, pp. 1399–1400. International Foundation for Autonomous Agents and Multiagent Systems (2009)
28. Padró, L., Stanilovsky, E.: Freeling 3.0: towards wider multilinguality. In: LREC 2012 (2012)
29. Pennington, J., Socher, R., Manning, C.D.: Glove: global vectors for word representation. In: EMNLP, vol. 14, pp. 1532–1543 (2014)
30. Riek, L.D., Rabinowitch, T.C., Bremner, P., Pipe, A.G., Fraser, M., Robinson, P.: Cooperative gestures: effective signaling for humanoid robots. In: 2010 5th ACM/IEEE International Conference on Human-Robot Interaction (HRI), pp. 61–68. IEEE (2010)
31. Robinson, H., MacDonald, B., Broadbent, E.: The role of healthcare robots for older people at home: a review. Int. J. Soc. Robot. **6**(4), 575–591 (2014)
32. Rogalla, O., Ehrenmann, M., Zollner, R., Becher, R., Dillmann, R.: Using gesture and speech control for commanding a robot assistant. In: Proceedings of the 11th IEEE International Workshop on Robot and Human Interactive Communication, pp. 454–459. IEEE (2002)
33. Salem, M., Kopp, S., Wachsmuth, I., Joublin, F.: Towards meaningful robot gesture. In: Ritter, H., Sagerer, G., Dillmann, R., Buss, M. (eds.) Human Centered Robot Systems, pp. 173–182. Springer, Heidelberg (2009)
34. Salem, M., Kopp, S., Wachsmuth, I., Joublin, F.: Towards an integrated model of speech and gesture production for multi-modal robot behavior. In: RO-MAN 2010, pp. 614–619. IEEE (2010)
35. Stone, M., DeCarlo, D., Oh, I., Rodriguez, C., Stere, A., Lees, A., Bregler, C.: Speaking with hands: creating animated conversational characters from recordings of human performance. ACM Trans. Graph. (TOG) **23**, 506–513 (2004). ACM
36. Sugiyama, O., Kanda, T., Imai, M., Ishiguro, H., Hagita, N.: Natural deictic communication with humanoid robots. In: IEEE/RSJ International Conference on Intelligent Robots and Systems, IROS 2007, pp. 1441–1448. IEEE (2007)
37. Tepper, P., Kopp, S., Cassell, J.: Content in context: generating language and iconic gesture without a gestionary. In: Proceedings of the Workshop on Balanced Perception and Action in ECAs at AAMAS, vol. 4, p. 8 (2004)
38. Ting, C.H., Yeo, W.H., King, Y.J., Chuah, Y.D., Lee, J.V., Khaw, W.B.: Humanoid robot: a review of the architecture, applications and future trend. Res. J. Appl. Sci. Eng. Technol. **7**, 1364–1369 (2014)
39. Voutilainen, A.: Part-of-speech tagging. In: The Oxford Handbook of Computational Linguistics, pp. 219–232 (2003)

Deep Learning

A Deep Learning Approach for Underwater Image Enhancement

Javier Perez(✉), Aleks C. Attanasio, Nataliya Nechyporenko, and Pedro J. Sanz

Department of Computer Science and Engineering, Jaume I University, Castellón de la Plana, Spain
{japerez,al366204,al365957,sanzp}@uji.es

Abstract. Image processing in underwater robotics is one of the most challenging problems in autonomous underwater robotics due to light transmission in water. Although image restoration techniques are able to correctly remove the haze in a degraded image they need many images from the same location making impossible to use it in a real time system. Taking into account the great results of deep learning techniques in other image processing problems such as colorizing images or detecting objects a deep learning solution is proposed. A convolutional neural network is trained with image restoration techniques to dehaze single images outperforming other image enhancement techniques. The proposed approach is able to produce image restoration quality images with a single image as input. The neural network is validated using images from different locations and characteristics to prove the generalization capabilities.

Keywords: Underwater robotics · Deep learning · Image dehazing

1 Introduction

One of the most challenging problems in underwater robotics is the processing of underwater images. Besides the well known problems to automatically interpret an image in order to interact with the environment, underwater robotics needs to deal with additional problems caused by the degradation of the image due to the light transmission in water.

A correct interpretation of the camera input is crucial to build autonomous robots capable to move and interact in an unknown environment. In the case of underwater robotics, there are many applications related to the underwater industry and, unfortunately, maritime disasters such as shipwrecks, leaks on offshore or aircraft accidents. These interventions are usually performed by Remote Operated Vehicles (ROVs) controlled by expert pilots through an umbilical communication cable. Nevertheless, in the last few years, a more autonomous architecture has been developed: Intervention Autonomous Underwater Vehicles (IAUV) [4]. This architecture has many advantages such as the absence of delay between commands and vehicle reaction.

J.M. Ferrández Vicente et al. (Eds.): IWINAC 2017, Part II, LNCS 10338, pp. 183–192, 2017.
DOI: 10.1007/978-3-319-59773-7_19

Usually, the first step in this kind of systems consists in processing the input of the cameras to be able to localize the system, safely navigate and identify the targets of interest. Due to the nature of light transmission in the underwater environment, described in [15], images suffer from different degradation effects such as absorption, scattering, marine snow or vignetting. These effects make interpreting the scene a really challenging problem.

Absorption reduces the amount of light as the robot goes deeper or further from the camera, colors drop off one by one depending on their wavelengths. This effect is the cause of the bluish color of underwater images as this wavelength is the least attenuated in the medium. The scattering effect changes the direction of the light to the camera generating a characteristic veil that superimposes itself on the image and hides the scene blurring the objects. Besides this effects, a common problem is the presence of small floating particles known as marine snow, that also increase the amount of scattered light. Finally, vignetting is a light fade-out in terms of intensity in the corners of the image caused by the geometry of the lens and sometimes by the lens housing.

For this reasons a preprocessing step is needed in order to restore the original colors and enhance the image for further processing. This can be addressed from two points of view. Image restoration that aims to recover a degraded image using a model of the degradation and of the acquired image: it is essentially an inverse problem. The second option, image enhancement, consists in using qualitative subjective criteria to produce a more visually pleasing image. Both methods have their own advantages and drawbacks, but the main difference is image restoration produces more realistic results but requires to estimate or measure several parameters thus it is difficult to use in a real time system.

In this work a hybrid solution is proposed: using a deep learning architecture to learn an image enhancement function from image restoration techniques. A dataset of pairs of raw and restored images is used to train a convolutional network, thus it is able to produce restored images from degraded inputs. The results are compared with other image enhancement methods using the image restoration as groundtruth of the system.

The paper is organized as follows. In the next section a review of state of the art techniques for image dehazing is presented. Section 3 describes the deep learning method. The experiments and results of the proposed approach are showed in Sect. 4. Finally, in Sect. 5 conclusions and further work are given.

2 State of the Art

Restoring degraded underwater images requires modelling and estimating many parameters such as water absorption, scattering and distance to objects (depthmap). This kind of inputs are difficult to estimate from a single image. For this reason, a large set of images from the same location or a combination of different sensors are typically used for this purpose. There is a large amount of work on restoring underwater images, [20] offers a detailed review.

The work in [1] uses a whole dataset of images and depthmaps from the same intervention to accurately estimate the water, light and camera parameters in order to restore the colors of the image. The main drawback of this approach is, it requires a medium sized dataset of images and depthmaps of the same area, which may not be available making impossible to use it in real time applications.

Similarly, the authors in [21] propose a method using a depthmap and use it with a single image to estimate the rest of the parameters to restore the image. However, this method depends on a dense depthmap that may not be available when the environment is not textured enough.

Other works like [25], use specific hardware that dynamically mixes the illumination of an object in a distance dependent way by using a controllable multicolor light source in order to compensate color loss. This approach achieves a great color correction, but the main problem is the need of a specific hardware to solve the problem. Similarly, in order to deal with scattering some methods use specific hardware such as structured illumination [16] or polarizers [24].

In the context of single image dehazing there are a big family of algorithms that use the dark channel prior as [10]. Dark Prior techniques are based on the observation that in most of the non-background patches of outdoor haze-free images, at least one color channel has some pixels whose intensity is very low and close to zero. This has been proved to work in most outdoor air images and has also been adapted to underwater environments in [3] or [6]. The main disadvantage of this method is that it is based on a statistical observation that may not be valid for some cases.

In terms of image enhancement, a histogram equalization is typically used as described in [7]. This techniques analyse the histogram and transform it to accomplish a determined distribution that produces visually pleasing images. The main drawback of this approach is it amplifies the noise in homogeneous regions and creates false colours. Some research lines work to palliate this problems like [9,12] combining different techniques.

2.1 Deep Learning

In the last few years there have been a great variety of studies demonstrating the effectiveness of deep learning methods in different application domains. In addition to the classic Mixed National Institute of Standards and Technology (MNIST) handwriting challenge [5] many applications have been studied such as image classification [17] or speech recognition [11] and many others.

The growth of available data in computers for processing [19] combined with the increasing processing capabilities of computers initiated this revolution. Deep learning is the process that allows patterns to be found, discovered or learned in large, complex data. Although applications are not restricted to image processing tasks, this is the domain that has seen the biggest change in response to the introduction of these deep learning methods.

In the case of neural network for image dehazing there are only a few works and none of them, to the best of the authors knowledge, are tested in underwater environments. In [2,13] authors propose a deep learning solution to estimate transmission. In the case of [22], it uses a random forest and several haze-relevant features to estimate the transmission. The approaches proposed in [18,27] perform a similar step generating synthetic images from non-hazy ones, but they also create a synthetic depth-map to produce the training images.

The main drawback of this learning approaches is they use synthetic images created from non-hazy images to train a neural network that estimates transmission due to the difficulty of finding hazy and non-hazy pairs. These images ignore many problems of real images and difficult its use in a real situation.

Other learning techniques have also been explored in this context, [23] has examined the use of Markov Random Fields (MRF) and a training stage to learn how to assign the most probable color to each pixel. The MRF is trained using pairs of input and output images learning transforms from a patch of degraded colors to restored colors. In order to acquire the desired output images, a light source is used, obtaining a better image to train. However, the method relies on a illumination system that obtains "groundtruth" images to train the system.

3 Proposed Method

The approach proposed in this work uses a convolutional neural network to learn the transformation from raw acquired images to enhanced images thus it can be used as input for other vision algorithms. In order to train and evaluate the system the images have been processed using the method in [1].

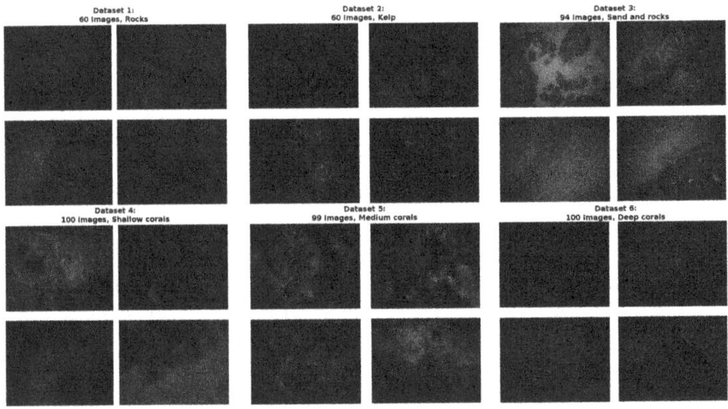

Fig. 1. Images of the different datasets used in the work.

The images used to train the neural network have been taking by an underwater camera mounted in an autonomous underwater vehicle [26] during different real underwater interventions. The images have been divided in 6 sets depending on the characteristics of the images, as Fig. 1 shows. Furthermore, the images have been chosen to cover a wide variety of textures at different depths in order to train different kind of images.

These dataset division allows to train with some sets of images and validate the neural network with images from a different intervention. Thus it is possible to test the system in the case of a different intervention. Besides this, each dataset has been organised in a training and testing set with images randomly selected to measure the training performance.

Several architectures have been tested to train the system, but the one proposed can be seen in Fig. 2. As can be seen, the neural net takes as input the whole image and goes through 6 convolutional steps. In the first one, the image size is reduced in an additional pooling step that extracts the most relevant features. Besides this, every convolutional step but the last one also includes a Rectifier Linear Unit (ReLU) layer as activation function.

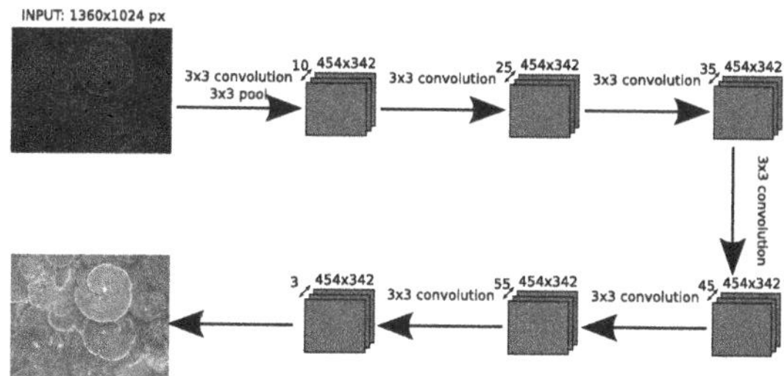

Fig. 2. Architecture of the convolutional network used to dehaze.

With each convolutional layer the number of features extracted increase from the 3 initial of the raw image (RGB) to 55 after five steps. At this moment the features are combined in the last neural network step to produce a matrix of 3 features that corresponds to the restored image.

In order to train the parameters in the neural network, the Adam optimizer, a gradient descent method, has been used with a $l2$ loss function as minimization function. The $l2$ loss function is a commonly used function that computes the squared sum of the differences between the estimated x and groundtruth y values: $l2 = \sum_{i=0}^{n}(y_i - x_i)^2$. In this case minimizing the l2 loss means minimizing the differences of intensities between the restored image and the ones estimated by the neural network.

As a consequence, the neural network learns to perform the same transform applied with the restoration methodology. However, the restoration method used to train requires a depthmap and a whole dataset of images while the neural network will need to do it with just a single image.

4 Results

Two experiments have been conducted to evaluate the precision of the neural network estimations. In the first case all the datasets have been used to train and evaluate it with the test images. However, this is not a realistic situation as training images for the intervention location are not usually available. For this reason, the second experiment simulates this situation training with all but one dataset that is used to validate the system.

In order to evaluate the precision of the neural network predictions the images have been enhanced with two commonly used techniques and compared with the proposed approach. The first, histogram equalization, analyses the histogram of the raw image and displaces it to follow the desired distribution. The histogram equalization used in this paper is the most commonly used, modifies the pixel intensities to follow a normal distribution for every channel.

The second compared algorithm is an Automatic Color Enhancement (ACE), as explained in [8], that is also used in underwater environments in [14]. This technique enhances the image based on a simple model of the human visual system, inspired by different techniques such as gray world transformation, white patch assumption, lateral inhibition and local global adaptation. The main drawback of this technique is it is computationally complex, each image requires around 1.5 s in a i5 at 3.2 Ghz with a Geforce 960GTX while the time to process a single image in a neural network is 0.013 s.

4.1 Experiment 1

In this experiment all the datasets have been used to train the neural network keeping a few images of each in order to evaluate it. The system has been trained for 1700 epochs, reaching a 5.6% training error. This error is the mean difference between each intensity pixel and its groundtruth counterpart. In order to show percent errors intensities are transformed from 0–255 to 0–1 range.

The results for the test images of each dataset can be seen in Table 1 together with ACE and histogram equalization techniques. As can be seen the proposed method obtains the best results in all cases. This is not surprising as it is training with images from the same survey, thus it has similar examples that help to dehaze the raw image. But it is important that the neural network is able to learn the transform and correctly apply it to new images.

Table 1. Results for the experiment 1: training with every dataset.

Technique	Rocks	Kelp	Rocks-sand	Deep	Medium	Shallow
Proposed	3.5%	6.5%	5.1%	4.1%	3.4%	3.2%
ACE	6.8%	9.1%	15.3%	15.7%	7.5%	9.1%
Histeq	25.6%	37.9%	29.4%	20.5%	27.6%	27.5%

Another interesting result is ACE is obtaining results closer to the target image than the histogram equalization. Although the histogram equalization is enhancing the raw images is still far from the restored image. This means the colors generated by the histogram equalization are exacerbated producing false colors that were not present in the real objects.

It is also important to notice that the techniques perform very differently depending on the datasets. ACE has around 130% higher error in the case of deep corals or rocks-sand than in rocks dataset. However, in the case of histogram equalization deep corals is the best case scenario according to the used metric. This means the technique performance depends on the characteristics of the input images such as object colors or noise.

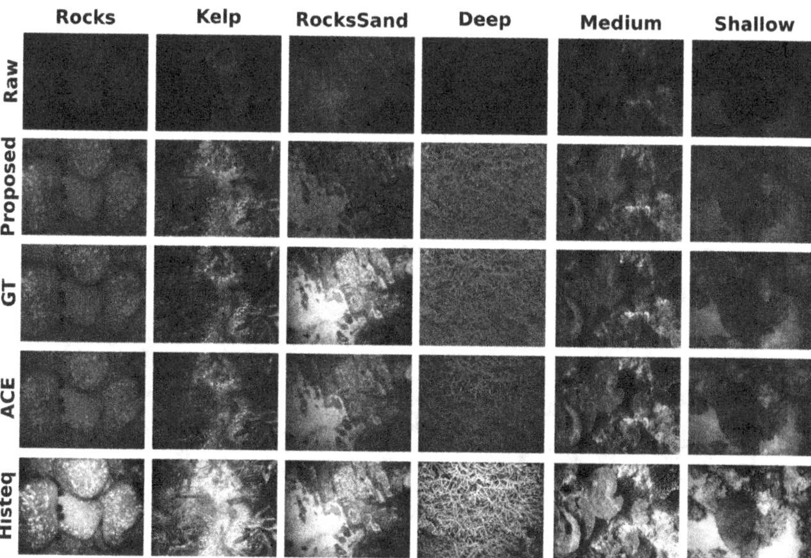

Fig. 3. Comparison of the image dehazing using different techniques in the first experiment. (Color figure online)

The visual results that can be seen in Fig. 3 reflect the numerical results. A test image of every dataset for each compared technique is showed together with the raw and groundtruth (GT). As can be seen the proposed method and the groundtruth images are indistinguishable in most cases, and in the cases that are different such as RocksSand dataset it is difficult to decide which one is better.

The ACE methodology obtains slightly uncorrected images. The algorithm is not able to completely remove the haze obtaining bluish or greenish images depending on the input. However the images are greatly enhanced. On the other hand, histogram equalization overcorrect the images producing unnatural images with extreme colours in some cases such as the kelp dataset, but it shows at least part of the error comes from the fact that the images are brighter than the produced by the restoration method.

4.2 Experiment 2

The results of the previous experiment show the system is able to learn dehaze transformations given training images, but a generalization experiment is needed.

Taking this into account the second experiment focus on training with all but one dataset and use this last dataset as validation.

The deep corals dataset has been chosen as validation dataset as it seems to be the most complex for other techniques, thus it is a more challenging dataset. For this reason the resting datasets are included in the training scheme and a new neural network has been trained with them.

The results in this case are closer to the ACE performance, but the neural network still performs better. The neural network obtained a 14.1% error in the validation set while maintaining a 5% in the validation set. This is close to the 15.7% error of the ACE technique. However, processing an image with ACE requires 1.5 s making difficult to use it in a real time environment while the neural network needed 0.013 s per image. The histogram equalization is far from this results producing a 20.5% error for the validation set.

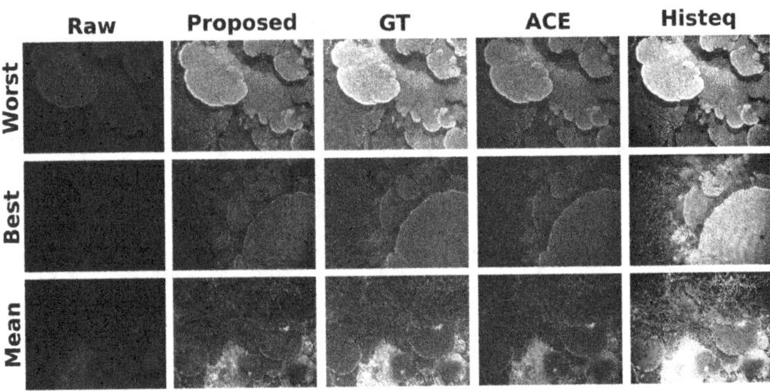

Fig. 4. Comparison of the image dehazing using different techniques in the second experiment. (Color figure online)

The visual results are displayed in Fig. 4. In this case three images from the validation set are showed, the worst and best performing images have been chosen together with one close to the mean error. As can be seen the neural network solution slightly overcorrects the images compared with the groundtruth result. In the case of ACE, images are not completely corrected showing a greenish color. Finally histogram equalization overcorrects inputs even more than the proposed image resulting in colors very different from the target with too dark and too bright zones.

This experiment proves the neural network performance is good, although numerical results are close to the ACE performance visual results look much more natural. Furthermore, the computation time is extremely shorter allowing to include it in a real time system as a preprocessing step. Finally, it is important to remark that the training never saw an image of the validation dataset permitting to use images to train in a different location from the intervention.

5 Conclusions and Future Work

In this work a real time deep learning solution for image dehazing is proposed and compared with other state of the art alternatives. The system is trained with other restoration methodologies that require several inputs that are hard to estimate at the intervention time. However, when the system is trained it is able to correctly dehaze images in real time with only a still raw image as input.

The results show that the system is able to generalize and learn to dehaze with images from a location and be used in a different location. However, in this situation the results are slightly worse, but still outperform other state of the art alternatives for real time dehazing.

Furthermore, when images from the same location as the final intervention are available to include in the training stage the results are visually indistinguishable from restoration techniques. This allows to obtain restoration results with only a single image as input in real time.

Acknowledgments. This work has been partially funded by Spanish Ministry under grant DPI2014-57746-C3 (MERBOTS Project), Generalitat Valenciana grant PROMETEO/2016/066 and Universitat Jaume I grant PREDOC/2012/47. The authors would like to acknowledge the Australian Centre for Field Robotics' marine robotics group for providing the data used in this work.

References

1. Bryson, M., Johnson-Roberson, M., Pizarro, O., Williams, S.B.: True color correction of autonomous underwater vehicle imagery. J. Field Robot. **33**(6), 853–874 (2016)
2. Cai, B., Xu, X., Jia, K., Qing, C., Tao, D.: Dehazenet: an end-to-end system for single image haze removal. IEEE Trans. Image Process. **25**(11), 5187–5198 (2016)
3. Chiang, J.Y., Chen, Y.C.: Underwater image enhancement by wavelength compensation and dehazing. IEEE Trans. Image Process. **21**(4), 1756–1769 (2012)
4. De Novi, G., Melchiorri, C., García, J., Sanz, P., Ridao, P., Oliver, G.: A new approach for a reconfigurable autonomous underwater vehicle for intervention. In: 2009 3rd Annual IEEE Systems Conference, pp. 23–26. IEEE (2009)
5. Deng, L.: The MNIST database of handwritten digit images for machine learning research. IEEE Sig. Process. Mag. **29**(6), 141–142 (2012)
6. Drews, P., Nascimento, E., Moraes, F., Botelho, S., Campos, M.: Transmission estimation in underwater single images. In: Proceedings of the IEEE International Conference on Computer Vision Workshops, pp. 825–830 (2013)
7. Garg, R., Mittal, B., Garg, S.: Histogram equalization techniques for image enhancement. Int. J. Electron. Commun. Technol. **2**(1), 107–111 (2011)
8. Getreuer, P.: Automatic color enhancement (ACE) and its fast implementation. Image Process. On Line **2**, 266–277 (2012)
9. Ghani, A.S.A., Isa, N.A.M.: Underwater image quality enhancement through integrated color model with rayleigh distribution. Appl. Soft Comput. **27**, 219–230 (2015)
10. He, K., Sun, J., Tang, X.: Single image haze removal using dark channel prior. IEEE Trans. Pattern Anal. Mach. Intell. **33**(12), 2341–2353 (2011)

11. Hinton, G., Deng, L., Yu, D., Dahl, G.E., Mohamed, A.R., Jaitly, N., Senior, A., Vanhoucke, V., Nguyen, P., Sainath, T.N., et al.: Deep neural networks for acoustic modeling in speech recognition: the shared views of four research groups. IEEE Sig. Process. Mag. **29**(6), 82–97 (2012)
12. Hitam, M.S., Awalludin, E.A., Yussof, W.N.J.H.W., Bachok, Z.: Mixture contrast limited adaptive histogram equalization for underwater image enhancement. In: 2013 International Conference on Computer Applications Technology (ICCAT), pp. 1–5. IEEE (2013)
13. Hussain, F., Jeong, J.: Visibility enhancement of scene images degraded by foggy weather conditions with deep neural networks. J. Sens. **16**, 1–9 (2016)
14. Iqbal, K., Abdul Salam, R., Osman, M., Talib, A.Z., et al.: Underwater image enhancement using an integrated colour model. IAENG Int. J. Comput. Sci. **32**(2), 239–244 (2007)
15. Jaffe, J.S.: Computer modeling and the design of optimal underwater imaging systems. IEEE J. Oceanic Eng. **15**(2), 101–111 (1990)
16. Jaffe, J.S.: Enhanced extended range underwater imaging via structured illumination. Opt. Express **18**(12), 12328–12340 (2010)
17. Krizhevsky, A., Sutskever, I., Hinton, G.E.: Imagenet classification with deep convolutional neural networks. In: Advances in Neural Information Processing Systems, pp. 1097–1105 (2012)
18. Mai, J., Zhu, Q., Wu, D., Xie, Y., Wang, L.: Back propagation neural network dehazing. In: 2014 IEEE International Conference on Robotics and Biomimetics (ROBIO), pp. 1433–1438. IEEE (2014)
19. McAfee, A., Brynjolfsson, E., Davenport, T.H., Patil, D., Barton, D.: Big data. The management revolution. Harvard Bus. Rev. **90**(10), 61–67 (2012)
20. Raimondo, S., Silvia, C.: Underwater image processing: state of the art of restoration and image enhancement methods. EURASIP J. Adv. Sig. Process. **2010**, 746052 (2010)
21. Roser, M., Dunbabin, M., Geiger, A.: Simultaneous underwater visibility assessment, enhancement and improved stereo. In: 2014 IEEE International Conference on Robotics and Automation (ICRA), pp. 3840–3847. IEEE (2014)
22. Tang, K., Yang, J., Wang, J.: Investigating haze-relevant features in a learning framework for image dehazing. In: 2014 IEEE Conference on Computer Vision and Pattern Recognition (CVPR), pp. 2995–3002. IEEE (2014)
23. Torres-Méndez, L.A., Dudek, G.: Color correction of underwater images for aquatic robot inspection. In: Rangarajan, A., Vemuri, B., Yuille, A.L. (eds.) EMMCVPR 2005. LNCS, vol. 3757, pp. 60–73. Springer, Heidelberg (2005). doi:10.1007/11585978_5
24. Treibitz, T., Schechner, Y.Y.: Active polarization descattering. IEEE Trans. Pattern Anal. Mach. Intell. **31**(3), 385–399 (2009)
25. Vasilescu, I., Detweiler, C., Rus, D.: Color-accurate underwater imaging using perceptual adaptive illumination. Auton. Robots **31**(2–3), 285–296 (2011)
26. Williams, S.B., Pizarro, O.R., Jakuba, M.V., Johnson, C.R., Barrett, N.S., Babcock, R.C., Kendrick, G.A., Steinberg, P.D., Heyward, A.J., Doherty, P.J., et al.: Monitoring of benthic reference sites: using an autonomous underwater vehicle. IEEE Robot. Autom. Mag. **19**(1), 73–84 (2012)
27. Zhu, Q., Mai, J., Shao, L.: A fast single image haze removal algorithm using color attenuation prior. IEEE Trans. Image Process. **24**(11), 3522–3533 (2015)

A Deep Learning Approach to Handwritten Number Recognition

Victoria Ruiz, Maria T. Gonzalez de Lena, Jorge Sueiras, Angel Sanchez, and Jose F. Velez(✉)

Universidad Rey Juan Carlos, c/Tulipan sn, Mostoles, Madrid, Spain
{victoria.ruiz.parrado,mariateresa.gonzalezdelena,jorge.sueiras, angel.sanchez,jose.velez}@urjc.es

Abstract. Nowadays, Deep Learning is one of the most popular techniques which is used in several fields like handwriting text recognition. This paper presents our propose for a handwritten digit sequences recognition system. Our system, based in two stage model, is composed by Convolutional Neural Networks and Recurrent Neural Networks. Moreover, it is trained using on-demand scheme to recognize numbers from digits of the MNIST dataset. We will see that, with these training samples is not necessary segment or normalize the input images. Average recognition results were on 88,6% of accuracy in numbers of variable-length, between 1 and 10 digits. This accuracy is independent on the number length. Moreover, in most of the wrongly predicted numbers there was only one digit error.

Keywords: Handwritten character recognition · Synthetic number database · Advanced convolutional neural networks · Recurrent Neural Networks · Deep learning

1 Introduction

Handwriting style is a personal behavior characteristic which can differentiate between individuals and consequently can be used as a biometric modality. Handwriting text recognition (HTR) is still an open research problem today due the multiple difficulties to be analyzed in an automatic form [18,23]. For example, the intrapersonal and interpersonal variabilities in handwriting make the task quite difficult. That means not everyone writes with the same style and the same person could not write in the same way at each time and situation. Also, it is very common to capture some noise in the image that could produce classification errors while performing this task in an automatic method.

The handwriting recognition problem uses two approaches based on data capture process: on-line and off-line recognition [18]. The data available in the on-line recognition are time series of coordinates, representing the movement of the pen. In the off-line case the data are only an image of the text. Because the data available are more detailed and noised free, the on-line recognition

J.M. Ferrández Vicente et al. (Eds.): IWINAC 2017, Part II, LNCS 10338, pp. 193–202, 2017.
DOI: 10.1007/978-3-319-59773-7_20

obtains generally better results [19]. For the off-line case, there are also two main approaches: holistic and segmentation-based ones [15,22]. While in the holistic (or global) approach the classification is carried out using directly the whole word image, in the segmentation-based case, the isolated characters are extracted before performing their classification.

Typically, a HTR system has five main steps: pre-processing, segmentation, feature extraction, training, recognition and post-processing [17]. In the segmentation-based case and previous to character extraction, it is a frequent practice to normalize the text images to reduce their variability in order to achieve better recognition results. Although there are several techniques which handle isolated characters, and some new techniques which recognize large vocabulary with the help of some dictionaries or grammars [12], there are still few works that consider the problem of recognizing long character sequences. In this paper, we present a new method for such handwriting text recognition problem, which is focused on the off-line approach and does not need from any normalization or segmentation stage. Our approach was tested using variable-length digit sequence images.

Despite the fact that there are many improvements in the HTR problem, especially in the on-line case, there are still several open problems to be solved [12,17]. The possible high variability in the text words and the image noise presence must also be taken into account. In particular, length variability in words may difficult the character segmentation task, and the presence of noise can cause the system wrongly isolates some characters.

One additional important problem we have to deal with, is the variable length of words (or digits in numbers). There exist some systems which produce very good recognition results on isolated characters (or digits), but their performance drop down when dealing with large words or numbers [12]. For example, different methods are applied to classify isolated characters [7,17] from the MNIST database [14]. One of these latest methods, proposed by Ciresan et al. [5], achieved a 99.77% of accuracy. These methods used Hidden Markov Models (HMM), Neural Netwoks (NN), Hybrid NN/HMM and Convolutional Networks (CNN) as classifiers [2,16]. More recently, some other proposals [9] aimed to recognize complete text words using Recurrent Neural Networks (RNN) [3,7,9] such as the Long-Short Term Memory (LSTM) [10,11], complemented with some types of language models.

Normalizing the images is one of the most common way to reduce the variability in handwritten text. As it is shown by Arica et al. [1], skew normalization and baseline extraction, slant normalization, size normalization and contour smoothing are some of the most common techniques for reducing text variability and simplify the practical problem. In our approach, for the sake of producing a more realistic solution, we avoid this image normalization through increasing the training database through data augmentation. Moreover, we generate the inputs 'on demand' from a handwritten numbers database, as it will be explained in the next Section.

For the above referred normalization-based methods, after that step a segmentation algorithm is applied in order to get isolated characters. One of the most used ones consists on splitting the words into connected components which are classified as characters [15]. As our method does need neither from normalization nor segmentation, the text and noise variability conditions will be higher and this makes it more difficult the recognition task as happens in many practical situations.

In this paper, we describe a new deep learning approach for handwritten number recognition. Our method has been successfully tested on large numbers (i.e. long chains of digits). The proposed system learns by an 'on demand' basis which generate an infinite number of samples, instead of using a standard fixed-length database.

The paper is organized as follows. Section 2 describes the building of our experimental number database produced using the MNIST dataset. Section 3 outlines the system architecture for the considered problem. Experimental results are presented and explained in Sect. 4. Finally, the last Section summarizes the conclusions of this work.

2 Handwritten Digit Database

The samples used to train and test our system are built on the well-known MNIST database [6]. This database consists of by 70.000 digit images, which of 60.000 are used for training and the remaining 10.000 are for tests. All of these samples are black and white images, centered and size-normalized (with 28×28 pixels). We use these images to create the new sample, as follows:

1. By combining randomly the MNIST digits to create variable-length numbers, a of digits which will be the data of our sample datasets.
2. Move and transform the generated sequenced in order to add variability.

Figure 1 shows the process of sample generation.

2.1 Generation of Sequence Numbers from MNIST Database

To develop our handwriting number recognition system, we have created a generator of numbers from the MNIST database images. In this generator it is possible to choose the numbers length with a maximum of 10 digits, the number of classes which are in the sequence, and the transformation applied to the images. So that:

1. First, the number of digits of the sequence is randomly chosen and an empty image of size 28×280 is created.
2. Second, the allowed digit classes are also randomly chosen.
3. Third, the following processes are performed as many times as number of digits the new sequence has:

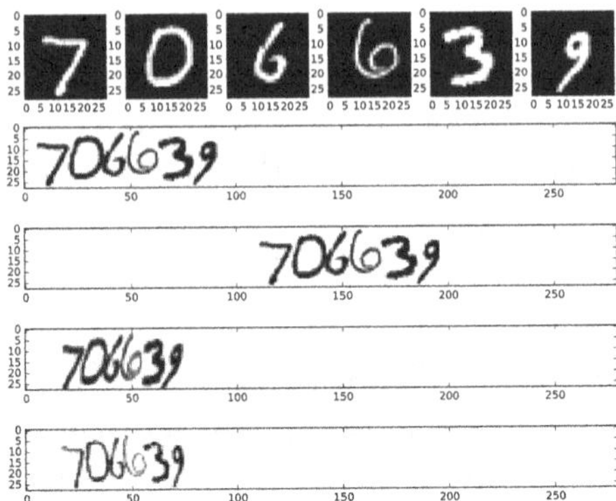

Fig. 1. Example of a generated number sequence. The first row shows the original MNIST digits, the second row show a generated digit sequence and the rest of rows shows some transformations which can be applied to the image sequence

   (a) Random choice of the digit between the allowed classes
   (b) The new digit is added to the 28×280 image. This digit is placed as close as possible to the remaining digits of the sequence
4. As the digits are joined without spaces, the width of the created number is less than 280, so it is possible to move the image around the free pixels. So that, if it is chosen, the digits can be randomly moved.

2.2 Transformations Applied to Images

To add variability and produce a potentially infinite sample, some transformations are applied to the created image. The generator can choose whether the following transformations are applied:

1. Affine transformations to the right or to the left in order to rotate the images.
2. Increase the scale of the digits by width or height.
3. Morphological erosions.
4. Morphological dilations.
5. Translate the positions of digits.

After these transformations a random background (with pixels between 240–255 gray values) is added to avoid the noise which is produced when a transformation is applied. Note that it is possible to apply more than one transformation into the same generated sequence. On the other hand, in the translation transformation, the sequence will be displaced to the right randomly or by a fixed scalar. Moreover, as we explain in the next Section, our system has two different models: a convolution neural network which is used to feature extraction, and a recurrent neural network which predicts the digit ordering of the sequence. In the convolution model the random translate transformation has been applied, while in the recurrent model the images were moved 8 pixels.

3 Classification

The proposed number recognition system (see Fig. 2) includes two main steps: (1) Convolutional Neural Network model (CNN) to obtain image digit features and (2) Long-Short Term Memory (LSTM) Network to recognize the digit sequence. Convolutions for feature extraction have been used formerly in works like Bluche [2] who applied them to predict the states of a Hidden Markov Model. In our system, we get the digits features by predicting the existing digits of the sequence in a CNN model based on the VGG architecture [21]. For that, the target of that model is an array of size 10 which outputs 1 if the number is in the image or 0, otherwise. Note that the CNN model only detect the presence of digits classes in the number sequence, but not their positions.

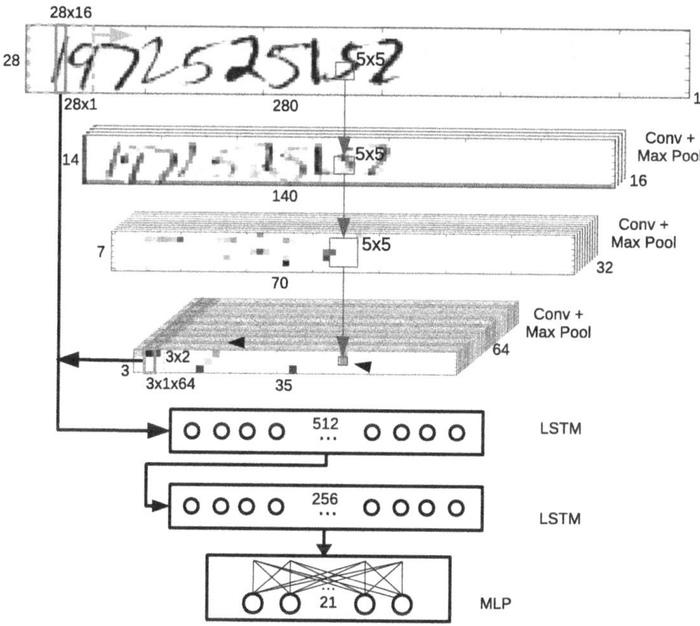

Fig. 2. General model architecture. Blue boxes correspond to the convolution masks. Green boxes correspond to the sliding window. Red boxes correspond to the tensors which are the inputs of the LSTM model. (Color figure online)

As the positions of the digits are important to get the number, a LSTM model placed at the output of the CNN model is applied to perform local predictions about positions of existing digits in the number. Moreover, to distinguish two or more consecutive identical digits, we transform each class in two classes. Instead of having class 0 we have class 'beginning of 0' (b0) and class 'end of 0' (e0), and so on with the rest of the classes. With this type of target, when we present the sequence 22 to the LSTM model, we get the output 'b2e2b2e2'. We use also and extra class which correspond to the 'blank' class, which is similar to Graves et al. uses [8]. Figure 2 shows the general model architecture of our system.

The CNN model is a simpler version of the VGG architecture and aims to predict just if a digit is present or not in the number. This model was trained in an incremental process where the number of classes were increased slowly. The training process of the CNN model had 10 phases:

1. In the first phase, the inputs had a variable length between 1 and 10. Moreover, each input only contains random patterns from one class. This first phase ended when the training error was lower than 1%.
2. In the second phase, the process was the same, but random patterns were chosen between 1 or 2 different classes.
3. We repeat this incremental process until the last phase, where all the classes could be present in the numbers.

Table 1 shows examples of the CNN model inputs. As it is shown in Fig. 3, the final CNN model is composed by three groups of two convolution layers followed by a sub sampling (in particular max-pooling) layer, and two dense layers. In the first dense layer we used a dropout [20] of 60%. All the convolutions layers have a stride of 3×3 (which is equivalent to have a stride of 5×5 due to there are two consecutive convolution layers) and zero-padding. Also, all the neurons have ReLU [13] as activation function.

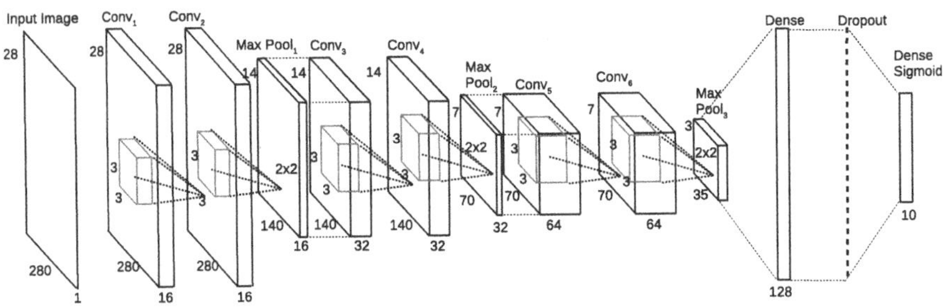

Fig. 3. CNN model architecture.

By the other hand, the inputs of the LSTM model come from a sliding window over the original image merged with the last convolutional layer of the CNN model. We chose the last convolutional layer, instead of the last dense layer, because we are interested in the local information obtained from the convolutions. To build the LSTM inputs, we scored each image and reshape the obtained $64 \times 3 \times 35$ tensors in a 192×35 vector. In the next step, we merge the convolutions with the original image, joining each column of the image (28 values) with its corresponding columns of the convolution layers (192), obtaining 220 values. Finally, each input sample for the LSTM training process is composed of a sliding window of 16 columns, and so of 220×16 values.

The LSTM model that we built has two LSTM layers and a dense layer as it is shown at the bottom of Fig. 2. For each input tensor, the output is a new tensor of 1×21. As the original image has a width of 280, we append the 280 outputs to get the output sequence of 'beginnings' and 'ends'. The final step is to convert the 'beginning-end' label sequence in the final digit sequence. Note that, the final softmax output give us different possibilities for each class, and we need only one. So, we select the combination that maximize the sum of the selected classes, taking into account two rules:

1. If there is a 'beginning' of a number it is necessary to have an 'end' of the same number.
2. The 'blank' can be applied only after an 'end'.

Table 1. Example of phases. In every phase the generated numbers have between 1 and 10 digits. In Phase 1 there is only 1 different class, in Phase 2 two classes, and so on until phase 10 where all the classes are can be present in the same sequence.

Phase	Example 1	Example 2
Phase 1		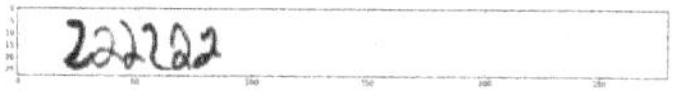
Phase 2		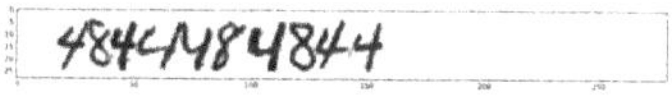
Phase 3		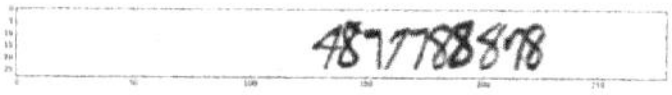
...	...	...
Phase 10		

4 Experimental Results

Experiments have been carried out in two stages. In the first one, the CNN model was trained in several phases as it was explained in previous Section. We use a learning rate of 0.01 and the Stochastic Gradient Descent (SGD) [4] algorithm as optimizer and we need 60 epochs to train the whole model. To achieve the error classification we build a test number sequence dataset with 1000 images, which was created with the same algorithm as in the training case, except that in the test case no transformation was applied on images. Figure 4(a) shows an example of an original test image, and the scores that we got with the CNN+LSTM model. In the example is how increase the 'beginning' and the 'end' of each number.

The CNN model produced 99% Character Accuracy Rate (CAR) and a 90% of Sequence Accuracy Rate (SAR), which means that in 90% of the cases all the digits were correctly found. By the other hand, in the global CNN+LSTM model, there is a 98,4% of accuracy in CAR and an 88,6% of accuracy in SAR. To measure how the CNN model improves the final results, we trained a LSTM model with the same architecture, but only with the original image as input data. The results were a few worse than the presented system as we obtained 86,2% of accuracy in SAR. These results are shown by Table 2.

Figure 4(b) shows the comparison between a perfect model, which would predict successfully all the numbers, and our system. This graphic is built sorting the tested numbers by their confidence and counting how many numbers are successfully predicted. It is seen that if we would predict just the 20% of the tested numbers with more confidence all the digits would be successfully classified. If we would predict the numbers with less confidence numbers, the accuracy would start to decrease until the 88,6% (i.e. the accuracy that we achieved when owe predicted all the numbers of the test sample).

Finally, in Fig. 5(a) shows the distribution of the edit distance on the test numbers. It shows that 88,6% of the tested numbers have 0 as edit distance

Table 2. Summary of recognition results of our system for isolated digits (CAR column) and variable-length numbers (SAR column)

	CAR	SAR
CNN+ LSTM model	98,4%	88,6%
Only LSTM	98,0%	86,2%

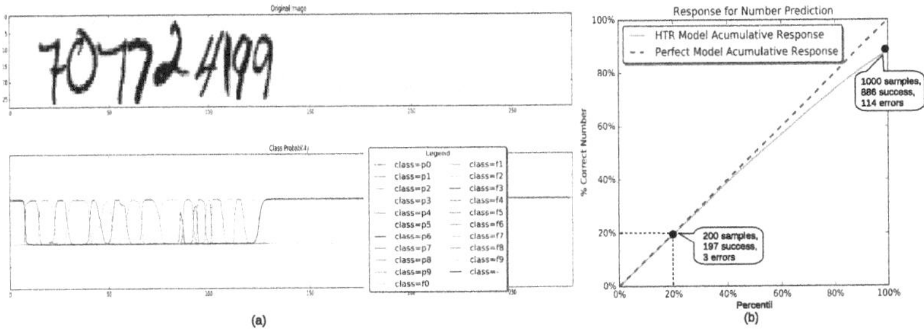

Fig. 4. (a) Example of an test image and their scores with the CNN+LSTM model. (b) Comparison between the accumulative response in a perfect model and our system.

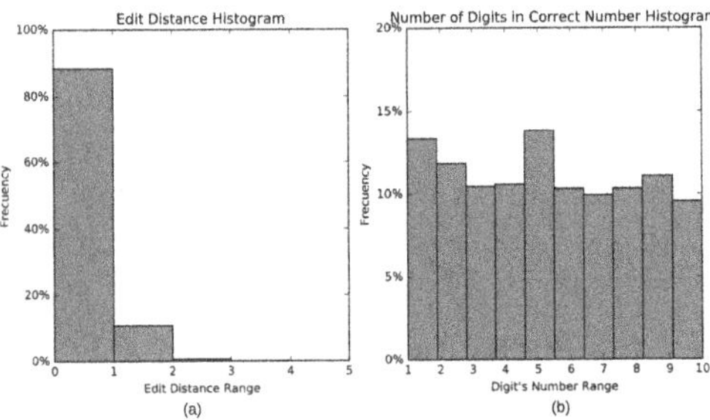

Fig. 5. Recognition results: (a) frequency of tested numbers by their edit distance and (b) frequency of well classified test number by their number length

(that means that they were correctly predicted), an 11% have edit distance of 1 (and just 1 digit were wrongly predicted), and a 0.4% have han edit distance of 2 or more. Figure 5(b) shows that the distribution of the successfully recognized numbers is uniform over the number length. So that, it was not relevant the number of digits in the sequences for our classifications results.

5 Conclusion

This paper describes a new automatic system for recognizing numbers of variable length. This system is based on deep learning neural models and was trained using an 'on demand' scheme to produce numbers using digit images of the MNIST dataset. We avoid the normalization step of many handwriting recognition systems. Moreover, our solution does not need to segment the digits and classifies the whole sequence as a number. Our model architecture was divided in two steps. In the first step a Convolutional Neural Network (CNN) model was trained to extract the digit features. This model was trained in several phases where the number of digits and classes were increased as well as the architecture of the model. In the second step, the convolutions were used with the original image by a LSTM model in order to predict the beginning and the end of each digit. Finally, the obtained digit sequence was transformed in the recognized number. Using this system, an 88,2% of the test numbers were correctly predicted. Moreover, we noticed that the lengths of the numbers do not influence in the classification and, when a number was misclassified, only one digit of it was wrongly predicted.

In the future, we would like to improve these models for longer numbers as well as to train them for arbitrary types of sequence of characters.

Acknowledgements. This work was funded by the Spanish Ministry of Economy and Competitiveness under grant number TIN2014-57458-R.

References

1. Arica, N., Yarman-Vural, F.T.: An overview of character recognition focused on off-line handwriting. Syst. Man Cybern. **31**(2), 216–233 (2001)
2. Bluche, T., Ney, H., Kermorvant, C.: Feature extraction with convolutional neural networks for handwritten word recognition. In: 12th International Conference on Document Analysis and Recognition, pp. 285–289 (2013)
3. Bluche, T., Ney, H., Kermorvant, C.: A comparison of sequence-trained deep neural networks and recurrent neural networks optical modeling for handwriting recognition. In: Besacier, L., Dediu, A.-H., Martín-Vide, C. (eds.) SLSP 2014. LNCS, vol. 8791, pp. 199–210. Springer, Cham (2014). doi:10.1007/978-3-319-11397-5_15
4. Bottou, L., Bousquet, O.: The tradeoffs of large scale learning. Adv. Neural Inf. Process. Syst. **20**, 161–168 (2008)
5. Ciresan, D., Meier, U., Schmidhuber, J.: Multi-column deep neural networks for image classification. Conf. Comput. Vis. Pattern Recognit. **2012**, 3642–3649 (2012)

6. Deng, L.: The MNIST database of handwritten digit images for machine learning research. In: IEEE Signal Processing Magazine, pp. 141–142 (2012)
7. Graves, A., Eck, D., Beringer, N., Schmidhuber, J.: Isolated digit recognition with LSTM recurrent networks. In: First International Workshop on Biologically Inspired Approaches to Advance Information Technology (2003)
8. Graves, A., Fernandez, S., Gomez, F., Schmidhuber, J.: Connectionist temporal classification: labelling unsegmented sequece data with recurrent neural networks. In: International Conference on Machine Learning, pp. 369–376 (2006)
9. Graves, A., Schmidhuber, J.: Offline handwriting recognition with multidimensional recurrent neural networks. Adv. Neural Inf. Process. Syst. **21**, 545–552 (2009)
10. Graves, A., Liwicki, M., Fernandez, S., Bertolami, R., Bunke, H., Schmidhuber, J.: A novel connectionist system for improved unconstrained handwriting recognition. IEEE Trans. Pattern Anal. Mach. Intell. **31**(5), 855–868 (2014)
11. Hochreiter, S., Schmidhuber, J.: Long short-term memory. Neural Comput. **9**(8), 1735–1780 (1997)
12. Koerich, A.L., Sabourin, R., Suen, C.Y.: Large vocavulary off-line handwriting recognition: a survey. Pattern Anal. Appl. **6**(2), 97–121 (2003)
13. Krizhesvky, A., Sutskever, I., Hinton, G.E.: ImageNet classification with deep convolutional neural networks. In: 26th Advances in Neural Information Processing Systems (NIPS), pp. 1097–1105 (2012)
14. LeCun, Y., Cortes, C., Burges, C.J.C.: The MNIST database of handwritten digits. http://yann.lecun.com/exdb/mnist (1998)
15. Lu, Y., Sridhar, M.: Character segmentation in handwritten words-an overview. Pattern Recognit. **29**(1), 77–96 (1995)
16. Matan, O., Burges, C.J.C., LeCun, Y., Denker, J.S.: Multi-digit recognition using a space displacement neural network. Neural Inf. Process. Syst. **4**, 488–495 (1992)
17. Patel, M., Thakkar, S.P.: Handwritten character recognition in english: a survey. Int. J. Adv. Res. Comput. Commun. Eng. **4**(2), 345–350 (2015)
18. Plamondon, R., Srihari, S.N.: On-line and off-line handwriting recognition: a comprehensive survey. Pattern Anal. Mach. Intel. IEEE Trans. **22**(1), 63–84 (2000)
19. Seiler, R., Schenkel, M., Eggimann, F.: Off-line cursive handwriting recognition compared with on-line recognition. In: Proceedings of the International Conference on Pattern Recognition IV-7472, pp. 505–509 (1996)
20. Srivastava, N., Hinton, G., Krizhesvsky, A., Sutskever, I., Salakhutdinov, R.: Dropout: a simple way to prevent neural networks from overfitting. J. Mach. Learn. Res. **15**, 1929–1958 (2014)
21. Symonian, K., Zisserman, A.: Very deep convolutional networks for large scale image recognition. In: 3rd International Conference on Learning Representation, pp. 1–14 (2015)
22. Vinayakumar, R., Paul, V.: A survey on recognition and analysis of handwrittten document. Int. J. Comput. Sci. Eng. Technol. **6**, 19–23 (2016)
23. Vinciarelli, A.: A survey on off-line cursive script recognition. Pattern Recognit. **35**(7), 1433–1446 (2002)

Deep Learning-Based Approach for Time Series Forecasting with Application to Electricity Load

J.F. Torres, A.M. Fernández, A. Troncoso, and F. Martínez-Álvarez(✉)

Division of Computer Science, Universidad Pablo de Olavide, 41013 Seville, Spain
{jftormal,amfergom}@alu.upo.es, {ali,fmaralv}@upo.es

Abstract. This paper presents a novel method to predict times series using deep learning. In particular, the method can be used for arbitrary time horizons, dividing each predicted sample into a single problem. This fact allows easy parallelization and adaptation to the big data context. Deep learning implementation in H2O library is used for each subproblem. However, H2O does not permit multi-step regression, therefore the solution proposed consists in splitting into h forecasting subproblems, being h the number of samples to be predicted, and, each of one has been separately studied, getting the best prediction model for each subproblem. Additionally, Apache Spark is used to load in memory large datasets and speed up the execution time. This methodology has been tested on a real-world dataset composed of electricity consumption in Spain, with a ten minute frequency sampling rate, from 2007 to 2016. Reported results exhibit errors less than 2%.

Keywords: Deep learning · Time series · Forecasting · Apache spark

1 Introduction

Time series forecasting is a task of utmost relevance that can be found in almost any scientific discipline. Electricity is not an exception, and much work is devoted to predict both demand and prices [10]. Achieving accurate demand forecasts is critical since it can be used in production planning, inventory management, or even in evaluating capacity needs. In other words, it may lead to insufficient or excessive energy production, thus reducing profits.

A novel approach based on deep learning [5,12] is proposed in this article to forecast time series, with application to electricity demand. Deep learning is an emerging branch of machine learning that extends artificial neural networks. One of the main drawbacks that classical artificial neural networks exhibit is that, with many layers, its training typically becomes too complex [9]. In this sense, deep learning consists of a set of learning algorithms to train artificial neural networks with a large number of hidden layers. Deep learning models are also sensitive to initialization and much attention must be paid at this stage [13].

The main idea underlying the method is dividing the number of samples to be simultaneously predicted (horizon of prediction) into different subproblems.

J.M. Ferrández Vicente et al. (Eds.): IWINAC 2017, Part II, LNCS 10338, pp. 203–212, 2017.
DOI: 10.1007/978-3-319-59773-7_21

Every subproblem is independently solved making use of different pieces of the historical data. The implementation of the deep learning method used is that of the well-known H2O library, which is open source and designed for a distributed environment [2].

It is worth noting that this strategy is particularly suitable for parallel implementations and it is ready to be used for big data environments. Furthermore, in order to speed up the whole process, Apache Spark is used to load the data in memory.

The performance of the approach has been assessed in real-world datasets. Electricity consumption in Spain has been used as case study, by analyzing data from 2007 to 2016 in the usual 70–30% training-test sets structure.

The rest of the paper is structured as follows. Relevant related works are discussed in Sect. 2. The methodology proposed in this paper is introduced and described in Sect. 3. The results of applying the approach to Spanish electricity data are reported and discussed in Sect. 4. Finally, the conclusions drawn are summarized in Sect. 5.

2 Related Works

This section reviews relevant works in the context of time series forecasting and deep learning.

Some studies are currently applying deep learning to prediction problems. Ding et al. [4] proposed a method for event driven stock market prediction. They used a deep convolutional neural network, at a second stage, to model both short-term and long-term stock price fluctuations. Results were assessed on S&P 500 stock historical data.

A novel deep learning architecture for air quality prediction was first introduce in [8]. The authors evaluated spatio-temporal correlations by first applying a stacked autoencoder model for feature extraction. Comparisons to other models confirmed that the method achieved promising results.

A meaningful attempt to apply a data-driven approach to forecasting transportation demand can be found in [1]. In particular, a deep learning model to forecast bus ridership at the stop and stop-to-stop levels was there adopted. As main novelty, the authors claim that, for the first time, the method is only based on feature data.

Deep learning based studies can be found for classification as well. Image processing has been shown to be one of the most fruitful fields of deep learning application. A successful approach for image classification with deep convolutional neural networks was introduced in [7]. They classified 1.2 million high-resolution images achieving top errors in the ImageNet LSVRC-2010 contest.

The authors in [3] proposed a deep learning-based classifier for hyperspectral data. The hybrid method (it is also combined with principal component analysis and logistic regression) was applied to extract deep features for such kind of data, achieving competitive results.

Tabar and Halici [14] introduced an approach based on deep learning for classification of electroencephalography (EEG) motor imagery signals. In particular, the method combined convolutional neural networks and stacked autoencoders and showed to be competitive when compared to other existing techniques.

Finally, some works relating to electricity demand forecasting are also discussed. Talavera et al. [15] proposed a forecasting algorithm to deal with Spanish electricity data. The algorithm was developed under the Apache Spark which is an engine for large-scale data processing framework [16], and was applied to big data time series. Satisfactory results were reported.

Electricity demand profiles were discovered as initial step for forecasting purposes in [11]. Spanish data were also analyzed and, as happened in the afore discussed study, the method was designed to be able to evaluate big time series data. Relevant patterns were discovered, distinguishing between different seasons and days of the week.

Grolinger et at. [6] explored sensor-based forecasting in event venues, a scenario with typically large variations in consumption. They authors paid particular attention to the relevance of the size of the data and on the temporal granularity impact. Neural networks and support vector regression were applied to 15-minute frequency data for Ontario, Canada.

As it can been seen after the analysis of updated state-of-the-art, deep learning is being currently applied into a variety of problems. However, to the authors' knowledge, no method has been developed to forecast electricity-related time series and has been conceived for big data time series forecasting. Therefore, the conduction of this research is justified.

3 Methodology

This section describes the methodology proposed in order to forecast time series. Apache Spark has been used to load data in memory and a deep learning implementation in R language, within the H2O package, has been applied to forecast time series.

The objective of this study consists in predicting h next values for a time series, expressed as $[x_1,\ldots,x_t]$, being h the horizon of prediction, depending on a historical window composed of w values. This can be formulated as:

$$[x_{t+1}, x_{t+2}, \ldots, x_{t+h}] = f(x_t, x_{t-1}, \ldots, x_{t-w-1}) \quad (1)$$

where f is the model to be found in the training phase by the deep learning algorithm. However, the package chosen does not support the multivariate regression, therefore, multi-step forecasting is not supported either.

The solution for this is splitting the problem into h forecast subproblems, which can formulated as:

$$x_{t+1} = f_1(x_t, x_{t-1}, \ldots, x_{t-w-1}) \quad (2)$$
$$x_{t+2} = f_2(x_t, x_{t-1}, \ldots, x_{t-w-1}) \quad (3)$$
$$\ldots \quad (4)$$
$$x_{t+h} = f_h(x_t, x_{t-1}, \ldots, x_{t-w-1}) \quad (5)$$

That is, given w samples used as input for the deep learning algorithm, h values are simultaneously forecasted. Based on this formulation, each estimation is made separately, thus avoiding the consideration of previously predicted samples and, consequently, removing the error propagation. In other words, if the prediction of previous values would be used to predict the next value, the error would be higher because the error would be accumulated in each iteration of the prediction horizon. Also, to create a model for each h value could involve a higher computational cost than building just a model to predict all values.

The last step consists in obtaining the best model for each subproblem by applying deep learning and varying the number of hidden layers and neurons per layer. Once the training for each subproblem is complete, the test set is predicted.

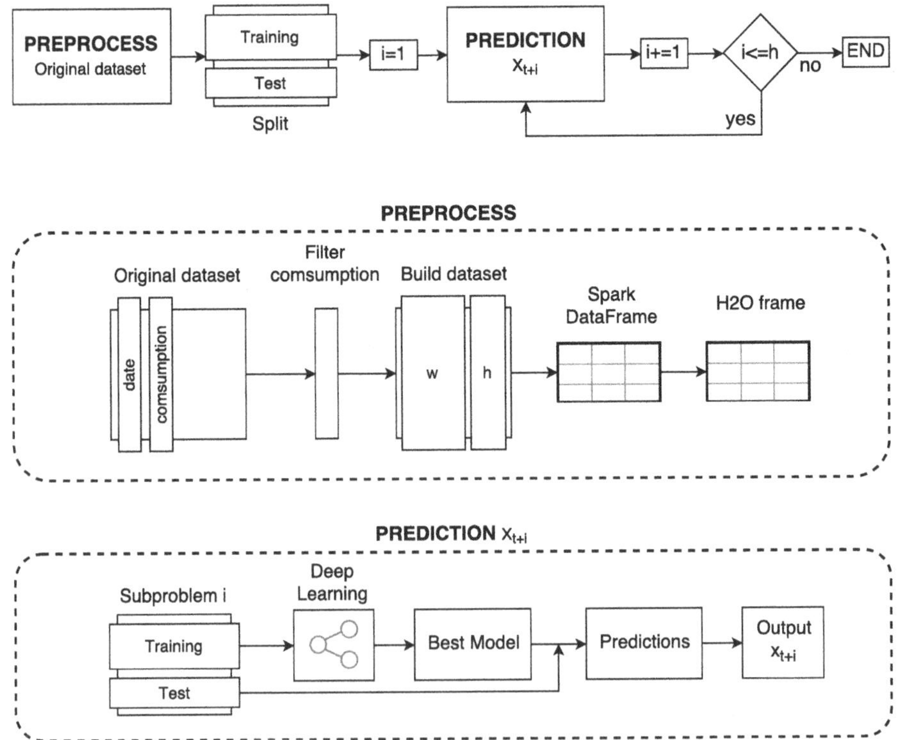

Fig. 1. Illustration of the proposed methodology.

Figure 1 shows the full study's flow, starting with input dataset and ending with aggregated output. It can be seen that, in its current implementation, an iterative strategy has been followed since each subproblem is solved after the previous one is done. However, it is easy to figure out that this strategy can be easily parallelized and adapted to a big data environment.

It is important to highlight that H2O frame can be created without Spark dataframe conversion, but this step allocates data in memory and makes the access more quickly. Also it is important to note that deep learning algorithm on H2O library has a lot of parameters to adjust the execution. In this study, some of this parameters have been used. They will be thoroughly discussed in Sect. 4.2

4 Results

As previously mentioned, a study to forecast a time series of electricity consumption has been conducted. This section presents the results obtained. First, Sect. 4.1 describes the dataset used for the study. Second, Sect. 4.2 provides the experimental setup carried out and, finally, Sect. 4.3 discusses results obtained.

4.1 Dataset Description

The dataset considered in this study provides electricity consumptions readings in Spain from January 2007 to June 2016 with a measure every 10 min, i.e., the time series is composed of 497832 measurements.

In study, the dataset was only filtered by consumption and redistributed in a matrix depending of the window size and prediction horizon. The values of these parameters were set to 168 and 24, respectively. After this preprocessing, the final dataset has 20736 rows and 192 columns into a 23.9 MB file which was recorded for further studies.

To perform the entire experimentation, the dataset has been split into 14515 instances for training (70%) and 6221 for test (30%).

4.2 Design of Experiments

In order to assess the performance of the algorithm, the well-known mean relative error (MRE) measure has been selected. For a matrix of data, the formula is:

$$MRE = \frac{1}{r * c} \sum_{i=1}^{r} \sum_{j=1}^{c} \frac{|v_{pred} - v_{actual}|}{v_{actual}} \tag{6}$$

where r and c represents the number of rows and columns on the test set, v_{pred} stands for the predicted values and v_{actual} for the actual values.

As discussed in previous sections, it is necessary to define and initialize several variables. Variable values have been set to:

1. The size of the window (w) represents the length of the historical data considered to predict the target subsequence. It has been set to 168, which represents 7 blocks of 4 h (1 day and 4 h, in total). This parameter was set during the training phase with values 24, 48, 72, 96, 120, 144 and 168, and was found to be the one with minimum error.
2. As for the prediction horizon (h), it was set to $h = 24$ (4 h). Considering a higher h would turn the problem into a long-term forecasting one, and some others consideration should then be taken into consideration.
3. To apply deep learning, it is necessary to set the number of hidden layers and number of neurons. The number of hidden layer was set to 3 and the number of neurons for each one was set to an interval ranging from 10 to 100 with a step of 10, using a validation set composed of the 30% of the training set. Then, only the best value was chosen for the analysis.
4. λ was set to 0.001. This parameter is used for regularization of the dataset.
5. Also, two different parameters were set to describe the adaptive rate. These were ρ and ϵ, which were set to 0.99 and $1.0E-9$, which are default values for those parameters, respectively.
6. The activation function chosen was the hyperbolic tangent function.
7. As for the distribution function, Poisson distribution was the one chosen.

These parameters were chosen based on several tests varying values. Some relevant results are shown in Table 1, in which it can be seen MRE values obtained for some parameters. For instance, Poisson distribution offers better results than other options.

Table 1. Errors varying deep learning parameters.

Lambda	Rho	Epsilon	Activation	Distribution	MRE (%)
1	0.9	1.0E-9	Tanh	Poisson	2.56
1	0.99	1.0E-9	Tanh	Poisson	2.43
1	0.999	1.0E-9	Tanh	Poisson	2.49
1	0.9	1.0E-9	Tanh	Gaussian	15.61
1	0.99	1.0E-9	Tanh	Gaussian	15.61
1	0.999	1.0E-9	Tanh	Gaussian	15.57
0.001	**0.99**	**1.0E-9**	**Tanh**	**Poisson**	**1.84**
1	0.99	1.0E-9	Tanh	Tweedie	4.21
10	0.99	1.0E-9	Tanh	Poisson	2.69
1	0.99	1.0E-9	Tanh	Huber	15.63
1	0.99	1.0E-9	Tanh	Laplace	15.63

The algorithm has been executed using the dataset described in Sect. 4.1. The computer used to complete this execution has been an Intel Core i7-5820K at 3.30 GHz, 15 MB cache, 12 cores and 16 GB of RAM memory working, under Ubuntu 16.04.

Finally, the dataset was loaded from Apache Spark to allocate it in memory instead of in disk, thus accessing to the data more efficiently and quickly.

4.3 Electricity Consumption Time Series Forecasting

This section describes the results obtained after applying the algorithm proposed to the dataset, which were described in Sect. 4.1 over the machine described in Sect. 4.2. This test provides a total of 20736 instances and 192 attributes, resulting in 149305 forecast values.

As forecasting are divided in h subproblems (in this case, h is 24), it is possible to use different neuron values in each subproblem to obtain smaller errors. In this study, it was decided to set the possible neurons combinations to 3 hidden layers, each one with a interval of neurons (10 to 100 with a step of 10), as discussed in the previous section. Table 2 shows the neuron configurations that are optimum for each subproblem:

Table 2. Optimum neurons configuration for each subproblem.

Subproblem	Hidden layers	Neurons	Error	Subproblem	Hidden layers	Neurons	Error
1	3	30	0.77	13	3	40	1.83
2	3	80	1.13	14	3	80	1.81
3	3	90	1.15	15	3	90	2.11
4	3	60	1.18	16	3	40	1.93
5	3	60	1.35	17	3	70	2.50
6	3	100	1.36	18	3	70	2.09
7	3	40	1.50	19	3	70	2.17
8	3	80	1.71	20	3	60	2.14
9	3	30	1.88	21	3	90	2.43
10	3	80	1.76	22	3	70	2.56
11	3	50	1.66	23	3	100	2.42
12	3	100	2.07	24	3	100	2.77

Table 2 summarizes the errors for each subproblem depending of the optimum number of neurons per layer. This error tends to increase as the subproblem increases because there exists a gap between the first sample in the historical data and the sample to be predicted, that is, there immediately after values of the target sample are missing and omitted during the forecasting process.

Using this configuration of neurons and the other deep learning parameter values mentioned in Sect. 4.2 the final value of MRE to predict the full data test has been 1.84%.

Figures 2 and 3 are depicted for illustrative purposes. They represent the best and the worst comparison between actual and predicted consumption on a

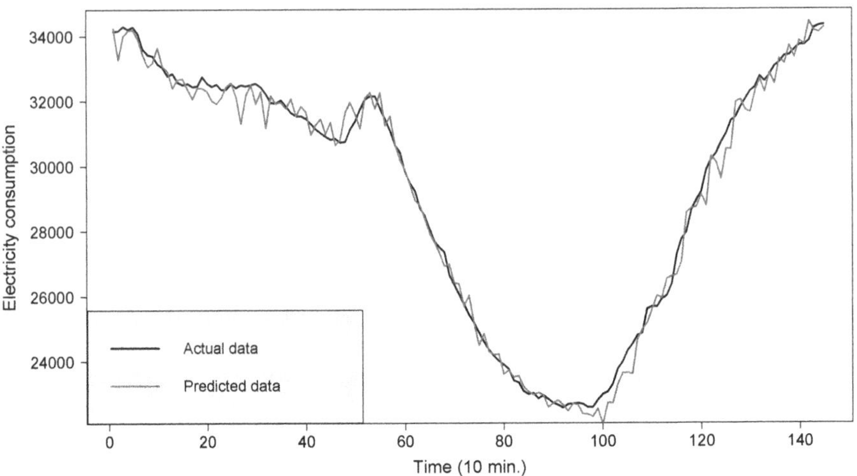

Fig. 2. The best forecast achieved for a full day.

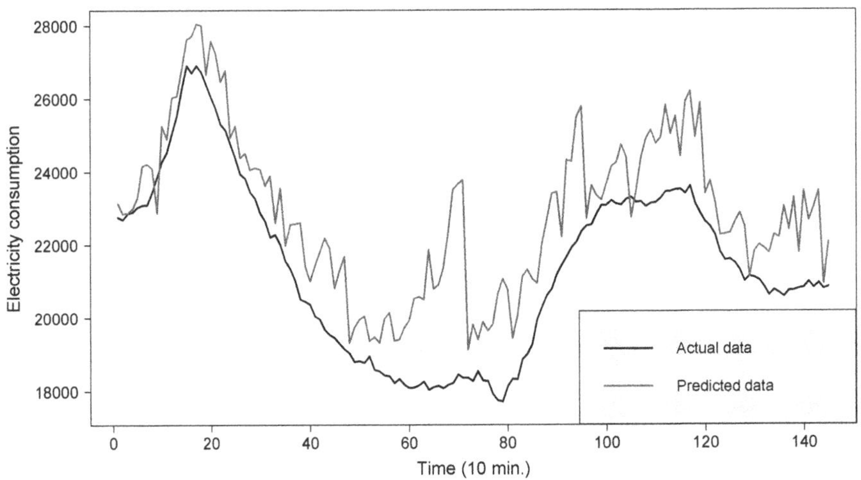

Fig. 3. The worst forecast achieved for a full day.

full day (144 measures) in the test set, respectively. It must be noted that some ripple in predicted data that is present not only in days depicted in the figures, but in almost the entire test set. This fact is justified because every sample is independently estimated. A feasible and successful post-processing could consist in the automatic application of any filter. In short, such a shape for the output must be further studied in future works.

5 Conclusions

This work describes a new approach to use deep learning methods as regressors and forecast the electricity consumption for the next twenty four values. It uses Apache Spark framework to load data in memory and the H2O library to apply the algorithm developed in R language. On this preliminary study, the results obtained can be considered satisfactory since errors are smaller than 2%. However, future works will be directed towards the improvement of the selection of the best parameters to forecast time series and to scale it to be applied to big data using a cluster of machines. Also, some post-processing seems to be necessary to reduce the ripple in forecasted values.

Acknowledgments. The authors would like to thank the Spanish Ministry of Economy and competitiveness and Junta de Andalucía for the support under projects TIN2014-55894-C2-R and P12-TIC-1728, respectively.

References

1. Baek, J., Sohn, K.: Deep-learning architectures to forecast bus ridership at the stop and stop-to-stop levels for dense and crowded bus networks. Appl. Artif. Intell. **30**(9), 861–885 (2016)
2. Candel, A., LeDell, E., Parmar, V., Arora, A.: Deep Learning with H2O. H2O.ai Inc., California (2017)
3. Chen, Y., Lin, Z., Zhao, X., Wang, G., Gu, Y.: Deep learning-based classification of hyperspectral data. IEEE J. Sel. Top. Appl. Earth Obs. Remote Sens. **8**(6), 2094–2107 (2014)
4. Ding, X., Zhang, Y., Liu, T., Duan, J.: Deep learning for event-driven stock prediction. In: Proceedings of the International Joint Conference on Artificial Intelligence, pp. 2327–2334 (2015)
5. Goodfellow, I., Bengio, Y., Courville, A.: Deep Learning. MIT Press, Cambridge (2016)
6. Grolinger, K., L'Heureux, A., Capretz, M.A.M., Seewald, L.: Energy forecasting for event venues: big data and prediction accuracy. Energy Buildings **112**, 222–233 (2016)
7. Krizhevsky, A., Sutskever, I., Hinton, G.E.: Imagenet classification with deep convolutional neural networks. In: Advances in Neural Information Processing Systems, pp. 1097–1105 (2012)
8. Li, X., Peng, L., Hu, Y., Shao, J., Chi, T.: Deep learning architecture for air quality predictions. Environ. Sci. Pollut. Res. Int. **23**, 22408–22417 (2016)
9. Livingstone, D.J., Manallack, D.T., Tetko, I.V.: Data modelling with neural networks: advantages and limitations. J. Comput.-Aided Mol. Des. **11**, 135–142 (1997)
10. Martínez-Álvarez, F., Troncoso, A., Asencio-Cortés, G., Riquelme, J.C.: A survey on data mining techniques applied to energy time series forecasting. Energies **8**, 1–32 (2015)
11. Pérez-Chacón, R., Talavera-Llames, R.L., Troncoso, A., Martínez-Álvarez, F.: Finding electric energy consumption patterns in big time series data. In: Omatu, S., et al. (eds.) Proceedings of the International Conference on Distributed Computing and Artificial Intelligence. AISC, vol. 474, pp. 231–238. Springer, Cham (2016)

12. Schmidhuber, J.: Deep learning in neural networks: an overview. Neural Netw. **61**, 85–117 (2015)
13. Sutskever, I., Martens, J., Dahl, G.E., Hinton, G.E.: On the importance of initialization and momentum in deep learning. In: Proceedings of the International Conference on Machine Learning, pp. 1139–1147 (2013)
14. Tabar, Y.R., Halici, U.: Deep learning-based classification of hyperspectral data. J. Neural Eng. **14**(1), 016003 (2016)
15. Talavera-Llames, R.L., Pérez-Chacón, R., Martínez-Ballesteros, M., Troncoso, A., Martínez-Álvarez, F.: A nearest neighbours-based algorithm for big time series data forecasting. In: Martínez-Álvarez, F., Troncoso, A., Quintián, H., Corchado, E. (eds.) HAIS 2016. LNCS, vol. 9648, pp. 174–185. Springer, Cham (2016). doi:10.1007/978-3-319-32034-2_15
16. Zaharia, M., Chowdhury, M., Franklin, M.J., Shenker, S., Stoica, I.: Spark: cluster computing with working sets. In: Proceedings of the International Conference on Hot Topics in Cloud Computing, pp. 1–10 (2010)

Deep Learning and Bayesian Networks for Labelling User Activity Context Through Acoustic Signals

Francisco J. Rodríguez Lera[1(✉)], Francisco Martín Rico[2], and Vicente Matellán[3]

[1] AI Robolab, University of Luxembourg, Luxembourg, Luxembourg
francisco.lera@uni.lu

[2] Universidad Rey Juan Carlos, Madrid, Spain

[3] Robotics Group, Universidad de León, León, Spain

Abstract. Context awareness in autonomous robots is usually performed combining localization information, objects identification, human interaction and time of the day. We think that gathering environmental sounds we can improve context recognition. With that purpose, we have designed, developed and tested an Environment Recognition Component (ERC) that provides an extra input to our Context-Awareness Component (CAC) and increases the rate of labeling correctly users' activities. First element, the Environment Recognition Component (ERC) uses convolutional neural networks to classify acoustic signals and providing information to the Context-Awareness Component (CAC) which infers the user activity using a hierarchical Bayesian network. The work described in this paper evaluates the results of the labeling process in two HRI scenarios: robot and user sharing room and robot, and when the human and the robot are in different rooms. The results showed better accuracy when the ERC uses acoustic signals.

1 Introduction

In order to produce natural responses to human behaviors, a robot should understand user's context. In this way to recognize and label the user activity is a cornerstone in HRI [21].

Activity context identification enhances the overall performance of the deliberative system [12] and favors a natural robot-user experience. Adding the ability to identify the context to autonomous robots will also help them to understand the environment where it inhabits and be aware of the situations that happens around it.

It is possible to define two procedures to infer and label the user activity. On the one hand, direct procedure, for instance a dialog system on the robot (through conversations or gestures) or using a software application connected to robot.

This work was partially supported by Spanish Ministry of Economy and Competitivity under grant TIN2016-76515-R.

J.M. Ferrández Vicente et al. (Eds.): IWINAC 2017, Part II, LNCS 10338, pp. 213–222, 2017.
DOI: 10.1007/978-3-319-59773-7_22

On the other hand, indirect procedure, that are based on inference approaches using sensors or wearables devices [21]. Nevertheless, these procedures assume that robots and humans share the physical space, but robots working in long time missions, as for instance home assistance, do not have to.

This challenge scenario could be faced through the deployment of new sensors in the robot platform or in the environment, notwithstanding, this research proposes a solution based on gathering environmental sounds using the robot's microphone, due to the microphone range surpass occupied room.

To the best of our knowledge, environmental acoustic information is mainly used for two tasks in the interaction with humans: automatic speech recognition (ASR), and environmental sound recognition (ESR). Both provides an important set of inputs for the decision taking of an autonomous robots. ASR is usually processed using Hidden Markov Models [19] and efficient programming search techniques [8]. ESR has been less faced in the literature [3], and although there are well defined taxonomies [14], they have not been extended and refined as ASR.

We present here a method for improving the activity-context labeling system recognizing acoustic sounds of the environment. The first contribution of this research is the performance improvement of a generic Context Recognition Component (CRC) based on localization, perception and timers caused by the use of the Environment Recognition Component (ERC).

The second contribution is the use of a convolutional neural network for classify the sound detected by the robot. First works on Convolutional Neural Networks (CNN) date back to the early 1980s [5], but nowadays are receiving a great attention [10]. CNN have been widely used for visual recognition contexts, and also successfully applied in music analysis [4], speech [2] and our domain, domestic sound classification [18].

The remainder of this paper is organized as follows. Section 2 presents the proposed framework integrated on an generic hybrid architecture. Section 3 shows the experiment setup and the description of the experiments to test it. Section 4 presents the discussion about the overall experiments. Finally conclusions and future work are presented in Sect. 5.

2 Context-Awareness Framework

In order to achieve the goals of this research we need to propose a framework able to be integrated in any control architecture. In that manner we propose a hybrid approach (Reactive-Deliberative) based on a motivational principles, this means that the decisions are not taking only with sensor information, but also internal motivations as battery status or robot role.

Very briefly, our framework is made up by two components levels: the ERC (Environment Recognition Component) and the Context-Awareness Component (CAC). Both components are deployed in the reactive subsystem which is divided in three blocks: data gathering, data preprocessing/fusion, and low-level reasoning. The ERC is a new element in the data gathering layer of the system, it works directly with low-level data from sensors along with perception nodes. The CAC

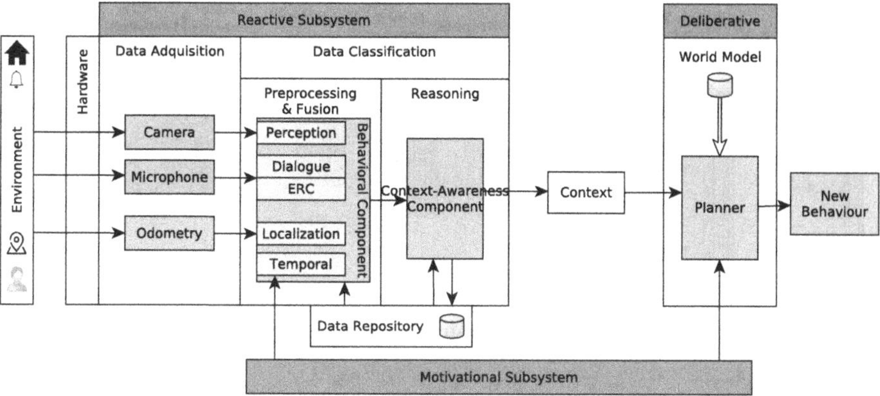

Fig. 1. ERC and CAC components integrated in a generic motivational architecture.

is a preprocessing-data fusion component that uses information from different data acquisition sources. It is deployed along with Natural Language Processing Components or Human recognition Components

Figure 1 shows the input stream associated to low-level sensors: perception, dialogue, ERC (Environment Recognition Component), localization and the timeline of the robot in the environment. Sections below describe in detail the environment-recognition component, in charge of the natural acoustic signal recognition and the CAC.

2.1 Environment Recognition Component

The Environment Recognition Component (ERC in Fig. 1) identifies the sounds perceived by robot microphones. It classifies the environmental sounds using a convolutional deep neural network. It has been developed to identify 14 different relevant sounds, associated to locations or scenarios, grouped into classes:

- General: Door bell, Entry Door, Phone, Door, Silence, Window
- Bathroom: Cistern, tap
- Kitchen: Induction, Fridge, Kettle, Microwave, Oven Alarm

We have used a convolutional neural network to implement this system, using both the sound and its variation. The topology of the neuronal network is shown in Fig. 2. It is composed by these layers:

- The input is a 60×200 matrix. Each of the elements of the matrix is a tuple of the spectrogram value and its variation in time (delta).
- The first convolution ReLU (Rectified Linear Units [6]) layer of 80 filters of shape (57×6) and stride (1×1).
- A max pooling layer of shape (57×6) and stride (1×3).
- We use a dropout layer with probability of 0.5 to reduce over-fitting.

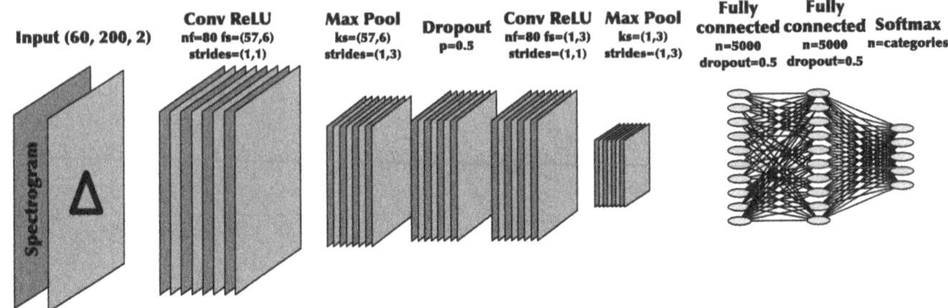

Fig. 2. Convolutional neural network topology

- A second convolution ReLU layer of 80 filters of shape (1×3) and stride (1×1).
- A second max pooling layer of shape (1×3) and stride (1×3).
- A second dropout layer with probability of 0.5.
- Two fully connected hidden layer of 5000 ReLUs each.
- A SoftMax output layer with a neuron for each category of sounds.

The network topology is similar to successful works, like [16], with some differences:

- A silence category which improves the classification results.
- Using a more appropriate duration in the input sound clips, attending to the characteristics of the sound and the robot operation.
- Implementation in TensorFlow [1], which let us to try a great variety of learning algorithms.
- Integration of the trained net in ROS nodes [17] to on board evaluation of sounds while robot operation.

The audio files from database are divided into clips of 2.95 s (200 frames). We think that this is enough to classify domestic sounds whose main characteristic is the monotonous repetition with different intervals, alarms or telephone tones.

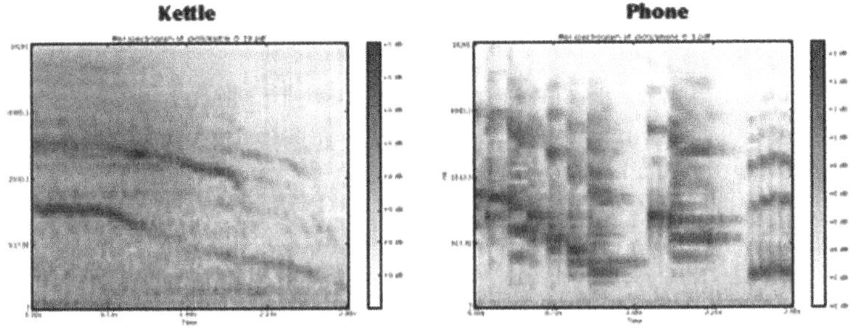

Fig. 3. Examples of normalized and log-scaled spectrograms.

These segments are processed to extract the input patterns for training and evaluating the net:

- Log-scaled mel-spectrograms *spec*, resampled to 22050 Hz and normalized with window size of 1024, hop length of 512 and 60 mel-bands, using the *librosa*[1] implementation. Figure 3 shows examples of the spectrogram of some of the categorized objects.
- The variation in time of this spectrogram $\Delta = \frac{\partial spec}{\partial t}$, computed with default settings.

2.2 Context Awareness Component (CAC)

Many researchers have faced the context awareness inference based on logic based models [13], ontologies [20] or probabilistic approaches [22]. We will formalize it using Bayesian methods [9,15], in particular, our inference system is supported on a Bayesian network approach.

A Bayesian network (BN) is a probabilistic directed acyclic graph generated from a group of random variables and their dependencies. Nodes (random variables) which are connected by arcs (conditional dependencies) compose it.

The definition of the variables of our BN is based on the American Occupational Therapy Association, Inc. (AOTA)[2]. We have determined three hierarchical layers for our BN: (1) class activities, (2) activities, and (3) Observations. These three levels of abstraction allowed us to identify and formalize the elements involved during the daily user activity, the notation used is:

- Observations: represent the information acquired by the robot. We denoted these nodes as; $O = \{o_1, o_2, \ldots, o_n\}$ where the n is the total number of observation defined in our system.
- Activities: These nodes identify the daily activities made by the users. For instance, meal preparation (cooking) or health management (medication control). Each activity is defined by a subset of observations: We denote this as: $P(A|O) = P(a_i|o_1, o_2, o_3, \ldots, o_n)$.
- Class Activities: These nodes identify the class of activity used in the system. In our case we used the eight AOTA class activity definition (ADLs, IADLs, rest,..).

The system works as follows: The robot processes a set of observations. Each activity has set of observations associated which different levels of probability, that identifies the user activity context. With this information we calculate the conditional distribution, the joint probability of all the nodes in our proposal is defined by:

$$P(ClassActivity, Activity, Observation) =$$
$$P(Observation) \cdot P(Activity|Observation) \cdot P(ClassActivity|Activity, Observation)$$

[1] librosa: v0.3.1 library by B. McFee et al., doi:10.5281/zenodo.12714.

[2] https://www.aota.org/.

At this point we have a set of contexts with different level of probabilities. This information is then used in the behavioral or the deliberative level to take decisions or generate new robot behaviors.

3 Experimental Validation

In the experiments, we wanted to measure the likelihood of positively labeling the user activity context using just classical methods based on Localization, Dialogue and Time of day (LDT) versus the use of environmental sound recognition in addition to the classical methods.

The robot assumes a place at home (kitchen or living room). In two cases, the user is talking to the robot, in a third one there is no user speaking with the robot. In each case, we trigger three of our previously defined acoustic signal during the dialogue scene between user and robot. If ERC has recognized the signal the context subsystem infers the context. In order to analyze the performance of the CAC using the LDT procedure we also performs the same test without using acoustic signals.

3.1 ERC

As we presented in Sect. 2.1, the dataset is composed by sound clips belonging to 14 categories of domestic sounds: door bell, cistern, tap, induction plaque, fridge, entry phone bell, kettle, phone, entry door bell, microwave alarm, door closing, window closing, silence and oven alarm. The clips of each category have different lengths, in a range of [55–371] seconds. To generate the segments of the input data, we have split the whole clip into 88.5% overlapping segments of 2.95 s, with a step of 1 s.

The dataset used for the training phase is balanced, so we use 52 segments (the size of the smaller category) of each category, 95% for training and 5% for validation.

As we previously mentioned, we used TensorFlow framework to train and evaluate the network. For the training process, we used a Stochastic Gradient Descent algorithm with a learning rate of 0.002 a learning rate decay of 0.96 with a decay step of 1000. The training took 14 h in a i7-4960HQ CPU 8 cores @ 2.60 GHz and 16 GB RAM computer for 300 epochs. The result is a net with an accuracy of 86%. The prediction result for the entire dataset is:

```
DB  CI   TA  IP   FR   EP   KE   PH   ED   MW   DO   WI   SI   OV
Door Bell [ 63  5    0    2    0    3    0    0    0    0    0    0    0    0  ]
Cistern   [ 3   162  0    0    0    0    0    0    0    1    0    0    0    0  ]
Tap       [ 3   9    555  3    0    0    62   0    1    0    10   5    2    0  ]
Induc Pla [ 0   0    0    301  0    0    0    0    0    0    0    0    0    0  ]
Fridge    [ 0   0    0    0    99   0    0    0    0    3    1    0    0    0  ]
Entry Pho [ 2   0    0    0    3    95   0    0    0    0    0    0    0    0  ]
Kettle    [ 0   0    0    16   1    0    183  0    0    0    0    0    0    0  ]
Phone     [ 0   0    0    0    0    0    0    104  0    0    0    0    0    0  ]
Entry Door[ 5   26   0    0    3    0    0    11   192  24   9    3    0    0  ]
Microwave [ 0   0    0    22   228  0    0    0    0    558  1    0    0    60 ]
Door      [ 0   0    0    0    0    0    0    0    0    0    224  0    0    0  ]
Window    [ 0   0    0    0    0    0    0    0    0    0    14   130  0    0  ]
Silence   [ 0   0    0    0    0    0    0    0    0    0    0    0    371  0  ]
Oven Alarm[ 0   0    0    0    0    0    0    0    0    0    10   0    3    184]
```

3.2 CAC

Having in mind @home competitions as RoboCup or ERL, we have been tried to formalize a set of scenarios where the dialogue, localization, time of day and acoustic sounds are involved. The proposal divides the tests in six scenarios: (1) and (4) the robot and human stayed at the same location and they have a conversation about an activity which can be performed in their location; (2) and (3) the robot and human stayed at the same place and they have a conversation about an activity which can be performed in other location at home; and (5) and (6) the robot and the human do not have a conversation nor share location context.

Under these six scenarios, the characteristics of the LDT+ Acoustic sounds are:

(a) Dialogue: we reduced the dialogue possibilities to just two, one related to cook something and one related with an upcoming visit.
(b) Localization: robot and user could stay in two places, kitchen and living room, or each one in one place.
(c) Time of day: we fixed the time at 12:00 PM.
(d) Acoustic sounds: we used the signals previously defined and recognized in the ERC section.

We defined three activity contexts: Meal (M) preparation context, that is the probabilities to be cooking something are high. Emergency context (E), the circumstances present a context where something is going wrong, so the user has to make a decision; and Social Interaction (I) context, meaning that the probabilities of interaction with other human are high.

We have used Elvira [11] to evaluate the inferences. Table 1 outlines the results. We have set a threshold to label the context. We have defined a base limit of 50%, under that value we do not recognize the case.

Table 1. Context classification results.

	Kitchen (Robot & Human)				Living Room (Robot & Human)			
Env. Signal	(O)	(F)	(D)	(-)	(O)	(F)	(D)	(-)
D:Dinner	*M*(99%)	*M*(97%)	*M*(97%)	*M*(97%)	*M*(98%)	M(15%)	M(15%)	M(15%)
	E(1%)	*E*(50%)	E(5%)	E(1%)	E(24%)	*E*(25%)	E(5%)	E(5%)
12:00pm	I(1%)	I(1%)	*I*(41%)	I(1%)	I(5%)	I(5%)	*I*(45%)	I(5%)
	Scenario 1				Scenario 2			
D:Visit	*M*(95%)	M(5%)	M(5%)	M(5%)	*M*(83%)	M(1%)	M(1%)	M(1%)
	E(24%)	*E*(50%)	E(5%)	E(1%)	E(24%)	E(25%)	E(5%)	E(5%)
12:00pm	*I*(94%)	*I*(94%)	*I*(98%)	*I*(94%)	*I*(95%)	*I*(95%)	*I*(99%)	*I*(95%)
	Scenario 3				Scenario 4			
Dialogue	Kitchen (Robot alone)				Living Room (Robot alone)			
D:(-)	*M*(95%)	M(5%)	M(5%)	M(1%)	*M*(83%)	M(1%)	M(1%)	M(1%)
	E(24%)	*E*(50%)	E(5%)	E(5%)	E(24%)	*E*(25%)	E(5%)	E(5%)
12:00pm	I(1%)	I(1%)	*I*(41%)	I(5%)	I(5%)	I(5%)	*I*(45%)	I(5%)
	Scenario 5				Scenario 6			

4 Discussion

The experiments in controlled scenarios have shown that the system is very reliable. It was able to successfully recognize the context more than 85% of the times even when random noise was added to the ambient.

In summary, we have developed a functional system for recognizing different acoustic signals in real world and we have identified two main issues. First, environmental noises as loud music or people shouting (this situation is common in robotics competitions) contaminates the ambient sound, thus it increases the number of false positives. Second, the microphone model and position in the robot is a key decision, for instance a directional microphone has drawbacks in indoors environments.

The context recognition component showed positive results in the six scenarios proposed (S1–S6) (Table 1). On the one hand, we have those cases where the robot is able to infer the context using LDT: scenarios S1, S3 and S4. It happens even when there is no acoustic signal triggered. The acoustic signal slightly improve the probability (they are depicted as dark gray cells): the oven increases a 2% the context probability in scenario S1; the doorbell increases 4% context probability in scenario in scenarios S3 and S4. In addition, the acoustic signals provided extra information about the human activity in these scenarios (black cells), with a likelihood within our threshold (fifty percent or more).

We have defined and additional case called *valuable information*. These cases are produced when the final probability is within a threshold between 25% and 50%. Even though these cases should not be used directly to the decision making process, it can be used to generate alternative sub-tasks, for instance the robot can ask about this special case.

Scenario S1 under doorbell signal presents this situation (41%), the robot should ask about if the user is cooking because it is going to receive visits, thus it is able to increase or decrease this probability.

On the other hand, we find those cases where the robot is not able to infer the situation using LDT method: scenarios S2, S5, S6. These cases show overall best results through our proposal.

The robot is not able to infer actual or future activity context of the user using LDT on the scenario S2. However, if the oven signal is recognized the robot knows that there is an activity related with meal preparation running. This scenario has two cases with *valuable information*, fridge signal presents a 25% of an emergency and doorbell shows a 45% of a visit context.

Finally, we have the scenarios S5 and S6 where the robot is not able to infer the situation using LDT because it is not sharing location or dialogue. In these scenarios, our proposal presents better results. We have 95% of certainty in S5 and 83% in S6 if the oven signal is recognized. We have 50% of certainty in S5 that there is an emergency context if the fridge signal is recognized. We also have three cases of *valuable information* that although we do not have the certainty about the context, they give to the robot information about what is happen or what will happen at home.

5 Conclusions

We present a two components framework to recognize and label user activity context in indoor environments based on four elements: Localization Dialogue, timers and acoustic signals. Two major contributions are presented in this paper: a component (ERC) for recognizing environmental acoustic signals and a context-awareness component (CAC) that is able to recognize user activities even when the scenario is not shared between robot and user. The ERC uses a deep convolution neural network for the Environment Recognition Component, that provides 87% of accuracy in the recognition of acoustic signals.

As other authors have pointed out [7] modeling user contexts may seem unnatural if the context consists of problems with solutions. However, the relevance of this information for getting autonomous robots is beyond doubt as we observed in those cases where human and robot do not share space.

The scalability of this solution depends of previous knowledge of user daily life but not by learning. If we propose a solution by learning, we should care about to store historical context data on runtime. In terms of memory, it would generate an uncontrolled growth of past context information.

As future work we are going to add an automatic learning component into ERC able to incorporate new user's environment acoustic signals. As well as a routine analysis system, to extract daily information to predict future context schedule attending user tasks.

References

1. Abadi, M., Agarwal, A., Barham, P., Brevdo, E., Chen, Z., Citro, C., Corrado, G.S., Davis, A., Dean, J., Devin, M., Ghemawat, S., Goodfellow, I., Harp, A., Irving, G., Isard, M., Jia, Y., Jozefowicz, R., Kaiser, L., Kudlur, M., Levenberg, J., Mané, D., Monga, R., Moore, S., Murray, D., Olah, C., Schuster, M., Shlens, J., Steiner, B., Sutskever, I., Talwar, K., Tucker, P., Vanhoucke, V., Vasudevan, V., Viégas, F., Vinyals, O., Warden, P., Wattenberg, M., Wicke, M., Yu, Y., Zheng, X.: TensorFlow: large-scale machine learning on heterogeneous systems (2015). Software available at http://tensorflow.org/
2. Abdel-Hamid, O., Mohamed, A., Jiang, H., Penn, G.: Applying convolutional neural networks concepts to hybrid NN-HMM model for speech recognition. In: Proceedings of the IEEE International Conference on Acoustics, Speech and Signal Processing (ICASSP), pp. 4277–4280. IEEE (2012)
3. Chachada, S., Kuo, C.C.J.: Environmental sound recognition: a survey. In: Signal and Information Processing Association Annual Summit and Conference (APSIPA), 2013 Asia-Pacific, pp. 1–9. IEEE (2013)
4. Dieleman, S., Brakel, P., Schrauwen, B.: Audio-based music classification with a pretrained convolutional network. In: Proceedings of the IEEE International Conference on Acoustics, Speech and Signal Processing (ICASSP), pp. 669–674. IEEE (2011)
5. Fukushima, K.: Features for content-based audio retrieval. Biol. Cybern. **36**(4), 193–202 (1980)

6. Glorot, X., Bordes, A., Bengio, Y.: Deep sparse rectifier neural networks. In: Proceedings of the 14th International Conference on Artificial Intelligence and Statistics, vol. 15, pp. 315–323 (2011)
7. Göker, A., Myrhaug, H.I.: User context and personalisation. In: Workshop proceedings for the 6th European Conference on Case Based Reasoning (2002)
8. Jiang, H.: Confidence measures for speech recognition: a survey. Speech Commun. **45**(4), 455–470 (2005)
9. Korpipaa, P., Mantyjarvi, J., Kela, J., Keranen, H., Malm, E.J.: Managing context information in mobile devices. IEEE Pervasive Comput. **2**(3), 42–51 (2003)
10. Krizhevsky, A., Sutskever, I., Hinton, G.E.: Imagenet classification with deep convolutional neural networks. In: Advances in Neural Information Processing Systems, pp. 1097–1105 (2012)
11. Lacave, C., Luque, M., Díez, F.J.: Explanation of Bayesian networks and influence diagrams in Elvira. Syst. Man Cybern. Part B: Cybern. IEEE Trans. **37**(4), 952–965 (2007)
12. Liao, L., Fox, D., Kautz, H.: Location-based activity recognition. Adv. Neural Inf. Process. Syst. **18**, 787 (2006)
13. McCarthy, J., Buvac, S.: Formalizing context (expanded notes) (1997)
14. Mitrović, D., Zeppelzauer, M., Breiteneder, C.: Features for content-based audio retrieval. Adv. Comput. **78**, 71–150 (2010)
15. Moore, D.J., Essa, I.A., Hayes, M.H.: Exploiting human actions and object context for recognition tasks. In: The Proceedings of the Seventh IEEE International Conference on Computer Vision, 1999, vol. 1, pp. 80–86. IEEE (1999)
16. Piczac, K.: Enviromental sound classification with convolutional neuronal network. In: Proceedings of the 2015 IEEE International Workshop on Machine Learning for Signal Processing. IEEE (2015)
17. Quigley, M., Conley, K., Gerkey, B.P., Faust, J., Foote, T., Leibs, J., Wheeler, R., Ng, A.Y.: ROS: an open-source robot operating system. In: ICRA Workshop on Open Source Software (2009)
18. Salamon, J., Bello, J.P.: Deep convolutional neural networks and data augmentation for environmental sound classification. IEEE Signal Process. Lett. (2017)
19. Trentin, E., Gori, M.: A survey of hybrid ann/hmm models for automatic speech recognition. Neurocomputing **37**(1), 91–126 (2001)
20. Wang, X.H., Zhang, D.Q., Gu, T., Pung, H.K.: Ontology based context modeling and reasoning using OWL. In: Proceedings of the Second IEEE Annual Conference on Pervasive Computing and Communications Workshops, 2004, pp. 18–22. IEEE (2004)
21. Zhu, C., Sheng, W.: Motion-and location-based online human daily activity recognition. Pervasive Mobile Comput. **7**(2), 256–269 (2011)
22. Ziebart, B.D., Maas, A.L., Dey, A.K., Bagnell, J.A.: Navigate like a cabbie: probabilistic reasoning from observed context-aware behavior. In: Proceedings of the 10th International Conference on Ubiquitous Computing, pp. 322–331. ACM (2008)

Deconvolutional Neural Network for Pupil Detection in Real-World Environments

F.J. Vera-Olmos(✉) and N. Malpica

Universidad Rey Juan Carlos, Madrid, Spain
{javier.vera,norberto.malpica}@urjc.es

Abstract. Eyelid identification provides key data that can be used in several application such as controlling gaze-based HMIs (human machine interfaces), the design of new diagnostic tools for brain diseases, improving driver safety, drowsiness detection, research on advertisement, etc. We propose a novel eyetracking algorithm by learning a deep deconvolutional neural network. To train and test our method, we use several data sets with hand-labeled eye images from real-world tasks. Our method outperforms previous eye tracking methods, improving the results of the current state of the art in a 19%.

1 Introduction

A robust pupil detection that can work with different conditions is needed for several application such as controlling gaze-based HMIs (human machine interfaces), the design of new diagnostic tools for brain diseases, improving driver safety, drowsiness detection, research on advertisement, etc. With the development of head-mounted eye trackers, the number of studies conducted in real-world scenarios, such as in sports, while driving a car, or shopping are increasing. Such eye trackers consist of two or more cameras, recording the subjects eyes from close-up and the scenery from the ego-perspective. The essential step for analyzing the data recorded by such devices is the accurate identification of the center of the pupil in the camera image. The state of the art in eye tracking is the ElSe algorithm [4], which is based on edge filtering, ellipse evaluation and pupil detection, but as other methods implemented before it, it is based on hand-crafted features and these methods have been recently outperformed by machine learning in most scenarios [1,6,8]. Taking this into account, we propose an algorithm based on convolutional neural networks (CNN), which is the current state of the art in machine learning. We propose an architecture with a feature extraction step based on convolutions and max-pooling, followed with an upsampling step based on deconvolutions (more technically transpose convolutions). In order to obtain the segmented pupil from the image, we implement two networks, one for obtaining a ROI with the pupil and another to obtain a fined position of the pupil's center, in a way similar to the work of Fuhl et al. [3]. This type of architecture has been used in other applications such as PASCAL VOC 2012 or multiple sclerosis lesion segmentation (Hyeonwoo Noh et al. [9],

J.M. Ferrández Vicente et al. (Eds.): IWINAC 2017, Part II, LNCS 10338, pp. 223–231, 2017.
DOI: 10.1007/978-3-319-59773-7_23

Richard McKinley et al. [8]), with the difference that they use unpooling to upsample the feature map, while we have used deconvolutions with stride 2 as proposed by Jonathan Long et al. [7]. First we describe the data set, then the architecture of our model, the steps that we have done to train it, and finally we evaluate it and present a comparison with the state of the art.

2 Data Sets

In order to train and test our networks we employed several data sets provided by Futhl et al. [2,4]. Figure 1 shows some examples of the data sets. Among these, data sets XVIII–XXII were filmed while driving [5] and data sets XXIII and XXIV were recorded in-door with asian subjects. Data sets I–XVII were recorded during an on-road driving experiment [5] and during a supermarket search task. The challenges in the data sets are related to motion blur artifacts, reflections, low pupil contrast to the surrounding area and dark regions around the pupil. The data sets were recorded with different subjects and contain overall 94,161 images (resolution 384×288 pixels). These data set can be downloaded at https://www.ti.uni-tuebingen.de/Pupil-detection.1827.0.html?&L=1.

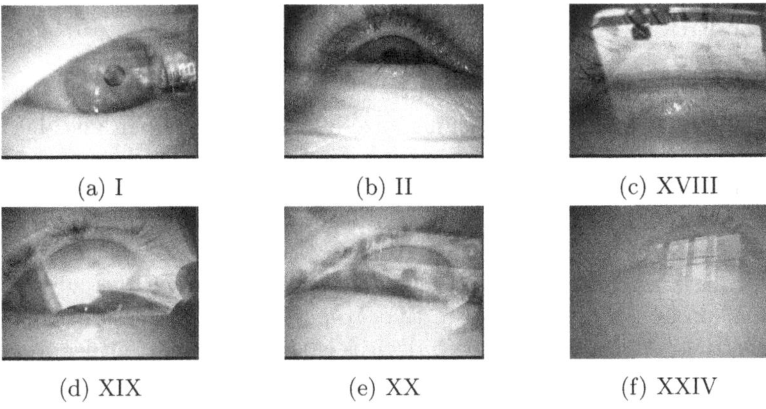

(a) I (b) II (c) XVIII (d) XIX (e) XX (f) XXIV

Fig. 1. Examples of images from the data sets.

3 Architecture

A convolutional network corresponds to a feature extractor that transforms the input image into a multidimensional feature map. Traditionally, after this network a classifier, commonly a multilayer perceptron, is used to label the image, but recent works have demonstrated the power of an upsampling step to generate an object segmentation from the features extracted by the convolutional phase [8–10]. In this case, the final output of the network is a probability map with the same size as the input image, that provides the probability of the pixel belonging to the background or to the object. Based on this definition, we create our own network that takes an eye image as input and returns the segmentation of the pupil center. Figure 2 illustrates the configuration of our network.

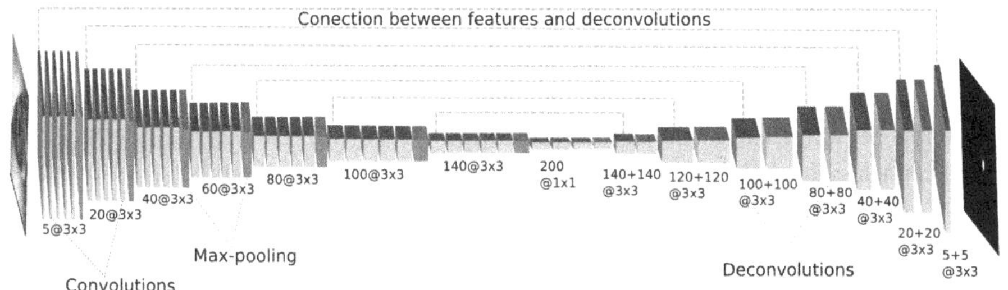

Fig. 2. Architecture of coarse network

In order to obtain a precise center of the pupil we have used two networks with a similar architecture, a coarse network and a fine network. The coarse network receives as input the whole image of the camera, an image of 384×288 pixels, to obtain a coarse segmentation of the pupil. We then crop this segmentation with a ROI of 80×80 and use it as input with the fine network, which will give a fined segmentation of the pupil's center. A schematic image of the architecture can be shown in Fig. 3.

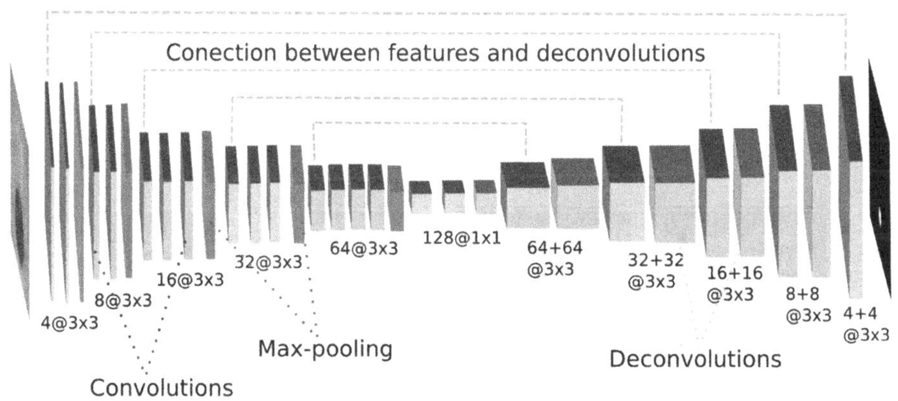

Fig. 3. Architecture of fine network.

In detail, both networks consists of two main parts: the feature extraction phase, usually named encoding step, and the upsampling phase named decoding step. Our networks are composed with convolutions with zero padding so that the output size (spatial) remains the same as the input, max-pooling 2×2 to reduce to a half the input and deconvolution with stride 2×2 to double the size of the input. The coarse network consists of 35 layers of convolutions and 7 of max-pooling in the encoding phase, and 10 convolution layers and 7 deconvolutions with 2×2 stride in the decoding phase, to perform the upsampling. We have also connected the results after every pooling operation in the encoding phase with the output of every deconvolution so that high resolution features from the first part can be used as extra inputs for the decoding step [10]. In order to give a probabilistic result in the output of the network we perform a softmax operation between the two classes (pupil and background). The fine network is a smaller version of the coarse network, with 14 convolution and 5 max-pooling 2×2 in the encoding and 7 convolutions and 5 deconvolutions with 2×2 stride in the decoding phase.

4 Training

In this section we describe the steps that we performed to train the networks.

4.1 Training Data

First of all we need to generate the ground truth output of the coarse network, as we just have the coordinate of the pupil center. To do this, we start with a zero valued image of the same size as the input image and set the value of the pixel in the coordinates of the pupil to one. Then we apply a Gaussian filter with sigma = 3 and we threshold the result, to obtain a mask with value one within the region affected by the gaussian filtering. Figure 4 shows some examples.

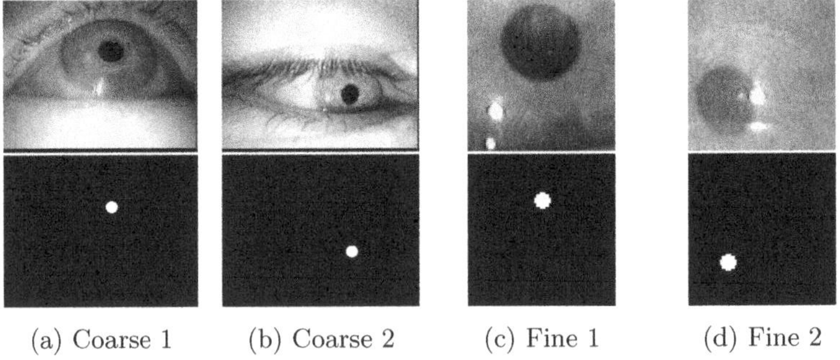

(a) Coarse 1 (b) Coarse 2 (c) Fine 1 (d) Fine 2

Fig. 4. Examples of input and ground truth for fine and coarse networks.

To generate the ground truth for the fine network we crop a ROI of 80×80 in the original image using as center of the ROI the center of the pupil plus a random offset. We also compute a thresholded gaussian filtering but with sigma = 1. Examples of this are shown in Fig. 4.

Another problem we have faced is the large variability in the amount of samples of the datasets, the smaller dataset being comprised of only 270 samples while the larger contains 13,476 samples. So we decided to harmonize the amount of samples by picking 3000 samples with repetition of every dataset to conform the training pools.

Summarizing, to train the two networks we generated two collection of samples: one with full images and its output with the gaussian in the pupil and a second with 80×80 crops of the eye along side with 80×80 output with a smaller gaussian in the center of the pupil. And both with the same numbers of training samples, obtained using sampling with replacement.

4.2 Objective Function

We used the cross-entropy as objective function, which forces us to have two values per pixel in the output of the deconvolutional phase. The first value will be the mask generated before and the second will be the opposite of that mask so that we have zeros in the thresholded gaussian and ones in the background.

4.3 Weights for Training

If we train the network using the ground truth output generated as explained above, we will end with a naive solution were all images are zeros in the first value of the output and ones in the second. The reason is that the pixels within the gaussian are so few, that the increase in the cross-entropy when detecting those pixels correctly is very small. In order to correct this, we have created a weights mask that multiplies the cross-entropy value, to give more weight to the pupil region in the computation of the cross-entropy [10]. We calculate the weight following the simple Eqs. 1 and 2, in a zero image with same size as the input image, N being the number of pixels in the image, N_{gauss} the number of pixels in the thresholded gaussian and N_{bg} the number of pixels in the background.

$$W_{gauss} = P_1 * N/N_{gauss} \tag{1}$$

$$W_{bg} = P_2 * N/N_{bg} \tag{2}$$

We used $P_1 = P_2 = 0.5$ with the aim of giving the same importance to the background pixels and to the gaussian pixels. We used this weights correction only for the coarse network.

4.4 Training Process

Once we have the ground truth and the weight mask we can perform the training. We have trained each network independently with the collections created before. We used RMSprop as optimization method and we run the training in a Nvidia Tesla K40. The training took 3–4 h for the coarse network and 1 h for the fine network.

4.5 Output Analysis

As explained above, in the output of our networks we will have 2 values per pixel, with the probability of the pixel belonging to the thresholded gaussian and to the background. We apply a threshold to define a mask, in the output we put as ones all values with a probability of being part of the thresholded gaussian greater than 0.9 in the coarse network and 0.5 in the fine network. We show some examples in Fig. 5. After this step, we apply a blob analysis to extract the bigger blob with a convexity of at least 0.7. We crop a 80×80 ROI around the blob of the coarse network, to use it as input to the fine network. The final center of the pupil is computed as the center of the blob obtained from the fine network.

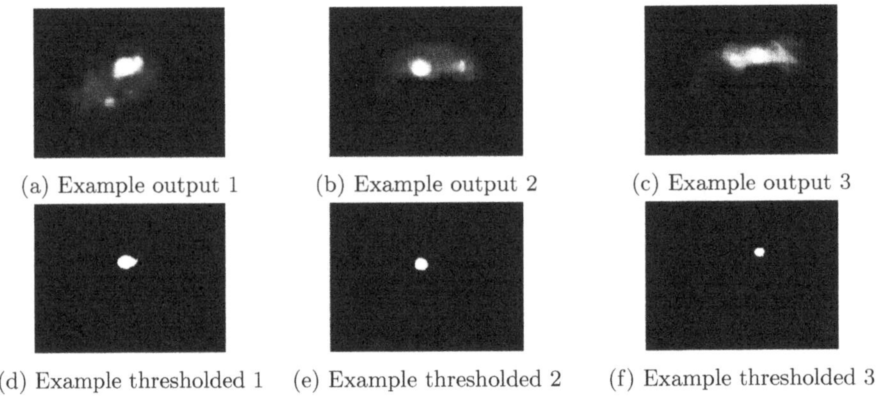

(a) Example output 1 (b) Example output 2 (c) Example output 3

(d) Example thresholded 1 (e) Example thresholded 2 (f) Example thresholded 3

Fig. 5. Examples of thresholding.

5 Experiments and Results

First we randomly separate the frames of all data sets in two groups, training and test, with the same amount of samples. We compare our results with ElSe [4], which is the current state of the art in eyetracking. The performance was measured in terms of the detection rate for different pixel errors. The pixel error represents the Euclidean distance between the hand labeled coordinates of the pupil and the coordinates provided by the algorithm. Figure 6 presents the performance in terms of the detection rate for different pixel error rates. More specifically, Fig. 6 shows two different results: the weighted detection rate which is the percentage of correctly detected pupil centers for all samples in the test collection and the unweighted detection rate, that depicts the detection rate as the average over all data sets with each data set weighted equally (due to different data set sizes).

In a second experiment, we performed a cross validation between data sets. We used as test all samples from a data set and use as training collection all

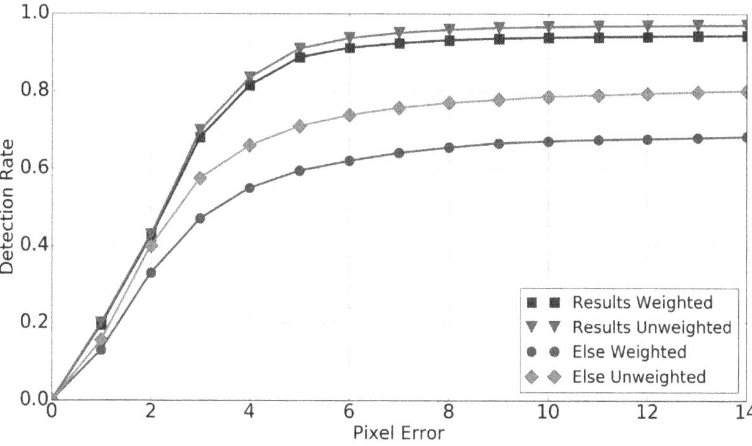

Fig. 6. Average detection rates at different pixel distances with random sampling

remaining data sets. This test will give us information about the ability of our model to generalize. Table 1 summarizes the performance results for ElSe and our model in terms of the detection rate up to an error of five pixels for all data sets, and Fig. 7 presents the performance in terms of the detection rate for different pixel distance, averaging the results in all samples (weighted and unweighted).

In both experiments our model clearly outperformed ElSe. In the first experiment the results are much better, but this probably due to training with the half of all samples as the samples in a data set tend to be similar among them. In the cross validation experiment the results are not as good as in the first, but our model still outperforms ElSe, improving the results of this method by 30% for unweighted and by 19% for the weighted result.

Table 1. Performance comparison among data sets between ElSe and our proposal in terms of detection rate up to an error of five pixels.

Data set	I	II	III	IV	V	VI	VII	VIII
ElSe %	85.52	65.35	63.6	83.24	84.87	77.52	59.51	68.41
Results %	87.04	69.50	84.98	90.99	96.11	92.97	82.41	83.33
Data set	IX	X	XI	XII	XIII	XIV	XV	XVI
ElSe %	86.72	78.93	75.27	79.39	73.52	84.22	57.30	59.95
Results %	88.76	90.04	76.48	82.44	76.17	96.16	78.23	71.68
Data set	XVII	XVIII	XIX	XX	XXI	XXII	XXIII	XXIV
ElSe %	89.55	50.86	33.04	67.90	41.47	48.98	94.34	52.97
Results %	98.13	65.14	64.19	89.33	87.43	82.43	96.38	57.02

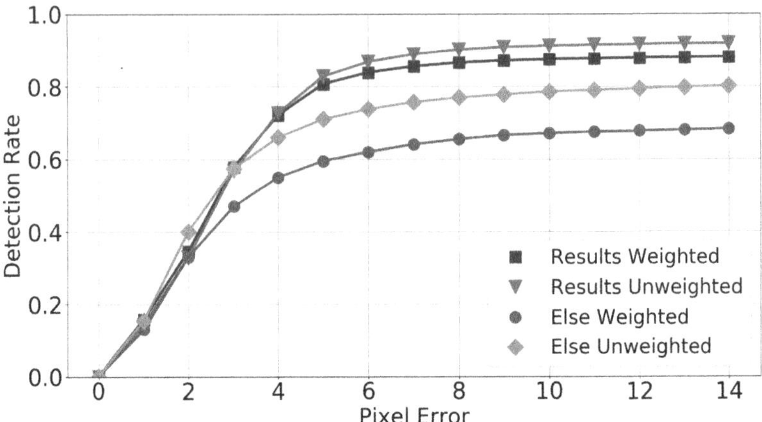

Fig. 7. Average detection rates at different pixel distances in the cross validation.

6 Conclusions

We have proposed a deep learning algorithm that outperforms the state of the art in eyetracking, improving the results in every data set that we have tested. Our method has been tested with a Nvidia Tesla k40 GPU in a desktop setup for training and test, due to it has 11 Gb of memory. It can run the model at 28 fps but we also have run the algorithm in a laptop with a Nvidia GTX 1060 reaching 25 fps. We have developed this algorithm mainly for offline analysis of high frame rate videos, but with some changes in the networks (reducing the deep and the amount of variables), it could work at a good frame rate with less hardware in an online context.

Acknowledgement. This work was partially funded by project DPI2015-68664-C4-1-R of the Spanish Ministry of Economy and by Banco de Santander and Universidad Rey Juan Carlos Funding Program for Excellence Research Groups ref. Computer Vision and Image Processing (CVIP). We gratefully acknowledge the support of NVIDIA Corporation with the donation of the Nvidia Tesla K40 GPU used for this research.

References

1. Esteva, A., Kuprel, B., Novoa, R.A., Ko, J., Swetter, S.M., Blau, H.M., Thrun, S.: Dermatologist-level classification of skin cancer with deep neural networks. Nature **542**(7639), 115–118 (2017)
2. Fuhl, W., Kübler, T., Sippel, K., Rosenstiel, W., Kasneci, E.: ExCuSe: robust pupil detection in real-world scenarios. In: Azzopardi, G., Petkov, N. (eds.) CAIP 2015. LNCS, vol. 9256, pp. 39–51. Springer, Cham (2015). doi:10.1007/978-3-319-23192-1_4
3. Fuhl, W., Santini, T., Kasneci, G., Kasneci, E.: Pupilnet: convolutional neural networks for robust pupil detection. arXiv preprint arXiv:1601.04902 (2016)

4. Fuhl, W., Santini, T.C., Kübler, T., Kasneci, E.: Else: ellipse selection for robust pupil detection in real-world environments. In: Proceedings of the Ninth Biennial ACM Symposium on Eye Tracking Research and Applications, pp. 123–130. ACM (2016)
5. Kasneci, E., Sippel, K., Aehling, K., Heister, M., Rosenstiel, W., Schiefer, U., Papageorgiou, E.: Driving with binocular visual field loss? a study on a supervised on-road parcours with simultaneous eye and head tracking. PLoS One **9**(2), e87470 (2014)
6. Krizhevsky, A., Sutskever, I., Hinton, G.E.: Imagenet classification with deep convolutional neural networks. In: Advances in Neural Information Processing Systems, pp. 1097–1105 (2012)
7. Long, J., Shelhamer, E., Darrell, T.: Fully convolutional networks for semantic segmentation. In: The IEEE Conference on Computer Vision and Pattern Recognition (CVPR), June 2015
8. McKinley, R., Gundersen, T., Wagner, F., Chan, A., Wiest, R., Reyes, M.: Nabla-net: a deep dag-like convolutional architecture for biomedical image segmentation: application to white-matter lesion segmentation in multiple sclerosis. In: MSSEG Challenge Proceedings: Multiple Sclerosis Lesions Segmentation Challenge Using a Data Management and Processing Infrastructure, p. 37 (2016)
9. Noh, H., Hong, S., Han, B.: Learning deconvolution network for semantic segmentation. In: Proceedings of the IEEE International Conference on Computer Vision, pp. 1520–1528 (2015)
10. Ronneberger, O., Fischer, P., Brox, T.: U-Net: Convolutional Networks for Biomedical Image Segmentation. ArXiv e-prints, May 2015

Air Quality Forecasting in Madrid Using Long Short-Term Memory Networks

Esteban Pardo(✉) and Norberto Malpica

Universidad Rey Juan Carlos, Madrid, Spain
esteban.pardo@urjc.es

Abstract. European and Spanish legislation set hourly limits for Nitrogen Dioxide, NO_2, that are enforced with traffic restrictions. In this context it is important to warn the citizens in advance, which can only be done if the NO_2 levels are forecasted. In this paper we propose a deep learning based air quality forecasting system that uses air quality and meteorological data to produce NO_2 forecasts up to 24 h with a root mean squared error, RMSE, of 10.54 $\mu g/m^3$. We also compare our results with the model based system CALIOPE.

Keywords: Air quality forecasting · Long short-term memory

1 Introduction

Air pollution in the city of Madrid is a problem that has grown in interest recently. Since the year 2015, the city council of Madrid has started enforcing the hourly NO_2 limit of 200 $\mu g/m^3$ set by the Environment Ministry [1] with a series of traffic restrictions. These restrictions include, depending on the severity of the air quality level, limiting the speed to 70 km/h on the M30 (the main ring higway of the city), forbidding the use of parking lots managed by the city council, or plate number based rationing [2]. Since cars remain one of the most popular forms of transport in Madrid, where the total number of cars registered as of 2015 was 1447786 [3], these restrictions resulted in sudden increases of Google searches related to pollution during the peaks; the relative search interest for the last 5 years is shown in Fig. 2. Despite this interest, there is not a lot of literature studying the case of pollution in Madrid, being the 2 most notable approaches to NO_2 forecasting the SERENA [4], and the CALIOPE [5] systems.

SERENA is the official system used by the city council of Madrid, consisting of a neural network regressor model that uses NO_2 measurements provided by the sensor network deployed across the city to forecast the pollution levels in the area around each sensor, up to 24 h ahead with an hourly resolution. The main drawback of the SERENA system is that there is no public information regarding its error rate and, when this information was requested to the city council in 23/12/2016, they were unable to answer it despite contacting both the air quality department, and the environment councilor[1]; another drawback

[1] As of 05/03/2017 we have not received any information regarding the error rate of the system.

J.M. Ferrández Vicente et al. (Eds.): IWINAC 2017, Part II, LNCS 10338, pp. 232–239, 2017.
DOI: 10.1007/978-3-319-59773-7_24

of the system is that, although multiple publications [6,7], have suggested that meteorological information improves the air quality prediction power, this system does not use it.

CALIOPE is a forecasting system that uses the WRF [8], HERMES [9], CMAQ [10] and BSC-DREAM8b [11] models to perform a high resolution ($4\,km^2$) simulation of the Iberian Peninsula; although a lot of effort has been put into developing these high fidelity models, inaccuracies in the simulation result in performance loss when compared to state of the art machine learning methods as we will see in the results section.

Several machine learning based air quality forecasting systems have been used to forecast air quality in China. In [12] the authors propose a spatiotemporal deep learning (STDL)-based air quality prediction method that inherently considers spatial and temporal correlations. This approach shows promising results between when forecasting PM2.5 levels, but it has not been applied to NO_2 forecasting, it uses no meteorological information and the forecasting error has only been reported for the next hour.

Zheng et al. [7] proposed a composite forecasting system that uses current meteorological data, weather forecasts, and air quality data to perform a 48 h PM2.5 forecast for China. One drawback of their approach is that training multiple forecasting models that work together can be cumbersome when compared to more unified solutions; the application to pollutants other than PM2.5 and to other cities also remains to be studied.

The application of ensemble artificial intelligence classifiers to forecast daily maximum ozone threshold exceedances in the Hong Kong area was analyzed in [6]; one important aspect of this study is that they highlight the importance of meteorological variables when forecasting air quality levels. Despite their success, classifier approaches to detecting threshold excedances may be too restrictive for some real world scenarios since they need to be trained for every threshold the users want to forecast, and do not account for how much time the threshold is exceeded.

In our method, we use publicly available air quality and meteorological information to forecast NO_2 levels for the next 24 h in the city of Madrid. Following the results from [13] we use a sequence of 2 long short-term memory (LSTM) nodes and 2 fully connected layers to analyze the time series; LSTMs have been shown to achieve high performance at temporal modeling, while fully connected layers usually perform good at feature mapping. We have decided not to use convolutional networks to reduce frequency variations since our approach uses data updated every hour, thus having a update frequency several orders of magnitude lower than audio recordings.

We test our approach using air quality data from Madrid's open data portal and meteorological data from Meteogalicia's WRF simulation for the time period 2011–2016. We achieve an average RMS error of $10.54\,\mu g/m^3$ for the air quality monitoring stations listed in Fig. 4, this stations have been selected for this study since they reported the most surpasses of the $200\,\mu g/m^3$ threshold during the analyzed period.

Our results indicate that our system may be more suitable than CALIOPE for pollution forecasting in Madrid since it requires less computational resources and also has a lower RMS error (Fig. 1).

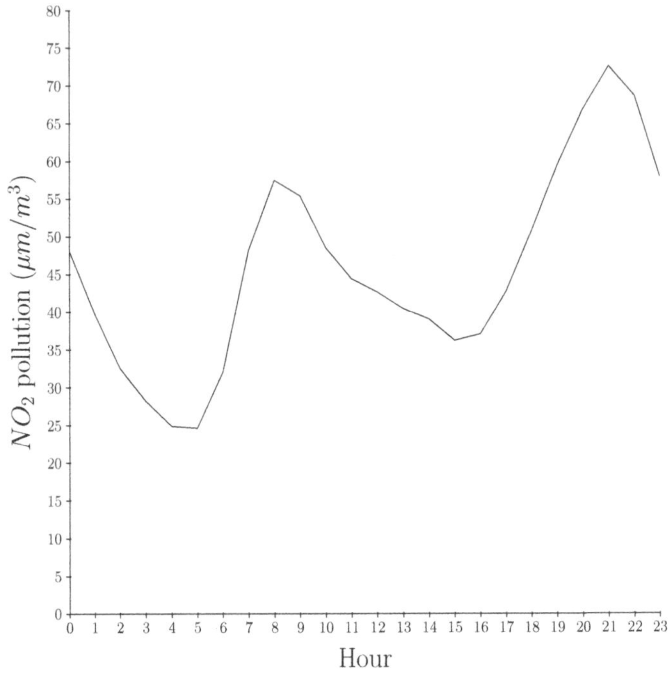

Fig. 1. Average daily pollution values for 2016. Since NO_2 levels peak at 21.00 and the city council of Madrid notifies at 12.00 the traffic restrictions that will take place the following day, it is important to develop a forecasting system that can be executed close to the notification time with a low computational footprint and has low forecasting error.

2 Data Sources

In this project we have decided to explore openly available air quality and meteorological datasets. The city council of Madrid has a total of 24 air quality monitoring stations scattered across the region of Madrid. These stations provide hourly measurements of air pollutants such as NO_2 that can be accessed through Madrid's open data portal [14]. NO_2 is measured using the chemiluminescence technique which involves getting NO from NO_2, mixing the resulting NO with O_3 and measuring the light that results from the chemical reaction using photomultiplier tubes [15], the resulting value is then converted to $\mu g/m^3$. Although the measurement error for the air quality monitoring stations is not reported, publications such as [16] report that conventional chemiluminescence monitors can have interferences of up to 50% in their observations.

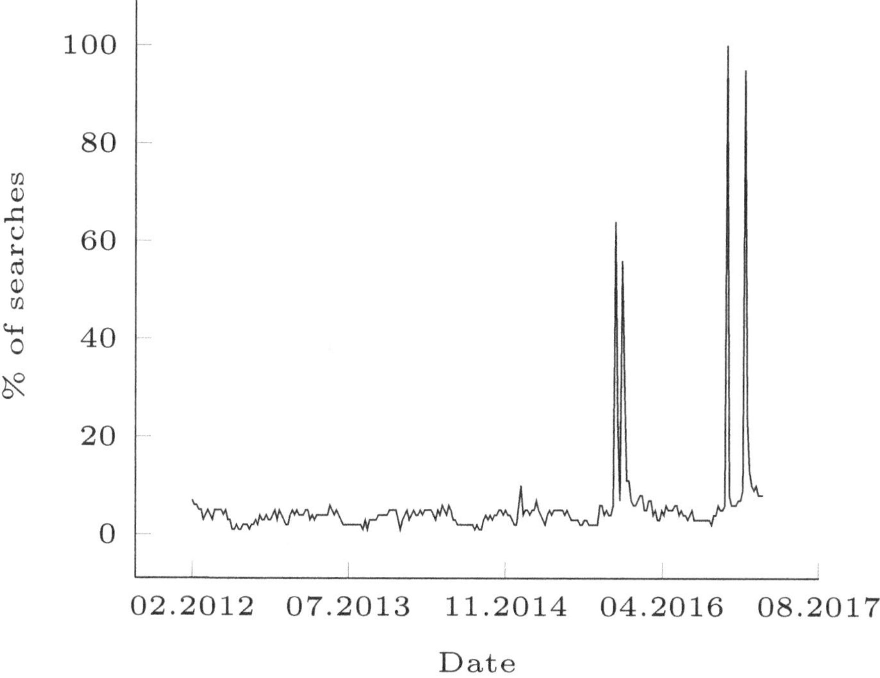

Fig. 2. Percentage of searches each day relative to the maximum number of searches in a day for the term "Contaminación" (Spanish for "pollution") in Madrid. Sudden increases in searches can be seen in 8.11.2015–14.11.2015, 29.11.2015–5.12.2015, 30.10.2016–5.11.2016 and 25.12.2016–31.12.2016; this dates match high pollution events that resulted in traffic restrictions.

On the other hand, MeteoGalicia, one of the official institutions that performs meteorological forecasts in Spain, provides the results from their WRF simulations free of charge through an instance of the THREDDS data server [17]. Contrary to Madrid's air quality monitoring stations, the performance of the WRF model run by MeteoGalicia is documented by comparing the predicted maximum and minimum temperature, wind direction and speed to measurements of sensors placed across the community of Galicia [18]. Although this dataset is rich in information, we have selected a subset of meteorological variables that intuitively should have a high impact in the transport of air particles; the selected variables are wind speed and direction, cloud cover at low altitudes, pressure, accumulated precipitation between each simulation, relative humidity and temperature.

With this data, we have created an hourly time series from 01-01-2011 to 31-12-2016 for each air quality station. Each time series is formed by the respective NO_2 reading, and the average of each of the previously mentioned meteorological variables across the 4 points that fall on the region of Madrid for each time step. At this point it is important to note that, although part some of the variables we are using are the result of a forecasting simulation, we are using them as if we had acquired them from a sensor and, for each time step in the time series, we use only the corresponding time step of the simulation closest to the time point in the time series.

3 Model

Following the successful combination of LSTMs and fully connected layers to the analysis audio sequences of [13], we propose a similar architecture to forecast NO_2 pollution. Our model is comprised of 2 LSTM layers which capture temporal information, followed by 2 dense layers which perform the feature mapping from the internal LSTM representation to the desired pollution forecast; our LSTM layers have 512 hidden units each while the fully connected layers have 1024 units.

We approach the forecast problem by first preparing a sequence of 120 sequential time steps comprised of the variables described in the data sources section; we then feed the data through the proposed architecture ignoring the network output until the last time step; finally, at the last time step, we compute the L2 distance between the output and the target NO_2 level and backpropagate the error. When training the network with time steps t_0 through t_n the forecasted level will be the one at time step t_{n+g} being g the temporal gap in the forecast; we thus train a different model for every station and every temporal gap.

An overview of this model can be seen in Fig. 3.

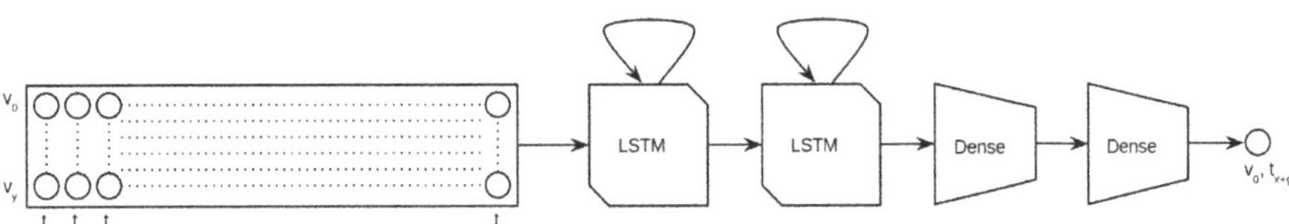

Fig. 3. Architecture of our approach. NO_2 readings V_0 and meteorological variables ($V_1..V_y$) are fed into the network at each time step. The network is comprised of 2 LSTM nodes that perform temporal modeling, followed by 2 fully connected layers that perform the feature mapping that results in the desired forecast. Once the last time step t_x is processed, the network output will be the desired NO_2 forecast at time step t_{x+g} being g the temporal gap in the forecast (1..24)

4 Experiments and Results

We analyzed the predictive power of our system for the period 2011–2016.

To this end, we first selected the 3 air quality monitoring stations that reported NO_2 levels above 200 $\mu g/m^3$ for the most time; information on these stations is shown in Fig. 4. We divided the time series in 5-day overlapping time frame and, once the time frames were extracted, they were shuffled and divided in

Station Name	Latitude	Longitude	Altitude	Times surpassed
Barrio del Pilar	40 28' 41,62"N	3 42' 41,55"W	674	362
Pza. Fernndez Ladreda	40 23' 05,87"N	3 43' 07,42"W	604	329
Avda. Ramn y Cajal	40 27' 05,31"N	3 40' 38,48"W	708	276

Fig. 4. Information about the analyzed stations. The station name and location was retrieved from the "Calidad del aire: Estaciones de control" dataset located at [14]; we also show how many hours each station reported NO_2 levels higher than 200 $\mu g/m^3$

a 95% training set, and 5% validation set. Finally, we trained our system to forecast the NO_2 levels for the next 24 h by performing different training sessions, each setting the regression target to be the NO_2 measurement at the desired time step for each of the 24 time steps; we report the error on the validation set.

Although we did not have access to the raw output of the CALIOPE system due to budget constraints, the Barcelona Supercomputing Center performs yearly reports on the error of their system which can be downloaded at [19]. We have used this information to compare it with the results of our system. We present our results in Fig. 5, it shows the RMS error of our system when setting a forecast gap of 8, 16 and 24 h and compares it to the average RMS error of CALIOPE for the period 2011–2016.

We have also tested the predictive performance of our LSTM based approach when using only the NO_2 readings as input data. For this purpose we performed the previous experiment again, this time without using meteorological information. Results indicate that, on average, the meteorological information we used reduced the error a 12%.

Station	$RMS_{g=8}$	$RMS_{g=16}$	$RMS_{g=24}$	$RMS_{CALIOPE}$
Barrio del Pilar	10.24	10.59	10.18	26,08
Pza. Fernndez Ladreda	11.22	10.53	10.75	26.3
Avda. Ramn y Cajal	10.61	10.16	10.61	26.08

Fig. 5. Forecasting error for the period 2011–2016. We trained the proposed architecture to forecast NO_2 levels at time steps +8 +16 and +24, and evaluated it on the validation set. The table also includes the average RMS error for the 24 h forecast reported by the Barcelona Supercomputing Center for the same time period and station. The CALIOPE error values for each year and station can be consulted at [19], however as of 05/03/2017 the 2016 reports for the stations "Av. Ramn y Cajal" and "Pza. Fernndez Ladrea" were incomplete and, because of this, removed from the RMS computation.

5 Conclusions and Future Work

In this work we have described an LSTM based approach for NO_2 forecasting in the city of Madrid that uses openly available air quality and meteorological datasets to perform a forecast for the next 24 h.

Arguably the most important outcome of this work is to show some disadvantages of using model simulation based systems when compared to machine learning based methods. Our results highlight the low performance of the Barcelona Supercomputing Center model when compared to LSTM based approaches, which are not only more accurate, but require less computational resources. Model simulation may still be an important area of research when trying to understand the dynamics of pollution since simulations can be performed with varying temporal and spatial resolutions; however, when researchers are interested in a low error forecasting system with fixed time steps for the area around a specific measuring station, machine learning based forecasting systems may be more appropriate.

Another important contribution is to show that meteorological information increases the predictive performance of machine learning based forecasting systems for NO_2 levels in Madrid. As we have previously mentioned, we have used the results of a WRF simulation as our meteorological information and, although these simulation is not error free [18], they are accurate enough to provide an significant, 12%, reduction of the RMS forecasting error.

Finally, the relative simplicity of our approach suggests that the prediction error could be further reduced by using more advanced techniques such as dropout [20], batch normalization [21] or data augmentation [22]; by using more elaborate network architectures having a wider and deeper structure; or by using complimentary datasets such as traffic information, or weather data that is not simulated. In future works, we will analyze other public available datasets and more advanced architectures to further reduce the predictive error; this will help to enable a more efficient and effective planning before high pollution points occur in the city of Madrid.

Acknowledgments. This work was partially funded by Banco de Santander and Universidad Rey Juan Carlos in the Funding Program for Excellence Research Groups ref. "Computer Vision and Image Processing (CVIP)". We gratefully acknowledge the support of NVIDIA Corporation with the donation of the Tesla K40 GPU used for this research. We would also like to thank the Barcelona Supercomputing Center and the Madrid city council for their support during our research.

References

1. Real Decreto 102/2011, de 28 de enero, relativo a la mejora de la calidad del aire
2. PROTOCOLO DE MEDIDAS, A ADOPTAR DURANTE EPISODIOS DE ALTA CONTAMINACIN POR DIXIDO DE NITRGENO (2016). http://www.madrid.es/UnidadesDescentralizadas/UDCMedios/noticias/2016/01Enero/21Jueves/Notasprensa/Nuevo%20protocolo%20contaminaci%C3%B3n/ficheros/Protocolo_NO2.pdf. Accessed 5 Mar 2017
3. DGT statistics for Madrid. http://www.dgt.es/informacion-municipal/2015/individuales/madrid/28079_Madrid.pdf. Accessed 5 Mar 2017
4. Sistema de Prediccin. http://www.mambiente.munimadrid.es/opencms/opencms/calaire/SistemaIntegral/SistPrediccion.html. Accessed 5 Mar 2017

5. Baldasano, J.M., Jorba, O., Gass, S., Pay, M.T., Arevalo, G.: CALIOPE: sistema de pronstico operacional de calidad del aire para Europa y Espaa
6. Gong, B., Ordieres-Mer, J.: Prediction of daily maximum ozone threshold exceedances by preprocessing and ensemble artificial intelligence techniques: case study of Hong Kong. Environ. Model. Softw. **84**, 290–303 (2016)
7. Zheng, Y., Yi, X., Li, M., Li, R., Shan, Z., Chang, E., Li, T.: Forecasting fine-grained air quality based on big data. In: Proceedings of the 21th ACM SIGKDD International Conference on Knowledge Discovery and Data Mining, pp. 2267–2276. ACM, August 2015
8. Michalakes, J., Dudhia, J., Gill, D., Klemp, J., Skamarock, W.: Design of a next-generation regional weather research and forecast model. Towards Teracomput. 117–124 (1998)
9. Guevara, M., Martnez, F., Arvalo, G., Gass, S., Baldasano, J.M.: An improved system for modelling Spanish emissions: HERMESv2. 0. Atmos. Environ. **81**, 209–221 (2013)
10. Byun, D.W., Ching, J.K.S. (eds.): Science algorithms of the EPA Models-3 community multiscale air quality (CMAQ) modeling system, p. 727. US Environmental Protection Agency, Office of Research and Development, Washington, DC (1999)
11. Prez, C., Nickovic, S., Pejanovic, G., Baldasano, J.M., Özsoy, E.: Interactive dustradiation modeling: a step to improve weather forecasts. J. Geophys. Res.: Atmos. **111**(D16) (2006)
12. Li, X., Peng, L., Hu, Y., Shao, J., Chi, T.: Deep learning architecture for air quality predictions. Environ. Sci. Pollut. Res. **23**(22), 22408–22417 (2016)
13. Sainath, T.N., Vinyals, O., Senior, A., Sak, H.: Convolutional, long short-term memory, fully connected deep neural networks. In: 2015 IEEE International Conference on Acoustics, Speech and Signal Processing (ICASSP), pp. 4580–4584. IEEE, April 2015
14. City council of Madrid open data portal. http://datos.madrid.es/portal/site/egob. Accessed 5 Mar 2017
15. ANALIZADORES Y TECNICAS DE ANALISIS. http://www.mambiente.munimadrid.es/opencms/export/sites/default/calaire/Anexos/aparatos_de_medida.pdf. Accessed 5 Mar 2017
16. Dunlea, E.J., Herndon, S.C., Nelson, D.D., Volkamer, R.M., San Martini, F., Sheehy, P.M., Allwine, E.J.: Evaluation of nitrogen dioxide chemiluminescence monitors in a polluted urban environment. Atmos. Chem. Phys. **7**(10), 2691–2704 (2007)
17. Unidata, 2015: THREDDS Data Server [Version 4.6.2 - 2015–06-09T15:16:47–0600]. Boulder, CO: UCAR/Unidata Program Center. doi:10.5065/D6N014KG
18. WRF error for August 2008. http://www.meteogalicia.gal/datosred/infoweb/meteo/docs/modelos/meteoDeterminista_es.pdf. Accessed 5 Mar 2017
19. CALIOPE evaluation reports. http://www.bsc.es/projects/earthscience/v_FCST_EVAL/files/new/NRT/KF/. Accessed 5 Mar 2017
20. Zaremba, W., Sutskever, I., Vinyals, O.: Recurrent neural network regularization. arXiv preprint arXiv:1409.2329 (2014)
21. Cooijmans, T., Ballas, N., Laurent, C., Gülçehre, Ç., Courville, A.: Recurrent batch normalization. arXiv preprint arXiv:1603.09025 (2016)
22. Parascandolo, G., Huttunen, H., Virtanen, T.: Recurrent neural networks for polyphonic sound event detection in real life recordings. In: 2016 IEEE International Conference on Acoustics, Speech and Signal Processing (ICASSP), pp. 6440–6444. IEEE, March 2016

Values Deletion to Improve Deep Imputation Processes

Adrián Sánchez-Morales[1(✉)], José-Luis Sancho-Gómez[1], and Aníbal R. Figueiras-Vidal[2]

[1] Department of Information and Communications Technologies, Universidad Politécnica de Cartagena, Plaza del Hospital, 1, 30202 Cartagena (Murcia), Spain
adrian.sm91@gmail.com
[2] Signal Theory and Communications Department, Universidad Carlos III de Madrid, Madrid, Spain

Abstract. Most machine learning algorithms are based on the assumption that available data are completely known, nevertheless, real world data sets are often incomplete. For this reason, the ability of handling missing values has become a fundamental requirement for statistical pattern recognition. In this article, a new proposal to impute missing values with deep networks is analyzed. Besides the real missing values, the method introduces a percentage of artificial missing ('deleted values') using the true values as targets. Empirical results over several UCI repository datasets show that this method is able to improve the final imputed values obtained by other procedures used as pre-imputation.

1 Introduction

Nowadays, regardless of the industry you work in, data plays an important role. However, it has been shown through the literature the wide range of drawbacks which can appear when one faces real applications. One of the most common is the presence of unknown data so that data processing is a necessity. Otherwise, missing values may cause false results on the main problem [1].

Trying to find out the best method to handle missing attributes in a database is another issue studied by many authors [2,3], and it depends in most cases on the kind of missing is being dealt with. Although there exist several ways of handling this problem, imputation has become one of the most studied due to missing treatment is independent of the learning algorithm used in a following stage. This technique consists of filling unknown values with estimated ones, and there is a wide family of this methods, from simple imputation techniques like mean substitution to those which analyze the relationships between attributes like support vector machines [2].

In this paper, we will consider the high representation capacity of Autoencoders (AE) to create an efficient method of imputation based on a deep architecture. In particular, Denoising Autoencoders (DAEs) will be used to form a Stacked Denoising Autoencoder (SDAE) through a layer-wise procedure [4].

J.M. Ferrández Vicente et al. (Eds.): IWINAC 2017, Part II, LNCS 10338, pp. 240–246, 2017.
DOI: 10.1007/978-3-319-59773-7_25

Moreover, this imputation method is able to leverage all the available information in a data set, including that which is in incomplete instances. We will show how our method is able to improve the final imputed values obtained by other procedures used as pre-imputation and that in general give good results. We use for that some of the UCI repository data sets where different amount of missing values will be artificially inserted in order to compute the error between real and final imputed values.

The remainder of this paper is structured as follows: in Sect. 2 details of the proposed deep learning technique are given and the learning algorithm is presented. Experiments of applying the proposed method to solve some synthetic problems and a review of the used pre-imputation techniques are shown in Sect. 3. Finally, the paper is closed by the conclusions and future related works in Sect. 5.

2 Proposed Method

As we have already mentioned above, an imputation method based on deep architectures is presented in this paper. Researchers have demonstrated how in a well-trained deep neural network, the hidden layers learn a good representation of the input data [5–7], and it is also widely known the capability of reconstruction of DAEs. If we review the concept of *denoising*, a neural network is constructed to provide 'clean' outputs from noisy inputs, which are obtained adding noise to the original patterns [4]. Learning is done through unsupervised training where the "clean" inputs are used as target.

These concepts will be used in order to carry out an efficient imputation procedure. Therefore, as a first approach, a SDAE will be created by stacking DAEs; then, it will be checked if the results can be improved by applying a new technique based on deleting samples.

2.1 SDAE Imputation Method

In most machine learning imputation techniques, the model is trained only using complete instances what implies a lost of information that could be critical in the problem. However, this issue will be overcome thanks to a simple modification of the Stochastic Gradient Descent (SGD) algorithm when it is used to train a SDAE.

Let us consider an unsupervised training data set with the form $\{\mathbf{x}_n, \mathbf{m}_n\}_{n=1}^{N}, n = 1, ..., N$, where $\mathbf{x}_n$ is the n-th pattern and $\mathbf{m}_n$ is a vector with the same dimension which indicates whether $\mathbf{x}_n$ presents missing values through:

$$m_{nd} = \begin{cases} 1, x_{nd} \textit{ is a known value}, \\ 0, x_{nd} \textit{ is missing}, \end{cases} \tag{1}$$

where d ($1 \leq d \leq D$) denotes component. These missing values are firstly filled in by one of the pre-imputation methods we will present in next section. Then, a SDAE is trained to reconstruct a noisy version of the input by minimizing a *Mean Squared Error* (MSE) function and overlooking error corresponding to missing values. This noise is inserted in every sample except those with missing, and weights in networks are iteratively updated to minimize

$$E = \sum_{n=1}^{N} \| (\mathbf{z}_n - \mathbf{x}_n) \odot \mathbf{m}_n \|^2 \qquad (2)$$

where $\mathbf{z}_n$ is the output of the SDAE which depends on the weights of the network and $\odot$ represents the direct product, also called Hadamard product.

Therefore, through an unsupervised layer-wise training and a subsequent fine tunning, a deep DAE is constructed by stacking DAEs. The training process to construct SDAEs is the same as that followed in [4]. This neural network is able to reproduce the input in its output layer, taking into account not only the complete instances but also the known characteristics of the incomplete patterns. The idea is to impute unknown values at the same time as it is learnt to denoise input data.

2.2 Deleting Values

In the approach mentioned above, the SDAE is trained to make predictions for missing values and reconstruct noisy versions of the input patterns.

Deleting some input values (values in some features of the input patterns) is now proposed so that the network can learn the true ones, i.e., some known input values are deleted –they can be considered as an artificial missing values– being these known values used as targets. In this way, a deep neural network can be trained to reconstruct noisy inputs, predicts both 'real' missing values and "deleted" values. Thus, due to the fact that deleted values are treated as missing but its targets are known, real missing values can be predicted more accurately.

Let us suppose we face a data problem with missing values in a particular characteristic (the extension to more characteristics is direct). The idea described above is to suppress a percentage of known values of that characteristic, playing with the advantage that the actual values are known and can be used to guide learning by using them as targets. Thus, if we define μ as the percentage of missing values and ε as the percentage of deleted samples, we will have $(\mu + \varepsilon)N$ samples with unknown values in the training set while there are only μN missing samples in the test set.

3 Experiments

The main objective of the experiment conducted in this work is to see how the imputation of missing values provided by several well-known methods can be improved by means of our proposed algorithm based on SDAEs.

Three datasets are selected from UCI repository [8] corresponding to classification and regression problems. In the UCI database, these sets are referred to as Cloud Dataset, Blood Transfusion Service Center and Boston Housing.

Table 1. Datasets.

	Samples		
	Total	Classes	Features
Cloud dataset	1024	-	10
Blood transfusion	683	2	4
Boston housing	506	-	13

While the descriptive features of these sets are shown in Table 1, a more detailed description of the sets can be found in [8].

Only complete datasets are considered to artificially insert a variety of missing values in order to compute the error between true and imputed values. Moreover, missing values will be inserted in continuous features.

Every architecture in this survey has been trained according to the techniques mentioned in the previous section. In all cases, SDAEs are constructed to have three hidden layers with 25%–75% of expansion and the number of hidden nodes is set by executing a 5-fold cross validation process applied with 50 different training runs (i.e., different network weights initialization). In order to do that, every data set is split into training (80%) and test (20%). During experiments, several missing percentages μ and different amounts of deleted samples ε are treated to test the performance of our strategy within different situations. More specifically, values of 10%, 20% and 30% of missing are explored while a percentage from 25% to 100% of the rest of samples in the same characteristic is deleted. Thus, for each missing percentage introduced, 25%, 50%, 75% and 100% of deleted samples are explored.

3.1 Pre-imputation Methods

Some of the well-known methods that have been widely studied in the literature are selected to be implemented in the pre-imputation stage. To demonstrate wether the capacity of the pre-imputation technique is key to getting better the final result, three methods with different levels of complexity are used. These are as follows:

- *Zero Imputation (Z).* A simple and general imputation procedure which consist of initializing unknown values to zero. This is perhaps the simplest method and one of the most carried out in practice, even though it does not take into account the correlation structure of the data. For this reason, it tends to yield poor imputation results.
- *K-Nearest Neighbour Imputation (K).* The K method is an imputation procedure based on the principle that the instances with similar properties in a data set are close to each others. This mechanism is one of the most popular approaches for solving incomplete data problems. Basically, given an unknown value, its K nearest neighbours are obtained among the training cases with

known values in the attribute to be imputed. Then, the missing value is filled in with an estimation calculated by using those K values. The optimal value of K is computed by cross validation in this work.

- *Support Vector Machine Imputation (S).* According to this technique, a SVM can be used to impute missing values as regression analysis. A different SVM is used to learn every feature with missing values. Therefore, every complete training example $\mathbf{x}$ is used to train the network in the following way. Without loss of generality, suppose we have a data set with missing values only in the j-th feature. Then the input pattern to train the SVM will be composed of $x_1, x_1, \ldots, x_{j-1}, x_{j+1}, \ldots, x_D$, and the target value by x_j. After the network is trained, it is used to perform regression on the instances which have unknown values.

3.2 Results

For each data set, the MSE between real and imputed values is shown in a table where the three pre-imputation methods mentioned above are distinguished. Missing is introduced in one feature randomly selected between the continuous features. Results show mean and standard deviation for 50 runs. As it has been said before, values within $\{0.1, 0.2, 0.3\}$ are explored for μ and $\{0.25, 0.5, 0.75, 1\}$ for ε. In addition, best result of a family of pre-imputations is shown in italic and the global minimum for a missing percentage in bold (in some cases, there is more than one bold value for each percentage (columns) because there is no statistical difference between them).

Cloud Dataset. In this set, both missing and deleted samples are inserted in the feature 7. Results can be seen in Table 2.

Table 2. Results for Cloud dataset.

Procedure	μ		
	0.1	0.2	0.3
Z	1.19 ± 0.17	0.98 ± 0.25	1.09 ± 0.17
Z-SDAE	0.35 ± 0.03	0.42 ± 0.06	0.4 ± 0.02
Z-SDAE (ε)	*0.08 ± 0.04 (0.25)*	*0.04 ± 0.02 (0.75)*	*0.07 ± 0.03 (1)*
K	0.20 ± 0.02	0.37 ± 0.01	0.51 ± 0.01
K-SDAE	0.08 ± 0.01	0.12 ± 0.007	0.17 ± 0.008
K-SDAE (ε)	*0.02 ± 0.01 (0.75)*	**0.02 ± 0.01 (0.5)**	**0.02 ± 0.007 (0.75)**
S	0.14 ± 0.01	0.29 ± 0.012	0.31 ± 0.016
S-SDAE	0.06 ± 0.02	0.14 ± 0.015	0.13 ± 0.01
S-SDAE (ε)	**0.01 ± 0.009 (0.75)**	**0.02 ± 0.007 (0.5)**	**0.02 ± 0.015 (1)**

Blood Transfusion Service Center. In this case, missing and deleting is inserted in characteristic number 2. Results are shown in Table 3.

Table 3. Results for Blood Transfusion dataset.

Procedure	μ		
	0.1	0.2	0.3
Z	0.81 ± 0.08	0.8 ± 0.05	0.81 ± 0.05
Z-SDAE	0.54 ± 0.09	0.46 ± 0.09	0.69 ± 0.15
Z-SDAE (ε)	*0.04 ± 0.03 (0.5)*	*0.07 ± 0.015 (1)*	*0.04 ± 0.016 (0.75)*
K	0.03 ± 0.025	0.04 ± 0.012	0.04 ± 0.01
K-SDAE	0.012 ± 0.006	0.025 ± 0.01	0.02 ± 0.006
K-SDAE (ε)	**0.005 ± 0.002 (1)**	**0.006 ± 0.004 (1)**	*0.006 ± 0.003 (1)*
S	0.0158 ± 0.01	0.02 ± 0.005	0.026 ± 0.01
S-SDAE	0.012 ± 0.005	0.016 ± 0.01	0.016 ± 0.005
S-SDAE (ε)	**0.004 ± 0.003 (1)**	**0.005 ± 0.002 (1)**	**0.004 ± 0.001 (1)**

Boston Housing. For this dataset, different values for μ and ε are inserted in feature number 13, and results are presented in Table 4.

Table 4. Results for Boston Housing dataset.

Procedure	μ		
	0.1	0.2	0.3
Z	1.41 ± 0.05	1.09 ± 0.03	1.15 ± 0.03
Z-SDAE	0.83 ± 0.03	0.93 ± 0.05	0.8 ± 0.02
Z-SDAE (ε)	*0.69 ± 0.04 (1)*	*0.62 ± 0.03 (1)*	*0.7 ± 0.01 (1)*
K	0.74 ± 0.05	0.69 ± 0.03	0.78 ± 0.02
K-SDAE	0.58 ± 0.04	0.45 ± 0.02	0.48 ± 0.01
K-SDAE (ε)	**0.46 ± 0.02 (0.75)**	**0.43 ± 0.02 (0.75)**	**0.39 ± 0.015 (1)**
S	0.61 ± 0.04	0.54 ± 0.016	0.64 ± 0.016
S-SDAE	**0.45 ± 0.018**	0.49 ± 0.014	*0.43 ± 0.016*
S-SDAE (ε)	**0.46 ± 0.03 (1)**	**0.45 ± 0.02 (0.75)**	0.51 ± 0.016 (1)

4 Discussion

From the results shown in the tables, it is observed that for each family of algorithms (Z, K and S), the best imputation result (in italic) is always obtained when deleting samples is introduced ($\varepsilon \neq 0$). There is only one case where this does not occur, in the Boston Housing with $\mu = 0.3$ where the best result is obtained with S-SDAE procedure. In addition, the best overall result (in bold) is always obtained by deleting samples and with high values of ε (mostly 0.75 and 1). This allow us to infer that the elimination of samples makes the machine able to learn a reconstruction of the missing values with greater precision.

It can also be observed that the method of imputation used is decisive for the final results: the better the method of pre-imputation, the better results are obtained.

5 Conclusions

In this paper, a new deep learning-based imputation technique has been presented. Although the unsupervised layer-wise training with Autoencoders (AEs) has been widely studied through the literature, we have carried out a method which allows a better imputation by stacking several Denoising AEs (DAEs). The proposed imputation method is able to leverage all the available information in a data set, including that which is in incomplete instances. Moreover, by means of inserting artificial missing values ('deleted' values), the quality of the imputed values is improved. Empirical results over several UCI repository datasets show that our method is able to improve the final imputed values obtained by other procedures used as pre-imputation.

References

1. García-Laencina, P.J., Sancho-Gómez, J.L., Figueiras-Vidal, A.: Pattern classification with missing data: a review. Neural Comput. Appl. **9**(1), 1–12 (2009)
2. Batista, G., Monard, M.C.: An analysis of four missing data treatment methods for supervised learning. Appl. Artif. Intell. **17**, 519–533 (2003)
3. Luengo, J., García, S., Herrera, F.: On the choice of the best imputation methods for missing values considering three groups of classification methods. Knowl. Inf. Syst. **32**(1), 77–108 (2012)
4. Vincent, P., Larochelle, H., Lajoie, I., Bengio, Y., Manzagol, P.-A.: Stacked denoising autoencoders: learning useful representations in a deep network with a local denoising criterion. J. Mach. Learn. Res. **11**(11), 3371–3408 (2010)
5. Bengio, Y.: Learning deep architectures for AI. Technical report, Dept. IRO, Universite de Montreal (2009)
6. Deng, L., Yu, D.: Deep learning: methods and applications. Found. Trends Sig. Process. **7**(3–4), 197–387 (2014)
7. Bengio, Y., Lamblin, P., Popovici, D., Larochelle, H.: Greedy layer-wise training of deep networks. Adv. Neural Inf. Process. Syst. **19**, 153 (2007). (NIPS06), (B. Scholkopf, J. Platt, and T. Hoffman, eds.)
8. Lichman, M.: UCI machine learning repository (2013). http://archive.ics.uci.edu/ml

Machine Learning Applied to Big Data Analysis

Big Data Infrastructure: A Survey

Jaime Salvador[1], Zoila Ruiz[1], and Jose Garcia-Rodriguez[2(✉)]

[1] Universidad Central del Ecuador, Ciudadela Universitaria, Quito, Ecuador
{jsalvador,zruiz}@uce.edu.ec

[2] Universidad de Alicante, Ap. 99, 03080 Alicante, Spain
jgarcia@dtic.ua.es

Abstract. In the last years, the volume of information is growing faster than ever before, moving from small datasets to huge volumes of information. This data growth has forced researchers to look for new alternatives to process and store this data, since traditional techniques have been limited by the size and structure of the information. On the other hand, the power of parallel computing in new processors has gradually increased, from single processor architectures to multiple processor, cores and threads. This latter fact enabled the use of machine learning techniques to take advantage of parallel processing capabilities offered by new architectures on large volumes of data. The present paper reviews and proposes a classification, using as criteria, the hardware infrastructures used in works of machine learning parallel approaches applied to large volumes of data.

Keywords: Machine learning · Big data · Hadoop · MapReduce · GPU

1 Introduction

Machine Learning tries to imitate human being intelligence using machines. Machine learning algorithms (supervised and unsupervised) use data to train the model. Depending on the problem modeled, the data may be of the order of gigas. For this reason an optimized storage system for large volumes of data (Big Data) is indispensable.

In the last years, the term Big Data has become very popular because of the large amount of information available from many different sources. The amount of data is increasing very fast and the technology to manipulate large volumes of information is the key when the purpose is the extraction of relevant information. The complexity of the data demands the creation of new architectures that optimize the computation time and the necessary resources to extract valuable knowledge from the data [44].

Traditional techniques are oriented to process information in clusters. With the evolution of the graphic processor unit (GPU) it appeared alternatives to take full advantage of the multiprocess capacity of this type of architectures. Graphic processors are in transition from processors specialized in graphic acceleration to general purpose engines for high performance computing [7]. This type

J.M. Ferrández Vicente et al. (Eds.): IWINAC 2017, Part II, LNCS 10338, pp. 249–258, 2017.
DOI: 10.1007/978-3-319-59773-7_26

of systems are known as GPGPU (General Purpose Graphic Processing Units). In 2008, Khronos Group introduced the OpenCL (Open Computing Language) standard, which was a model for parallel programming. Subsequently appeared its main competitor, NVidia CUDA (Computer Unified Device Architecture). CUDA devices increase the performance of a system due to the high degree of parallelism they are able to control [27].

This document reviews platforms, languages, and many other features of the most popular machine learning frameworks and offers a classification for someone who wants to begin in this field. In addition an exhaustive review of works using machine learning techniques to deal with Big Data is done, including its most relevant features.

The remainder of this document is organized as follows. Section 2 describes the techniques of machine learning and the most popular platforms. Next, an overview about Big Data Processing is presented. Section 3 presents a summary table with several classification criteria. Finally, in Sect. 4 some conclusions and opportunities for future work are presented.

2 Machine Learning for Big Data

This section reviews Machine Learning and Big Data processing platforms concepts. The first part presents a classification of the machine learning techniques to later summarize some platforms oriented to the implementation of the algorithms.

2.1 Machine Learning

The main goal of machine learning is to create systems that learn or extract knowledge from data and use that knowledge to predict future situations, states or trends [29].

Machine Learning techniques can be grouped into the following categories:

- *Classification algorithms.* A system is able to learn from a set of sample data (labeled data), from which a set of classification rules called model is built. This rules are used to classify new information [34].
- *Clustering algorithms.* It consists on the formation of groups (called clusters) of instances that share common characteristics without any prior knowledge [34].
- *Recommendations algorithms.* It consists of predicting patterns of preferences and the use of those preferences to make recommendations to the users [36].
- *Dimensionality Reduction Algorithms.* It consists on the reduction in the number of variables (attributes) of a dataset without affecting the predictive capacity of the model [14].

Scalability is an important aspect to consider in a learning method. Such capacity is defined as the ability of a system to adapt to the increasing demands in terms of information processing. To support this process onto large volumes of data, the platforms incorporate different forms of scaling [43]:

- *Horizontal scaling*, involves the distribution of the process over several nodes (computers).
- *Vertical scaling*, involves adding more resources to a single node (computer).

Machine Learning Libraries. In this section we present the description of several libraries that implement some of the algorithms included in the previous classification. The use of these libraries is proposed using as criteria the integration with new systems but not and end user tool criteria.

Apache Mahout[1] provides implementations for many of the most popular machine learning algorithms. It contains implementation of clustering algorithms, classification, and many others. To enable clustering, it uses Apache Hadoop [2].

MLlib[2] is part of the Apache Spark project that implements several machine learning algorithms. Among the groups of algorithms that it implements we can find classification, regression, clustering and dimensionality reduction algorithms [30].

FlinkML[3] is the Flink machine learning library. It's goal is to provide scalable machine learning algorithms. It provides tools to help the design of machine learning systems [2].

Table 1 describes the libraries presented above. For each one, the supported programming language is detailed:

Table 1. Machine learning tool by language

Tool	Java	Scala	Python	R
Apache Mahout	x			
Spark MLlib	x	x	x	x
FlinkML	x	x		

As shown above, the most used language is Java, which shows a tendency when implementing systems that integrate machine learning techniques.

Table 2 describes each library and the support for scaling when working with large volumes of data:

Table 2. Machine learning tool scaling

Tool	H+V	Multicore	GPU	Cluster
Apache Mahout	x	x		x
Spark MLlib	x	x	x	x
FlinkML	x	x		x

[1] http://mahout.apache.org/.
[2] http://spark.apache.org/mllib/.
[3] https://ci.apache.org/projects/flink/flink-docs-release-1.2/dev/libs/ml/index.html.

In the table we can see that the scaling techniques are combined with others to obtain platforms with better performance.

2.2 Platforms for Big Data Processing

Big Data is defined as a large and complex collection of data, which are difficult to process by a relational database system. The typical size of the data, in this type of problems, is of the order of tera or peta bytes and they are in constant growth [23].

There are many platforms to work with Big Data, among the most popular we can mention Hadoop, Spark (two open source projects from the Apache Foundation) and MapReduce.

MapReduce [9] is a programming model oriented to the process of large volumes of data [16]. Problems addressed using MapReduce should be problems that can be separated into small tasks to be processed in parallel [26]. This programming model is adopted by several specific implementations (platforms) like Apache Hadoop and Spark.

Apache Hadoop[4] is an open source project sponsored by the *Apache Software Fundation.* It allows distributed processing of large volumes of data in a cluster [21]. It consists of three fundamental components [19]: HDFS (storage component), YARN (resource planning component) and MapReduce.

Apache Spark[5] is a cluster computing system based on the MapReduce concept. Spark supports interactive computing and its main objective is to provide high performance while maintaining resources and calculations in memory [29].

H_2O[6] is an open source framework that provides libraries for parallel processing, information analysis and machine learning along with data processing and evaluation tools [29].

Apache Storm[7] is an open source system for real time distributed computing. An application created with Storm is designed as a directed acyclic graph (DAG) *topology.*

Apache Flink[8] is an open source platform for batch an stream processing.

Table 3 compares the platform with the type of processing supported and the storage system used.

As can be seen, all the platforms support all varieties of storage. However in large implementations the local storage (or pseudo-cluster) is not an option to consider.

---

[4] http://hadoop.apache.org/.
[5] http://spark.apache.org/.
[6] http://www.h2o.ai/h2o/.
[7] http://storm.apache.org/.
[8] https://flink.apache.org/.

Table 3. Platform scaling

	Scaling				Storage		
Tool	HV	Multicore	GPU	Cluster	IM[a]	Local	DFS[b]
Apache Hadoop	x	x		x		x	x
Apache Spark	x	x	x	x	x	x	x
H2O	x	x	x[c]	x	x	x	x
Apache Storm	x	x		x	x	x	x
Apache Flink	x	x		x	x	x	x

[a]In-memory
[b]Distributed File System.
[c]Through Deep Water (http://www.h2o.ai/deep-water/) in beta state.

3 Machine Learning for Big Data Review

This section proposes a classification of research works that use Big Data platforms to apply machine learning techniques based on three criteria: language (programming language supported), scaling (scalability) and storage (supported storage type).

The combination of these three factors allows the proper selection of a platform to integrate machine learning techniques with Big Data. Scaling is related to the type of storage. In the case of using horizontal scaling, a distributed file system must be used.

Table 4 shows the classification based on the above mentioned criteria.

3.1 Language

The supported programming language is an important aspect when selecting a platform. Taking into account that this work is oriented to platforms that are not end user (tools like Weka[9], RapidMiner[10], etc. are not considered), the following programming languages are considered: Java, Scala, Python, R.

The most common language in this type of implementations is Java. However over time appeared layers of software that abstract access to certain technologies. With these news technologies is possible to use the platforms described in this document with different programming languages.

3.2 Scaling

Scaling focuses on the possibility of including more process nodes (horizontal scaling) or include parallel processing within the same node (vertical scaling) by using of graphics cards. This document consider horizontal, vertical, cluster and GPU scaling.

[9] http://www.cs.waikato.ac.nz/ml/weka/.
[10] https://rapidminer.com/.

Table 4. Language-scaling-storage LSS classification

Article[a]	Language	Scaling	Storage
Al-Jarrah et al. [1]		V	DFS, IM
Aridhi and Mephu [2]	Scala, Java	Cluster	DFS, IM
Armbrust et al. [3]	Scala, Java, Python	Cluster	Local, DFS, IM
Bertolucci et al. [4]	Java	Cores, Cluster	DFS, IM
Borthakur [5]	Java	Cluster	Local, DFS
Castillo et al. [6]		Cluster	
Catanzaro et al. [7]		Cluster, GPU	DFS, IM
Crawford et al. [8]	Scala, Java, Python		Loca,IM
Dhingra and Professor [10]	Java	Cluster	Local, DFS
Fan and Bifet [11]	Java	Cluser, GPU	DFS
Gandomi and Haider [12]		Vertical	
Ghemawat et al. [13]		Cluster	DFS
Hafez et al. [15]	Scala, Java, Python	Cluster	DFS, IM
Hashem et al. [16]	Java	H, V, Cluster, GPU	DFS, IM
He et al. [17]		V, Cluster	DFS, IM
Hodge et al. [18]	Scala, Java	Cluster	DFS
Issa and Figueira [20]	Java, Python	H, Cluster	DFS, IM
Jackson et al. [21]	Java, Python	Cluster	DFS
Jain and Bhatnagar [22]	Java	Cluster	DFS
Jiang et al. [23]	Java, Python	Cluster, GPU	DFS, IM
Kacfah Emani et al. [24]	Scala, Java	Cluster	DFS, IM
Kamishima and M. [25]			
Kiran et al. [26]	Java	Cluster	DFS, IM
Kraska et al. [28]	Scala	Cluster	DFS, IM
Landset et al. [29]	Scala, Java		DFS, IM
Meng et al. [30]	Scala, Java	Cluster	DFS
Modha and Spangler [31]		Cluster	DFS
Naimur Rahman et al. [32]	Java	Cluster	DFS
Namiot [33]	Scala, Java	Cluster	DFS
Norman et al. [35]		Cluster	DFS
Pääkkönen [37]	Scala, Java, Python	Cluster	DFS
Ramírez-Gallego et al. [38]	Scala	Core, Cluster	DFS
Saecker and Markl [39]		H, V, Cluster, GPU	DFS
Salloum et al. [40]	Scala, Java	Cluster, Paralell	DFS
Saraladevi et al. [41]	Java	Cluster	DFS
Seminario and Wilson [42]	Java	Cluster	Local, IM, DFS
Singh and Reddy [43]	Scala, Java		Local, IM, DFS
Singh and Kaur [44]	Java	H, V, Cluster	DFS
Walunj and Sadafale [45]	Java		Local, DFS
Zaharia et al. [46]	Scala, Java	Cluster	DFS

[a]Some articles only deal one of the criteria mentioned above, but in any case all the articles are included in the table.

As can be seen in Table 4, and in the above tables, all the platforms scale horizontal by using a DFS that in most cases corresponds to Hadoop. However platforms that work with data in memory are becoming more popular (like Spark).

3.3 Storage

Depending on the amount of information and the strategy used to process the information, it is possible to decide the type of storage: local, DFS, in-memory. Each type involves the implementation of hardware infrastructure to be used. For example, in the case of a cluster implementation, it is necessary to have adequate equipment that will constitute the cluster nodes.

For proof of concepts it is acceptable to use a pseudo-cluster that simulates a cluster environment on a single machine.

4 Conclusions

In this document, a brief review on the machine learning techniques was carried out, orienting them to the processing of large volumes of data. Then, some of the platforms that implement several of the techniques described in the document were analyzed. Most of the reviewed articles use techniques, languages and scaling described in this document.

In general, we can conclude that all these techniques are scalable in one way or another. It is possible to start from a local architecture (or pseudo-cluster) for a proof of concept test and progressively scale to more complex architectures like a cluster, evidencing the need for distributed storage (DFS). The programming language should not be a factor when selecting a platform, since nowadays there are interfaces that allow the use of the mentioned platforms in a growing variety of languages.

Future work may be proposed to perform a similar study considering the *time* factor. This factor determines two forms of processing: batch and online processing. Finally, streaming processing could be incorporated into the study, which is a fundamental part of some of the platforms described in this document.

Acknowledgements. This work has been funded by the Spanish Government TIN2016-76515-R grant for the COMBAHO project, supported with Feder funds.

References

1. Al-Jarrah, O.Y., Yoo, P.D., Muhaidat, S., Karagiannidis, G.K., Taha, K.: Efficient machine learning for big data: a review. Big Data Res. **2**(3), 87–93 (2015)
2. Aridhi, S., Mephu, E.: Big graph mining: frameworks and techniques. Big Data Res. **6**, 1–10 (2016)

3. Armbrust, M., Ghodsi, A., Zaharia, M., Xin, R.S., Lian, C., Huai, Y., Liu, D., Bradley, J.K., Meng, X., Kaftan, T., Franklin, M.J.: Spark SQL: relational data processing in spark michael. In: Proceedings of the ACM SIGMOD International Conference on Management of Data - SIGMOD 2015, pp. 1383–1394 (2015)
4. Bertolucci, M., Carlini, E., Dazzi, P., Lulli, A., Ricci, L.: Static and dynamic big data partitioning on apache spark. Adv. Parallel Comput. **27**, 489–498 (2016)
5. Borthakur, D.: HDFS architecture guide. Hadoop Apache Project, 1–13 (2008). https://hadoop.apache.org/docs/r1.2.1/hdfs_design.pdf
6. Castillo, S.J.L., del Castillo, J.R.F., Sotos, L.G.: Algorithms of machine learning for K-clustering. In: Demazeau, Y., et al. (eds.) Trends in Practical Applications of Agents and Multiagent Systems. AISC, vol. 71, pp. 443–452. Springer, Heidelberg (2010)
7. Catanzaro, B., Sundaram, N., Keutzer, K.: Fast support vector machine training and classication on graphics processors. In: Machine Learning, pp. 104–111 (2008)
8. Crawford, M., Khoshgoftaar, T.M., Prusa, J.D., Richter, A.N., Al Najada, H.: Survey of review spam detection using machine learning techniques. J. Big Data **2**(1), 23 (2015)
9. Dean, J., Ghemawat, S.: MapReduce: simplified data processing on large clusters. In: Proceedings of 6th Symposium on Operating Systems Design and Implementation, pp. 137–149 (2004)
10. Nagina, Dhingra, S.: Scheduling algorithms in big data: a survey. Int. J. Eng. Comput. Sci. **5**(8), 17737–17743 (2016)
11. Fan, W., Bifet, A.: Mining big data: current status, and forecast to the future. ACM SIGKDD Explor. Newslett. **14**(2), 1–5 (2013)
12. Gandomi, A., Haider, M.: Beyond the hype: big data concepts, methods, and analytics. Int. J. Inf. Manag. **35**(2), 137–144 (2015)
13. Ghemawat, S., Gobioff, H., Leung, S.: Google file system (2003)
14. Guller, M.: Big Data Analytics with Spark (2015). ISBN 9781484209653
15. Hafez, M.M., Shehab, M.E., El Fakharany, E., Abdel Ghfar Hegazy, A.E.F.: Effective selection of machine learning algorithms for big data analytics using apache spark. In: Hassanien, A.E., Shaalan, K., Gaber, T., Azar, A.T., Tolba, M.F. (eds.) AISI 2016. AISC, vol. 533, pp. 692–704. Springer, Cham (2017). doi:10.1007/978-3-319-48308-5_66
16. Hashem, I.A.T., Anuar, N.B., Gani, A., Yaqoob, I., Xia, F., Khan, S.U.: MapReduce: review and open challenges. Scientometrics **109**(1), 1–34 (2016)
17. He, Q., Li, N., Luo, W.J., Shi, Z.Z.: A survey of machine learning for big data processing. Moshi Shibie yu Rengong Zhineng/Pattern Recogn. Artif. Intell. **27**(4), 327–336 (2014)
18. Hodge, V.J., Keefe, S.O., Austin, J.: Hadoop neural network for parallel and distributed feature selection. Neural Netw. **78**, 24–35 (2016)
19. Holmes, A.: Hadoop in Practice. Manning, 2nd edn. (2015). ISBN 9781617292224
20. Issa, J., Figueira, S.: Hadoop and memcached: performance and power characterization and analysis. J. Cloud Comput.: Adv. Syst. Appl. **1**(1), 10 (2012)
21. Jackson, J.C., Vijayakumar, V., Quadir, M.A., Bharathi, C.: Survey on programming models and environments for cluster, cloud, and grid computing that defends big data. Procedia Comput. Sci. **50**, 517–523 (2015)
22. Jain, A., Bhatnagar, V.: Crime data analysis using pig with Hadoop. Phys. Procedia **78**(December 2015), 571–578 (2016)
23. Jiang, H., Chen, Y., Qiao, Z., Weng, T.H., Li, K.C.: Scaling up MapReduce-based big data processing on multi-GPU systems. Cluster Comput. **18**(1), 369–383 (2015)

24. Kacfah Emani, C., Cullot, N., Nicolle, C.: Understandable big data: a survey. Comput. Sci. Rev. **17**, 70–81 (2015)
25. Kamishima, T., Motoyoshi, F.: Learning from cluster examples. Mach. Learn. **53**(3), 199–233 (2003)
26. Kiran, M., Kumar, A., Mukherjee, S., Ravi Prakash, G.: Verification and validation of MapReduce program model for parallel support vector machine algorithm on Hadoop cluster. Int. Conf. Adv. Comput. Communi. Syst. (ICACCS) **4**(3), 317–325 (2013)
27. Kirk, D., Hwu, W.-M.W.: Processors, Programming Massively Parallel: A Hands-on Approach (2010). ISBN 0123814723
28. Kraska, T., Talwalkar, A., Duchi, J., Griffith, R., Franklin, M., Jordan, M.: MLbase: a distributed machine-learning system. In: 6th Biennial Conference on Innovative Data Systems Research (CIDR 2013) (2013)
29. Landset, S., Khoshgoftaar, T.M., Richter, A.N., Hasanin, T.: A survey of open source tools for machine learning with big data in the Hadoop ecosystem. J. Big Data **2**(1), 24 (2015)
30. Meng, X., Bradley, J., Yavuz, B., Sparks, E., Venkataraman, S., Liu, D., Freeman, J., Tsai, D.B., Amde, M., Owen, S., Xin, D., Xin, R., Franklin, M.J., Zadeh, R., Zaharia, M., Talwalkar, A.: MLlib: machine learning in apache spark. J. Mach. Learn. Res. **17**, 1–7 (2016)
31. Modha, D.S., Spangler, W.S.: Feature weighting in k-means clustering. Mach. Learn. **52**(3), 217–237 (2003)
32. Naimur Rahman, M., Esmailpour, A., Zhao, J.: Machine learning with big data an efficient electricity generation forecasting system. Big Data Res. **5**, 9–15 (2016)
33. Namiot, D.: On big data stream processing. Int. J. Open Inf. Technol. **3**(8), 48–51 (2015)
34. Nguyen, T.T.T., Armitage, G.: A survey of techniques for internet traffic classification using machine learning. IEEE Commun. Surveys Tutorials **10**(4) (2008)
35. Spangenberg, N., Roth, M., Franczyk, B.: Evaluating new approaches of big data analytics frameworks. In: Abramowicz, W. (ed.) BIS 2015. LNBIP, vol. 208, pp. 28–37. Springer, Cham (2015). doi:10.1007/978-3-319-19027-3_3
36. Owen, S., Anil, R., Dunning, T., Friedman, E.: Mahout in Action. Manning (2012). ISBN 9781935182689
37. Pääkkönen, P.: Feasibility analysis of AsterixDB and Spark streaming with Cassandra for stream-based processing. J. Big Data **3**(1), 6 (2016)
38. Ramírez-Gallego, S., Mouriño-Talín, H., Martínez-Rego, D., Bolón-Canedo, V., Benitez, J.M., Alonso-Betanzos, A., Herrera, F.: Un Framework de Selección de Características basado en la Teoría de la Información para Big Data sobre Apache Spark
39. Saecker, M., Markl, V.: Big data analytics on modern hardware architectures: a technology survey. In: Aufaure, M.-A., Zimányi, E. (eds.) Business Intelligence. LNBIP, vol. 138, pp. 125–149. Springer, Heidelberg (2013). doi:10.1007/978-3-642-36318-4_6
40. Salloum, S., Dautov, R., Chen, X., Peng, P.X., Huang, J.Z.: Big data analytics on Apache Spark. Int. J. Data Sci. Anal. **1**(3), 145–164 (2016)
41. Saraladevi, B., Pazhaniraja, N., Paul, P.V., Basha, M.S.S., Dhavachelvan, P.: Big data and Hadoop-a study in security perspective. Procedia Comput. Sci. **50**, 596–601 (2015)
42. Seminario, C.E., Wilson, D.C.: Case study evaluation of mahout as a recommender platform. CEUR Workshop Proc. **910**(September 2012), 45–50 (2012)

43. Singh, D., Reddy, C.K.: A survey on platforms for big data analytics. J. Big Data **2**(1), 8 (2015)
44. Singh, R., Kaur, P.J.: Analyzing performance of Apache Tez and MapReduce with Hadoop multinode cluster on Amazon cloud. J. Big Data **3**(1), 19 (2016)
45. Walunj, S.G., Sadafale, K.: An online recommendation system for e-commerce based on apache mahout framework. In: Proceedings of the Annual Conference on Computers and People Research, pp. 153–158 (2013)
46. Zaharia, M., Chowdhury, M., Franklin, M.J., Shenker, S., Stoica, I.: Spark: cluster computing with working sets. In: HotCloud 2010 Proceedings of the 2nd USENIX Conference on Hot Topics in Cloud Computing, p. 10 (2010)

A Survey of Machine Learning Methods for Big Data

Zoila Ruiz[1], Jaime Salvador[1], and Jose Garcia-Rodriguez[2](✉)

[1] Universidad Central Del Ecuador, Ciudadela Universitaria, Quito, Ecuador
{zruiz,jsalvador}@uce.edu.ec
[2] Universidad de Alicante, Ap. 99, 03080 Alicante, Spain
jgarcia@dtic.ua.es

Abstract. Nowadays there are studies in different fields aimed to extract relevant information on trends, challenges and opportunities; all these studies have something in common: they work with large volumes of data. This work analyzes different studies carried out on the use of Machine Learning (ML) for processing large volumes of data (Big Data). Most of these datasets, are complex and come from various sources with structured or unstructured data. For this reason, it is necessary to find mechanisms that allow classification and, in a certain way, organize them to facilitate to the users the extraction of the required information. The processing of these data requires the use of classification techniques that will also be reviewed.

Keywords: Big Data · Machine learning · Classification · Clustering

1 Introduction

In recent years there has been an accelerated growth in the volume of information available on the network. Likewise, several alternatives have appeared for processing these large volumes of data (Big Data) and their storage [18]. There are many studies oriented to the processing of Big Data and extraction of relevant information that allows to generate knowledge [17]. The different techniques of Machine Learning allow to achieve this purpose, therefore, several studies have been devoted to replace the statistical analysis by ML techniques. For this reason, it's necessary to study the main data characteristics, such as: heterogeneity, autonomy, complexity and evolution [40].

Nowadays, presenting alternatives for processing large volumes of data is undoubtedly the main goal of many works or projects [32]. The ability to process information with savings in computational costs "maximizing the relevance and reliability of the information obtained" is a real challenge [2]. Machine Learning techniques are a good alternative to solve problems related to Big Data. In this document we review some algorithms used in different works, combination of techniques or proposals of hybrid techniques used to process large volumes of data.

J.M. Ferrández Vicente et al. (Eds.): IWINAC 2017, Part II, LNCS 10338, pp. 259–267, 2017.
DOI: 10.1007/978-3-319-59773-7_27

This document is organized as follows. Section 2 introduces the Big Data concept summarizing its characteristics; later, some classification techniques and algorithms are described. Section 3 presents a discussion about the criteria for choosing a classification technique. Finally, Sect. 4 presents some conclusions and opportunities for future work.

2 Big Data

This section describes the most common datasets used for verifying certain algorithms. Some of the most relevant classification algorithms are reviewed below.

Big Data is present in all areas and sectors worldwide. However, it's complexity exceeds the processing power of traditional tools. Because of this, high-performance computing platforms are required to exploit the full power of Big Data [36]. These requirements have undoubtedly become a real challenge. Many studies focus on the search of methodologies that allow lowering computational costs with an increase in the relevance of extracted information. The need to extract useful knowledge has required researchers to apply different machine learning techniques, to compare the results obtained and to analyze them according to the characteristics of the large data volumes (volume, velocity,veracity and variety, the 4V's) [26].

2.1 Datasets

With the growth of data size, it is essential to consider techniques to find complex relationships between samples and models always considering the evolution of data over time [39]. In this way, we can build systems whose design allows unstructured data to be linked through relationships. This will allow us to obtain valid patterns through which trends can be predicted or a phenomenon can be better understood.

Table 1 briefly describes some types of popular datasets used to validate different methods commonly used in processing large volumes of data.

Table 1. Features present in popular datasets

Dataset	Features		
	Velocity	Volume	Variety
Repository of the ML databases [16]		X	X
Social computing [26]	X	X	X
Synthetic interval datasets [9]	X	X	
Sociodemographic data [24]		X	X
Real database [12]	X	X	X

As we observed in the previous table, there are datasets that can be used for the verification, validation, comparison and previous training of the algorithms to process the data. Many of these algorithms require training to properly process the data. Each dataset has features that allow you to choose the ones that best fit the actual data [30].

2.2 Classification Techniques

In this section we introduce the most relevant algorithms for classification and its relationship with Big Data platforms. First, a classification of machine learning techniques is presented, later we describe some classification algorithms.

The classification algorithms are divided into:

- *Supervised.* The main task is to determine to which class each new data belongs. This is achieved based on a training-classification scheme using previously established sample sets. These techniques can only be used if the number of classes is known a priori. Examples of these algorithms are Neighborhood Based, Decision Trees (DT) and Support Vector Machines (SVM).
- *Unsupervised.* They are used when training sets are not available. Therefore, they use grouping algorithms to construct groups, so that the data belonging to the group has a high level of similarity. Among the most used algorithms we can find K-Means, Sequential Grouping, ISODATA or Adaptive method.

The main problem found in different studies oriented to the processing of large volumes of data resides in the selection of suitable techniques for variable selection and classification. The technique chosen depends on the type of information analyzed, this allows to obtain higher quality information, reduces the computational cost and improves processing times. Some of the most used criteria are: the dimensionality of the data, the relevant features [14] and the veracity of the information obtained. With these considerations we can select the most appropriate Machine Learning techniques that allow us to optimize the results obtained.

2.3 Classification Algorithms

The following are some of the most relevant classification algorithms:

- *K-Means:* Simple and efficient, it needs only one initial parameter (k) and its results depend on the initial selection of the clusters centroids [1].
- *K-Medoids:* It is considered a K-Means variation. Its goal is to determine the best representative of the center of each cluster (medoide) [29].
- *Support Vector Machine (SVM):* Given a training set with a labeled class (through training), SVM can build a model that predicts the class of a new sample [31].
- *k-Nearest Neighbor (KNN):* It is simple and local. You need to specify an appropriate metric to measure proximity. It is noise and dimensionality sensitive [7].

- *Expectation-Maximization (EM):* It provides a maximum likelihood iterative solution. It converges to a local maximum and is sensitive to the choice of the initial values [20].
- *Self Organized Map (SOM):* It groups data from the input set according to different criteria from a training process. An intuitive description of the similarity between data can be observed through a map [22].
- *DBSCAN:* Automatically determines the number of clusters. Points with low density are classified as noise and are omitted, so there is no complete clustering [6].
- *Decision Tree (DT):* It is recursevely constructed following a hierarchical descending strategy [11].

In several works we find "as the used methodology" a variation of these Machine Learning algorithms. These variations allow, in a certain way, to eliminate or minimize the limitations present in each one. Sometimes they depend directly on the data set used in the experimentation stage or on the initialization parameters of each algorithm, among others. In other cases they propose a technique [42] or hybrid strategy for processing large volumes of data.

Table 2 summarizes different studies that propose the combination of algorithms, metrics or pre-processing of data using another algorithm. This contributes to improving the processing of information (minimizing computational costs and maximizing the relevance of extracted information).

Table 2. Combining algorithms

Algorithm	EM	Fuzzy	PSO[a]	Bisection	GA[b]	KNN
K-Means [10]	X	X	X	X	X	X
K-Medoids [35]		X	X		X	X
SVM [44]	X	X	X	X	X	X
KNN [13]	X	X	X		X	
SOM [21]	X	X	X		X	X
DBSCAN [15]		X	X		X	X
DT [37]	X	X	X		X	X

[a]Particle Swarm Optimization
[b] Genetic Algorithm

Table 3 shows some hybrid techniques or strategies. Different methods are used for similarity calculation. They combine different ML techniques to create more efficient classification methods.

In the reviewed papers, a distinction was found between implementing hybrid techniques or strategies. The first case is based on introducing in the algorithm some technique different from the one usually used for the internal calculation of some parameter. In the second case, a certain limitation of a technique is strengthened in the pre-processing stage. For example, if it is not suitable for

Table 3. Techniques and hybrid strategies

Technique	Hybrid techniques	Hybrid strategy
Hybrid Bisect K-Means [27]	X	X
HOPACH [a] [38]	X	
DHG [b][12]	X	X
K-mean and KHM [c] [19]	X	
K-Means - GA [3]	X	
HcGA [d] [5]		X
HFS [e] [43]		X
MAM - SOM		X
K-ICA [28]	X	
GKA [f][33]	X	
NKMC [g] [8]	X	
HSRS [h] [34]		X
HC-HOSVD [i] [23]	X	

[a]Hierarchical Ordered Partitioning And Collapsing Hybrid
[b]Density-based Hierarchical Gaussian
[c]K-Harmonic Mean
[d]Hybrid Cellular Genetic Algorithms
[e]Hybrid feature selection scheme
[f]Genetic K-means Algorithm
[g]Naive multi-view K-means
[h]Hybrid sequential-ranked searches
[i]Hybrid clustering via Higher-order singular value decomposition

processing large volumes of data, the data is first partitioned with an appropriate technique and then the resulting technique is applied to each resulting partition.

Among the most outstanding studies we can mention the one of Mishra and Raghavan [25], comparison of optimization algorithms, Al-Sultan and Khan [4], about algorithms like K-means, SA[1], TS[2] and GA, Xiaowei and Ester [41] among others.

From these works three main conclusions can be drawn:

- No method outperforms the other methods in regards to performance when working with one-dimensional or multi-dimensional data.
- Solutions found by TS, GA and SA outperform K-Means, but this is much faster. GA is the fastest finding the best solution, while SA is the fastest in converging.
- The problem with these algorithms is that they do not work properly for large volumes of data, only K-means and Kohonen Maps have been successfully applied to large datasets.

[1] Simulated Annealing.
[2] Tabu search.

3 Discussion

In this section we analyze the usual criteria taken into account when choosing a Machine Learning algorithm to efficiently process information. This allows a greater comprehensibility and interest of the extracted data.

The proposal of new perspectives in the classification methods allows to open new lines of investigation. Considering different metrics to establish similarity between groups or combine techniques for parameter adjustment, allow to improve the results obtained by directly applying a technique. The considerations that are analyzed prior to choosing a classification technique are:

- Data to be processed
- Limitations and parameters to each algorithm

3.1 Data to be Processed

The high dimensionaly of data features is one of the problems that must be considered when working with large volumes of data. The reduction of the data dimensionality is considered, for which the feature selection is very important; to take this into account, algorithms of feature selection and extraction are usually applied. Another valid consideration is the structure and specific features of the data.

3.2 Algorithms Limitations and Accurate Parameterization

Some algorithms are more suitable to process large volumes of data but are not necessarily faster to find the best solution or the least costly; however, by analyzing different algorithms we can obtain important considerations and propose improvements that exceed the limitations of each algorithm. For example, replacing the sequential search of the winning unit for a faster and more efficient search (MAM-SOM).

With this previous analysis, we can pre-select the most adequate techniques for processing our data. However, depending on the data characteristics and the planned objectives, in most cases it requires a combination of techniques, preprocessing of the data, modification of the inner calculations of the algorithms, or hybrid strategies to achieve optimal results.

To verify its behavior, performance and favorable parameters for optimal performance, it is necessary to evaluate each algorithm and compare the results through experimentation. The best way is to use different types of datasets, considering that there are algorithms that work better with categorical data and others do with quantitative data, but very few manage data that have both characteristics simultaneously.

We need to evaluate the validity, stability and scalability in the results obtained in each algorithm.

- Validity: Determining the precision of an algorithm for data clustering.
- Stability: The variation of results obtained in different executions must be similar to each other.
- Scalability: The capacity of clustering big volumes of data in an efficiently way.

4 Conclusions

Machine Learning algorithms have a series of advantages and disadvantages that are reflected in execution times, computational requirements, convergence capacity, complexity levels, their implementation or parameter adjustment among others. Therefore, in many studies it has been decided to combine algorithms to solve problems when processing large volumes of data, depending on their characteristics and goals. It is possible to take advantage of the characteristics of two or more techniques, at the same time, to provide versatile tools in the processing of Big Data.

Despite the existence of a large number of ML techniques, most have some limitations. Problems such as overlap between groups, presence of noise or irregular structures are usually treated using hybrid techniques or strategies. The replacement of an internal calculation by another ML technique allows to overcome the limitations of the algorithms.

As future work, it is intended to test each technique and combination presented with public datasets on various platforms. To test the scalability, computational cost and response time of the different techniques. We should consider parallelization as an alternative to improve aspects such as: response time, computational capacity required by some algorithms or the ability to process large volumes of data.

Acknowledgements. This work has been funded by the Spanish Government TIN2016-76515-R grant for the COMBAHO project, supported with Feder funds.

References

1. Agrawal, A.: Global K-means (GKM) clustering algorithm: a survey. Int. J. Comput. Appl. **79**(2), 20–24 (2013)
2. Al-Jarrah, O.Y., Yoo, P.D., Muhaidat, S., Karagiannidis, G.K., Taha, K.: Efficient machine learning for big data: a review. Big Data Res. **2**(3), 87–93 (2015)
3. Al Malki, A., Rizk, M.M., El-Shorbagy, M.A., Mousa, A.A., Malki, A.A., Rizk, M.M., Mousa, A.A., Mousa, A.A.: Hybrid genetic algorithm with K-means for clustering problems. Open J. Optim. **5**(02), 71 (2016)
4. Al-Sultana, K.S., Khan, M.M.: Computational experience on four algorithms for the hard clustering problem. Pattern Recogn. Lett. **17**(3), 295–308 (1996)
5. Arellano-Verdejo, J., Alba, E., Godoy-Calderon, S.: Efficiently finding the optimum number of clusters in a dataset with a new hybrid differential evolution algorithm: DELA. Soft. Comput. **20**(3), 895–905 (2016)

6. Backlund, H., Hedblom, A., Neijman, N.: A density-based spatial clustering of application with noise. Data Mining TNM033, pp. 11–30 (2011)
7. Bobadilla, J., Ortega, F., Hernando, A., de Rivera, G.G.: A similarity metric designed to speed up, using hardware, the recommender systems k-nearest neighbors algorithm. Knowl.-Based Syst. **51**, 27–34 (2013)
8. Cai, X., Nie, F., Huang, H.: Multi-view K-means clustering on big data. In: IJCAI International Joint Conference on Artificial Intelligence, pp. 2598–2604 (2013)
9. De Carvalho, F.A.T.: Fuzzy c-means clustering methods for symbolic interval data. Pattern Recogn. Lett. **28**(4), 423–437 (2007)
10. Cui, X., Potok, T.E.: Document clustering analysis based on hybrid PSO + K-means algorithm. J. Comput. Sci. **27**(special issue), 33 (2005)
11. Dai, W., Ji, W.: A MapReduce implementation of C4. 5 decision tree algorithm. Int. J. Database Theory Appl. **7**(1), 49–60 (2014)
12. Pascual, D., Pla, F., Sánchez, J.S.: A density-based hierarchical clustering algorithm for highly overlapped distributions with noisy points. In: CCIA, vol. 220, pp. 183–192 (2010)
13. Derrac, J., Chiclana, F., García, S., Herrera, F.: Evolutionary fuzzy k-nearest neighbors algorithm using interval-valued fuzzy sets. Inf. Sci. **329**, 144–163 (2016)
14. Fan, W., Bifet, A.: Mining big data : current status, and forecast to the future. ACM SIGKDD Explor. Newsl. **14**(2), 1–5 (2013)
15. Feng, X., Wang, Z., Yin, G., Wang, Y.: PSO-based DBSCAN with obstacle constraints. J. Theor. Appl. Inf. Technol. **46**(1), 377–383 (2012)
16. Hatamlou, A.: Black hole: a new heuristic optimization approach for data clustering. Inf. Sci. **222**, 175–184 (2013)
17. Ho, R.: Big data machine learning: patterns for predictive analytics. DZone Refcardz **158**, 1–6 (2012)
18. Jadhav, D.K.: Big data: the new challenges in data mining. Int. J. Innov. Res. Comput. Sci. Technol. **1**(2), 39–42 (2013)
19. Jain, R.: A hybrid clustering algorithm for data mining, pp. 387–393 (2012). arXiv preprint arXiv:1205.5353
20. Jiang, M., Ding, Y., Goertzel, B., Huang, Z., Zhou, C., Chao, F.: Improving machine vision via incorporating expectation-maximization into deep spatio-temporal learning. In: Proceedings of the International Joint Conference on Neural Networks, pp. 1804–1811 (2014)
21. Jin, H., Shum, W.-H., Leung, K.-S., Wong, M.-L.: Expanding self-organizing map for data visualization and cluster analysis. Inf. Sci. **163**(1–3), 157–173 (2004)
22. Kohonen, T.: Essentials of the self-organizing map. Neural Netw. **37**, 52–65 (2013)
23. Liu, X., Lathauwer, L., Janssens, F., Moor, B.: Hybrid clustering of multiple information sources via HOSVD. In: Zhang, L., Lu, B.-L., Kwok, J. (eds.) ISNN 2010. LNCS, vol. 6064, pp. 337–345. Springer, Heidelberg (2010). doi:10.1007/978-3-642-13318-3_42
24. Luo, W., Nguyen, T., Nichols, M., Tran, T., Rana, S., Gupta, S., Phung, D., Venkatesh, S., Allender, S.: Is demography destiny? application of machine learning techniques to accurately predict population health outcomes from a minimal demographic dataset. PLoS ONE **10**(5), e0125602 (2015)
25. Mishra, S.K., Raghavan, V.V.: An empirical study of the performance of heuristic methods for clustering. In: Pattern Recognition in Practice IV - Multiple Paradigms, Comparative Studies and Hybrid Systems, pp. 425–436. Elsevier BV (1994)
26. Mujeeb, S., Naidu, L.K.: A relative study on big data applications and techniques. Int. J. Eng. Innov. Technol. (IJEIT) **4**(10), 133–138 (2015)

27. Murugesan, K., Jun, Z.: Hybrid bisect K-means clustering algorithm. In: International Conference on Business Computing and Global Informatization (BCGIN), pp. 216–219. IEEE (2011)
28. Niknam, T., Fard, E.T., Pourjafarian, N., Rousta, A.: An efficient hybrid algorithm based on modified imperialist competitive algorithm and k-means for data clustering. Eng. Appl. Artif. Intell. **24**(2), 306–317 (2011)
29. Park, H.-S., Jun, C.-H.: A simple and fast algorithm for k-medoids clustering. Expert Syst. Appl. **36**(2), 3336–3341 (2009)
30. Parsons, L., Haque, E., Liu, H.: Subspace clustering for high dimensional data. ACM SIGKDD Explor. Newsl. **6**(1), 90–105 (2004)
31. Qi, Z., Tian, Y., Shi, Y.: Robust twin support vector machine for pattern classification. Pattern Recogn. **46**(1), 305–316 (2013)
32. Rebentrost, P., Mohseni, M., Lloyd, S.: Quantum support vector machine for big data classification. Phys. Rev. Lett. **113**(3), 1–5 (2014)
33. Roy, D.K., Sharma, L.K.: Genetic k-Means clustering algorithm for mixed numeric and categorical data sets. Int. J. Artif. Intell. Appl. **1**, 23–28 (2010)
34. Ruiz, R., Riquelme, J.C., Aguilar-Ruiz, J.S., García-Torres, M.: Fast feature selection aimed at high-dimensional data via hybrid-sequential-ranked searches. Expert Syst. Appl. **39**(12), 11094–11102 (2012)
35. Sheng, W., Liu, X.: A genetic k-medoids clustering algorithm. J. Heuristics **12**(6), 447–466 (2006)
36. Shim, K.: MapReduce algorithms for big data analysis. In: Madaan, A., Kikuchi, S., Bhalla, S. (eds.) DNIS 2013. LNCS, vol. 7813, pp. 44–48. Springer, Heidelberg (2013). doi:10.1007/978-3-642-37134-9_3
37. Tsai, M.-C., Chen, K.-H., Su, C.-T., Lin, H.-C.: An Application of PSO algorithm and decision tree for medical problem. In: 2nd Internatonal Conference on Intelligent Computational System, pp. 124–126 (2012)
38. van der Laan, M.J., Pollard, K.S.: A new algorithm for hybrid hierarchical clustering with visualization and the bootstrap. J. Stat. Plann. Infer. **117**, 275–303 (2003)
39. Venkatesh, H., Perur, S.D., Jalihal, N.: A study on use of big data in cloud computing environment. Int. J. Comput. Sci. Inf. Technol. (IJCSIT) **6**(3), 2076–2078 (2015)
40. Wu, X., Zhu, X., Wu, G.-Q., Ding, W.: Data mining with big data. IEEE Trans. Knowl. Data Eng. **26**(1), 97–107 (2014)
41. Xu, X., Ester, M., Kriegel, H.-P., Sander, J.: A distribution-based clustering algorithm for mining in large spatial databases. In: 14th International Conference on Data Engineering (ICDE 1998) (1998)
42. Yang, F., Sun, T., Zhang, C.: An efficient hybrid data clustering method based on k-harmonic means and particle swarm optimization. Expert Syst. Appl. **36**(6), 9847–9852 (2009)
43. Yang, Y., Liao, Y., Meng, G., Lee, J.: A hybrid feature selection scheme for unsupervised learning and its application in bearing fault diagnosis. Expert Syst. Appl. **38**(9), 11311–11320 (2011)
44. Zhang, H., Berg, A.C., Maire, M., Malik, J.: SVM-KNN: Discriminative nearest neighbor classification for visual category recognition. Proc. IEEE Comput. Soc. Conf. Comput. Vis. Pattern Recogn. **2**, 2126–2136 (2006)

Vehicle Type Detection by Convolutional Neural Networks

Miguel A. Molina-Cabello(✉), Rafael Marcos Luque-Baena, Ezequiel López-Rubio, and Karl Thurnhofer-Hemsi

Department of Computer Languages and Computer Science, University of Málaga, Bulevar Louis Pasteur, 35, 29071 Málaga, Spain
{miguelangel,rmluque,ezeqlr,karlkhader}@lcc.uma.es

Abstract. In this work a new vehicle type detection procedure for traffic surveillance videos is proposed. A Convolutional Neural Network is integrated into a vehicle tracking system in order to accomplish this task. Solutions for vehicle overlapping, differing vehicle sizes and poor spatial resolution are presented. The system is tested on well known benchmarks, and multiclass recognition performance results are reported. Our proposal is shown to attain good results over a wide range of difficult situations.

Keywords: Foreground detection · Background modeling · Convolutional neural networks · Probabilistic self-organizing maps · Background features

1 Introduction

Nowadays, research on video surveillance systems is considered a prolific area due to mainly the great amount of available data obtained from any corner of the world. Concretely, the automatic analysis of traffic scenes is particularly relevant since it is possible to detect and avoid traffic congestions, incident and some breaches of road worthiness requirements [11]. Thus, a high-level description of the road sequences which involves the position, speed and class of the vehicles is sufficient to provide useful information about road traffic [9].

Foreground detection is the first step in any generic traffic video surveillance system. There are many algorithms which can model the background. For example, the background of a general scene can be modeled by using a single Gaussian distribution [15] or with a self-organizing neural network [8]. Furthermore, if the scenario is well-known, different techniques can be applied in order to improve the performance. For example, in this particular case of a traffic sequence, there are techniques which consider several facets like foggy or snow conditions [13].

Once an object is detected and tracked along the sequence, a simple labeling task, which identify the type of the object in motion, could be carried out. However, this process is not as straightforward as it seems to be, because a

J.M. Ferrández Vicente et al. (Eds.): IWINAC 2017, Part II, LNCS 10338, pp. 268–278, 2017.
DOI: 10.1007/978-3-319-59773-7_28

feature extraction task is required to identify uniquely each class. This module should extract as many significant characteristics of the objects as possible, which are the inputs of the label detector or classifier, which the aim of improving the predicted class. Texture or brightness variations are features that can be employed for this purpose [14]. Recently, the use of deep learning networks has managed to alleviate the feature detection problem, performing this process in an intrinsic way in the first layers of the neural network [4].

Thus, in this work a new proposal for vehicle type detection in traffic videos is presented. Our proposed system is an enhancement of our previous vehicle tracking system [7]. A new module is added to this system in order to detect the type of the vehicles which appear in the scene. To this end a special kind of Convolutional Neural Network (CNN) has been used, namely AlexNet [5]. It has been previously used in traffic monitoring tasks [1,16]. The standard procedure to employ CNNs (AlexNet in particular) to object recognition, provides the neural network with an input image where the object of interest occupies most of the image area. If there are occlusions, they must be caused by objects that can not be confused with the objects to be recognized. For example, it is allowed that trees partially block the sight of a vehicle [1]. In current applications of CNNs to vehicle detection, either the camera footage is manually segmented to ensure that these conditions are fulfilled [1], or a special sensor arrangement is implemented so that the acquired images always satisfy them [16].

However, in many practical situations the preprocessing of the video footage prior to processing by the CNN is a challenge of paramount importance. In this work we focus on this key issue for the specific application of vehicle type detection in traffic scenes. This kind of video sequences often exhibit vehicles which partially occlude other vehicles. Hence a segmentation procedure must be put in place in order to separate the foreground regions from the background, and split those regions into vehicles. After that, rectangular windows must be determined which contain only one vehicle, and an appropriate resizing has to be carried out to honor the image size requirements of the CNN (in the case of the AlexNet, 227×227 pixel RGB images). The situation is substantially worsened by two factors. First of all, the size of the vehicles varies largely from motorbikes to trucks, which means that it is difficult to find an appropriate scaling of the original video data in order to fit the CNN size requirement while maintaining a high recognition rate. Secondly, traffic videos typically have a poor resolution, so that the segmented vehicles are given by a rather small number of pixels. Obviously, this hampers the recognition ability of the CNN. Here we study these issues and propose new solutions for them.

The rest of the paper is organized as follows: Sect. 2 presents the system architecture where this approach is integrated and Sect. 3 sets out the classification framework describing how the convolutional neural network is applied. Section 4 shows the experimental results over a public traffic surveillance sequence and Sect. 5 concludes the article.

2 System Architecture

The proposed vehicle tracking system (Fig. 1) can be divided in three different stages: an initial stage where the objects are detected from the sequence of frames, a second one where the objects are tracked, and finally, they are classified according to the different types of vehicles considered.

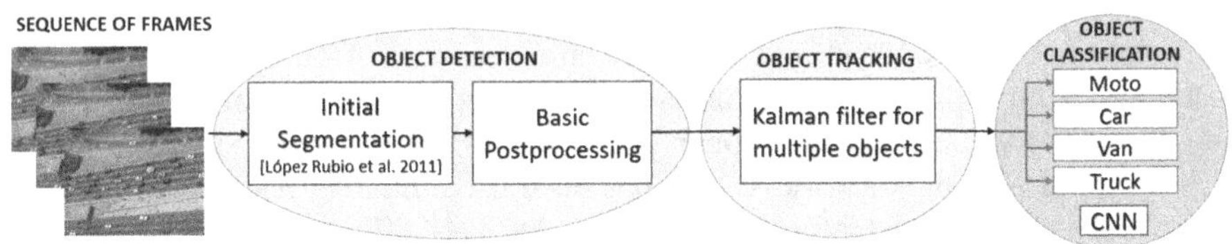

Fig. 1. Scheme of the proposed vehicle tracking system.

Initially, it is performed an initial segmentation based on the method proposed in [6], which it is based on the use of mixtures of uniform distributions and multivariate Gaussians with full covariance matrices, and it features an update process of the model that is based on stochastic approximation. One Gaussian component is used to model the background and one uniform component for the foreground, and when this probabilistic model is applied the Robbins–Monro stochastic approximation algorithm is used for the update equations [12]. It has been tested that it is a robust method for background modeling, and the stochastic framework has been proved to be suitable and effective as a learning method for real time algorithms with discarding data.

Then it is carried on a postprocessing applying some basic operators such as erosion and dilation. The first one carries out a superficial elimination of the borders of the objects. Thus, we can remove the false positives that are present in the segmented image, and also the false negatives which can appear inside the objects. Then, a dilation is applied to recover the original size of the objects. In many cases, objects that are very close to each other are represented with a single blob after the motion detection. These overlapping regions undergo a process that divides them to separate each individual vehicle. The final aim is to improve the quality of the segmented images and remove spurious objects.

In the tracking stage, a version of the Kalman filter for multiple objects has been implemented [10]. This statistical model computes the next position of the object using only information of the previous frame. In order to find the previous objects tracked, first the features of the objects detected in the new frame are extracted, and then a search over a window narrow centered in the centroids is performed. This Kalman model has as input the output obtained from the previous segmentation step.

At the end, the vehicles present in the image are classified depending on their features in four classes: moto, car, van and truck. This classification has carried out using the CNN as it is proposed in the following section.

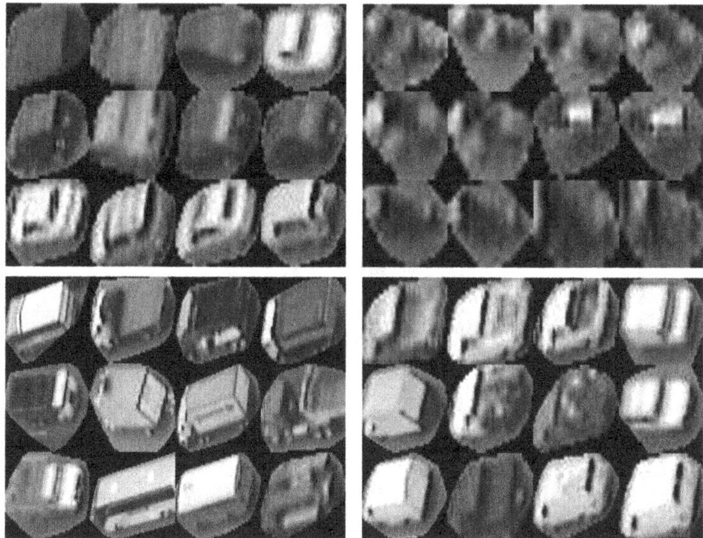

Fig. 2. Types of vehicles. A resize operation is applied in order to display them conveniently. First row shows cars and motorcycles, and second row reports trucks and vans, respectively.

3 Classification Framework

The CNN that we have employed in this work is AlexNet [5]. This net was developed in order to classify the IMAGENET dataset[1], which is a set of high-resolution images. Alexnet is composed by 5 convolutional layers and 3 fully-connected layers, where neurons which belong to a fully-connected layer have connections with all input neurons. In addition, normalization layers are used after the two first convolutional layers and its aim is that the excited neurons moderate their neighbor neurons. Finally, after these normalization layers and the fifth convolutional layer, the pooling layers have been placed. A Caffe replication of the original model is used in this work[2]. We have considered a set of input samples to train the network and this set presents the same number of samples for each vehicle class. On the other hand, the images have been selected from the testing sequence and each one of them show a motion vehicle from the video. Several vehicles from this dataset are shown in Fig. 2 ordered by its type.

In order to train the CNN, a dataset with all the images with the same size (256×256 pixels) is required. However, the vehicle samples does not have the same dimensions (e.g. trucks are bigger than motorcycles) which implies that all the image regions should be resized to serve as input to the neural network. So that, we need to apply a process to adapt the dataset to the needed size.

---

[1] http://www.image-net.org.

[2] https://github.com/BVLC/caffe/tree/master/models/bvlc_alexnet.

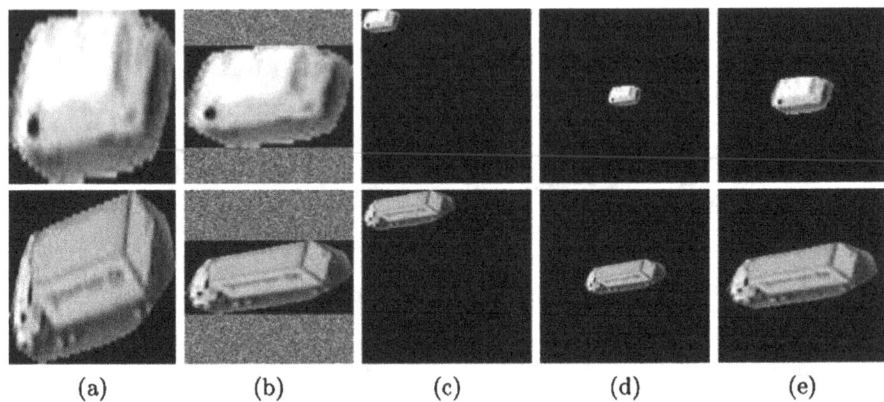

Fig. 3. Resizing region approaches for 256 × 256 pixels. (a) Standard resize. (b) Resize preserving the aspect ratio. (c) Non-resize and non-centered. (d) Non-resize and centered. (e) Resize with scale and centered. First row presents a van while second row shows a truck. It is possible to observe that the two first strategies lose the size relation between the two vehicles, while the rest of approaches keep this visual proportion.

In this point, we have considered some different kinds of strategies in order to get the best possible performance. The first one is that we have noted the standard resize (*Standard*), where all the images have been resized to the required size, independently of its ratio. The second considered process (noted as *Fill*) applies an resize over the columns and it centers the vehicle, filling the rest of the pixels with noise. The third proposal (*Non-Centered*) considers the original size and fill the rest of the pixels with black color, placing the vehicle on the top left corner. The fourth approach (*Centered*) is like the previous one, but centered the vehicle on the image. The last suggested process (*Centered Scale*) resizes the images applying a scale preserving the ratio between the original images, placing it in the center of the image and the rest of the pixels are filled with black color. All of this proposals are reported in Fig. 3.

Deep learning networks work best if the number of input patterns is high. In cases where this circumstance is not fulfilled, it is possible to carry out a process called data augmentation. In this work we will take 10 regions of 227 × 227 pixels of each sample that will serve as input to the network, where each region will have a random displacement over the original region of 256 × 256 pixels. In addition to modifying the input of the network, it is necessary to modify the output. The only variation in this point is to change the number of output classes to 4, because there will be four types of vehicles to detect: cars, motorcycles, trucks and vans.

4 Experimental Results

In this section we report the different tests that we have carried out and its results. In order to test the proposal we show in this work, we have chosen a

Table 1. Quantitative measures of the results. Each row is a measure and each column presents the mean and the standard deviation. Best results are highlighted in **bold**.

Measure	Standard	Fill	Non-Centered	Centered	Centered Scale
Accuracy	0.684 ± 0.02	0.670 ± 0.01	0.772 ± 0.02	0.862 ± 0.01	$\mathbf{0.865 \pm 0.01}$
Mean Square Error	1.471 ± 0.11	1.387 ± 0.09	1.117 ± 0.07	0.913 ± 0.08	$\mathbf{0.893 \pm 0.11}$
Rand Index	0.764 ± 0.01	0.759 ± 0.01	0.822 ± 0.02	0.876 ± 0.01	$\mathbf{0.879 \pm 0.01}$
Hubert's Gamma	0.336 ± 0.03	0.327 ± 0.02	0.503 ± 0.04	0.650 ± 0.01	$\mathbf{0.651 \pm 0.03}$
Overall Cluster Entropy	0.622 ± 0.03	0.634 ± 0.01	0.461 ± 0.04	0.293 ± 0.01	$\mathbf{0.292 \pm 0.03}$
Overall Class Entropy	0.559 ± 0.03	0.560 ± 0.02	0.405 ± 0.04	$\mathbf{0.251 \pm 0.00}$	0.265 ± 0.02
Overall Entropy	0.590 ± 0.03	0.597 ± 0.01	0.433 ± 0.04	$\mathbf{0.272 \pm 0.01}$	0.279 ± 0.02

sequence which shows a highway with different kinds of vehicles moving on it and it presents some troubles like occlusions or overlapping objects. The selected video is named *US-101 Highway*. This sequence is taken from the dataset of Next Generation Simulation (NGSIM) program, provided by the Federal Highway Administration (FHWA).

Our proposal tries to classify the detected vehicles of the sequence into 4 different classes depending on the characteristics of the vehicle. The possible classes are motorcycle, car, van and truck. In order to train the network and test it, we have selected several vehicles with its trajectory and we have labeled them. The trajectory of a segmented object O_i is a set of features $\{\boldsymbol{x}_i^f \in \mathbb{R}^4 \mid f \in [1..MaxFrame]\}$ that it is composed by all the frames where this vehicle appears in the whole video. Then, we form a set of images that we use to train and test the performance of our proposal. The images of this set corresponds to images of each selected trajectories previously.

In order to obtain a robust performance of the goodness of the proposal we have employed a 10-fold strategy, where the training set has the 90% of the data and the test set has the 10 remaining percent. Furthermore, each set has the same number of images of each class. In this way, we have repeated the process 10 times. The next step is the training of the network applying the different resizing region approaches that we have described in the section before.

After the training, we use the test set to measure the performance of the approach. In order to compare the proposals among themselves from a quantitative point of view, we have selected some different well-known measures. The most important considered measures in this work are the Accuracy (Acc), which attains values in the interval $[0, 1]$, where higher is better, and it represents the percentage of hits of the system; and the Mean Square Error (MSE), which is a positive real number, where lower is better, and it calculates the error of the model when it predicts a class for an object.

Table 2. Accuracy values for each labeled class (higher is better). Each row represents a different type of vehicle (car, motorcycle, truck and van). The studied resizing region proposals are shown from the second to the fifth columns. Last column displays the global accuracy for all the classes.

Class	Standard	Fill	Non-Centered	Centered	Centered Scale
Car	0.671 ± 0.02	0.683 ± 0.03	0.804 ± 0.03	0.803 ± 0.01	$\mathbf{0.829 \pm 0.03}$
Moto	0.883 ± 0.01	0.820 ± 0.05	0.811 ± 0.03	$\mathbf{0.994 \pm 0.01}$	0.992 ± 0.01
Truck	0.546 ± 0.03	0.578 ± 0.02	$\mathbf{0.918 \pm 0.02}$	0.893 ± 0.02	0.909 ± 0.01
Van	0.653 ± 0.05	0.614 ± 0.04	0.595 ± 0.03	$\mathbf{0.808 \pm 0.03}$	0.777 ± 0.04
All	0.684 ± 0.02	0.670 ± 0.01	0.772 ± 0.02	0.862 ± 0.01	$\mathbf{0.865 \pm 0.01}$

Let K be the existing objects and k the observed object, we note as $\mathbf{x}_k$ and $\mathbf{w}_k$ the real and the predicted class of the object k, respectively, where $\mathbf{x_k}, \mathbf{w_k} \in \{1, 2, 3, 4\}$, corresponding $1 = car, 2 = moto, 3 = truck$ and $4 = van$. Moreover, if the model succeeds the classification of the object k, (that is, $\mathbf{x_k} = \mathbf{w_k}$), we note this as $\mathbf{q}_k = 1$; and we note as $\mathbf{q}_k = 0$ when the model makes a mistake in its prediction (that is, $\mathbf{x_k} \neq \mathbf{w_k}$). So that, the definition of the Accuracy and the Mean Square Error are:

$$Acc = \frac{1}{K}\sum_{k=1}^{K} \mathbf{q}_k \qquad MSE = \frac{1}{K}\sum_{k=1}^{K} (\mathbf{x}_k - \mathbf{w}_k)^2 \tag{1}$$

We have selected other measures which can be employed in order to complete the comparison of the classification performance of the proposed models. One of them is the Rand Index [3], which is a value between 0 and 1, and higher value is better. We have also considered the Hubert's Gamma Statistic [3], whose values are in the interval $[-1, 1]$ and higher values are better. Finally, we have included some entropy measures: the Overall Cluster Entropy, the Overall Class Entropy and the Overall Entropy [2]. This measures are values between 0 and 1, where lower is better.

The performance of each proposal according to these measures is reported in Table 1. As it can be observed, the Centered Scale process achieves the best performance in five of the seven considered measures. The Centered process also obtains a good performance, with the best result in the other two measures and similar values in the rest of the measures. These results reflect that the sizing strategies that preserve the difference in size between classes, are able to improve the accuracy values of the classification process. Therefore, a good performance is achieved despite the fact that the small number of labeled data and its low quality and size.

In addition, a comparative between each approach and its performance with each vehicle class is shown in Table 2. In this case, the Centered process gets the best performance in two of the four considered vehicle types. Nevertheless, the Centered Scale obtains the best mean from all the classes. As may be evident,

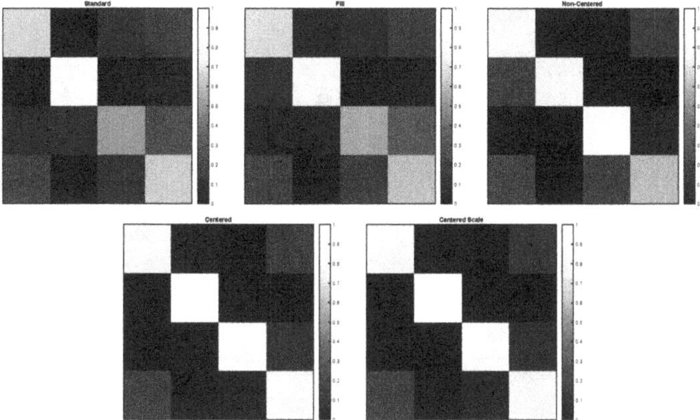

Fig. 4. Confusion matrices for the resizing region approaches, namely: Standard, Fill and Non-Centered (first row); Centered and Centered Scale (second row). The order of the classes for both columns and rows is: car, motorcycle, truck and van. The row dimension indicates the real class while the column dimension reflects the predicted class. The clearer the blocks on the diagonal the greater the accuracy of the method.

the greater complexity lies in the distinction between the Car and Van classes (80% of success on average), because of its undeniable similarity. In fact, visually there may be doubts in its correct classification, mainly due to the low resolution of the regions (see Fig. 3).

The confusion matrices for each resizing strategy, which show the errors between the predicted class by the model and the real class of a vehicle, are shown in Fig. 4. The clearer the blocks on the diagonal the greater the accuracy of the method. If a block outside the diagonal is not very dark, it implies that, given an image of a vehicle, there is an error between the output of the network (prediction) and the actual class to which it belongs. For example, it is noted that the blocks relating to the classes Car and Van display more orange tones than blocks relating to the classes Car and Motorcycle. In this way, both the Centered and the Centered Scale approaches provide visually the best result.

Additionally, another important result is that the distinction between vans and trucks cause certain difficulty. is very difficult. This is because there are some trucks which have a similar size with respect to a van. Moreover, the segmentation and the tracking processes cause negative effects in the reported results. This two steps introduce mistakes and occasionally provide a wrong segmentation, so that it produces a bad classification.

Finally, the best trained classification model has been integrated in the developed video surveillance traffic system previously described. Some qualitative results are reported in Fig. 5, where the online vehicle classification can be observed in several tested frames.

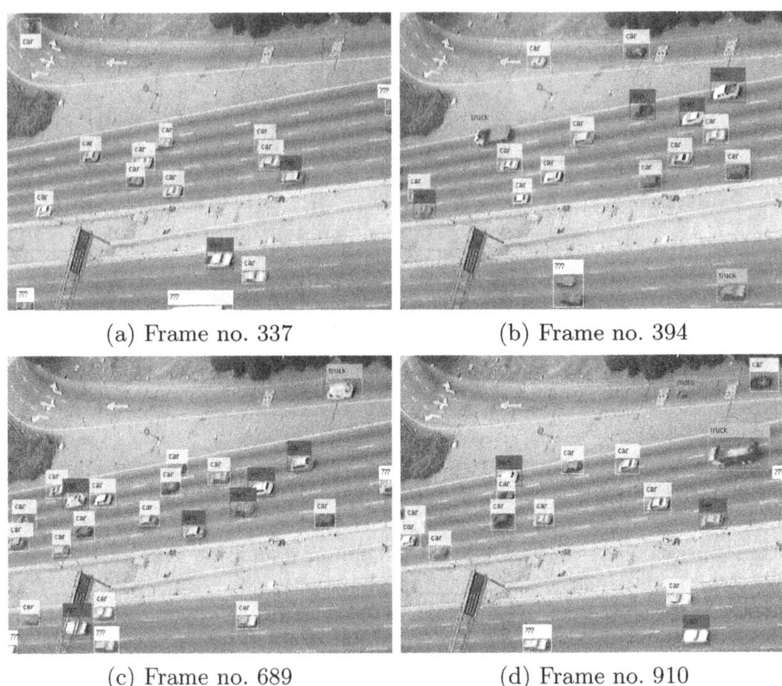

(a) Frame no. 337 (b) Frame no. 394

(c) Frame no. 689 (d) Frame no. 910

Fig. 5. Online vehicle classification of the sequence *S-101 Highway*.

5 Conclusions

We have proposed an approach employing a Convolutional Neural Network (CNN) AlexNet network model to classify the vehicles that are presented in traffic sequences. The system assigns each detected vehicles to a class: car, motorcycle, truck or van. Because the AlexNet network needs a training image dataset where all the images have the same size, different resizing region approaches have been considered to transform the dataset to adapt the size of its images to the required size. A quantitative comparison between these proposals have been studied. The reported results show the noted Centered Scale method as the best classifier with a high accuracy. In addition, the low resolution of the training dataset and the considered difference between classes car and van affect negatively to the obtained performance. Finally, we have integrated the best classification proposal to our previous developed vehicle tracking system with an online strategy in order to complete a real-time classification of the vehicles.

Acknowledgments. This work is partially supported by the Ministry of Economy and Competitiveness of Spain under grant TIN2014-53465-R, project name Video surveillance by active search of anomalous events. It is also partially supported by the Autonomous Government of Andalusia (Spain) under projects TIC-6213, project name Development of Self-Organizing Neural Networks for Information Technologies; and

TIC-657, project name Self-organizing systems and robust estimators for video surveillance. All of them include funds from the European Regional Development Fund (ERDF). Karl Thurnhofer-Hemsi is funded by a PhD scholarship from the Spanish Ministry of Education, Culture and Sport under the FPU program. The authors thankfully acknowledge the computer resources, technical expertise and assistance provided by the SCBI (Supercomputing and Bioinformatics) center of the University of Málaga. They also gratefully acknowledge the support of NVIDIA Corporation with the donation of the Titan X GPU.

References

1. Amato, G., Carrara, F., Falchi, F., Gennaro, C., Meghini, C., Vairo, C.: Deep learning for decentralized parking lot occupancy detection. Expert Syst. Appl. **72**, 327–334 (2017)
2. He, J., Tan, A.H., Tan, C.L., Sung, S.Y.: On quantitative evaluation of clustering systems. In: He, J., Tan, A.-H., Tan, C.-L., Sung, S.-Y. (eds.) Clustering and Information Retrieval, pp. 105–133. Springer, New York (2004)
3. Jain, A.K., Dubes, R.C.: Algorithms for Clustering Data. Prentice-Hall, Inc., Upper Saddle River (1988)
4. Kato, N., Fadlullah, Z.M., Mao, B., Tang, F., Akashi, O., Inoue, T., Mizutani, K.: The deep learning vision for heterogeneous network traffic control: proposal, challenges, and future perspective. IEEE Wirel. Commun. (2016)
5. Krizhevsky, A., Sutskever, I., Hinton, G.: ImageNet classification with deep convolutional neural networks. In: Advances in Neural Information Processing Systems 25, pp. 1097–1105 (2012)
6. López-Rubio, E., Luque-Baena, R.M.: Stochastic approximation for background modelling. Comput. Vis. Image Underst. **115**(6), 735–749 (2011)
7. Luque-Baena, R.M., López-Rubio, E., Domínguez, E., Palomo, E.J., Jerez, J.M.: A self-organizing map to improve vehicle detection in flow monitoring systems. Soft. Comput. **19**(9), 2499–2509 (2015)
8. Maddalena, L., Petrosino, A.: A self-organizing approach to background subtraction for visual surveillance applications. IEEE Trans. Image Process. **17**(7), 1168–1177 (2008)
9. Mithun, N., Howlader, T., Rahman, S.: Video-based tracking of vehicles using multiple time-spatial images. Expert Syst. Appl. **62**, 17–31 (2016)
10. Reid, D.: An algorithm for tracking multiple targets. IEEE Trans. Autom. Control **24**(6), 843–854 (1979)
11. Ren, J., Chen, Y., Xin, L., Shi, J., Li, B., Liu, Y.: Detecting and positioning of traffic incidents via video-based analysis of traffic states in a road segment. IET Intel. Transport Syst. **10**(6), 428–437 (2016)
12. Robbins, H., Monro, S.: A stochastic approximation method. Ann. Math. Stat. **22**(3), 400–407 (1951)
13. Sen-Ching, S.C., Kamath, C.: Robust techniques for background subtraction in urban traffic video. In: Electronic Imaging 2004, pp. 881–892. International Society for Optics and Photonics (2004)
14. Wang, K., Liu, Y., Gou, C., Wang, F.Y.: A multi-view learning approach to foreground detection for traffic surveillance applications. IEEE Trans. Veh. Technol. **65**(6), 4144–4158 (2016)

15. Wren, C., Azarbayejani, A., Darrell, T., Pentl, A.: Pfinder real-time tracking of the human body. IEEE Trans. Pattern Anal. Mach. Intell. **19**(7), 780–785 (1997)
16. Wshah, S., Xu, B., Bulan, O., Kumar, J., Paul, P.: Deep learning architectures for domain adaptation in HOV/HOT lane enforcement. In: IEEE Winter Conference on Applications of Computer Vision (WACV), pp. 1–7 (2016)

Motion Detection by Microcontroller for Panning Cameras

Jesús Benito-Picazo[1(✉)], Ezequiel López-Rubio[1], Juan Miguel Ortiz-de-Lazcano-Lobato[1], Enrique Domínguez[1], and Esteban J. Palomo[1,2]

[1] Department of Computer Languages and Computer Science, University of Málaga, Bulevar Louis Pasteur, 35, 29071 Málaga, Spain
{jpicazo,ezeqlr,jmortiz,enriqued,ejpalomo}@lcc.uma.es
[2] School of Mathematical Sciences and Information Technology, University of Yachay Tech, Hacienda San José s/n, San Miguel de Urcuquí, Ecuador
epalomo@yachaytech.edu.ec

Abstract. Motion detection is the first essential process in the extraction of information regarding moving objects. The approaches based on background difference are the most used with fixed cameras to perform motion detection, because of the high quality of the achieved segmentation. However, real time requirements and high costs prevent most of the algorithms proposed in literature to exploit the background difference with panning cameras in real world applications. This paper presents a new algorithm to detect moving objects within a scene acquired by panning cameras. The algorithm for motion detection is implemented on a Raspberry Pi microcontroller, which enables the design and implementation of a low-cost monitoring system.

Keywords: Foreground detection · Background modeling · Probabilistic self-organizing maps · Background features

1 Introduction

Moving object detection is very important for video surveillance. This task is known to be a significant and difficult research problem in many real environments. Motion detection consists of detecting a change in the position of an object relative to its surroundings or a change in the surroundings relative to an object.

Video surveillance systems have become an extremely active research area due to increasing levels of social conflict and public awareness about security issues. This has led to motivation for the development of robust and precise automatic video surveillance systems, which are essential tools for safety and security in both public and private sectors.

J.M. Ferrández Vicente et al. (Eds.): IWINAC 2017, Part II, LNCS 10338, pp. 279–288, 2017.
DOI: 10.1007/978-3-319-59773-7_29

One of the most common algorithms is to compare the current frame with the previous one. If the pixel difference is bigger than a predefined alarm level or threshold, a motion event alarm is generated. The estimated background is just the previous frame. It clearly works under easy conditions of foreground objects, motion speed and frame rate but it is very sensitive to the threshold so that for a noisy image, motion will be detected in many places even if there is no motion at all. If the object is moving smoothly, a small change, which is less than the predefined threshold, is obtained. Therefore, the moving object would not be detected.

Microcontroller boards are economic, small and flexible hardware devices. They are frequently employed in motion detection systems due to their low energy consumption and reduced cost. Kinetically challenged people can benefit from microcontroller based input devices specifically designed for them, which measure motion on a plane in real time [11]. A flexible Printed Board Circuit (PCB) prototype which integrates a microcontroller has been proposed to estimate motion and proximity [5]. In this prototype, eight photodiodes are used as light sensors. The efficiency of solar energy plants can be improved by low power systems which estimate cloud motion [6]. The approximation of the cloud motion vectors is carried out by an embedded microcontroller, so that the arrangement of the solar panels can be optimized for maximum electricity output. Energy-saving street lighting for smart cities can be accomplished by low power motion detection systems equipped with low consumption microcontrollers and wireless communication devices [1]. This way, the street lamps are switched on when people are present in their surroundings. Finally, a motion detection algorithm based on Self-Organizing Maps (SOMs) was developed in an Arduino DUE board [10]. The implementation of the SOM algorithm was employed as a motion detector for static cameras in a video surveillance system.

Research on computer vision systems based on pan-tilt-zoom (PTZ) cameras has been intense for many years [2,4,8,13]. Nevertheless, there is a lack of a comprehensive theory which sets the foundations for the development of practical systems. Fragmentary approaches that are limited to some parts of the problem are available, but it is still not clear how to combine them to yield complete and reliable systems that can be deployed in many situations. In the present work we focus on the panning movement of a PTZ camera, which is able to cover the entire environment of the camera.

In this paper, we propose a motion detection algorithm and its real-time implementation on an inexpensive microcontroller. The system is able to detect motion by analyzing the output of a panning PTZ camera with the help of a feed forward neural network. Section 2 presents the motion detection algorithm for panning cameras. Section 3 outlines the hardware part of the system, which is based on the Raspberry Pi 3 model B microcontroller, and the employed software architecture. Experimental results on real video footage are reported in Sect. 4. Finally, Sect. 5 contains our conclusions.

2 Methodology

As mentioned before, our goal is to detect the motion of foreground objects while a PTZ camera is moving. Let us consider the image acquired by the camera:

$$f : \mathbb{R}^3 \to \mathbb{R}^3 \tag{1}$$

$$f(x_1, x_2, t) = (y_1, y_2, y_3) \tag{2}$$

where $\mathbf{x} = (x_1, x_2) \in [-A, A] \times [-B, B]$ are the video frame coordinates in pixels, with $(0, 0)$ at the center of the image and frame size $(2A) \times (2B)$ pixels; t is the time instant; and $\mathbf{y} = (y_1, y_2, y_3)$ comprises the color tristimulus values at the frame location and instant of interest.

For a PTZ camera moving in the horizontal direction one can write:

$$\begin{aligned} &(x_1, x_2), (x_1 + \delta, x_2) \in [-A, A] \times [-B, B] \Rightarrow \\ &f(x_1, x_2, t) \approx f(x_1 + \delta, x_2, t + \epsilon) \end{aligned} \tag{3}$$

where δ is the observed horizontal displacement of the image as ϵ units of time have elapsed, and the equality does not hold due to optical effects such as lens aberration, and the motion of foreground objects in the scene. The precondition means that the approximation applies to those points in the scene that are visible both at time t and $t + \epsilon$; the remaining pixels in the video frame must be ignored for our purposes. Then the error in the approximation can be computed as follows:

$$\mathcal{E}(x_1, x_2, t) = f(x_1, x_2, t) - f(x_1 + \delta, x_2, t + \epsilon) \tag{4}$$

For given values of ϵ and the camera speed, the value of δ can be estimated experimentally by finding the value of δ which minimizes $\|\mathcal{E}\|$, where $\|\cdot\|$ stands for any suitable norm. Now it is important to realize that the error comes from two sources, namely optical effects and the presence of foreground objects:

$$\mathcal{E}(x_1, x_2, t) = \mathcal{E}_{optical}(x_1, x_2, t) + \mathcal{E}_{objects}(x_1, x_2, t) \tag{5}$$

where the optical effects can be assumed to be small with respect to the foreground objects effect, if those objects are present:

$$Fore(t) \Leftrightarrow \|\mathcal{E}_{optical}(x_1, x_2, t)\| \ll \|\mathcal{E}_{objects}(x_1, x_2, t)\| \tag{6}$$

where $Fore(t)$ means that there are foreground objects in motion at time t. Moreover, if there are no foreground objects, then the associated error is zero:

$$Fore(t) \Leftrightarrow \mathcal{E}_{objects}(x_1, x_2, t) \neq 0 \tag{7}$$

Therefore, the expectation of the error norm should be larger when foreground objects are present:

$$E[\|\mathcal{E}(x_1, x_2, t)\| \mid Fore(t)] > E[\|\mathcal{E}(x_1, x_2, t)\| \mid \neg Fore(t)] \tag{8}$$

Our proposal takes advantage of this by training a feed forward neural network classifier in order to estimate the probability that foreground objects are present, $P(Fore(t))$. To this end, the error norm is summarized by pixel columns, so that the sum of the norms of the differences of the pixels at columns x_1 and $x_1 + \delta$ is computed. Then the error norm sums are added for contiguous pixel columns, so that a reduced set of sums of error norms are obtained. These sums are provided as inputs to the neural network, while the desired output $z(t)$ is 1 whenever $Fore(t)$ holds, and -1 otherwise. The probability is then estimated as follows:

$$P(Fore(t)) = \frac{1}{2}(z(t) + 1) \tag{9}$$

Subsequently a probability threshold θ is applied in order to declare whether foreground object motion has been detected:

$$Detection(t) \Leftrightarrow P(Fore(t)) > \theta \tag{10}$$

Next the details of the implementation of the above proposal are described.

3 System Architecture

Hardware choice is such an important issue when it comes to microcontroller-powered computer vision applications. In general, projects involving real-time motion detection should consume a minimal amount of computing power, but at the same time, they must be affordable and low-energy consuming insofar as a certain amount of them may be required to monitor a medium sized building or building complex and the spots they are going to be placed in may not have access to the general power network. All these reasons present Raspberry Pi class microcontrollers as a good choice for our project. Hence, we have chosen a Raspberry Pi 3 model B microcontroller (Fig. 1), running under Linux Raspbian distribution.

Fig. 1. Raspberry Pi 3 model B overview

This device features an ARM CortexV8 Quad Core CPU running at 1200 MHz, 1 GB RAM, and a 8 GB micro-SD data storage card. It can be powered by a 5.1 V power source and its power consumption reaches 1.2 Amps/h approximately at max operating load.

The second component of our system architecture is a PTZ camera software emulator called *Virtual PTZ* [3]. This software consists of a C++ library that simulates the functionality of an actual Sony SNC-RZ50N PTZ camera from spherical panoramic video footage. In particular, the experiments in this paper employ sequences obtained by a *Point Grey Ladybug 3 Spherical camera* (Fig. 2).

Fig. 2. 360° spherical images supplied by the *Point Grey Ladybug 3 Spherical camera.*

When it comes to PTZ cameras, *Virtual PTZ* software has been proposed as a valid framework for researching because of its capability of substituting a real PTZ camera by providing the user with the possibility of moving the virtual camera through an almost-spherical 360° video frame that can be totally controlled and that is not affected by dynamical issues or physical limitations. Since the only output our system requires from the PTZ camera is real-time video streaming from a panning-capable camera, the virtual PTZ software stands as a convenient framework for this project.

4 Experimental Results

As explained in Sect. 2, our motion detection system can be regarded as a classifier which consists of an algorithm that is in charge of obtaining training samples from a set of consecutive images and supplying them to a multilayer perceptron that will decide whether there are foreground moving objects in the video frames supplied by a PTZ camera. Because of its speed and ease of use, the multilayer perceptron implementation chosen for this project is the fast artificial neural network from Nissen [9]. In order to increase our control over the experimentation process, tests have been performed from videos supplied by the Virtual PTZ camera. For the same reason, as the video frame rate is about 16 fps, camera rotation speed has been adjusted to a constant rate of 16 degrees per second to the left. After performing several tests, the δ value has been estimated as 5 pixels/degree and Mean Squared Error (MSE) has been considered as the error norm $\|\mathcal{E}\|$ (see Sect. 2). All set up, to perform the comparison of two frames, the process described in Fig. 3 has been carried out.

First, frame $n+1$ is shifted δ pixels to the left with respect to frame n to compensate camera rotation. Next, both frames are divided into 63-pixel wide stripes (all but the last stripe, which will be 68-pixel wide) and the mean squared error is calculated for each stripe of the two frames. Finally, a 30 component

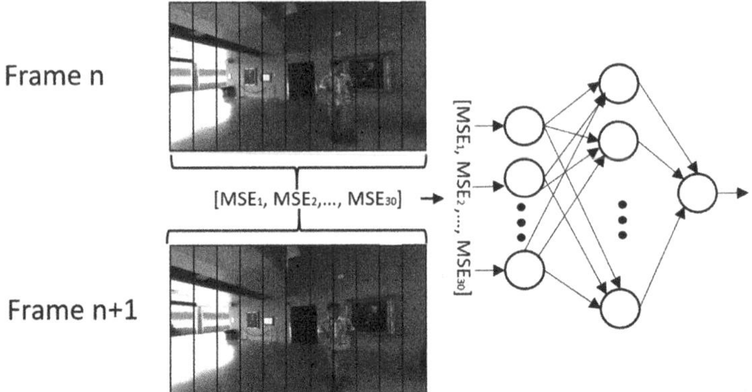

Fig. 3. Example of how samples are obtained and supplied to the perceptron.

vector (10 for each RGB color channel) plus one number, which will be 1 if the sample is positive and −1 if the sample is negative, will be saved as a sample for perceptron training, validation and testing.

In order to evaluate system performance and accuracy when it comes to detecting movement in video streams supplied by the Virtual PTZ, several tests have been performed. These tests involve multilayer perceptron general performance values measured for various different network topologies.

Multilayer perceptrons can be calibrated by modifying several parameters with the objective of achieving better performance rates. However, since the number of parameter combinations would eventually grow exponentially, testing the system by varying every parameter would not be practical. Therefore, for this work, perceptron training and performance comparisons are done just by modifying the number of neurons in its hidden layer, while keeping fixed the rest of them. Thus, the neural network used for this system will have the characteristics listed in Table 1.

Table 1. Test parameters for multilayer perceptron

Neural network class	Multilayer perceptron
Number of inputs	30
Number of neurons in hidden layer	50–600
Number of outputs	1
Learning algorithm	Backpropagation
Max training epochs	10000
Learning rate	0.7

In order to guarantee a correct neural network performance evaluation as much as possible, a 10-fold cross-validation procedure has been established for our system, so separate sample sets have been used for the training, validation and test phases. For this purpose, it is well known that several measures are available. Because of its simplicity, one of the most popular ones is the classification accuracy, which computes the number of correct predictions divided by the total amount of test samples [12]. The networks have been trained with a class-balanced set of 576 samples. Figure 4 shows the accuracy values for the training, validation and test sets versus the number of neurons in the hidden layer of the perceptron.

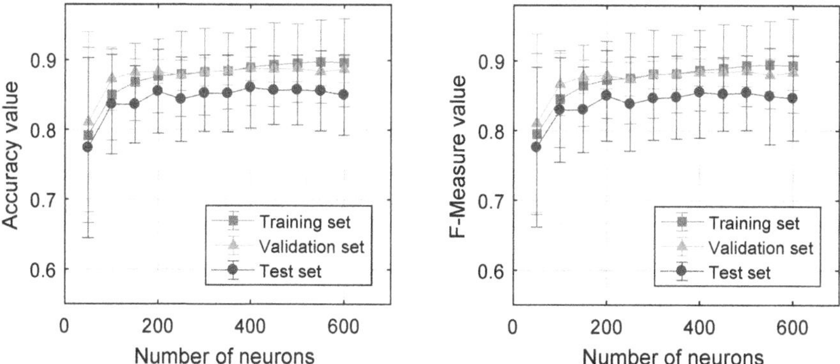

Fig. 4. Accuracy and F-measure error bar chart for training, validation and test sets (higher is better).

Even though accuracy is widely accepted as an acceptable performance measuring criterion, specially in cases like the one presented here, where the number of positive and negative samples is balanced, it is interesting to extend our experimental results with the F-measure performance (Fig. 4), as F-measure is considered as another valid performance measure which eventually can be even more reliable than accuracy [12].

As both accuracy and F-measure limit their performance measurement to one single threshold value, it has been considered that a measurement that integrates all possible threshold values is necessary in order to complement the results represented in the above charts [7]. For this purpose the AUC *Area under the Curve*, has been calculated for every neural network model. So, in Fig. 5 the AUC values for our model can be seen.

All three charts illustrate how the model reaches high performance levels from 200 hidden layer neurons on, and increases its stability as the number of hidden layer neuron number grows higher. Results also show that for test samples in configurations comprehending 200 neurons or more, all three performance measures are above 80%. It is also remarkable that in order to prevent image data loss, all the results above were obtained by just processing images as they come from the Virtual PTZ. This means that no further image processing has been done to correct neither camera sensor noise nor camera lens aberration.

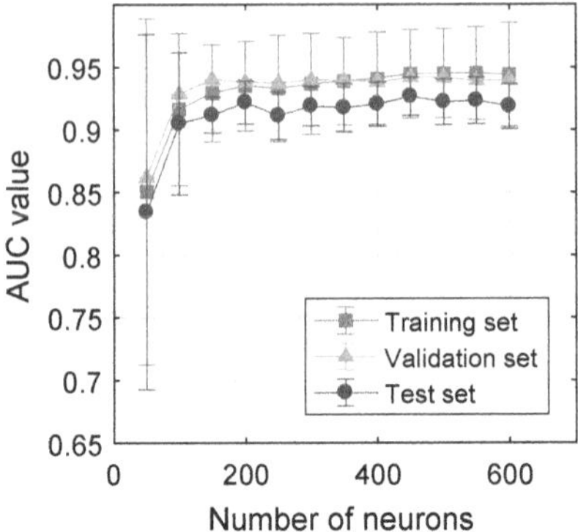

Fig. 5. AUC error bar chart for training, validation and test sets (higher is better).

Time consumption is an absolutely critical issue when it comes to real-time video processing, not to say when using microcontrollers to undertake artificial neural network processes which involve real-time presence detection from a panning camera as the one explained here does. Therefore, the algorithm not only has to be reliable but it also has to prove that the training time stays within acceptable limits and sample classifying is fast enough to provide real-time presence detection when being deployed in a Raspberry Pi. In Table 2, both training average time and single sample average classifying time versus hidden layer neuron number can be observed when executing the algorithm in a Raspberry Pi microcontroller with the features enunciated in Sect. 3. To give a clearer idea about our system performance, Table 2 also includes the average speed (measured in frames per second, fps) the system can work at, when receiving a video stream from the Virtual PTZ.

Training average time has been calculated from the values obtained by launching the training process 90 times, each one corresponding to the same number of neurons in the hidden layer. Single sample average time and processing speed in fps have been calculated from the values obtained by passing 72 different samples through the algorithm explained above, combined with each trained neural network. As can be seen in Table 2, processing speed is approximately 50 frames per second which is an excellent frame rate for real-time video processing.

Table 2. Training average time and sample processing average time versus number of neurons in the hidden layer.

# Neurons	50	100	200	300	400	500	600
Training avg. time (s)	39.49777	26.49671	36.32062	53.55619	54.05586	62.48622	93.27951
Processing avg. time (s)	0.01959	0.01963	0.01969	0.01975	0.01982	0.01988	0.01995
Fps	51.03369	50.95048	50.78488	50.62035	50.45434	50.29447	50.13059

5 Conclusions

A microcontroller-based real-time motion detection system for video surveillance panning cameras has been proposed. It features an algorithm that processes a sequence of images streamed from a PTZ camera simulation software by dividing every image in a set of stripes and comparing each one with the equivalent stripe in the next frame in order to obtain a vector of numbers that will be fed as training, validation or test samples to a multilayer perceptron that will be in charge of pointing out whether there is movement in the video stream. With the objective of increasing system power efficiency and portability, it has been deployed in a Raspberry Pi type microcontroller.

Tests have been performed by varying the number of neurons in the hidden layer of the perceptron. They indicate that it is possible to achieve good results according to several well known classification performance measures. Time tests indicate as well that the movement detection system proposed here shows acceptable training times and when it comes to video processing, reaches processing speeds higher than 50 fps, confirming it as a valid alternative for real-time movement detection when combined with panning cameras.

Acknowledgments. This work is partially supported by the Ministry of Economy and Competitiveness of Spain under grant TIN2014-53465-R, project name Video surveillance by active search of anomalous events. It is also partially supported by the Autonomous Government of Andalusia (Spain) under projects TIC-6213, project name Development of Self-Organizing Neural Networks for Information Technologies; and TIC-657, project name Self-organizing systems and robust estimators for video surveillance. Finally, it is partially supported by the Autonomous Government of Extremadura (Spain) under the project IB13113. All of them include funds from the European Regional Development Fund (ERDF). The authors thankfully acknowledge the computer resources, technical expertise and assistance provided by the SCBI (Supercomputing and Bioinformatics) center of the University of Málaga. They also gratefully acknowledge the support of NVIDIA Corporation with the donation of the Titan X GPU used for this research.

References

1. Adnan, L., Yussoff, Y., Johar, H., Baki, S.: Energy-saving street lighting system based on the waspmote mote. Jurnal Teknologi **76**(4), 55–58 (2015)
2. Boult, T., Gao, X., Micheals, R., Eckmann, M.: Omni-directional visual surveillance. Image Vis. Comput. **22**(7), 515–534 (2004)
3. Chen, G., St-Charles, P., Bouachir, W., Bilodeau, G., Bergevin, R.: Reproducible evaluation of pan-tilt-zoom tracking. In: Proceedings - International Conference on Image Processing (ICIP), pp. 2055–2059, December 2015
4. Ding, C., Song, B., Morye, A., Farrell, J., Roy-Chowdhury, A.: Collaborative sensing in a distributed PTZ camera network. IEEE Trans. Image Process. **21**(7), 3282–3295 (2012)
5. Dobrzynski, M.K., Pericet-Camara, R., Floreano, D.: Vision tape-a flexible compound vision sensor for motion detection and proximity estimation. IEEE Sens. J. **12**(5), 1131–1139 (2012)

6. Fung, V., Bosch, J.L., Roberts, S.W., Kleissl, J.: Cloud shadow speed sensor. Atmos. Measur. Tech. **7**(6), 1693–1700 (2014)
7. Ling, C.X., Huang, J., Zhang, H.: AUC: a statistically consistent and more discriminating measure than accuracy. In: IJCAI International Joint Conference on Artificial Intelligence, pp. 519–524 (2003)
8. Micheloni, C., Rinner, B., Foresti, G.: Video analysis in pan-tilt-zoom camera networks. IEEE Signal Process. Mag. **27**(5), 78–90 (2010)
9. Nissen, S.: Fast Artificial Neural Network (2016). http://leenissen.dk/fann/wp/. Accessed 10 Jan 2017
10. Ortega-Zamorano, F., Molina-Cabello, M.A., López-Rubio, E., Palomo, E.J.: Smart motion detection sensor based on video processing using self-organizing maps. Expert Syst. Appl. **64**, 476–489 (2016)
11. Papadimitriou, K., Dollas, A., Sotiropoulos, S.N.: Low-cost real-time 2-D motion detection based on reconfigurable computing. IEEE Trans. Instrum. Meas. **55**(6), 2234–2243 (2006)
12. Parker, C.: An analysis of performance measures for binary classifiers. In: Proceedings - IEEE International Conference on Data Mining, ICDM, pp. 517–526 (2011)
13. Song, K.T., Tai, J.C.: Dynamic calibration of pan-tilt-zoom cameras for traffic monitoring. IEEE Trans. Syst. Man Cybern. B Cybern. **36**(5), 1091–1103 (2006)

Data Visualization Using Interactive Dimensionality Reduction and Improved Color-Based Interaction Model

P.D. Rosero-Montalvo[1,2(✉)], D.F. Peña-Unigarro[3], D.H. Peluffo[1,4], J.A. Castro-Silva[5], A. Umaquinga[1], and E.A. Rosero-Rosero[1]

[1] Universidad Técnica Del Norte, Ibarra, Ecuador
pdrosero@utn.edu.ec
[2] Instituto Tecnológico Superior 17 de Julio, Ibarra, Ecuador
[3] Universidad de Nariño, Pasto, Colombia
[4] Corporación Universitaria Autónoma de Nariño, Pasto, Colombia
[5] Universidad Surcolombiana, Neiva, Huila, Colombia

Abstract. This work presents an improved interactive data visualization interface based on a mixture of the outcomes of dimensionality reduction (DR) methods. Broadly, it works as follows: The user can input the mixture weighting factors through a visual and intuitive interface with a primary-light-colors-based model (Red, Green, and Blue). By design, such a mixture is a weighted sum of the color tone. Additionally, the low-dimensional representation space produced by DR methods are graphically depicted using scatter plots powered via an interactive data-driven visualization. To do so, pairwise similarities are calculated and employed to define the graph to simultaneously be drawn over the scatter plot. Our interface enables the user to interactively combine DR methods by the human perception of color, while providing information about the structure of original data. Then, it makes the selection of a DR scheme more intuitive -even for non-expert users.

Keywords: Color-based model · Data visualization · Dimensionality reduction · Pairwise similarity

1 Introduction

The advance of technology can be observed through the integration into everyday human activities in devices like sensors, mobile applications, web pages and companies integrated systems that allows the collection of user data for the purpose of finding valuable information. Subsequently, such information can be converted into useful knowledge for humans to finally make proper decisions [1]. As a consequence, there had been an increasing volume of data generating then the need for computational systems become more robust by incorporating machine learning algorithms, so that knowledge generation can be reached in an optimal way (i.e. by avoiding information redundancy and noise) mainly for unstructured and multivariate databases [2,3].

J.M. Ferrández Vicente et al. (Eds.): IWINAC 2017, Part II, LNCS 10338, pp. 289–298, 2017.
DOI: 10.1007/978-3-319-59773-7_30

The dimensionality reduction (DR) is one of the approaches to make data perceivable in a simpler and compact way, since representing a set of high dimensional data increases the complexity of user's understanding due that the information may become abstract specially, regarding the manner to describe objects being non-physical [4].

DR methods are able to simplify the description of the data set that can represent large volumes of information at optimal processing times, while keeping the same properties of the complex high-dimensional data. As a result, it favors compression, elimination of redundancy and improves the processes with the implementation of machine learning algorithms. Then, it also reduces the computational cost. In virtue of the above, the user obtain a better analysis with an effective pattern recognition and considering a smaller number of dimensions [2].

Once performed the DR stage, the interactive visualization takes place to create an interface between the human beings and the computational processes with their algorithms of machine learning. Such an interface allows to generate efficient forms of mathematical and statistical processes to the user's understanding, where he can manipulate the information until to determine the best method in each specific information type. However, presenting data in an understandable, dynamic and intuitive way with transparent mathematical processes to the user becomes a challenge [4,5]. The visualization of data only succeeds when it can encodes the information in a way that our eyes can discern and our brains can understand. To achieve this objective is more a science than an art, which can only be achieved through the study of human perception [6].

Some works [2,3,7,8] have accomplished interfaces with methods of dimensionality reduction with different approaches and ways of generating mixtures between the different DR algorithms, so that the user can intuitively select the most appropriate in a visual way. [9] also has a pairwise similarities to determinate the affinity for the DR method mixture result but all these works does not focus in the interface design and reason to applies the color inside the data visualization. The present work is an improved approach to those cited works by optimizing the user interaction with the interface by associating DR methods with colors and RGB bars that are easier to associate with processes previously learned by user with the aim of create more intuitive environments.

For experiments, we used the spherical data set in 3-D, the evaluation of the performance of the mixture was considered conventional methods of DR such as: multidimensional classical scaling (CMDS) [10], locally linear embedding (LLE) and t-Student distributed (TSNE) [11,12], in addition to provide more interactivity to the user can control color bars tone by varying their parameter, also integrates a slider to control and visualize the affinity of the points of the 2-D graphic in relation to the 3-D graphic. To perform the mixing of methods the user has the RGB bars (Red, Green, Blue) in order to modify the color tone in a container with scale from 0 to 255, for weights factors are performed by an average in relation to the tonality summation of the RGB bars, as a result the 2-D circumference is graphically observed in a friendly and interactive way [6].

The remaining of the paper is organized as follows: In Sect. 2, Data visualization via dimensionality reduction is outlined. Section 3 introduces the proposed interactive data visualization scheme. Experimental setup and results are presented in Sects. 4 and 5, respectively. Finally, Sect. 6 gathers some final remarks as conclusions and future work.

2 Data Visualization via Dimensionality Reduction

The data visualization means the interaction between the human and the system (interface) which handle thousands of complex data sets records. This allowing an in depth knowledge and pattern recognition in such a way that they become information comprehensible for the user. The 2- or 3-dimensional representation maybe can the most intuitive ways of visualizing large volumes numerical data for analyzing and find information when strong hypotheses about data are not yet available [13], besides can be readily represented using a scatter plot, giving the facility to the human eye for its interpretation, since they can see easily in two dimensions and the brain is in charge of calculating the distance between the object, giving the perception of third dimension [14]. In this way, dimensionality reduction methods are born from the need to obtain a simple representation of the complexity or relationship of big volume of data into a low dimension space, with the least loss of information possible [15]. So, when performing a DR method, a more realistic and intelligible visualization for the user is expected [11]. More technically, the goal of dimensionality reduction is to embed a high dimensional data matrix $\boldsymbol{Y} = [\boldsymbol{y}_i]_{1 \leq 1 \leq N}$ such that $\boldsymbol{y}_i \in \mathbb{R}^D$ into a low-dimensional, latent data matrix $\boldsymbol{X} = [\boldsymbol{x}_i]_{1 \leq 1 \leq N}$ being $\boldsymbol{y}_i \in \mathbb{R}^d$, where $d < D$ [11,16]. Figure 1 depicts an instance where a manifold (3-dimensional sphere) is embedded into a 2-D representation, which resembles to an unfolded version of the original manifold.

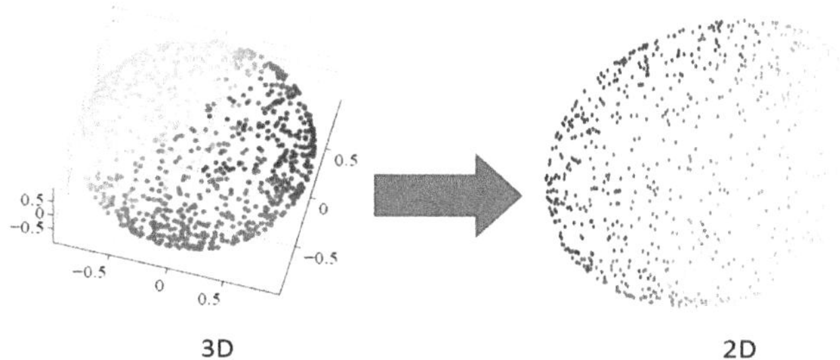

Fig. 1. Dimensionality reduction effect over an artificial (3-dimensional) spherical shell manifold. Resultant embedded (2-dimensional) data is an attempt to unfolding the original data.

3 Interactive Data Visualization Scheme

The proposed visualization improve approach, here so-called DataVisSim, involves three main stages: mixture of DR outcomes, interaction, and visualization, as depicted in the block diagram of Fig. 2. One of the most important contributions of this work is that information on the structure of the input high-dimensional space is added to the visual final representation, by using a pairwise-similarity-based scheme and the greater accuracy of the proportion of DR methods, giving the user the knowledge of their DR mixture in percentages according to the color's tonality.

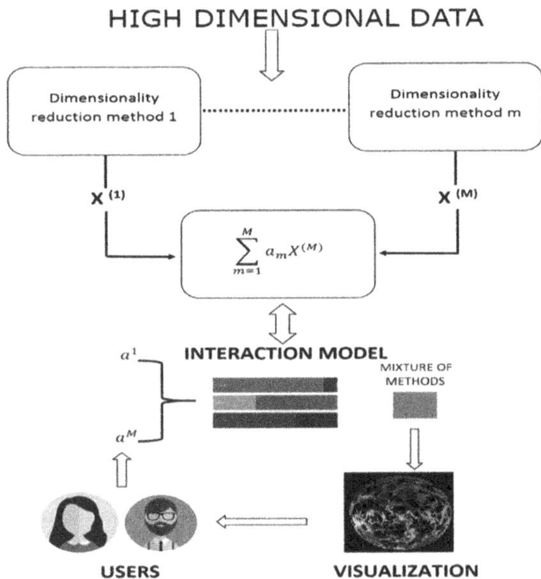

Fig. 2. Block diagram of proposed interactive data visualization using dimensionality reduction and similarity-based representations (DataVisSim). It works as follows: First the interface loads the database of high dimension and reduced dimension, in second step the user can manipulate the color bars for performs a mixture between DR methods, at third step when the user has decided the weighting factors for the aforementioned mixture we can validate his choice with a novel similarity-bases approach, and finally the embedded representation can be saved. (Color figure online)

3.1 Mixture

Let us suppose that the input matrix $\boldsymbol{Y}$ is reduced by using $\mathbf{M}$ different DR methods, yielding then a set of lower-dimensional representations: $\{\boldsymbol{X}^{(1)}, \cdots, \boldsymbol{X}^{(M)}\}$. Herein, we propose to perform a weighted sum in the form:

$$\bar{\boldsymbol{X}} = \sum_{m=1}^{M} \alpha_m \boldsymbol{X}^{(m)}, \tag{1}$$

where $\{\alpha_1, \cdots, \alpha_M\}$ are the weighting factors. To make the selection of weighting factors intuitive, we use probability values so that $0 \leq \alpha_m \leq 1$ and $\sum_{m1=1}^{M} \alpha_m = 1$, and therefore all matrices $\boldsymbol{X}^{(m)}$ should be normalized to rely within a unit hypersphere.

3.2 Interaction Model

An appropriate design of an interface, allows to the user to create own mental models that help to understand the information on the screen of a computer. Through previous experiences and expectations the user shapes perceptions. The interaction between the user and the system must be a fluid dialogue in the style of the interface where the senses of vision, hearing and touch interact [17]. This work emphasizes touch and vision based on an additive synthesis model that emits light directly to the source of illumination of some kind, representing a color by mixing the 3 primary RGB light colors (Red, Green, Blue) [18]. This form of representation and creation of color is used since the human eye has photoreceptors, approximately 64% of the cones (photosensitive cells) contains photo pigments (light sensitive proteins), 32% contain green and only about 2% contains photo blue pigments [6]. Consequently the human eye has greater sensitivity RGB colors based on human perception and the combination between light, object and observer [17].

The proposed interface allows the process between luminescence, contrast, color and movement that allows a sensation of physical stimuli to the human being and can pay attention to the mixture of DR. The HSV model (Hue, Saturation and Value) represented in a computer according to Fig. 3. The user can to manipulate the values of the bars of tone of the RGB colors, the increase or decrease of their value is given according to the saturation of the bar, giving the feeling of filling or emptying it [6,18]. The interface works as follows: the user loads the sphere in third dimension, once visualized the figure has the RGB bars that can modify the percentage of tone of the same, so the user change the weight of the DR methods and they can be observed the 2-D figure about the existing blend and the resulting color of the RGB. Finally, the work can be save for later analysis of the new data set.

For the sake of interactivity, the values of every α_m -required to calculate $\bar{\boldsymbol{X}}$ according to Eq. (1)- are to be defined by the users using an color saturation-bar available in the interface. Within a friendly-user and intuitive environment, in the case than more DR methods is selected, weighting factors can be readily imputed by just select values from bars and choose the color saturation between RGB color bars are definite by fundamental counting principle, which given a set of n elements, is defined as an arrangement of n in order of k ($k <= n$) to each tuple that can be formed by taking k different elements among n given. The user can move the bars when they consider suitable.

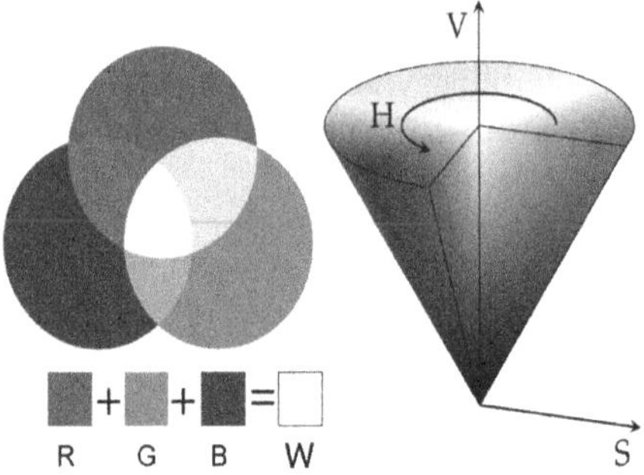

Fig. 3. The picture in the left side explain the way of the RGB color can make others colors, the right side show the saturation and hue with model HSV and the interaction with RGB color for visualize different color tone (Color figure online)

3.3 Similarity-Based Visualization

The most used method to visualize 2- or 3-dimensional data is the scatter plot. In this work, we introduce a similarity-based visualization approach with the aim to provide a visual hint about the structure of the high-dimensional input data matrix $\boldsymbol{Y}$ into the scatter plot of its representation in a lower-dimensional space To do so, we use a pairwise similarity matrix $\boldsymbol{S} \in \mathbb{R}^{N \times N}$, such that $\boldsymbol{S} = [\boldsymbol{s}_{ij}]$. In terms of graph theory, entries $\boldsymbol{s}_{ij}$ defines the similarity or affinity between the $i - th$ and $j - th$ data point from $\boldsymbol{Y}$. Doing so, we can hold the structure of original input space in a topological fashion, specifically in terms of pairwise relationships. For visualization purposes, such a similarity is used to define graphically the relationship between data points by plotting edges. In order to control the amount of edges and make an appealing visual representations, the value of $\boldsymbol{s}_{ij}$ is constrained as $\boldsymbol{s}_{ij} > \boldsymbol{s}_{max}$, being $\boldsymbol{s}_{max}$ a maximum admissible similarity value to be given by the users as well. In other words, our visualization approach consists of building a graph with constrained affinity values.

4 Experimental Setup

Database: In order to visually evaluate the performance of the DataVisSim approach, we use an artificial spherical shell (N = 1000 data points and D = 3), as depicted in Fig. 1.

Parameter Settings and Methods: In order to capture the local structure for visualization, i.e. data points being neighbors, we utilize the Gaussian similarity given by: $\boldsymbol{s}_{ij} = -exp(-0.5\|\boldsymbol{y}_{(i)} - \boldsymbol{y}_{(j)}\|^2/\sigma^2)$. The parameter is a bandwidth value set as 0.1, being the 10% of the hypersphere ratio (applicable once matrices are normalized as discussed in Sect. 3.1. To perform the dimensionality reduction we consider $M = 3$ DR methods, namely: CMDS, LLE, and t-SNE. All of them are intended to obtain spaces in dimension $d = 2$.

Performance Measure: To quantify the performance of studied methods, the scaled version of the average agreement rate $R_{NX}(K)$ introduced in [19] is used, which is ranged within the interval [0, 1]. Since $R_{NX}(K)$ is calculated at each perplexity value from 2 to $N-1$, a numerical indicator of the overall performance can be obtained by calculating its area under the curve (AUC). The AUC assesses the dimension reduction quality at all scales, with the most appropriate weights.

5 Results

Figure 4 shows the scatter plots for the resultant low-dimensional spaces obtained by the considered dimensionality reduction methods for the interface. These DR methods has been insert doing relationship with eye perception in front of the computer.

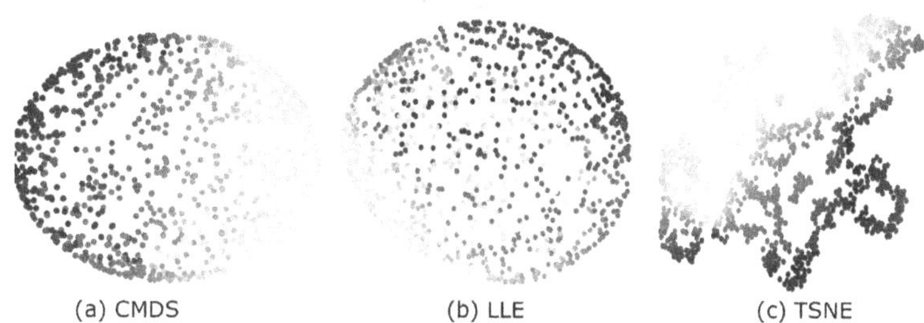

Fig. 4. The effects of dimensionality reduction methods considered on the 3-D sphere. The results are embedded data represented in a bi-dimensional space.

The interface was developed in Processing in virtue of the ease of represent information in a visual way, the interface shows all the content in relation of pixels, of this way all the data points must be modify and change only to positive points. In the Fig. 5 shows the final interactive interface with RGB model.

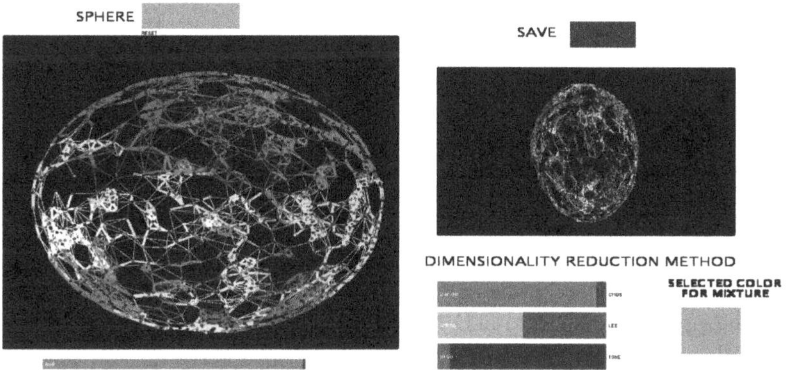

Fig. 5. Finally interface developed in Processing with interactive RGB model. Sample video https://sites.google.com/site/intelligentsystemsrg/home/gallery/

Figure 6 shows the result with the interaction between the user and the interface in three important aspects: RGB mixture color, the 2-D visualization and the mixture performance. As seen, $R_{NX}(K)$ measure allows for assessing both the different mixtures and the methods independently Since the area under its curve represents a representation quality measure of the low-dimensional space, is in turn a visual and intuitive indicator that helps the user to find the best either a single DR method or the proper mixture [9].

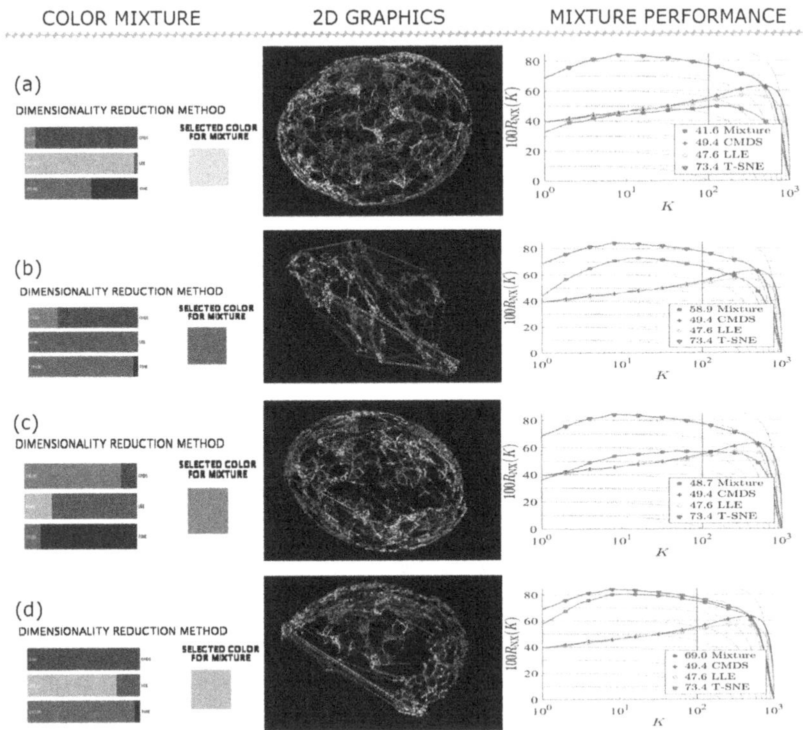

Fig. 6. The picture show four results of the interaction between interface and the user and how they find their mixture, in some cases the mixture had been with good performance and others do not.

As well, the interface incorporates a slider bar to dynamically draw the edges between nodes. This is useful for visual analysis given that it allows to relate the structure of high-dimensional data (original data) within the visualization of the low-dimensional representation space, the thickness line amounts to relation between the points in 2-D and 3-D dimension. Therefore, is easy to see by the user the DR mixture quality, as the picture shows in Fig. 7.

This follows from the interaction between the user and the interface, which shows greater preferences in blends of blue and green in men, while in women it changes its selection to yellow and pink colors. This indicates that the most

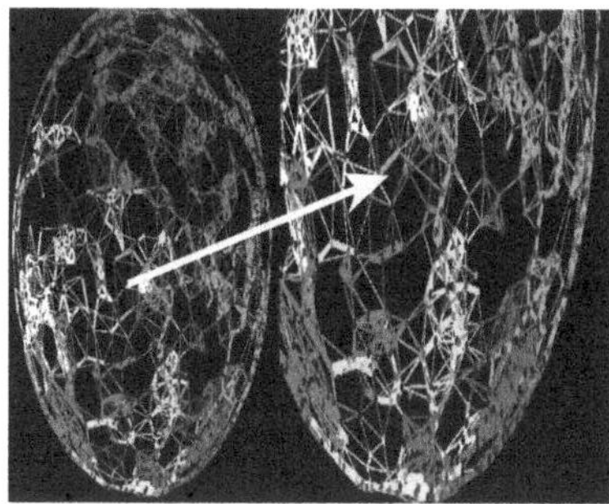

Fig. 7. The figure indicates the affinity of the points by making the relation with the thickness of the lines that join to each other. (Color figure online)

widely used method is CMDS and T-SNE, respectively. In addition, the affinity bar allows the verification of the result of the mixture, giving the opportunity to change the result by observing the distance of the points increases when plotting them with The RGB mix.

6 Conclusions and Future Work

This paper presents an improved visualization method, which is based on the mixture of dimensionality reduction methods by following a color-human-perception criterion and enables users to have mental structures on the performance of the obtained results by visualizing a similarity measure calculated at the high dimension data. Particularly, the mixture is performed as a weighted sum whose weights are defined as the average of the tonality of the primary light colors of RGB.

As a future work, other dimensionality reduction methods are to be integrated into the interface and improve intuitive way of generate mixture DR methods. The interface needs more mathematical developments regarding the way to perform the mixture of DR methods.

Aknowledgments. The authors would like to thank the project "Desarrollo de una metodología de visualización interactiva y eficaz de información en Big Data" supported by VIPRI from Universidad de Nariño - Colombia, as well as Universidad Técnica del Norte - Ecuador.

References

1. Ward, M.O., Grinstein, G., Keim, D.: Interactive Data Visualization: Foundations, Techniques, and Applications. CRC Press, Boca Raton (2010)
2. Salazar-Castro, J., Rosas-Narváez, Y., Pantoja, A., Alvarado-Pérez, J.C., Peluffo-Ordóñez, D.H.: Interactive interface for efficient data visualization via a geometric approach. In: 2015 20th Symposium on Signal Processing, Images and Computer Vision (STSIVA), pp. 1–6. IEEE (2015)

3. Peña-Unigarro, D.F., Salazar-Castro, J.A., Peluffo-Ordóñez, D.H., Rosero-Montalvo, P.D., Oña-Rocha, O.R., Isaza, A.A., Alvarado-Pérez, J.C., Theron, R.: Interactive visualization methodology of high-dimensional data with a color-based model for dimensionality reduction. In: 2016 XXI Symposium on Signal Processing, Images and Artificial Vision (STSIVA), pp. 1–7, August 2016
4. Alvarado-Pérez, J.C., Peluffo-Ordóñez, D.H., Therón, R.: Visualización y métodos kernel: integrando inteligencia natural y artificial (2016)
5. Dai, W., Hu, P.: Research on personalized behaviors recommendation system based on cloud computing. Indones. J. Electr. Eng. Comput. Sci. **12**(2), 1480–1486 (2013)
6. Dastan, M.: The role of visual perception in data visualization. J. Vis. Lang. Comput. **13**(6), 601–622 (2002)
7. Peluffo-Ordóñez, D.H., Alvarado-Pérez, J.C., Lee, J.A., Verleysen, M., et al.: Geometrical homotopy for data visualization. In: European Symposium on Artificial Neural Networks (ESANN 2015). Computational Intelligence and Machine Learning. (2015)
8. Díaz, I., Cuadrado, A.A., Pérez, D., García, F.J., Verleysen, M.: Interactive dimensionality reduction for visual analytics. In: Proceedings of the 22th European Symposium on Artificial Neural Networks, Computational Intelligence and Machine Learning (ESANN 2014), pp. 183–188. Citeseer (2014)
9. Rosero-Montalvo, P., Diaz, P., Salazar-Castro, J.A., Peña-Unigarro, D.F., Anaya-Isaza, A.J., Alvarado-Pérez, J.C., Therón, R., Peluffo-Ordóñez, D.H.: Interactive data visualization using dimensionality reduction and similarity-based representations. In: Beltrán-Castañón, C., Nyström, I., Famili, F. (eds.) CIARP 2016. LNCS, vol. 10125, pp. 334–342. Springer, Cham (2017). doi:10.1007/978-3-319-52277-7_41
10. Borg, I., Groenen, P.J.: Modern Multidimensional Scaling: Theory and Applications. Springer Science & Business Media, New York (2005)
11. Peluffo-Ordóñez, D.H., Lee, J.A., Verleysen, M.: Short review of dimensionality reduction methods based on stochastic neighbour embedding. In: Villmann, T., Schleif, F.-M., Kaden, M., Lange, M. (eds.) Advances in Self-Organizing Maps and Learning Vector Quantization. AISC, vol. 295, pp. 65–74. Springer, Cham (2014). doi:10.1007/978-3-319-07695-9_6
12. Belkin, M., Niyogi, P.: Laplacian eigenmaps for dimensionality reduction and data representation. Neural Comput. **15**(6), 1373–1396 (2003)
13. Park, Y., Cafarella, M., Mozafari, B.: Visualization-aware sampling for very large databases. In: 2016 IEEE 32nd International Conference on Data Engineering (ICDE), pp. 755–766, May 2016
14. Emberson, L.L., Amso, D.: Learning to sample: eye tracking and fMRI indices of changes in object perception. J. Cogn. Neurosci. **24**(10), 2030–2042 (2012)
15. Bertini, E., Lalanne, D.: Surveying the complementary role of automatic data analysis and visualization in knowledge discovery. In: Proceedings of the ACM SIGKDD Workshop on Visual Analytics and Knowledge Discovery: Integrating Automated Analysis with Interactive Exploration, pp. 12–20. ACM (2009)
16. Peluffo-Ordóñez, D.H., Lee, J.A., Verleysen, M.: Generalized kernel framework for unsupervised spectral methods of dimensionality reduction. In: 2014 IEEE Symposium on Computational Intelligence and Data Mining (CIDM), pp. 171–177. IEEE (2014)
17. Levkowitz, H.: Color Theory and Modeling for Computer Graphics, Visualization, and Multimedia Applications. Springer, New York (1997)
18. Dix, A.: Human-Computer Interaction. Springer, New York (2009)
19. Lee, J.A., Renard, E., Bernard, G., Dupont, P., Verleysen, M.: Type 1 and 2 mixtures of Kullback-Leibler divergences as cost functions in dimensionality reduction based on similarity preservation. Neurocomputing **112**, 92–108 (2013)

Bayesian Unbiasing of the *Gaia* Space Mission Time Series Database

Héctor E. Delgado(✉) and Luis M. Sarro

Dpto. de Inteligencia Artificial, UNED, Juan del Rosal 16, 28040 Madrid, Spain
hed_up@iasystems.org, lsb@dia.uned.es

Abstract. 21st century astrophysicists are confronted with the herculean task of distilling the maximum scientific return from extremely expensive and complex space- or ground-based instrumental projects. This paper concentrates in the mining of the time series catalog produced by the European Space Agency *Gaia* mission, launched in December 2013. We tackle in particular the problem of inferring the true distribution of the variability properties of Cepheid stars in the Milky Way satellite galaxy known as the Large Magellanic Cloud (LMC). Classical Cepheid stars are the first step in the so-called distance ladder: a series of techniques to measure cosmological distances and decipher the structure and evolution of our Universe. In this work we attempt to unbias the catalog by modelling the aliasing phenomenon that distorts the true distribution of periods. We have represented the problem by a 2-level generative Bayesian graphical model and used a Markov chain Monte Carlo (MCMC) algorithm for inference (classification and regression). Our results with synthetic data show that the system successfully removes systematic biases and is able to infer the true hyperparameters of the frequency and magnitude distributions.

Keywords: Astrostatistics · Bayesian · Data analysis · Hierarchical model · Markov chain Monte Carlo · Catalogues

1 Introduction

Gaia [5] is a European Space Agency (ESA) space mission, launched in December 2013, whose main objective is to compile a large-scale astronomical survey of about one billion stars (≈1%) of our Galaxy and its Local Group. The satellite will scan the entire sky for about 5 years yielding an unprecedented catalog in both size and precision of positions, distances and proper motion measures. Additionally, it will perform multi-epoch photometry (70 transits per object on average) which renders the satellite suitable too for studies of stellar variability. Amongst the many variability types present in the stellar zoo, one in particular is of paramount importance: the Classical Cepheids. Classical Cepheids represent the first calibrator in the cosmic distance ladder used to infer the structure and evolution of our Universe, and our current knowledge about the Big Bang, the inflationary period, the dark matter problem or dark energy relies on the

J.M. Ferrández Vicente et al. (Eds.): IWINAC 2017, Part II, LNCS 10338, pp. 299–311, 2017.
DOI: 10.1007/978-3-319-59773-7_31

period-luminosity relation for Classical Cepheids [14]. Therefore, a precise and accurate understanding of the population of Classical Cepheids is central to all cosmological studies.

In this paper we address the problem of inferring the true properties of this population of variable stars from the petabyte-size *Gaia* catalog. In order to populate the catalog, and as part of a much larger framework to deliver a data set of scientific quality, the Data Processing and Analysis Consortium (DPAC[1]) developed a pipeline to characterize the time series observed and classify them. A key element of this process is that the time sampling of stellar brightness time series will have the imprint of the satellite intrinsic frequencies (amongst other, the spinning and precessing frequencies, a description of which is out of the scope of this paper). As a consequence, some (but not all) of the derived frequencies will be affected by aliasing which results in biased samples.

The objective is to characterize the phenomenon of *aliasing* in the *Gaia* catalog, correct for it, and reconstruct the real distribution of LMC Classical Cepheids properties. In order to achieve these goals, we tackle the problem under the Bayesian paradigm [6,7] and adopt the knowledge representation language of Bayesian Networks (BN) [8,11]. This framework allows a hierarchical representation of the problem in which the time series gathered by Gaia are the product of a generative process which ultimately depends on the parameters of the population of stars. Given that the computation of the posterior probabilities of our model are analytically intractable, the inference mechanism of our proposal is founded in Markov chain Monte Carlo (MCMC) simulation techniques [13].

We have validated our models using a data base of 36688 synthetic Classical LMC Cepheids time series generated according to controlled prescriptions based on current understanding of the true distributions and the satellite characteristics. Our results prove that we are ready for the second *Gaia* data release expected for 2018. This will be the first data release to include photometric time series (although this still needs to be confirmed).

The structure of the rest of the paper is as follows. In Sect. 2 we describe our model and the MCMC technique used for the inference of the parameters of interest. In Sect. 3 we validate the model with the simulated data base in a scenario of extreme aliasing and describe the results of this validation procedure. Finally, in Sect. 4 we summarize the contributions of this work and some of its limitations, and give pointers to future developments.

2 Hierarchical Modelling of the Distribution of Pulsation Properties of Classical Cepheid Variable Stars

2.1 The Hierarchical Model

Figure 1 and Table 1 depict the structure of the DAG associated to the model and summarize the meanings of the nodes and the types of their distributions.

[1] The DPAC (Data Processing and Analysis Consortium) is the consortium responsible for building and making accessible the GAIA catalogue.

We classify the nodes into a hierarchy of three levels. The hierarchy distinguishes between evidential nodes (observations), the rest of nodes inside the rectangle or *plate*, which is replicated N times (one per star), and the nodes outside the rectangle. In the following paragraphs we describe the parameters and probability distributions for each level and its contribution to the joint probability distribution.

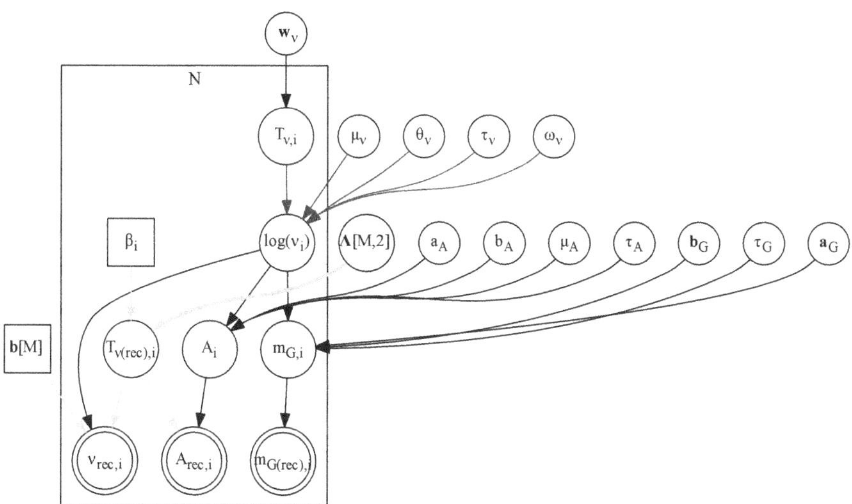

Fig. 1. Graph structure of our proposed Bayesian Graphical Model (BGM). Most fixed parameters are not included in the graph, with the exception of those enclosed inside a square. See the text and Table 1 for node descriptions.

2.1.1 Likelihood

In the bottom level of our graph we present the *evidential nodes*, that is, the variables measured directly or derived by the DPAC

$$\mathcal{D} = (\nu_{\mathrm{rec},i}, A_{\mathrm{rec},i}, m_{G_{\mathrm{rec}},i}) \,. \tag{1}$$

These nodes, depicted by double circles, are the output/recovered frequency $\nu_{\mathrm{rec},i}$, the amplitude $A_{\mathrm{rec},i}$ and the apparent G-magnitude $m_{G_{\mathrm{rec}},i}$ for the i-th star.

Recovered Frequencies. Most of the pairs $(\nu_{\mathrm{input}}, \nu_{\mathrm{rec}})$ in the simulated data base fall on straights lines of the form:

$$\nu_{\mathrm{rec}} = \pm\nu_{\mathrm{input}} \pm k_1\nu_s \pm k_2\nu_p, \tag{2}$$

where $k_1 \in \{0, 3, 7\}$, $k_2 \in \{0, \ldots, 19\}$, $\nu_s \approx \frac{1}{0.25} = 4\mathrm{d}^{-1}$ is the rotational frequency of Gaia and $\nu_p = \frac{1}{63}\mathrm{d}^{-1}$ is its precessional frequency. We refer to each line as a *locus/category* of recovered frequencies. Excluding the line $\nu_{\mathrm{rec}} = \nu_{\mathrm{input}}$,

Table 1. Description of parameters. NI = non informative

Node	Description	Type of distribution
τ_G	Precision	Gamma NI prior
$\mathbf{a}_G$	Slopes	Gaussian NI prior
$\boldsymbol{b}_G$	Intercepts	Gaussian NI prior
$m_{G,i}$	Input apparent G magnitude	Gaussian
$m_{G,\text{rec},i}$	Recovered apparent G magnitude	Gaussian
μ_A	Mean	Gaussian NI prior
τ_A	Precision	Gamma NI prior
a_A	Slope	Gaussian NI prior
b_A	Intercept	Gaussian NI prior
A_i	Input amplitude	Gaussian
$A_{\text{rec},i}$	Recovered amplitude	Mixture of skewed Cauchy
$\boldsymbol{w}_\nu$	Mixing proportions	Gamma NI prior
T_{ν_i}	Category of $\log(\nu_i)$	Categorical
μ_ν	Mean	Non informative
$\boldsymbol{\theta}_\nu$	Mean perturbations	Gaussian NI prior
τ_ν	Precision	Non informative
ω_ν	Precision perturbations	Uniform prior
$\log(\nu_i)$	Input frequency $\left[d^{-1}\right]$	Mixture of Gaussian
Λ	Logistic R. coefficients	Student t prior
$T_{\nu_{\text{rec},i}}$	Category of $\nu_{\text{rec},i}$	Categorical
$\nu_{\text{rec},i}$	Recovered frequency	Mixture of Gaussian

all these *loci* correspond to spurious (aliased) frequencies. Based on that, we parameterize the i-th recovered frequency as the following mixture of Gaussian distribution

$$f\left(\nu_{\text{rec},i} \mid \log(\nu_i), T_{\nu_{\text{rec},i}}\right) = \sum_{j=1}^{M} \delta^{j}_{T_{\nu_{\text{rec},i}}} \mathsf{N}\left((-1)^{j-1}\, 10^{\log(\nu_i)} + b_j, \tau_{\nu_{\text{rec}}}\right). \quad (3)$$

In Eq. 3 the Kronecker deltas $\delta^{j}_{T_{\nu_{\text{rec},i}}}$ dictate the Gaussian component to which $\nu_{\text{rec},i}$ belongs according to the value of the categorical variable $T_{\nu_{\text{rec},i}}$ (described in Sect. 2.1.2). The mean of each component represents the *locus* in which the input frequency has been recovered, i.e. the identity locus, with $b_j = 0$ for $j = 1$, or some locus of spurious (aliased) frequencies for $j > 1$. We assume the same precision $\tau_{\nu_{\text{rec}}} = 10000$ for all components.

Recovered Amplitudes. To gain insight into the form of the conditional distribution of the recovered amplitude given the input amplitude we have checked the hypothesis that recovered amplitudes are also biased by the aliasing phenomenon, just as recovered frequencies are. By analysing the relationship between *loci* of frequencies and pairs $(A_{\text{input}}, A_{\text{rec}})$, we have discovered that for a perfect recovery the distribution $A_{\text{rec}} \mid A$ is skewed to lower amplitudes with a central parameter approximately equal to the input amplitude. Otherwise, for *loci* of aliased frequencies we have observed that the skewness of the recovered amplitude increases as the input amplitude does according to a certain slope to be determined as part of the model. To account for this fact we have fitted two linear regression models

$$A_{\text{rec},i} = \beta_1^j A_{\text{in},i} + \beta_0^j + \epsilon_i^j, \; j = 1, 2, \tag{4}$$

with $j = 1$ corresponding to the identity locus and $j = 2$ to the *loci* $\nu_{\text{rec}} = \pm\nu_{\text{in}} + 7\nu_s - 3\nu_p$[2]. For the identity locus, we have assumed a skewed Student t distribution [2] with one degree of freedom (skewed Cauchy) for the error component $\epsilon_i^1 \sim \mathsf{st}(0, \omega, \alpha, 1)$ where ω and α denote respectively the shape and scale parameters. For the *locus* $\nu_{\text{rec}} = \pm\nu_{\text{in}} + 7\nu_s - 3\nu_p$ we have assumed that $\epsilon_i^2 \sim \mathsf{t}(0, \omega, 1)$. Based on that, we model the conditional distribution for the recovered amplitude $A_{\text{rec},i}$ by means of the mixture of two skewed Student t distributions

$$\begin{aligned} f\left(A_{\text{rec},i} \mid A_i, T_{\nu_{\text{rec},i}}\right) = & \; \delta^1_{T_{\nu_{\text{rec},i}}} \mathsf{ST}\left(A_i, 0.020, -2.395, 1\right) \\ & + \sum_{j=2}^{M} \delta^j_{T_{\nu_{\text{rec},i}}} \mathsf{ST}\left(0.749 \cdot A_i, 0.0266, 0, 1\right), \end{aligned} \tag{5}$$

where the location parameters $\xi_1 = A_i$, $\xi_j = 0.749 \cdot A_i, \forall j = 2, \ldots, M$, the scale ω and the shapes α have been obtained from the fitting of the two linear models of Eq. 4 and taken as constants in our BGM.

Recovered Apparent Magnitudes. We parameterize the distribution of the i-th recovered apparent G magnitude by means of a Gaussian distribution with mean $m_{G,i}$ and precision $\tau_{G(rec)} = 2.5\text{E}{+}5$ (to be adjusted when real *Gaia* data become available)

$$f\left(m_{G_{rec},i} \mid m_{G,i}\right) = \mathsf{N}\left(m_{G,i}, \tau_{G_{rec}}\right). \tag{6}$$

The conditional distribution of the data given their parents is then given by

$$\begin{aligned} p\left(\mathcal{D} \mid \boldsymbol{\theta}_1\right) = & \prod_{i=1}^{N} f_1\left(\nu_{\text{rec},i} \mid \log(\nu_i), T_{\nu_{\text{rec},i}}\right) \cdot f_2\left(A_{\text{rec},i} \mid A_i, T_{\nu_{\text{rec},i}}\right) \\ & \cdot f_3\left(m_{G_{\text{rec}},i} \mid m_{G,i}\right). \end{aligned} \tag{7}$$

2.1.2 First Level Random Parameters

These are

$$\boldsymbol{\theta}_1 = \left(\log\left(\nu_i\right), A_i, m_{G,i}, T_{\nu_{\text{rec},i}}, T_{\nu_i}\right). \tag{8}$$

[2] We only select these particular *loci* of aliased frequencies because they are the most frequent *loci* located far away from the identity *locus* and because the model does not work well if we include more *loci* located close to them.

In $\boldsymbol{\theta}_1$, we distinguish two classes of nodes. The *input nodes* are, for the i-th star, the real frequency $\log(\nu_i)$, the real amplitude A_i and the real apparent G-magnitude $m_{G,i}$. The *categorical nodes* $T_{\nu_{\text{rec},i}}$ and T_{ν_i} determine the component of a node modelled by a mixture of distributions. T_{ν_i} and $T_{\nu_{\text{rec},i}}$ are respectively associated with the real frequency and the recovered frequency and amplitude. In Fig. 1 all the nodes at this level replicate with the plate. They depend on (amongst other) non informative orphan nodes outside the plate.

Categories of Recovered Frequencies. The node $T_{\nu_{\text{rec},i}}$ takes a value $j \in \{1, \ldots, M\}$ if the i-th frequency has been recovered in the j-th locus, which occurs with a probability π_{ij}. In this paper we assume that the main factor determining the aliasing phenomenon in Gaia is the ecliptic latitude β of the stars. The influence of β over the rate of correct detections of periodic signals by *Gaia* has been studied in [4] where it is shown that for high values of β, typical of LMC sources, the relation between the rate of correct detections and β is approximately linear with a negative slope. Based on that, we make π_{ij} depend on the ecliptic latitude β_i and parameterize this dependence by a multinomial logistic regression submodel with a *softmax* transfer function. We model the conditional distribution of $T_{\nu_{\text{rec},i}}$ as

$$p\left(T_{\nu_{\text{rec},i}} \mid \{\boldsymbol{\lambda}_j\}_{j=2}^{M}\right) = \mathsf{Cat}\left(M, \{\pi_{ij}\left(\beta_i', \boldsymbol{\lambda}_j\right)\}_{j=1}^{M}\right), \tag{9}$$

with

$$\pi_{ij}\left(\beta_i', \boldsymbol{\lambda}_j\right) = \frac{e^{\boldsymbol{\lambda}_j^T \cdot (1, \beta_i')}}{\sum_{l=1}^{M} e^{\boldsymbol{\lambda}_l^T \cdot (1, \beta_i')}}, \tag{10}$$

where we have rescaled the predictor β_i by subtracting the mean and dividing by two times the standard deviation, i.e. $\beta_i' = \frac{\beta_i - \overline{\beta}}{2 \cdot \text{sd}(\beta)}$, which guaranties that the mean and the standard deviation are respectively 0 and 0.5.

Input Frequencies and Categories. The marginal distribution of the (decadic) logarithm of the input frequency in the synthetic data set created by the DPAC Quality Assessment group was sampled from a mixture of five Gaussian distributions [1]. In our BGM, we parameterize it by the mixture of only three components[3]

$$\begin{aligned} f\left(\log(\nu_i) \mid T_{\nu_i}, \mu_\nu, \boldsymbol{\theta}_\nu, \tau_\nu, \boldsymbol{\omega}_\nu\right) = {} & \delta_{T_{\nu_i}}^1 \mathsf{N}\left(\mu_\nu, \tau_\nu\right) \\ & + \delta_{T_{\nu_i}}^2 \mathsf{N}\left(\mu_\nu + \sqrt{\tau_\nu^{-1}}\theta_{\nu 1}, \tau_\nu \omega_{\nu 1}^{-2}\right) \\ & + \delta_{T_{\nu_i}}^3 \mathsf{N}\left(\mu_\nu + \sqrt{\tau_\nu^{-1}}\theta_{\nu 1} + \sqrt{\tau_\nu^{-1}}\omega_{\nu 1}\theta_{\nu 2}, \tau_\nu \omega_{\nu 1}^{-2}\omega_{\nu 2}^{-2}\right). \end{aligned} \tag{11}$$

In Eq. 11, μ_ν and τ_ν denote, respectively, the mean and the precision of the first component of the mixture. $(\theta_{\nu 1}, \theta_{\nu 2})$ and $(\omega_{\nu 1}, \omega_{\nu 2})$ denote, respectively, the perturbation parameters which affect the mean and the scale parameter of a

[3] We rely on the Occam's razor principle.

given component to obtain the mean and scale parameter of the next component [12]. The Kronecker deltas $\delta^j_{T_{\nu_i}}$ have the same role as in Eq. 3 but now the categorical variable T_{ν_i} represents the class of the real frequency. For T_{ν_i} we assign the distribution

$$p\left(T_{\nu_i}\right) = \mathsf{Cat}\left(3, w_{\nu 1}, w_{\nu 2}, w_{\nu 3}\right), \tag{12}$$

where $w_{\nu j}$ are the mixing proportions of the mixture.

Input Amplitudes. This distribution has been simulated based on the OGLE III catalogue of Classical Cepheids [15], as

$$f\left(A \mid \log\left(\nu\right)\right) = \begin{cases} \mathsf{N}\left(-0.5 \cdot \log\left(\nu\right) + 0.2, 0.15\right) & \log\left(\nu\right) < -1 \\ \mathsf{N}\left(0.7, 0.15\right) & \log\left(\nu\right) > -1 \end{cases} \tag{13}$$

In our BGM we parameterize this variable as

$$\begin{aligned} f\left(A_i \mid \log(\nu_i), a_A, b_A, \mu_A, \tau_A\right) = & \mathbf{1}_{\{\log(\nu_i)<-1\}} \mathsf{N}\left(a_A \cdot \log\left(\nu_i\right) + b_A, \tau_A\right) \\ & + \mathbf{1}_{\{\log(\nu_i)>-1\}} \mathsf{N}\left(\mu_A, \tau_A\right), \end{aligned} \tag{14}$$

where $\mathbf{1}_S$ denotes the indicator function of a subset S, a_A and b_A are, respectively, the slope and the intercept of the regression line of A on $\log(\nu)$ when $\log(\nu) < -1$, μ_A denotes the mean of the amplitude when $\log(\nu) > -1$, and τ_A denotes the precision, which we take equal in both cases.

Input Apparent G Magnitudes. Based on Eqs. 12 and 13 of [14] and discarding the distance r to the sources, we parameterize this node as

$$\begin{aligned} & f\left(m_{G,i} \mid \log\left(\nu_i\right), a_{G1}, b_{G1}, a_{G2}, b_{G2}, \tau_G\right) \\ & = \mathbf{1}_{\{\log(\nu_i)<-1\}} \mathsf{N}\left(a_{G1} \cdot \log\left(\nu_i\right) + b_{G1}, \tau_G\right) \\ & + \mathbf{1}_{\{\log(\nu_i)>-1\}} \mathsf{N}\left(a_{G2} \cdot \log\left(\nu_i\right) + b_{G2}, \tau_G\right). \end{aligned} \tag{15}$$

The conditional distribution of the first level of random parameters given the parameters of the top level is then

$$\begin{aligned} p\left(\boldsymbol{\theta}_1 \mid \boldsymbol{\theta}_2\right) = \prod_{i=1}^{N} & g_1\left(T_{\nu_{rec,i}} \mid \{\boldsymbol{\lambda}_j\}_{j=2}^{M}\right) \cdot g_2\left(A_i \mid \log(\nu_i), a_A, b_A, \mu_A, \tau_A\right) \\ & \cdot g_3\left(m_{G,i} \mid \log(\nu_i), \mathbf{a}_G, \mathbf{b}_G, \tau_G\right) \cdot g_4\left(\log\left(\nu_i\right) \mid T_{\nu_i}, \lambda_\nu, \boldsymbol{\theta}_\nu, \tau_\nu, \boldsymbol{\omega}_\upsilon\right) \\ & \cdot g_5\left(T_{\nu_i} \mid \boldsymbol{w}_\nu\right) \end{aligned} \tag{16}$$

2.1.3 Top Level Random Parameters

These hyperparameters are

$$\boldsymbol{\theta}_2 = \left(a_A, b_A, \mu_A, \tau_A, \mathbf{a}_G, \mathbf{b}_G, \tau_G, \mu_\nu, \boldsymbol{\theta}_\nu, \tau_\nu, \boldsymbol{\omega}_\nu, \boldsymbol{w}_\nu, \Lambda\right). \tag{17}$$

$\boldsymbol{\theta}_2$ include the orphan nodes in the graph. We only have a vague (or non informative) prior knowledge about their distributions. The nodes denoted by a and b represent the slopes and intercepts of the distributions of the real amplitude and apparent G-magnitude given the frequency. The nodes denoted by τ and μ represent precisions and means. The nodes denoted by Λ represent the coefficients of the logistic regression submodel of Eq. 10. The rest of nodes are associated with the parameterization of the real frequency of Eq. 11. For these latter hyperparameters we take the non informative priors

$$p(\boldsymbol{w}_\nu) = \mathsf{Dir}(1,1,1) \tag{18}$$

$$p(\mu_\nu) = \mathsf{N}(0, 0.001) \tag{19}$$

$$p(\theta_{\nu j}) = \mathsf{N}(0, 0.01) \tag{20}$$

$$p(\tau_\nu) = \mathsf{Gamma}(0.001, 0.001) \tag{21}$$

$$p(\omega_{\nu j}) = \mathsf{U}(0,1) \tag{22}$$

For the hyperparameters of the logistic regression submodel of Eq. 10 $\boldsymbol{\lambda}_j = (\lambda_{0j}, \lambda_{1j})$ with $j \in \{2, \ldots, M\}$, we assign the weakly informative priors $p(\lambda_{kj}) = \mathsf{t}\left(0, \frac{1}{2.5^2}, 7\right), k \in \{0,1\}$. This election provides a minimal prior information to constrain the range of coefficients λ_{kj} once the covariate β_i has been rescaled [6]. This approximation is used to enhance the convergence rate of our model.

For the parameters a_A, b_A, λ_A of the input amplitude distribution of Eq. 14 and the parameters $a_{G1}, b_{G1}, a_{G2}, b_{G2}$ of the input apparent G magnitude of Eq. 15 we take $\mathsf{N}(0, 0.001)$ non informative priors. And for the precisions τ_A and τ_G we take $\mathsf{Gamma}(0.001, 0.001)$ priors. For all these priors the full conditional distribution of the node is available in closed form.

The distribution (hyperprior) of the top level parameters is then

$$\begin{aligned} p(\boldsymbol{\theta}_2) = {} & h_1(a_A) \cdot h_2(b_A) \cdot h_3(\mu_A) \cdot h_4(\tau_A) \cdot h_5(\mathbf{a}_G) \cdot h_6(\mathbf{b}_G) \cdot h_7(\tau_G) \\ & \cdot h_8(\boldsymbol{w}_\nu) \cdot h_9(\mu_\nu) \cdot h_{10}(\boldsymbol{\theta}_\nu) \cdot h_{11}(\tau_\nu) \cdot h_{12}(\boldsymbol{\omega}_\nu) \cdot h_{13}(\Lambda). \end{aligned} \tag{23}$$

2.1.4 Joint Distribution of the Parameters and Data

From Eqs. 7, 16 and 23 we formulate the joint PDF associated to the graphical mode by

$$p(\boldsymbol{\theta}, \mathcal{D}) = p(\mathcal{D} \mid \boldsymbol{\theta}) \cdot p(\boldsymbol{\theta}) = p(\mathcal{D} \mid \boldsymbol{\theta}_1) \cdot p(\boldsymbol{\theta}_1 \mid \boldsymbol{\theta}_2) \cdot p(\boldsymbol{\theta}_2). \tag{24}$$

2.2 Computation

The joint posterior distribution of the $22+5N$ parameters of the model described in Sect. 2.1 is given by

$$\pi^*(\boldsymbol{\theta}) = \pi(\boldsymbol{\theta} \mid \mathcal{D}) \propto \mathcal{L}(\boldsymbol{\theta}_1) \cdot p(\boldsymbol{\theta}_1 \mid \boldsymbol{\theta}_2) \cdot p(\boldsymbol{\theta}_2). \tag{25}$$

Our goal is to infer the marginal *a posteriori* distribution $\pi^*(\boldsymbol{\theta}_2)$ of the top level hyperparameters[4]. The marginalization to obtain samples from $\pi^*(\boldsymbol{\theta}_2)$

[4] In the case of the logarithm of the frequency distribution $\log(\nu)$ we are interested in the means and standard deviations of each Gaussian component, but obtaining these parameters from those in Eq. 11 by deterministic relationships is straightforward.

can be accomplished by a general MCMC procedure in which, once a sample for the joint posterior has been obtained, the procedure retains only the values of $\boldsymbol{\theta}_2$ and discards the rest. The joint posterior distribution of Eq. 25 can be efficiently sampled by means of a Gibbs sampling scheme (see Sect. 4.2 of [9]). To reduce our model to the programming language level we have used the BUGS [10] probabilistic language and the OpenBUGS software environment.

3 Application to the *Gaia* Simulated Database of Classical Cepheids

In this section we evaluate the effectiveness of our model to infer the real distributions of hyperparameters in an extreme scenario of systematic biases in the recovered data. In order to do so, we have constructed a dataset $\mathcal{T} = \{(A_{\mathrm{rec},i}, \nu_{\mathrm{rec},i}, m_{G,\mathrm{rec},i})\}_1^{854} \subsetneq \mathcal{D}$ composed of 500 randomly selected instances from the *locus* $\nu_{\mathrm{rec}} = \nu_{\mathrm{in}}$ and all instances (354) from the *locus* $\nu_{\mathrm{rec}} = \pm\nu_{\mathrm{in}} + 7\nu_S - 3\nu_p$. Figure 2 shows the systematic biases for the empirical frequency distribution (histogram) vs the true probability density function (PDF) and for the empirical conditional distributions of the recovered amplitude given the input amplitude for the three *loci* (the identity locus and the $\nu_{\mathrm{rec}} = \pm\nu_{\mathrm{in}} + 7\nu_S - 3\nu_p$ *loci*), whose observed parameters are included in the training set.

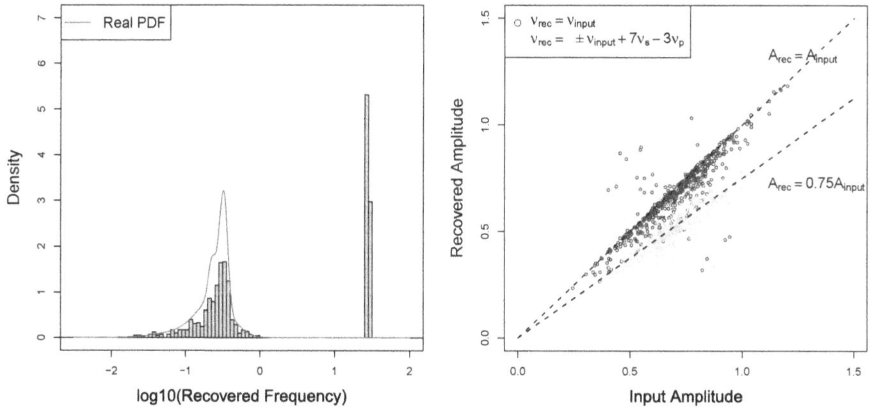

Fig. 2. Biases in the frequencies (left) and amplitudes (right) present in the training set.

We have trained the model using the OpenBUGS MCMC engine. We have divided the training in two stages and generated three Markov chains (more properly realizations) in each, with a total of 30000 iterations. We have used the first 20000 iterations as a *burn-in* phase, and discarded them after using them for convergence assessment. Thereafter, we obtain 10000 samples from each chain in a second stage (30000 in total). We will assume that these samples were drawn from the posterior distribution of the parameters of interest.

Table 2. Summary statistics of parameters of interests.

θ	$\overline{\text{ACR}}$	GRB	$\overline{\theta}$	2.5–97.5% Perc.	Real value
$w_{\nu 2}$	0.39	1.09	0.03	$0.01, 0.05$	-
$w_{\nu 1}$	0.18	1.03	0.41	$0.32, 0.50$	-
$w_{\nu 3}$	0.16	1.01	0.57	$0.47, 0.66$	-
$\mu_{\nu 2}$	0.60	1.16	−1.50	$-1.61, -1.37$	-
$\mu_{\nu 1}$	0.19	1.01	−0.66	$-0.71, -0.61$	-
$\mu_{\nu 3}$	0.05	1.01	−0.53	$-0.54, -0.51$	-
$\sigma_{\nu 2}$	0.83	1.25	0.14	$0.10, 0.20$	-
$\sigma_{\nu 1}$	0.25	1.01	0.28	$0.25, 0.33$	-
$\sigma_{\nu 3}$	0.09	1.02	0.09	$0.08, 0.10$	-
a_A	0.04	1.00	−0.43	$-0.67, -0.21$	−0.5
b_A	0.03	1.00	0.28	$-0.02, 0.57$	0.2
μ_A	0.00	1.00	0.62	$0.58, 0.66$	0.7
σ_A	0.00	1.00	0.15	$0.14, 0.16$	0.15
a_{G1}	0.25	1.04	2.55	$2.22, 2.91$	-
b_{G1}	0.23	1.03	16.76	$16.38, 17.17$	-
a_{G2}	0.01	1.00	3.01	$2.96, 3.06$	-
b_{G2}	0.01	1.00	17.16	$17.13, 17.19$	-
σ_G	0.00	1.00	0.10	$0.09, 0.11$	-
λ_{02}	0.00	1.00	−1.132	$-1.314, -0.955$	-
λ_{03}	0.00	1.00	−0.981	$-1.156, -0.816$	-
$\lambda_{\beta 2}$	0.00	1.00	−0.766	$-1.140, -0.395$	-
$\lambda_{\beta 3}$	0.00	1.00	−0.743	$-1.091, -0.385$	-

3.1 Convergence Analysis

To evaluate the convergence within and between the three chains we have selected the first 20000 iterations of the algorithm and computed the mean autocorrelation (ACR) (after 200 lags) and the upper bound of a credible interval (at 95%) for the corrected GR statistic [3]. The results of the analysis are summarized in the second and third columns of Table 2. Since the ACR function should decrease to zero as the lag increases and the upper bound for the corrected scale reduction factor (CSRF) should approach unity if the chain is reaching its stationary distribution, we conclude that the worst scenario (high autocorrelation) is encountered in the chains of the parameters specifying the second Gaussian component of $\log(\nu)$, namely the mixing proportion $w_{\nu 2}$, the mean $\mu_{\nu 2}$ and the standard deviation $\sigma_{\nu 2}$. In particular, chains for $\sigma_{\nu 2}$ show the worst behaviour with a mean ACR after 200 lags of about 0.8 and a CSRF upper bound of 1.25. In contrast, the best scenario is found in the chains of the parameters of the conditional distributions of apparent G-magnitude and amplitude (given the frequency) when $\log(\nu) > -1$, and by chains of logit coefficients. For the slope a_{G2}, the intercept b_{G2}, the mean μ_A and the logit coefficients $\lambda_{\beta j}, \lambda_{0j}, j \in \{1,2\}$ the mean ACR is nearly zero after lags greater than 50 and the CSRF bound is close to unity.

3.2 Posterior Distributions and Comparison with Real Parameters

In this section we evaluate the ability of our model to retrieve the real distributions of the frequency, amplitude and apparent G-magnitude of the simulated Cepheids sample from the recovered values in the training set $\mathcal{T}$. We first compute summary statistics (means and 2.5–97.5% percentiles) for the samples of the posterior distributions of the hyperparameters inferred by the model. Then, we have compared the posterior means with the parameters of the real theoretical distributions used to generate the simulated sample. Finally, we have constructed theoretical distributions using the posterior means and compared them with the true theoretical distributions and the empirical distribution in the set $\mathcal{I} = \{(A_{\text{in},i}, \nu_{\text{in},i}, m_{G,\text{in},i})\}_1^{854}$.

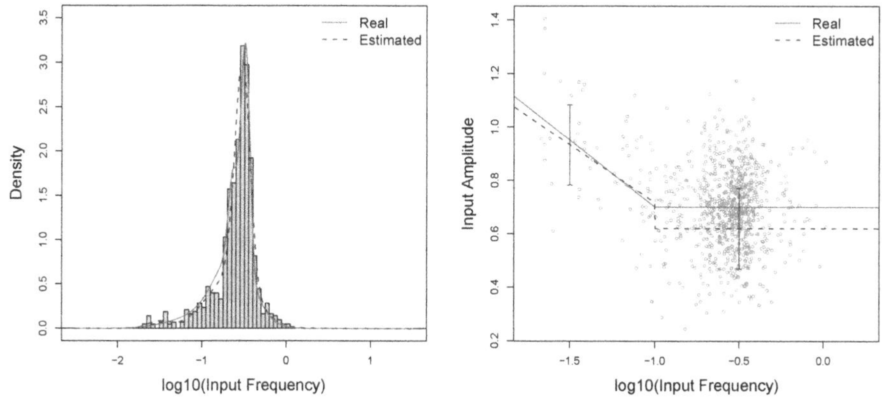

Fig. 3. Posterior versus real distributions.

The results of our analysis are shown in Table 2 and Fig. 3. We do not include in the table the parameters used to generate the real frequency $\log(\nu)$, because it is difficult to make a correspondence with the inferred parameters due to the different number of Gaussian components. But if we observe the comparison graph to the left of Fig. 3, we conclude that the fitting of $\log(\nu)$ with three components (dotted line), reconstructs the real PDF (solid line) successfully.

For the parameters of the conditional distribution $A_{\text{in}} \mid \log(\nu_{\text{in}})$ we fitted the piecewise linear model of Eq. 14. The middle rows of Table 2 and the graph at the right of Fig. 3 show that the system underestimates the true value of the mean μ_A when $\log(\nu_{\text{in}}) > -1$.

4 Summary and Conclusions

We have presented a two-level BGM to infer the real distributions of amplitude, frequency and apparent G-magnitude of the Large Magellanic Cloud population of Classical Cepheids from the values recovered by the *Gaia* DPAC pipeline. We have modelled the real frequency by a mixture of three Gaussian distributions and used piecewise linear models (with a fixed knot value depending on the frequency) to model the dependency of the true amplitude and G-magnitude on the true frequency. We have tackled the problem of aliasing in the DPAC frequency recovery module which arises as a result of the Gaia scanning law. We have modelled the recovery probabilities in various *loci* of aliased frequencies using a logistic regression submodel based on the ecliptic latitude predictor. We have modelled the recovered frequencies and amplitudes as generated from mixtures of distributions where the mixing proportions are the recovery probabilities. Although our model has not yet solved completely the aliasing problem (we have only used some predefined configurations of aliased data, and we have restricted the application to a very narrow range of ecliptic latitudes in which the relationship between the recovery probability of aliased frequencies and the ecliptic latitude is monotone) it represents a major step forward. The next step will necessarily consist in extending the analysis to the full celestial sphere by clustering the full variety of time samplings (and corresponding window functions) into discrete bands of ecliptic longitudes and latitudes.

References

1. Antonello, E., Fugazza, D., Mantegazza, L.: Variable stars in nearby galaxies VI. Frequency-period distribution of Cepheids in IC 1613 and other galaxies of the local group. Astron. Astrophys. **388**, 477–482 (2002)
2. Azzalini, A., Genton, M.G.: Robust likelihood methods based on the skew-t and related distributions. Int. Stat. Rev. **76**(1), 106–129 (2008)
3. Brooks, S.P., Gelman, A.: General methods for monitoring convergence of iterative simulations. J. Comput. Graph. Stat. **7**(4), 434–455 (1998)
4. Eyer, L., Mignard, F.: Rate of correct detection of periodic signal with the Gaia satellite. Mon. Not. R. Astron. Soc. **361**(4), 1136–1144 (2005)
5. Gaia Collaboration, Prusti, T., de Bruijne, J.H.J., Brown, A.G.A., Vallenari, A., Babusiaux, C., Bailer-Jones, C.A.L., Bastian, U., Biermann, M., Evans, D.W., et al.: The Gaia mission. Astron. Astrophys. **595**, A1 (2016)
6. Gelman, A., Jakulin, A., Pittau, M.G., Su, Y.S.: A weakly informative default prior distribution for logistic and other regression models. Ann. Appl. Stat. **2**(4), 1360–1383 (2008)
7. Gelman, A., Shalizi, C.R.: Philosophy and the practice of Bayesian statistics. B. J. Math. Stat. Psychol. **66**, 8–38 (2013)
8. Lauritzen, S.: Graphical Models. Oxford University Press, Oxford (1996)
9. Lunn, D., Jackson, C., Best, N., Thomas, A., Spiegelhalter, D.: The BUGS Book: A Practical Introduction to Bayesian Analysis. CRC Texts in Statistical Science, Chapman & Hall. CRC Press, Boca Raton (2012)
10. Lunn, D., Spiegelhalter, D., Thomas, A., Best, N.: The bugs project: evolution, critique and future directions. Stat. Med. **28**(25), 3049–3067 (2009)

11. Pearl, J.: Probabilistic Reasoning in Intelligent Systems: Networks of Plausble Inference. Morgan Kaufmann Publishers, Burlington (1988)
12. Robert, C.P., Mengersen, K.L.: Reparameterisation issues in mixture modelling and their bearing on MCMC algorithms. Comput. Stat. Data Anal. **29**(3), 325–343 (1999)
13. Robert, C., Casella, G.: Monte Carlo Statistical Methods, 2nd edn. Springer, New York (2004)
14. Sandage, A., Tammann, G., Reindl, B.: New period-luminosity and period-color relations of classical Cepheids II. Cepheids in LMC. Astron. Astrophys. **424**, 43–71 (2004)
15. Soszynski, I., Poleski, R., Udalski, A., Szymanski, M.K., Kubiak, M., Pietrzynski, G., Wyrzykowski, L., Szewczyk, O., Ulaczyk, K.: The optical gravitational lensing experiment. The OGLE-III catalog of variable stars I. Classical Cepheids in the large magellanic cloud. Acta Astronomica **58**, 163–185 (2008)

Computational Intelligence in Data Coding and Transmission

Adapting Side Information to Transmission Conditions in Precoding Systems

Josmary Labrador, Paula M. Castro(✉), Adriana Dapena, and Francisco J. Vazquez-Araujo

Department of Computer Engineering, University of A Coruña, Campus de Elviña 8, 15071 A Coruña, Spain
pcastro@udc.es

Abstract. This work proposes an hybrid precoding method in a Multiple-Input/Multiple-Output Frequency Division Duplex (MIMO FDD) system with the objective of reducing the load associated to transmit side information needed to adapt precoding matrices in both the transmitter and the receiver. The type of precoding is determined at the transmitter by using a simple rule that takes into account a receive Signal–to–Noise Ratio (SNR) estimate. The receiver computes the magnitude of the channel level fluctuations and determines the time instants when long pilot sequences are needed to estimate the precoding matrices. Using a low cost feedback channel, the receiver indicates to the transmitter both the type of precoder and transmit frames to be used.

1 Introduction

Computational Intelligence (CI)-based approaches have been widely used to solve different problems in digital communications and networking such as call admission control, management of resources and traffic, routing, multi casting, media encoding, and synchronization [5]. CI paradigms include supervised and unsupervised learning, reinforcement learning, fuzzy logic, evolutionary computation, etc. In this paper, we propose to include a decision-based learning in precoding systems to improve the transmission rate.

Precoding is an effective strategy to equalize the channel before transmission, and is included in most of the recent wireless standards with the aim of simplifying the receiver equipment by moving the equalization task to the transmitter. Linear and nonlinear precoding techniques have been widely studied in the literature. Tomlinson-Harashima Precoding (THP) is one of the best known nonlinear precoding techniques due to its adequate compromise between performance and computational complexity. THP computational complexity is still 1.6 times higher than the linear counterpart, which will be referred to as Linear Precoding (LP), as shown in [8]. In [10] we show that the combination of both precoders, which is referred to as Hybrid Precoding (HP), allows us to improve the overall system performance.

Precoding needs Channel State Information (CSI) at the transmitter, which must be obtained at the receiver by channel estimation and sent back to the

J.M. Ferrández Vicente et al. (Eds.): IWINAC 2017, Part II, LNCS 10338, pp. 315–324, 2017.
DOI: 10.1007/978-3-319-59773-7_32

transmitter by means of a feedback channel, usually available in recent standards for Frequency Division Duplex (FDD) systems. However, this feedback channel is not necessary in Time Division Duplex (TDD) systems because the channel can be obtained by the transmitter in the uplink using reciprocity. This Partial CSI (PCSI) affects the system performance since the design of the precoding filters are based on the channel estimate and, therefore, linear and non-linear precoders will need a good channel estimate under time-varying environments [3]. Classical estimation methods are based on the sending from the transmitter of pilot symbols that are used by the receiver to obtain the channel estimate. The performance achieved with such methods, also known as *supervised learning based-methods*, is high, but the use of pilots affects throughput, spectral efficiency, and transmission energy consumption of the system [1,12]. In this work, we propose to mitigate these limitations by using reinforcement learning in which the optimal policy will be determined to minimize the total pilot transmissions.

We assume that both the transmitter and the receiver are two individual entities with some capacity for decision, communication, and adaptation. The receiver is able to acquire channel information from the environment and then makes decisions as a consequence of these measurements. More specifically, this decision uses rules based on measurements of both the quality of the received signal (measured in terms of Signal–to–Noise Ratio (SNR)) and the channel fluctuations (measured according to an ad hoc metric also proposed in this work). The decisions will be communicated via the aforementioned low-cost feedback channel to the transmitter, which will send pilots symbols when a significant channel fluctuation is detected at the receiver. Then, with the information provided by the pilots, the receiver estimates the channel and sends this estimate to the transmitter. Both the transmitter and the receiver will adapt their precoding filters using the linear or the non-linear approaches as indicated by the receiver according to its receive SNR measurement. Therefore, we have an adaptive system that guarantees good performance with low complexity.

This work is organized as follows. Section 2 describes the signal and channel models, and shows the designs of the linear and non-linear precoders most commonly used in the literature. Section 3 briefly describes the supervised method for channel estimation used in this work. Section 4 explains the proposed scheme for minimizing the number of pilot symbols required by the receiver. Illustrative computer simulation results are presented in Sects. 5, and 6 contains the conclusions.

2 System Model

Figure 1 shows a MIMO system with N_t TX antennas and N_r RX antennas. In this paper we will assume $N_\mathrm{t} = N_\mathrm{r} = N$. We can model the received observations as

$$\boldsymbol{y}[n] = \boldsymbol{H}[q]\boldsymbol{x}[n] + \eta[n], \tag{1}$$

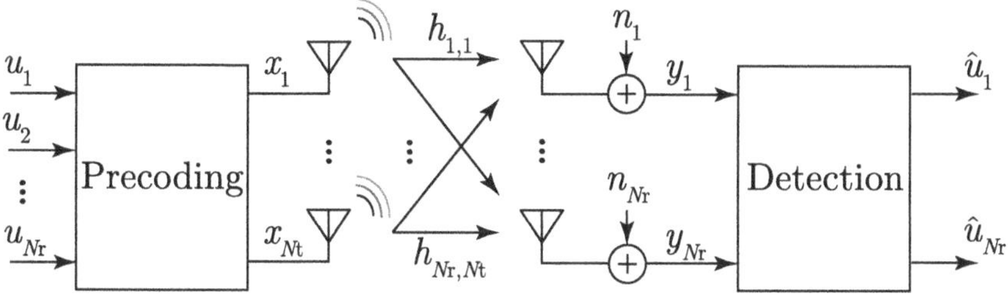

Fig. 1. Scheme of a MIMO system with precoding.

where $n = 0, 1, 2, \ldots$ corresponds to the sample index. Given that the channel remains constant during several frames of N_B symbols, we use $\boldsymbol{H}[q]$ to denote the time–varying flat block fading channel.

The equalization task can be performed at the TX and thus the channel is pre-equalized or *precoded* before the transmission with the goal of simplifying the requirements at the RX. Such an operation is only possible when a centralized TX is employed (e.g. the base-station of the downlink of a cellular system). We have considered the linear and non-linear precoding schemes more commonly used in the literature: Wiener LP and THP, respectively.

2.1 Linear Precoder

We assume hereinafter that the RX filter is an identity matrix (multiplied by a scalar $\beta[q]$, with $\beta[q] \in \mathbb{C}$), which allows the use of decentralized RX (see, for instance, [6]). Clearly, the restriction that all receivers apply the same scalar weight $\beta[q]$ is not necessary for decentralized receivers, but it ensures closed–form solutions for the design of the filters. The goal is to find the optimum TX filter $\boldsymbol{F}[q] \in \mathbb{C}^{N \times N}$ and the RX filter $\boldsymbol{G}[q] = \beta[q]\boldsymbol{I} \in \mathbb{C}^{N \times N}$. The data symbols $\boldsymbol{u}[n]$ are passed through the transmit filter $\boldsymbol{F}[q]$ to form the transmitted signal $\boldsymbol{x}[n] = \boldsymbol{F}[q]\boldsymbol{u}[n] \in \mathbb{C}^N$. Note that the constraint for the transmitted energy must be fulfilled, $\mathrm{E}\left[\|\boldsymbol{x}[n]\|_2^2\right] \leq E_\mathrm{tx}$, where E_tx is the fixed total transmitted energy. The received signal is thus given by

$$\boldsymbol{y}[n] = \boldsymbol{H}[q]\boldsymbol{F}[q]\boldsymbol{u}[n] + \eta[n], \tag{2}$$

where $\boldsymbol{y}[n] \in \mathbb{C}^N$, $\boldsymbol{H}[q] \in \mathbb{C}^{N \times N}$, and $\eta[n] \in \mathbb{C}^N$ is the Additive White Gaussian Noise (AWGN). After multiplying by the receive gain $\beta[q]$, we get the estimated symbols $\hat{\boldsymbol{u}}[n] = \beta[q]\boldsymbol{H}[q]\boldsymbol{F}[q]\boldsymbol{u}[n] + g\eta[n]$, where $\hat{\boldsymbol{u}}[n] \in \mathbb{C}^N$.

Wiener Filtering (WF) is a very powerful transmit optimization that minimizes the Mean Square Error (MSE) with a transmit energy constraint [2,7,11], and therefore the linear precoders of our proposal will be obtained according to that optimization.

2.2 Tomlinson-Harashima Precoder

In this subsection, we will briefly describe the Tomlinson-Harashima (TH) non-linear precoder, which will be used in this paper. This precoder employs two filters: one, denoted by $\boldsymbol{F}[q]$, placed at the transmitter to suppress parts of the interference linearly, and another one, given by $\boldsymbol{I} - \boldsymbol{B}[q]$, inside a feedback loop and also at the transmitter to subtract the remaining interferences non-linearly, with $\boldsymbol{B}$ being strictly lower triangular to ensure the causality of the feedback process. Since the order of precoding has an important effect on performance, the data signal $\boldsymbol{u}[n]$ is reordered by means of the permutation filter $\boldsymbol{P}[q] = \sum_{i=1}^{N} \boldsymbol{e}_i \boldsymbol{e}_{n_i}^{\mathrm{T}}$, where $\boldsymbol{e}_i$ is the i-th column of the $N \times N$ identity matrix and n_i is the index of the i-th data stream to be precoded [8]. The signal $\boldsymbol{P}[q]\boldsymbol{u}[n]$ is first passed through the feedback loop to get the output $\boldsymbol{v}[n]$. The nonlinear modulo operator $\mathrm{M}(\bullet)$ of the feedback loop limits the amplitude of $\boldsymbol{v}[n]$ and thus, the power of the transmit signal $\boldsymbol{x}[n]$. The received signal is expressed as

$$\boldsymbol{y}[n] = \mathrm{M}\left(g[q]\boldsymbol{H}[q]\boldsymbol{F}[q]\boldsymbol{v}[n] + g\eta[n]\right), \tag{3}$$

because the modulo operator is applied again at the receiver to invert its effect at the transmitter [11]. The receive weight $g[q]$ directly follows from the transmit energy constraint. The resulting estimate of $\boldsymbol{u}[n]$ is denoted again by $\hat{\boldsymbol{u}}[n]$.

The Wiener THP for flat fading channels results from the minimization of the MSE and the restriction of a spatially causal feedback filtering. The filters obtained from that minimization are determined column by column [8,9,11], and each column requires one matrix inverse which results in a total complexity order of $O(N^4)$. With the decomposition described in [4,13], the complexity is reduced to $O(N^3)$. In addition, some heuristic ordering strategies can be applied as described in [8].

3 Supervised Channel Estimation

Channel estimation is crucial in wireless communication systems. In this work CSI is acquired at the receiver and sent back to the transmitter via a feedback channel so that the precoding filters can be updated at both link sides. This channel estimation can be performed by means of pilot symbols, also called *training sequences*.

When pilots are employed, the received signal $\boldsymbol{Y}[q]$ is a linear combination of the transmitted signals $\boldsymbol{S}[q]$ as follows

$$\boldsymbol{Y}[q] = \boldsymbol{S}[q]\boldsymbol{H}[q] + \eta[q] \in \mathbb{C}^{K \times N}, \tag{4}$$

where K is the length of the pilot sequence. The matrix $\eta[q] \in \mathbb{C}^{K \times N}$ is the AWGN with covariance matrix denoted as $\boldsymbol{C}_{\eta}$. Thus, the channel estimate is obtained as

$$\hat{\boldsymbol{H}}[q] = \boldsymbol{W}[q]\boldsymbol{Y}[q], \tag{5}$$

where $\boldsymbol{W}[q] \in \mathbb{C}^{N \times K}$ is the matrix that calculates the estimate from the observations.

The Linear Minimum Mean Square Error (LMMSE) channel estimation minimizes the average MSE between the channel and its estimate, which leads to the final expression for the MMSE linear filter

$$\boldsymbol{W}[q] = \boldsymbol{C}_{\boldsymbol{HY}}\boldsymbol{C}_{\boldsymbol{Y}}^{-1}, \tag{6}$$

where $\boldsymbol{C}_{\boldsymbol{HY}} = \boldsymbol{C}_{\boldsymbol{H}}\boldsymbol{S}^{\mathrm{H}}[q]$ and $\boldsymbol{C}_{\boldsymbol{Y}} = \boldsymbol{S}[q]\boldsymbol{C}_{\boldsymbol{H}}\boldsymbol{S}^{\mathrm{H}}[q] + \boldsymbol{C}_{\eta}$, being $\boldsymbol{C}_{\boldsymbol{H}} = N\mathbf{I}$. Therefore, the channel estimate can be obtained as

$$\hat{\boldsymbol{H}}[q] = \boldsymbol{C}_{\boldsymbol{H}}\boldsymbol{S}^{\mathrm{H}}[q](\boldsymbol{S}[q]\boldsymbol{C}_{\boldsymbol{H}}\boldsymbol{S}^{\mathrm{H}}[q] + \boldsymbol{C}_{\eta})^{-1}\boldsymbol{Y}[q]. \tag{7}$$

4 Decision-Aided Precoding System

In this section we propose a MIMO system with decision-aided precoding that requires the updating of the precoding filters depending on the channel fluctuations. This system will be referred to as Decision-aided Precoding (DP) in the following. The goal of this solution is to reduce the computational complexity of the overall system without penalizing in a significant way its performance. In standard systems, the pilots are transmitted in all the frames, which produces a strong degradation of performance, spectral efficiency, and transmit energy. With our approach we will be able to minimize the loss of effective transmission rate or the channel overload produced by the sending of pilot symbols.

We will consider that the transmitter sends two types of frames: *classic* and *user frames*. The *classic frames* contain a long pilot sequence and user data symbols. The *user frames* contain a short pilot sequence and user data symbols.

For determining if the channel variations are important enough to request the sending of classic frames and the updating of the precoding filters, we propose a metric that compares the estimate of the channel matrix corresponding to the current frame, denoted by $\hat{\boldsymbol{H}}[n]$, and that estimated in the previous frame, denoted by $\hat{\boldsymbol{H}}[n-1]$. Both estimates are obtained by the receiver using the short pilot sequence of the user frames, which will calculate for each transmit frame the matrix $\boldsymbol{\Gamma}[n] = (\hat{\boldsymbol{H}}[n])^{-1}\hat{\boldsymbol{H}}[n-1]$. In particular, we will use the error measurement, denoted as ϵ_{CSI}, as follows

$$\epsilon_{\mathrm{CSI}} = \frac{1}{N}\sum_{i=1}^{N}\sum_{j=1,j\neq i}^{N}\left(\frac{|\gamma_{ij}[n]|^2}{|\gamma_{ii}[n]|^2} + \frac{|\gamma_{ji}[n]|^2}{|\gamma_{ii}[n]|^2}\right), \tag{8}$$

where $\gamma_{ii}[n]$ is the i–th diagonal entry of the matrix $\boldsymbol{\Gamma}[n]$. Thus, this value, that shows the distance between $\boldsymbol{\Gamma}[n]$ and the identity matrix, gives us a measurement of the channel time variations. If ϵ_{CSI} is high, the channel is suffering from significant fluctuations and therefore, the receiver will request a classic frame including a long pilot sequence to the transmitter. The receiver will estimate the channel from pilots using LMMSE and the updated coefficients will be sent to the transmitter using the feedback channel. Transmit and receive precoding filters will be updated at both link sides. Otherwise, if ϵ_{CSI} is low, the precoding filters remain unchanged as had been used in the previous frame.

Moreover, in [10] we have demonstrated that LP is better than THP for low SNRs, and vice versa. Therefore, we propose to include a decision rule at the receiver to determine the action to be performed by our system, as follows

State 1: A user frame is received
Actions:
Estimate $\hat{\boldsymbol{H}}[q]$ using the pilot sequence in the supervised algorithm
Compute $\epsilon_{CSI}[q]$, estimate the receive SNR, and determine $p_{i,\mathrm{SNR}}$
If $\epsilon_{CSI}[q] \geq p_{i,\mathrm{SNR}}$, require a classic frame
otherwise, require an user frame.

State 2: A classic frame is received
Actions:
Estimate $\hat{\boldsymbol{H}}[q]$ using the pilot symbols in the supervised algorithm
Estimate the receive SNR
If SNR > SNR_l, update THP using $\hat{\boldsymbol{H}}[q]$;
otherwise, update LP using $\hat{\boldsymbol{H}}[q]$
Send $\hat{\boldsymbol{H}}[q]$ to the transmitter and require an user frame

Notice that $p_{i,\mathrm{SNR}}$ and SNR_l are the two thresholds of our decision-aided algorithm that will be determined in a training step prior to real transmission.

5 Simulation Results

In this section we will show some results obtained from computer simulations. First, the time-varying channel will be modeled as follows

$$\boldsymbol{H}[q] = \begin{cases} \dfrac{(1-\alpha)\,\boldsymbol{H}[q-1] + \alpha \boldsymbol{H}_{\mathrm{R}}[q]}{\sqrt{(1-\alpha)^2 + \alpha^2}} & \textbf{if } q = bF,\ b = 1, 2, \ldots \\ \boldsymbol{H}[q-1] & \textbf{otherwise}, \end{cases} \tag{9}$$

where F is the number of frames in which the channel remains unchanged. $\boldsymbol{H}_{\mathrm{R}}[q]$ is randomly generated following a Rayleigh distribution. The α parameter determines the speed in channel variations. If $\alpha = 0$ the channel is constant, whereas for $\alpha = 1$ the channel changes randomly from one block to another.

Additionally, the following simulation parameters are considered: $N = 4$ transmit and receive antennas; 1000 independent experiments; 128 channel realizations in each experiment; 512 frames of 128 symbols; $F = 4$ frames in which the channel remains unchanged; $P_l = 12$ QPSK pilot symbols per long pilot sequence; $P_s = 4$ QPSK per short pilot sequence; LMMSE channel estimation, and $\alpha = 0.2$ in (9).

5.1 Training Step

In a training step prior to transmission we have evaluated the distance between the performance, evaluated in terms of Bit Error Rate (BER), obtained with both precoders, LP and THP, when the channel information is partially known at the transmitter. Classic frames are transmitted so that the long pilot sequence included in these frames are used to obtain the CSI via LMMSE estimation.

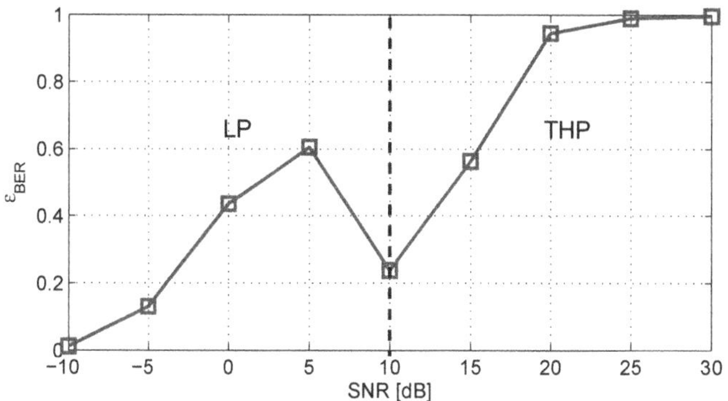

Fig. 2. Training step: SNR_l for using LP or THP.

Therefore, the range of application of each type of precoder is determined by using the following distance measurement

$$\epsilon_{\text{BER}} = \frac{|\text{BER}_{\text{LP}} - \text{BER}_{\text{THP}}|}{\text{BER}_{\text{LP}}}. \tag{10}$$

Figure 2 shows this merit figure as a function of the receive SNR. Taking into account these results, we have decided to consider an SNR threshold, denoted as SNR_l, of 10 dB in (4), so that LP is used for SNR values equal or less than 10 dB and THP for SNR higher than that value.

Otherwise, we need to calculate the threshold values $p_{i,\text{SNR}}$ of (4) to decide if pilot symbols are required or not for channel estimation. For this purpose, for each SNR we consider only the values of $\epsilon_{\text{CSI}}[q]$ obtained every 4 frames, i.e. when the channel changes. Then, we calculate the threshold as the i–th percentile, where the $i\%$ of those values are lower than this threshold, and the $100 - i\%$ are greater. Table 1 shows the threshold values $p_{i,\text{SNR}}$ as a function of receive SNR. We have selected the percentiles 1, 2, and 5 to illustrate the performance of our decision-aided system. These percentiles will be respectively denoted as $p_{1,\text{SNR}}, p_{2,\text{SNR}}$, and $p_{5,\text{SNR}}$.

5.2 Transmission Step

In our experiment we will consider an $\text{SNR}_\text{l} = 10\,\text{dB}$ and the values of $p_{i,\text{SNR}}$ in Table 1, obtained during the training step.

Figure 3 (top) shows the performance in terms of BER of the proposed DP scheme for $p_{1,\text{SNR}}, p_{2,\text{SNR}}$ and $p_{5,\text{SNR}}$. Notice that the floor effect is produced

Table 1. $p_{i,\text{SNR}}$ thresholds.

SNR [dB]	−10	−5	0	5	10	15	20	25	30
$p_{1,\text{SNR}}$	0.6285	0.5537	0.3292	0.1418	0.0570	0.0295	0.0210	0.0179	0.0169
$p_{2,\text{SNR}}$	0.7290	0.6493	0.3933	0.1680	0.0682	0.0350	0.0249	0.0211	0.0201
$p_{5,\text{SNR}}$	0.9180	0.8200	0.5228	0.2241	0.0903	0.0464	0.0328	0.0276	0.0264

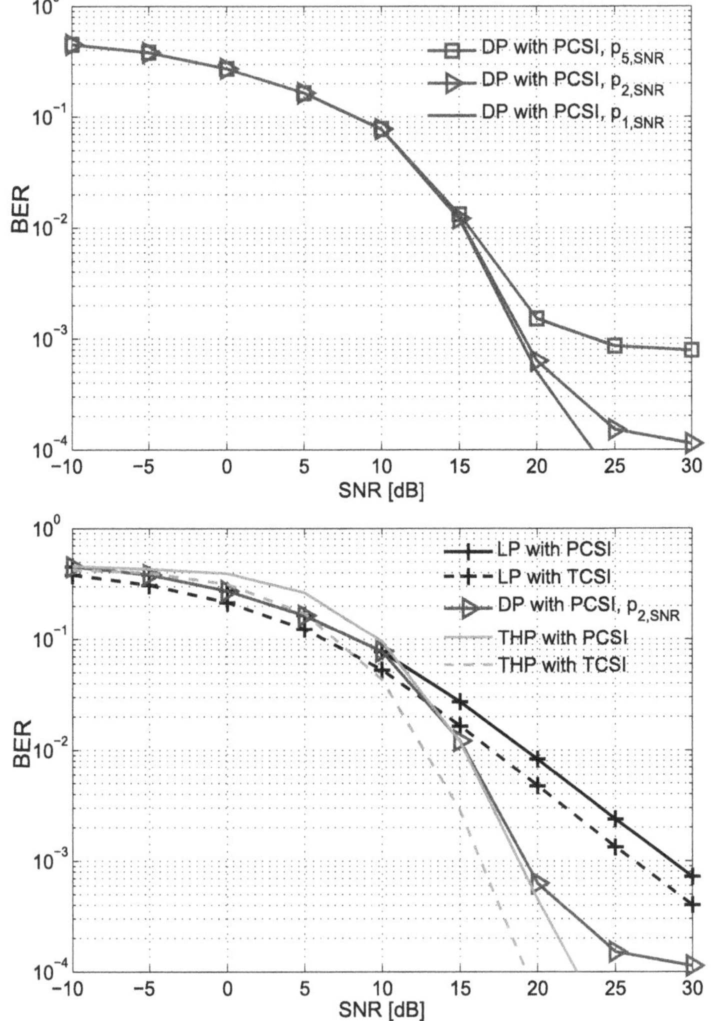

Fig. 3. BER vs. SNR for LP, THP, and DP.

by the use of a precoder that is not adapted to the actual channel state due to the channel fluctuations not being strong enough to trigger a filter update. The curve corresponding to DP for $p_{2,\text{SNR}}$ exhibits a medium performance with a floor

Table 2. Percentage of precoder updates and pilot reduction as a function of receive SNR in dB.

SNR [dB]	−10	−5	0	5	10	15	20	25	30
Precoder updates [in %]	98.05	97.86	97.75	97.09	94.77	85.28	62.41	40.41	30.21
ϵ_{pilot} [in %]	34.30	34.43	34.50	34.94	36.49	42.81	58.06	72.73	79.53

effect for SNRs higher than 30 dB. In Fig. 3 (bottom), we compare the results for LP, THP, and the proposed DP. As boundary cases, we have included the curves for LP and THP with Total CSI (TCSI), i.e. perfect CSI at the transmitter. The curve corresponding to DP for $p_{2,\text{SNR}}$ exhibits a medium performance, close to that achieved with LP for low SNR and to that obtained with THP for high SNR, according to the decision rule of (4).

Considering a threshold $p_{2,\text{SNR}}$, Table 2 shows the percentage of filter updates and the reduction in pilot symbols computed using the following expression

$$\epsilon_{\text{pilot}} = \left(1 - \frac{N_u P_s + N_c P_l}{(N_u + N_c) P_l}\right) \times 100, \qquad (11)$$

where N_u and N_c are the number of user frames and classic frames, respectively. We can see that the reduction of pilot symbols is higher than 34% for all SNRs. The reduction is considerable for SNR higher than 15 dB. In addition, for SNR higher than 15 dB, the THP filter is updated in a reduced number of times which implies a considerable improvement in terms of computational load.

6 Conclusions

In this paper a decision-aided MIMO hybrid precoding system with partial transmit CSI is proposed. The system increases the effective data rate (or spectral efficiency) by minimizing the overhead caused by the transmission of pilot symbols. This is achieved by means of limiting the number of updates of the precoding filters to the time instants in which the channel significantly varies according to a given threshold, which is fixed prior to transmission in a training step. As shown with simulation results, the loss in performance is not very significant, especially if adequate decision thresholds are selected.

Acknowledgments. This work has been funded by the Galician Government under grants ED431C 2016-045 and ED341D R2016/012 as well as by the Spanish Government under grants TEC2013-47141-C4-1-R (RACHEL project) and TEC2016-75067-C4-1-R (CARMEN project).

References

1. Castro, P.M., Garca-Naya, J.A., Dapena, A., Iglesia, D.: Channel estimation techniques for linear precoded systems: supervised, unsupervised, and hybrid approaches. Sig. Process. **91**(7), 1578–1588 (2011). http://www.sciencedirect.com/science/article/pii/S0165168411000028

2. Choi, R.L., Murch, R.D.: New transmit schemes and simplified receiver for MIMO wireless communication systems. IEEE Trans. Wirel. Commun. **2**(6), 1217–1230 (2003)
3. Fischer, R.F.H.: Precoding and Signal Shaping for Digital Transmission. Wiley, Hoboken (2002)
4. Golub, G.H., Van Loan, C.F.: Matrix Computations, vol. 3. JHU Press, Baltimore (2012)
5. Guturu, P.: Computational intelligence in multimedia networking and communications: trends and future directions. In: Hassanien, A.-E., Abraham, A., Kacprzyk, J. (eds.) Computational Intelligence in Multimedia Processing Recent Advances, pp. 51–76. Springer, Heidelberg (2008)
6. Hunger, R., Joham, M., Utschick, W.: Extension of linear and nonlinear transmit filters for decentralized receivers. In: European Wireless 2005, vol. 1, pp. 40–46, April 2005
7. Karimi, H.R., Sandell, M., Salz, J.: Comparison between transmitter and receiver array processing to achieve interference nulling and diversity. In: Proceedings of the PIMRC, vol. 3, pp. 997–1001 (1999)
8. Kusume, K., Joham, M., Utschick, W., Bauch, G.: Efficient Tomlinson-Harashima precoding for spatial multiplexing on flat MIMO channel. In: Proceedings of the International Conference on Communications, Seoul, Korea, vol. 3, pp. 2021–2025, May 2005
9. Kusume, K., Joham, M., Utschick, W., Bauch, G.: Cholesky factorization with symmetric permutation applied to detecting and precoding spatially multiplexed data streams. IEEE Trans. Signal Process. **55**(6), 3089–3103 (2007)
10. Labrador, J., Castro, P.M., Vazquez-Araujo, F.J., Dapena, A.: Hybrid precoding scheme with partial CSI at the transmitter. In: 16th International Conference on Knowledge-Based and Intelligent Information and Engineering Systems (KES 2012), September 2012
11. Nossek, J.A., Joham, M., Utschick, W.: Transmit processing in MIMO wireless systems. In: Proceedings of the 6th IEEE Circuits and Systems Symposium on Emerging Technologies: Frontiers of Mobile and Wireless Communication, Shanghai, China, pp. I-18 - I-23, May/June 2004
12. Scharf, L.L.: Statistical Signal Processing: Detection, Estimation, and Time Series Analysis. Addison-Wesley, Boston (1991)
13. Schnorr, C.P., Euchner, M.: Lattice basis reduction: improved practical algorithms and solving subset sum problems. Math. Program. **66**(1), 181–199 (1994). http://dx.doi.org/10.1007/BF01581144

Energy Based Clustering Method to Estimate Channel Occupation of LTE in Unlicensed Spectrum

Daniel Malafaia[1(✉)], José Vieira[1,2], and Ana Tomé[2]

[1] Instituto de Telecomunicações, Universidade de Aveiro, Aveiro, Portugal
danielmalafaia@ua.pt

[2] IEETA, Universidade de Aveiro, Aveiro, Portugal

Abstract. In this article we propose a subtractive histogram clustering method to estimate the number of LTE users based on the uplink energy probability density distribution sensed by an RF front-end. The energy of the signal is estimated and its histogram is analyzed to determinate the number of different distributions. As the energy estimation of the sensed LTE uplink can be modeled by a Gaussian mixture, this allow us to have *a priori* information that help us to determine the number of users. The lowest value Gaussian distribution can be used to accurately estimate the noise floor and the remaining distributions allow us to estimate the number of LTE users and their received power.

Keywords: Multiuser detection · 4G mobile communication · Detection algorithms · Radio spectrum management

1 Introduction

Unlicensed spectrum is one of society's most valuable resources. Certified devices can operate in it, under the legal regulations and radiated power limits without the obligation of paying license fees and with minimal license administration. These advantages make it very attractive model for low power and short range communications.

There is a current trend of implementing telecommunication protocols that used to be confined to licensed frequency bands, in the unlicensed spectrum. One of these implementations is Long-Term Evolution (LTE) in the unlicensed spectrum [8]. LTE on unlicensed spectrum allows an easier proliferation of smaller base stations with better spectral efficiency, easier network integration and better traffic load management. The critical aspect of LTE in unlicensed band is to ensure that it can co-exist with current access technologies such as WiFi. A fundamental necessity will then be the implementation of coexistence mechanisms that permits the best channel selection scenario for every protocol using the unlicensed spectrum.

In order for a communication protocol to take an informed decision of which band of the unlicensed spectrum to use, it should be able to determine the

J.M. Ferrández Vicente et al. (Eds.): IWINAC 2017, Part II, LNCS 10338, pp. 325–332, 2017.
DOI: 10.1007/978-3-319-59773-7_33

channel occupation. The dynamical allocation of unlicensed channels must take into account the number of users that in each moment is using each channel.

The LTE uplink of the standard air interface transmission scheme is based on a Single-Carrier Frequency Division Multiple Access (SC-FDMA) which converts a wideband channel into a set of sub-channels called resource blocks [2]. For each User Equipment (UE) a number of resource blocks are attributed according to the user's needs.

The energy of the LTE uplink air interface channel can be used to detect the presence of a UE in an spatial region without the need for signal demodulation. It is expected that different users will be received with different powers levels, due to path loss and multi-path effect [9]. Therefore, it is possible to discriminate each individual LTE uplink UEs by the received energy level and estimate the numbers of users in the channel.

For the noise floor, in order to obtain a good estimation, we need to ensure that we have a time-slot where no users are transmitting. In the LTE uplink it should be expected in each uplink frame, free Resource Elements (REs). These free time/frequency resources can be used to dynamically obtain an estimation of the noise floor.

As the LTE uplink is a shared medium, at a given moment an RE can be either free or occupied. When none of the users has the RE allocated, then the slot is free and only the noise floor will be present (produced by the environment and by the RF front-end itself). When a user transmits in a RE the transmitted signal will have an approximately constant power. The PDF of a resource block will then be a mixture of both noise and the users PDF.

By using an energy estimator, that averages a large number of samples, then by the central limit theorem, more specifically De Moivre Laplace theorem [4], the histogram of each transmitting user will converge toward a Gaussian distribution. Therefore the sum of all users signal Gaussian distributions is considered a Gaussian Mixture Model (GMM). The lowest mean component will be the noise floor and the other components of the mixture are related with the signals transmitted by different users.

2 Proposed Method to Determine the Number of Users

In order to determine the number of users, their power level and the channel occupation we propose a subtractive histogram method. The proposed subtractive histogram method is a clustering technique capable of determining the number of transmissions, during a given time interval, based on an energy estimation analysis of a multiple user RF shared medium. The method requires the energy, of the sampled RF data, to be estimated as explained in Subsect. 2.1. The histogram of the energy estimation is then analysed as a GMM and its components are extracted with a subtractive histogram as explained in Subsect. 2.2.

2.1 Energy Estimation

The RF acquired data is sampled in In-phase and Quadrature (I/Q) and its energy is estimated in order to obtain its energy modeled by a Gaussian distribution as seen in Fig. 1.

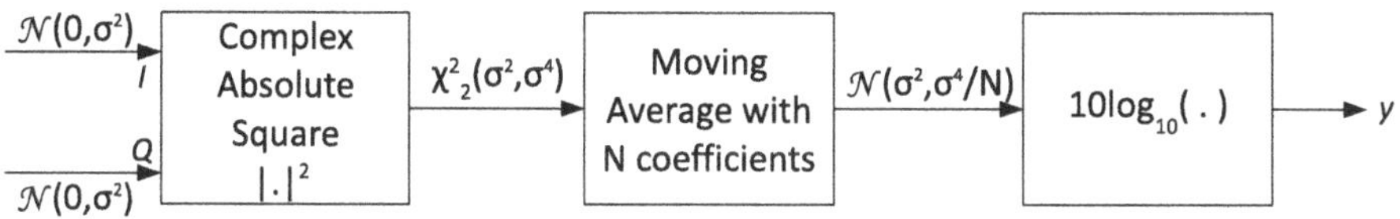

Fig. 1. Functional diagram of the energy estimator.

The complex I/Q data is assumed to be from a single user and can be approximately modeled by a Gaussian distribution with zero mean and a variance given by σ^2. The I/Q signal is squared in order to obtain its instant energy, resulting in a signal with a Chi-Square distribution of second order. By analyzing the squared signal with an energy estimator of order N it is obtained, as previously mentioned, an approximate Gaussian distribution. The energy estimation is then converted to a dB scale.

For a moving average of high order N and assuming that the moving average energy output is concentrated around its mean, it can be demonstrated that the energy estimator output y, has the following statistical proprieties [5]:

$$E[y] \approx 10\log_{10}(\sigma^2) - \frac{10}{2Nln(10)} \tag{1}$$

$$var[y] = v \approx \frac{100}{Nln(10)^2}. \tag{2}$$

For a estimation using a large N, the mean value of the estimation is approximately the dB of the input signal energy and its variance will be mainly a function of the estimation order N. The energy estimation of a single user transmission will then be $y \sim \mathcal{N}(\sigma_x^2, \frac{\sigma_x^4}{N})$. In a scenario where the number K of users are transmitting in the RF channel in a time multiplexing way, the energy y can be model as a GMM with $K+1$ components that includes the background noise.

2.2 Subtractive Histogram Method

Most of the existing algorithms available in the literature to get the parameters of each component in a GMM assumes that the number of components K is known [1]. In this work this number is unknown and may change with time. To overcome this problem we propose a greedy algorithm that iteratively search for the signals with higher probability and stops with the background noise component. To analyse the channel PDF we start by evaluating histogram of y.

In the obtained histogram, the received signal from each user will be a Gaussian component with the average energy, in dB, being its mean value. The histogram will then be a mixture of at most K Gaussian distributions, where K is the number of different UE received transmissions with unique power plus the noise floor.

The subtractive method iteratively searches, one by one, the Gaussian distribution components in the histogram of the y energy. Searching by the maximum value of the histogram and then using it as a starting value for a Gaussian fit. The method obtains then the mixture model that will better fit the y histogram and also estimates the number K of Gaussian distributions in the GMM.

The method iterates till most of the histogram y, that is defined as 90%, is fitted. The first step is to detect the maximum value on the histogram under evaluation, this will give us the user signal that occurs more often, or the most frequent contribution in the observation for the GMM. After determining the peak value, the coefficient of determination R^2 is obtained,

$$R^2 = 1 - \frac{\sum_{i=1}^{n}(h_i - \hat{h}_i)^2}{\sum_{i=1}^{n}(h_i - \bar{h})^2} \tag{3}$$

where n is the number of bins of the histogram being evaluated, h_i is the Gaussian distribution PDF for each i energy value, $\bar{h}$ is it mean and $\hat{h}_i$ is the y histogram [6]. The R^2 is calculated for multiple fitting Gaussian distributions, with a fixed v variance and a variable M mean. The tested interval for M is given by:

$$M \in [p - v, p + v] \tag{4}$$

where p is the detected peak value of the histogram. The value of M that generates the distribution with the closest fit to the original PDF (having a higher R^2) is selected and defined as the mean value that generates the closest Gaussian distribution fit for that energy interval. For this goodness of fit evaluation, it is defined an interval of three times the theoretical standard variation, where 97.7% of the Gaussian distribution energy is concentrated [3]. This interval around the detected peak is then used for analyzing the R^2.

The difference between the calculated fit and the histogram data in that interval is calculated, if it is an acceptable fit, defined as R^2 being higher than a threshold value of 0.7, then the Gaussian is identified as an transmitting user or the noise floor. If the determined R^2 is low, then the analyzed data does not represent a Gaussian of the GMM and the obtained peak value position is ignored. Nevertheless the calculated Gaussian distribution, that fits the detected peak, is subtracted from the original histogram. The value of $\hat{h}_i$ is updated by removing the Gaussian fit in the following manner:

$$\hat{h}_i^{(k)} \leftarrow \hat{h}_i^{(k-1)} - h_i^{(k-1)}, \tag{5}$$

where k is the iteration number. The algorithm will iterate and detect the next maximum value position till $\hat{h}_i^{(k)}$ reaches the majority of the y histogram data is fit by the method. After k iterations, if the remaining data is less than 10% of the original histogram data then the method ends.

3 Experimental Setup

To validate the proposed algorithm with real signals we performed a test using LTE FDD signals. These are composed by three Physical Uplink Shared Channel (PUSCH) symbols of the type TS36.104 Uplink FRC A3-3 [7] that occupy 15 Resource Blocks (RB) with a total of 3 MHz bandwidth. Each symbol is generated with an individual UE, a unique Radio Network Temporary Identifier and a data block containing random data. The modulation used is QPSK and the symbols are scheduling so that the three users are allocated in three sequential resource blocks on the same frequency band.

The complete frame used in this experiment as the following composition:

1. A blank resource block that has the same length as the PUSCH subframe;
2. The first user PUSCH subframe;
3. The second user's PUSCH subframe with 4 times higher amplitude than the first user;
4. The third user with a PUSCH subframe with 16 times higher amplitude than the first user.

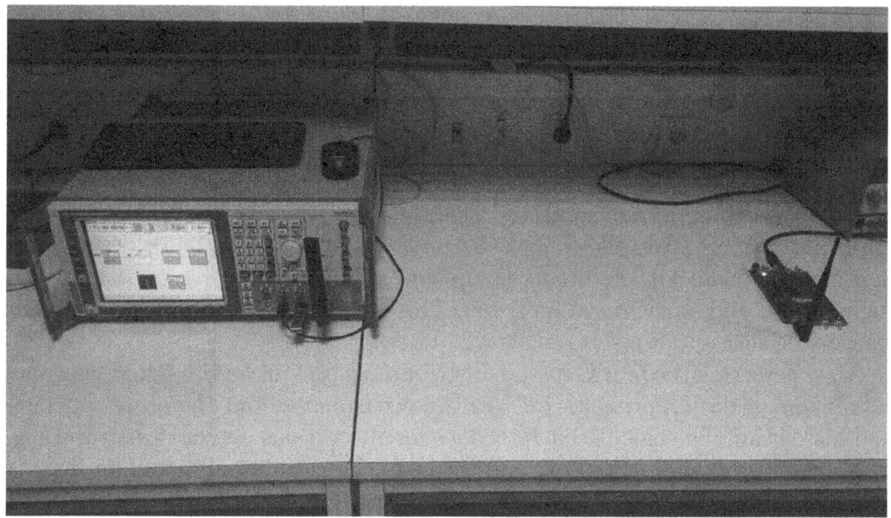

Fig. 2. The experimental setup to simulate multiple UE uplink transmissions.

The generated frame is transmitted by a Rohde & Schwarz SMJ100A at −25 dBm, centered at channel 1 Uplink (1950 MHz) and is intended to simulate the usage of the LTE uplink by three different UEs. The data will be received by the detection unit, an ETTUS USRP B210 connected trough USB3 to a personal computer as seen in Fig. 2. The B210 is configured to operate at 4MSPS in the same central frequency as the LTE signal is transmitted. The received signal has 8900 samples and is analyzed with an energy estimator of order 50. This energy estimator has a theoretical variance of 0.38 given from Eq. 2. The output of the power estimator can be seen in Fig. 3. This data is then analysed using a histogram with a thousand bins and the algorithm from Sect. 2 is used with a threshold of 10% of the total energy of the histogram. Distributions with a goodness of fit, $R^2 < 0.7$ are ignored.

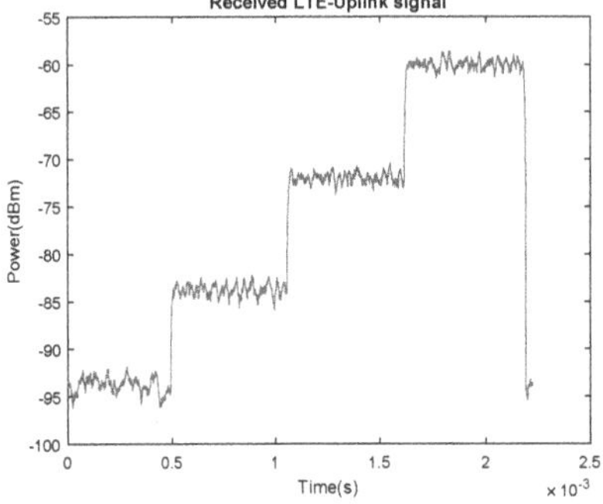

Fig. 3. Energy estimation of the received LTE-Uplink signal.

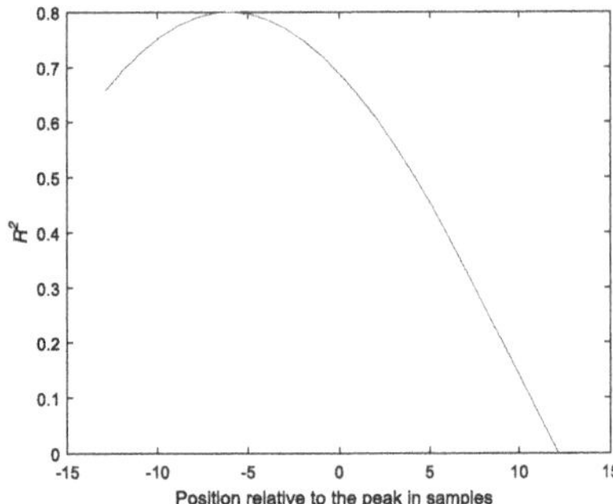

Fig. 4. Variation of the coefficient of determination around the first detected peak bin.

The first histogram peak value, is detected at −72 dBm and the fit iof the mean value is illustrated in Fig. 4. The curve obtained by the coefficient of adaptation, shows that the first detected peak is approximately six bins away from the local optimum, this allows for a better fit than only use the detected maximum as the mean for the fitting Gaussian. This fit is then removed from the original PDF and a new iteration is run. This iterations of the applied algorithm can be seen in Fig. 5.

After detecting the four Gaussian distributions present on the signal segment, the remaining data represents 7.8% of the occurrences from the original generated histogram. The calculated R^2 values for the various detected distributions are the following: 0.8; 0.86; 0.92 and 0.86. As the remaining histogram data is bellow the defined threshold of 10%, the algorithm concludes the iterations. If that wouldn't be the case, then the next distribution that would be detected, by ignoring the data remaining threshold, would reduce the data left in the histogram to 6.6%. This detection would have a coefficient of determination of 0.04 that would be ignored by the method due to the low R^2.

From the obtained distributions it is then possible to have a power estimation for the noise floor, that is given by the lowest detected power distribution. The other three detected distributions refer to the number of transmitting UE present on the shared medium.

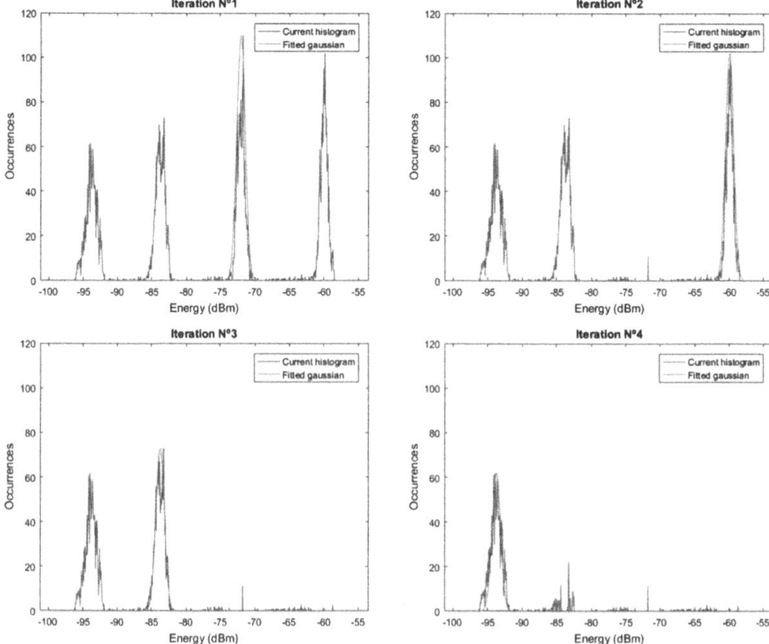

Fig. 5. Iterations of the subtractive histogram method for the LTE-Uplink data.

4 Conclusion

The subtractive histogram method proposed in this article was able to correctly determine the number of users and their power in a LTE channel using simulated PUCSH transmitted data using a signal generator and received in a software defined radio kit. This is done by analysing the data with an energy estimation method and an analysis based on fixed variance Gaussian distribution model. The method was also able to give a power estimation for the noise floor obtained in the detection unit.

Acknowledgment. This work was funded by the European Defence Agency under the pilot project grant with agreement number PP-15-INR-02_02_SPIDER.

References

1. El-Zaart, A.: Expectation-maximization technique for fibro-glandular discs detection in mammography images. Comput. Biol. Med. **40**(4), 392–401 (2010)
2. Holma, H., Toskala, A.: LTE for UMTS - OFDMA and SC-FDMA Based Radio Access. Wiley, Hoboken (2009)
3. Katayama, T., Sugimoto, S.: Statistical Methods in Control & Signal Processing. CRC Press, Boca Raton (1997)

4. Loève, M.: Fundamental limit theorems of probability theory. Ann. Math. Stat. **21**(3), 321–338 (1950)
5. Malafaia, D., Vieira, J., Tomé, A.: Adaptive threshold spectrum sensing based on EM algorithm. Phys. Commun. **21**, 60–69 (2016)
6. Renaud, O., Victoria-Feser, M.P.: A robust coefficient of determination for regression. J. Stat. Plann. Infer. **140**(7), 1852–1862 (2010)
7. Technical Specification: LTE; Evolved Universal Terrestrial Radio Access (E-UTRA); Base Station (BS) conformance testing (3GPP TS 36.141 version 10.1.0 Release 10). Technical report (2011)
8. Syrjälä, V., Valkama, M.: Coexistence of LTE and WLAN in unlicensed bands: full-duplex spectrum sensing. In: Weichold, M., Hamdi, M., Shakir, M.Z., Abdallah, M., Karagiannidis, G.K., Ismail, M. (eds.) CrownCom 2015. LNICST, vol. 156, pp. 725–734. Springer, Cham (2015). doi:10.1007/978-3-319-24540-9_60
9. Zuniga, M., Krishnamachari, B.: Analyzing the transitional region in low power wireless links. In: 2004 First Annual IEEE Communications Society Conference on Sensor and Ad Hoc Communications and Networks, IEEE SECON 2004, pp. 517–526 (2004)

Cellular Automata-Based Image Sequence Denoising Algorithm for Signal Dependent Noise

Blanca Priego[1(✉)], Richard J. Duro[1], and Jocelyn Chanussot[2]

[1] Integrated Group for Engineering Research, Universidade da Coruna, A Coruña, Spain
blanca.priego@udc.es

[2] GIPSA-Lab, Grenoble Institute of Technology, Grenoble, France

Abstract. This work deals with the problem of denoising sequences of multi-dimensional images that are corrupted by different types of noise. The denoising is performed through a cellular automata based filtering structure (4DCAF) that jointly considers spectral, spatial and temporal information by means of a three-dimensional neighborhood when each pixel of the sequence is processed. The novelty of the proposed method is its capacity to contemplate information concerning the type of noise by using as training data specific image sequences to tune the algorithm. The 4DCAF structures outperform selected state-of-the-art algorithms on both single band and multi-dimensional image sequences corrupted by different sources of noise.

Keywords: Cellular automata · Signal dependent noise · Spatio-spectro-temporal denoising · Hyperspectral denoising

1 Introduction

Temporal sequences of images captured by real-world imaging devices can be corrupted by specific noise depending on several factors such as the particularities of distinct sensors, the acquisition technology, the spectral range involved in the acquisition process or the capturing conditions.

Out of the different noise reduction techniques one can find in the literature, many neglect any information about the nature of the noise present, assuming as a general approach a model with zero-mean additive Gaussian noise for ease of computation and mathematical simplicity. However, in many cases, knowledge about the noise model is crucial for the process of denoising. On the other hand, those specialized denoising algorithms designed taking into account some specific noise models such as Impulse, Poisson or Speckle models can be strongly affected when images exhibit noise resulting from mixed noise models.

In addition, the majority of algorithms are focused on denoising single images [1,2,4,8,11,14] or on denoising single-band video sequences [3,9,12]. When considering multidimensional image sequences, in particular hyperspectral images,

J.M. Ferrández Vicente et al. (Eds.): IWINAC 2017, Part II, LNCS 10338, pp. 333–342, 2017.
DOI: 10.1007/978-3-319-59773-7_34

we find very limited contributions towards the denoising of whole hyperspectral datasets, being most of the algorithms devoted to the denoising of still hyperspectral images [5–7,10,13,15,17].

Thus, in view of the state of the art related to temporal denoising, there is an evident lack of denoising algorithms able to adapt to the multidimensional nature of the data (temporary and spectrally-wise), and at the same time to the specific type of noise models that may corrupt the sequences.

At this juncture, in this work we address the denoising of image sequences of different spectral dimensions corrupted by singular or different types of mixed noise models. The denoising is performed by locating and applying a cellular automaton over each pixel of the image sequence. The cellular automaton transforms or denoises the multidimensional pixel value according to a predefined set of rules, taking information from a dynamically established variable-sized spatial and temporal neighborhood.

The novelty of the method which we have called 4DCAF (4-dimensional cellular automata based filtering) relies on the procedure for selecting the transition rules that govern the denoising behavior of the CAF structure, which are tuned following an evolutionary process called ECAF (evolutionary method for obtaining cellular automata filters). This evolutionary procedure is adjusted using synthetic multi-dimensional image sequences as training datasets, which are created reflecting similar characteristics in terms of noise to those of the real image sequences to be denoised.

The rest of the paper is organized as follows. Sections 2 and 3 present a brief description of the proposed 4DCAF method which is tuned using synthetic image sequences that have been noised following a particular noise model, depending on the real single-band or multi-band image sequences that it aims to denoise. Sections 3 and 4 present the procedure followed in order to build the synthetic image sequences, based on a preliminary noise model analysis applied to the real dataset. Section 4 addresses the experimental results of applying the denoising algorithms over both synthetic and real image sequences. Finally, some concluding remarks are summarized in Sect. 5.

2 Cellular Automata Based Filtering Structures

A cellular automaton (CA) is a dynamic system consisting of a regular spatially distributed grid of cells, each of which can be in a certain state. The state of every cell is updated based on the their current state, the state of neighboring cells and a set of transition rules. The key to achieving a particular result in the execution of a CA lies in the adequate selection of this set of transition rules, so that after successive changes of state, the CA generates the desired behavior.

For the CAs used in this paper, a cell of the automaton is placed over each pixel of the image sequence and the state of the cell ($\mathbf{s_i}$) is given by an N–band spectrum, each band taking values in the range $[0, 1]$. In the case of a single-band, RGB or image sequences of any other dimensionality, the value of N will correspond to one, three and the number of spectral bands, respectively. The CA is executed K times over a section of the image sequence centred on a temporal image frame f. Once a frame is properly denoised by gradually modifying the cell states while converging towards a denoised version of it, the CA is moved to the next frame, performing again the denoising operation.

The updating of each cell, which involves the denoising of the pixel value, consists in applying one out of a set of M transition rules that control the automaton behavior. This selection is performed based on the state of the cell and on the states of the $N_S \times N_S \times N_T$ closest neighboring cells, where N_S and N_T are the sizes considered for the spatio-temporal neighborhood window centered over each cell. This information on cell states is combined in the form of spatio-temporal gradients applied to measurements of distance between each evaluated cell and its neighbors. For this implementation, when the method deals with multiple-band image sequences (RGB, multispectral or hyperspectral sequences), we have chosen the spectral angle normalized between 0 and 1 to measure distances between cell states. The normalized spectral angle, $\alpha_{i,j}$ between the spectrum of a cell i and that of its neighboring cell j is defined as:

$$\alpha_{i,j} = \frac{2}{\pi} cos^{-1} \left(\frac{\sum \boldsymbol{s_j} \boldsymbol{s_i}}{\sqrt{\sum \boldsymbol{s_j}^2} \sqrt{\sum \boldsymbol{s_i}^2}} \right) \tag{1}$$

where the summation is performed over the components of the state of $\boldsymbol{s_i}$.

On the other hand, when the 4DCAF method deals with single-band image sequences, the spatio-temporal gradients are obtained by directly using the intensity pixel values for each cell.

Then, in order to select a particular rule from the transition ruleset, a gradient vector ($\mathbf{G}$) is calculated taking into account the spectral angle (or the intensity pixel value) between the evaluated pixel and its neighbours contained in the $N_S \times N_S \times N_T$ 3-dimensional window. For this calculation, a set (containing 3 masks in the examples presented here) of different 3-dimensional masks are applied to the pixel, obtaining this way three gradient components: G_X, G_Y and G_T.

The value of $\mathbf{G}$ when 4DCAF is applied to a multi-dimensional image sequence is calculated as:

$$G_{X_{N_{S_i}}} = \sum_{j=1} \alpha_{i,j} \cdot M_{X_{N_{S_j}}}; G_{Y_{N_{S_i}}} = \sum_{j=1} \alpha_{i,j} \cdot M_{Y_{N_{S_j}}}; G_{T_{N_{T_i}}} = \sum_{j=1} \alpha_{i,j} \cdot M_{T_{N_{T_j}}} \tag{2}$$

where $\alpha_{i,j}$ denotes the normalized spectral angle between a cell i and its neighboring cell j in a $N_S \cdot N_S \cdot N_T$ window.

4DCAF takes the information of the spatial projection of the gradient vector ($\rho_P = \sqrt{G_X^2 + G_Y^2}$) and the absolute value of the temporal component (G_T) in order to select one rule out of the set of transition rules. A plane perpendicular to the gradient direction is defined based on this gradient vector dividing the neighborhood into two parts: a positive and a negative one. Once the transition rule is selected, based on this rule, the CA will decide which pixels on each side are going to participate in the modification of the cell state and how they are going to contribute to this cell state updating process.

The transition rules are made up of five parameters (2 state parameters + 3 updating parameters):

$$CA = \begin{Bmatrix} \rho_{rP_1} & G_{rT_1} & S_{rWS_1} & T_{rWS_1} & b_{r1} \\ \vdots & \vdots & \vdots & \vdots & \vdots \\ \rho_{rP_k} & G_{rT_k} & S_{rWS_k} & T_{rWS_k} & b_{rk} \\ \vdots & \vdots & \vdots & \vdots & \vdots \\ \rho_{rP_M} & G_{rT_M} & S_{rWS_M} & T_{rWS_M} & b_{rM} \end{Bmatrix} \quad (3)$$

with $b_{r_k} \in [0,1], \rho_{P_{r_k}} \in [0,1], G_{rT_k} \in [0,1]$, $S_{rWS_k} \in \{1,3,5,\ldots,N_S\}$ and $T_{rWS_k} \in \{1,3,5,\ldots,T_S\}$ where ρ_{rP_k} and G_{rT_k} are the state parameters (they define which pixels will use this rule) and are related to the spatial and temporal projection of the vector gradient; S_{rWS_k} and T_{rWS_k} denote the spatial and temporal size of the updating window which will define which pixels will be used to calculate the updated state of the current cell; b_{r_k} indicates the contribution of the pixels used from the positive and negative sides to the updating process. Subindex r is used here to avoid confusing rule parameters with the values of the gradient vectors extracted from the neighborhood information of a cell.

As mentioned before, ρ_P and G_T, are obtained from projections of a gradient vector calculated within a 3-dimensional spatio-temporal $N_S \times N_S \times N_T$ window. In order to select a rule, the automaton will take the rule whose first two parameters $\left(\{\rho_{rP_1}, G_{rT_1}\}, \{\rho_{rP_2}, G_{rT_2}\}, \ldots, \{\rho_{rP_M}, G_{rT_M}\}\right)$ are most similar in Euclidean terms to $\{\rho_P, G_T\}$. The selected rule, q, establishes the spatial and temporal window size $\left(\{S_{rWS_q}, T_{rWS_q}\}\right)$ of the pixels that are taking part in the cell state updating process and the value of the updating parameter b_{r_q}.

The updating process of the new cell state in the 4DCAF structure is given by the following updating formula:

$$\mathbf{s_{i,t+1}} = \mathbf{\bar{p}_{i,t}} \cdot b_{r_q} + \mathbf{\bar{n}_{i,t}} \cdot (1 - b_{r_q}) \quad (4)$$

where $\mathbf{s_{i,t+1}}$ is the new spectrum of cell i and $\mathbf{\bar{p}_{i,t}}$ and $\mathbf{\bar{n}_{i,t}}$ denote the averaged spectra of all the pixels contained in the positive and negative sides of the spatio-temporal window defined by $\left\{S_{rWS_q}, T_{rWS_q}\right\}$.

This procedure is iteratively applied to all the cells of every frame producing, in the end, an updated and denoised image sequence.

3 Obtaining the Transition Rule Set

The behavior of the CA in its application to the multi-temporal denoising problem depends on how the set of transition rules has been constructed. Setting the values of the parameters that make up the transition rules is a complex problem to solve manually. 4DCAF relies on an automatic rule adjustment procedure based on evolutionary algorithms that encode the CAF rule set (Eq. 3).

The methodology permits adapting the procedure to particular noise characteristics of the sequences to be denoised.

Any evolutionary algorithm could be used, but here we will just consider a GA based solution operating over a population of data structures that encode the solutions to the problem. One of the keys for evolving 4DCAF structures adapted to denoising sequences corrupted by specific noise models is to provide the evolutionary algorithm with suitable training image sequence datasets that allow determining the fitness of each candidate CA. These should reflect the spatial and temporal properties of the real image sequences that need denoising, as well as particular characteristics of the type of corrupting noise that corrupts those real sequences. As real training sets are rare and difficult to label, the methodology presented here makes use of synthetic images that reflects the types of noise and structures that need to be dealt with, which are obtained from a preliminary analysis of the real images to be denoised.

When a individual of the population is evaluated, the cellular automaton it encodes is executed over the noised synthetic training image sequences and the denoising result is compared to the desired denoised version in the training set. This comparison is performed in terms of mean squared error (MSE) between the original and denoised sequences, which is used as fitness function of the GA:

$$MSE = \frac{1}{X \cdot Y \cdot N \cdot F} \sum_{f=1}^{F} \sum_{b=1}^{N} \sum_{x=1}^{X} \sum_{y=1}^{Y} [I(x,y,b,f) - I'(x,y,b,f)]^2 \tag{5}$$

where $I(x,y,b,t)$ and $I'(x,y,b,t)$ represent the b-band spectral value of pixel (x,y) in frame f for the original and denoised sequences; X and Y are the spatial dimensions of the image, N is the number of bands and F is the number of frames of the sequences.

4 Results and Discussion

This section is devoted to the presentation of the experimental results obtained from applying the procedure presented in the previous sections to single-band and multi-band image sequences corrupted by different types of noise, and to its comparison to successful methods from the state of the art. In particular, we have considered four different types of real image sequences acquired from distinct acquisition sources: X-ray single-band image sequences, IR single-band image sequences, single-band image sequences acquired under low light conditions and hyperspectral image sequences covering the thermal spectral domain.

Previous to the application of the denoising method, a study of the noise model has been carried out for each type of image sequence, in order to construct the synthetic training image dataset. This analysis has been performed by representing the variance (σ) versus the intensity (μ) of the pixels from the sequences. The σ and μ values were obtained by means of a temporal average of selected frames without motion or objects moving. The results of this analysis are shown in Fig. 1 for some of the images. The circles in these graphs represent the density of elements in each range of intensity that exhibit a certain noise variance value. It can be noticed that the noise/signal representation in Fig. 1a fits a Poisson-distributed noised model, while the result observed in Fig. 1b corresponds to a mixed noise model. On the other hand, in the case of the hyperspectral image sequence 1c it can be observed that the noise behaves completely different, since the σ values decrease with augmenting μ values.

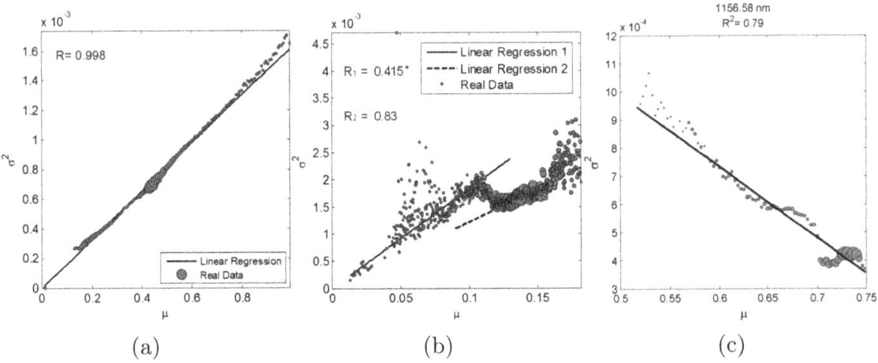

Fig. 1. Representation of the noise variance vs. intensity signal value from the noisy real X-ray sequence shown in Fig. 2(a), the highly noisy real IR sequence from Fig. 3(b) as well as for 1156.58 nm band of the real hyperspectral image shown in Fig. 5(c)

In order to cover the casuistry considered with these sequences, we have created three synthetic image sequence training datasets to evolve three different CAF structures that will be used in order to denoise both synthetic and real single-band and hyperspectral images: the first one consists of sequences of single-band images corrupted by a Poisson-distributed noise model; the second dataset of synthetic sequences follows a $\sigma - \mu$ distribution consisting in a mixed noise model similar to the shown in Fig. 1b. Finally, a third dataset is constructed considering hyperspectral image sequences of 131 spectral bands corrupted by a signal dependent noise similar to the one reflected in Fig. 1c.

4.1 Application to Real Image Sequences

The following tests have been carried out using real single-band X-Ray, IR and low-illuminated image sequences, as well as a hyperspectral image sequence to consider a multi-band case.

As the use of real images suffers from the lack of a ground truth (denoised sequence) against which to measure the performance of the denoising, the evaluation of the results has to be carried out by means of visual inspection. In the next subsection we will provide quantitative denoising results using a synthetic image sequence with a well characterized ground truth.

The denoising results of the proposed algorithm for the single-band image sequences will be visually compared to those of ST-GSM [16] and VBM3D [3]

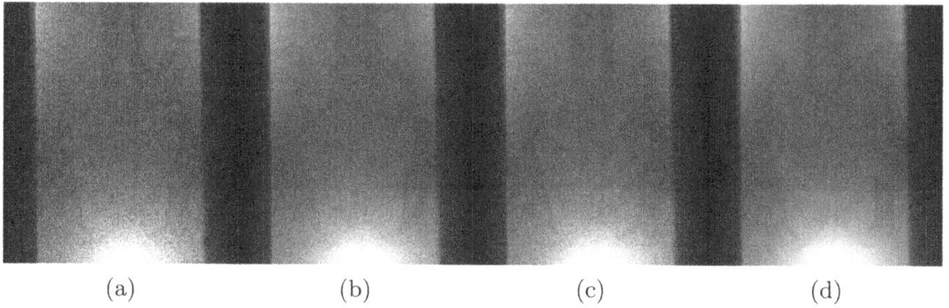

(a) (b) (c) (d)

Fig. 2. (a) Frame of a highly noisy real sequence, and denoised frames using: (b) VBM3D, (c) STGSM and (d) 4DCAF

methods. In the case of the hyperspectral sequence, the comparison will be carried out with respect to MTSNMF [17], K-SVD [1], BM3D [3], BM4D [9] and DNTDL [10]. K-SVD and BM3D treat each frame and spectral band separately. This has been called frame-wise band-wise (fw-bw) processing, whereas MTSNMF, BM4D and DNTDL are applied frame-wise (fw).

Performing a visual analysis of a selected X-ray denoised frame (Fig. 2), a qualitative observation reveals that 4DCAF reduces the noise more significantly in light regions without losing sharpness, avoiding blurring existing structures in the original image sequence. Also when denoising the IR and low-illuminated image sequences (Figs. 3 and 4), the denoising improvement of 4DCAF over VBM3D and STGSM can be noticed: the background areas are more homogeneous while the sharpness of the structures and edges is preserved.

In the case of the application of the method to real multi-dimensional (hyperspectral) image sequences, the dispersion of a chemical plume acquired by a LWIR sensor has been considered. The sequence consists of 25 frames, each one containing 129 spectral bands in the [853, 1.280] nm range. Figure 5 demonstrates that the 4DCAF method produces the most satisfactory result: the background appears more homogeneous, whereas the shape of the plume looks sharper than in the case of the other methods.

(a) (b) (c) (d)

Fig. 3. (a) Frame of a noisy IR real sequence, denoised frame using: (b) VBM3D, (c) STGSM and (d) 4DCAF

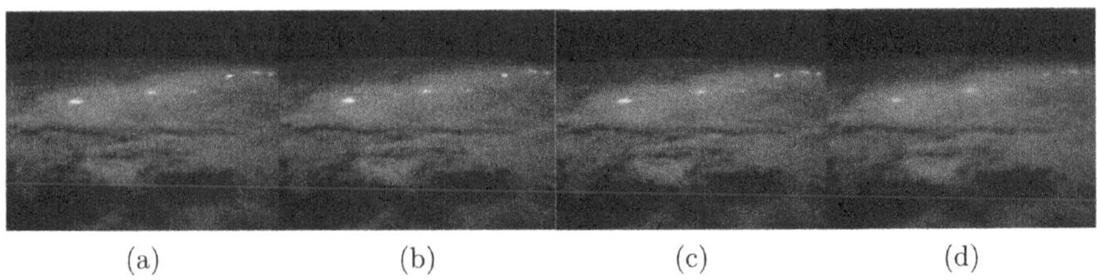

Fig. 4. (a) Frame of a noisy real sequence under low light conditions, denoised frame using: (b) VBM3D, (c) STGSM and (d) 4DCAF

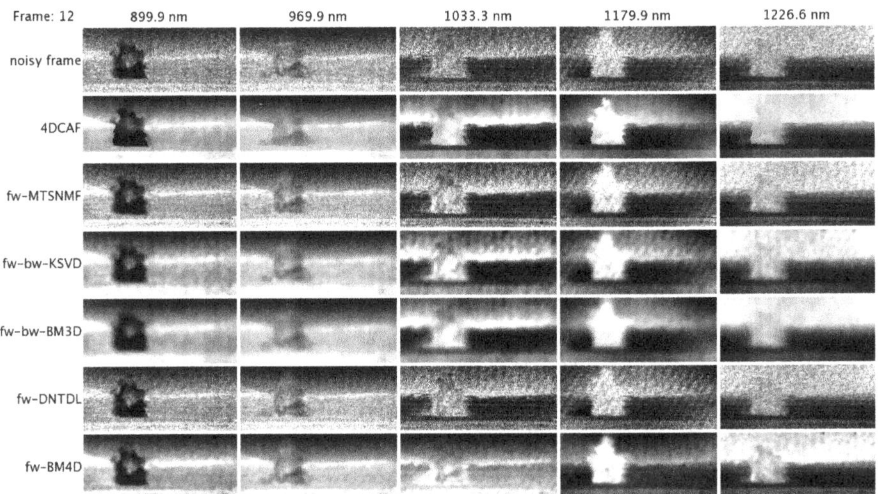

Fig. 5. Noisy and denoised images of a selected frame from a real hyperspectral image sequence representing a chemical plume using the different methods mentioned in the text. Only five bands (out of 129) are shown

4.2 Quantitative Analysis

Finally, in order to quantitatively analyze the performances of the method proposed here, a 25 frame sequence of 129-band synthetic images has been created using realistic spectral signatures. In order to evaluate the performances of the algorithms, we have obtained four quantitative picture quality indices (PQI), including peak signal-to-noise ratio (PSNR), structure similarity (SSIM), feature similarity (FSIM) and spectral angle mapper (SAM).

The quantitative results from these comparisons are shown in Table 1. The picture quality indices demonstrate that 4DCAF is able to efficiently operate over noisy hyperspectral image sequences consistently providing values for the indices that are much better than those given by the other methods.

Table 1. PQI comparison of the proposed 4DCAF, fw-bw-KSVD, fw-bw-BM3D, fw-DNTDL and fw-BM4D applied to a synthetic image sequence corrupted by signal dependent noise

Method	PSNR	SSIM	FSIM	SAM
4DCAF	**49.62**	**0.993**	**0.982**	**0.003**
fw-MTSNMF [17]	46.02	0.986	0.957	0.007
fw-bw-KSVD [1]	41.36	0.972	0.932	0.010
fw-bw-BM3D [3]	42.85	0.976	0.924	0.009
fw-DNTDL [10]	44.99	0.983	0.971	0.006
fw-BM4D [9]	44.01	0.984	0.958	0.010

5 Conclusions

This paper has described a methodology for obtaining cellular automata based filtering structures (4DCAF) that can be used for denoising multi-dimensional image sequences. It jointly considers spectral, spatial and temporal information during the denoising process by means of a three-dimensional neighborhood structure. It is also able to easily contemplate information about the type of noise through the use of easily obtainable synthetic image sequences to train or tune the algorithm. The approach has been visually and quantitatively compared to other state of the art techniques found in the literature, outperforming them over both, single band and multi-dimensional image sequences corrupted by different sources of noise.

Acknowledgements. This work has been partially funded by the MINECO of Spain as well as by the Xunta de Galicia and the European Regional Development Funds through grants TIN2015-63646-C5-1-R and redTEIC network (ED341D R2016/012).

References

1. Aharon, M., Elad, M., Bruckstein, A.: K-SVD: an algorithm for designing overcomplete dictionaries for sparse representation. IEEE Trans. Signal Process. **54**(11), 4311–4322 (2006)
2. Buades, A., Coll, B., Morel, J.M.: A non-local algorithm for image denoising. In: 2005 IEEE Computer Society Conference on Computer Vision and Pattern Recognition, vol. 2, pp. 60–65. IEEE (2005)
3. Dabov, K., Foi, A., Egiazarian, K.: Video denoising by sparse 3D transform-domain collaborative filtering. In: Proceedings of the 15th European Signal Processing Conference, vol. 1, p. 7 (2007)
4. Dabov, K., Foi, A., Katkovnik, V., Egiazarian, K.: Image denoising with block-matching and 3D filtering. In: Electronic Imaging 2006, p. 606414. International Society for Optics and Photonics (2006)
5. Lam, A., Sato, I., Sato, Y.: Denoising hyperspectral images using spectral domain statistics. In: 2012 21st International Conference on Pattern Recognition, pp. 477–480. IEEE (2012)

6. Liao, C.S., Choi, J.H., Zhang, D., Chan, S.H., Cheng, J.X.: Denoising stimulated Raman spectroscopic images by total variation minimization. J. Phys. Chem. C **119**(33), 19397–19403 (2015)
7. Liu, X., Bourennane, S., Fossati, C.: Denoising of hyperspectral images using the PARAFAC model and statistical performance analysis. IEEE Trans. Geosci. Remote Sens. **50**(10), 3717–3724 (2012)
8. Luisier, F., Blu, T.: SURE-LET multichannel image denoising: interscale orthonormal wavelet thresholding. IEEE Trans. Image Process. **17**(4), 482–492 (2008)
9. Maggioni, M., Katkovnik, V., Egiazarian, K., Foi, A.: Nonlocal transform-domain filter for volumetric data denoising and reconstruction. IEEE Trans. Image Process. **22**(1), 119–133 (2013)
10. Peng, Y., Meng, D., Xu, Z., Gao, C., Yang, Y., Zhang, B.: Decomposable non-local tensor dictionary learning for multispectral image denoising. In: 2014 IEEE Conference on Computer Vision and Pattern Recognition, pp. 2949–2956. IEEE (2014)
11. Portilla, J., Strela, V., Wainwright, M.J., Simoncelli, E.P.: Image denoising using scale mixtures of Gaussians in the wavelet domain. IEEE Trans. Image Process. **12**(11), 1338–1351 (2003)
12. Priego, B., Veganzones, M.A., Chanussot, J., Amiot, C., Prieto, A., Duro, R.J.: Spatio-temporal cellular automata-based filtering for image sequence denoising: application to fluoroscopic sequences. In: 2013 20th IEEE International Conference on Image Processing, pp. 548–552. IEEE (2013)
13. Renard, N., Bourennane, S., Blanc-Talon, J.: Denoising and dimensionality reduction using multilinear tools for hyperspectral images. Geosci. Remote Sens. Lett. **5**(2), 138–142 (2008)
14. Rudin, L.I., Osher, S., Fatemi, E.: Nonlinear total variation based noise removal algorithms. Physica D: Nonlinear Phenom. **60**(1), 259–268 (1992)
15. Salmon, J., Harmany, Z., Deledalle, C.A., Willett, R.: Poisson noise reduction with non-local PCA. J. Math. Imaging Vis. **48**(2), 279–294 (2014)
16. Varghese, G., Wang, Z.: Video denoising based on a spatiotemporal Gaussian scale mixture model. IEEE Trans. Circuits Syst. Video Technol. **20**(7), 1032–1040 (2010)
17. Ye, M., Qian, Y., Zhou, J.: Multitask sparse nonnegative matrix factorization for joint spectral-spatial hyperspectral imagery denoising. IEEE Trans. Geosci. Remote Sens. **53**(5), 2621–2639 (2015)

Applications

Robust Step Detection in Mobile Phones Through a Learning Process Carried Out in the Mobile

R. Iglesias[1(✉)], C.V. Regueiro[2], S. Barro[1], G. Rodriguez[3], and A. Nieto[3]

[1] CiTIUS, University of Santiago de Compostela, Santiago de Compostela, Spain
roberto.iglesias.rodriguez@usc.es
[2] Department of Electronics and Systems, University of A Coruña, A Coruña, Spain
[3] Situm Technologies S.L., Santiago de Compostela, Spain

Abstract. In this paper we describe an strategy to obtain a robust pedometer in mobile phones through a learning process that is carried out in the mobile itself. Using the vertical component of the acceleration, dynamic time warping and data collected on the mobile, we achieve a model able to detect steps and which exhibits an important robustness to the way the mobile is being carried out. We believe this robustness is due to the fact that the model, learnt on the mobile, requires less heuristic parameters and is linked to specific characteristics of the user and the hardware. We have tested our strategy in real experiments carried out at our research centre.

1 Introduction

Most mobile phones are equipped with inertial sensors like accelerometers, gyroscopes or magnetometers. These inertial sensors are being used in increasing number of applications in many fields – health care, agriculture, education – Nevertheless, the diversity of the hardware installed in the mobile phones, together with the specific noise inherent to these sensors, or other issues related with the fact that mobile phones can be carried freely by users – in the pocket, hand, etc.–, create serious problems regarding software development. Step detection is a good example of this. Almost any application aimed at detecting steps with the mobile phone, will have to deal with the accelerometer and in some cases the gyrometer. Nevertheless, it is difficult to achieve a robust solution, since the mobile phone can experience many movements that have nothing to do with the physical displacement of the user, and that's without considering other aspects such as differences in walking speed, processing power of the unit, etc.

The detection of steps with mobile phones is relevant for tasks such as indoor positioning, guiding, gait analysis for health applications, biometric identification, measurement of physical activity, etc. There are algorithms developed to detect steps with a low computational burden – zero velocity update (ZUPT), or other thresholds-based alternatives –. Nevertheless these solutions are not valid,

J.M. Ferrández Vicente et al. (Eds.): IWINAC 2017, Part II, LNCS 10338, pp. 345–354, 2017.
DOI: 10.1007/978-3-319-59773-7_35

or will show a poor performance when they are applied to mobile phones, due to the fact that they rely on a specific attachment of the sensors to different parts of the body (feet, hip, etc.).

We believe that one good option consists on the learning of models in the mobile itself. These models should gather the specific characteristics of both, the mobile and the user, and therefore will not be easily transferable amongst different mobiles or users. In the rest of the article we will describe our proposal (Sect. 2), the experimental results attained so far (Sect. 3), and finally we will point out some of our conclusions.

2 Description of Our Proposal

We have developed a system able to detect when the user is walking and count the steps. Our solution, aimed for mobile phones, should be robust to the step frequency and the dynamics of the phone, especially to the relative movement of the phone with respect to the body.

The strategy we have developed works on three stages: first, our proposal will ask the user to move normally. During this first stage, our application will collect some basic statistics of the information provided by the accelerometer and will collect samples corresponding to a set of steps. From this initial set of steps our proposal will build a model (second stage), and the user will be able to test it and to decide whether the performance is good enough. Finally, a further improvement in the model can be carried out through a third and final stage in which the user records false positives (by simply moving the mobile in the arm but without walking).

2.1 Attitude Estimation

Although some studies detect steps just using the module of the acceleration signal acquired with the accelerometer [], in our case we think that these solutions might be too sensitive to the relative motion of the mobile with respect to the body. Another possibility is working with the perpendicular component of the accelerations experienced by the phone, but in this case we will need to translate the readings (acquired in a local frame) to an inertial frame (fixed with respect to earth). Therefore, in this paper we will deal with the *earth frame* and the *body frame*. The earth frame more commonly known as Earth-Centred Earth-Fixed (ECEF) frame [1] is a reference system where the x-axis points from the Earth's centre of mass towards the equator, the z-axis points from the centre towards the North Pole, and the y-axis completes the right handed orthogonal system (pointing towards the East). This will be our inertial reference system. On the contrary, the body frame is a local reference system, i.e., it is a coordinate frame that remains fixed with respect to the phone. The x-axis points forward, the z-axis points downwards and the y-axis completes the right-handed orthogonal system. We want to project the accelerations experienced by the phone and which are given in the body frame (readings acquired with the accelerometer) into the earth frame. To carry out this transformation we will employ the gradient descent algorithm described by Madgwick in [2,3]. We will try to summarize this algorithm in this section to make this article comprehensible. This algorithm works with the quaternion algebra [3–6]. A quaternion describes a rotation [4] in the three dimensional space. In particular it represents the rotation of an angle $\theta \in]-pi, pi]$ with respect to an axes u (being u an unit vector):

$$\mathbf{q} = \begin{pmatrix} cos\theta \\ sin\theta \quad u \end{pmatrix} \tag{1}$$

Hence, a quaternion is four-dimensional vector $\mathbf{q} = [q1, q2, q3, q4]$ that can be used to represent the relative orientation amongst two coordinate frames a and b. Any vector x expressed in frame b can be translated into frame a:

$$^{a}x =^{b}_{a} q \otimes^{b} x \otimes^{b}_{a} q^{*} \tag{2}$$

where q^{b}_{a} represents the rotation from frame a to frame b. $\otimes$ represents the product of two quaternions, and $^{b}_{a}q^{*}$ is the conjugate of $^{b}_{a}q$.

Hence, this quaternion arithmetic can be used to represent the transformation amongst our inertial reference system (the earth frame aforementioned), and the body frame (local frame linked to the phone):

$$^{b}_{e}\widehat{q}_{t+1} = f(^{b}_{e}\widehat{q}_{t}, a_{t}, g_{t}) \tag{3}$$

The previous Eq. 3 represents the fact that the current estimation of the orientation of the inertial reference system with respect to the body frame, quaternion $^{b}_{e}\widehat{q}_{t+1}$, is obtained from the previous estimation $^{b}_{e}\widehat{q}_{t}$, and the current readings of the tri-axis acelerometer a_t and the tri-axis gyroscope g_t. In this work in particular we will not use the magnetometer.

The tri-axis gyroscope measures the angular rate about the x, y, and z axes of the body frame (w_x, w_y, w_z). These values (in $rads^{-}1$) are arranged into the vector S_w: $S_w = [0, w_x, w_y, w_z]$. These values can be used to follow the evolution of the rotation between the two frames:

$$^{b}_{e}\dot{q}_{t+1} = \frac{1}{2} * {}^{b}_{e}\widehat{q}_{t} \otimes S_{w_t} \tag{4}$$

Thus, integrating Eq. 4, it is possible to obtain the current estimation of the orientation of the body frame:

$$^{b}_{e}\widehat{q}_{t+1} =^{b}_{e} \widehat{q}_{t} + \left(\frac{1}{2} * {}^{b}_{e}\widehat{q}_{t} \otimes S_{w_t}\right) * \Delta t \tag{5}$$

where Δt is the sampling period. On the other hand, in absence of other external forces, the accelerometer will ideally measure only gravity. Hence, in this case, the quaternion should be the one that minimizes the expression provided in Eq. 6

$$^{b}_{e}\widehat{q} = argmin_{^{b}_{e}\widehat{q} \in \Re^{4}} (^{b}_{e}\widehat{q}^{*} \otimes E_g \otimes^{b}_{e} \widehat{q} - s_a) \tag{6}$$

where $E_g = [0, 0, 0, 1]$ is the four dimensional vector associated to the gravity force (for the computation with quaternions), and $s_a = [0, a_x, a_y, a_z]$ is the four dimensional arrangement of the values provided by the tri-axis accelerometer (a_x, a_y, a_z). In Eq. 6 the expression ${}^b_e\widehat{q}^* \otimes E_g \otimes^b_e \widehat{q}$ represents the projection of E_g into the body frame, which, in absence of other external forces than gravity, should coincide with s_a. Therefore, Madgwick et al. [2] formulates this as an optimisation problem where the orientation of the body frame ${}^b_e\widehat{q}$ is found as that which aligns a predefined reference direction of the gravity in the earth frame, E_g, with the measured field in the body frame, s_a:

$$ {}^b_e\widehat{q}_{t+1} = {}^b_e \widehat{q}_t - \mu * \frac{\nabla({}^b_e\widehat{q}^* \otimes E_g \otimes^b_e \widehat{q} - s_a)}{\|({}^b_e\widehat{q}^* \otimes E_g \otimes^b_e \widehat{q} - s_a)\|} \tag{7} $$

Finally, we can combine Eqs. 5 and 7 to get the expression to update the orientation of the body frame with respect to the earth frame, using the information provided by the accelerometer and the gyroscope [2,3]:

$$ {}^b_e\widehat{q}_{t+1} = {}^b_e \widehat{q}_t + \gamma * \left(-\mu * \frac{\nabla({}^b_e\widehat{q}^* \otimes E_g \otimes^b_e \widehat{q} - s_a)}{\|({}^b_e\widehat{q}^* \otimes E_g \otimes^b_e \widehat{q} - s_a)\|} \right) + (1-\gamma) * \left(\frac{1}{2} * {}^b_e\widehat{q}_t \otimes S_{w_t} \right) * \Delta t \tag{8} $$

The obtaining of this quaternion will allow the projection of the acceleration detected in the body frame to the inertial reference systems, and thus obtain the vertical component of the acceleration ${}^e a_z$:

$$ [{}^e a_x, {}^e a_y, {}^e a_z] = {}^e \mathbf{a} = {}^b_e \widehat{q} \otimes s_a \otimes^b_e \widehat{q}^*, \quad where \quad s_a = [{}^b a_x, {}^b a_y, {}^b a_z] \tag{9} $$

2.2 First Stage: Segmenting the Time Series to Detect Steps

As we pointed out before, initially our application will ask the user to walk for a while to obtain an initial sequence of steps from which obtain a first model. Obviously we count on the collaboration of the user during this phase. Usually, the movement of walking gives rise to a very characteristic vertical acceleration signal which looks very similar to sinusoidal waves [7]. This is the reason why in this stage we will use a simple version of what is known as peak detection [8] to identify steps. As it is shown in Algorithm 1, in our case we do not use adaptive thresholds or sophisticated approaches to identify the steps, the reason why we decided to do this is because we assume that we will count on the collaboration of the user during this phase. In fact, the problem with peak-detection based algorithms is that they tend to bee to sensitive to the relative movements of the phone with respect to the body. Just moving the arm is quite often enough to get the system confused and counting false steps.

Algorithm 1 will be used to detect *step candidates*. For us a *step candidate* is the acceleration signal obtained in a time interval and that might reflect the fact that the user has given a step. Therefore this algorithm chops the acceleration signal into segments that might reflect steps. The thresholds Th_{valley} and Th_{peak} that appear in Algorithm 1 are computed from the average and the standard deviation σ of the initial acceleration samples: $Th_{peak} = \overline{{}^e a_z} + \alpha\sigma$, $Th_{valley} = \overline{{}^e a_z} - \alpha\sigma$.

```
counter = 0 ;
A = [] ;
T = [] ;
initial_time = current_time_stamp ;
last_state="not_identified";
while process is not finished do
    Sc="neither_peak_nor_valley";
    if ^e a_z(t) >= max(^e a_z(t-1), ^e a_z(t+1))&(^e a_z(t) > Th_peak) then
        Sc="peak";
    else if ^e a_z(t) <= min(^e a_z(t-1), ^e a_z(t+1)&(^e a_z(t) < Th_valley) then
        Sc="valley";
    end
    if Sc="peak" then
        last_state="peak"
    end
    if Sc="valley" & last_state="peak" then
        last_state="valley" ;
        steps=steps+1 ;
        counter = 0 ;
        initial_time = current_time_stamp ;
        Analise_wheter_step(A,T) ;
    end
    A[counter] =^e a_z ;
    T[counter] = current_time_stamp - initial_time;
    counter = counter + 1 ;
end
```

Algorithm 1. Detection of peaks and *step candidates*

2.3 Second Stage: Obtaining of a Model

As it was pointed out at the beginning of Sect. 2, our system will build a first model starting from a set of N initial *potential* steps collected while the user moves. Since most probably the walking speed of user will not be constant, we must assume that the number of data points in every gait cycle is not identical. Algorithm 1 shows how through the peak segmentation of the first stage we obtain a set of accelerations A for each step, as well as the time instants that these accelerations occurred. Therefore, to build a model, the time-scale of all the steps is normalized, i.e., $T'_j[i] = T_j[i]/max\{T_j[]\}$, $\forall j = 1, \ldots, N$. After this normalization all acceleration samples have a time stamp in the interval $[0, 1]$, being 0 the time associated to the first sample and 1 the times stamp corresponding to the last acceleration sample. The purpose of this is to achieve a solution that is, somehow, robust to differences in walking speed.

Once all acceleration time series have been normalized, we will look for a template, i.e., a representative step that can be used for template matching in order to decide when a step might have occurred. In order to determine the most representative step we need a similarity measurement. In this case we have used *Dynamic Time Warping* (DTW) and in particular FastDTW [9].

Dynamic Time Warping is suitable to match temporal series, basically it finds the optimal alignment between the samples corresponding to two different time series, minimizing the distance amongst them. Therefore it allows the comparison of time series even if one of them may be *warped* non-linearly by stretching or shrinking it along its time axis [9].

There is another issue we had to deal with, and that is related with whether it is convenient or not normalizing the time series, i.e. working with steps made up by the same number of samples. According to [10] length normalization reduces the recognition accuracy in application domains where the length of the compared time series matters for their classification. In our case we do not want such a dependency since it might lead to solutions that are too sensitive to gait frequency. Another study [11] claims that making the sequences to be of the same length has no detrimental effect on the performance of DTW. Due to all this, we have opted for normalizing the time series that are going to be compared, i.e., when they are of different lengths, one of them must be reinterpolated.

The step that is going to be used as template for the matching processes, is determined automatically from the N *potential* steps collected while the user moves:

$$rep = arg\,min_{j\in[1,N]}\{max_{\forall k=1,\ldots,N}\{dtw_{j,k}\}\} \tag{10}$$

where $dtw_{j,k}$ represents the warping distance amongst time series (steps) j and k. According to Eq. 10, the pattern that is going to be used as template is the step that minimizes the distance to the furthest of the N − 1 remaining steps in the collection. The matching radius ρ_{rep} is determined as $\rho_{rep} = max_{j\in[1,\ldots,N]}\{dtw_{j,rep}\}$. Any new pattern exhibiting a distance to the template rep lower than ρ_{rep} will be considered as a valid step, while otherwise it will no be considered as a step.

2.4 Third Stage: Improving of the Model

Finally, when one template is not enough, it is possible to improve the model after collecting false positives. In this case, the user is asked to move the arm trying to get our application counting steps but without walking at all. On this way, a second set of M false positives is collected. Using the two sets: (1) the N true positives and, (2) the M false positives, the model is improved (Algorithm 2). The application of this algorithm will issue a new model formed by the minimum number of templates (each one with its own radius), so that all the N initial steps are properly recognized but none of the M false positives is misidentified.

3 Experimental Results

We have carried out two experiments to analyze the performance of our approach.

```
// Set of true positives
TP = {A_p[1], A_p[2], ..., A_p[N]};
// Set of false positives
FP = {A_fp[1], ..., A_fp[M]};
templates = { };
// Initialize the set "left" as a copy of the set of true positives
left = TP = {A_p[1], A_p[2], ..., A_p[N]};
while cardinal_of{left} ≠ ∅ do
    // Select the "true" positive with the highest number of
       neighbours belonging to the set TP
    // A true positive "A" is considered neighbour of B when the
       DTW-distance amongst A and B is less that the distance from A
       to any false positive
    w = arg max_{i∈TP}{cardinal_of{A_p[j] ∈ left | dtw_{i,j} < dtw_{i,l}, ∀l ∈ FP}} ;
    // Set the validity radius of w
    // Half way amongst the distance to the furthest neighbouring
       true positive and the distance to the closest false positive
    R_w = (max_{j∈left}{dtw_{w,j} | dtw_{w,j} < dtw_{w,l}, ∀l∈FP} + min{dtw_{w,l}, ∀l∈FP}) / 2 ;
    // Increase the set of templates with w and its radius
    templates = templates + {(w, R_w)} ;
    // Remove w and its neighbouring true positives from the set left
    left = left − {w} ;
end
```

Algorithm 2. Improving the model

3.1 Experiment 1

In the first experiment the model is obtained from noisy data, i.e., the initial set of steps to obtain the model are collected under a wide variety of circumstances: the user walks with the mobile in his hand, swings it, simulates a phone call, keeps the mobile in the pocket and walks with it, gesticulates while walking, puts the mobile facing upwards in the palm of his hand, touches the screen, etc. This is done, without following any kind of regular pattern and during 100 steps. Once this initial set of steps are collected for training, then first model is obtained and tested when the user follows a particular 5-stage-sequence (Fig. 1): (a) 20 steps walking with the mobile in the left hand, (b) 20 steps swinging the mobile, (c) 20 steps with the mobile in the ear (simulating a phone call), (d) 20 steps during which the user keeps the mobile in the right pocket and walks with it in the pocket (the user does not stop walking at any moment), (e) finally, after these 80 steps, the user stops and removes the mobile from the pocket (no steps should detected here) and checks the screen of the mobile to see how many steps have been detected. Obviously 80 steps is the desired output. Table 1 (first column) shows the output of the model when it is formed by only 1 template. In general we clearly see that our application counts a higher number of steps than the desired output. After this, and for each one of these experiments we carried out the third stage (model refinement). In this case initially the user collects false positives without walking and by moving the mobile in the arm sideways, up and down, keeping the mobile in the pocket, touching the screen, etc. The second column of Table 1 shows the number of false positives collected in each experiment. With this set, the model is refined adding new templates (third column of Table 1). This model is tested once again following the 5-stage-sequence aforementioned, the number of steps counted this time is shown in the last column of Table 1. As we can see the results are very accurate, as the numbers of steps that have been counted with our application are very close to the real case.

Table 1. Results obtained for five different experiments following the 5-stage-sequence described in the text.

Steps counted	False positives	Number of templates after refinement	Steps counted
101 (80)	57 FP	22T	80 (80)
96 (80)	51 FP	21T	81 (80)
103 (80)	44 FP	15T	84 (80)
95 (80)	57 FP	20T	79 (80)
95 (80)	52 FP	22T	75 (80)

3.2 Experiment 2

In this case during the initial collection of 100 steps the user walked with the mobile placed in the palm of his left hand (Fig. 1A). After this, then the model is obtained and tested (Table 2). We run 10 experiments. During the first five experiments we observe the output of the model when the user follows the 5-stage-sequence described in the previous subsection (Fig. 1). In this case we observe that the model misses a significant number of steps (second column of Table 2). Nevertheless the model is able to recognize perfectly the steps given by the user when the mobile is in his palm (columns 4 and 6 of Table 2, the desired output is 50, we tested the model when is formed by 1 template (4 column), or after correction (column 6). Nevertheless, if we correct the model once again and test it with the 5-stage-sequence, the number of steps missed is even worse than before (column 8). The reason is due to the fact that the model is tuned to recognize a specific way of walking. Hence, when the model detects an step it is correct in all cases (low number of false positives, it filters out all the relatives movements of the arm), but it also misses too many steps when the user moves in a different way from what it is expected and to what the model has been trained for (high number of false negatives). This can be useful for specific applications like guiding inside buildings, where the expected position of the mobile might be restrained, but for the general case is better to follow the procedure described in the previous experiment.

Table 2. Results when the model is tuned to recognize a specific way of walking

Exp.	Output	Exp.	Output (1)	False pos.	Output (2)	False pos.	Output (3)	Templates
Exp 1	78 (80)	Exp 6	49 (50)	44 FP	55 (50)	20 FP	46 (80)	9T
Exp 2	59 (80)	Exp 7	49 (50)	15 FP	49 (50)	18 FP	40 (80)	5T
Exp 3	75 (80)	Exp 8	50 (50)	166 FP	49 (50)	97 FP	35 (80)	10T
Exp 4	78 (80)	Exp 9	50 (50)	4 FP	49 (50)	2 FP	63 (80)	2T
Exp 5	62 (80)	Exp 10	50 (50)	6 FP	49 (50)	9 FP	50 (80)	4T

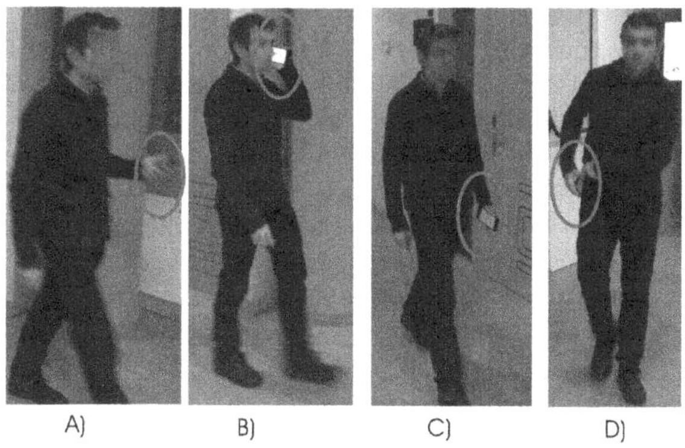

Fig. 1. Part of the sequence of movements followed during the experiments: the user carried the mobile in his palm looking upwards (A), he also walked with the mobile in his ear (simulating a phone call) (B), in his hand (swinging the mobile) (C), and finally he walked keeping the mobile in his pocked and also with it in the pocket (D)

4 Summary

In this article, we have described a novel mechanism to get a robust pedometer for mobile phones. The solution achieved shows an considerable robustness to the way the mobile is carried by the user thanks to a learning process that is carried out in the mobile itself. Our strategy involves a three stage procedure: first, data is collected while the user moves normally. On a second stage fast dynamic time warping is applied to find the most representative step together with a similarity radius. Finally, in a third stage, it is possible to refine the model including new templates by using a set of false positives. After this three-stage procedure, we achieve solutions that have proved to be robust even when the user changes significantly the position of the mobile while walking. In general we have noticed that when the data collected for the learning process (first stage) is noisy, the solutions are in general the most robust to the way the user carries the mobile. On the contrary, the models can be tuned for certain specific situations (for example we can assume that the mobile is going to be placed in the user's palm). In this case the model is very robust to this particular way of carrying out the mobile, filtering out all the noisy easily, but missing more steps when the user changes its behaviour or way of carrying the phone.

Acknowledgements. This work has received financial support from the Consellería de Cultura, Educación en Ordenación Universitaria (accreditation 2016–2019, ED431G/08 and reference competitive group 2014–2017 GRC2014/030) and the European Regional Development Fund (ERDF).

References

1. Rahim, K.A.: Heading drift mitigation for low-cost inertial pedestrian navigation. Ph.D. thesis, The University of Nottingham, UK (2012)
2. Madwick, S.O.H., Harrison, A.J.L., Vaidyanathan, R.: Estimation of IMU and MARG orientation using a gradient descent algorithm. In: IEEE International Conference on Rehabilitation Robotics. IEEE (2011)
3. Madwick, S.O.H.: An efficient orientation filter for inertial and inertial/magnetic sensor arrays. Technical report, University of Bristol, UK (2010)
4. Renaudin, V., Combettes, C.: Magnetic, acceleration fields and gyroscope quaternion. Sensors **14**, 22864–22890 (2014)
5. Yun, X., Bachmann, E., Mcghee, R.: A simplified quaternion-based algorithm for orientation estimation from earth gravity and magnetic field measurements. IEEE Trans. Instrum. Meas. **57**, 638–650 (2008)
6. Sabatini, A.: Quaternion-based extended Kalman filter for determining orientation by inertial and magnetic sensing. IEEE Trans. Biomed. Eng. **53**, 1346–1356 (2006)
7. Jang, H.-J., Kim, J.W., Hwang, D.H.: Robust step detection method for pedestrian navigation systems. IET Electron. Lett. **43**, 749–751 (2007)
8. Lee, H., Choi, S., Lee, M.: Step detection robust against the dynamics of smartphones. Sensors **15**, 27230–27250 (2015)
9. Salvador, S., Chan, P.: FastDTW: toward accurate dynamic time warping in liner time and space. Intell. Data Anal. **11**, 561–580 (2007)
10. Henninger, O., Mller, S.: Effect of time normalization on the accuracy of dynamic time warping. In: First IEEE International Conference on Biometrics: Theory, Applications and Systems. IEEE (2007)
11. Ratanamahatana, C.A., Keogh, E.: Everything you know about dynamic time warping is wrong. In: 3rd Workshop on Mining Temporal and Sequential Data, in Conjunction with 10th ACM SIGKDD International Conference on Knowledge Discovery and Data Mining (KDD-2004) (2004)

Predicting Trust in Wikipedia's Vote Network Using Social Networks measures

J. David Nuñez-Gonzalez and Manuel Graña(✉)

Computational Intelligence Group, UPV-EHU, San Sebastian, Spain
manuel.grana@ehu.es

Abstract. Predicting trust is an emerging topic in Social Networks research area. This problem tries to guess wheter an actor should trust another actor or not. The information used for this prediction can be extracted from different sources, such as the user profile, information extracted from the Web of Trust (WoT). The WoT contains the user explicit trust declarations about trust and distrust opinions about other actors (trustees). We propose a trust prediction experiment building features based on social networks measures to train different classifiers. Those features are extracted from the involved actors.

1 Introduction

Online Social Network (OSN) structures are represented by a graph $G(V, E)$ where nodes V correspond to users and edges E correspond with relationships among users. Sometimes those relationships contain information that must be included in the OSN graph, Thus, we have the $G(V, E, W)$ graph where W are the weights associated to edges. A special case is the Web of Trust (WoT) where users explicitly state their trust degree over other users [12,13]. In this case, W represent trust values among users. In this paper, the WoT obtained from the Wikipedia Voted Newtork the graph shows voting results among users. The trust value a user A gives to a user B indicates the trust degree (in this case, positive or negative) from A to B to give to B administration privileges on Wikipedia.

Several attemps have been done to predict trust values among users making experimental work with Wikipedia Voted Network database. Thus, previous works have dropped information in order to obtain such fixed size reputation vectors, fixed size probabilistic descriptors of the reputation information as discriminant features and high order reputation features [14]. In this work we propose fixed size arrays using social network measures in order to build the reputation features database to predict trust values given by users. Then, we perform cross-validation experiments in order to evaluate the quality of the proposed features with a variety of classifiers.

Contents of the Paper. This paper is organized as follows: Sect. 2 reviews some related work. Section 3 describes the proposed work and used database for experimentation. In Sect. 4 we show results and we compare them we previous works. Finally, Sect. 5 concludes this paper proposing future work.

J.M. Ferrández Vicente et al. (Eds.): IWINAC 2017, Part II, LNCS 10338, pp. 355–363, 2017.
DOI: 10.1007/978-3-319-59773-7_36

2 Related Work

Different works about Trust have been proposed in the literature to present properties, definitions, metrics, models and taxonomies i.e. [1–3, 5, 8, 15] Previous work on this database has been reported in the literature. Theories of signed social networks are investigated in those works as well as the underlying mechanisms that determine the signs of links in large social networks where interactions can be both positive and negative [9, 10].

This work has been inspired in [11] where verdict outcomes have been modeled using social network measures analysing members of a criminal (binary) datasets. In this work three different machine learning classifiers are used to model the verdicts in two real–world cases: the U.S. Watergate Conspiracy of the 1970's and the now–defunct Canada–based international drug trafficking ring known as the Caviar Network. Different social network measures are used to perform the feature matrix.

In this paper we work with ternary datasets using the following social networks measures:

- In/Out degree centrality defined as an agent in/out–flow communication edge [16]. A formal definition is: $grade(v_i) = \sum_i a_{ij}$being a_{ij}each element of the adjacency. $a_{ij} = 1$if a link exists from node v_i to node v_j.
- Betweeness centrality defined as across all agent pairs that have the shortest path containing the player, the percentage that pass through the player [4]. A formal definition is: $C_{BET}(i) = \sum_{j,k} \frac{b_{jik}}{b_{jk}}$ where b_{jk} is the number of shortest paths from node j to node k, and b_{jik} is the number of shortest paths from j to k that pass through node i.
- Clustering coefficient defined as density of the agent's ego network, which is subgraph induced by its immediate neighbours [17]. A formal definition is: $C_i = \frac{|\{e_{jk}\}|}{k_i(k_i-1)} : v_j, v_k \in N_i, e_{jk} \in E$ where the local clustering coefficient C_i for a vertex v_i is then given by the proportion of links between the vertices within its neighbourhood divided by the number of links that could possibly exist between them. For a directed graph, e_{ij} is distinct from e_{ji}, and therefore for each neighbourhood N_i there are $k_i\,(k_i - 1)$ links that could exist among the vertices within the neighbourhood (k_i is the number of neighbours of a vertex) (Fig. 1).

3 Proposed Approach

3.1 Preprocessing the Original Database

Wikipedia is a collaboratively edited, multilingual, free-access, free content Internet encyclopedia that is supported and hosted by the non-profit Wikimedia Foundation. Many people contribute writing articles[1]. When a Request for

[1] http://en.wikipedia.org/wiki/Wikipedia.

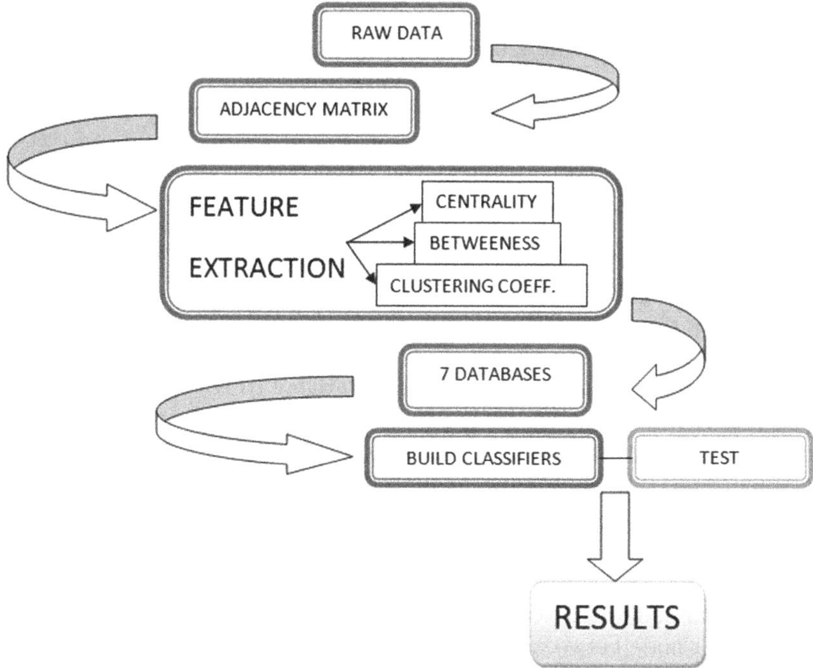

Fig. 1. Pipeline of the experiment

adminship is generated, users are able to propose and vote candidates. Chosen candidates are voted positively, negatively, blank or reciving no vote. About 7000 users have the right to participate in the elections and more than 100,000 votes are given. The dataset has a 5-tuple structure: elector resulted in promotion, time election, user identification of editor that is being considered for promotion, user identification of the nominator and the vote. As mention before, the vote can be possitive (1) to support the candidate; neutral (0) and negative (–1) to oppose it. We are interested in two vote values: 1 (support) and –1 (oppose). We ignore the vote "0". For this reason, we reorganize the database as follows: each row has three attributes $[A, B, v]$, that are user identifcation of editor that is being considered for promotion, user identification of the nominator and the vote. Before performing feature extraction from this database we make a random selection of 4,000 users for experimentation. In summary, we obtain a social network Trust database containing 61,979 instances (79.93% for class "1" and 20.07% for class "–1").

3.2 Feature Extraction

The problem we want to solve is described as follows: we want to predict the vote of a user A will give to a user B. For each instace we built an array of

20 features based on social networks measures to complete the feature matrix M. There are 3 groups of measures: related with the degree centrality, related with node betweeness, and related with clustering coefficient. Due to we have a ternary adjacency directed matrix (–1, 0 and 1 values) we transform it in 3 binary adjacency matrix: the first matrix takes only positive votes ($Adj^{pos}(M)$); the second matrix takes only negative votes ($Adj^{neg}(M)$); the third matrix takes both positive and negative as they were unique ($Adj^{tot}(M)$).

1. The first group of measures are 8 features related with the degree centrality:
   (a) d_in_–_A: degree of nodes pointing negatively to A.
   (b) d_in_–_B: degree of nodes pointing negatively to B.
   (c) d_in_+_A: degree of nodes pointing positevely to A.
   (d) d_in_+_B: degree of nodes pointing negatively to B.
   (e) d_out_–_A: degree of nodes pointed negatively by A.
   (f) d_out_–_B: degree of nodes pointed negatively by B.
   (g) d_out_+_A: degree of nodes pointed positively by A.
   (h) d_out_+_B: degree of nodes pointed positively by B.
2. The second group of measures are 6 features related with node betweeness:
   (a) BN_+_A: node betweeness of node A from $Adj^{pos}(M)$.
   (b) BN_+_B: node betweeness of node B from $Adj^{pos}(M)$.
   (c) BN_–_A: node betweeness of node A from $Adj^{neg}(M)$.
   (d) BN_–_B: node betweeness of node B from$Adj^{neg}(M)$.
   (e) BN_×_A: node betweeness of node A from $Adj^{tot}(M)$.
   (f) BN_×_B: node betweeness of node B from $Adj^{tot}(M)$.
3. The third group of measures are 6 features related with clustering coefficient:
   (a) CC_+_A: clustering coefficient of node A from $Adj^{pos}(M)$.
   (b) CC_+_B: clustering coefficient of node B from $Adj^{pos}(M)$.
   (c) CC_–_A: clustering coefficient of node A from $Adj^{neg}(M)$.
   (d) CC_–_B: clustering coefficient of node B from $Adj^{neg}(M)$.
   (e) CC_×_A: clustering coefficient of node A from $Adj^{tot}(M)$.
   (f) CC_×_B: clustering coefficient of node B from $Adj^{tot}(M)$.

4 Experimental Results

We run experiments using Weka[2] software to build some classifiers. We propose seven datasets from features proposed before. In fact, we propose as many databases (seven) as combinations can be made with the three groups of features. Table 1 shows how are they built. We build classifiers using Naive Bayes (NB), Multilayer Precepton with only hidden layer (MPLC), Radial Basis Function Classifier (RBFC), Multilayer Precepton (MP), 1-Nearest Neighbourhood (KNN-1), AdaBoost (AB) and Random Forest (RF). Because of the nature of the original database, all datasets are not well balanced. Instaces of the positive class are more than instances of negative class. We use 10-fold cross-validation process for testing.

[2] http://www.cs.waikato.ac.nz/ml/weka/.

Table 1. Proposed datasets and their contents

	Group 1	Group 2	Group 3
DB1	X		
DB2		X	
DB3			X
DB4	X	X	
DB5	X		X
DB6		X	X
DB7	X	X	X

Evaluated metrics when building classifiers are as follows where TP, TN, FP and FN are typicall elements of the confusion matrix corresponding with True Positives, True Negatives, False Positives and False Negatives. Notice that we will show results for both positive and negative class of Recall and Precision. Results are expresed in percentage.

- Overall accuracy (OA): $\frac{TP+TN}{TP+FP+TN+FN}$
- Recall (R): $\frac{TP}{TP+FN}$
- Precision (P): $\frac{TP}{TP+FP}$
- Matthews Correlation Coefficient (MCC):
$\frac{TP*TN-FP*FN}{\sqrt{(TP+FP)+(TP+FN)+(FP+TN)+(FN+TN)}}$
- ROC Area (ROC): $\frac{1}{2}\left(\frac{TP}{TP+FN}+\frac{TN}{TN+FP}\right)$

From Tables 2, 3, 4, 5, 6, 7 and 8 results are shown using the group(s) of measures specified in the bottom of each table to build the feature matrix. Best accuracy as well as other parameters is given by Random Forest in all experiments.

Table 2. Results for DB1. Using only first group of measures to build feature matrix

	OA	R+	R–	P+	P–	MCC	ROC
Naive Bayes	79.59	94.5	20.2	82.5	20.2	21.1	80.3
MPLC	86.71	96.6	47.5	88.0	77.6	53.8	89.5
RBFC	85.59	94.6	49.8	88.2	69.8	50.7	85.8
Multilayer Precepton	88.32	95.3	60.6	90.6	76.3	61.1	92.7
1-NN	85.08	90.9	61.8	90.5	63.1	53.2	76.4
AdaBoost	85.40	**98.2**	34.4	85.6	**82.7**	47.2	84.2
Random Forest	**88.84**	94.4	**66.9**	**91.8**	74.8	**63.9**	**93.3**

Table 3. Results for DB2. Using only second group of measures to build feature matrix

	OA	R+	R–	P+	P–	MCC	ROC
Naive Bayes	78.58	95.5	11.4	81.1	38.6	11.6	64.4
MPLC	80.08	**99.3**	3.4	80.4	56.4	10	71.3
RBFC	80.30	99.1	5.5	80.7	60.0	13.6	70.5
Multilayer Precepton	80.71	97.6	13.4	81.8	58.5	21.1	72.8
1-NN	76.53	86.6	**36.3**	84.4	40.5	23.9	61.5
AdaBoost	80.24	59.7	2.9	80.3	**67.8**	11.2	69.8
Random Forest	**82.54**	95.0	32.9	**84.9**	62.3	**36.3**	**82.1**

Table 4. Results for DB3. Using only third group of measures to build feature matrix

	OA	R+	R–	P+	P–	MCC	ROC
Naive Bayes	81.51	96.0	23.8	83.4	59.9	29.3	71.7
MPLC	83.25	97.4	26.9	84.1	72.2	37.0	69.2
RBFC	81.20	99.4	8.5	**91.2**	79.2	22	69.1
Multilayer Precepton	84.59	97.1	34.6	85.6	75.0	44.0	82.6
1-NN	80.87	88.7	49.6	87.5	52.5	39.2	69.2
AdaBoost	82.76	**99.6**	15.9	82.5	**90.1**	33.5	76.7
Random Forest	**86.10**	94.7	**51.8**	88.7	71.7	**52.7**	**88.4**

Table 5. Results for DB4. Using first and second groups of measures to build feature matrix

	OA	R+	R–	P+	P–	MCC	ROC
Naive Bayes	78.88	93.4	30.9	82.5	44.5	19.7	79.4
MPLC	86.92	95.7	51.9	88.8	75.2	55.2	89.7
RBFC	85.59	95.1	47.6	87.8	71.1	50.1	85.0
Multilayer Precepton	88.41	95.0	62.1	90.9	75.8	61.7	92.4
1-NN	84.97	90.8	61.7	90.4	62.8	52.8	76.2
AdaBoost	85.40	**98.2**	34.4	85.6	**82.7**	47.2	84.2
Random Forest	**88.62**	94.4	**65.4**	**91.6**	74.7	**63.0**	**93.8**

AdaBoost is sometimes the winner in other parameteres in all experiments. 1-NN, RBFC and MPLC give best results in some parameters eventually. Notice that Multilayer Precepton gives in general the second best results in many situations in all experiments.

Table 9 sumarizes the best results of each database. Best accuracy as well as other three parameters is given by Database 5 which use degree centrality

Table 6. Results for DB5. Using first and third groups of measures to build feature matrix

	OA	R+	R–	P+	P–	MCC	ROC
Naive Bayes	81.28	91.4	41.0	86.0	64.5	36.2	79.5
MPLC	86.89	95.7	51.7	88.8	75.2	55.1	90.0
RBFC	85.75	94.8	49.6	88.2	70.6	51.2	85.9
Multilayer Precepton	88.20	92.8	62.1	90.9	74.8	61.1	92.5
1-NN	87.78	91.0	60.0	90.1	62.6	51.8	75.5
AdaBoost	85.40	**98.2**	34.4	85.6	**82.7**	47.2	84.2
Random Forest	**89.40**	95.2	**66.4**	**91.9**	77.5	**65.4**	**94.0**

Table 7. Results for DB6. Using second and third groups of measures to build feature matrix

	OA	R+	R–	P+	P–	MCC	ROC
Naive Bayes	81.01	94.0	29.4	84.1	55.0	30.3	72.8
MPLC	83.98	97.4	30.4	84.8	74.9	40.7	79.7
RBFC	82.15	98.9	15.6	82.3	77.4	29.4	73.8
Multilayer Precepton	85.07	96.2	40.9	86.6	72.8	47.0	85.5
1-NN	81.78	89.3	51.9	88.1	54.9	42.0	70.6
AdaBoost	82.72	**99.2**	16.1	82.5	**87.9**	33.1	80.2
Random Forest	**86.48**	94.3	**55.2**	**89.3**	71.0	**54.7**	**89.5**

Table 8. Results for DB7. Using all groups of measures to build feature matrix

	OA	R+	R–	P+	P–	MCC	ROC
Naive Bayes	80.95	91.9	37.2	85.4	53.6	33.7	79.6
MPLC	86.90	95.2	53.8	89.1	73.8	55.5	90.1
RBFC	85.72	95.2	47.9	87.9	71.6	50.6	85.4
Multilayer Precepton	88.52	95.1	62.5	91.0	76.1	62.1	92.5
1-NN	84.71	91.0	59.7	90.0	62.5	51.6	75.4
AdaBoost	85.40	**98.2**	34.4	85.6	**82.7**	47.2	84.2
Random Forest	**89.23**	95.2	**65.6**	**91.7**	77.3	**64.8**	**94.0**

and clustering coeficient as features. Database 3 gives best results for recall of positive class and precision of negative class. In contrast, Database 1 gives best results for recall of negative class.

Table 9. Comparison among datasets

	OA	R+	R–	P+	P–	MCC	ROC
DB1	88.84	98.2	**66.9**	91.8	82.7	63.9	93.3
DB2	82.54	99.3	36.3	84.9	67.8	36.3	82.1
DB3	86.10	**99.6**	51.8	91.2	**90.1**	52.7	88.4
DB4	88.62	98.2	65.4	91.6	82.7	63.0	93.8
DB5	**89.40**	98.2	66.4	**91.9**	82.7	**65.4**	**94.0**
DB6	86.48	99.2	55.2	89.3	87.9	54.7	89.5
DB7	89.23	98.2	65.6	91.7	82.7	64.8	**94.0**

5 Conclusions and Future Work

We propose a trust prediction experiment based on social network measures using ternary adjacency matrix for feature extraction process. Results achieve a good accuracy using machine learning classifiers. In this work, node betweeness is not significant as feature in the way of getting good results. In fact, Databases 2 and 6, where node betweeness participates as feature, show the worst results of the experimental work. Comparing Databases 1, 5 and 7 we could discuss about the interest of need to handle large amount of data to get little improvements in results (in terms of overall accuracy).

In social networks is also important a good accuracy on the negative class in order to predict users whose bad behaviors could badly feed the knowledge generated by users of the network [7]. Thus, we achieve an accuracy of 66.9% using Database 1 that improve results from other works found in the literature [6].

Future work will be done experimenting with other social network databases as well as using more social network measures.

References

1. Abassi, R., El Fatmi, S.G.: Towards a generic trust management model. In: 2012 19th International Conference on Telecommunications (ICT), pp. 1–6 (April 2012)
2. Chadwick, D.W., Young, A.J., Cicovic, N.K.: Merging and extending the PGP and PEM trust models-the ICE-TEL trust model. IEEE Netw. **11**(3), 16–24 (1997)
3. Fachrunnisa, O., Hussain, F.K.: A methodology for maintaining trust in industrial digital ecosystems. IEEE Trans. Ind. Electron. **60**(3), 1042–1058 (2013)
4. Freeman, L.C.: A set of measures of centrality based on betweenness. Sociometry, pp. 35–41 (1977)
5. Golbeck, J.: Computing with trust: denition, properties, and algorithms. In: Securecomm and Workshops, 2006, pp. 1–7, 28 2006 September 1 2006
6. Graña, M., Nuñez-Gonzalez, J.D., Ozaeta, L., Kaminska-Chuchmala, A.: Experiments of trust prediction in social networks by articial neural networks. Cybern. Syst. **46**, 19–34 (2015). (cited By 4)

7. Graña, M., Nuñez-Gonzalez, J.D., Apolloni, B.: A discussion on trust requirements for a social network of eahoukers. In: Pan, J.-S., Polycarpou, M.M., Woźniak, M., Carvalho, A.C.P.L.F., Quintián, H., Corchado, E. (eds.) HAIS 2013. LNCS, vol. 8073, pp. 540–547. Springer, Heidelberg (2013). doi:10.1007/978-3-642-40846-5_54
8. Josang, A., Ismail, R., Boyd, C.A.: A survey of trust and reputation systems for online service provision. Decis. Support Syst. **43**(2), 618–644 (2007)
9. Leskovec, J., Huttenlocher, D., Kleinberg, J.: Predicting positive and negative links in online social networks. Proceedings of the 19th International Conference on World Wide Web. WWW 2010, pp. 641–650. ACM, New York (2010)
10. Leskovec, J., Huttenlocher, D., Kleinberg, J.: Signed networks in social media. Proceedings of the SIGCHI Conference on Human Factors in Computing Systems. CHI 2010, pp. 1361–1370. ACM, New York (2010)
11. Masias, V.H., Valle, M., Morselli, C., Crespo, F., Vargas, A., Laengle, S.: Modeling verdict outcomes using social network measures: the watergate and caviar network cases. PloS One **11**(1), 1–24 (2016)
12. Nuñez-Gonzalez, J.D., Graña, M.: On the effect of high order reputation information on trust prediction in wikipedia's vote network, pp. 59–62, cited By 0 (2014)
13. Nuñez-Gonzalez, J.D., Graña, M.: Graph-based learning on sparse data for recommendation systems in social networks. In: Ferrández Vicente, J.M., Álvarez-Sánchez, J.R., de la Paz López, F., Toledo-Moreo, F.J., Adeli, H. (eds.) IWINAC 2015. LNCS, vol. 9108, pp. 61–68. Springer, Cham (2015). doi:10.1007/978-3-319-18833-1_7
14. Nuñez-Gonzalez, M., Graña, J.D., Apolloni, B.: Reputation features for trust prediction in social networks. Neurocomputing **166**, 17 (2015). (cited By 2)
15. Viriyasitavat, W., Martin, A.: A survey of trust in workows and relevant contexts. IEEE Commun. Surv. Tutor. **14**(3), 911–940 (2012)
16. Wasserman, S., Faust, K.: Social Network Analysis: Methods and Applications, vol. 8. Cambridge University Press, Cambridge (1994)
17. Watts, D.J., Strogatz, S.H.: Collective dynamics of "small-world"networks. Nature **393**(6684), 440–442 (1998)

Acceleration of Moving Object Detection in Bio-Inspired Computer Vision

José L. Sánchez[1,2], Raúl Viana[1], María T. López[1,2], and Antonio Fernández-Caballero[1,2(✉)]

[1] Instituto de Investigación en Informática de Albacete, Universidad de Castilla-La Mancha, 02071 Albacete, Spain
antonio.fdez@uclm.es
[2] Departamento de Sistemas Informáticos, Universidad de Castilla-La Mancha, 02071 Albacete, Spain

Abstract. Computer vision is a great interest field offering relevant information in a wide variety of areas. Different video processing techniques, for instance, allow us to detect moving objects from image sequences of fixed surveillance cameras. Lateral Interaction in Accumulative Computation is a classical bio-inspired method that is usually applied for detecting moving objects in video processing. This method achieves high precision but also requires a high processing time. This paper introduces a parallel code capable of keeping a high performance in terms of accuracy and runtime for the method. For some of the image sequences tested, a speed-up of 67× over the sequential counterpart is achieved.

Keywords: Motion detection · Acceleration · Graphics Processing Unit · Lateral Interaction in Accumulative Computation

1 Introduction

The design of computer vision algorithms has been greatly inspired by studies in biological vision [1–3]. It is well known that quite simple biological systems efficiently and quickly solve most of the difficult computational problems that are still challenging for artificial systems. Despite the efforts put into biological vision as source for designing computer vision, the rich dynamics of feedback and lateral interactions are usually ignored [4].

Lateral Interaction in Accumulative Computation (LIAC) is a classical bio-inspired method exploiting the concepts of feedback and lateral interactions [5,6]. Mainly, the LIAC method has been applied in the last decade to the typical problem of detecting moving objects in video processing. Although the accuracy and precision of the LIAC method in detecting moving objects has been proven in manifold applications (see [7] for a review), the real-time performance has remained a serious drawback until now. In fact, algorithmic simplifications [8] and hardware implementations [9] have aimed to reach real-time performance, but not with an efficiency close enough to biological vision.

J.M. Ferrández Vicente et al. (Eds.): IWINAC 2017, Part II, LNCS 10338, pp. 364–373, 2017.
DOI: 10.1007/978-3-319-59773-7_37

Current technological advances make Graphics Processor Units (GPUs) one of the most promising alternatives for accelerating applications by exploiting the intrinsic parallelism they have [10]. These devices have a high computational power, which allows very significant time reductions as long as there exists sufficient parallelism in the method at hand.

In this paper, the complete biologically inspired LIAC algorithm for moving object detection is parallelised to accelerate the processing runtime. Firstly, the LIAC algorithm is revisited in Sect. 2. Then, Sect. 3 offers an overview of the architecture of the NVIDIA's GPUs and the programming model offered by the Compute Unified Device Architecture (CUDA). Section 4 describes the parallel algorithm implemented starting from the sequential version of the LIAC method. The experimental set up and the excellent results obtained are explained in detail in Sect. 5. Lastly, we provide some conclusions in Sect. 6.

2 Lateral Interaction in Accumulative Computation

LIAC Temporal Motion Detection. This initial phase firstly covers the need to segment each input image I into a pre-set group of grey level bands (n), according to Eq. (1):

$$x_k(i,j;t) = \begin{cases} 1, \text{if } I(i,j;t) \in [\frac{256}{n} \cdot k, \frac{256}{n} \cdot (k+1) - 1] \\ 0, \text{otherwise} \end{cases} \quad (1)$$

This formula assigns pixel (i,j) to grey level band k. Then, the accumulated charge value related to motion detection at each input image pixel is obtained, as shown in formula (2):

$$y_k(i,j;t) = \begin{cases} v_{dis}, \text{if } x_k(i,j;t) = 0 \\ v_{sat}, \text{if } (x_k(i,j;t) = 1) \cap (x_k(i,j;t-\Delta t) = 0) \\ \max[x_k(i,j;t-\Delta t) - v_{dm}, v_{dis}], \\ \qquad \text{if } (x_k(i,j;t) = 1) \cap (x_k(i,j;t-\Delta t) = 1) \end{cases} \quad (2)$$

The charge value at pixel (i,j) is (i) discharged down to v_{dis} when no motion is detected, (ii) is saturated to v_{sat} when motion is detected at t, and, (iii) is decremented by a value v_{dm} when motion goes on being detected in consecutive intervals t and $t - \Delta t$.

LIAC Spatial-Temporal Recharging. This second phase is thought to reactivate the charge values of those pixels partially loaded (charge different from v_{dis} and v_{sat}) and that are directly or indirectly connected to saturated pixels (whose charge is equal to v_{sat}). Formula (3) explains these issues, where v_{rv} is precisely the recharge value.

$$y_k(i,j;t+l\cdot\Delta\tau) = \begin{cases} v_{dis}, & \text{if } y_k(i,j;t+(l-1)\cdot\Delta\tau) = v_{dis} \\ v_{sat}, & \text{if } y_k(i,j;t+(l-1)\cdot\Delta\tau) = v_{sat} \\ \min[y_k(i,j;t+(l-1)\cdot\Delta\tau) + v_{rv}, v_{sat}], & \\ \qquad \text{if } v_{dis} < y_k(i,j;t+(l-1)\cdot\Delta\tau) < v_{sat} & \end{cases} \quad (3)$$

This phase occurs in an iterative way in a different space of time $\tau \ll t$. The value of $\Delta\tau$ will determine the number of times the mean value is calculated.

LIAC Spatial-Temporal Homogenisation. In this phase, the charge is distributed among all connected neighbours holding a minimum charge (greater than θ_{min}), according to Eq. (5).

$$\begin{aligned} y_k(i,j;t+m\cdot\Delta\tau) = & \frac{1}{1+\delta_{i-1,j}+\delta_{i+1,j}+\delta_{i,j-1}+\delta_{i,j+1}} \\ & \times[y_k(i,j;t+(m-1)\cdot\Delta\tau)+ \\ & \delta_{i-1,j}\cdot y_k(i-1,j;t+(m-1)\cdot\Delta\tau)+ \\ & \delta_{i+1,j}\cdot y_k(i+1,j;t+(m-1)\cdot\Delta\tau)+ \\ & \delta_{i,j-1}\cdot y_k(i,j-1;t+(m-1)\cdot\Delta\tau)+ \\ & \delta_{i,j+1}\cdot y_k(i,j+1;t+(m-1)\cdot\Delta\tau)] \end{aligned} \quad (4)$$

where

$$\forall(\alpha,\beta)\in[i\pm 1,j\pm 1],\delta_{\alpha,\beta}=\begin{cases}1, & \text{if } y_k(\alpha,\beta;t+(m-1)\cdot\Delta\tau)>\theta_{min}\\ 0, & \text{otherwise}\end{cases} \quad (5)$$

Lastly, we take the maximum value of all outputs of the k grey level bands to show the silhouette of a moving object (Eq. (6)). The result is filtered with a second threshold, namely θ_{max}, eliminating noisy pixels pertaining to non-moving objects, as shown in formula (7):

$$O(i,j;t)=\arg\max_k z_k(i,j;t) \quad (6)$$

$$O(i,j;t)=v_{dis}, \quad \text{if } (O(i,j;t)=\theta_{min})\cup O(i,j;t)>\theta_{max}) \quad (7)$$

3 Graphic Processor Unit

This section includes an overview of the architecture of NVIDIA GPUs and the programming model offered by CUDA [11] to programmers for producing efficient code for these devices.

The GPU architecture is composed of several multiprocessors, each consisting of several scalar processors. All multiprocessors can access the same on-board global memory through a high bandwidth bus. The hierarchical memory system is completed with several on-chip memories, such as caches, shared memory and a large number of registers. A program running on the CPU (the host) must explicitly or implicitly manage data transfers from host memory to device memory, and vice versa, to feed the processors and collect results, respectively. The part of the program that runs on the device is called *kernel*, and consists of a sequential code executed by a large set of threads on the GPU multiprocessors. All threads that are created when the kernel is invoked are organised into a grid of thread blocks. The programmer specifies the number of blocks and threads per block, taking into account some restrictions. Blocks are distributed among the multiprocessors, in such a way that threads within a block cooperate with each other by sharing data through the low latency shared memory of each multiprocessor. However, threads from different blocks scheduled on different multiprocessors can only coordinate their execution through the high latency global memory.

At execution level, threads are grouped into warps, that is, groups of 32 threads scheduled together on a single multiprocessor. Threads of a warp are simultaneously executed on the processors of a single multiprocessor in lock-step. Higher performance is achieved when all the threads in a warp execute the same instructions most of the time. However, they have their own instruction address counter and register state, and therefore are free to branch and execute independently.

A single multiprocessor generally executes multiple warps, interleaving their executions to hide stalls, mainly due to global memory accesses. A change of context has a practically null overhead since a large number of registers is available in each multiprocessor (up to 64 K in current GPUs). So, it is possible to keep many active warps. However, this model introduces a high pressure on the memory bus bandwidth. Therefore, it is still important to reduce global memory accesses, for instance, by using shared memory to exploit thread locality and data reuse.

To summarise, the programmer needs to partition the code into host and GPU code. In the best case, CPU and GPU work simultaneously, although a more usual situation is that once the control has been given to the GPU, the CPU waits for results. Threads assigned to different blocks communicate through global off-chip memory, whereas threads assigned to the same block do it through on-chip shared memory. The applications must exhibit a high degree of data parallelism for obtaining a high performance. In addition, data locality should be efficiently exploited in the register file and the local shared memories to reduce bandwidth requirements.

4 Parallel Algorithm

In the different phases of the previously described LIAC method, some kind of pixel-based processing is performed for each image in the video when it is received, and of the intermediate images generated throughout the processing. In most cases, this processing consists of modifying, under certain conditions, the pixel's charge, which is a numerical value between v_{dis} (completely discharged) and v_{sat} (saturated). In other cases, the algorithm processes some auxiliary structures associated with the pixels.

It can be observed that, in general, pixel computation could be performed simultaneously on all pixels, since there is no dependency on such processing. Actually, only certain information specific to that pixel is checked when modifying or not the charge of a pixel. There are some cases where this is not so obvious and requires further analysis. In particular, sometimes certain information from the four neighbouring pixels is necessary to obtain the new charge value of a pixel. Therefore, it is clear that there exists some level of parallelism in the operations of the LIAC method used for moving object detection. Consequently, it is expected that this fact can be exploited by using some kind of parallel platform, in particular one based on GPU. Let us review the different phases of the LIAC method to find out that parallelism.

In first place, in phase *LIAC Temporal Motion Detection*, from a given image of the sequence, n new images are obtained, one for each band considered. The calculation of the value of all the pixels for any of these n images can be done simultaneously. Moreover, there is no dependence between the n images, thus allowing to generate the n images at the same time. Afterwards, in the same phase, there exists dependence between consecutive images when processing the pixels. The charge value of a pixel in image ι $(1 \leq \iota \leq n)$ is obtained, in some case, from its value in that image ι and the value of that pixel in image $\iota - \Delta t$ in the sequence. Therefore, for this calculation parallelism should be exploited in the same way than in the previously described segmentation sub-phase. Then, in order to reactive the charge value of partially charged pixels connected to saturated pixels, a communication between each pixel and its neighbours is needed, making it difficult to overlap communication and computing. Consequently, communication is completely performed before starting computation. However, each step can be developed concurrently at pixel level.

In the other two phases of the method, namely *LIAC Spatial-Temporal Recharging* and *LIAC Spatial-Temporal Homogenisation*, operations similar to those discussed above are performed. Therefore parallelism is exploited in the same manner.

From this analysis, and the decisions taken, a baseline CUDA code has been obtained, such that: (a) the kernel is composed of all the operations that have to be performed on a single pixel or a set of pixels (this will be discussed in Sect. 5); (b) a kernel invocation allows to concurrently process all the pixels in an image; and, (c) as a consequence, as many kernels will be launched as images have to be processed in the source sequence.

5 Experimental Results

This section includes all the relevant details on the evaluation process carried out to check the performance of the CUDA code developed to reduce the execution time of the sequential moving object detection algorithm (sequential version of LIAC method). The tests performed, the configurations of the algorithm and the processed image sequences are described. In addition, the results obtained and the analysis of those results are also included. Before all this, the most important characteristics of the used hardware/software platform are indicated.

Hardware/Software Platform. An NVIDIA GPU Tesla K40 based on Kepler architecture has been used. It incorporates 2,880 cores, at 745 MHz, divided in 15 multiprocessors with 192 cores, 15 MB L2 cache, 49 KB of shared memory and 64 K registers. The off-chip memory device has a capacity of 12 GB, at 3 GHz with 384-bit memory bus. The host CPU, where the sequential code has been run is an Ivy Bridge architecture Intel Xeon E5-2660v2 2.20 GHz, with 64 GB main memory. Regarding the software, we have used CentOS Linux operating system release 7.2.1511 (Core), gcc/g++ compiler version 4.8.5, for the sequential code, and nvcc compiler for the parallel code, CUDA 7.5, and OpenCV versions 3.0 and 2.4.13 for image processing.

Image Sequences. Two different image sequences have been used in this work. In both cases a person moves from one position to another, and therefore he/she is the object/entity that has to be detected:

- Sequence A: images obtained with a fixed security camera of our university campus. The sequence consists of 100 240×320 grey-level images. Figure 1 includes the first image (left) and the last (right) image of this sequence captured by an infrared camera.
- Sequence B: images from a sequence belonging to the well-known PETS-ECCV 2004 CAVIAR test case scenarios (http://www.dai.ed.ac.uk/homes/rbf/CAVIAR/). The sequence consists of 100 288×384 colour images. Figure 2 includes the first (left) and last (right) images.

Configurations. The considered model manages several parameters, some of which are used to obtain a good fit of the algorithm. The parameters belonging to the LIAC method have been tuned in accordance with our previous experience [12]. In addition to the previous ones, other aspects related to CUDA implementation have been considered:

Fig. 1. Image sequence A. (a) First image, (b) last image

Fig. 2. Image sequence B. (a) First image, (b) last image

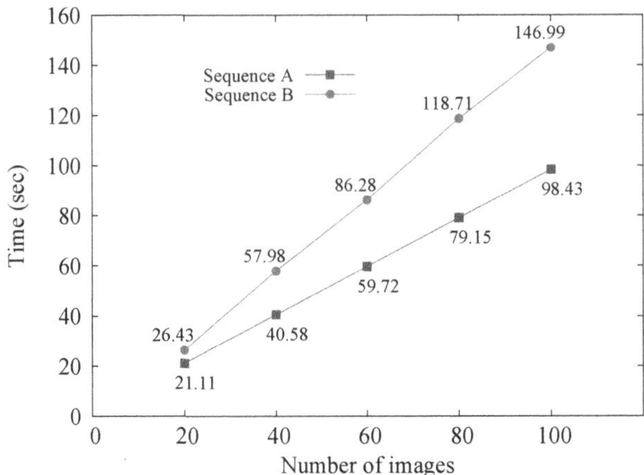

Fig. 3. Total runtime of the sequential algorithm for several number of images

- Task granularity: determines the operations being executed by a single thread. Different task sizes are considered: fine-grain (a thread processes only one pixel), medium-grain (a thread processes a row or column of pixels) and coarse-grain (a thread processes a group of rows, or a group of columns, or a sub-block of rows and columns of pixels).
- Number of threads per block: blocks with different number of threads organised in one or two dimensions are considered: 10×10 threads, 16×16, 20×20, and so on.
- Type of memory: global memory has been used to store the images, but also shared memory has been used to reduce the memory access latency.

Results. First, the sequential program was run to check its behaviour. Figure 3 shows the total runtime when varying the number of processed images. Two conclusions are obvious: time is directly proportional to the number of images considered, and time increases with the size of the images. The most important result is that the time is too high, rates of one image per second are gotten at best (sequence A), which is insufficient to process the images properly.

Regarding the parallel version of the LIAC moving object detection algorithm, we performed several tests that consider different granularity of the tasks and size of the thread blocks. The parallel algorithm was evaluated, taking into account fine grain and medium grain tasks. In view of the results it was not necessary to test with coarse-grained tasks.

In Fig. 4 you may observe that the total runtime for processing the 100 images of the sequences is smaller (between 15% and 20%) when a thread is considered to process a single pixel. Since the images are not too large, this means that a reasonable number of threads can be created when the kernel is invoked, without introducing overhead into the system.

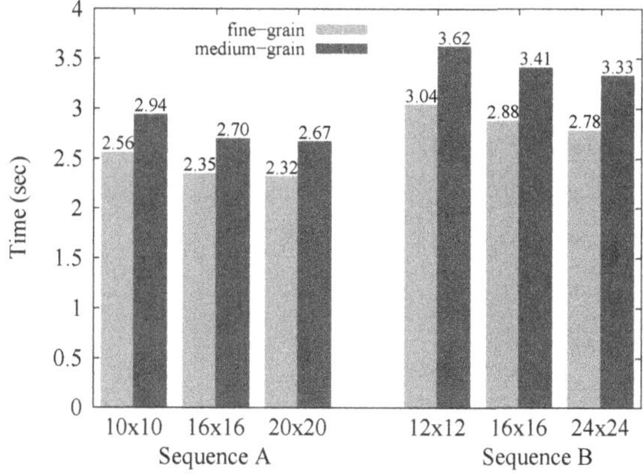

Fig. 4. Total runtime of the parallel algorithm for different task size, considering 100 images for both sequences

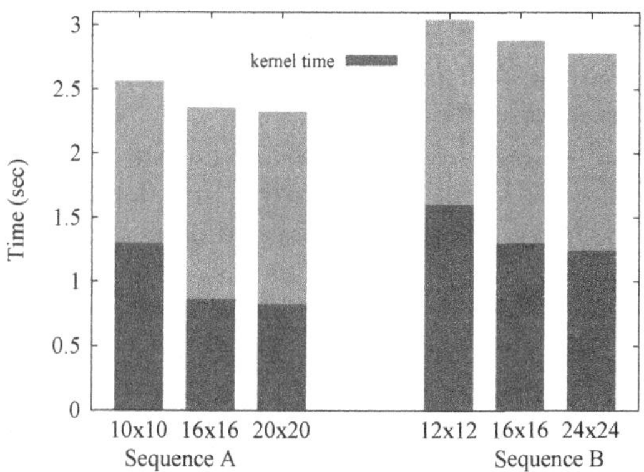

Fig. 5. Kernel time versus total runtime, considering 100 images for both sequences

From Fig. 4, it can also be verified that the LIAC parallel algorithm behaves better when considering more threads per block. We considered three cases in which each block has 100, 256 and 400 threads, for sequence A, and 144, 256 and 576 for sequence B[1]. Not always a greater number of threads translates into a better performance, and, for that reason, it is convenient to establish the most adequate block size in each case through experimentation.

These same results have been collected in Fig. 5, which also shows another important detail: there is an important proportion of the total runtime that is not dedicated to processing (kernel), and that is mainly due to data transfer between host and device.

[1] Note that these numbers have been selected so that all blocks have the same number of threads, i.e. the number of pixels in the images is multiple of these numbers.

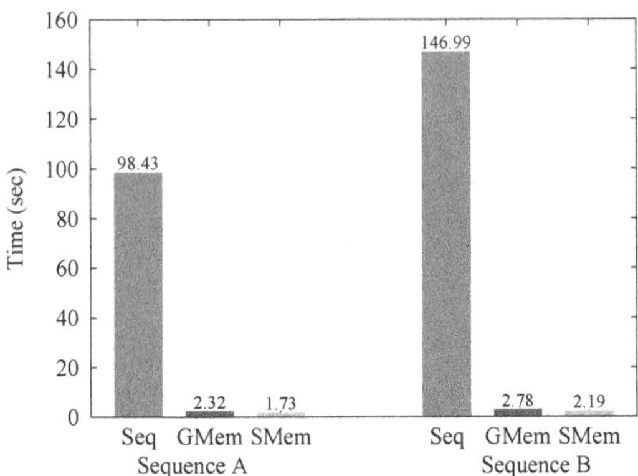

Fig. 6. Total runtime of the sequential and parallel codes, considering 100 images for both sequences

From here on, we consider fine-grained tasks (one thread processes one pixel) and thread blocks with a high number of threads (400 and 576 for processing sequence A and B, respectively).

The previous results have been obtained with a parallel code that exclusively uses the global memory (GMem) in the device. In order to try to further reduce the total time, a new version of the parallel code was programmed. It also uses the shared memory, which, as we know, has much less latency than the global memory. This type of memory is useful when the carried data is frequently used and/or utilised by different threads of a block. In our case, there are several phases of the LIAC algorithm in which the update of a pixel requires the charge of its neighbours. This means that the same data is used as many times as neighbours it has. It is not much, but it can reduce the total time. The images have been stored into the shared memory in sub-blocks, because this memory does not have much capacity.

As shown in Fig. 6, when shared memory (SMem) is used, runtime reductions around 25% are obtained in case of sequence A, and 22% for sequence B. According to the aforementioned, we consider that this is more than a significant runtime reduction. Finally, in the same figure, the runtime of the parallel code can be compared with the time obtained with the sequential code. The reduction of time is very important and when using shared memory, reaching 57× and 67× factors, for sequences A and B, respectively. In this way, a rate of approximately 50 images per second can be processed.

6 Conclusions

Image processing offers excellent possibilities to be accelerated by parallel computer systems due to their intrinsic parallelism exhibited. For many applications, acceleration is achieved by using simple and cost-efficient servers equipped with accelerators, such as graphic processing units. CUDA code has allowed to reach real-time performance for the bio-inspired LIAC moving object detection task.

The parallel code speeds up to 60× over the sequential code. It could still be improved by exploiting other properties of the heterogeneous platform used. From the results, it is also observed that the data transfers between host and device have an important contribution in the runtime. Therefore, it will be the next task in our work to reduce the overhead. The objective is to eliminate some of the transfers and reduce the runtime contribution of the inevitable ones.

Acknowledgements. This work was partially supported by Spanish Ministerio de Economía, Industria y Competitividad, Agencia Estatal de Investigación (AEI)/ European Regional Development Fund under DPI2016-80894-R grant.

References

1. Ullman, S., Assif, L., Fetaya, E., Harari, D.: Atoms of recognition in human and computer vision. PNAS **113**(10), 2744–2749 (2016)
2. Kriegeskorte, N.: Deep neural networks: a new framework for modeling biological vision and brain information processing. Ann. Rev. Vis. Sci. **1**, 417–446 (2015)
3. Cox, D.D., Dean, T.: Neural networks and neuroscience-inspired computer vision. Curr. Biol. **24**(18), R921–R929 (2014)
4. Medathati, N.V.K., Neumann, H., Masson, G.S., Kornprobst, P.: Bio-inspired computer vision: towards a synergistic approach of artificial and biological vision. Comput. Vis. Image Underst. **150**, 1–30 (2016)
5. Fernández-Caballero, A., Mira, J., Fernández, M.A., Delgado, A.E.: On motion detection through a multi-layer neural network architecture. Neural Netw. **16**(2), 205–222 (2003)
6. Fernández-Caballero, A., Mira, J., Delgado, A.E., Fernández, M.A.: Lateral interaction in accumulative computation: a model for motion detection. Neurocomputing **50**, 341–364 (2003)
7. Fernández-Caballero, A., López, M.T., Carmona, E.J., Delgado, A.E.: A historical perspective of algorithmic lateral inhibition and accumulative computation in computer vision. Neurocomputing **74**(8), 1175–1181 (2011)
8. Delgado, A.E., López, M.T., Fernández-Caballero, A.: Real-time motion detection by lateral inhibition in accumulative computation. Eng. Appl. Artif. Intell. **23**(1), 129–139 (2010)
9. Fernández-Caballero, A., López, M.T., Castillo, J.C., Maldonado, S.: Real-time accumulative computation motion detectors. Sensors **9**(12), 10044–10065 (2009)
10. Kirk, D., Hwu, W.-M.: Programming Massively Parallel Processors, 2nd edn. Morgan Kaufmann, Burlington (2012)
11. NVIDIA Corporation. CUDA C Best Practices Guide, v8.0, ed. (2017)
12. Fernández-Caballero, A., Fernández, M.A., Mira, J., Delgado, A.E.: Spatio-temporal shape building from image sequences using lateral interaction in accumulative computation. Pattern Recognit. **36**(5), 1131–1142 (2003)

Supervised Metaplasticity for Big Data: Application to Pollutant Concentrations Forecast

J. Fombellida(✉), M.J. Alarcon, S. Torres-Alegre, and D. Andina

Group for Automation in Signals and Communications,
Universidad Politécnica de Madrid, Madrid 28040, Spain
jfv@alumnos.upm.es, d.andina@upm.es

Abstract. Artificial Metaplasticity Multilayer Perceptron is a training algorithm implementation for Artificial Neural Networks inspired in biological metaplasticity property of neurons and Shannon's information theory. It is based on the hypothesis that a higher amount of information from a Data Set is included in the most atypical data. Using this theory basis a supervised algorithm is developed giving more relevance to the less frequent patterns and subtracting relevance to the more frequent ones. This algorithm has achieved deeper learning on several mutidisciplinar data sets without the need of a Deep Network. The application of this algorithm to a key nowadays environmental problem: the pollutant concentrations prediction in cities, is now considered. The city selected is Salamanca, Mexico, that has been ranked as one of the most polluted cities in the world. The concerning registered pollutants are particles in the order of 10 µm or less (PM_{10}). The prediction of concentrations of those pollutants can be a powerful tool in order to take preventive measures such as the reduction of emissions and alerting the affected population. In this paper the results obtained are compared with previous recent published algorithms for the prediction of the pollutant concentration. Discussed and conclusions are presented.

Keywords: Metaplasticity · Big Data · Plasticity · MLP · AMP · Pollutant concentration · Artificial neural network

1 Introduction

Atmospheric pollution is currently one of the most important environmental problems at global scale [1] that affects all societies independently of its development status impacting on human health in a very damaging way. According to a recent study, carried out by the European Environmental Agency, atmospheric pollution is the environmental factor with the greatest impact on human health in Europe and is responsible for the greatest number of environmentally related illnesses. The estimation presented on this study shows that more than 20 million European citizens may suffer from pollutant related health problems every day [2].

J.M. Ferrández Vicente et al. (Eds.): IWINAC 2017, Part II, LNCS 10338, pp. 374–383, 2017.
DOI: 10.1007/978-3-319-59773-7_38

The air quality in cities is highly impacted depending on the degree of industrialization, population density, traffic density, topographical characteristics and meteorological variables [7,8,12] and many other social and environmental characteristics. Among the different aspects that have influence on this problem it has been demonstrated that the global and regional variations in the climate together with the topographical conditions of the studied area highly affect the transport and dispersion of pollutants [11,14]. Parallel studies are focused on the appearance of severe episodes of pollution due not only to sudden increases in the concentration of the pollutants but also to certain meteorological conditions that reduce the ability of the atmosphere to disperse the concentrations [9,13].

Among the meteorological parameters that have influence on the pollutant concentrations wind patterns, clouds, rain and temperature can affect how quickly pollutants move away from an area. As a consequence of the alterations in the pollutant concentrations the changes in the chemical composition of the atmosphere may produce changes in climate, bring acid rain, destroy the ozone layer and affect the Earth's biodiversity. So it is proved that air quality is decisive for human health and the environment. These problems have attracted the interest of researchers, which have developed different forecasting strategies.

In this research we continue with our previous works [6]. The object under study in this article is the prediction of concentrations of PM_{10} for the city of Salamanca (Mexico), where they frequently exceed the legislated air quality standards [5]. We propose a model for the prediction of the average concentration of PM_{10} for the next 24 h. In the experiments that have been performed in the frame of this investigation several neural networks belonging to the multiplayer perceptron type has been used to classify the patterns in the available databases.

To check the possible improvements on the results of pollutant concentration prediction, based on the application of Shannon's theory in this work networks training has been performed using two supervised training methods: first the basic one is a backpropagation method (BPA), and additionally a variation based in the artificial neural metaplasticity theory have been applied.

The first step is to optimize the parameters used in the nominal BPA algorithm to be sure that the results obtained with the modifications of the method are compared with the best performance obtained by the classic method. For the second step it is needed to apply probability information about the input patterns, the second experiment uses an estimation of *a priori* knowledge of the probability of the input distribution considering a Guassian probability distribution in order to improve the results of the basic training method.

Based in the theory exposed in [4] less frequent patterns provide more information to the training than the more frequent ones. Considering an *a priori* estimation of the input distribution the experiment uses the Artificial Metaplasticity Multilayer Perceptron (AMMLP) algorithm giving more or less relevance to the pattern for the learning process If the input is less frequent we assume the pattern has relevance and then we increase the learning ratio in this iteration, if the input is more frequent then we reduce the learning ratio. This algorithm is applicable to ANNs in general, although here it is applied to a MLP.

For assessing this algorithm's accuracy of classification, we used the most common performance measures: MSE and MAE. The results obtained were validated using the 10-fold cross-validation method.

The remainder of this paper is organized as follows. Section 2 presents a detailed description of the database and the algorithms. In Sect. 3 the experimental results obtained are present. A brief discussion of these results is showed in Sect. 4. Finally Sect. 5 summarizes the main conclusions.

2 Materials and Methods

2.1 Study Area

Salamanca city is located in the state of Guanajuato, Mexico, and it has an approximate population of 260 769 inhabitants. The city is 340 km northwest from Mexico City, with coordinates 20°34'09" North latitude, and 101°11'39" West longitude. The Automatic Environmental Monitoring Network (AEMN) was installed in Salamanca in 2007. The system has the necessary instrumentation to measure the concentration of criteria pollutants as well as the meteorological variables. The measured meteorological variables are: wind direction (WD), wind speed (WS), temperature (T), relative humidity (RH), atmospheric pressure (AP), precipitation (P) and solar radiation (SR).

2.2 Methodology

The proposed model predicts the average concentration of PM_{10} for the next 24 h based on the information provided by the AEMN. The model combines artificial neural networks with clustering algorithms that have been previously applied in order to find relationships among pollutant and meteorological variables. These relationships that are expressed as groups there the inputs are pre-classified help us to get additional information in order to obtain a more accurate prediction model. The clustering algorithm is not part of the study of this article, only the results are used as an input to the network, details can be found on [6].

2.3 Data Preparation

Due to the large amount of signaling information included in the database as well as to the random erroneous measurements, it is necessary to review and refine the gathered information. Interpolation method was used to replace the missing data. For the pre-processing of the data based on different clustering algorithm (K-Means and FCM) PM_{10} pollutant concentrations, wind direction, wind speed, temperature and relative humidity were used to create patterns. These patterns were created as follows:

$$P = [C_{PM_{10}}, WS, WDI, T, HR] \tag{1}$$

where, $C_{PM_{10}}$ is PM_{10} concentration, WS is wind speed, WDI is the Wind Direction Index, T is temperature and HR is the relative humidity.

The final network input patterns will contain a label corresponding to the result of the clustering algorithm. In order to compare the results obtained with the ones presented by [6] the same input patterns original groups have been used:

- K-Means: Prediction based on 1 previous day using 8 clusters.
- FCM: Prediction based on 1 previous day using 7 clusters.

In both cases the total amount of patterns of the network is 962.

To obtain results statistically independent of the distribution of the patterns a 10 fold cross validation evaluation method has been considered. Using this method the possible dependence of the results with the distribution of the samples in the training or performance evaluation sets is eliminated: all the samples are used to train the networks and all the samples are used to evaluate the performance. For these experiment we have created ten data groups as initial sets to create 10 different final folders. In each one of these final folder the training set that will be used in the experiments as inputs to the networks for training the system and evaluating the evolution of the error in the classification will consists in 9 of the previous 10 groups. The final evaluation of the performance of the network will use the other element. The 10 folders will be created with the variation of the initial set. This is the mathematical basis of the 10 fold cross validation method.

50 initial networks are created using random values. The networks are trained from the same initial conditions (same initial values for weights and biases of the neurons) presenting the information corresponding to each of the 10 folders. Finally the mean values of the results will be calculated to eliminate the possible statistical influence in the results due to the concrete fixed selection of some patterns to train the system and the fixed selection of other patterns to evaluate the results.

2.4 Artificial Metaplasticity Neural Network Model

Based on the theory and applications presented on [3,10,15], for these experiments multiplayer perceptron neural networks have been used with a input composed by 6 attributes contained in each single pattern, a hidden layer composed by 3 neurons (in previous experiments it has been proved that 3 neurons is enough to get a good level of flexibility to define the decision regions), and an output layer with just 1 neuron (that will give us the final result of the prediction).

The activation function used in all the neurons of the system is sigmoid logarithmic. For the experiments we have considered that the input values of the patterns x_i have to be normalized. The initialization of the weights of the neurons is random but included in an interval $[-0.8, +0.8]$, parameter value σ is constant and equal to 1. Doing this so the range of inputs to the activation function $\sigma \sum \omega_i x_i$ will be limited to the interval $[-4.8, +4.8]$. Then the initial part of the training is compliant with the premise of not saturating the output of the neurons.

To analytically introduce AMP in an arbitrary MLP training based on classic BP training, all that has to be done is to introduce the weighting function $\frac{1}{f_X^*}$

in the MLP learning equation that has the properties of a probability density function.

$$w_{ij}^{(s)}(t+1) = w_{ij}^{(s)}(t) - \eta \frac{\partial E^*[W(t)]}{\partial w_{ij}^{(s)}} = w_{ij}^{(s)}(t) - \eta \frac{1}{f_X^*} \frac{\partial E[W(t)]}{\partial w_{ij}^{(s)}} \tag{2}$$

So, as the pdf weighting function proposed is the distribution of the input patterns that does not depend on the network parameters, the AMMLP algorithm can then be summarized as a weighting operation for updating each weight in each MLP learning iteration as

$$\Delta^* w = w^*(x)\, \Delta w \tag{3}$$

being $\Delta w = w(t+l) - w(t)$ the weight updating value obtained by usual BPA and $w^*(x)$ the realization of the described weighting function $w^*(x)$ for each input training pattern x.

Metaplasticity Influence Based on the Probability Distribution. The idea is to use the existing information of the distribution of probability of the inputs to the network to improve the classification results and the speed of the learning curve (being able to use a smaller number of patterns as inputs to the network to obtain the same results, that can be very useful to avoid overspecialization if the data base contains very few available patterns).

In this article we consider that the probability distribution is known *a priori*: One suboptimal solution tested in this paper for $f_X^*(x)$ is

$$f_X^*(x) = \frac{A}{\sqrt{(2\pi)^N} \cdot e^{B \sum_{i=1}^{N} x_i^2}} = \frac{1}{w_X^*(x)} \tag{4}$$

where $w_X^*(x)$ is defined as $1/f_X^*(x)$, N is the number of neurons in the MLP input, and parameters A and $B \in R^+$ are algorithm optimization values which depend on the specific application of the AMLP algorithm. These concrete values will be evaluated in the second part of the experiment. Equation 4 is a gaussian distribution, so it has been assumed that X pdf is Gaussian (if it is not the case, the real X pdf should be used instead). Then, $w_X^*(x)$ has high values for unfrequent x values and close to 1 for the frequent ones and can therefore be straightforwardly applied in weights updating procedure to model the biological metaplasticity during learning.

3 Results

3.1 Network Characteristics

Structure of the network

- Number of inputs: equal to the number of attributes of the input pattern (6).
- Number of hidden layers: 1.

- Number of neurons included in the hidden layer: Based on previous experience [6] it has been considered that 3 neurons are considered ideal for a tradeoff between the flexibility in the definition of the decision regions and the complexity of the system.
- Number of neurons in the output layer: 1.
- Activation function: Sigmoid logarithmic with an output included in the interval $[0, 1]$.

Conditions considered to finalize the network training:

- Reach a predefined number of inputs presented to the network: 200 iteration (each iteration the whole set is presented to the network). The errors are calculated at the end of each iteration.

3.2 Evaluation Method

The ANN model performance was evaluated through the following parameters: Mean Absolute Error (MAE) and Mean Square Error (MSE):

$$MAE = \frac{1}{N}\sum_{i=1}^{N}|X_i - Y_i| \tag{5}$$

$$MSE = \frac{1}{N}\sum_{i=1}^{N}|X_i - Y_i|^2 \tag{6}$$

3.3 Experiments Using K-Means Clustered Inputs

Nominal Backpropagation Algorithm. According to the existing literature due to the fact the inputs have been normalized to a hypersphere of radius 1 in order to have a training method considered convergent it is necessary that the learning rate is included in the interval $(0, 1]$. Based on this premise the value 1 will be considered as the upper limit for the learning rate in the nominal backpropagation experiments. In this first part of the training we will study the behavior of the nominal backpropagation method maintaining the learning rate inside the theoretical limits. The best results obtained for MSE and MAE corresponds to value $\eta = 1$:

- % MSE = 0.0012
- % MAE = 0.0270

Evolution of MSE error during the training phase is shown in Fig. 1.

Gaussian Function Experiment. The Gaussian function has two parameters to be optimized: A and B. The experiments show that the optimum values selected are $A = 10$ and $B = 0.55$, the results obtained are:

- % MSE = 0.0010
- % MAE = 0.0245

Evolution of MSE error during the training phase is shown in Fig. 2.

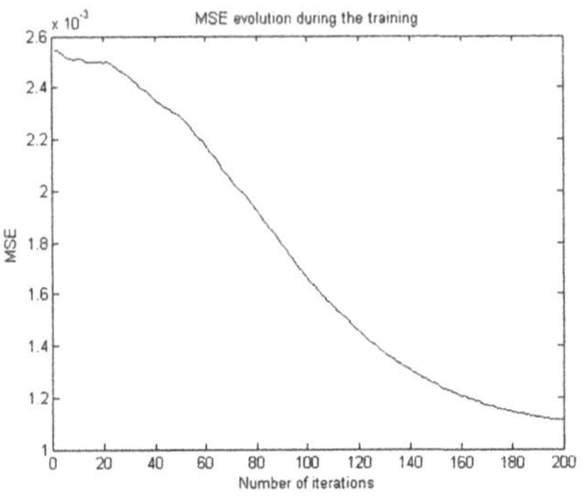

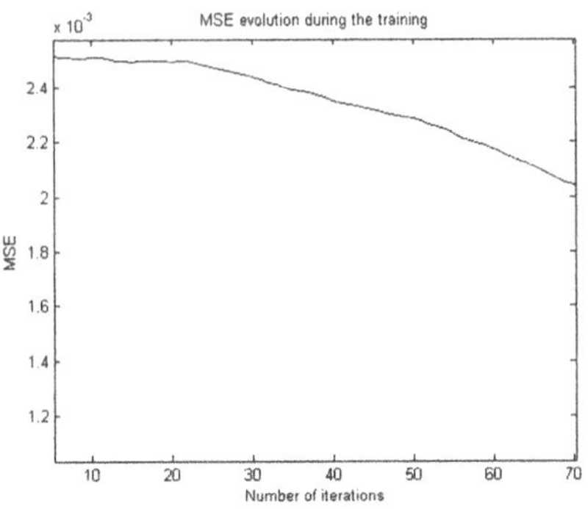

Fig. 1. K-Means - evolution of the MSE error (detail in right figure) $\eta = 1$ - nominal backpropagation

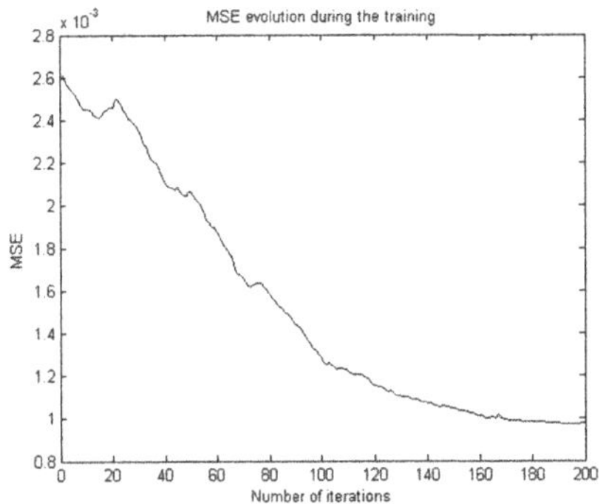

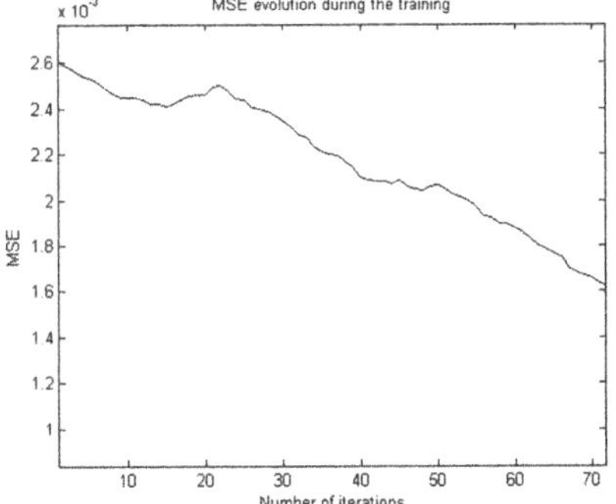

Fig. 2. K-Means - evolution of the MSE error (detail in right figure) $A = 10$ $B = 0.55$ - Gaussian

3.4 Experiments Using Fuzzy C-Means Clustered Inputs

Nominal Backpropagation Algorithm. The best results obtained for MSE and MAE corresponds to value $\eta = 1$:

- % MSE = 0.0012
- % MAE = 0.0267

Evolution of MSE error during the training phase is shown in Fig. 3.

Gaussian Function Experiment. The optimum values selected are $A = 10$ and $B = 0.55$, the results obtained are:

- % MSE = 0.0010
- % MAE = 0.0245

Evolution of MSE error during the training phase is shown in Fig. 4.

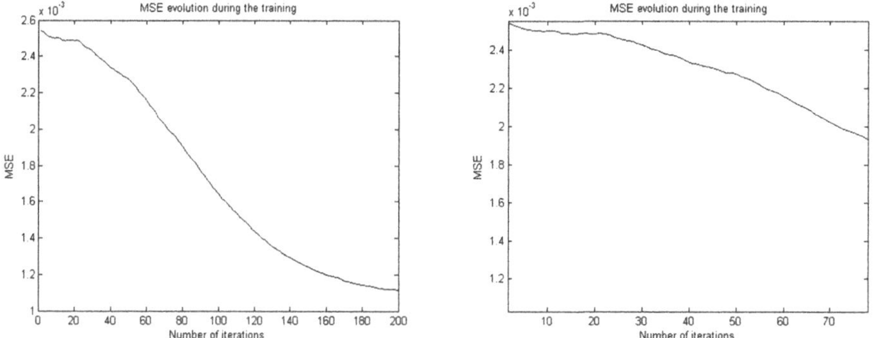

Fig. 3. Fuzzy C-Means - evolution of the MSE error (detail in right figure) $\eta = 1$ - nominal backpropagation

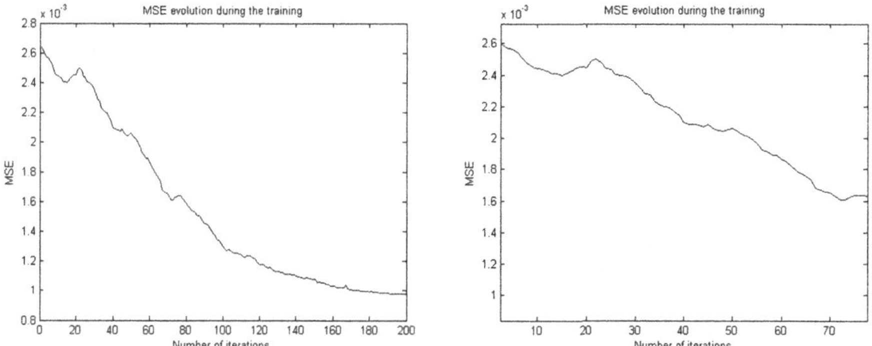

Fig. 4. Fuzzy C-Means - evolution of the MSE error (detail in right figure) $A = 10$ $B = 0.55$ - Gaussian

4 Discussion

- The results obtained from the Gaussian metaplasticity improve those recently obtained in [6] both MSE and MAE. We can confirm then that a deeper learning is obtained form the same Data Set just by applying the Bio-inspired Metaplasticity. The hypothesis that the patterns with less occurrence frequency (atypical data) contain more information than the patterns with more frequency is so reinforced, and this information can be applied in ANN learning to improve the prediction results.
- The results obtained from the variants K-Means and Fuzzy C-Means are very similar between them once the different parameters have been optimized. Differences are considered negligible in both MSE and MAE. The amount of information provided by both types of clustering can be considered similar.
- In the detail of the evolution of the error it can be observed that the evolution is much faster using metaplasticity and also the asymptotic final performance, so it can be extended to a very high improvement method in case of general

Big Data, where atypical patterns have usually irrelevant impact in the overall learning while being responsible of relevant information, as it must happen with the influence of atypical patterns in the PM_{10} concentrations.

5 Conclusions

In this paper, the artificial metaplasticity, a Bio-inspired method implemented on classical MLP, has been applied to the nowadays problem of pollutant concentration risk estimation. The goal of this research was to improve the accuracy of the prediction in previous recent published results while reducing the training time. The results show that the use of the AMMLP algorithm is an option for accurate pollutant concentration prediction and could be used as a computer aided system for taking decisions protecting public health. It also con be concluded that atypical patterns in the continuously growing Data Set of measures can be responsible of significant changes in PM_{10}, and most similar prediction methods are not considering properly their value for the overall performance of the prediction.

References

1. U.S.EPA: U.S. Environmental Protection Agency (2012). www.epa.gov/air/airpollutants.html
2. SESA: Spanish acronym for Spanish Society of Environmental Health (2008). http://www.sanidadambiental.com/2008/08/19/environment-and-health/
3. Andina, D., Ropero-Pelaez, J.: On the biological plausibility of artificial metaplasticity learning algorithm. Neurocomputing (2012). doi:10.1016/j.neucom.2012.09.028
4. Andina, D., Alvarez-Vellisco, A., Jevtic, A., Fombellida, J.: Artificial metaplasticity can improve artificial neural network learning. Intell. Autom. Soft Comput. Spec. Issue Signal Process. Soft Comput. **15**(4), 681–694 (2009)
5. Barron-Adame, J.M., Cortina-Januchs, M.G., Vega-Corona, A., Andina, D.: Unsupervised system to classify SO_2 pollutant concentrations in Salamanca, Mexico. Expert Syst. Appl. **39**, 107–116 (2012)
6. Cortina-Januchs, M.G., Quintanilla-Dominguez, J., Vega-Corona, A., Andina, D.: Development of a model for forecasting of PM_{10} concentrations in Salamanca, Mexico. Atmos. Pollut. Res. **6**, 626–634 (2015). doi:10.5094/APR.2015.071
7. Celik, M., Kadi, I.: The relation between meteorological factors and pollutants concentration in Karabuk city. G.U. J. Sci. **20**, 89–95 (2007)
8. D'Amato, G., Cecchi, L., D'Amato, M., Liccardi, G.: Urban air pollution and climate change as environmental risk factors of respiratory allergy: an update. J. Investig. Allergol. Clin. Immunol. **20**, 95–102 (2010)
9. Elminir, H.K.: Dependence of urban air pollutants on meteorology. Sci. Total Environ. **350**, 225–237 (2005)
10. Fombellida, J., Torres-Alegre, S., Piñuela-Izquierdo, J.A., Andina, D.: Artificial metaplasticity for deep learning: application to WBCD breast cancer database classification. In: Ferrández Vicente, J.M., Álvarez-Sánchez, J.R., de la Paz López, F., Toledo-Moreo, F.J., Adeli, H. (eds.) IWINAC 2015. LNCS, vol. 9108, pp. 399–408. Springer, Cham (2015). doi:10.1007/978-3-319-18833-1_42

11. Lee, S.H., Sung, Y.H., Lee, H.W.: Impact of regional trans-boundary ozone associated with complex terrain on urban air quality. Atmos. Environ. **42**, 7384–7396 (2008)
12. Nagendra, S.M.S., Khare, M.: Artificial neural network based line source models for vehicular exhaust emission predictions of an urban roadway. Transp. Res. Part D-Transp. Environ. **9**, 199–208 (2004)
13. Pearce, J.L., Beringer, J., Nicholls, N., Hyndman, R.J., Tapper, N.J.: Quantifying the influence of local meteorology on air quality using generalized additive models. Atmos. Environ. **45**, 1328–1336 (2011)
14. Perez, P., Trier, A., Reyes, J.: Prediction of $PM_{2.5}$ concentrations several hours in advance using neural networks in Santiago, Chile. Atmos. Environ. **34**, 1189–1196 (2000)
15. Ropero-Pelaez, J., Andina, D.: Do biological synapses perform probabilistic computations? Neurocomputing (2012). http://dx.doi.org/10.1016/j.neucom.2012.08.042

Towards Hospitalization After Readmission Risk Prediction Using ELMs

Jose Manuel Lopez-Guede[1(✉)], Asier Garmendia[1], Manuel Graña[1], Sebastian Rios[2], and Julian Estevez[1]

[1] Computational Intelligence Group, Basque Country University (UPV/EHU), San Sebastian, Spain
jm.lopez@ehu.es
[2] Business Intelligence Research Center (CEINE), Industrial Engineering Department, University of Chile, Beauche 851, Santiago 8370456, Chile

Abstract. A criteria to evaluate the performance of Emergency Departments (ED) is the number of readmissions and hospitalizations short time after discharge of patients because the problem was not solved in the first admission. Such events contribute to overload the care system and to worsening the health of patients. In this paper we address the problem of predicting hospitalization events after readmission in ED, facing it as a classification problem and using Extreme Learning Machines (ELM). We have carried out experiments with a dataset with 45,089 admission events of 21,269 pediatric patients recorded in the Hospital José Joaquín Aguirre of the University of Chile during 3 years and 4 months, improving the state-of-the-art sensitivity results on the same dataset by 17%.

1 Introduction

There is a growing concern about Emergency Department (ED) readmissions within a short period of time after a previous patient discharge, since they are indicative of either a bad quality of healthcare service, or structural problems in the healthcare systems. So there is a growing need for sensitive predictive tools in this scope to improve planning and distribution of resources. Some of to date efforts address specific populations, as geriatric patients [1] or specific fragile populations [2–4], while others focus on general healthcare services [5] or institution specific prediction models [6].

This paper deals with the problem of pediatric hospitalization after readmission prediction taking 3 days as time threshold, which has received little attention in the literature, posing this problem as a classification one.

The structure of the paper is as follows: Sect. 2 gives a background on the state-of-the-art approaches to readmission and hospitalization in ED and on ELMs. The problem faced in this paper is formally stated in Sect. 3, and the experimental design is described in Sect. 4 while Sect. 5 discusses the obtained results. Finally our main conclusions are given in Sect. 6.

J.M. Ferrández Vicente et al. (Eds.): IWINAC 2017, Part II, LNCS 10338, pp. 384–393, 2017.
DOI: 10.1007/978-3-319-59773-7_39

2 Background

This section is devoted to give a brief background on the state of the art in the scope of the readmission and hospitalization risk prediction in Subsect. 2.1, and in Extreme Learning Machines in Subsect. 2.2.

2.1 State-of-the-Art in Readmission and Hospitalization Risk Prediction Methods

Prediction of readmission and hospitalization after readmission risks have been addressed from a number of points of view, many times developing the studies focusing on specific types of populations, as shown in [7]. Usually the approaches combine physiological, biochemical, psychological, administrative and demographic data to compute a risk index. There are differences among care centers when implanting their electronic medical records and recording patient information, which lead to institution specific risk prediction models, i.e., computed with institution specific data [6], or even specific healthcare networks [5], in such a way that risk indices are limited to specific and aforementioned subpopulations, such as people suffering from Chronic Obstructive Pulmonary Disease [2]. Usually, the highest rates of readmission in ED, the longest stays, and the greatest resources are invested in ancillary tests corresponding to adults above 75 years old [3,8]. Although this intense use of resources, this kind of patients often leave the ED unsatisfied and with higher rates of misdiagnosis and medication errors, compared to younger patients. Additionally, they have a higher risk of ED readmission, hospitalization after readmission and death [9]. So, readmission risk prediction is critical for this subpopulation of patients [10]. Some specific characteristics as medication regime are less predictive than expected, but clustering patients have been found to improve prediction [4]. There are a number of methods to predict this and other risks in this scope, some of which are the following:

- The most typical approach is carried out through the LACE readmission index [11], developed from data collected by a network of Canadian hospitals. It has been defined based on logistic regression analysis of demographic and physiological data of a sample of near to 50,000 patients.
- A posterior approach, the LACE+ [12], uses administrative data to improve the risk prediction.
- Closely related to LACE, the HOMR (Hospital patient One year Mortality Risk) approach by [13] is a more recent model for predicting death within one year after hospital admission, as its name states. In this case, the authors pursued to predict long-term survival after admission to hospital, being the used variables included in the following categories: health status (Charlson comorbidity index, number of visits to hospital emergency, etc.), acuity disease (emergency admissions, direct intensive care unit admissions, etc.) and demographics (age, gender, etc.). The dataset used for the development and validation of this model consisted of more than three million instances obtained from several hospitals in the areas of Ontario, Alberta and Boston.

- An approach based on classification by Support Vector Machines (SVM) [6] allows to tune the prediction model for a particular population, avoiding to apply a risk index developed on a specific population characteristics to potentially very different populations.
- The same approach was followed by [14] in order to obtain prediction values specific for the pediatric patients of a specific hospital (Hospital José Joaquín Aguirre of the University of Chile), using four classification algorithms, namely Multilayer Perceptron (MLP), Decision Trees (DT), k-Nearest Neighbors (k-NN), and Naive Bayes (NB), reporting an accuracy of 0.78 and a sensitivity of 0.34. Details of the algorithms are well known and can be found in [15,16].

2.2 Extreme Learning Machines

Extreme Learning Machines (ELMs) [17,18] are classified as Single-Hidden Layer Feedforward Networks (SLFNs). They can be trained without iterative tuning, which confers them several interesting characteristics compared to classical back-propagation algorithm: they are easy to use, they require minimal human intervention, they have a faster learning speed and a higher generalization performance, and they are suitable for several nonlinear activation functions. The ELM approach to SFLN training consists of the following two steps:

1. Generate randomly the hidden layer weights $\mathbf{W}$, computing the hidden layer output $\mathbf{H} = g(\mathbf{WX})$ for the given data inputs $\mathbf{X}$, where $g(x)$ denotes the hidden units activation function, which can be sigmoidal, Gaussian or even the identity.
2. Solve the linear problem $\mathbf{H}\boldsymbol{\beta} = \mathbf{Y}$, where $\mathbf{Y}$ are the outputs of the data sample, and $\boldsymbol{\beta}$ the weights from the hidden layer to the output layer, by the mean least squares approach. Therefore $\hat{\boldsymbol{\beta}} = \mathbf{H}^{\dagger}\mathbf{Y}$, where $\mathbf{H}^{\dagger}$ is the pseudo-inverse.

3 Statement of the Problem

The problem that we are facing in this paper is to design a predictor of hospitalizations after a readmission of a patient in a ED 3 days after the discharge, in such a way that given a set of attributes or variables described in Subsect. 4.1, the predictor indicates whether the patient will be hospitalized or not. The predictor will be specific for a given population, namely of the Hospital José Joaquín Aguirre of the University of Chile.

4 Experimental Design

This section is devoted to explain the experimental design that has been implemented in order to get the objective of the paper. In Subsect. 4.1 we make a brief analysis of the dataset in order to obtain a summary of its more outstanding characteristics, while Subsect. 4.2 describes the ELM training process.

4.1 Dataset Analysis

The anonymized dataset used in this paper was recorded in the electronic medical record system of the Hospital José Joaquín Aguirre of the University of Chile between January 1st, 2013 and April 30, 2016, i.e., during 3 years and 4 months. The raw dataset is composed of ED 45,089 admission events of 21,269 pediatric patients.

At admission time a set of 17 variables were collected, including physiological values (e.g. temperature, breath rate, heart rate and blood pressure), biochemical values (e.g. glucose level) and demographic values (e.g. gender, age, fragility index). Besides, there are five triage levels to distribute the patients and the nurse had to select a motive for the admission, which is a categorical value among 500. If the time between visits to the ED falls below the readmission threshold, then it is a readmission event, otherwise it is an unrelated event. Readmission thresholds vary between countries for political or economical reasons, and we have considered a threshold of only 3 days because it is the regular value in Chile (the origin of the dataset).

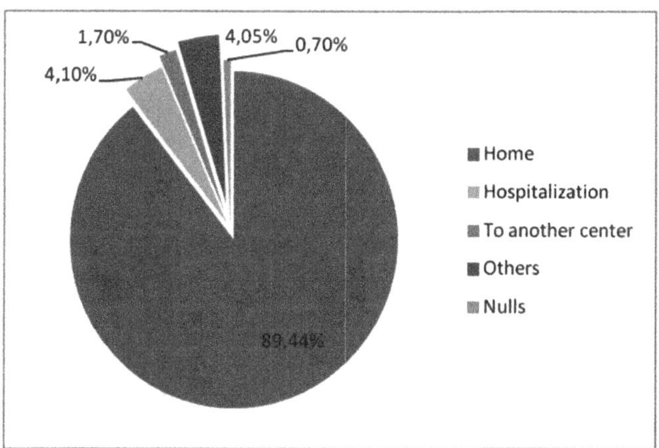

Fig. 1. Options for pediatric patients after discharge

As Fig. 1 shows, there is a variety of options at discharge: patients can go home (89.44 %), be hospitalized (4.10%), translated to another center (1.70%), or other situations (4.05%) including left without being seen (0.70%). It is a relevant event the hospitalization of a patient as a result of readmission, because it involves some lack of diagnosis or treatment leading to a worse condition of the patient.

The distribution of readmission events for a threshold of 3 days is shown in Fig. 2, where we can see that the 7.13% of ED admissions are in fact readmissions, implying the 11.73% of the patients.

The distribution of hospitalization events for a readmission threshold of 3 days is shown in Fig. 3. Though these events are rare compared to the total ED

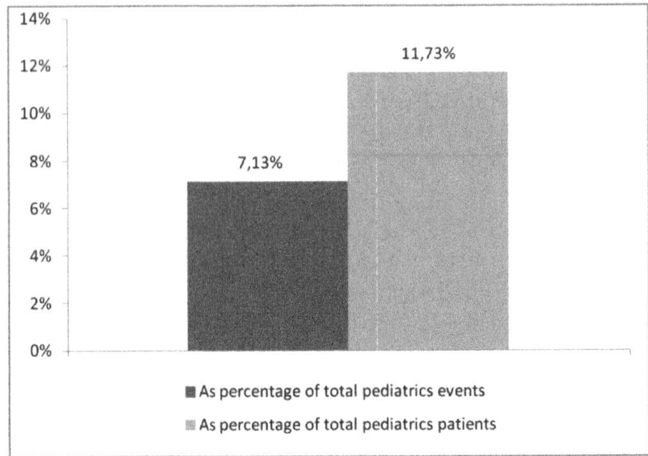

Fig. 2. Distribution of the number of pediatric readmissions

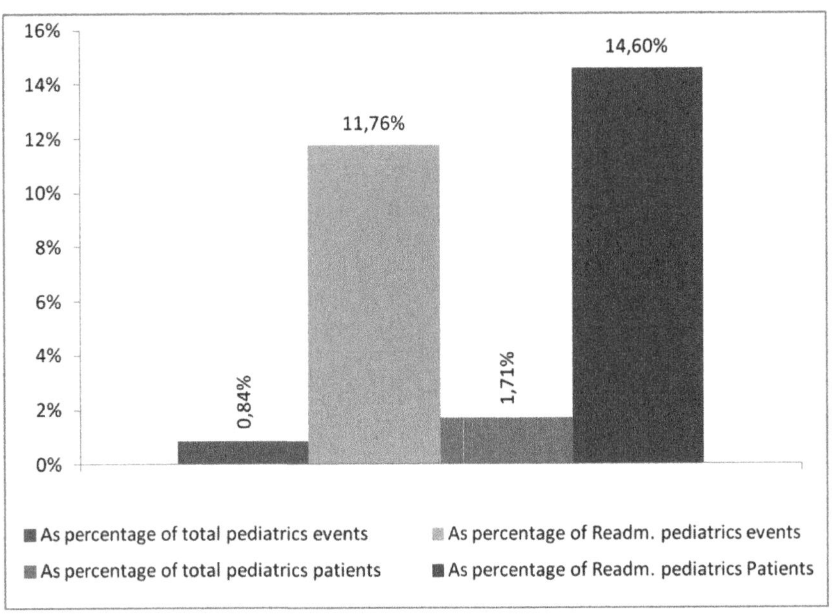

Fig. 3. Distribution of the number of pediatric admissions leading to hospitalization

events (0.84%), they are significant relative to the readmission events (11.76%), and the same can be stated regarding patients: the hospitalized patients are the 1.71% of the total but the 14.60% of the readmitted patients.

The most frequent (those accounting for 0.5% of the cases or more) readmission and hospitalization motives are provided in Table 1, for the patients that end up hospitalized after readmission, according to the readmission threshold of 3 days. The non-informative category OTHER is the most frequent, pointing to

Table 1. Distribution of the most salient motives for (a) readmissions, and (b) readmissions that lead to hospitalizations. (1/3DF: fever between 1 and 3 days, 24HF: fever <24 h, GAP: general abdominal pain, T: throwing up, D:diarrhea, 4/7DF: fever between 4 and 7 days, AD: acute disnea, FP3: pediatric fever 3 years, HA: headache, GD: general discomfort, EP: epigastric pain, LegP: leg pain, LuP: lumbar pain, IFPr: pain in the right iliac fossa, RFPl: pain in the left renal fossa, RFPr: pain in the right renal fossa)

Total Readmissions	
Motive	%
OTHERS	45.60
1/3DF	10.36
COUGH	7.59
24HF	6.78
GAP	4.92
T	4.89
D	3.39
4/7DF	2.49
FP3	1.06
NAUSEA/T	1.06
EXANTH	1.00
EARACHE	0.90
HA	0.87
AD	0.68
DYSURIA	0.62

(a)

Readmissions leading to Hospitalization	
Motive	%
OTHERS	39.42
COUGH	9.52
1/3DF	8.73
GAP	7.41
T	7.14
D	5.03
24HF	4.76
AD	3.70
4/7DF	2.65
NAUSEA/T	1.59
CC	1.06
HA	0.79
AAP	0.53
IFPr	0.53
F>1W	0.53

(b)

excessive workload on the nurses or difficulty to assess precisely the predefined categories. It can be observed that the distribution of motives is similar for both the readmissions and hospitalizations, with little variations in their ordering for the main motives, covering more than the 80% of the cases. The feature set is composed of the numerical codification of the variables measured at admission time, being this codification trivial in all variables, except for the motive. There are two possibilities regarding its codification. The first one to encode the motive is to define a binary variable per value, ending up with a feature space of more than 500 dimensions very sparsely populated, which poses many difficulties for training predictors. The other one has been used in this paper encoding the motive in a single numerical feature whose value is computed in one of two ways: (i) the percentage of hospitalizations for a given motive relative to the number of readmissions for this motive, and (ii) the position of the motive in the ranking of readmissions.

4.2 Predictor Training Process

In this paper we have posed the hospitalization prediction problem as a classification one into two classes. The class distribution in the dataset is strongly unbalanced, i.e., the number of samples of one class is much more greater than the other. Most classifier building approaches are biased towards the majority class, so that they achieve high classification accuracy but low sensitivity on the minority class, which is often the interesting one as in this case because the target hospitalization event is much more scarce than the admission. Therefore, accuracy is less relevant as a measure of performance than other measures focused on the positive minority class prediction. So, we pay attention to the indices defined by Eqs. 1, 2 and 3:

$$Accuracy = \frac{TP + TN}{N} \tag{1}$$

$$Sensitivity = \frac{TP}{TP + FN} \tag{2}$$

$$Specificity = \frac{TN}{TN + FP} \tag{3}$$

where N is the total elements of the prediction, TP is the number of true positives, TN is the number of true negatives, FP is the number of false positives and FN is the number of false negatives.

In order to build a predictor of hospitalization after readmission, the first step is to fix the structure of the network to train, being in this case a regular ELM. As explained in Sect. 3, the input of the network is the complete set of attributes of the electronic medical record of the readmission, while there is only one output indication if the readmission will lead to hospitalization. Another aspect to decide is how to use the gathered data in order to carry out the learning process. In this case, all the input data appear at once in a batch. They are used directly as obtained from the electronic record, avoiding to run any normalization nor preprocess. Both the input and target vectors have been divided into two sets using interleaved indices generating a partition where the 75% are used for training and the remaining 25% are used as a completely independent test of network generalization (i.e., for test). Regarding the activation function used in the hidden nodes, we have tried sigmoidal, sine, hardlim, triangular basis function and radial basis function. After carrying out a number of trials in a heuristical way we have decided to perform a pseudo-random search in the number of nodes search space, making 10 different trials for each of one of the selected number of nodes.

5 Experimental Results

This section is devoted to discuss the results that we have obtained following the training process described in Sect. 4. We are going to carry out the analysis of the obtained results in a comparative fashion, taking as reference the pediatric specific published results of [14] because in this reference the authors dealt with exactly the same dataset.

Table 2. Summary of the obtained results

	Test Sensitivity	Test Accuracy	Test Specificity	Learning time [s]
[14]	0.34	**0.78**	Not given	Not given
This work	**0.51**	0.58	**0.59**	**6.25**

As stated before in the paper, the hospitalization is a rare event, so we have paid much more attention to *Sensitivity* than to *Accuracy*, and besides we have computed the *Specificity*. Following this criteria, Table 2 shows a comparative study between the results obtained in [14] and the results of this paper, obtained using an ELM of 2,300 hidden nodes with the *sine* activation function, being the best result for each dimension in bold. We can see that we have improved the test sensitivity from 0.34 to 0.51 (true positives detection), at the expense of worsening the accuracy results from 0.78 to 0.58, while the specificity (true negatives detection) is 0.59. The learning time is 6.25 seconds, meaning that it is quasi-immediate to execute again a training process with this predictor in order to add new knowledge.

It is obvious that there is still work to do in order to improve these results, and some ideas on how to tackle this issue are the following:

- The dataset used to train the network is composed of raw and non-preprocessed data (un-normalized data).
- The dataset used to train the network has not been balanced, although paying attention to Table 1 it is obvious that not all the motives have the same importance.

6 Conclusions

The readmissions ratio is sometimes used as a measure of the quality of service of emergency departments (ED), implying any kind of penalization by the insurance companies if that event takes place under a time threshold, e.g., 3 days in Chile. The paper has started reviewing the state-of-the-art on the field of readmission and hospitalization prediction, where a number of different approaches have been used. We have faced this problem as a classification one, using a dataset of 45,089 admission events of 21,269 pediatric patients gathered during more than 3 years with a time threshold of 3 days, achieving a sensitivity of 0.51, a value better than the previous references of the literature for the same datast, but it is clear that there is a room for improvement.

Acknowledgments. The research was supported by the Computational Intelligence Group of the Basque Country University (UPV/EHU) through Grant IT874-13 of Research Groups Call 2013–2017 (Basque Country Government).

References

1. Besga, A., Ayerdi, B., Alcalde, G., Manzano, A., Lopetegui, P., Graña, M., González-Pinto, A.: Risk factors for emergency department short time readmission in stratified population. BioMed Res. Int. **2015** (2015)
2. Nguyen, H.Q., Chu, L., Amy Liu, I.L., Lee, J.S., Suh, D., Korotzer, B., Yuen, G., Desai, S., Coleman, K.J., Xiang, A.H., Gould, M.K.: Associations between physical activity and 30-day readmission risk in chronic obstructive pulmonary disease. 1 Department of Research and Evaluation, Kaiser Permanente Southern California, Pasadena, California. FAU - Chu, Lynna
3. Pereira, L., Choquet, C., Perozziello, A., Wargon, M., Juillien, G., Colosi, L., Hellmann, R., Ranaivoson, M., Casalino, E.: Unscheduled-return-visits after an emergency department (ed) attendance and clinical link between both visits in patients aged 75 years and over: a prospective observational study. PLoS One **10**(4), 1–13 (2015)
4. Olson, C.H., Dey, S., Kumar, V., Monsen, K.A., Westra, B.L.: Clustering of elderly patient subgroups to identify medication-related readmission risks. Int. J. Med. Inform. **85**(1), 43–52 (2016)
5. Hao, S., Wang, Y., Jin, B., Shin, A.Y., Zhu, C., Huang, M., Zheng, L., Luo, J., Hu, Z., Fu, C., Dai, D., Wang, Y., Culver, D.S., Alfreds, S.T., Rogow, T., Stearns, F., Sylvester, K.G., Widen, E., Ling, X.B.: Development, validation and deployment of a real time 30 day hospital readmission risk assessment tool in the maine healthcare information exchange. PLoS One **10**(10), 1–15 (2015)
6. Yu, S., Farooq, F., van Esbroeck, A., Fung, G., Anand, V., Krishnapuram, B.: Predicting readmission risk with institution-specific prediction models. Artif. Intell. Med. **65**(2), 89–96 (2015). http://dx.doi.org/10.1016/j.artmed.2015.08.005
7. Kansagara, D., Englander, H., Salanitro, A., et al.: Risk prediction models for hospital readmission: a systematic review. JAMA **306**(15), 1688–1698 (2011). http://dx.doi.org/10.1001/jama.2011.1515
8. Silverstein, M.D., Qin, H., Mercer, S.Q., Fong, J., Haydar, Z.: Risk factors for 30-day hospital readmission in patients=65 years of age. In: Proceedings (Baylor University Medical Center), vol. 21, no. 4, pp. 363–72, October 2008. pT: J; TC: 62; UT: MEDLINE:18982076
9. Carpenter, C.R., Heard, K., Wilber, S., Ginde, A.A., Stiffler, K., Gerson, L.W., Wenger, N.S., Miller, D.K.: Research priorities for high-quality geriatric emergency care: medication management, screening, and prevention and functional assessment. Acad. Emerg. Med. **18**(6), 644–654 (2011)
10. Deschodt, M., Devriendt, E., Sabbe, M., Knockaert, D., Deboutte, P., Boonen, S., Flamaing, J., Milisen, K.: Characteristics of older adults admitted to the emergency department (ed) and their risk factors for ed readmission based on comprehensive geriatric assessment a prospective cohort study. BMC Geriatr. **15**(1), 54 (2015). http://dx.doi.org/10.1186/s12877-015-0055-7
11. van Walraven, C., Dhalla, I.A., Bell, C., Etchells, E., Stiell, I.G., Zarnke, K., Austin, P.C., Forster, A.J.: Derivation and validation of an index to predict early death or unplanned readmission after discharge from hospital to the community. Can. Med. Assoc. J. **182**(6), 551–557 (2010). pT: J; TC: 144; UT: WOS:000275978300007
12. van Walraven, C., Wong, J., Forster, A.J.: Lace+ index: extension of a validated index to predict early death or urgent readmission after hospital discharge using administrative data. Open Med.: Peer-Rev. Indep. Open-Access J. **6**(3), e80–e90 (2012). pT: J; TC: 15; UT: MEDLINE:23696773

13. van Walraven, C., McAlister, F.A., Bakal, J.A., Hawken, S., Donze, J.: External validation of the hospital-patient one-year mortality risk (homr) model for predicting death within 1 year after hospital admission. Can. Med. Assoc. J. **187**(10), 725–733 (2015). pT: J; TC: 1; UT: WOS:000371005500009
14. Garmendia, A., Graña, M., Lopez-Guede, J.M., Rios, S.: Predicting patient hospitalization after emergency readmission. Cybern. Syst. **48**(3), 182–192 (2017). http://www.tandfonline.com/doi/abs/10.1080/01969722.2016.1276772
15. Graña, M., Nuñez-Gonzalez, J.D., Ozaeta, L., Kaminska-Chuchmala, A.: Experiments of trust prediction in social networks by artificial neural networks. Cybern. Syst. **46**(1–2), 19–34 (2015). http://dx.doi.org/10.1080/01969722.2015.1007725
16. Haykin, S., Networks, N.: A Comprehensive Foundation, 2nd edn. Prentice Hall PTR, Upper Saddle River (1998)
17. Huang, G.-B., Zhu, Q.-Y., Siew, C.-K.: Extreme learning machine: theory and applications. Neurocomputing **70**(1–3), 489–501 (2006)
18. Huang, G.-B., Wang, D., Lan, Y.: Extreme learning machines: a survey. Int. J. Mach. Learn. Cybern. **2**(2), 107–122 (2011)

Probabilistic Classifiers and Statistical Dependency: The Case for Grade Prediction

Bakhtiyor Bahritidinov and Eduardo Sánchez(✉)

Grupo de Sistemas Inteligentes (GSI),
Centro Singular de Investigación en Tecnologías de la Información (CITIUS),
Universidad de Santiago de Compostela,
15782 Santiago de Compostela, Spain
bakhtiyor.bahriddinov@gmail.com, eduardo.sanchez.vila@usc.es

Abstract. The research presented here aims at predicting grades by means of a set of relevant student's variables. To solve this problem, a probabilistic approach was applied in which we assume that the probability of obtaining a certain grade is conditioned on the personal attributes of each student. A Bayesian classifier was the natural choice to include the student's attributes in the estimation of the likelihood. However, a striking result was observed when the accuracy of the bayesian prediction was lower than the one provided by a baseline predictor based on student's clustering. A follow-up analysis explains the reason behind this result and provides a guideline for similar classification problems.

Keywords: Probabilistic models · Bayesian classifier · Statistical dependency · Education

1 Introduction

The ability to predict academic success is a key tool to evaluate the performance of learning programs [2]. Numerous explanatory factors have been proposed: partial grades and current performance [4], demographic characteristics and intermediate grades [6], level of attendance, study techniques and previous academic experience in the field [9], and grades in previous courses, academic level of the professor, and demographic attributes [7], to name a few. From a methodological point of view, the prediction models proposed so far mainly rely on machine learning techniques [5]: Bayesian classifiers [2], neural networks [4], decision networks [2,7,9], and regression methods [6,8].

In this article we explore the optimality of naive Bayesian classifiers to correctly predict student's grades. In what follows, we present the hypothesis underlying the research work, the experiment carried out to gather the data, the results in terms of accuracy of the Bayesian classifier and its comparison with a clustering-based model, and finally, the application of the mutual information measure to understand why the accuracy results did not confirm our prior expectations.

J.M. Ferrández Vicente et al. (Eds.): IWINAC 2017, Part II, LNCS 10338, pp. 394–403, 2017.
DOI: 10.1007/978-3-319-59773-7_40

2 Hypothesis

The naive Bayesian classifier is an optimal technique when the "naive" assumption, i.e. the attributes are independent, is satisfied. It can be shown that the misclassification rate is minimized when applying a "maximum a posteriori" (MAP) estimation to choose the class that maximizes the posterior probability [1]. Considering this background, we expected the grade prediction problem could be solved efficiently if the gathered student's attributes happen to be independent. The work shown here pretends to confirm this hypothesis.

3 Probabilistic Models

3.1 Experiment

The data were obtained from the course called "Design of Advanced Web Applications" (DAWA) corresponding to the third year of the Bachelor of Computer Science at the University of Santiago de Compostela. The experiment was held on two consecutive courses of 2013 and 2014 years, and therefore we have two sets of data, DAWA-13 and DAWA-14, the first with 19 students and the second with 33 students. The DAWA course is part of the Web Engineering specialty and is a continuation of an earlier course "Design of Web Applications" which is a mandatory course and that all students of DAWA have completed it. For each student the following information is known: (1) two attributes or variables of state, "Grade of DAW" and "level of previous knowledge" (2) two attributes or variables of context, "Availability to attend the class" and "The number of enrolled courses", (3) the utility of educational material for the practices of the course, and (4) the final grade. Table 1 describes these variables as well as their available values. Furthermore, the students assessed the utility of the activities and resources of the course using a Likert scale. Figure 1 illustrates a snapshot of the questionnaire used to gather this information.

3.2 Bayesian Classifier

In machine learning, the naive Bayes classifier is a powerful probabilistic technique that relies on the popular Bayes' theorem as well as on the assumption of independency between the attributes. From the Bayes' theorem, the posterior probability of getting grade G_i given a student S can be estimated as follows:

$$P(G_i|S) = \frac{P(S|G_i) * P(G_i)}{P(S)} \quad (1)$$

If a student S is characterized by means of independent attributes A_j, then the likelihood $P(S|G_i)$ could be computed through the following formula:

$$P(S|G_i) = \prod_j P(A_j|G_i) \quad (2)$$

Table 1. The attributes (variables) of the students used in the prediction model.

Attribute	Variable symbol	Categorical values	Numerical values
Availability to assist to theoretical classes and practices	a_1	Did not have conflict with any other courses	1
		Had to miss some sessions by coincidence with other courses	2
		Had to miss many sessions by coincidence with other courses	3
Which grade did you get in DAW	a_2	Suspended	1
		Passed	2
		Good	3
		Outstanding	4
		MH	5
Level of knowledge of web technologies	a_3	Low	1
		Medium	2
		Good	3
Number of enrolled courses in the semester	a_4	Less than 6	1
		Equal to 6	2
		More than 6	3
Utility	u	1, 2, 3, 4, 5	1, 2, 3, 4, 5
Final grade	g	Suspended	1
		Passed	2
		Good	3
		Outstanding	4
		MH	5

Substituting (2) in (1), we have:

$$P(G_i|S) = \frac{\prod_j P(A_j|G_i) * P(G_i)}{P(S)} \tag{3}$$

Now, if we consider the law of total probability, we can represent $P(S)$, the normalized term, as follow:

$$P(S) = \sum_i P(S|G_i) * P(G_i) \tag{4}$$

Substituting (4) in (3), we have:

$$P(G_i|S) = \frac{\prod_j P(A_j|G_i) * P(G_i)}{\sum_i P(S|G_i) * P(G_i)} \tag{5}$$

QUESTIONNAIRE FOR EVALUATION OF THE UTILITY OF COURSE ACTIVITIES
"DESIGN OF ADVANCED WEB APPLICATIONS"

1. STUDENT PROFILE: GOALS, INITIAL STATE AND PERSONAL CONTEXT

- **First and last name:**

- **What was your motivation before starting the course?**

Learn the Basics of Web Application Design	
Go deeper into Web Application Design concepts	

- **What was your goal regarding the grade before starting the course?**

Basically pass the course	
To get a good grade in the course	

- **Which grade did you get in DAW?**

Did you pass DAW?	YES NO
Which grade did you get in DAW (Suspended, Passed, Good, Outstanding, MH)	

- **What was your level of knowledge of web technologies before starting the course?**

Low (Basically what have been learnt in DAW)	
Medium (DAW and some personal experience)	
High (Personal and work experience)	

- **Work load during the semestr**

Number of credits of enrolled courses in the semester	
Number of enrolled courses in the semester	

- **Availability to assist to theoretical classes and practices**

Did not have conflict with any other courses	
Had to miss some sessions by coincidence with other courses	
Had to miss many sessions by coincidence with other courses	

2. EVALUATION OF PRACTICE 3

- Indicate the utility grade of previous activities for successfully carry out the practice 3.

Activity/Utility grade	**1**	**2**	**3**	**4**	**5**
Assist to theoretical class of subject 1 "Understanding the concept of web application"					
Assist to theoretical class of subject 2 "Modularizing web applications MVC1"					
Assist to theoretical class of subject 3 "Modularizing web applications MVC3"					
Perform exercise on MVC1 and beans: "Bean design for travel agency"					
Perform exercise on MVC2: "Design of travel agency with MVC2"					
Perform practice 1: "Refactoring and installation of work environment"					
Perform practice 2 "MVC1"					
Individual work					
Working with a partner					
Working in a group					
Search the web for additional resources					
Search in the library for additional resources					

1

Fig. 1. Snapshot of DAWA questionnaire

And applying (2) in (5), our final equation becomes:

$$P(G_i|S) = \frac{\prod_j P(A_j|G_i) * P(G_i)}{\sum_i \prod_j P(A_j|G_i) * P(G_i)} \tag{6}$$

This equation allows to derive $P(G_i|S)$ based on known data. $P(A_j|G_i)$ is the conditional probability of finding the attribute A_j given the grade G_i, and $P(G_i)$ is the probability of finding a student with a grade G_i in the dataset.

Now, we want to test if the attribute variables are independent or not. Two random variables X and Y are said to be independent if the probability distribution of one variable is not affected by the presence of another. We resorted to the following statistical techniques in order to prove/reject the independency of variables:

- Chi-square test of independence.
- Analyzing second-order correlations.
- Principal Component Analysis.

In a Chi-square test for independence, a null hypothesis is specified. In our case, we set as null hypothesis that variables A and B are independent. In addition the significance level of the test was set to 0.05. It means that if the cumulative probability based on chi-square distribution $P(X^2 \leq CV)$ is less than the significance level (0.05), we reject the null hypothesis, thus inferring that the alternative hypothesis, i.e. variables A and B are dependent, is correct. Tables 2 and 3 show the p-values of the Chi-square test on the 4 variables we use in our prediction model. From these data we conclude that all variables are independent in DAWA-13. The picture is slightly different in DAWA-14, in which the test between variables "Availability to assist to theoretical classes and practice" and "Grade of DAW" yields a p-value of $P(X^2 \leq CV) = 0.006$, and between "Level of knowledge of web technologies" and "Number of enrolled courses", a p-value of $P(X^2 \leq CV) = 0.03$. As these figures are less than the significance value, we should reject the null hypothesis for these specific cases and consider these variables as statistically dependent. In summary, the Chi-square test demonstrates that the variables are independent in the majority of cases. The analysis carried out with PCA and second-order correlations, not shown here, allow us to conclude that the independence assumption is met.

Table 2. Chi-square test of DAWA-13.

Variables	a_1	a_2	a_3	a_4
a_1	-	$0.18 > 0.05$	$0.86 \geq 0.05$	$0.4 > 0.05$
a_2	-	-	$0.39 > 0.05$	$0.42 > 0.05$
a_3	-	-	-	$0.75 > 0.05$
a_4	-	-	-	-

Table 3. Chi-square test of DAWA-14.

Variables	a_1	a_2	a_3	a_4
a_1	-	$0.006 < 0.05$	$0.05 \geq 0.05$	$0.34 > 0.05$
a_2	-	-	$0.31 > 0.05$	$0.12 > 0.05$
a_3	-	-	-	$0.03 < 0.05$
a_4	-	-	-	-

3.3 Baseline: Clustering-Based Classifier

To provide a comparative baseline, a clustering-based classifier was also built. First, the set of M students $S = s_m$, $m = 1..M$, was clustered into K groups or clusters. The clustering process relied on exploratory data analysis (EDA), a paradigm whose primary objective is the visual inspection of the data in order to detect possible patterns and correlations [10]. In this work we have used classical graphical techniques such as bars (Fig. 2), probability density graphics (Fig. 3), and box plots, among others, to identify the student's clusters. Second, the conditional probability of a student in cluster c_j obtaining grade g_i, $P(g_i|c_j)$, was estimated for all g_i and c_j. At the prediction stage, for any new student s_k, the cluster to which the student belongs, c_j^*, was identified. The conditional probability of obtaining a certain grade g_i for cluster c_j^*, $P(g_i|c_j^*)$, was then computed. Finally, once the conditional probabilities were calculated for each

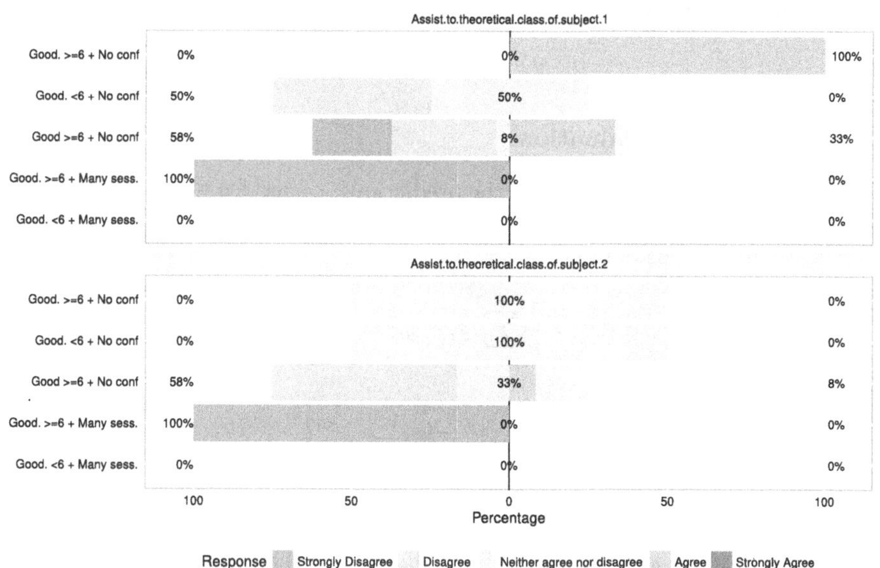

Fig. 2. Bar graphs show the utility degree of classroom activities for one of the projects of the course. Each horizontal line summarizes the results for each group (left legend)

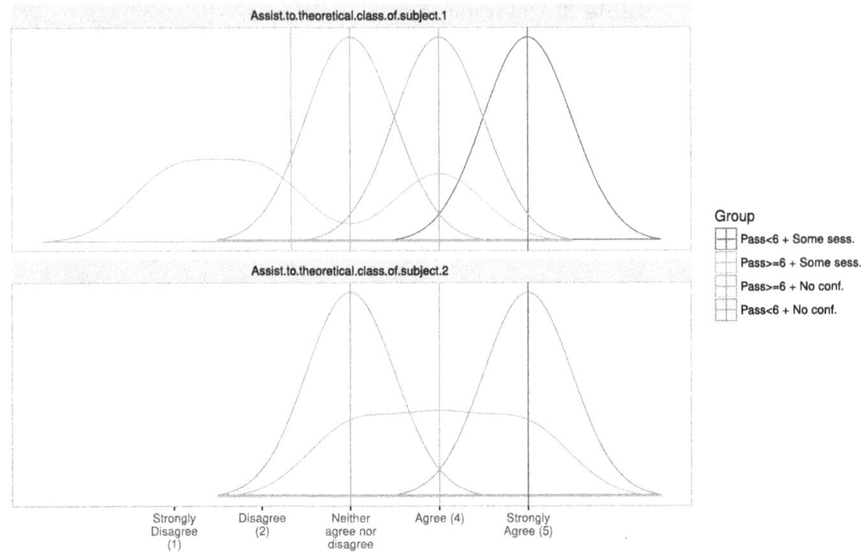

Fig. 3. Probability density graphics associated with utility of classroom activities for one of the projects of the course. The color of each density identifies a group of students (right legend). (Color figure online)

grade g_i, we made the prediction by choosing grade g^*, which maximizes the conditional probability:

$$g^* = arg_g max(P(g_i|c_j^*)) \tag{7}$$

3.4 Performance Evaluation

In order to evaluate the accuracy of the predictions, we used standard measures of error: the mean absolute error (MAE) and the root mean-squared error (RMSE). These measures are calculated as follows:

$$MAE = \frac{1}{n}\sum_{i=1}^{n}|f_i - y_i| = \frac{1}{n}\sum_{i=1}^{n}|e_i| \tag{8}$$

$$RMSE = \sqrt{\frac{\sum_{t=1}^{n}(\check{y}_t - y_t)^2}{n}} \tag{9}$$

3.5 Results

Tables 4 and 5 show the results of the evaluation of the probabilistic models in datasets DAWA-13 and DAWA-14:

- Bayesian - using a Bayesian classifier.

Table 4. The evaluation of model M-13 constructed by the dataset of DAWA-13, using the dataset of DAWA-14

	Clustering-based	Bayesian
MAE	0.5152	0.6667
RMSE	0.8257	0.9535

Table 5. The evaluation of model M-14 constructed by the dataset of DAWA-14, using the dataset of DAWA-13

	Clustering-based	Bayesian
MAE	0.4211	0.5555
RMSE	0.7255	0.8819

- Clustering-based - the clusters were created manually using exploratory data analysis. The following variables were used for clustering (see Table 1): a_1, a_2, a_3 and a_4.

In both datasets (DAWA-13 and DAWA-14) the clustering-based classifier yields more accurate predictions (lower MAE and RMSE) than the Bayesian classifier, i.e. the prediction model constructed with Bayesian classifier is weaker than the basic baseline model.

4 Why Bayesian Classifier Does Not Work? Relationship Between Explanatory and Response Variables

We wanted to understand the reason why the prediction accuracy of the Bayesian classifier is worse than the clustering-based baseline. A line of research was to analyze the degree of dependency between the explanatory and the response values of both models. While the response value is the same for both classifiers, i.e. the final grade, the explanatory variables are different: four student's attributes for Bayesian classifier, and one student's cluster for the clustering-based approach.

4.1 Mutual Information Measure

The mutual information measure was used to quantify the degree of statistical dependence between each explanatory variable and the response variable. The mutual information between two random variables X and Y is defined as follows:

$$I(X;Y) = H(X) + H(Y) - H(X,Y) \tag{10}$$

where $H(X)$ and $H(Y)$ are the marginal entropies and $H(X,Y)$ is the joint entropy of the random variables. In information theory, entropy is the average

Table 6. Mutual information between student's attributes (a_1 to a_4) and final grade (g) of courses DAWA-13 and DAWA-14.

	a_1	a_2	a_3	a_4
g(DAWA-13)	0.1254	0.4550	0.2459	0.1254
g(DAWA-14)	0.2346	0.5673	0.2556	0.2549

Table 7. Mutual information between student's clusters and final grade (g) of courses DAWA-13 and DAWA-14

	Clusters (EDA)
g(DAWA-13)	0.8914
g(DAWA-14)	1.0235

amount of information contained in each message received. It is calculated using following formula:

$$H(X) = -\sum_i P(x_i) * log_b P(x_i) \tag{11}$$

where b is the base of the logarithm used. Common values of b are 2, Euler's number e, and 10. In our analysis we used $b = 2$. When the joint entropy equals the sum of the marginal entropies, $I(X;Y)$ is zero, which means that variables X and Y are fully independent. On the other hand, positive values of $I(X;Y)$ indicate a degree of dependence: the higher the value of $I(X;Y)$, the larger the dependency between X and Y.

4.2 Results

Table 6 presents the analysis of mutual information between the student's attributes and the final grade of both courses DAWA-13 and DAWA-14. A low degree of dependence is observed for all variables. The results are different in the case of the relationship between student's clusters and the final grade. Table 7 shows that the dependency between clusters, considered as a random variable, and the final grade is surprisingly high. These figures would explain the reason why the clustering-based classifier performs better than the Bayesian classifier. In the next section a detailed discussion of this finding is provided.

5 Discussion

Probabilistic classifiers seem to be good candidates to solve the grade prediction problem. The task is complex and the degree of uncertainty is high as the same student can behave quite differently on different subjects depending on personal and context factors. Among the family of probabilistic models, the naive Bayesian classifier is a natural choice in order to include the observed student's attributes in the estimation of the likelihood. After analyzing and confirming that the attributes were independent, we expected that the problem might be solved efficiently through the Bayes' approach. However, the comparison with a clustering-based classifier, which was built as a baseline, proved this hypothesis to be wrong. This finding was at odds with the fact that the clustering-based classifier does not handle specific student's information, but an aggregated knowledge synthesized in the cluster to which the student is assigned. In order to analyze and understand this contradiction, a measurement of the degree of dependency between explanatory and response variables was carried out. The estimation of the mutual information shed light on the problem and revealed that the clustering process was in fact creating a new random variable, the cluster coefficient, with a significant degree of statistical dependence with the response variable, i.e. the final grade. This relationship explains the superior performance in our setting of the clustering-based classifier. It also points out the benefits of EDA as a tool to explore patterns and relationships in the data before choosing any particular classification technique from the available library or toolkit.

Acknowledgments. This work has received financial support from the Ministry of Science and Innovation of Spain under grant TIN2014-56633-C3-1-R as well as from the Consellería de Cultura, Educación e Ordenación Universitaria (accreditation 2016–2019, ED431G/08) and the European Regional Development Fund (ERDF).

References

1. Domingos, P., Pazzani, M.: On the optimality of the simple Bayesian classifier under zero-one loss. Mach. Learn. **29**, 103–130 (1997)
2. Edin, O., Mirza, S.: Data mining approach for predicting student performance. Econ. Rev. - J. Econ. Bus. **X**(1), 3–12 (2012)
3. Friedman, N., Geiger, D., Goldszmidt, M.: Bayesian network classifiers. Mach. Learn. **29**, 131–163 (1997)
4. Gedeon, T.D., Turner, H.S.: Explaining student grades predicted by a neural network. In: Proceedings of 1993 International Joint Conference on Neural Networks, IJCNN 1993, Nagoya, vol. 1, pp. 609–612 (1993)
5. Klosgen, W., Zytkow, J.: Handbook of Data Mining and Knowledge Discovery. Oxford University Press, New York (2002)
6. Kotsiantis, S.B., Pintelas, P.E.: Predicting students marks in Hellenic Open University. In: Fifth IEEE International Conference on Advanced Learning Technologies, ICALT 2005, pp. 664–668 (2005)
7. Qasem, A.A., Emad, M.S., Mustafa, I.N.: Mining student data using decision trees. In: International Arab Conference on Information Technology (2006)
8. Rutger, K., Henk, F.: Predicting academic success in higher education: what's more important than being smart? Eur. J. Psychol. Educ. **27**(4), 605–619 (2012)
9. Superby, J.F., Vandamme, J-P., Meskens, N.: Determination of factors influencing the achievement of the first-year university students using data mining methods. In: Proceedings of the Workshop on Educational Data Mining at the 8th International Conference on Intelligent Tutoring Systems, pp. 37–44 (2006)
10. Tukey, J.W.: Exploratory Data Analysis. Pearson, London (1977)

OntoLexmath: An Ontology for Dealing with Mathematical Lexicon

M. Angélica Pinninghoff J.[1], Angel Castillo C.[1], Pedro Salcedo L.[2], and Ricardo Contreras A.[1](✉)

[1] Department of Computer Science, University of Concepción, Concepción, Chile
{mpinning,rcontrer}@udec.cl

[2] Research and Educational Informatics Department, University of Concepción, Concepción, Chile
psalcedo@udec.cl

Abstract. This work is aimed to the design and implementation of an ontology, for helping to quantify and describe the lexicon of students in a particular location, focused on mathematics. The idea is to build a tool that can help to share, via Internet, this particular lexicon, encouraging new research efforts pointing to support new educational systems. The final product, the resulting ontology, was evaluated taking into account different parameters as suggested by the selected methodology, showing that results satisfy the initial goals of the project.

Keywords: Ontology · Mathematical lexicon

1 Introduction

The key idea of this work focuses in the learning process of students. Even if students are capable of handling a lexicon that allows the communication among them, this lexicon is not rich enough, sometimes, to ensure the understanding of texts in a specific topic. A typical example of that is the form in which students deal with a text of mathematics. As students are in the process of learning to use the language, that increases according to the typical scholar advance, there is a set of new terms that need to be acquired by the students. However, an important part of the set of new terms cannot be successfully transferred to the students.

Different authors propose that increasing the students lexicon can improve the learning process performance and, at the same time, can enhance their ability to deal with any communicative situation. There is a general agreement in the sense that humans have a mental dictionary, the lexicon, that consists of a set of lexical units, which can behave dynamically and that are influenced by the context around the individual, and by the time period in which the individual is present. LEXMATH [10] is an example of a tool that allows for studying the lexicon, measuring the lexicon and extracting some relevant indexes.

J.M. Ferrández Vicente et al. (Eds.): IWINAC 2017, Part II, LNCS 10338, pp. 404–412, 2017.
DOI: 10.1007/978-3-319-59773-7_41

LEXMATH is a tool that accomplish three key tasks:

- It quantifies and describes the lexicon of high school level students in the interests topics of numbers (arithmetic), algebra, geometry probabilities and statistics.
- It elaborates a didactical proposal to develop an adaptive hypermedia, in the sense of being a software capable of storing documents (in the form of texts, audios, videos and graphics) for a non convention al access, i.e., offering a free navigational style. The hypermedia defined in the previous way allows to increase the lexical availability in the previously mentioned topics.
- In creates an on-line computational lexicon that, under the paradigm of the semantic web, shares latent and available lexicons, as well as the statistical indexes and the graphs that represent the corresponding semantic relationships.

The third task is relevant for the present work, because it is necessary to have an ontology for sharing the set of available lexicons stored. The key issue here is the knowledge representation under the concept of semantic web.

An ontology is a simple and abstract model of a particular phenomena, in which it is possible to identify the fundamental concepts and entities for the phenomena, the relationships existing among them and the constraints that rule those relationships. An ontology needs to be readable for humans and computers, where the represented knowledge is not property of a particular individual, but it is accepted by a group or community.

An ontology defines a common lexicon for those who need to share information about a particular domain. It contains basic concept definitions end their relationships and can be interpreted by a machine. The reasons for developing an ontology are: (i) to share the common understanding among people or software agents, (ii) to allow the re-use of existing knowledge in a domain, (iii) to make explicit suppositions about a domain, and (iv) to analyze the available knowledge for the domain.

This work aims to develop ontology to allow the implementations of applications or systems that use the knowledge stored in LEXMATH. In other words, an ontology for the LEXMATH project is developed, and the considered domains are the mathematical lexicons for a group of students in a particular geographic location, where lexicons are obtained taking into account different topics.

This article is structured as follows; the first section is the present introduction. Second section present a summarized theoretical frame, describing the context of the problem. The third section presents the proposal. Section four describes some results and finally, in section five, conclusions are presented.

2 Theoretical Frame

The term ontology is used to denote the philosophical study of the nature of being, becoming, existence or reality as well as the basic categories of being and their relations. In other words, it describes the science of being, the types and structures of objects, their properties, events, processes and relationships in every aspect of reality [11]. In artificial intelligence, or more precisely in knowledge representation, the term ontology is used to describe a set of basic concepts definition and the fundamental relationships that form teethe lexicon in a specific topic, and the rules for combining terms and relationships to define the lexicon extensions. According to Gruber [4], an ontology is *a explicit specification of a concept.* This definition indicates that an ontologies supplies a structure an the explicit contents to describe a reality and the corresponding (implicit) rules. In 1997 Borst introduced a modification to the previous definition: ontologies are defined as a formal specification of a shared conceptualization [1].

Based on the definitions of Gruber and Borst, Struder et al. added more expressivity through new terminology:

- Conceptualization. Refers to a simple and abstract model representing some phenomena, resulting of the identification of relevant entities and concepts of the phenomena, and the detection of the existing relationships.
- Explicitation. Refers to the fact that that the used concepts and the constraints that rule their use are explicitly defined.
- Formalization. An ontology should be readable or legible by people and processable by computers.
- Sharing. It reflects the fact that an ontology captures consensual knowledge, i.e., knowledge that is accepted by a group or community.

In an ontology, definitions associate entity names that belong to a domain containing classes, relationships, functions or other objects, describing the meaning of the names, and the axioms that rule the interpretation and use of these terms [4]. In other words, an ontology allows to make explicit the objects that belong to a particular universe, their properties and their constraints, and the way in which the objects are organized based on their existing relationships; i.e., an ontology introduces a structure for the domain and introduces limits to the valid interpretations.

2.1 Ontology Components

Common components in every ontology are concepts, properties, relationships, axioms and instances [2,4,7].

A concept is a thing about which something can be assessed. It may be a physical object (a dog, a house) or an abstracto object (a function, a strategy). Concepts are represented as a set of classes that are relevant for the domain and are described by specifying the conditions that must be fulfilled for belonging to that class. A class may be divided into subclasses, representing more specific concepts. A typical example is *Educational Institution.* This class represents the set of all possible educational institution in the context of the ontology defined for the country (Chile).

A property is a set of specifications, characteristics or attributes of a class. The values associated to the specifications, to the valid intervals and to the constraints, are those that describe the classes of an ontology. A typical example is *Type of Institution*, considering values like private institution, state institution, or other.

A relationship represents the interaction that exists among the concepts of a domain. Ontologies normally contain binary relationships. A typical example of this type of relationship is *belongs to a state*, that represents the set of educational institutions that belongs to a particular state.

Axioms contain rules and constraints to the values of classes or to the values a property, in a relationship, can hold. Axioms are true assessments valid in a domain and can be denoted in terms of first order logic. Additionally, axioms can be structural or not. Structural axioms establish conditions related to the hierarchies of an ontology. Non structural axioms are used to describe relationships among attributes of a concept and are specific for the domain. A typical example is: an educational institution can belong only to one type of institution.

Instances represents specific elements of a class. Instances cannot be divided into parts and are grouped into classes. A typical example of instance for the class *State* could be (to use a known geographic location) New York, Indiana, Nevada, etc.

2.2 Ontologies Use

Ontologies help to the communication process, because they supply a common domain understanding. It allows for avoiding misunderstandings of terms and concepts. Additionally, there exists the capability of reusing knowledge in a specific domain by making visible assumptions about this domain, or by analyzing this knowledge [7].

In [13] appears a classification of ontologies applications, for helping developers to understand specific stages of ontologies use. Every stage includes a general view that identify the purpose of the ontology, the role of the ontology, the necessary participants (actors) and the technological support. Three different stages are identified: (i) *Neutral authorship.* An information artifact is created in a language and translated to different formats for being used in different systems. This approach includes the knowledge reuse, maintenance improvement, and long term knowledge storage. The artifact can be an ontology or a set of operational data. (ii) *Common information access.* Information is requested by one or more persons or applications, but the format is unfamiliar or non accesible. The ontology helps to answer the requested information in a readable format. The benefits of this approach include inter-operability and a more effective use and reuse of knowledge. (iii) *Ontology search-based.* The ontology is used to search for a particular information source (documents, web pages, etc.). The main advantage of this approach is a fast access to information resources.

2.3 LEXMATH and Types of Lexicon

It is necessary to introduce some fundamental concepts related to lexical availability: (i) *mental lexicon*, that can be understood as a lexical units storage that a speaker can use or recognize in written or spoken format. The mental lexicon represents an individual knowledge and it is probably a subset of a community lexicon; (ii) *available lexicon*, is the set of words that immediately comes to the speaker mind when dealing with a specific topic; (iii) *interest center*, that are words used to trigger the mental lexicon of a speaker in a lexical availability test; (iv) *lexical unit*, the basic unit used to count the number of concepts a speaker stores in his mental lexicon; the lexical units may contain one or more words; and (v) *lexical availability index*, is a value that indicates the degree of availability of a term in the speaker mind; it is used to describe the difficulty level to get a concept for a speaker that needs to use it.

LEXMATH is a software that helps to deal with lexical availability. The software allows to realize on-line lexical availability test, to generate reports containing the necessary indexes for a particular interest center study. Among the indexes, perhaps the most relevant is the lexical availability index (LAI) for every word which, when ordered in descending order, represents the mental lexicon of a community.

LEXMATH allows to quantify and to describe the lexicon of high school students in different interest topics in mathematics (geometry, algebra and others). The software can create an on-line lexicon for studying and sharing it through the use of Internet. Additionally, the software permits an automatic available lexicon update for different geographic locations. Because of these characteristics, the software can be used for developing other educational systems and for supporting other research projects to include new geographic locations, new interest centers and other thematic areas.

3 The Proposal

When representing something through an ontology, some desirable characteristics should be established. An ontology is expected to communicate and, for this reason definitions should be as clear as possible. Every definition needs a natural language description. An ontology allows to make inferences that are consistent with the definitions, i.e., there is a set of logically consistent axioms.

An ontology is built to support new terms definition based on the current vocabulary. The quantity of assumptions must be reduced, the diversification of considered hierarchies is assumed to be a tool for increasing the multiple heredity mechanisms. Additionally, similar concepts are grouped for representing them as elements of a subclass, and are defined by using the same set of primitive rules. Finally, it is a good practice to define rules for names' creation, a simple agreement that helps when maintaining an ontology.

To develop any ontology, it is necessary to adopt a specific methodology. Among the set of available methodologies there is no agreement to accept a standard one. Every developing group has used their own set of principles, design criteria and the sequence of stages for building an ontology. Nevertheless, there exist some methodologies that have been commonly used according the available literature: Cyc, proposed by Lenat and Cuga in 1990 [6]; the methodology proposed by Uschold and King [12]; the method proposed by Gruninger and Fox [5]; the Methontology method proposed by a group of the Madrid Polytechnic University in 1996 [3] and the Ontology Development 101 methodology, a proposal from the Stanford University [7].

The Ontology Development 101 methodology was selected in this work, because the simplicity to explain concepts through examples, giving a starting point that helps new ontology designers during the development stage. As they say, there is not a correct and simple methodology for designing ontologies, but it presents useful ideas based on the experience in the process of building ontologies. Fundamental recommendations in this methodology are: specify the domain and the scope for the ontology, the intended use of the ontology, re-use ontologies and existing lexicons, enumerate the relevant terms in the domain, to define the class hierarchy, and create the corresponding instances.

Development tools are those that help for new ontologies construction, or for reusing existing ontologies. We selected Protégé [8], based on a set of interesting features, it is an open code tool, free, is periodically updated and it offers an important number of plugins that allow to develop queries, visualize and validate ontologies. There is a community of users and developers that support their use and because their popularity, most of tutorial and guides are based on this tool.

There are three fundamental tasks for obtaining the necessary knowledge from the domain. The first task deals with the search process in the existing documentation, mainly diagrams and data models that describe the domain. The second task is devoted to retrieve, from experts, rules or cases of use that are not contained in the documentation, but are necessary during the implementation stage. The third task considers other sources useful for understand and describe the domain, mainly public databases that contain statistical information.

The information model for Lexmath describes the lexicon for students in a particular city (Concepción, Chile) in mathematics. The lexicon corresponds to lexical units obtained through surveys by considering a given topic which is partitioned into sub-topics with more specific contents.

The students lexicon consists of lexical units obtained through a set of surveys, under the context of a given thematic center. Every thematic center belongs to an interest center and, if necessary, a thematic center can be partitioned into thematic sub-centers containing more specific information. The lexicon presents a series of characteristics to establish a relationship between the interest center and the students, the students level or their geographic location. The lexicon also contains a lexical availability index for every lexical unit, a value that can be modified as a results of new surveys.

The W3C Web Ontology Language (OWL) is a Semantic Web language designed to represent rich and complex knowledge about things, groups of things, and relations between things. The THING class is the set that contains all the individuals and hence is the root of every taxonomic three. All existing classes are sub-classes under THING. Under THING we can find the eight classes that are part of OntoLexmath, and from that starting point we obtain the thirty-seven subclasses that compose this ontology. The seven classes are: (i) EducationalInstitution, (ii) Lexicon, (iii) EducationalLevel, (iv) Person, (v) LexicalAvailabilityIndex, (vi) Topic, (vii) GeographicLocation and (viii) LexicalUnit.

The class *EducationalInstitution* represents any organizational unit which serves to an educative purpose. This class is divided into five sub-classes according to the Chilean Educational System, ranging from technical formative level to university level. This class *EducationalInstitution* is illustrated in Fig. 1.

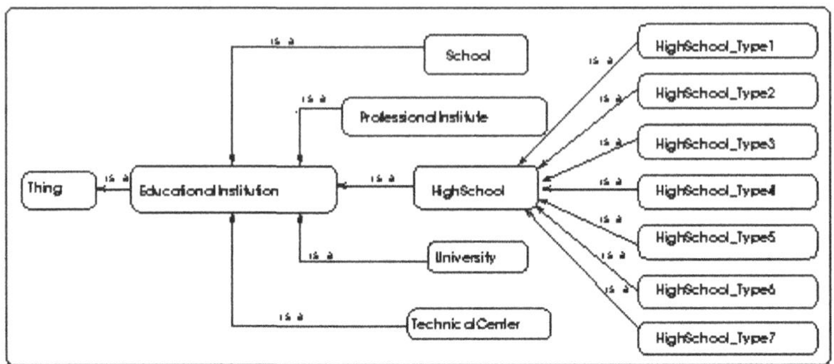

Fig. 1. The structure for class EducationalInstitution

In every class there exist some constraints, that rules the way in which the properties are considered in a class instance. There are some constraints that indicate the values to be used (property constraint) and others that indicate the quantity of values that a property can hold (cardinality constraint).

4 Results

To evaluate the quality of an ontology, we adopted the proposal of Ramos [9], which considers four elements: (i) the use of the adequate language, (ii) taxonomical accuracy, (iii) the vocabulary validity and, (iv) the capability of answering to requirements. This is illustrated in Fig. 2.

During the evaluation process, different tools were employed, the ontologies editor Protégé; Fact++, a descriptive logic classifier for extracting the knowledge from the concepts defined in an ontology and to infer new relationships that are not explicit in the original model; Pellet, a classifier which allows to validate the ontology consistence; Hermit, an open code classifier for OWL ontologies. Fact++, Pellet and Hermit are included as part of Protégé; in summary they allow to verify the ontology from the taxonomic point of view and allow to carry on the inference process. SPARQL is a query language for RDF graphs. In Protégé, SPARQL questions are supported by a complement called SPARQL Query, which offers a user interface to write a query and to visualize results.

Related to the first element, the use of the adequate language, the use of OWL language guarantees that conclusions are computable and computations are loved in finite time. As a result of using Protégé, there are no syntactic inconsistencies and the generated code satisfies the standard.

Related to the second element, by using Fact++, Pellet and Hermit, it was possible to verify the absence of inconsistencies. Additionally, the hierarchical

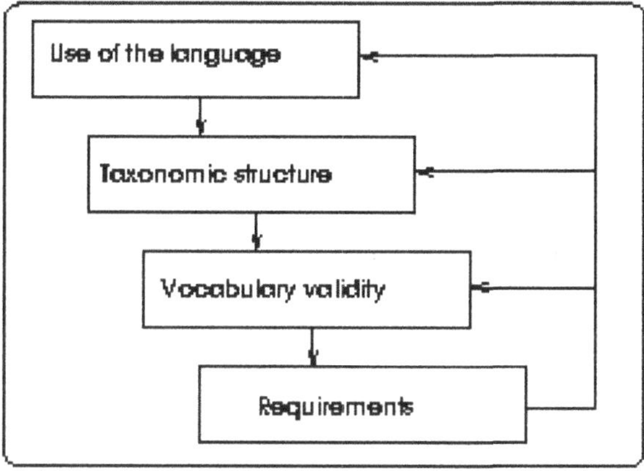

Fig. 2. A typical schema for the ontology evaluation

structure defined corresponds to the hierarchical structure considered the input to the system.

Taking into account the third element, the vocabulary validity, and by considering the selected corpus, the value for *precision* indicates that 100% of the terms coded into the ontology exist into the corpus. The result for *recall* indicates that 100% of terms present in the corpus exist in the ontology.

5 Conclusions

Taking into account that an ontology is created by considering different elements from different information sources, the adequate selection ensures the quality model. The selected elements were validated with the help of experts in the domain and the domain was extended as new requirements appeared. It allows to have an ontology that reflects the knowledge contained in LEXMATH, satisfying the expected quality.

To evaluate an ontology is a relevant process. In this work, the evaluation schema produced a set of results that satisfy the requirements defined during the development stage, which indicates that the ontology contains the required elements to model the domain and allows to carry on valid inferences respect to the knowledge present in LEXMATH.

References

1. Borst, W.N.: Construction of engineering ontologies for knowledge sharing and reuse. Ph.D. thesis, University of Twente (1997)
2. Farquhar, A., Fikes, R., Rice, J.: Tools for assembling modular ontologies in Ontolingua. In: Proceedings of Fourteenth American Association for Artificial Intelligence Conference (AAAI 1997) (1997)

3. Gómez-Pérez, A., Fernández, M., Vicente, A.: Towards a method to conceptualize domain ontologies. In: Budapest: ECAI96 Workshop on Ontological Engineering (1996)
4. Gruber, T.R.: Toward Principles for the design of ontologies used for for knowledge sharing. Stanford Knowledge System Laboratory (1993)
5. Grüninger, M., Fox, M.: Methodology for the design, evaluation of ontologies. In: Montreal: Workshop on Basic Ontological Issues in Knowledge Sharing (1995)
6. Lenant, D., Guha, R.: Building Large Knowledge-Based System: Representation and Inference in the Cyc Proyect. Addison-Wesley, Boston (1990)
7. Noy, N., McGuiness, D.: Ontology development 101: a guide to creating your first ontology. Stanford knowledge systems laboratory technical report KSL-01-05 and Stanford medical informatics technical report SMI–0880 (2001)
8. Protégé V.4.3. http://protege.stanford.edu/. Accessed Aug 2016
9. Ramos, E., Núñez, H., Casañas, R.: Esquema para evaluar ontologías únicas para un dominio de conocimiento. Revista Venezolana de Información, Tecnología y Conocimiento (2009)
10. Salcedo Lagos, P., del Valle, M., Contreras Arriagada, R., Pinninghoff, M.A.: LEX-MATH - a tool for the study of available lexicon in mathematics. In: Ferrández Vicente, J.M., Álvarez-Sánchez, J.R., de la Paz López, F., Toledo-Moreo, F.J., Adeli, H. (eds.) IWINAC 2015. LNCS, vol. 9108, pp. 11–19. Springer, Cham (2015). doi:10.1007/978-3-319-18833-1_2
11. Smith, B.: Ontology. In: Blackwell Guide to the Philosophy of Computing and Information, pp. 155–166. Blackwell, Oxford (2004)
12. Uschold, M., King, M.: Towards a methodology for building ontologies. In: Montreal: IJCAI95 Workshop on Basic Ontological Issues in Knowledge Sharing (1995)
13. Uschold, M., Jasper, R.: A framework for understanding and classifying ontology applications. In: Stockholm: Proceedings of the IJCAI 1999 Workshop on Ontologies and Problem Solving Methods (KRR5) (1999)

A Propose Architecture for Situated Multi-agent Systems and Virtual Simulated Environments Applied to Educational Immersive Experiences

O. Calvo, Jose M. Molina, Miguel A. Patricio, and A. Berlanga(✉)

Applied Artificial Intelligence Group, University Carlos III of Madrid, Madrid, Spain
miguelangel.patricio@uc3m.es, aberlan@ia.uc3m.es

Abstract. Education and *Multiagent Systems* share a common space on *Virtual Immersive Environments*. To build a new type of *Educational Experience*, a framework called *SSR-Hub* has been implemented following the *Deployment Representation Model* here proposed. We will describe the details of this educational experience stressing the synergies found on MASs over IVE systems. Finally the results of the experiment will be evaluated. Also, next steps to this research line and educational virtual laboratory platform strengths are discussed.

1 Introduction

The confluence between the teaching activity and the artificial intelligence has several uncharted points. One of those is how Education can benefit of the *Multi-agent Systems* (commonly referred as MAS) field of study. This task seems to be complicated for the different natures of both worlds, aside of teaching proper MAS discipline techniques itself.

But in the last years a branch into the MAS field has emerged stressing the importance of the *environment* and embedded this concept in the core of the MAS architecture, developing what has been called *Situated* MAS (MASs in short). The *environment* has been consolidated as a fundamental layer of abstraction in the construction of any complex MAS [1–4]. One special case of MASs is those whose *environments* are embedded into a *Virtual Immersive Environment* (VIE). The VIEs are itself a perfect playground where *Intelligent Agents* can interact with humans in a huge range of possibilities, one of the most important is *Education*.

One of the clearest and most direct use cases is the virtual recreation of classrooms and auditoriums for remote-learning use. For instance, many *in-world* services are provided by the MAS intelligence like students guidance, assistance monitoring or facilities orientation.

But in many cases the implementation of the MASs are incomplete or tailored for a very particular purpose. The cause for this lack of maturity is the absence of theoretical models [5] to follow at the time of designing and developing those systems.

J.M. Ferrández Vicente et al. (Eds.): IWINAC 2017, Part II, LNCS 10338, pp. 413–423, 2017.
DOI: 10.1007/978-3-319-59773-7_42

Along several years of working with MASs over IVE systems we have developed what we called *Deployment Representation Model.* This theoretical model has been proved in various projects, one of them related to an Educational experience related to computer simulation techniques will be exposed in this paper.

2 Related Work

There are numerous teaching experiences in which VIE technology has been used to facilitate access to training remotely or to increase the intuitive understanding in some complex subjects such as mathematics or 3D geometry.

In year 2000 [6] several teachers documented the experience with the tool [7–9] Studierstube (http://studierstube.icg.tugraz.at/main.php). The goal is to provide students with advanced geometric understanding and spatial visualization, that is, how the mathematical functions with which they are working abstractly are expressed in 3D space. The result was quite positive as the students showed a quick understanding of the user interface and were able to solve the problem in its entirety. Evidences were found that everyone evaluated as much easier to understand the matter through the 3D tool than in a 2D media such as paper or screen. On the other hand, six of the students became dizzy, which is commonly referred to as *cybersickness*.

In 2006, Rizzo et al. [10] presented the use of a virtual classroom to treat the cases of children with Attention-Deficit/Hyperactivity Disorder (ADHD). The study indicates that in a traditional way the treatment of these diseases is based on the observation of the patients in a functional environment in the real world. The use of VIEs allows to recreate the functional environments in a much more flexible and quick way. Through the use of VIEs it is possible to expose the patient to complex situations, to observe the behavior directly, to execute a rehabilitation technique immediately and to return the patient to the same situation in order to observe the effectiveness of the technique. Another advantage of VIE is that sometimes it is impossible to use a specific environment either for its inherent danger (driving a car) or because of its special nature (an airborne plane). Prior to the existence of the VIEs, the construction of these complex functional environments was carried out by means of "models" or scenarios where a consensus of reality was reached. However a complete branch of opinion within psychology questioned the "ecological validity" (how valid are) of the therapies performed in non-real environments whether in VIE or in models. Although this vision continues to exist today, the continuous improvements of the VIE are making this option gain followers. Apart from the clinical conclusions of the study, the authors assert that the use of VIE technologies allow much more effectiveness of the time spent with the patients, as well as a reduction in the cost of the treatments.

In 2008 Limniou et al. [11] proposed an educational experience based in the use of CAVE. This device is a kind of virtual reality human interface device consisting in four transparent walls with external projectors. One person gets inside the square room and projectors put the corresponding image on the walls giving the sense of full immersion of that subject. In the context of this paper it is not relevant how this device works, instead focus on the results of the teaching experience. In chemistry, it is very complex to intuitively understand the 3D shapes of the molecules in a chemical component. The students of that subject complains on how inefficient are the 2D book images to depict how a chemical reaction affects the molecules geometrical formation in space. Thus, this experience pursues to solve this problem giving the possibility to the students of experiment in first hand the illusion of being in the very middle of a chemical reaction, with the possibility of control the timing of the formulation and get back and forth as many times as needed to complete the proper understanding of the problem.

From the years 2008 to 2011 one of the most popular Internet public VIE services up to the date centered all the educational activities in virtual worlds: Second Life http://secondlife.com/. In 2009 Warburton studies [12] reflected the big mass media impact that Second Life had during those years. In his paper focused on the analysis of the service in three components: technical, immersive and social. Also typified the possible educational experiences possible and enunciated the greatest barriers for that service.

Also in Second Life service, Wiecha [13] describes the experience using second life for medical education. That experience was prepared for postgraduate medical education program to explore the potential of VIEs in medical education and get feedback from the students to measure the success of the experience. Results were significantly good, suggesting VIEs can be applied to postgraduate professional development.

Once summarized the most significant experiences in the area it is remarkable the fact that no-one of the experiences had a bad feedback. The first experiences took place when the hardware and the software required to have a good VIE experience simply didn't exist. That caused a drawback in some occasions due to the poor overall experience. Although, if we follow the sequence along the years, the more recent experiment, the more richer feedback is received. With the latest advances in VR devices the immersive potential was grown dramatically. Something similar happened with the *in-world* overall quality. In the first stages the objects were plain, without detail or with very limited interactive capacities. In the last years, since the appearance of Second Life and his open source successor OpenSim, the potential of the quality of the experiments is raising day by day. Now, within those kind of VIEs it is now possible start speaking of real Multiagent Systems able to do real interesting work. Nevertheless all the experiences presented are in a very early stage of maturity, being little more than mere proof of concept. The robustness of the underlying architecture is very limited, and the solutions are fully tailored for a single objective. This situation discourages in many occasions a more widespread use, being only used in the academic environment and totally nonexistent in the industry or business.

3 A Proposed Architecture for Situated Multi Agent Systems. The Deployment/Representation Model

The present model has been developed based on the work of multiple expert authors in the field and following the guidance of the experience obtained during more than ten years in MASs experimentation. By *Deployment Structure* we mean the part of a MASs that is closely tied to physical low level. A key concept is the *Environment Provider*, since it disconnects the system from the environment which it is built in. This abstraction layer allows the model not to be tied to a single simulator or even the real world. On the other side of the scale we have the "*Symbolic Spatial Representation*" layer: a set of services that are published to the Deployment Structure and put into disposition of Agents. The model has several different functional modules: *Agent Management (AM), Virtual Spatial Representation (VSR), Augmented Environment (AE) and System Status (SS).*

3.1 Deployment Structure

Through the *Deployment Structure(DS)* we can lay the foundations of the entire multi-agent system for a specific problem. Before the construction or design of the agents we have to define the characteristics of the problem. Likewise, non-functional requirements should also be reflected. We can therefore say that the *Deployment Structure(DS)* consists of: one or more environment providers, a set of internal services, a set of external services and a set of metrics for success. Specifically, the actions to be taken when analyzing a deployment structure are the following:

- Identify the **environment providers**: the context where agents develops themselves. In other words, is the scenario where agents will be able to use their sensing, motor and communicative capacities.
- Identify the **internal services** to the environment: communications connections, motor types or characteristics of the sensory agents. We could assimilate the purely reactive behaviors in this type of services.
- Identify **external services** to the environment: all functions that escape from the environment because are of a higher level of abstraction.
- Identify **success metrics**: taken directly from the environment to avoid biased results.

It should be noted that while *internal services* may be different for each environment provider and that consequently these services are linked to each environment, *external services* must always maintain the same structure to ensure portability.

3.2 Spatial Symbolic Representation

The concept *Spatial Symbolic Representation (SSR)* is defined as a set of distributed hubs that collaboratively provide high-level services to a *Deployment*

Structure(DS) and all of its possible underlying environments. In our model will talk about *hubs* as the set of high level abstraction services on which a group of agents work. The Hub is composed by the following high level modules:

Augmented Symbolic Environment (ASE). As in augmented reality technology, existing spatial information is overlapped to enhance a real image, the knowledge of this module will allow the agents to complete the virtual representation of the environment. This module will be responsible to store all the information from the environment or any other source and format that data in order to help the Agents in their work.

Virtual Spatial Environmental Representation (VSER). Considering that all this model is designed exclusively for three-dimensional space environments, it is essential that the Hub has a representation of this space and make it accessible to agents. Although there's no restriction to the type of data this module must store and process.

Agent Management (AM). The Hub must have a strong knowledge and control of the Agents it is serving in every moment. This feature must be implemented in this module, as well as the Multi Agent typical functionality like yellow or white pages, usually assigned to a *facilitator agent.*

System Status (SS). Although all the information of the environment and the Hub is stored in the representation of the symbolic space, yet there are data that is outside the domain. Depending on the problem, these data may be more or less abundant, which means that the module will be larger or smaller. In many cases all the user interface module is implemented within this module (Fig. 1).

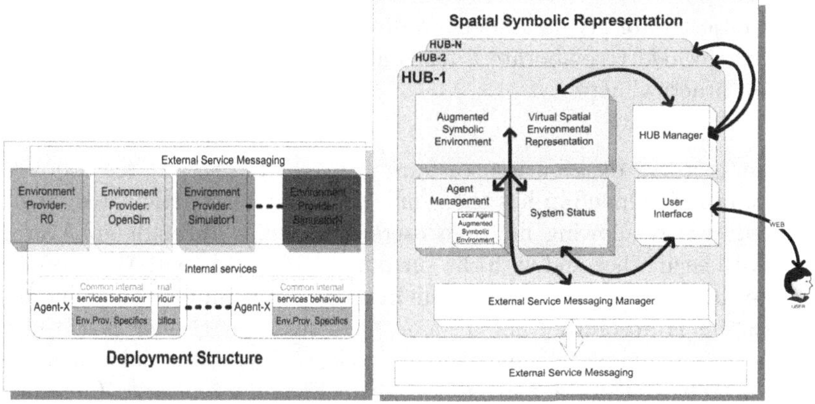

Fig. 1. Deployment Representation Model functional modules diagram

4 Probe of Concept: Simulation Experiment

4.1 Background

During the elaboration of the academic agenda for 2011 course of the **Computer Science and Technology Master, University Carlos III of Madrid** into the subject **Modeling, Simulation and Optimization** (usually abbreviated by **MSO**) it was decided to include a practical experiment to the students related to simulation techniques within virtual immersive environments. The main academic goal pursued was to put the students in touch with unusual ways to face high complexity problems using a simulation strategic approach and taking advantage of the possibilities of the virtual environments technologies at hand (Fig. 2).

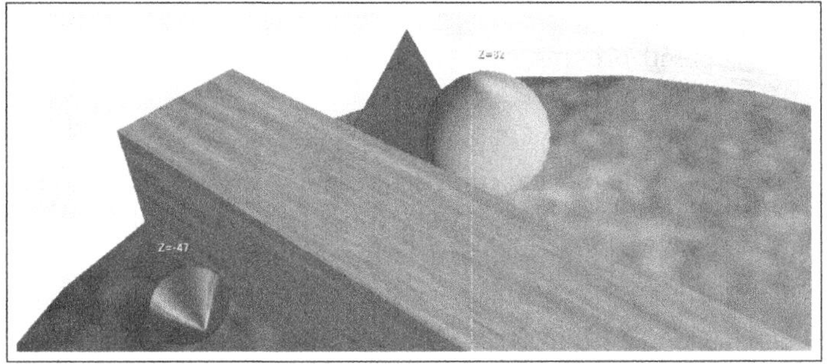

Fig. 2. VIE-MSO detail: some geometrical agents at the shaker

4.2 Practical Session Definition

With the objective of giving students a direct experience in the field of simulation, it was decided to elaborate a teaching activity consisting of a theoretical class and a practical activity.

OpenSim is a free distribution software evolved from the source code of the game *Second Life*. OpenSim has the same functional and participatory features as its predecessor, allowing multiple users, personified through an Avatar to interact with each other and with the surrounding environment. Moreover, users can create their own elements of the environment. It is important to emphasize that OpenSim is absolutely not a game, it is just a container platform that provides physical simulation and social services. Trying to make an analogy between a Web site and a Virtual World or *Virtual Immersive Environment (VIE)*: OpenSim would be similar to Apache. Just like any web page requires a web server to be experienced, a VIE requires a simulator to exist. And just like with Apache, there are different software products which offers the Web Pages

Fig. 3. VIE-MSO detail: two virtual laboratory views

Serving feature, there are also different simulation software that would allow you to run a VIE, although unfortunately there is not so much variety. The choice of OpenSim is due to its integral service and its freely access. The next option today, Unity, although more widespread and with higher graphic quality, lacks of a multi-user management layer since it is more orientated to build 3D games (Fig. 3).

4.3 System Built to Support Practical Session

In the first two practical sessions, the OpenSim server was hosted and executed on a University facilities server, allowing all students to enter the same VIE sharing the experimentation environment or virtual laboratory. This experience resulted very enriching since the students keep interacting while working on the practice, enhancing teamwork much more efficiently than simple mailing list or even chat rooms.

From the third year experimentation and on, students were also allowed to run their personal simulator on their own computer, being able to reconcile both worlds by taking advantage of the multi-environment capability of the *Display Representation Model*. With this strategy we solved the problem of resource sharing: in the proposed practice the students must use an object “shaker” for several hours, causing some conflicts. The common use now is: connect to the shared VIE to develop collaboratively and once the student's agent is performing well, use the personal VIE to let the experiment running for many hours or with many agents to get the better experimental results. In other words, we have a common laboratory where all students can share, test and experiment together and as many cloned labs as needed. This is one of the most clear advantages of virtual laboratories experimentation.

4.4 Practical Activity Articulations

A space agency is studying alternative designs for exploratory robots to be used in Solar System planets scouting. One of these designs bases on the premise of using a solid cover as homogeneous as possible. With this purpose, it is necessary to study how different three-dimensional geometric shapes evolve in the orientation

Fig. 4. VIE dev. desktop: students user interface to develop and construct

of their spatial axes in chaotic movement situations. Thus, it would be necessary to perform a statistical study of the angles for the X, Y and Z axes over time for a wide range of objects with different geometric shapes.

To simplify the scope of this practical session, we will limit the axes to be studied to the Z axis, and the geometric forms to that of a simple sphere (Fig. 4).

Description of the Experiment: Hypothesis states perfect sphere maintains equiprobability in all its axes. **Decision** variable: Z-axis value. **Events** to be described: the concrete value of the component Z over time in an iterative discrete sequence.

Enrich and Elaborate Model: Once the minimum requirements of the practice have been met, the enrichment of the model and conclusions drawn will be positively valued. Some suggestions in this regard: **Measure**, record and analyze the X and Y components of agents. **Extend**, the objects that are experienced: toroids, spindles, cylinders, etc. **Propose**, new devices or situations to generate random movement: double agitators, wells, spirals, etc. (Figs. 5 and 6).

Data Analysis: Storage, all samples sent by the Agents, regardless of whether they were generated in the common or personal VIE, will be stored on a hosted SSR server at the University facilities. **Retrieval**, these samples may be consulted at any time via the Web Console just taking note of the UUID (universal unique identifier code) of the Agent. This UUID is only known by the owner of the Agent so the confidentiality of the experiments is guaranteed. **Conversion**, once the student requested from the SSR Web Console a set of samples gathered from a specific Agent (in HTML or CSV format) can be imported into

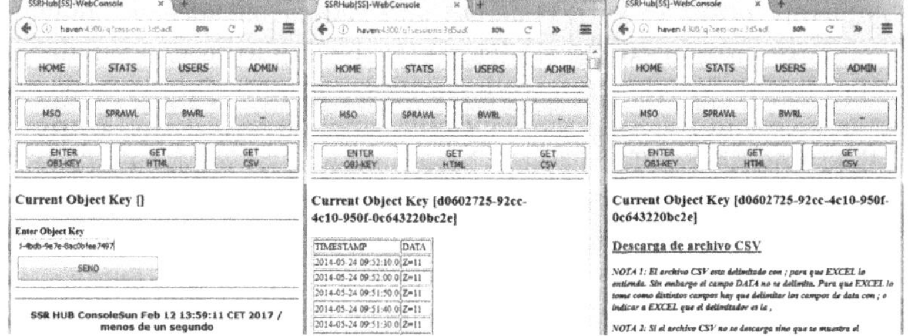

Fig. 5. SSR-MSO Web Console: student interface

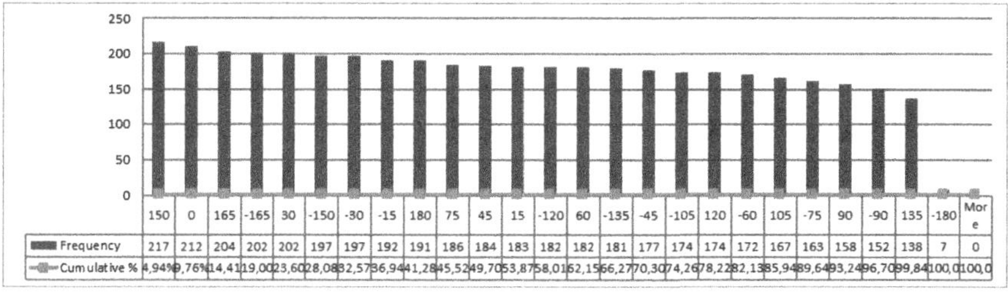

250
200
150
100
50
0
150 0 165 -165 30 -150 -30 -15 180 75 45 15 -120 60 -135 -45 -105 120 -60 105 -75 90 -90 135 -180 More
Frequency 217 212 204 202 202 197 197 192 191 186 184 183 182 182 181 177 174 174 172 167 163 158 152 138 7 0
Cumulative %

Fig. 6. Experimental result example: Z-axis angles histogram 15° arc

another tool (Excel, Matlab, etc.) **Study**, from that moment on, standard statistical techniques will be used to analyze the information received (frequency analysis, histograms, graphs, etc.) that will be the deliverable result of the practice, together with the conclusions regarding compliance or not of the working hypothesis.

4.5 Educational Feedback from Students

The experience of both theoretical practice and practice has been very well received. Students often find it stimulating to use unusual tools especially when they have a large visual component. Although in the first instance this fact can "distract" somewhat the attention of the student, mainly by its similarity to the classic aesthetics of "first person shooter" game, they quickly perceive the general spirit of the activity.

5 Conclusions and Future Work

In this paper we have presented a theoretical model. A multipurpose framework has been developed following this model. Taking advantage of this framework and the flexibility of the model we have built an educational experience. Through this practice we have achieved different formative goals. Overall experience has been completely positive, with concrete and significant success points: **Education**, we have introduced the students into the applied use of simulators and virtual laboratories. **Workteam**, the teamwork capabilities of the students, have been empowered and by using the multiuser capabilities of VIEs. **Experience**, the practical experience efficiency has been improved by implementing common and private virtual laboratories seamlessly. **Scientific**, practical use of scientific experimentation has been presented to the students: starting with an initial hypothesis, the description of an experiment, the implementation of a laboratory, the execution of the experiment, the collection and analysis of the data, and finally the elaboration of the results of the whole process. **Validation**, the proposed theoretical model has been validated by the framework success.

Year after year this educational experience is enriched by the participation of both teachers and students, and it is proposed to expand the range of experiments as well as be used in other subjects.

Acknowledgement. This work was partially funded by projects MINECO TEC2014-57022-C2-2-R, TEC2012-37832-C02-01.

References

1. Weyns, D.: Architecture-Based Design of Multi-agent Systems. Springer, Heidelberg (2010)
2. Weyns, D., Michel, F.: Agent Environments for Multi-agent Systems IV. LNCS. Springer, Heidelberg (2015)
3. Platon, E., Mamei, M., Sabouret, N., Honiden, S., Parunak, H.V.D.: Mechanisms for environments in multi-agent systems: survey and opportunities. Auton. Agent. Multi-agent Syst. **14**(1), 31–47 (2007)
4. Bandini, S., Manzoni, S., Simone, C.: Dealing with space in multi-agent systems: a model for situated MAS. In: Proceedings of the First International Joint Conference on Autonomous Agents and Multiagent Systems: Part 3, pp. 1183–1190. ACM (2002)
5. Weyns, D., Michel, F.: Agent environments for multi-agent systems – a research roadmap. In: Weyns, D., Michel, F. (eds.) E4MAS 2014. LNCS, vol. 9068, pp. 3–21. Springer, Cham (2015). doi:10.1007/978-3-319-23850-0_1
6. Kaufmann, H., Schmalstieg, D., Wagner, M.: Construct3D: a virtual reality application for mathematics and geometry education. Educ. Inf. Technol. **5**, 263–276 (2000)
7. Fuhrmann, A., Schmalstieg, D.: Concept and implementation of a collaborative workspace for augmented reality (1999)
8. Szalavári, Z., Schmalstieg, D., Fuhrmann, A., Gervautz, M.: "Studierstube": an environment for collaboration in augmented reality. Virtual Real. **3**, 37–48 (1998)
9. Schmalstieg, D., Fuhrmann, A., Szalavári, Z., Gervautz, M.: Studierstube-an environment for collaboration in augmented reality. In: CVE 1996 Workshop Proceedings, vol. 19 (1996)
10. Rizzo, A.A., Bowerly, T., Buckwalter, J.G., Klimchuk, D., Mitura, R., Parsons, T.D.: A virtual reality scenario for all seasons: the virtual classroom. CNS Spectr. **11**, 35–44 (2006)

11. Limniou, M., Roberts, D., Papadopoulos, N.: Full immersive virtual environment CAVE TM in chemistry education. Comput. Educ. **51**(2), 584–593 (2008)
12. Warburton, S.: Second life in higher education: assessing the potential for and the barriers to deploying virtual worlds in learning and teaching. Br. J. Educ. Technol. **40**(3), 414–426 (2009)
13. Wiecha, J., Heyden, R., Sternthal, E., Merialdi, M.: Learning in a virtual world: experience with using second life for medical education. J. Med. Internet Res. **12**(1), e1 (2010)

Phonation and Articulation Analyses in Laryngeal Pathologies, Cleft Lip and Palate, and Parkinson's Disease

J.C. Jiménez-Monsalve[1,2], J.C. Vásquez-Correa[2,3], J.R. Orozco-Arroyave[2,3], and P. Gomez-Vilda[4(✉)]

[1] Engineering Department, Owens Illinois, Medellín, Colombia
[2] Faculty of Engineering, Universidad de Antioquia, Medellín, Colombia
[3] Pattern Recognition Lab, Friedrich-Alexander-Universität Erlangen, Erlangen, Germany
[4] Neuromorphic Speech Processing Lab, Center for Biomedical Engineering, Universidad Politécnica de Madrid, Madrid, Spain
pedrogvilda@telefonica.net

Abstract. This study considers phonation and articulation measures to model voice disorders produced by three different pathologies: Laryngeal pathologies (LP), cleft lip and palate (CLP), and Parkinson's disease (PD). Different speech tasks are considered including sustained vowel phonations, isolated words, and read texts. The obtained accuracies, in terms of the area under the ROC curve (AUC), range between 55.7 and 99.2 depending on the pathology. The results suggest that phonation features are appropriate to model LP; however, for the case of CLP and PD, it seems like the articulation measures provide more information about the problems in moving and controlling the articulators of the vocal tract. This work is a step towards the development of methodologies for the automatic discrimination among different voice disorders.

1 Introduction

There are several diseases that produce different speech disorders, for instance children with cleft lip and palate (CLP) can develop hypernasality, laryngeal pathologies (LP) mainly produce breathy voice and hoarseness among other disorders, and neurological diseases like Parkinson's (PD) can produce abnormal vibration of vocal folds, monotonicity and loss of intelligibility. CLP is a facial and oral malformation that occurs during pregnancy. It affects the velar movement during phonation and produces changes in resonant properties of the nasal cavity. The main effect in the speech of CLP patients is called hypernasality which is characterized by an excess of air coming out through the nasal cavity [1]. LP is a group of disorders that affect the correct larynx function. LP may be the result of different diseases like cancer, polyps, and nodules. The main symptoms in the voice of LP patients are breathy voice, hoarseness, and abnormal vibration of the vocal folds [2]. PD is a neurological disorder that alters the function of the basal ganglia in the midbrain, affecting motor and non-motor abilities

J.M. Ferrández Vicente et al. (Eds.): IWINAC 2017, Part II, LNCS 10338, pp. 424–434, 2017.
DOI: 10.1007/978-3-319-59773-7_43

of the patients. The main symptoms of the speech of PD patients include reduced loudness, monopitch, monoloudness, hypotonicity, breathy, hoarse voice quality, and imprecise articulation. These symptoms are typically grouped and called *hypokinetic dysarthria* [3].

Several studies have analyzed phonatory impairments in pathological speech from the medical and engineering perspectives. Phonation deficits in CLP have been described in [4]. The authors claim that vocal nodules often occur in patients with a small velopharyngeal gap or with a nasal grimace. Additionally, they observed that breathiness appears as a compensatory strategy to mask the hypernasality. From the engineering perspective, phonation in CLP patients was studied in [5]. The authors evaluated different perturbation measures, noise contents and non-linear dynamics upon the speech signals in order to discriminate CLP patients vs. healthy controls (HC). The five Spanish vowels and two isolated words were considered, and accuracies of up to 95.4% were reported when the acoustic and non-linear features are combined. On the other hand, phonation in LP can be often characterized as an asymmetric change of fold masses, deficient closure, and alterations in vocal fold tension. LP is commonly studied analyzing features derived mainly from sustained vowels. For instance in [6] a non-linear model based on the fractal dimension computed on a three-level discrete wavelet transform was proposed to detect patients with LP. The method was evaluated only in utterances of the vowel /a/. According to the results, the spectrum from 1 Hz to 1562 Hz shows significant differences between pathological and healthy voices. The authors reported an AUC value of 0.9506 in LP vs. HC subjects. Additionally in [7], a longitudinal study was performed in 33 patients with laryngeal cancer and 32 HC. The patients were recorded every month while receiving voice therapy. The authors considered recordings of the sustained vowel /a/ and vowels extracted from a read text. Features related to period perturbation, noise content, and duration were computed. According to their results, an improvement in the speech quality was observed within the first six months after radiotherapy, indicating that voice rehabilitation has potentially positive effects in the patients. Regarding Parkinson's patients, their phonation is characterized by inadequate vocal fold closing and vocal folds bowing [8], producing problems in the stability and periodicity of the vibration. Besides, tremor should be added to these observables as a feature present in at least 80% of the cases. Phonation in PD has been analyzed in [9], where features related to perturbation, noise content, and non-linear dynamics are used to evaluate whether the response of 14 PD patients to the Lee Silverman voice treatment is "acceptable" or "unacceptable". The authors considered only information from the sustained vowel /a/, and reported accuracies close to 90% when discriminating between "acceptable" vs. "unacceptable" utterances. Finally, the study of multiple voice disorders was recently addressed in [10]. Different characterization methods were tested for the detection of PD, LP, and CLP. The authors used information only from sustained vowels and evaluated four different characterization approaches: stability and periodicity, noise measures, spectral wealth, and non-linear dynamics. The reported accuracies range from 70% to 99% depending on the pathology and on the feature set.

Articulation deficits in pathological voices have been addressed in several studies. Such deficits in CLP patients are described in [4]. The authors show that children with CLP make compensatory articulation errors, exhibit abnormal nasal emission, and produce nasalized consonants due to the velopharyngeal insufficiency. Such articulation phenomena are studied in [11], where different measures are extracted from the speech of CLP patients in order to detect four different states of the disease. The features are based on the fundamental frequency of voice, the energy content, and Mel-frequency cepstral coefficients (MFCC). The experiments are performed in syllables uttered by 567 children with CLP (Mandarin language speakers). The highest reported accuracy is 80%. For the case of LP patients, the articulation analysis is studied in [12]. The authors consider recordings of 34 patients with advanced head and neck cancer and analyzed 12 different phonemes including vowels and consonants. The patients received voice treatment and were recorded in three sessions: before the treatment, 10 weeks after the treatment, and one year later. The features are based on formant frequencies and energy in consonants. The authors observed a reduced vowel space, an increased nasalization, and deficits in the pronunciation of plosive sounds and fricative consonants in the first recording session. Finally, the articulation deficits in PD patients are mainly related to reduced amplitude and velocity of lip, tongue, and jaw movements [13]. It has been studied in several works. In [14] the authors evaluated possible correlations between vowel articulation, global motor performance, and the stage of the disease. A total of 68 patients and 32 HC are considered, and according to the results obtained in several statistical tests, the authors concluded that the vowel articulation index (VAI) is significantly reduced in PD speakers. In [15] six different articulatory deficits in PD were modeled: vowel quality, coordination of laryngeal and supra-laryngeal activity, precision of consonant articulation, tongue movement, occlusion weakening, and speech timing. The authors studied the rapid repetition of the syllables /pa-ta-ka/ pronounced by 24 Czech native speakers, and reported an accuracy of 88% discriminating between PD patients and HC.

According to the reviewed literature, most of the studies considering data of multiple voice disorders are performed only with sustained vowels. The information that can be provided by continuous speech signals, e.g., isolated words, syllabic sequences or phonated segments from running speech, have not been studied in this context so far; additionally, the problem of recognizing multiple voice disorders considering such information has not been addressed. In this study, phonation and articulation–based features are extracted from recordings of sustained vowels and running speech signals uttered by patients with LP, CLP, and PD. The phonation analysis includes measures related to periodicity, stability, and noise content. The analysis of articulation comprises measures related to vocal formant frequencies, MFCCs, and the modified group delay functions (MGDF). The aim of this study is to show which aspect of speech (phonation or articulation) is more suitable to discriminate HC speakers from patients with different voice disorders.

2 Methods

2.1 Phonation Analysis

Phonation features can be used to model abnormal patterns in vocal folds vibration. The modeling includes descriptors related to stability and noise measures. The stability measures include: *Jitter and shimmer*, which describe the variation of the fundamental period and amplitude of the voice signal, respectively; *pitch perturbation quotient (PPQ)*, which models long term perturbations of the fundamental period; *amplitude perturbation quotient (APQ)*, which models long term variability of the peak to peak amplitude of the signal. Additionally, the first and second derivatives of the fundamental frequency (F_0) are included along with the energy content of the signal. The set of noise measures includes: *Harmonics to noise ratio (HNR)* to describe the relation between the periodic components produced by the vocal fold vibration and the non-periodic components related to the glottal noise; *voice turbulent index (VTI)* which is the average ratio of the in-harmonic high frequency energy with respect to the spectral harmonic energy where the influence of the frequency and amplitude variations of the signal is minimal [16]; *soft phonation index (SPI)* defined as the average ratio between the lower frequency harmonic energy and the higher frequency harmonic energy [16]; *normalized noise energy (NNE)* to model the relation between the noise energy and the total energy of the speech signal [17]; and *glottal to noise ratio (GNE)* which is the relation between the vocal excitation due to the vocal folds vibration and the excitation produced by turbulent noise in the vocal tract [18]. APQ and PPQ are computed upon 100 ms frames with an overlap of 80 ms between frames, and the rest of phonation features are computed on 20 ms frames with an overlap of 15 ms between frames. Four statistical functionals are calculated per phonation feature (mean, standard deviation, skewness, and kurtosis), forming a 48–dimensional feature vector.

2.2 Articulation Analysis

Articulatory features are used to model changes in the position of the tongue, lips, velum, and other articulators involved in the speech production process. The analysis includes thirteen descriptors: *Formant frequencies* to represent resonances of the vocal tract. The first two formants (F_1 and F_2) and their first two derivatives are computed; *vowel space area (VSA)* is calculated to quantify the capability of speakers to put the tongue in certain positions during the sustained phonation of vowels /a/, /i/, and /u/. VSA is estimated as the area of the triangle formed by the vertex (F_1, F_2) obtained from the three vowels. Typically, people with low articulatory capability exhibit reduced VSA values [14]; *formant centralization ratio (FCR)* is also calculated and consists of calculating the center of the vocal triangle to increase the reliability in the comparison of speakers and detect drifts in articulation average positions due to illness [19]; *cepstral coefficients (MFCCs)* are computed as a smooth representation of voice spectrum that considers the human auditory perception according to the Mel scale [20].

Twelve MFCC coefficients are calculated along with their first and second derivatives. The *Teager energy operator (TEO)* is also calculated to model non-linear effects in the glottal cycle. TEO has been successfully used to evaluate different voice disorders [10]; and finally, the *modified group delay function (MGDF)* is calculated to obtain an alternative representation of the speech spectrum [5]. Twelve coefficients of the discrete cosine transform of the modified spectrum are calculated according to [21]. The feature vector with the articulation model comprises a total of 55 components.

2.3 Classification

The classification is performed using a support vector machine (SVM) with a Gaussian kernel. The SVM is trained following a 10-fold cross-validation strategy (speaker independent, i.e., non of the test speakers are included in the train process). The parameters of the machine C and γ are optimized in a grid search ($C \in \{10^{-5}, 10^{-4}, \dots 10^{4}\}$ and $\gamma \in \{10^{-6}, 10^{-5}, \dots 10^{2}\}$), and the selection criterion is based on the accuracy obtained from the train set. The performance is evaluated using the area under the receiver operating characteristic curve (AUC). These curves are typically used to display results in a more compact way [22].

3 Experimental Framework

3.1 Databases

1. *LP:* the database of *the Massachusetts Eye and Ear Infirmary (MEEI) Voice & Speech Lab* was used. It contains sustained phonations of the English Vowel /a/ and the readings of the rainbow passage. The database is formed with 53 healthy speakers and 173 patients with different laryngeal pathologies [23].
2. *CLP*: the database of *Grupo de Procesamiento y Recnocimiento de Señales* (GPRS) from *Universidad Nacional de Colombia* was used. It contains recordings of the five Spanish vowels and a set of five isolated words (/coco/, /gato/, /jugo/, /mano/, and /papa/) uttered by 59 healthy controls and 144 patients. The age of the participants range between 5 and 15 years [5].
3. *PD*: *PC-GITA* database was used [24]. It contains recordings of 50 PD patients and 50 HC. The speakers are balanced in age and gender. Recordings of the five Spanish vowels, 10 sentences, and a read text are considered in this study.

Note: three databases are sampled at 44.1 kHz with 16 bit-resolution.

3.2 Experiments

Figure 1 summarizes the general methodology which is being used to perform the experiments in this study. Phonation and articulation measures are extracted from recordings of the three databases. For the classification experiments two fusions are performed: at feature level, i.e., the feature vectors of phonation and articulation measures are combined, and at speech-task level, i.e., features from different speech tasks (vowels, words, sentences, or read text) are combined. Additionally, multi-class classification experiments are performed (not displayed in Fig. 1), thus the capability of the system to detect/discriminate one specific disease among the three considered here (LP, CLP and PD) is evaluated.

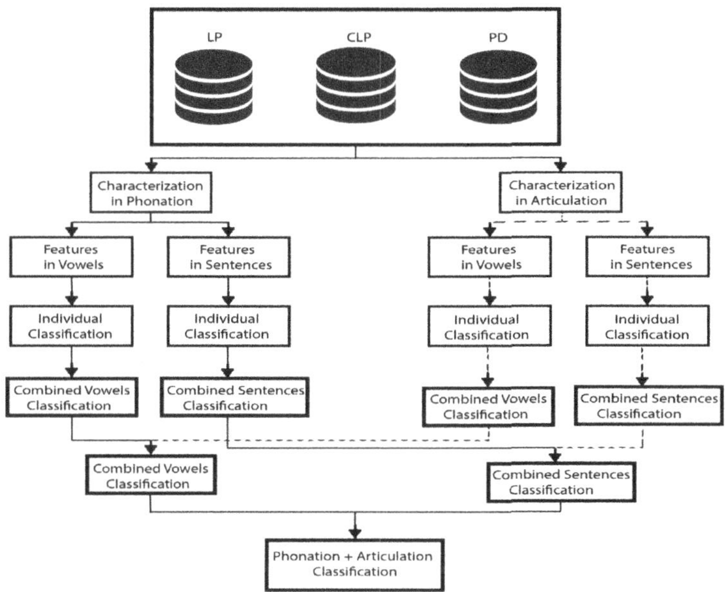

Fig. 1. General methodology.

4 Results and Discussion

Phonation Results. Results obtained with phonation and articulation features are displayed in Table 1. Note that the highest AUC values of phonation are obtained with the LP database in both cases, sustained vowels and continuous speech. The highest AUC in CLP is obtained when the five Spanish vowels are combined; regarding the isolated words the results are around 0.81. Finally, the AUC with PD is around 0.65 in both cases, sustained vowels and continuous speech signals. The results suggest that to improve the AUC values it is necessary to consider other features like the articulation ones. Note that the combination of /a-i-u/ task was only considered for articulation analysis to compute VSA and FCR.

Articulation Results. The results obtained with articulation features are higher than those obtained with phonation. For LP the AUC values are close to 100% in both cases. In CLP the AUC values are around 90%, while in PD the results are between 57% and 77% when vowels or sentences are considered.

Table 1. Phonation and articulation results

Pathology	Task	AUC phonation	AUC articulation
LP	/ah/	96.1	99.2
	/Rainbow/	92.6	99.8
CLP	/a/	89.9	89.1
	/e/	92.3	90.8
	/i/	91.8	83.2
	/o/	87.6	92.2
	/u/	81.4	87.7
	/aiu/	NA	93.4
	/aeiou/	93.0	97.2
	/coco/	80.8	95.6
	/gato/	81.6	90.6
	/jugo/	86.7	90.0
	/mano/	79.7	91.9
	/papa/	78.4	95.1
	/coco-papa/	84.1	97.3
PD	/a/	69.1	68.2
	/e/	67.7	57.9
	/i/	74.4	56.7
	/o/	67.5	64.6
	/u/	62.8	64.7
	/aiu/	NA	59.8
	/aeiou/	81.5	66.3
	/Sent. 01/	72.8	62.6
	/Sent. 02/	63.9	70.3
	/Sent. 03/	62.6	69.1
	/Sent. 04/	61.1	60.8
	/Sent. 05/	59.3	70.7
	/Sent. 06/	68.6	64.4
	/Sent. 07/	68.1	71.7
	/Sent. 08/	64.9	72.2
	/Sent. 09/	55.7	74.2
	/Sent. 10/	60.4	77.5
	/Read text/	68.0	82.9
	/Sent. 1–10 + read text/	70.8	94.4

When the read text is evaluated, the AUC increases to 82.9% and when data from the ten sentences and the read text are combined, the result is around 94%, indicating that such information is complementary, thus it is worth to combine different speech tasks in order to improve the classification results.

Fusion Results. In these experiments the combination of phonation and articulation features is performed. The obtained results are displayed in Table 2. Note that the AUC values improved in all cases. For LP the results are 99.6% and 99.7% for vowels and read text, respectively. For the case of CLP, the result evaluating sustained phonations is 96.7% (combining the five Spanish vowels). Finally, for PD all of the speech tasks are combined, i.e., five Spanish vowels, read sentences, and the red text. When only phonation features are considered the AUC value is 72.9%. The result when phonation and articulation features are combined is 92.1%. The result is similar when only articulation features are considered, which could find an explanation in the fact that PD is a movement disorder, thus the problems to move articulators and limbs are more prominent than those associated to phonation. Besides the results displayed in the table (left), the best results per pathology are summarized in the ROC curves on the right side. The curves were created by stacking the predicted values of the 10-folds cross-validation.

Table 2. Fusion results and ROC curves with the highest AUC values

Pathology	Task	AUC
LP Phon. + Art	/a/	99.7
LP Phon. + Art.	/Rainbow/	99.6
CLP Phon. + Art.	/aeiou/	96.7
CLP Phon. + Art.	/coco-papa/	98.1
PD Phon.	/aeiou/ + sent. + read	72.9
PD Art.	/aeiou/ + sent. + read	92.6
PD Phon. + Art.	/aeiou/ + sent. + read	92.1

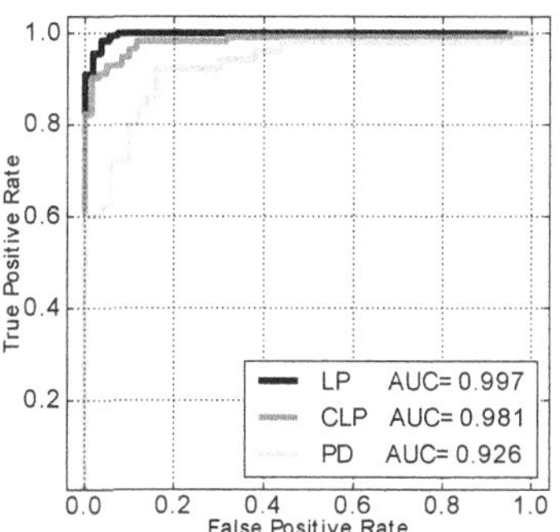

Multi-class Results. Table 3 displays the confusion matrix with the results of discriminating among the four groups of speakers (LP, CLP, PD, and HC). Results considering features of phonation, articulation, and the combination of both are included. The main idea of this experiment is to perform a fair comparison among the considered models to discriminate between diseases of different nature. As the only speech-task included in the three databases is the sustained vowel /a/, the experiments are performed considering such a task only. The Cohen's kappa coefficient (κ) is computed in order to measure the accuracy of the tests considering the class-unbalance in the databases. Regarding the classification results, note that as in the previous experiments, the best results are obtained when phonation and articulation features are combined. Note that in

CLP the results considering only articulation features is similar to those from fusion. For the case of LP and PD the combination improves the results. Regarding the detection of healthy speakers, the best result is obtained with articulation measures, and it is similar to the accuracy obtained combining both models (articulation and phonation).

Table 3. Confusion matrix: phonation, articulation, and their fusion

	Phon. $\kappa = 0.56$				Art. $\kappa = 0.64$				Phon.+Art. $\kappa = 0.65$			
	LP	CLP	PD	HC	LP	CLP	PD	HC	LP	CLP	PD	HC
LP	**71.6**	6.9	4.0	17.3	**64.8**	8.7	4.0	22.5	**74.0**	6.4	2.3	17.3
CLP	7.6	**80.6**	9.7	2.1	2.8	**95.8**	0.0	1.4	1.4	**95.8**	2.1	0.7
PD	14.0	34.0	**38.0**	14.0	12.0	34.0	**48.0**	6.0	10.0	32.0	**54.0**	4.0
HC	21.0	2.5	6.8	**69.7**	18.5	2.5	7.4	**71.6**	21.0	1.6	7.4	**71.0**

5 Conclusions

Phonation and articulation features are used in this study to model three different pathologies: LP, CLP, and PD. Different speech-tasks including sustained vowel phonations and read texts are considered. High accuracies in LP are obtained considering phonation and articulation features, indicating that not only the vocal fold vibration is important to model this pathology; in sight of the results, it seems that the movement of the articulators would be providing information related to laryngeal pathology as well; of course, this observation would require further investigation. The highest accuracies in CLP were obtained with articulation features. This result confirms the importance of modeling the articulators to study the velopharyngeal insufficiency and the resulting hypernasality. Regarding the PD set, the better results are obtained also with articulation features, which confirms that these patients develop problems to move several articulators including tongue, jaw, and lips. In all of the cases, the results improve when phonation and articulation features were combined. This fact may indicate that the information of phonation and articulation is complementary, thus it is worth consider both models together to obtain larger accuracies. The combination of speech tasks also improved accuracy. This result can be likely explained because more tasks include more sounds (vocal, consonants, plosives, etc.), thus the richness of the model is directly improved. Finally, the four groups of speakers are combined and a multi-class classification problem is addressed. In this case the results suggest that articulation features are more appropriate to discriminate among the four groups; however, as in the aforementioned experiments, the combination of phonation and articulation features also improved the results. For future work recordings of running speech from different pathologies are being collected. The idea is to work on the development of general methods for the automatic discrimination of different diseases and voice disorders.

Acknowledgments. This work is funded by CODI at Universidad de Antioquia, projects PRV16-2-01 and 2015-7683.

References

1. Kummer, A.W.: Cleft Palate and Craniofacial Anomalies: Effects on Speech and Resonance. Thomson Delmar Learning, Clifton Park (2008)
2. Hillenbrand, J., Houde, R.: Acoustic correlates of breathy vocal quality dysphonic voices and continuous speech. J. Speech Hear. Res. **39**(2), 311–321 (1996)
3. Logemann, J.A., Fisher, H.B., Boshes, B., Blonsky, E.R.: Frequency and cooccurrence of vocal tract dysfunctions in the speech of a large sample of Parkinson patients. J. Speech Hear. Disord. **43**(1), 47–57 (1978)
4. Kummer, A.W.: Speech evaluation for patients with cleft palate. Clin. Plast. Surg. **41**(2), 241–251 (2014)
5. Orozco-Arroyave, J.R., Vargas-Bonilla, J.F., et al.: Automatic detection of hypernasal speech of children with cleft lip and palate from spanish vowels and words using classical measures and nonlinear analysis. Rev. Fac. Ing. Universidad de Antioquia **79**, 69–82 (2016)
6. Ali, Z., Elamvazuthi, I., Alsulaiman, M., Muhammad, G.: Detection of voice pathology using fractal dimension in a multiresolution analysis of normal and disordered speech signals. J. Med. Syst. **40**(1), 1–10 (2016)
7. Karlsson, T., Tuomi, L., Andréll, P., Johansson, M., Finizia, C.: Effects of voice rehabilitation after radiotherapy for laryngeal cancer: a longitudinal study. Logop. Phoniatr. Vocol., 1–11 (2016). http://dx.doi.org/10.1080/14015439.2016.1250943
8. Hanson, D.G., Gerratt, B.R., Ward, P.H.: Cinegraphic observations of laryngeal function in Parkinson's disease. Laryngoscope **94**(3), 348–353 (1984)
9. Tsanas, A., Little, M.A., Fox, C., Ramig, L.O.: Objective automatic assessment of rehabilitative speech treatment in Parkinson's disease. IEEE Trans. Neural Syst. Rehabil. Eng. **22**(1), 181–190 (2014)
10. Orozco-Arroyave, J.R., Belalcazar-Bolaños, E.A., et al.: Characterization methods for the detection of multiple voice disorders: Neurological, functional, and laryngeal diseases. IEEE JBHI **19**(6), 1820–1828 (2015)
11. He, L., Zhang, J., et al.: Automatic evaluation of hypernasality based on a cleft palate speech database. J. Med. Syst. **39**(5), 61 (2015)
12. Jacobi, I., Van Rossum, M.A., Van Der Molen, L., Hilgers, F., Van Den Brekel, M.: Acoustic analysis of changes in articulation proficiency in patients with advanced head and neck cancer treated with chemo-radiotherapy. Ann. Otol. Rhinol. Laryngol. **122**(12), 754–762 (2013)
13. Ackermann, H., Ziegler, W.: Articulatory deficits in Parkinsonian dysarthria: an acoustic analysis. J. Neurol. Neurosurg. Psychiatry **54**(12), 1093–1098 (1991)
14. Skodda, S., Visser, W., Schlegel, U.: Vowel articulation in Parkinson's disease. J. Voice **25**(4), 467–472 (2011)
15. Novotnỳ, M., Rusz, J., Čmejla, R., Růžička, E.: Automatic evaluation of articulatory disorders in Parkinson's disease. IEEE ACM Trans. Audio Speech Lang. Process. **22**(9), 1366–1378 (2014)
16. Di Nicola, V., Fiorella, M., Spinelli, D., Fiorella, R.: Acoustic analysis of voice in patients treated by reconstructive subtotal laryngectomy. Evaluation and critical review. Acta Otorhinolaryngol. Ital. **26**(2), 59 (2006)

17. Kasuya, H., Ebihara, S., Chiba, T., Konno, T.: Characteristics of pitch period, amplitude perturbations in speech of patients with laryngeal cancer. Electron. Commun. Jpn. (Part I: Commun.) **65**(5), 11–19 (1982)
18. Michaelis, D., Gramss, T., Strube, H.W.: Glottal-to-noise excitation ratio-a new measure for describing pathological voices. Acta Acust. United Acust. **83**(4), 700–706 (1997)
19. Sapir, S., Ramig, L., Spielman, J., Fox, C.: Formant centralization ratio: a proposal for a new acoustic measure of dysarthric speech. J. Speech Lang. Hear. Res. **53**(1), 114–125 (2010)
20. Godino-Llorente, J.I., Gómez-Vilda, P., Blanco-Velasco, M.: Dimensionality reduction of a pathological voice quality assessement system based on gaussian mixture models and short-term cepstral parameters. IEEE Trans. Biomed. Eng. **53**(10), 1943–1953 (2006)
21. Murthy, H.A., Gadde, V.: The modified group delay function and its application to phoneme recognition. In: IEEE ICASSP, pp. 63–68 (2003)
22. Sáenz-Lechón, N., Godino-Llorente, J.I., Osma-Ruiz, V., Gómez-Vilda, P.: Methodological issues in the development of automatic systems for voice pathology detection. Biomed. Sig. Process. Control **1**, 120–128 (2006)
23. Parsa, V., Jamieson, D.: Acoustic discrimination of pathological voice sustained vowels versus continuous speech. J. Speech Lang. Hear. Res. **44**(2), 327–339 (2001)
24. Orozco-Arroyave, J.R., Vargas-Bonilla, J.F., et al.: New Spanish speech corpus database for the analysis of people suffering from Parkinson's disease. In: 9th LREC, pp. 342–347 (2014)

A Knowledge-Based Clinical Decision Support System for Monitoring Chronic Patients

Víctor Vives-Boix(✉), Daniel Ruiz-Fernández, Alberto de Ramón-Fernández, Diego Marcos-Jorquera, and Virgilio Gilart-Iglesias

Department of Computer Technology, University of Alicante, Alicante, Spain
{vvives,druiz,aderamon,dmarcos,vgilart}@dtic.ua.es

Abstract. Monitoring chronic patients represent one of the main challenges in healthcare and information technologies. Knowledge-based and decision support systems seek to facilitate the adherence of physicians to treatments and guidelines, while improving self-management and empowerment of patients. In this work, a knowledge-based clinical decision support system is proposed for monitoring chronic patients, whose knowledge is given beforehand by human experts in the domain application.

Keywords: Decision support system · Expert system · Knowledge base · Chronic diseases · Crohn's disease · High blood pressure

1 Introduction

Chronic diseases represents one of the main challenges for health institutions. According to the World Health Organization (WHO), they cause 63% of deaths worldwide and this fact will increase up to 88% in 2020. Those with the highest mortality rate in the world are: cardiovascular diseases (with 17 million deaths), respiratory diseases (with 7.6 million deaths) and diabetes (with 1.3 million deaths). All these numbers can be considerably reduced by controlling four risk factors: smoking, physical activity, alcohol consumption and diet [1].

Thus, in recent years, a new research area of information technologies has emerged to support patients with chronic diseases. Knowledge management systems in healthcare have been shown to improve physician adherence to evidence-based guidelines for treatments and reduce human errors while helping physicians to process new findings and guidelines in research [2]. Moreover, decision support systems are powerful solutions that can make life easier for patients [3].

Chronic patients often encounter a reduction in their quality of life that can be improved through empowerment and self-management [4]. The term self-management denotes the active participation of chronic patients in their treatment, which aim is to minimise the impact of a particular disease in their health status [5]. This includes self-care activities undertaken with the intention of preventing and limiting their disease for enhancing their health. Moreover, self-management support involves a patient-physician collaborative approach to

J.M. Ferrández Vicente et al. (Eds.): IWINAC 2017, Part II, LNCS 10338, pp. 435–443, 2017.
DOI: 10.1007/978-3-319-59773-7_44

promote patient empowerment, a process through which people reach greater control over decisions and actions affecting their health [6].

In this work we focus on patients with high blood pressure or Crohn's disease. High blood pressure, also known as hypertension, is defined by the World Health Organization (WHO) as a common and dangerous chronic condition in which the blood vessels have persistently raised pressure and the most important preventable cause of stroke and heart disease [7]. In contrast, Crohn's disease is not well defined yet, but is known to be related to the mutation of the NOD2 gene [8]. The most common symptoms of Crohn's disease are diarrhoea, abdominal cramping and pain, weight loss and, depending on the location along the gastrointestinal tract, vomiting and skin alterations [9].

Both diseases have several guidelines for their treatment and well-defined procedures for their monitoring. However, there are not technological solutions for reducing face-to-face medical consultation in any of theses chronic diseases. Thus, well-approached clinical decision support systems can improve the quality of life of both chronic patients and physicians.

The aim of the proposed knowledge-based clinical decision support system is monitoring patients from home by analysing physiological parameters and daily measurements using digital devices (blood pressure monitor, scale and wristband). In addition, we include empowerment and self-management by giving patients the option of choosing what kind of provided lifestyle changes are they willing to do. In this way, we can process patients' preferences and perform personalised recommendations by merging their selections with the stored knowledge given beforehand by physicians.

Some background about knowledge-based and clinical decision support systems is described below. The state of the art and related work is also described in detail. There is also a deeper explanation about the proposed system. Finally, conclusions and future work are presented.

2 Background

A clinical decision support system (CDSS) is a computer-based decision-making system applied to clinical practice to achieve medical knowledge [10]. This kind of systems should be able to provide appropriate services to the users satisfying different requirements. A CDSS is also able to process complex requirements of medical experts and can evaluate whether the results of previous measurements could influence patient treatment. This systems can include a knowledge-based system with a set of requirements established jointly with physicians.

Knowledge-based decision support systems (KBDSS) are decision support systems (DSS) that use relevant knowledge, in the form of a decision-making emulation of a human expert, as information base. KBDSS are designed to ensure more precise decision-making by effectively using timely and appropriate data, information and knowledge management [11]. Therefore, these systems are not designed to take decisions for users, but rather they provide relevant information in an efficient way that allow users to take more informed decisions. In addition, decision-making can be supported through recommendation techniques.

Knowledge-based decision support systems arose out of earlier expert systems (Fig. 1) and they consist of three types of sub-systems: (1) a knowledge base, (2) an inference engine and (3) a mechanism to communicate [12]. The knowledge base contains all the information (called facts) that encode the expertise of the system about a certain application domain. This expertise is encoded in the form of rules and associations of compiled data, given beforehand by human experts, which most often take the form of IF-THEN rules [13]. The inference engine is an automated reasoning system that evaluates the current state of the knowledge base, combines the rules with the current user's data and then asserts new facts and knowledge to the knowledge base. Last, the communication mechanism allows the system to collect information from the users and show them the results of evaluating their data, mostly in the form of recommendations.

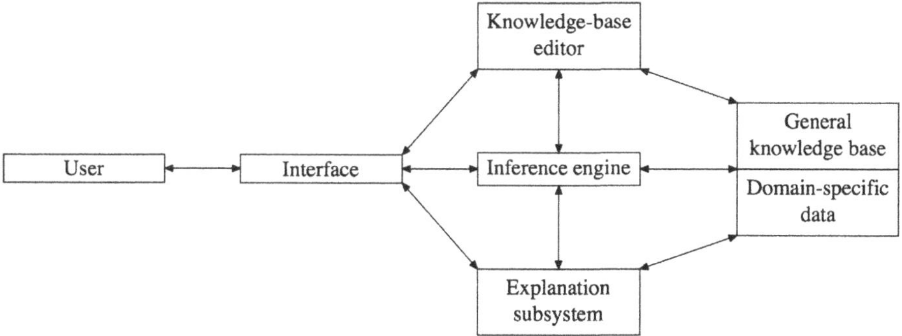

Fig. 1. Expert system architecture by Luger and Stubblefield [14]

Combining both concepts we get knowledge-based clinical decision support systems, where the aim is to build a computer program that could no longer simulate an expert's decision-making, but to assist patients to their own decision-making. This means, patients are expected to filter and discard information in which they are not interested, also to be active and to interact with the system and decide about their treatment rather than just be an observer [15].

3 Related Work

Clinical decision support systems are a current field of study in medical and health care [16]. Moreover, in [17] can be found a classification table with multiple examples of clinical decision support systems and data mining tools for healthcare. It is also said that one of the major differences between clinical decision support systems employing data mining tools and those that employ rule-based expert systems resides in the knowledge engine. In the decision support systems that use rule-based expert systems, the inference engine must be supplied with the facts and the rules associated with them.

Delving into chronic diseases, Huygens et al. in [18] collect the needs of patients with chronic diseases for using information and communication technologies in healthcare (also called eHealth or e-health) and they conclude that disease control is a key factor in the willingness of patients to use eHealth for self-management purposes. In addition, eHealth it is also shown in [19] to be a useful tool for both chronic patients to become aware of their own health status and caregivers to improve their relationship with patients.

On the other hand, in recent years some personalised self-management systems have been proposed and it has been shown that they improve lifestyle in patients with chronic diseases [12]. Telemedicine is also a current topic in the monitoring of chronic patients as shown in [20], where a telemedicine system has been developed to monitor three chronic pathologies: cardiac arrhythmia, hypertension and diabetes mellitus. However, it is not included any clinical decision support system in the chronic patients monitoring.

4 Method

4.1 Knowledge Base

Knowledge-based decision support systems in a clinical domain require a high-quality knowledge base, and its construction and maintenance can consume great efforts in broad domains as chronic diseases. In this project we have been working together with the Nursing Department within the Faculty of Health Sciences of the University of Alicante. They have been our experts during the knowledge base development, as they have a solid background in chronic disease treatment and patient monitoring with multiple publications in high impact journals [21].

First, blood pressure values are established according to the seventh report of the Joint National Committee (JNC) on prevention, detection, evaluation and treatment of hypertension (Fig. 1). In addition, guidelines for hypertension management in [22] are used to summarise different lifestyle changes that reduce blood pressure and cardiovascular disease (Table 2), with the aim of achieving an optimal situation based on estimated blood pressure reductions (Tables 1 and 3).

Table 1. Hypertension classification according to the seventh report of the JNC [23].

Blood pressure	Systolic (mmHg)		Diastolic (mmHg)
Normal	<120	and	<80
Prehypertension	120–139	or	80–89
Stage 1 of hypertension	140–159	or	90–99
Stage 2 of hypertension	≥ 160	or	≥ 100

Patients with Crohn's disease have different lifestyle changes depending on their period: remission or outbreak. However, they also need to have life habits regardless of the period in which they are (Table 4).

Table 2. Lifestyle changes that reduce blood pressure and cardiovascular disease.

Lifestyle changes that reduce blood pressure
Restriction of weight
Restriction of salt consumption
Limitation of alcohol consumption
Increase of physical activity
Increase of fruits and vegetables consumption
Reduction of total fat and saturated fat consumption
Lifestyle changes that reduce the risk of cardiovascular disease
Quit smoking
Reduction of total fat and saturated fat consumption
Adoption of a mediterranean diet

Table 3. Changes in lifestyle and effect on blood pressure.

Changes	Optimal situation	Estimated reduction
Weight	Maintain ideal weight (BMI 20–25 kg/m^2)	5–20 mmHg per 10 kg
Salt consumption	Reduce intake to below 100 mmol/day (6 g of salt, a teaspoon)	2–8 mmHg
Alcohol consumption	Limit consumption below 210 g/week (30 g/day) in men and 140 g (20 g/day) in women	2–4 mmHg
Healthy diet	Diet rich in fruits, vegetables and dairy products with total and saturated fat reduction	8–14 mmHg
Physical activity	Regular practice of aerobic exercise (at least 5 days a week)	4–9 mmHg

For all patients, many physiological and non-physiological parameters are used for the monitoring such as weight, height, body mass index, age, blood pressure, heart rate, daily activity or sleep quality. Moreover, patients are empowered by giving them the possibility of selecting, using the interface, what lifestyle changes they are willing to do and what changes they do not. These preferences selection infer directly in the recommendations given by the inference engine with the aim of achieve personalised solutions.

4.2 Inference Engine

The inference or reasoning engine maps the patient's signs and symptoms to those diseases and might suggest some lifestyle recommendations available for both, patient and physician [13]. This component of a knowledge-based CDSS

Table 4. Lifestyle changes for Crohn's patients.

Lifestyle changes in remission's period
Make rich meals in proteins, iron and calcium
Lifestyle changes in outbreak's period
Avoid food that contain fibre and fat
Avoid legumes, vegetables and fruit
Do not drink milk in case of intolerance
Make simple meals (boiled, iron, oven)
Common lifestyle changes (both periods)
Balanced diet (4–5 meals/day)
Eat slowly and chew well
Avoid certain medications: aspirins and non-steroidal anti-inflammatory drugs
Ensure vaccination against tetanus, diphtheria, poliomyelitis, rubella, measles, mumps, hepatitis B, chicken pox and influenza
Periodic review with the dermatologist

combines the input data and the information allocated in the knowledge base to have a result in the form of lifestyle recommendations. These combinations are made with IF-THEN rules, as knowledge is well-defined and don't include any probabilistic parameter in the decision-making process.

The reasoning method used is forward chaining, where the knowledge is developed by a data-driven search. Thus, the method starts with the available data and uses inference rules to extract more data until it finds a rule where the antecedent (IF clause) is known to be true. When such a rule is found, the engine infer the consequent (THEN clause) resulting in new data in the form of one or more personalised recommendations for the patient. Examples for blood pressure and Crohn's disease respectively are given below.

Example 1. **if** (change4.selected **and** state == prehypertesion **and** bmi $\geq$ 30) **then** addRecommendation (regular practice of aerobic exercise: at least 5 days a week walking fast for 45 min.)

Example 2. **if** (change2.selected **and** period == outbreak) **then** addRecommendation (avoid foods that contain fibre and fat: they are complicated to digest by the organism and can damage the bowel because of excessive movements.)

4.3 Interface

CDSS implementation often suffer from usability issues, which have a direct impact on the adherence of patients and the effectiveness of the treatment [24]. For this reason we have performed a user-centered design, given by Norman and explained in [25], with principles that have become widely used since then.

The interface has been built as a mobile application for smartphones that can automatically interact with multiple digital devices via Bluetooth LE (Low Energy), also called Bluetooth Smart. These digital devices are (1) a blood pressure monitor, (2) a scale and (3) a wristband. All these devices collect data automatically with no manual interaction required by the patient.

Moreover, the interface allows not only the automatic data collection, but also the patient preferences selection. In this way, the application also shows historical data and the evolution of the patients during their treatment, plus the personalised recommendations based on their current status and their previously selected lifestyle changes and preferences.

5 Conclusions

In the pursuit of greater life expectancy, advances in medicine have led to a high percentage of people who can live longer, by converting deadly diseases into chronic diseases. In this work we propose a knowledge-based clinical decision support system for monitoring chronic patients with the aim of controlling their disease and improve their quality of life. This system also empowers patients by including the possibility of selecting those lifestyle changes they are willing to do, thus using these preferences for making personalised recommendations.

In a future work, we contemplate the possibility of improving our expert system by including more chronic diseases in the knowledge base. For this to be possible, it is necessary to carefully analyse the clinical guidelines and processes associated to each of these new diseases with its corresponding human experts. In addition, this work is expected to be operational in a few months with a set of patients that we have already selected. After this experimental phase, we will be able to observe how this proposal works and what impact has on their lives.

Conflict of Interest

The authors declare no conflict of interest.

Acknowledgements. This work has been granted by the Ministerio de Economía y Competitividad of the Spanish Government (ref. TIN2014-53067-C3-1-R) and cofinanced by FEDER (Fondo Europeo de Desarrollo Regional).

References

1. World Health Organization: Global status report on noncommunicable diseases (2010)
2. Jamal, A., McKenzie, K., Clark, M.: The impact of health information technology on the quality of medical and health care: a systematic review. Health Inf. Manag. J. **38**(3), 26–37 (2009)
3. Sim, I., Gorman, P., Greenes, R.A., Haynes, R.B., Kaplan, B., Lehmann, H., Tang, P.C.: Clinical decision support systems for the practice of evidence-based medicine. J. Am. Med. Inform. Assoc.: JAMIA **8**(6), 527–534 (2001)

4. Nolte, E., McKee, M.: Caring for People with Chronic Conditions: A Health System Perspective. Open University Press, Maidenhead (2008)
5. Koch, T., Jenkin, P., Kralik, D.: Chronic illness self-management: locating the 'self'. J. Adv. Nurs. **48**(5), 484–492 (2004)
6. Goldstein, M.S.: The persistence and resurgence of medical pluralism. J. Health Polit. Policy Law **29**(4–5), 925–945 (2004)
7. World Health Organization: Hypertension (2013)
8. Abraham, C., Cho, J.H.: Inflammatory bowel disease. N. Engl. J. Med. **361**(21), 2066–2078 (2009)
9. Wilkins, T., Jarvis, K., Patel, J.: Diagnosis and management of Crohn's disease. Am. Fam. Physician **84**(12), 1365–1375 (2011)
10. Yang, J., Kang, U., Lee, Y.: Clinical decision support system in medical knowledge literature review. Inf. Technol. Manag. **17**(1), 5–14 (2016)
11. Chung, K., Boutaba, R., Hariri, S.: Knowledge based decision support system. Inf. Technol. Manag. **17**(1), 1–3 (2016)
12. Dinevski, D., Bele, U., Sarenac, T., Rajkovic, U., Sustersic, O., Berner, E.S.E., La Lande, T.J., Lande, T.J.: Overview of clinical decision support systems. Vasa **6**(1), 3–22 (2007)
13. Spooner, S.A.: Mathematical foundations of decision support systems. In: Berner, E.S. (ed.) Clinical Decision Support Systems: Theory and Practice, pp. 23–43. Springer International Publishing, Cham (2007)
14. Luger, G.F., Stubblefield, W.A.: Artificial Intelligence and the Design of Expert Systems. Benjamin/Cummings Publishing Company, San Francisco (1989)
15. Jimison, H.B., Sher, P.P., Jimison, J.J.B.: Decision support for patients. In: Berner, E.S. (ed.) Clinical Decision Support Systems, pp. 249–261. Springer International Publishing, Cham (2007)
16. Kilsdonk, E., Peute, L., Jaspers, M.: Factors influencing implementation success of guideline-based clinical decision support systems: a systematic review and gaps analysis. Int. J. Med. Inform. **98**, 56–64 (2017)
17. Hardin, J.M., Chhieng, D.C.: Data mining and clinical decision support systems. In: Berner, E.S. (ed.) Clinical Decision Support Systems, pp. 44–63. Springer, Heidelberg (2007)
18. Huygens, M.W.J., Vermeulen, J., Swinkels, I.C.S., Friele, R.D., Schayck, O.C.P.V., Witte, L.P.D.: Expectations and needs of patients with a chronic disease toward self-management and eHealth for self-management purposes. BMC Health Serv. Res. **16**(232), 1–11 (2016)
19. Talboom-Kamp, E.P., Verdijk, N.A., Harmans, L.M., Numans, M.E., Chavannes, N.H.: An eHealth platform to manage chronic disease in primary care: an innovative approach. Interact. J. Med. Res. **5**(1), e5 (2016)
20. Gonzalez-Fernandez, R.I., Mulet-Cartaya, M.L., Lopez-Cardona, J.D., Lopez-Reyes, A., Lopez-Rodriguez, R., Lopez-Creagh, R., Ledesma-Valdes, E.: A telemedicine system to follow-up the evolution of chronic diseases in the community. In: Jaffray, D.A. (ed.) World Congress on Medical Physics and Biomedical Engineering. IFMBE Proceedings, vol. 51, pp. 1431–1434. Springer, Heidelberg (2015)
21. García-Sanjuán, S., Lillo-Crespo, M., Sanjuán-Quiles, Á., Gil-González, D., Richart-Martínez, M.: Life experiences of people affected by Crohn's disease and their support networks: scoping review. Clin. Nurs. Res. **25**(1), 79–99 (2016)
22. Williams, B., Poulter, N.R., Brown, M.J., Davis, M., McInnes, G.T., Potter, J.F., Sever, P.S., Thom, S.M.: British Hypertension Society guidelines for hypertension management 2004 (BHS-IV): summary. BMJ **328**(7440), 634–640 (2004)

23. Chobanian, A.V., Bakris, G.L., Black, H.R., Cushman, W.C., Green, L.A., Izzo Jr., J.L., Jones, D.W., Materson, B.J., Oparil, S., Wright Jr., J.T., Roccella, E.J.: Seventh report of the joint national committee on prevention, detection, evaluation, and treatment of high blood pressure. Hypertension **42**(6), 1206–1252 (2003)
24. Gong, Y., Kang, H.: Usability and clinical decision support. In: Berner, E.S. (ed.) Clinical Decision Support Systems, pp. 69–86. Springer, Heidelberg (2016)
25. Bailey, B.: Paper Prototypes Work as Well as Software Prototypes (2005)

Using the Power Spectra of Images and Noise for Portal Imaging Systems Characterization

Antonio González-López[1(✉)] and Juan Morales-Sánchez[2]

[1] Servicio de Radiofísica y Protección Radiológica, Hospital Universitario Virgen de la Arrixaca, 30120 Murcia, Spain
antonio.gonzalez7@carm.es

[2] Dpto. Tecnologías de la Información y las Comunicaciones, Universidad Politécnica de Cartagena, 30202 Cartagena, Spain

Abstract. In this work an ensemble of portal images and noise images are wavelet transformed. The power distribution of the resulting coefficients is then calculated as a function of scale. Assuming statistical independence between noise and image, the noise power is subtracted to the image power, and the resulting power spectrum (averaged over orientations) is found to behave approximately as $f^{-\alpha}$, $\alpha = 3.2 \pm 0.1$, where f is the resolution (inverse of the scale). The power spectrum is calculated in the wavelet domain using a two-dimensional separable transform, with a Haar wavelet basis. No test objects are used in this determination. Clinical portal images and uniform images are the input to the method. In this way, the portal image system performance is studied on an ensemble of images with the same characteristics (contrast, noise and frequency content) as the images used in the clinical procedures.

1 Introduction

Detective quantum efficiency (DQE) is accepted as the standard determination procedure for the performance of the x-ray image detectors used in diagnostic radiology. DQE is defined as the square of the signal to noise ratio fraction that the system is able to transfer from its input to its output, and is usually calculated from the ratio of the system modulation transfer function (MTF) to the system noise power spectrum (NPS).

Treatment of MTF and NPS is not as simple with digital images as with analog ones. Aliasing of high frequency values into lower ones due to undersampling make noise equivalent quanta (NEQ) lose its meaning as maximum available SNR^2 at a given frequency. Also, MTF do not behave as transfer amplitude of a single sinusoid. In MTF calculation aliasing, resulting from sampling, is overcome by means of oversampling techniques, but these oversampling procedures are not possible in NPS calculation. Aliasing does not produce any visible artefacts on noise or uniform images, but alters the frequency content of the sampled signal.

The MTF is calculated by imaging slits [1], high density edges [2–4], pinhole arrays [5] or bar patterns [6]. All of them are intended to produce a high contrast

J.M. Ferrández Vicente et al. (Eds.): IWINAC 2017, Part II, LNCS 10338, pp. 444–452, 2017.
DOI: 10.1007/978-3-319-59773-7_45

image, with well-defined image irregularities as edges or peaks. The most widely used test object in diagnostic x-ray is the lead or tungsten edge as recommended by the International Electrotechnical Commission [7]. A problem has been associated to the use of these objects arising from the scattered radiation produced in the edge. The high density of the edge material allows for the required small thickness of the edge, but Pb characteristic x-rays scatter form the edge blurring the acquired image.

The problem for the MTF determination becomes worse when facing radiotherapy portal image. The high energy particles used in radiotherapy, produce a huge amount of scatter in every object used as test object. This makes very difficult to produce a well defined radiation pattern to irradiate the detector, making complex the analysis of the image system.

In this work an alternative way to measure the detector performance is presented. The image wavelet power spectrum (PS) is calculated in the wavelet domain as a function of scale. PS is calculated as the difference between image power and noise power, both averaged over an ensemble of portal images and noise images respectively. No test objects are used in this work. Instead, all the images representing signal in PS calculations are clinical portal images. On the other hand, noise is obtained from the analysis of uniform images. Previously, any not random trend is removed from these uniform images by an average-and-subtract process.

Image processing has been taken advantage of wavelet properties in several applications such as, for instance, image compression and image denoising. Image denoising methods, most of them developed on natural images, have been shown to be useful in other image modalities as Portal Imaging [8].

Among the properties that make wavelets popular in image processing, it's worth noting that the receptive fields of simple cells in the visual cortex of animals have been found to resemble wavelet functions [9, 10]. Decomposing images using wavelets leads to coefficients that are quite non-Gaussian, i.e. the histograms of wavelet coefficients display heavy tails, sharp cusps at the median and large correlations across different scales.

A wavelet transform decomposes an image into a multiscale representation [11], and this fits into the multiscale nature of images which contain information on objects at different scales. Wavelet basis functions are localized in space and are scaled versions of one mother wavelet, and a wavelet coefficient tells how much or the corresponding wavelet basis is present in the total image. This information is local in space and in frequency (or resolution, defined as the inverse of the scale), and shows where a singularity in the image is located, and how far it ranges.

It's also worth noting the sparsity of the wavelet decomposition. The decorrelating property of wavelet transforms leads to sparsity, and simplifies the statistical distribution of images in the wavelet domain. Sparseness means a representation where a small number of coefficients contain the most part of the image energy, and this makes a fundamental difference with noise (where energy is widely distributed between coefficients). For the same irradiation dose, energy (defined as the square of the image norm) is higger in an image containing irregularities (such as edges or peaks) than in an uniform one.

On the other hand, orthogonality guarantees numerically well conditioned transforms. Also, wavelet transform is a linear decomposition with linear complexity (can be implemented with fast algorithms).

Finally, decorrelated noise and signal are kept decorrelated under linear transformations, and in the case of orthonormal wavelet transforms the energy of the signal is also kept invariant.

2 Materials and Methods

Imaging System. The electronic portal image (EPID) studied in this work was the Portal Vision aS500 electronic portal imaging device, from Varian Medical Systems. The aS500 is equipped with an amorphous Silicon flat panel detector with an array of 384 × 512 elements. The pixel size is 0.784 mm × 0.784mm and the physical build-up of the amorphous Silicon detector is composed of a metal plate, a phosphor plate to transform x-rays to visible light and a pixel array on the a-Si plate to capture the light. Radiation beams used were 6 MV x-rays beams from a Clinac 2100 DHX linear accelerator (Varian Medical Systems).

Portal Images. A fundamental issue is the selection of the portal images for the ensemble. The images selected must include the image features looked for in portal imaging as, for instance, contrast between soft tissue and bone. On the other hand, all the images must be similar enough to produce similar results after the analysis. Therefore, some requirements are needed for the images in the ensemble:

- All of the images should correspond to the same anatomical location and projection. This location and projection will produce images containing the features of interest in portal images.
- Features not belonging to anatomy should be excluded. Such features could proceed from imaging the field limits, as in double exposure techniques, or from anatomy borders producing high contrast air-tissue interfaces, as in brain imaging.

For these reasons, images are acquired during open field single exposure, and images are cropped so no treatment field limits appear inside. Also the location and projection selected are pelvic and anteroposterior.

The Anatomical portal images analyzed in this work come from patient set-up procedures exclusively, and are obtained following the clinical procedure. The number of images in the ensemble is fifty nine. Figure 1 shows a sample of the images used in the calculation of energy density. Around every image it can be seen a number of peripheral non irradiated areas (shown as white bands). Before wavelet decomposition these white bands were detected and eliminated.

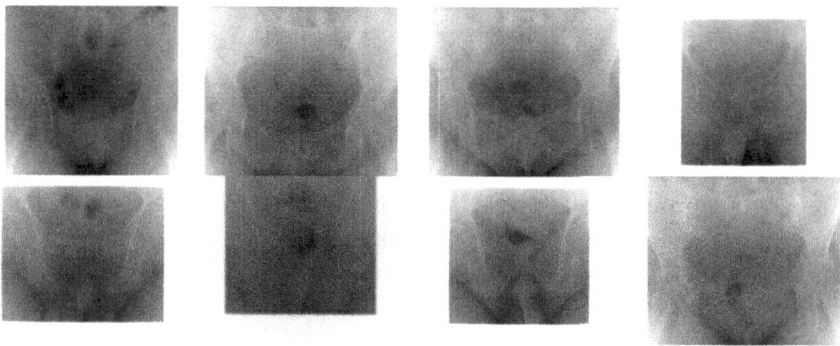

Fig. 1. A sample of the fifty nine portal images used in the power spectrum calculation.

Noise Images. Noise images are obtained from uniform images through an average and subtract process similar to that described in [12]. A PMMA slabs phantom uniformly irradiated was imaged sixteen times. The PMMA phantom was a 30 cm × 30 cm × 15 cm block of PMMA slabs, the nominal energy for the photon beam was 6 MV, and the collimator sizes were chosen to keep the field limits inside the detector area and the phantom body. The image acquisition was carried out following the clinical procedure. In this way the radiation dose delivered to the image detector in the case of phantom imaging is close to the radiation dose for anatomical portal images.

A mean uniform image was calculated and subtracted from each of the uniform images to obtain sixteen *noise images.* Peripheral pixels are excluded by cropping the image to a central region of 325 × 465 pixels. The noise images were later processed to eliminate low frequencies trends by means of subtraction of a second degree polynomial fit.

Wavelet Selection. Important question is which wavelet to choose for image processing. In order to obtain a sparse representation it is desirable a small support and a high number of vanishing moments N_v. Optimal wavelets for these requirement are the *daubechies* wavelets dbN_v [13], where N_v is the number of vanishing moments. The N_v selected in this work is one, and the discrete wavelet transform (DWT) used is a separable two-dimensional transform with a *Haar* wavelet basis. Haar wavelet has a drawback for image processing: its lack of regularity. This negative characteristic influences the visual quality of the processed image. But this is not a concern in the present context, as no processed image is produced.

Power Spectral Calculation. For each portal image I_n, $n = 1, \dots, N$ an eight levels two-dimensional DWT is carried out. Let $w_{In}(i, j, S, O)$ be the detail coefficient with coordinates (i, j) in the subband with orientation O, at level (or scale) S. The ensemble power spectrum (averaged over orientations) at scale S, is obtained by averaging the square of these detail coefficients over the portal images ensemble

$$EPS(S) = \frac{1}{3NN_SM_S}\sum_{n=1}^{N}\sum_{i,j=1}^{N_S,M_S}\sum_{O=H,V,D} w_{In}^2,\ S = 1,2,\ldots,8 \tag{1}$$

where N is the number of portal images, N_S and M_S are the dimensions of the subbands in scale S, and the orientations O are horizontal, vertical and diagonal.

An analogous procedure is carried out for the noise images in the calculation of the noise power spectrum $NPS(S)$ at scale S.

Assuming statistical independence for noise and image an image power spectrum (PS) is obtained subtracting noise power to image power

$$PS(S) = EPS(S) - NPS(S),\ S = 1,2,\ldots,8 \tag{2}$$

The number of scales used is $S = 8$, because no image investigated in this work has a size greater or equal than 512×512 pixels. Therefore, the scale ranges from 1.57 mm to 200.7 mm, and resolution (inverse of scale) ranges from 0.005 mm^{-1} to 0.638 mm^{-1}.

3 Results

The relevant statistical characteristics of the system noise are plotted in Fig. 2. The histograms of noise subbands are shown in Fig. 2(a), where the ordinate axis is represented in the logarithmic scale. The parabolic shape of the histogram in this representation shows the Gaussian nature of the noise distribution for all of the scales displayed. Similar results are obtained for the rest of scales and orientations. The width of the Gaussians remains almost constant for all the scales but the last, which means a flat energy spectrum for most of the frequencies in the range.

Figure 2(b) shows the noise power spectrum (radially averaged) of the portal imaging system, calculated in the frequency domain. This power spectrum in the frequency domain is estimated using

$$S(r,s) = \frac{a^2}{N_xN_y}\frac{1}{N}\sum_{n=1}^{N}\left|\sum_{k,l=1}^{N_x,N_y} I_n(k,l)e^{-2\pi i(rk/N_x+sl/N_y)}\right|^2 \tag{3}$$

where N_x and N_y are the dimensions (in pixels) of the noise images and a is the pixel spacing. Except for the very low frequencies, the curve shows a flat shape with a slightly descending slope.

These results make the system noise to resemble Gaussian uncorrelated noise. Figure 3 shows the power spectrum versus resolution curves obtained for the ensembles of noise and portal images. The abscissa and ordinate represent the base 10 logarithm of resolution and power respectively. It can be seen the variability of these curves, and how they cluster around a mean value.

The PS curve is shown in Fig. 4. A linear polynomial fit is also shown. The slope amplitude of the fitted curve is 3.17 ± 0.12, which means that the power spectrum of the portal images studied falls with a form $f^{-\alpha}$ with $\alpha \approx 3.17$ (where f stands for resolution).

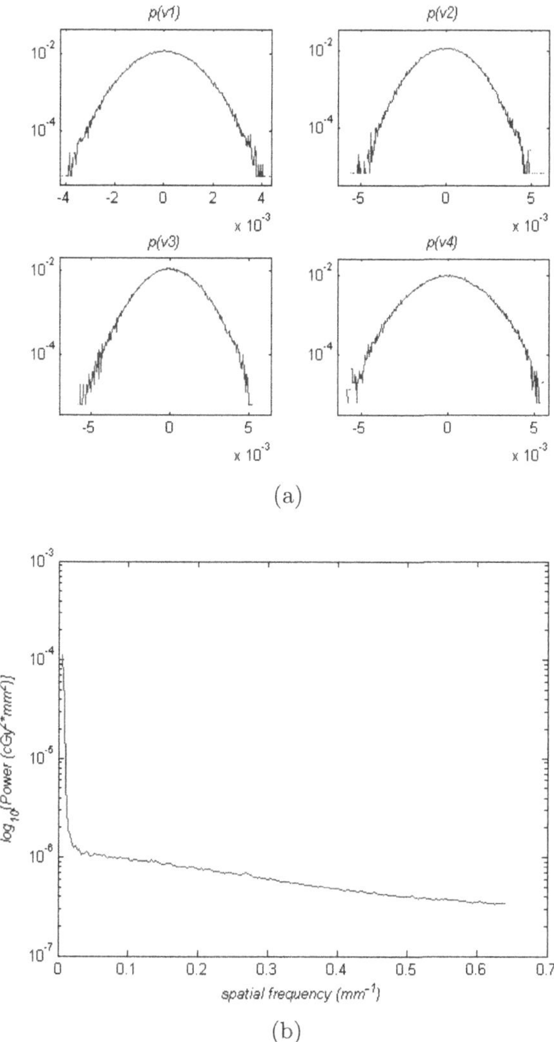

Fig. 2. (a) Experimental probability density function for the distribution of wavelet coefficients in the diagonal orientation (first four scales). (b) Power spectrum, in the frequency domain, for the noise in the portal imaging system.

4 Discussion and Conclusions

It has been presented a method to calculate the energy distribution of noise and signal in the wavelet domain, and it has been applied to a portal image system. The method uses clinical images and noise images obtained from uniform ones, no test objects either high contrast or low contrast have been used. The method is based on the energy conservation through orthonormal transforms, and the multirresolution feature of wavelets. Multirresolution allows the analysis of the

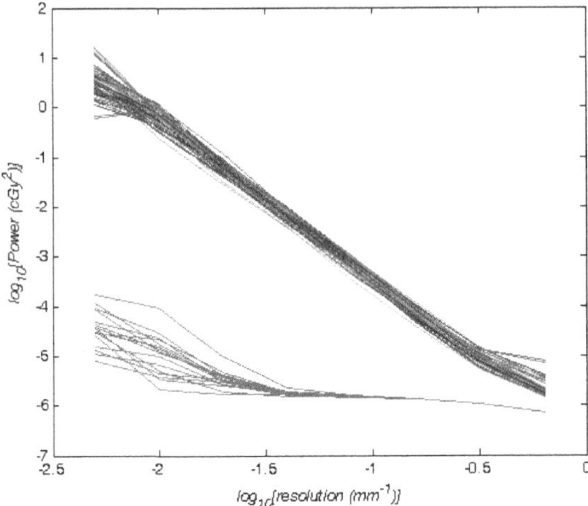

Fig. 3. Wavelet power spectrums for the portal images (upper cluster) and noise images (lower cluster) studied.

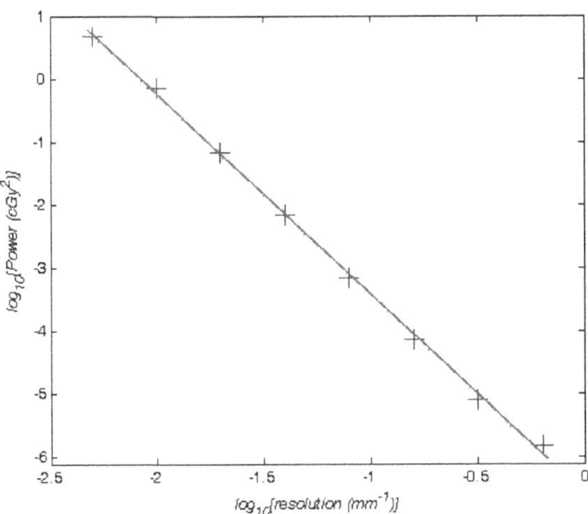

Fig. 4. Image wavelet power spectrum versus resolution curve for the ensemble of pelvic portal images, after noise power subtraction. A linear fit (continuous line) is also shown.

signal in scales that are multiples of 2 of the original pixel size. Therefore the image information content can be calculated at different resolutions.

The PS versus resolution curve can be compared to the energy spectrum for natural images obtained by several authors [14,15]. For ensembles of natural scenes Ruderman [15] mentions, as a highly robust statistical feature, the scale invariant exponential tails in the distribution of contrast gradients. Scale invariance means that the statistical properties of images should not change if one changes the scale at which observations are made. In particular, the power spectrum should not change shape under such rescaling. Field [16] points out that, if the power falls as f^{-2}, where f stands for spatial frequency, there will be equal energy in equal octaves. Therefore, in the natural world objects can appear at any scale in an image.

In portal imaging the energy is not invariant with scale. The system performance is limited in terms of spatial resolution, especially in radiotherapy where the high energy beams used have a large focus size, and the particles released in the image detector have a large range. The slope obtained for the portal images analyzed in this work is substantially greater than two, which means that high resolution objects have a lower probability to be found in these images. The slope of the PS versus resolution curve measures the loss of spatial resolution for the system and the images studied. This suggests that it can be used for the performance comparison between different equipments imaging the same type of portal images. The method presented here uses clinical images from the system under evaluation, and can be used to evaluate any particular type of images or acquisition techniques. The only requirement for implementing the method is the statistical independence of noise and image.

References

1. Fujita, H., Tsai, D.Y., Itoh, T., Doi, K., Morishita, J., Ueda, K., Ohtsuka, A.: A simple method for determining the modulation transfer function in digital radiography. IEEE Trans. Med. Imaging **11**(1), 34–39 (1992)
2. Dobbins, J.T., Ergun, D.L., Rutz, L., Hinshaw, D.A., Blume, H., Clark, D.C.: DQE of four generations of computed radiography acquisition devices. Med. Phys. **22**, 1581–1593 (1995)
3. Buhr, E., Gunther, S., Neitzel, U.: Accuracy of a simple method for deriving the presampled modulation transfer function of a digital radiographic system from an edge image. Med. Phys. **30**, 2323–2331 (2003)
4. Samei, E., Buhr, E., Granfors, P., Vandenbroucke, D., Wang, X.: Comparison of edge analysis techniques for the determination of the MTF of digital radiographic systems. Phys. Med. Biol. **30**, 1747–1757 (2005)
5. Fetterly, K., Hangiandreou, N., Schueler, B.: Measurement of the presampled two-dimensional modulation transfer function of digital imaging systems. Med. Phys. **50**(5), 913–921 (2002)
6. Droege, R.T., Rzeszotarski, M.S.: An MTF method immune to aliasing. Med. Phys. **6**, 721–725 (1985)
7. IEC 62220–1: Medical Electrical Equipment-Characteristics of Digital X-ray Imaging Devices - Part 1: Determination of the Detective Quantum Efficiency. IEC, Newark, NY (2003)
8. González-López, A., Morales-Sánchez, J., Verdú-Monedero, R., Larrey-Ruiz, J.R., Sancho-Gómez, J.L., Tobarra-González, B.: SURE-LET and BLS-GSM wavelet-based denoising algorithms versus linear Local Wiener Estimator in Radiotherapy portal image denoising. In: Dössel, O., Schlegel, W.C. (eds.) WC 2009. IFMBE Proceedings, vol. 25, no. 1, pp. 938–940. Springer, Heidelberg (2009)
9. Miller, K.D.: A model for the development of simple-cell receptive fields and the arrangement of orientation columns through activity dependent competetion between on- and off-center inputs. J. Neurosci. **14**, 409–441 (1994)

10. Olshausen, B.A., Field, D.J.: Sparse coding with an overcomplete basis set: a strategy employed by V1? Vis. Res. **37**(23), 3311–3325 (1997)
11. Mallat, S.G.: A theory for multiresolution signal decomposition - the wavelet representation. IEEE Trans. Pattern Anal. Mach. Intell. **11**, 674–693 (1989)
12. González-López, A.: Useful optical density range in film dosimetry: limitations due to noise and saturation. Phys. Med. Biol. **52**(15), N321–N327 (2007)
13. Daubechies, I.: Ten Lectures on Wavelets. SIAM, Philadelphia (1992)
14. Burton, G.J., Moorhead, I.R.: Color and spatial structure in natural scenes. Appl. Opt. **26**, 157–170 (1987)
15. Ruderman, D.L., Bialek, W.: Statistics of natural images: scaling in the woods. Phys. Rev. Lett. **73**(6), 814–817 (1994)
16. Field, D.J.: Relations between the statistics of natural images and the response properties of cortical cells. J. Opt. Soc. Am. **4**, 2379–2394 (1987)

Calculating the Power Spectrum of Digital X-ray Images in the Wavelet Domain

Antonio González-López[1(✉)] and Juan Morales-Sánchez[2]

[1] Servicio de Radiofísica y Protección Radiológica, Hospital Universitario Virgen de la Arrixaca, 30120 Murcia, Spain
antonio.gonzalez7@carm.es

[2] Dpto. Tecnologías de la Información y las Comunicaciones, Universidad Politécnica de Cartagena, 30202 Cartagena, Spain

Abstract. The multiresolution approximation decomposes an image in scales or frequency bands. The knowledge of the image power distribution in these bands is therefore important for understanding the performance of image processing algorithms. However the spectra calculated in the wavelet domain depend on the characteristics of the wavelet selected and the method used to extend the image. This extension must be done before convolving the image with the wavelet decomposition filters. On the other hand, the calculated spectrum depends on the number of vanishing moments of the wavelet and the symmetry of the wavelet filters. In this work the Fourier power spectrum and the power spectrum in the wavelet domain are compared for one ensemble of images. Highly non-symmetric *Daubechies* and very symmetric *symlet* wavelets of different vanishing moments N_v are used in combination with different extension methods. The best matching between spectrums is found for *symlet* wavelets and symmetric padding extension. Also, removing the extended part of the subbands before the power calculation improves the result.

1 Introduction

Wavelet analysis has been successfully used in a wide range of image processing applications including image compression, restoration and denoising. A wavelet transform is a linear decomposition with linear complexity, so it can be implemented with fast algorithms. Also the transform is well conditioned because of its orthogonality.

The multiresolution approximations [1] decomposes an image in scales so that the processing algorithms can be adjusted on each frequency band. The knowledge of the image power distribution in these bands is therefore important in order to better understand the performance of these algorithms. However the calculation of the power distribution in the wavelet domain depends on the particular wavelet selected and the method followed to extend the image.

Due to its finite size, it is necessary to extend the image in order to convolve it with the wavelet decomposition filters. There are different padding extension methods including zero padding, periodic padding and symmetric padding, and

J.M. Ferrández Vicente et al. (Eds.): IWINAC 2017, Part II, LNCS 10338, pp. 453–462, 2017.
DOI: 10.1007/978-3-319-59773-7_46

these extensions methods must be carefully applied in order to minimize the problem of border distortion. Border distortion may produce image discontinuities, and these discontinuities may result in high amplitude coefficients in the highest resolution subbands. In this way the power computation could be ruled by these foreign coefficients, created during pre-processing and not belonging to the image.

On the other hand, the characteristics of the wavelet filters also modify the calculated spectrum. In particular the number of vanishing moments of the wavelet and the symmetry of the wavelet decomposition filters affect the final result.

The power spectrum is a basic statistical feature of an ensemble of images and is usually calculated in the frequency domain [2]. The power spectrum in the frequency domain (or Fourier domain) decomposes the energy of an image in a series of coefficients, using trigonometric functions as the basis functions for decomposition. Trigonometric functions provide an intuitive decomposition, relating the "speed" of spatial variations to the independent variable (frequency) in the spectrum curve. Moreover the resulting spectrum has a great resolution in terms of frequency.

In order to guarantee that the spectrum calculated in the wavelet domain computes the image characteristics and is minimally affected by the calculation procedure, the wavelet spectrum must match the Fourier spectrum.

In this work the Fourier power spectrum and the wavelet power spectrum are compared for one ensemble of images. The differences observed are explained in base to the characteristic of the selected wavelet and decomposition procedure. Highly non-symmetric *Daubechies* and very symmetric *symlet* wavelets of different vanishing moments N_v are used in combination with different padding extension methods.

2 Materials and Methods

2.1 Ensemble of Images

The ensemble of computerized radiography (CR) images is comprised of 25 clips obtained from digital radiographies of various anatomical locations. The size of each clip is 512×512 pixels and the pixel spacing is $a = 0.143$ mm. Figure 1 shows a sample of the CR images used in the calculation of the power spectrum.

2.2 Multiresolution and Decomposition Filters

The approximation of a function f at scale 2^j is specified by a discrete grid of samples $\{a_j[n]\}$ that provides local averages of f over neighborhoods of size proportional to 2^j. In the multiresolution approximation [1], a fast wavelet transform is computed with a cascade of filterings with a low pass filter $\overline{h}$ and a high pass filter $\overline{g}$ followed by a factor 2 subsampling.

Daubechies wavelets dbN_v [3], where N_v is the number of vanishing moments, are used in this work because they have a support of minimum size for any

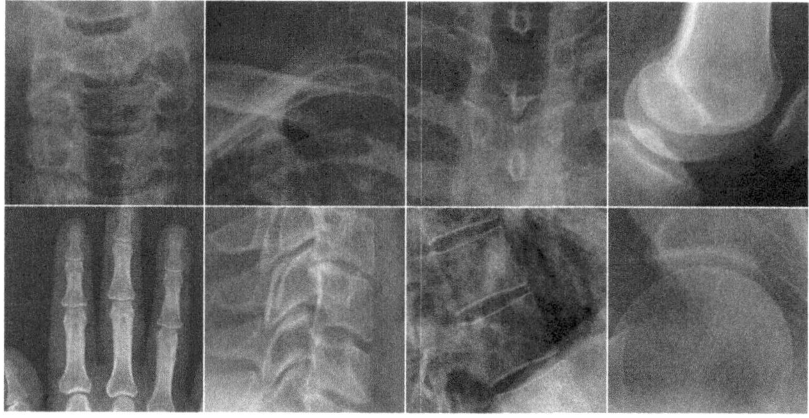

Fig. 1. A sample of the CR images used in the power spectrum calculation.

given number of vanishing moments. A small support and a high number of vanishing moments are important in order to obtain a sparse representation, and this feature has been shown very useful in a number of image processing applications [4–6]. Wavelets dbN_v are orthonormal, have a support of $2N_v - 1$ and are implemented with digital filters of length $2N_v$.

Filters $\overline{h}[n]$ and $\overline{g}[n]$ split the frequency spectrum in two overlapping bands. The overlapping area depends on the wavelet characteristics. Figure 2 shows the graphs of $|\widehat{h}(\nu)|^2$ and $|\widehat{g}(\nu)|^2$, where $h[n] = \overline{h}[-n]$ and $g[n] = \overline{g}[-n]$, for the *Daubechies* wavelets db1, db2, db4 and db8, and the *symlet* wavelets sym2, sym4, sym8 and sym16. The Fourier series of $x[n]$ is calculated as $\widehat{x}(\nu) = \sum_{n=-\infty}^{\infty} x[n]exp(-2\pi jn\nu)$. The overlapping of both filters $\overline{h}[n]$ and $\overline{g}[n]$ means that the spectrum division in frequency bands is not perfect. Figure 2 shows that, as the number of vanishing moments increases the filters $h[n]$ and $g[n]$ approaches to perfect low pass and high pass filters respectively. However, as the number of vanishing moments increases the filters length increases too.

Daubechies wavelets are very asymmetric because the decomposition filters have their energy optimally concentrated near the starting point of their support. The *symlet* filters still have a minimum support but the decomposition low pass filter $h[n]$ is more symmetric, as illustrated in Fig. 3(b).

Figure 3 shows a test signal and its successive approximations in a wavelet decomposition. The decomposition in Fig. 3(a) uses a db8 wavelet, and the one shown in Fig. 3(b) uses a sym16. Both use symmetric padding extension. Two important characteristics of a wavelet decomposition are shown. First, as the scale increases the relative importance of the extended part of the signal increases. For the approximation coefficients a_4 the extension is larger than the original signal approximation in both cases. The extended part of the signal must be excluded from the calculation of the subband power, because it includes the border distortion produced by zero padding and periodic padding.

For a db8 wavelet the approximation coefficients a_4 have lost the shape of the original signal (as the evident loss of symmetry shows). This is due to some of the

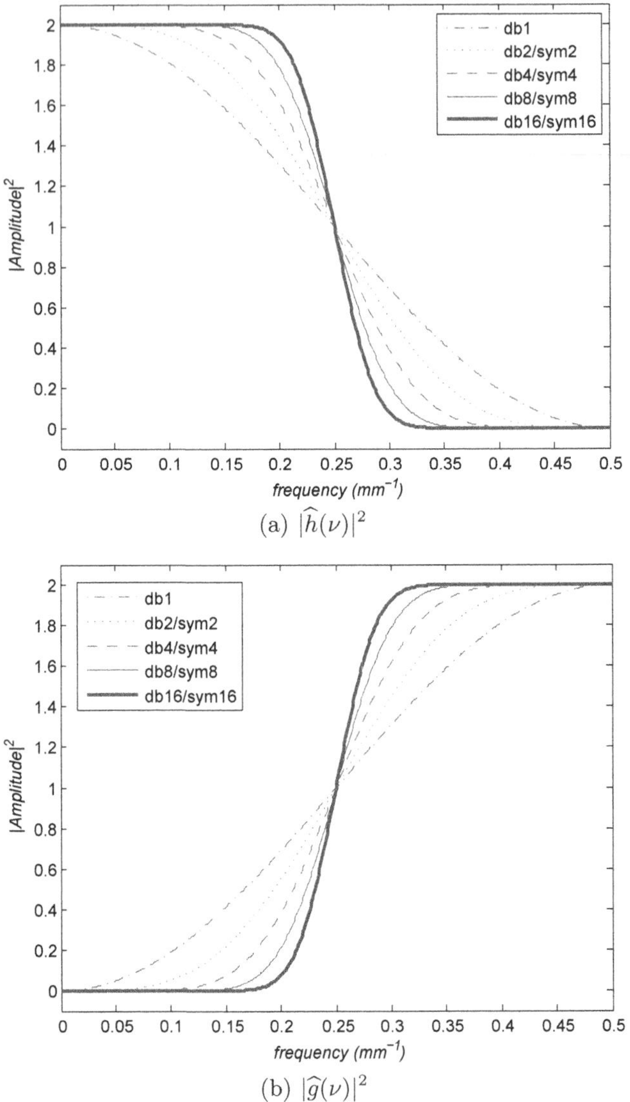

(a) $|\widehat{h}(\nu)|^2$

(b) $|\widehat{g}(\nu)|^2$

Fig. 2. Square of the modulus of the Fourier series of $h[n]$ and $g[n]$ for some *Daubechies* and *symlet* wavelets.

energy of the original signal being transferred into the extended part of the signal, and conversely, some energy of the extended part being transferred into the signal approximation. However, for the sym16 wavelet the loss is clearly smaller and the shape of the approximation is much closer to shape of the original signal.

The filter length is an important issue because, except for the *db*1 or *Haar* wavelet, it involves the extension of the analyzed image. Every border of the

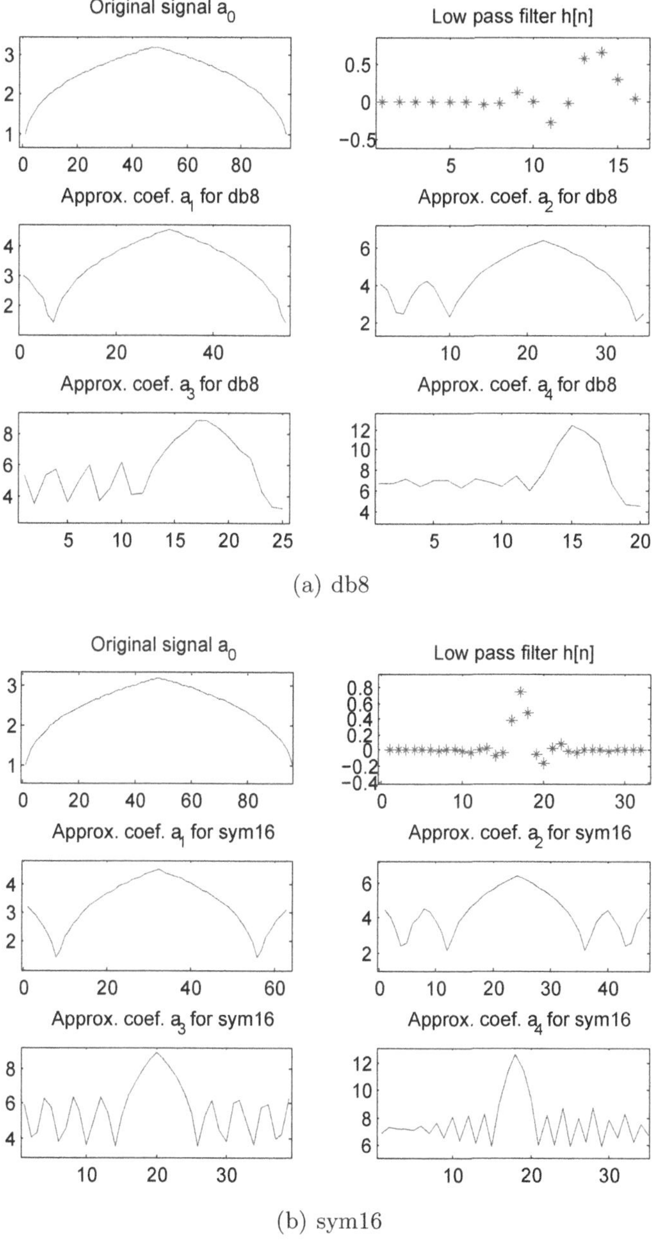

Fig. 3. Test signal, low pass filter and approximation coefficients (four first scales) for two discrete wavelet transforms (*Daubechies* db8 and *symlet* sym16) using symmetric extension.

image has to be extended $2N_v - 1$ pixels before the image is convolved with the decomposition filters. The effect of different extension methods on the power distribution calculation are investigated in this work. The extension methods analyzed are zero padding, periodic padding and symmetrical padding. Details on the rationale of these schemes can be found in [7].

2.3 Power Spectrum Calculations

For each image in the ensemble I_n, $n = 1, \ldots, N$ a nine levels two-dimensional decimated wavelet transform is carried out. Let $d_j(k, l, O, n)$ be the detail coefficient with coordinates (k, l) in the subband with orientation O, at scale $2^j a$ (where a is the pixel spacing). The wavelet power spectrum (averaged over orientations) at resolution $1/2^j a$, is obtained by averaging the square of these detail coefficients over the portal images in the ensemble (Eq. 1). In Eq. 1 N is the number of images in the ensemble, N_j and M_j are the dimensions of the subbands in scale $2^j a$, and the orientations O are horizontal, vertical and diagonal.

$$WPS(\frac{1}{2^j a}) = \frac{1}{3N_j M_j N} \sum_{n=1}^{N} \sum_{k,l=1}^{N_j, M_j} \sum_{O=H,V,D} d_j^2, \; j = 1, 2, \ldots, 9 \tag{1}$$

The average Fourier power spectrum is estimated using Eq. 2, where N_x and N_y are the dimensions (in pixels) of the images. In order to compare the Fourier spectrum with the wavelet spectrum, the quantity represented in Figs. 4 and 5 is the radially averaged spectrum divided by a^2.

$$PS(r, s) = \frac{a^2}{N_x N_y N} \sum_{n=1}^{N} \left| \sum_{k,l=1}^{N_x, N_y} I_n(k, l) e^{-2\pi i (\frac{rk}{N_x} + \frac{sl}{N_y})} \right|^2 \tag{2}$$

3 Results

Figure 4 shows the average power spectrum calculated for the CR ensemble of images for the different extension methods. The continuous line corresponds to the Fourier power spectrum divided by a^2 versus frequency, and the rest of plots correspond to the wavelet spectrums versus resolution. The wavelets used are a db8 and a sym8. Figure 4(a) shows how the border distortion created by zero padding and periodic padding results in an overestimate of the high frequency components. This effect is not observed in the case of symmetric extensions.

A db8 wavelet is used in the calculation of the spectrums in Fig. 4(a). Also, every pixel in each subband is used in the calculation. If these extensions are removed from the subbands before power calculations, then the spectrums are less dependent on the extension method, as can be seen in Fig. 4(b). In this figure a sym8 wavelet is used, because for symmetric wavelets the removal of the extended signal is easier (the original signal remains in the central part of each subband).

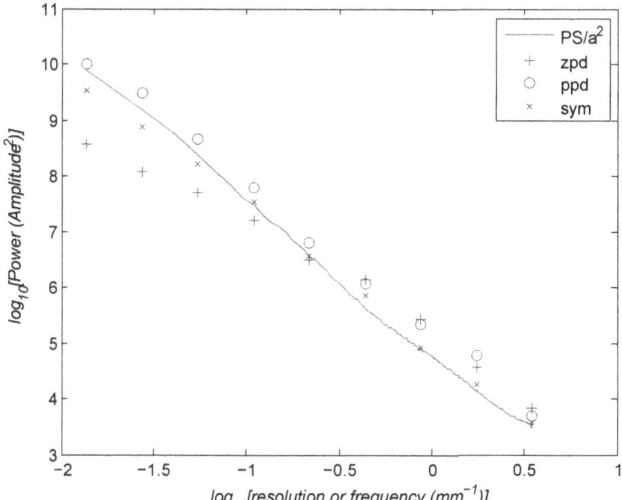

(a) Wavelet db8. Spectrum calculated using all the pixels in each subband

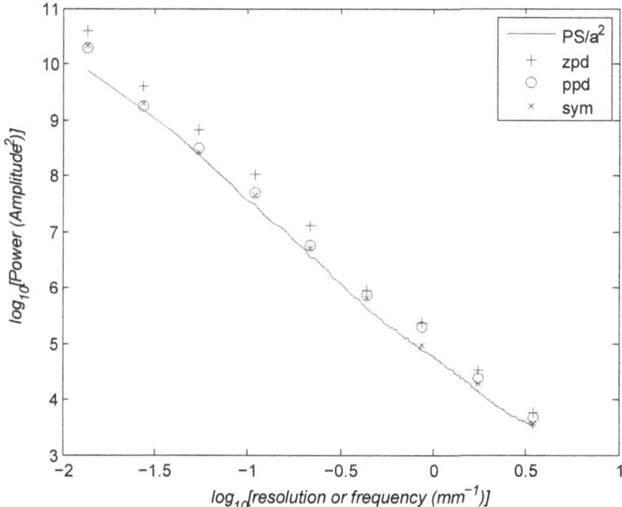

(b) Wavelet sym8. Spectrum calculated after removal of the extended part of each subband

Fig. 4. Average Fourier spectrum divided by a^2 (PS/a^2) and average wavelet power spectrums for the ensemble of CR images using different padding extension methods: Zero padding (zpd), periodic padding (ppd) and symmetric padding (sym).

In the case of symmetric padding the relative weight of the peripheral part of the images increases with the scale. This explains the drop of the wavelet power spectrum for symmetric padding at the lowest resolutions in Fig. 4(a).

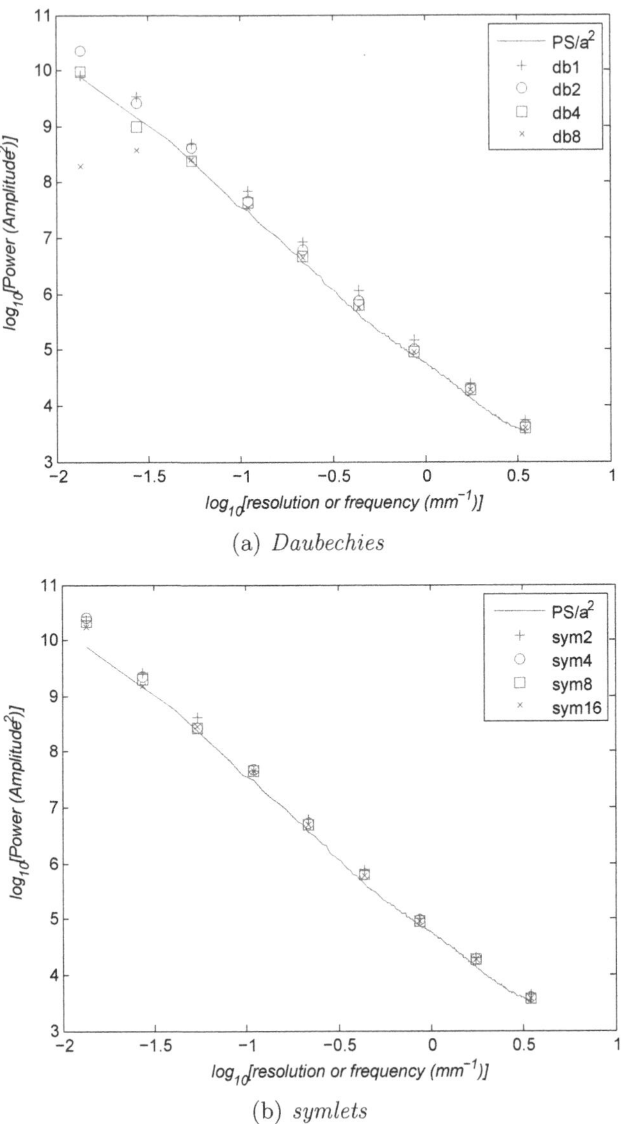

(a) *Daubechies*

(b) *symlets*

Fig. 5. Average Fourier power spectrum divided by a^2 (PS/a^2) and average wavelet power spectrum for different *Daubechies* and *symlets* wavelets for the ensemble of CR images. Wavelet transforms have been calculated using symmetric padding extensions and the extended part of each subband has been removed before the calculation of the power.

The power spectrums calculated for the ensemble of CR images using symmetric padding extension are shown in Figs. 5(a) and (b). Results obtained using *Daubechies* wavelets db1 (also called Haar), db2, db4 and db8 are plotted in

Fig. 5(a), and results obtained for *symlets* wavelets db2 (equal to sym2), sym4, sym8 and sym16 are plotted in Fig. 5(b).

For the calculation of the wavelet power spectrum represented in Fig. 5 each subband has been cropped before the calculation of the power. The cropping consists in removing the extended part of the image, required for its convolution with the decomposition filters. For *Daubechies* wavelets two strips situated toward the top and left sides of the image are removed, while for the *symlets* wavelets only the central part of each subband is kept for the calculation.

Figure 5(a) and (b) show how the symmetry of the wavelet filters affects the calculation of the spectrum. When the filters are symmetric the spectrum seems to be less dependent on the number of vanishing moments, particularly for the lowest resolutions and the highest values of N_v.

4 Conclusions

The knowledge of the image power distribution, in the frequency bands in which a multiresolution approximation decomposes an image, is important for a better understanding of the algorithms that work in the wavelet domain.

The basic algorithm for the discrete wavelet transform is based on a simple scheme of convolution and downsampling and, as the convolution is performed on finite size images, border distortions arise. To deal with border distortions, the border should be treated differently from the other parts of the image.

Figure 4 shows the effect of different extension methods in the calculation of the spectrum. The best matching between the wavelet and the Fourier spectrums is found for symmetric padding. Symmetric padding avoids the creation of artificial sharp edges that could rule the calculation of the image power. In contrast zero padding or periodic padding must be carefully applied, and their use is only appropriate in images with a very particular kind of borders, for instance images in which border pixels have values close to zero.

Another important fact shown in Fig. 4 is that removing the extended part of each subband before the power calculation results in a better matching between the wavelet and the Fourier spectrums. This improvement is due to the removal of the border distortion that is included in this extended part.

Last, as Fig. 2 shows, in a wavelet decomposition the energy interchange between high and low frequencies is smaller for wavelets with a high number of vanishing moments. Figure 5(b) shows how the wavelet spectrum approaches to the Fourier spectrum when N_v increases. In this figure symmetric wavelets *symlets* are used in combination with symmetric expansion. Also, the pixels in the extended part of each subband have been excluded from the calculation. Under these conditions, using non-symmetric *Daubechies* wavelets increases the dependence of the spectrum on number of vanishing moments (Fig. 5(a)). A larger N_v means a better matching at high resolutions but a worse matching at the low ones. This is a consequence of longer filters in an asymmetric wavelet.

References

1. Mallat, S.G.: A theory for multiresolution signal decomposition - the wavelet representation. IEEE Trans. Pattern Anal. Mach. Intell. **11**, 674–693 (1989)
2. Bracewell, R.N.: The Fourier Transform and Its Applications, 2nd edn. MacGraw-Hill, New York City (1986)
3. Daubechies, I.: Ten Lectures on Wavelets. SIAM, Philadelphia (1992)
4. Xu, Y., Weaver, J.B., Healy, D.M., Lu, J.: Wavelet transform domain filters: a spatially selective noise filtration technique. IEEE Trans. Image Proc. **3**(6), 747–758 (1994)
5. Donoho, D., Johnstone, J.M.: Adapting to unknown smoothness via wavelet shrinkage. J. Am. Stat. Assoc. **90**, 1200–1224 (1995)
6. Portilla, J., Strela, V., Wainwright, M.J., Simoncelli, E.P.: Image denoising using scale mixtures of Gaussians in the wavelet domain. IEEE Trans. Image Proc. **12**(11), 1338–1351 (2003)
7. Strang, G., Nguyen, T.: Wavelets and Filter Banks. Wellesley-Cambridge Press, Wellesley (1996)

Chaotic Encryption of 3D Objects

A. Martín del Rey(✉)

Department of Applied Mathematics,
Institute of Fundamental Physics and Mathematics,
University of Salamanca, Salamanca, Spain
delrey@usal.es

Abstract. In the recent years there has been an unstoppable rise of the use of 3D technologies in several branches of science and technology. In this sense it is mandatory to guarantee the privacy of 3D data since they are exposed to several cybersecurity threats. The main goal of this work is to introduce a novel protocol to encrypt 3D objects defined by voxels. The proposed protocol involves the iterative application of two phases: the confusion phase (based on a chaotic map), and the diffusion phase (governed by a three-dimensional cellular automata). It is shown to be secure against the most important cryptanalytic attacks.

Keywords: 3D data · Encryption · Cellular automata · Chaotic maps

1 Introduction

The potential applications of 3D technology in the different fields of science are huge. This has also contributed largely the great advances made in recent years in designing algorithms devoted to the acquisition and processing of three-dimensional data. For example, this new technology have made possible the development in the field of Biomedicine of new disciplines like Bioinformatics, Bioengineering, Biomechanics, etc.

The 3D objects, as well as other data, must be protected against several types of misuse [1]. Then, it is crucial to ensure at least the privacy (the digital data managed and transmitted on the information systems must be hidden from non-authorized parties, and the content of the digital records in a file system must be hidden) and integrity of such data (the digital data must not been malicious modified). This is the goal of cryptographic protocols. In this sense, although there have been proposed several protocols in order to guarantee the confidentiality and integrity of text and images [7], unfortunately few protocols dealing with the encryption of 3D data have been designed. The great majority (see, for example [2–5]) deals with hologram data and the encryption procedure is based on optics techniques. As far as we know, there is only one proposal introducing an encryption method for 3D objects defined by the aggregation of voxels (see [6]). It is not based on optic techniques but on discrete mathematical tools such as discretized chaotic maps and linear cellular automata.

J.M. Ferrández Vicente et al. (Eds.): IWINAC 2017, Part II, LNCS 10338, pp. 463–472, 2017.
DOI: 10.1007/978-3-319-59773-7_47

The main goal of this work is to improve the encryption method proposed in [6] by using non-linear techniques. This new protocol is given by means of an iterative process defined by two phases: the confusion phase and the diffusion phase. The confusion phase is ruled by a 3D chaotic map in order to permute the position of the voxels of the 3D object. On the other hand, the purpose of the diffusion phase is to change the values of the voxels using a reversible three-dimensional cellular automata (3D-CA for short) defined by a non-linear local transition rule. To de-correlate the relationship between adjacent voxels, there must be $N \geq 1$ permutation rounds in the confusion stage. Moreover, each confusion-diffusion round repeats M times to achieve good statistical and security properties.

The rest of the paper is organized as follows: In Sect. 2 the definition and characteristics of 3D Cat map are introduced; the basic theory about the three-dimensional cellular automata is presented in Sect. 3; in Sect. 4 the encryption protocol is introduced, and its security analysis is shown in Sect. 5. Finally, the conclusions and further work are presented in Sect. 6.

2 The 3D Chaotic Cat Maps

The chaotic map used in the confusion phase is the discretized 3D Cat map F. It is defined by $\left(x^{t+1}, y^{t+1}, z^{t+1}\right) = F\left(x^t, y^t, z^t\right)$, where:

$$\begin{pmatrix} x^{t+1} \\ y^{t+1} \\ z^{t+1} \end{pmatrix} = C \cdot \begin{pmatrix} x^t \\ y^t \\ z^t \end{pmatrix} (\bmod n), \quad C = \begin{pmatrix} c_{11} & c_{12} & c_{13} \\ c_{21} & c_{22} & c_{23} \\ c_{31} & c_{32} & c_{33} \end{pmatrix}, \tag{1}$$

such that:

$$\begin{aligned} c_{11} &= 1 + a_1 a_3 b_2,\ c_{12} = a_3,\ c_{13} = a_2 + a_1 a_3 + a_1 a_2 a_3 b_2, \\ c_{21} &= b_3 + a_1 b_2 + a_1 a_3 b_2 b_3,\ c_{22} = a_3 b_3 + 1, \\ c_{23} &= a_2 b_3 + a_1 a_2 a_3 b_2 b_3 + a_1 a_3 b_3 + a_1 a_2 b_2 + a_1,\ c_{31} = a_1 b_1 b_2 + b_2, \\ c_{32} &= b_1,\ c_{33} = a_1 a_2 b_1 b_2 + a_1 b_1 + a_2 b_2 + 1, \end{aligned} \tag{2}$$

with $a_1, a_2, a_3, b_1, b_2, b_3 \in \mathbb{Z}^+$. As $\mid C \mid = 1$ the Cat map is invertible; moreover, it exhibits a chaotic behavior when its leading Lyapunov exponent is strictly larger than 0.

3 Three-Dimensional CA

A three-dimensional cellular automaton is a very simple type of agent-based model constituted by $n \times n \times n$ cells that are uniformly arranged into a three-dimensional space $\mathcal{C}$. At every step of time t, the (i, j, k)-th cell is endowed with the state $s_{i,j,k}^t \in \mathbb{F}_2 = \{0, 1\}$. These states change synchronously in discrete steps of time according to a local transition function f, whose variables are the states at the previous step of time of m cells fixed beforehand: $s_{i_1,j_1,k_1}^{t-1}, s_{i_2,j_2,k_2}^{t-1}, \ldots, s_{i_m,j_m,k_m}^{t-1}$. Consequently:

$$\begin{gathered} f\colon \mathbb{F}_2^m \to \mathbb{F}_2 \\ \left(s_{i_1,j_1,k_1}^{t-1}, \ldots, s_{i_m,j_m,k_m}^{t-1}\right) \mapsto s_{i,j,k}^{t} = f\left(s_{i_1,j_1,k_1}^{t-1}, \ldots, s_{i_m,j_m,k_m}^{t-1}\right) \end{gathered} \tag{3}$$

for every $1 \leq i, j, k \leq n$.

As there is a finite number of cells, some type of boundary conditions must be established in order to assure a well-defined evolution of the cellular automaton: in this case null boundary conditions are stated: $s_{i,j,k}^{t} = 0$ if the cell $(i, j, k) \notin \mathcal{C}$. The three-dimensional array defined by all the states of the cellular space at time t is called configuration of the cellular automaton and denoted as follows:

$$C^t = \left(s_{i,j,k}^{t}\right)_{1 \leq i,j,k \leq n} \in \mathbb{F}_2^{n^3}. \tag{4}$$

The global transition function of the 3D-CA is a transformation that yields the configuration at the next time step during its evolution, that is:

$$\Phi\colon \mathbb{F}_2^{n^3} \to \mathbb{F}_2^{n^3}, C^{t-1} \mapsto C^t = \Phi\left(C^{t-1}\right) \tag{5}$$

A 3D-CA is reversible if it is possible to compute its inverse evolution. In this sense, Φ^{-1} will be the global transition function of the inverse 3D-CA. On the other hand, an m-th order memory 3D-CA is a cellular automaton where the state of each cell at a particular step of time not only depends on the state of its neighbor cells at the immediately preceding step of time, but also on the states of these neighbor cells at previous steps of time. The global transition function of an m-th order memory 3D-CA is:

$$\begin{gathered} \Phi\colon \mathbb{F}_2^{n^3} \times \ldots \times \mathbb{F}_2^{n^3} \to \mathbb{F}_2^{n^3} \\ \left(C^{t-1}, \ldots, C^{t-m}\right) \mapsto C^t = \Phi\left(C^{t-1}, \ldots, C^{t-m}\right) \end{gathered} \tag{6}$$

where configurations $C^0, C^1, \ldots, C^{m-1}$ are called initial configurations of the memory 3D-CA.

In this work we consider the 4-th order memory reversible 3D-CA whose global transition function is the following:

$$\begin{aligned} C^t = {} & C^{t-1} \circ C^{t-2} \oplus C^{t-1} \circ C^{t-3} \oplus C^{t-2} \circ C^{t-3} \oplus C^{t-1} \circ C^{t-2} \circ C^{t-3} \\ & \oplus C^{t-4} \oplus K, \end{aligned} \tag{7}$$

where, if $A = \left(a_{ijk}\right)_{1 \leq i,j,k \leq n}$ and $B = \left(b_{ijk}\right)_{1 \leq i,j,k \leq n}$, then:

$$A \circ B = \left(a_{ijk} \cdot b_{ijk}\right)_{1 \leq i,j,k \leq n}, \quad A \oplus B = \left(a_{ijk} \oplus b_{ijk}\right)_{1 \leq i,j,k \leq n}. \tag{8}$$

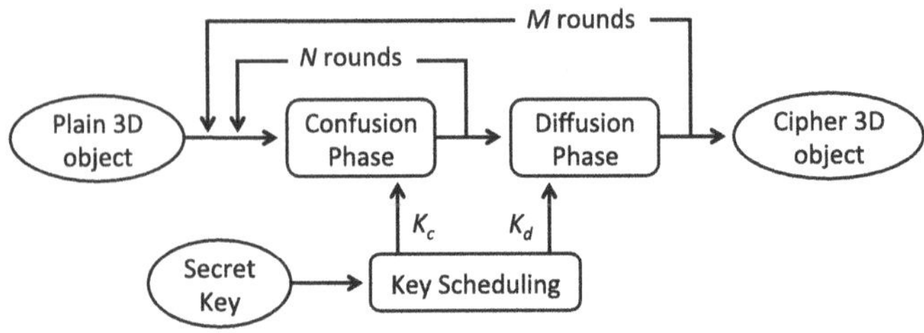

Fig. 1. The flow diagram of the encryption protocol

4 The Encryption Method

4.1 General Description

The 3D object of dimension $n \times n \times n$ to be ciphered can be interpreted as a 3D array $Q_0 = \left(q_{ijk}^0\right)_{1 \leq i,j,k \leq n}$ of dimension $n \times n \times n$ such that

$$q_{ijk}^0 = \begin{cases} 1 \text{ if the position } (i,j,k) \text{ is occupied} \\ 0 \text{ if the position } (i,j,k) \text{ is empty in the solid object} \end{cases} \tag{9}$$

Note that this is a configuration of a 3D-CA. The encryption protocol consists of two main phases: the confusion phase CP, and the diffusion phase DP. Moreover, also the key scheduling must be included in the protocol (see Fig. 1).

The encrypted 3D object, W, is computed from the following iterative process:

$$Q_i = \text{DP}\left(\text{CP}^N\left(Q_{i-1}, K_c\right), K_d\right), \ 1 \leq i \leq M, \quad W = Q_M, \tag{10}$$

where K_c is the confusion key and K_d is the diffusion key.

4.2 Key Scheduling

The secret key of this encryption scheme is defined by two subkeys: the confusion subkey K_{CF}, and the diffusion subkey K_{DF}. They hold the parameters used in both phases. K_{CP} gives the number of iterations of the confusion phase N and the six parameters used to compute the coefficients of the matrix associated to the chaotic 3D Cat map: $a_1, a_2, a_3, b_1, b_2, b_3$. On the other hand, K_{DP} determines the number of iterations of the diffusion phase M, the number of iterations of the 3D-CA, T_l, $1 \leq l \leq M$, and the pseudorandom three-dimensional arrays $\tilde{K}_{\text{DP}}^l$, $1 \leq l \leq M$, used in the local transition function of the 3D-CA.

The parameters involved in the protocol are computed by means of the pseudorandom bit generator ANSI X9.31 using AES with the 128-bit length seeds K_{CP} and K_{DP}.

4.3 The Confusion Phase

The main goal of this phase is to permute the positions of the voxels of the 3D objects $Q_l = \left(q_{ijk}^l\right)$, $0 \le l \le M-1$. To achieve this, these positions are permuted N times using the chaotic 3D Cat map F defined in (1). Specifically, the voxel q_{ijk}^l of Q_l, $0 \le l \le M-1$, changes its original position (i,j,k) to the new position $F(i,j,k)$.

4.4 The Diffusion Phase

Let $P_l = \mathrm{CP}^N(Q_{l-1}, K_{\mathrm{CP}}) = (p_{ijk})_{1\le i,j,k\le n}$ be the 3D array obtained after applying the N rounds of the confusion phase at stage l, $1 \le l \le M$. This 3D object is divided into the following four three-dimensional arrays (see Fig. 2):

$$P_{l,1} = (p_{ijk})_{1\le i\le \frac{n}{2}, 1\le j\le n, \frac{n}{2}+1\le k\le n}, \tag{11}$$

$$P_{l,2} = (p_{ijk})_{\frac{n}{2}+1\le i\le n, 1\le j\le n, \frac{n}{2}+1\le k\le n}, \tag{12}$$

$$P_{l,3} = (p_{ijk})_{1\le i\le \frac{n}{2}, 1\le j\le n, 1\le k\le \frac{n}{2}}, \tag{13}$$

$$P_{l,4} = (p_{ijk})_{\frac{n}{2}+1\le i\le n, 1\le j\le n, 1\le k\le \frac{n}{2}}. \tag{14}$$

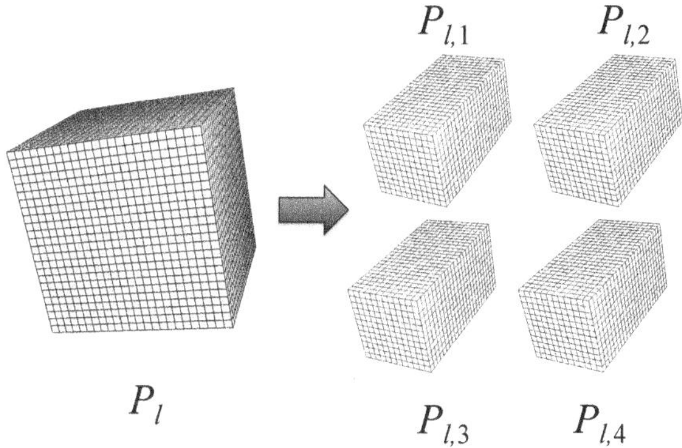

Fig. 2. Division of the three-dimensional array $P_l = \mathrm{CP}^N(Q_{l-1}, K_{\mathrm{CP}})$ into four three-dimensional arrays.

The diffusion phase is governed by means of a 4-th order memory reversible 3D-CA whose global transition function is defined as follows:

$$\begin{aligned} C^t = {} & C^{t-1} \circ C^{t-2} \oplus C^{t-1} \circ C^{t-3} \oplus C^{t-2} \circ C^{t-3} \oplus C^{t-1} \circ C^{t-2} \circ C^{t-3} \\ & \oplus C^{t-4} \oplus \tilde{K}_d^l, \end{aligned} \tag{15}$$

where $\tilde{K}_{\mathrm{DP}}^l$ is the pseudorandom three-dimensional array defined by the diffusion subkey. In this sense, the three-dimensional arrays $P_{l,1}, P_{l,2}, P_{l,3}, P_{l,4}$ stand for the initial configurations of this 3D-CA: $C^0 = P_{l,1}, C^1 = P_{l,2}, C^2 = P_{l,3}$, and $C^3 = P_{l,4}$.

The output of this phase, $Q_{l+1} = \text{DP}(P_l, K_{\text{DP}})$, is a $n \times n \times n$ 3D array constituted by the union of the configurations of the 3D-CA at times $T_l, T_l + 1$, $T_l + 2$ and $T_l + 3$: $C^{T_l}, C^{T_l+1}, C^{T_l+2}$, and C^{T_l+3}. Then, if

$$C^{T_l} = \left(s_{i,j,k}^{T_l}\right)_{1 \le i \le \frac{n}{2}, 1 \le j \le n, 1 \le k \le \frac{n}{2}}, C^{T_l+1} = \left(s_{i,j,k}^{T_l+1}\right)_{1 \le i \le \frac{n}{2}, 1 \le j \le n, 1 \le k \le \frac{n}{2}}, \quad (16)$$
$$C^{T_l+2} = \left(s_{i,j,k}^{T_l+2}\right)_{1 \le i \le \frac{n}{2}, 1 \le j \le n, 1 \le k \le \frac{n}{2}}, C^{T_l+3} = \left(s_{i,j,k}^{T_l+3}\right)_{1 \le i \le \frac{n}{2}, 1 \le j \le n, 1 \le k \le \frac{n}{2}},$$

we obtain that Q_{l+1} is a 3D array whose coefficient at position (i, j, k) is defined by:

$$(Q_{l+1})_{ijk} = \begin{cases} s_{i,j,k-\frac{n}{2}}^{T_l}, & \text{if } 1 \le i \le \frac{n}{2}, 1 \le j \le n, 1 + \frac{n}{2} \le k \le n \\ s_{i-\frac{n}{2},j,k-\frac{n}{2}}^{T_l+1}, & \text{if } 1 + \frac{n}{2} \le i \le n, 1 \le j \le n, 1 + \frac{n}{2} \le k \le n \\ s_{i,j,k}^{T_l+2}, & \text{if } 1 \le i \le \frac{n}{2}, 1 \le j \le n, 1 \le k \le \frac{n}{2} \\ s_{i-\frac{n}{2},j,k}^{T_l+3}, & \text{if } 1 + \frac{n}{2} \le i \le n, 1 \le j \le n, 1 \le k \le \frac{n}{2} \end{cases} \quad (17)$$

As an illustrative example, a 3D object and its corresponding encrypted object are shown in Fig. 3. Specifically, in Fig. 3-(a) a three-dimensional detail of a tumor growth is introduced. The encryption key parameters used are shown in Table 1.

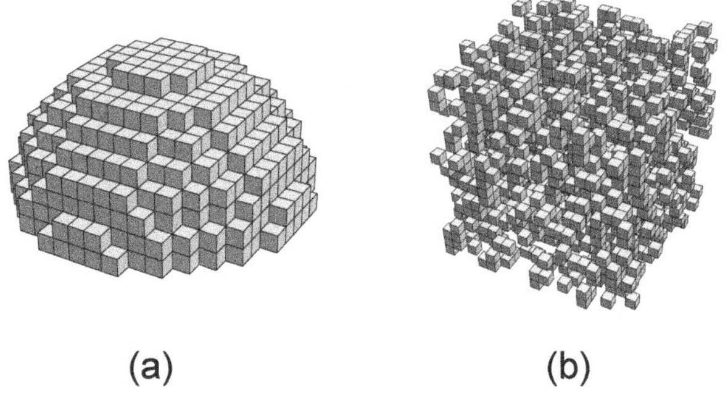

Fig. 3. (a) Digitalized 3D biomedical object (three-dimensional tumor growth). (b) Encrypted 3D object.

Table 1. Parameters used in the encryption protocol

n	N	C	Lyapunov exponent	M	T
20	5	$\begin{pmatrix} 2 & 1 & 5 \\ 3 & 2 & 8 \\ 2 & 1 & 6 \end{pmatrix}$	2.2252	10	(7, 9, 5, 10, 6, 9, 6, 9, 10, 7)

5 The Analysis of the Security

The analysis of the security aspects of the encryption method is shown in this section. Several simulations have been obtained from different original 3D objects but, for the sake of simplicity only one simple example is introduced and studied here (since all of the simulations exhibit the same behavior).

5.1 Statistical Analysis

The confusion and diffusion properties of the method must be studied by means of a statistical analysis. In our case the distribution of non-zero (occupied) positions in the original objects and their encrypted is checked. In addition the study of the balancedness of the configurations generated by the 3D-CA and the distribution of bits in the neighborhood of every position are analyzed.

Distribution of Occupied Positions. We study the occupied positions per x-column, y-column and z-column of a 3D object defined by the 3D array $Z = (z_{ijk})$. Consequently the matrices $\Lambda_x = (\lambda_x(j,k))_{1\leq j,k\leq n}$, $\Lambda_y = (\lambda_y(i,k))_{1\leq i,k\leq n}$ and $\Lambda_z = (\lambda_z(i,j))_{1\leq i,j\leq n}$ are computed such that:

$$\lambda_x(j,k) = \sum_{i=1}^{n} z_{ijk}, \lambda_y(i,k) = \sum_{j=1}^{n} z_{ijk}, \lambda_z(i,j) = \sum_{k=1}^{n} z_{ijk}. \tag{18}$$

The matrices associated to the original 3D objects and the corresponding encrypted objects are far different in all the simulations performed. For example in the case of the example introduced above (see Fig. 3), the distribution of the number of occupied positions per x-column, y-column, and z-column in the original 3D object and their corresponding encrypted 3D object are shown in Fig. 4. Note that the distributions of occupied positions are far apart: in the case of the original 3D object some clusters appears, whereas in the case of the 3D cyphered object the distributions seems to be homogeneously.

Balancedness. The encrypted objects computed exhibit a balanced number of empty and occupied voxels, that is, the number of 1's in the associated three-dimensional boolean arrays that define the configurations of the 3D-CA is approximately 50%. In Fig. 5 the evolution of the number of 1's in the configurations is shown when the last example is considered for $m = 100$ (all other parameters are the same).

Neighbor Analysis. The study the distribution of bits in the neighbor positions of a given one is an important security issue. If Moore neighborhoods are considered, the number of non-zero positions around every one is computed and some statistical parameters are obtained. The results are shown in Table 2; note that the encrypted objects exhibit good statistical properties.

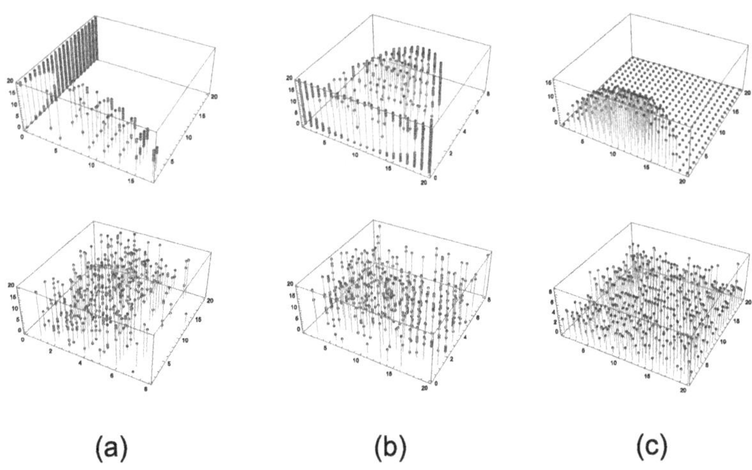

Fig. 4. Distribution of non-zero positions per column (top: original 3D object; bottom: encrypted 3D object). (a) x-column. (b) y-column. (c) z-column.

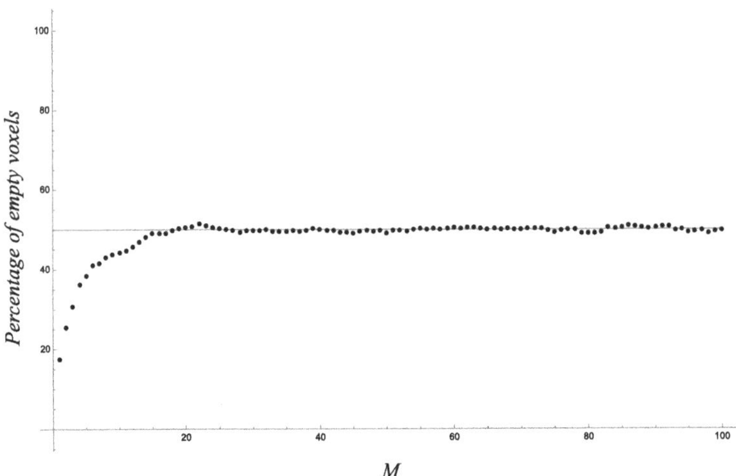

Fig. 5. Evolution of the number of 1's in the configurations generated by the 3D-CA in the diffusion phase.

Table 2. Statistical parameters associated to the neighborhoods

	Example	Encrypted 3D object
Mean	3.54488	12.0499
Mean deviation	5.57627	2.67244
Standard deviation	7.90187	3.32175
Median	0	12
Median deviation	0	2

5.2 Key Space

The key space of an encryption scheme should be large enough to resist brute-force attacks. As is mentioned in the section introducing the key scheming, the secret key used in this method is formed by two subkeys: the confusion subkey K_{CP}, and the diffusion subkey K_{DP}, each one of them holding the parameters of confusion and diffusion phases, respectively.

The 128-bit length confusion key gives the integer numbers N, $a_1, a_2, a_3, b_1, b_2, b_3$, and the 128-bit length diffusion subkey gives $M, T_1, T_2, \ldots, T_M$, and the $\frac{n^3}{4}$-bit sequences $\tilde{K}_{\mathrm{DP}}^1, \ldots, \tilde{K}_{\mathrm{DP}}^M$. Consequently, there are $2^{256} \simeq 1.15792 \cdot 10^{77}$, and the size of the key space is large enough to resist all kinds of brute-force attacks.

5.3 Sensitivity Analysis

As is well-known a desirable property of the encryption method is that small changes in the secret key should result in a significant change in the encrypted 3D object. For example, if we consider the example introduced in Fig. 3 the percentages of different voxels between the two encrypted objects are shown in Table 3. Specifically, these percentages are computed when the following parameters are modified: (1) N is modified changing from $N = 5$ to $N = 4$; (2) M is modified changing from $M = 10$ to $N = 10$; (3) The chaotic Cat map is modified changing from $a_1 = 1$ to $a_1 = 2$; and finally, (4) $\tilde{K}_{\mathrm{DP}}^1$ is modified changing its $\left(\frac{n}{4}, \frac{n}{2}, \frac{n}{4}\right)$-th position.

Table 3. Percentage of different voxels

Modified parameter	Percentage of different voxels
N	49.5625%
M	50.3875%
Cat map	50.0625%
$\tilde{K}_{\mathrm{DP}}^1$	50.0875%

As a consequence, it can be concluded that the encryption protocol is sensitive to secret key, that is, a small change of the key yields a different deciphered 3D object and no information about the original one is obtained.

6 Conclusions

The protection of digital 3D data is a priority in our society. Unfortunately, and as far as we know, there are so few protocols dealing with 3D objects defined by voxels. The goal of this work is to introduce a novel encryption algorithm for 3D digitalized 3D objects based on the aggregation of voxels. Such 3D objects can be mathematically characterized by means of three-dimensional boolean arrays and consequently, they can be processed using 3D discrete mathematical tools.

The method proposed in this work follows the standard paradigm to encrypt digital images; that is, it is based on the iteration of two different phases: the confusion phase governed by the 3D Cat map, and the diffusion phase based on the computation of the evolution of a 3D reversible memory cellular automata.

The protocol is shown to be secure against the most important cryptanalytic attacks.

Finally, further work aims at designing new cryptographic algorithms for 3D objects defined by voxels endowed with different states in order to take into account specific characteristics of these voxel.

Acknowledgments. This work has been supported by Ministerio de Economía y Competitividad (Spain) and the European Union through FEDER funds under grants TIN2014-55325-C2-2-R and MTM2015-69138-REDT.

References

1. Jang-Jaccard, J., Nepal, S.: A survey of emerging threats in cybersecurity. J. Comput. Syst. Sci. **80**(5), 973–993 (2014)
2. Kong, D.Z., Cao, L.C., Jin, G.F., Javidi, B.: Three-dimensional scene encryption and display based on computer-generated holograms. Appl. Opt. **55**(29), 8296–8300 (2016)
3. Lee, S.H., Kwon, K.R.: Multiple 3D medical data watermarking for healthcare data management. J. Med. Syst. **35**, 1573–1593 (2011)
4. Li, W.N., Shi, C.X., Piao, M.L., Kim, N.: Multiple 3D-object secure information system based on phase shifting method and single interference. Appl. Opt. **55**(15), 4052–4059 (2016)
5. Li, X.W., Wang, Q.H., Kim, S.T., Lee, I.K.: Encrypting 2D/3D image using improved lensless integral imaging in Fresnel domain. Opt. Commun. **381**, 260–270 (2016)
6. del Rey, A.M., Hernández Pastora, J.L., Rodríguez Sánchez, G.: 3D medical data security protection. Expert Syst. Appl. **54**, 379–386 (2016)
7. Stapleton, J.J.: Security Without Obscurity: A Guide to Confidentiality, Authentication, and Integrity. Auerbach Publications, Boca Raton (2014)
8. Wolfram, S.: A New Kind of Science. Wolfram Media Inc., Champaign (2002)

Architecture of a Monitoring System for Hipertensive Patients

Alberto de Ramón-Fernández(✉), Daniel Ruiz-Fernández, Javier Ramírez-Navarro, Diego Marcos-Jorquera, Virgilio Gilart-Iglesias, and Antonio Soriano-Payá

Department of Computer Technology, University of Alicante, Alicante, Spain
{aderamon,druiz,jramirez,dmarcos,vgilart,asoriano}@dtic.ua.es

Abstract. Hypertension is a chronic disease affecting eight out of ten over 65 years. Current medical systems focus on the monitoring of the hypertensive patient and, in some cases, on the diagnosis, making the doctor-patient communication more direct. However, these systems have a rigid structure that does not adapt neither to the patient's real needs nor to manage key aspects such as security, scalability, integration, flexibility, interoperability or standardisation data. Our proposal aims to create an integrative architecture that solves the different weaknesses that the current systems have.

Keywords: Hypertension · Web based architecture · RESTful services

1 Introduction

Chronic diseases represent the main cause of mortality in the world. In 2008, of the 58 million deaths, 36 were due to chronic diseases, mainly cardiovascular diseases, cancers, diabetes and chronic lung diseases. It should be noted that one fourth of these deaths occur before the age of 60. The vast majority of these deaths (80%) take place in countries with a medium/low income level. The cost of such diseases in human, social and economic terms is increasing rapidly, especially in countries with fewer resources [1]. However, the human and social impact of chronic diseases could be reduced by taking concrete, feasible and cost-effective measures.

Numerous papers focus their research on evaluating the impact of different factors on the mortality in cardiovascular diseases. According to the World Health Organization (WHO), hypertension is already a highly prevalent cardiovascular risk factor worldwide because of increasing longevity and prevalence of contributing factors such as obesity. It affects 80% of the population over 65 years and represnt the main cause of chronic disease seen in primary care (WHO). In [2], Lewington et al. studied the relationship between blood pressure and mortality in different age groups. Throughout the middle and advanced age, high blood pressure is strongly and directly related to vascular mortality.

J.M. Ferrández Vicente et al. (Eds.): IWINAC 2017, Part II, LNCS 10338, pp. 473–480, 2017.
DOI: 10.1007/978-3-319-59773-7_48

Low compliance with prescribed medical recommendations is an ever-present and complex problem, especially for patients with a chronic disease [3]. This paper has identified key factors such as the quality of the physician-patient relationship and patient's health beliefs, professional empathy and patient empowerment that can help improve adherence.

Knowing the priorities of patients can be useful to optimize the clinical processes. In this context, technology support begins to play a crucial role. eHealth has enormous (yet to be exploited) potential to improve the quality of health care [4]. In [5,6] it was evaluated the role of telemedicine and, in particular, home blood pressure telemonitoring (HBPT) of the hypertensive patients. The results of several randomized trials suggest that HBPT represents a promising tool for improving blood pressure control in hypertensive patients, particularly those at high risk. Most studies documented a significant reduction in blood pressure with regular HBPT compared to usual care. HBPT interventions showed a high degree of patient acceptance, helped improve patients' quality of life, and were associated with lower medical costs than standard care.

However, the most of these computer applications have significant shortcomings. They have rigid architecture systems, and they are not prepared to change along the process. Moreover, key aspects such as security or standardisation of clinical data are managed inefficiently in many of them.

Our proposal aims to create an integrative, flexible, scalable and secure system architecture to monitor hypertension patients throughout the clinical process. In the next sections, we detail some examples of technologies, methods and paradigms oriented to monitor hypertensive patients, our proposed architecture and final conclusions.

2 State of Art

Clinical guidelines have established high blood pressure as a risk factor for cardiovascular disease [7]. The implementation of IT in health has allowed the use of many applications aimed at improving the treatment of patients with chronic diseases. For the acquisition of data, there are a wide range of devices capable of measuring the different variables that have incidence throughout the clinical process. It is the case of smart wristbands, blood pressure monitors, scales, etc. However, many of these applications have shortcomings in meeting the requirements to integrate process support, information and knowledge management.

Regarding hypertension, there are some examples of architectures proposed for the monitoring of the disease. In [8] an application was made to remind the patient to take the prescribed medication and thus improve adherence. Logan et al. [9] developed a tele-monitoring system through a blood pressure monitor, a mobile device, and a server capable of processing the information. Data related to blood pressure is sent from the blood pressure monitor via Bluetooth to the mobile phone, which sends this information via general packet radio service network (GPRS) to the server. Application serves are responsible for sending medical reports and reminders to the patient. In this case, security is ensured by SSL encryption protocol. This solution is based on message communication which has a lack of standardization, transmission speed and separation of different business layers.

Other architectures, in addition to focusing on blood pressure monitoring and bi-directional communication of the actors involved in the process, have incorporated decision support systems to aid in diagnosis [10]. In this paper, a decision support system was implemented for the diagnosis of both hypertension and hypotension. The real-time and wireless vital signs monitoring system proposed with two-way audio/video conferencing enables medical professionals to provide much enhanced healthcare compared to traditional methods. Security and privacy of medical data and patient's personal identification is secured by using XML based messaging with first key exchange and streaming encryption. This security solution needs to have an encryption key control and keep a client state on the server.

In [11], it was intended to control hypertension induced by pregnancy. Basically, the architecture of this system consists of a monitoring terminal responsible for the acquisition of maternal blood pressure data and a computer system to perform analysis, processing, storage and data management tasks, such as an expert physician. In addition, it manages the feedback of the results of the analysis and send the appropriate recommendations to the user terminal. The GPRS network is in charge of communication between both parties. The computer system has a fixed IP address, ready to receive terminal GPRS connection request and to send parameters to monitoring terminal. This approach does not include any authentication nor authorization security methods. There is no standard data format to send and receive patient information and it is a centralized architecture.

The system architecture proposed in [12] consists of three main domains (user, data and service) connected via wireless or wired communication networks. The user, through a blood pressure monitor sends the information via wireless network (GSM and GPRS) to the data server located in the hospital. The decision support system performs some initial decisions on patient condition. By following these first recommendations, the clinicians make a final diagnosis and sent it directly to the patients. If some data is difficult to judge, one specialist would be informed to access to the system to offer their decisions on patient condition. If the blood pressure data show that a patient is in emergency condition, alarms would be sent to the first-aid station for emergent treatment, either to an ambulance when this patient is outside the hospital or to some healthcare staff when this patient is in hospital. This architecture is centralized with no security, scalability and data standardisation solution.

All these studies are focused on the monitoring of the hypertensive patient and in some cases on the diagnosis, making the doctor-patient communication more direct. However, these usually have a rigid structure that does not adapt patient's real needs. They focus on partial aspects of the infrastructure for the clinical process and do not manage key aspects such as security, scalability, integration, flexibility, interoperability or data standardization. Our proposal aims to create an integrative architecture that solves the different weaknesses that the current systems have. In the next section we detail this architecture.

3 Proposed Architecture

Current solutions have numerous inefficiencies for security, communication protocols, data errors, scalability, standardisation of clinical data and interoperability between different information systems. Our proposal aims to design an architecture that provides security, flexibility, scalability, standardisation of data and minimization of data errors in the clinical process of hypertension.

This architecture is designed based on a web application that follows the Model-View-Controller (MVC) design pattern. MVC divides a web application in three decopled and interconnected parts in order to separate internal representation of information from the way that information is presented to the user.

This pattern has the ability to provide multiple views (desktop, tablet, mobile device) and code duplication is very limited due to separation between model, business logic and view layer. The code software modifications do not affect the entire model because the different parts of the architecture are independent. This architecture also supports asynchronous technique to implement stateless RESTful services.

The purpose of this web application is provide security, scalability, integration, flexibility, interoperability and data standardization of the clinical process. The Fig. 1 shows what elements make up this architecture, as well as what technologies, protocols and languages are used for the development of the web application, in order to reach the proposed requirements.

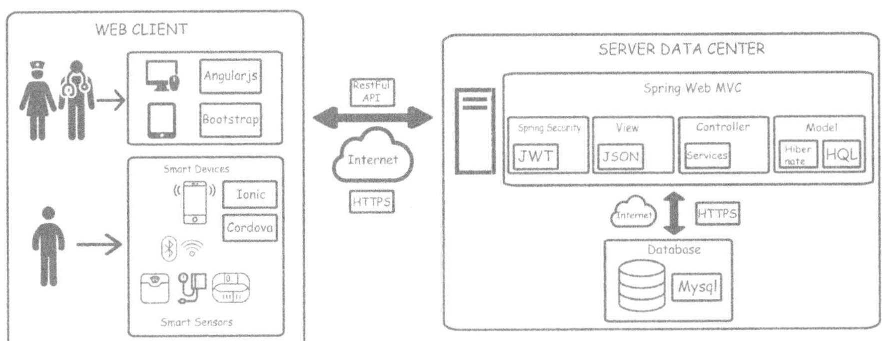

Fig. 1. Architecture of the proposed monitoring system

3.1 View Component

This part of the pattern is developed with the Angular and Bootstrap framework for desktops and tablets. Angularjs and Bootstrap are backed by Google and Twitter so it is used by a large community of developers. AngularJS supports data exchange formats in a standard way such as JavaScript Object Notation (JSON). Although Angular is also based on MVC, we use the view part to represent the data given from the RESTful API. We also use the controller part to communicate with the RESTful API and navigate between different application web pages.

To render the data we use HTML5, JavaScript and CSS3. These languages are widely used and are part of the standard of current web browsers. For mobile devices we develop the user interface with Ionic and Cordova frameworks to deploy native applications.

Ionic and Cordova allows software developers to build applications for mobile devices using CSS3, HTML5, and Javascript instead of using platform-specific APIs such as Android, iOS, or Windows Phone.

We use these frameworks and languages to standardise all the user interface logic with the different devices as desktops, tablets and mobiles. We also make the system flexible because it does not depend on a specific software to access data from the web application.

3.2 Controller Component

To develop this component we use Spring Web model-view-controller (MVC) framework due to flexibility, security, enterprise integration and data access. In this part we design a RESTful API to allow users to connect and interact with cloud services.

Controllers act as an interface between Model and View components. These controllers process all the business logic and incoming requests, manipulate data using the Model component and interact with the View component to send data for the final output. We also separate the controller layer from the model layer through services requests. This solution allows to connect in a flexible way the different layers of the model and offers a full integration between the MVC components of the web application.

3.3 Model Component

It specifies the logical structure of data in a software application and the high-level class associated with it. It is the domain-specific representation of the data which describes the working of an application. When a model changes its state, controller notifies its associated views, so they can refresh.

In our case, we use Hibernate which is an object-relational mapping tool for the Java programming language. It provides an object-oriented domain model to a relational database. This allows us to map Java classes to database tables and provides data query and retrieval facilities. This also supports greater scalability and integration with other existing systems since the model can be developed for different database management systems and not have a strong dependency between them.

We used MySQL database management system to store the clinical data referring to patients. In order to query database data we used Hibernate Query Language (HQL) which is fully object-oriented and understands notions like inheritance, polymorphism and association.

Using the HQL language we achieve a separation between the database management system data and the objects stored in the model component and allow us to make inquiries to different database management systems if necessary.

3.4 Integration and Standardisation Data

To standardise the data communication between the requests of the users and the response given by the server we use JavaScript Object Notation (JSON) which is easier to work with. JSON is a lightweight data-interchange format which reduces the amount of data transfer between user and web application. With the Angular framework is very easy to convert data given in JSON format to JavaScript objects and vice versa.

To avoid human errors entering patient's data we use two mechanism. On the one hand we use direct communication between different health devices and web application through Bluetooth protocol where patient just connect both parts. On the other hand patient can use web interface where data inputs are preformatted to avoid human errors.

3.5 Security

Clinical data are very sensitive and it is necessary to provide a safety component that ensures its protection. Moreover, users must be properly authorized and authenticated.

We use Spring Security Framework to provide user authentication and authorization to consume web application services. This framework allows us to set up some roles for users in order to authenticate them. The authentication mechanism we use is based on JSON Web Token (JWT) is a JSON-based open standard for passing claims between parties in web application environment. We use JWT to check that all requests are valid and come from authenticated users.

Our application is easily scalable as it allows integrating different authentication systems. For example we could access our system from the Google or Facebook authentication systems. JWT needs to be sent through an encrypted communication to prevent main-in-the-middle attacks. To avoid this kind of attacks we use Hyper Text Transfer Protocol Secure (HTTPS) to ensure that communication and sensitive data are transmitted in a secured channel.

With this role-based system we can also check which services can consume any profile associated to an user. There are some services that only can be accessed by certain profiles.

4 Conclusions

As a consequence of a higher human life expectancy, the advances in medicine and in medical treatments have achieved that a high percentage of people may live longer, turning potentially deadly diseases into chronic diseases. Currently, national health systems bear a higher economic and management load derived from these chronic diseases, which imply high health expenditure.

The aim of our proposal is to use some different frameworks and languages to design and develop a web application that is flexible, scalable, provides a safe environment to process sensitive data, standards health data and reduces errors in data stored. This architecture also provides a full integration of the clinical process where doctors and patients can access to health data immediately and allow greater control of patient pathology.

This architecture allows a fully integration of the monitoring devices into the clinical process and better patient empowerment with their disease. The daily health parameters are sent to the health centres to be available by medical teams which can detect possible anomalies in patient data faster.

Conflict of Interest

The authors declare no conflict of interest.

Acknowledgements. This work has been granted by the Ministerio de Economía y Competitividad of the Spanish Government (ref. TIN2014-53067-C3-1-R) and cofinanced by FEDER (Fondo Europeo de Desarrollo Regional).

References

1. World Health Organization: Global status report on noncommunicable diseases (2010)
2. Lewington, S., Clarke, R., Qizilbash, N., Peto, R., Collins, R.: Age-specific relevance of usual blood pressure to vascular mortality: a meta-analysis of individual data for one million adults in 61 prospective studies. Lancet **360**(9349), 1903–1913 (2002)
3. Vermeire, E., Hearnshaw, H., Van Royen, P., Denekens, J.: Patient adherence to treatment: three decades of research. A comprehensive review. J. Clin. Pharm. Ther. **26**(5), 331–342 (2001)
4. Lenz, R., Reichert, M.: IT support for healthcare processes - premises, challenges, perspectives. Data Knowl. Eng. **61**(1), 39–58 (2007)
5. Omboni, S., Ferrari, R.: The role of telemedicine in hypertension management: focus on blood pressure telemonitoring. Curr. Hypertens. Rep. **17**(4), 21 (2015)
6. AbuDagga, A., Resnick, H.E., Alwan, M.: Impact of blood pressure telemonitoring on hypertension outcomes: a literature review. Telemed. e-Health **16**(7), 830–838 (2010)
7. Foundation, N.H.: Guideline for the diagnosis and management of hypertension in adults (2016)
8. Patel, S., Jacobus-Kantor, L., Marshall, L., Ritchie, C., Kaplinski, M., Khurana, P.S., Katz, R.J.: Mobilizing your medications: an automated medication reminder application for mobile phones and hypertension medication adherence in a high-risk urban population. J. Diab. Sci. Technol. **7**(3), 630–639 (2013)
9. Logan, A.G., McIsaac, W.J., Tisler, A., Irvine, M.J., Saunders, A., Dunai, A., Rizo, C.A., Feig, D.S., Hamill, M., Trudel, M., Cafazzo, J.A.: Mobile phone-based remote patient monitoring system for management of hypertension in diabetic patients. Am. J. Hypertens. **20**(9), 942–948 (2007)

10. Baig, M.M., GholamHosseini, H.: A remote monitoring system with early diagnosis of hypertension and Hypotension. In: 2013 IEEE Point-of-Care Healthcare Technologies (PHT), pp. 34–37 (2013)
11. Zhang, K., Jiang, M., Ma, Z.: The monitoring system for Pregnancy-induced Hypertension based on Mobile Communication Technology. In: 2015 Seventh International Conference on Advanced Computational Intelligence (ICACI), pp. 263–266 (2015)
12. Lin, D., Zhang, X., Labeau, F., Kang, G.: A hypertension monitoring system and its system accuracy evaluation. In: 2012 IEEE 14th International Conference on e-Health Networking, Applications and Services, Healthcom 2012, pp. 132–137 (2012)

Combining Multiscale Filtering and Neural Networks for Local Rainfall Forecast

Fulgencio S. Buendia(✉), Gabriel Buendia Moya, and Diego Andina

Departamento de Señales, Sistemas y Radiocomunicaciones, E.T.S.I. Telecomunicación, Universidad Politécnica de Madrid, Madrid, Spain
fbuebue@gmail.com, fsbb@gmv.es, d.andina@upm.es

Abstract. Rainfall is one of the most important events of human life and society. Some rainfall phenomena like floods or hailstone are a threat to agriculture, business and even life. Predicting the weather has emerged as one of the most important areas of scientific endeavour. Nowadays, there is a big effort and great developments in long and mid-term rainfall forecasts, where qualitative improvements have been obtained both in forecasts and verification. This work proposes a diverse local rainfall forecasting system, using a long term local measurements registry. The forecast is performed estimating pressure time series and processing them with multispectral wavelet analysis and Neural Networks. The aim of the study is to provide complementary criteria based on the observed pressure wave pattern repetition. This method was proposed by expert meteorologists after observing these events during 40 years.

Keywords: Rainfall · Forecast · Wavelet · Neural networks · Multispectral analysis

1 Introduction

Since climate change is now widely accepted and there is a rapidly increasing realisation that it will affect every person in the world, the resources and efforts in weather investigation have been increased. One of the most important event of daily life is rainfall, predictions became more accurate, as a result weather forecasts has made society more and more dependent on them. Weather predictions are provided by Ensemble Prediction Systems (EPS). A ensemble is a collection of weather forecasts, properly named, are a set of numerical weather prediction (NWP) systems. The ensembles run the models many times from very slightly different initial conditions. Often the model physics is also slightly perturbed, and some ensembles use more than one model within the ensemble (multi-model EPS) or the same model but with different combinations of physical parameterization schemes (multi-physics EPS), see WMO (2012). Some European reference centres are the HIRLAM, ECMWF and the UK MET Office. The European Centre for Medium-Range Weather Forecasts (ECMWF) is supported by 34 states and specialised in prediction for the medium range (up to two weeks

J.M. Ferrández Vicente et al. (Eds.): IWINAC 2017, Part II, LNCS 10338, pp. 481–490, 2017.
DOI: 10.1007/978-3-319-59773-7_49

ahead), on the other side, the HIRLAM (HIgh Resolution Limited Area Model) is a research cooperation of European meteorological institutes that provides a numerical short-range weather forecasting based on an hydrostatic model. The main handicap of medium and long term forecasts, as in any kind of simulation, is that any uncertainty either in the measurements or in the model definition makes the temporal simulation diverge from the real evolution (Lorenz 1963, 2006; Lynch 2006). Since Richardson in 1942, performed the first NWP setting the equations of a particle in the atmosphere, the prediction systems have awesome evolved (Holton 2004; WMO 2012), but have the inherent limitation due to chaotic nature of weather. Regarded to this matter, Rodriguez (2008) stated the need to evolve the current forecast systems to overcome these limitations. Many other approximations based on stochastic models have been proposed (Cowpertwait et al. 1996; Burton et al. 2008). Lovejoy and Mandelbrot proposed a fractal model of rain fields, Lovejoy and Mandelbrot (1985). The use of ANN in weather forecast was first proposed by Hu (2004), and during last years, several authors have made different approximations to this subject, Dubey performs a good summary of Rainfall prediction using ANN (2015). The work proposes an approximation to local rainfall forecast based weather time series analysis and neural networks to complement current ensemble predictions.

2 Local Rainfall Forecast Proposal

2.1 Local Rainfall Forecast Model

During many years the observation in the Valladolid weather forecast of rainfall patterns repetition, motivated the registry twice a day of a selected set of data to characterize the rainfall events as an aid to the ensembles evolution prediction. As a result the rainfall events produced in Valladolid as the winds at surface and at 500 Hpa and different pressure waves were recorded in a time series during more of a decade. At a first analysis of the data, it was clearly seen the high dependence of rainfall events and precipitation amount with the combination of surface and height winds. On the other hand, the pressure waves situation can suggest, not so clearly as winds, the rainfall situation. These set of data evolution was used as an aid to the predictions. The idea is to automate the process and, given a situation, being able to predict the evolution of the data, but not by the models, but using the historical registry and a Neural Networks stage. This study started in Buendia et al. (2008). The system retreives the preasure and geostrophic winds from the national meteorological agencies, and filter them to make a forecast of these variables evolution with the historical database. In Buendia et al. (2008) there is explained the first stage of the work, how to filter the input data. Note, the stages of the system are (Fig. 1):

- A Capture Stage to retreive the input observations.
- Filtering stage, which prepares the data.
- Historical database.
- A time series forecaster to predict the evolution.
- A classification stage.

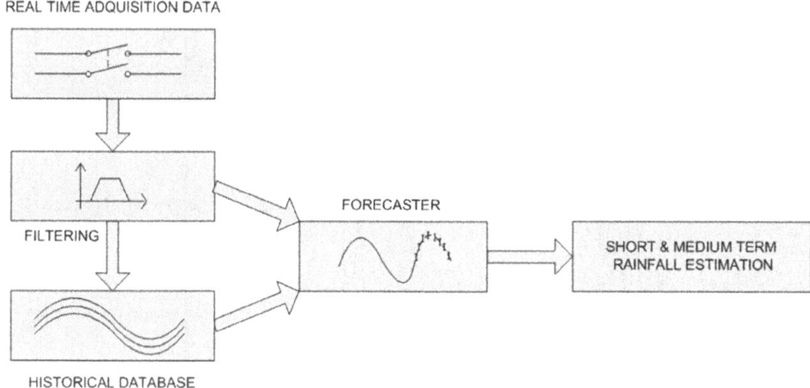

Fig. 1. System architecture

2.2 Vertical Profile of the Atmosphere Observation Time Series

As explained before, two sets of variables were selected. The first related to the height between certain pressure levels:

- **Pressure waves, measured in hecto pascals, Hpa.**
- **Geopotential height at 500 Hp, measured in metres.**
- **Thickness of the pressure layer from 500–1000 Hpa, measured in metres.**

Plotting these variables among time appear a set of time series, that can be seen as the evolution of the vertical profile of the atmosphere at sea level, 500 Hpa and 1000 Hpa over the observation. The evolution of the data shows the pass through of warm and cold fronts, and the other sinoptic situations, that are directly related to the rainfall events. The data have been captured twice a day during 10 years.

2.3 Geostrophic Winds Direction Observations

To complete the dataset, the direction of the geostrophic winds (GW) at sea level and at 500 Hpa has been registered.

The geostrophic wind is the resulting wind in the atmosphere under horizontal and hydrostatic movement without any acceleration or friction, actually at sea level is just theoretical due to the friction forces to the Earth.

As the geostrophic winds are registered each 12 h, this provides a time series that estimates the rainfall probability. This time series will be named p_{wind}. Next figure shows the p_{wind} probability time series for the eary 1999. It can be cuantitative seen that in the peaks of the signal there are several rainfalls clusters (Fig. 2).

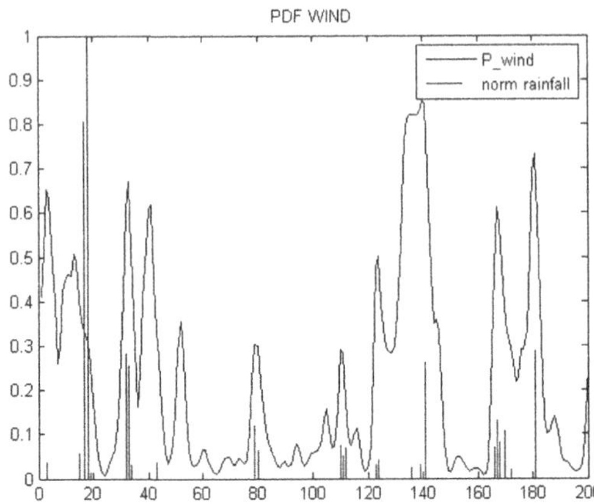

Fig. 2. Rainfall probability time series p_{wind} with rainfall events

3 Filtering Stage

3.1 Filtering Stage Design

This stage is designed to simplify and extract the useful information from the input data to:

- Obtain simple data where the rainfall information is contained.
- Obtain simple series easy to forecast individually.

The idea is, the simpler the time series the easier to forecast. So the input signals are decomposed using the multiscale analysis idea, using a family of convolution filters inspired in the time-scale wavelet concept; see Percibal and Walden (2002), Addison (2002), and Mallat (1999). The family of filters, $h(n)$, is a set of band-pass filters obtained subtracting two gaussian distributions:

$$h(n) = A\left(\exp\left\{-\left(\frac{n2^{s+2}}{N}\right)^2\right\} - \exp\left\{-\left(\frac{n2^{s+1}}{N}\right)^2\right\}\right) \quad (1)$$

Where A is a scaling coefficient, N is the number of input samples, n is an integer number (n = 1..N) and S represents the "scale" of the filter. This actually is the rest of two gaussian distributions. The responses of this family of filters in the time domain are represented in left side of Fig. 3 and the right figure shows it in the frequency domain. These have a frequency response similar to the Mexican Hat wavelet, Addison (2002).

With the family of filters, the scale used would depend on the temporal scale to observe. The filter, is Shift Invariant (as it is a convolution of a continuous signal), it means that the events represented in the different scales at the same position correspond to the same time instant (which is necessary to locate

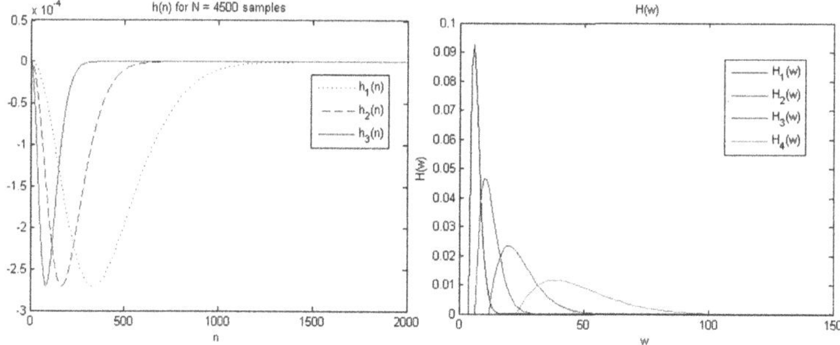

Fig. 3. Time and frequency response of the multiscale filter

events in time series using filtering stages). Some wavelet transforms, as the Continuous Wavelet Transform (CWT), the Maxima Overlap Wavelet Transform (MODWT), the Double Tree Wavelet transform (DWCWT) preserves also the invariance of the event location among the scales, and consequently, can be used. For example, the Discrete Wavelet Transform (DWT) is not shift invariant.

3.2 Filtering Application: P_{esc}, Z_{500} and H_{esc}

Three components can be expected in the time series analysis: an stationery periodic component in the low scales/frequencies, the non-stationary components in the middle and high scales/frequencies range. The stationary components of the pressure are well known due to cyclic contributions, and the high frequency scales the main contribution is due to the day/night pressure variations. The middle range variations can be attributed to frontal circulation.

Figure 4 shows the decomposition of the P_{esc} for scales 3, 4, 7 and 10 through 2002 to the end of 2011. Those signals are obtained filtering P_{esc} with the Eq. 1. The filtered signal, at a certain scale, holds the main variations of the signal at a range of time, for instance, scale 2–3 holds the main variations of the signal in one year scale approximately. The signals at scales 10 and above are quite sharp and therefore discarded.

Figure 5 the resulting of filtering P_{esc} at scales 7, 8 and 9. While in scale 7 the variation of the signal is to slow to fit the rainfall clusters, at scales 8 and 9 the signal enclose perfectly. The rainfall is bounded by the valleys of the pressure wave. The decomposition of the other time series (Z_{500} and H_{esc}) presents a similar pattern.

In the rest of the article, it is supposed that P_{esc}, Z_{500} and H_{esc}, are the signals filtered at scale $8+9$. Note that the selection of the scales is referred to the length of the input vector.

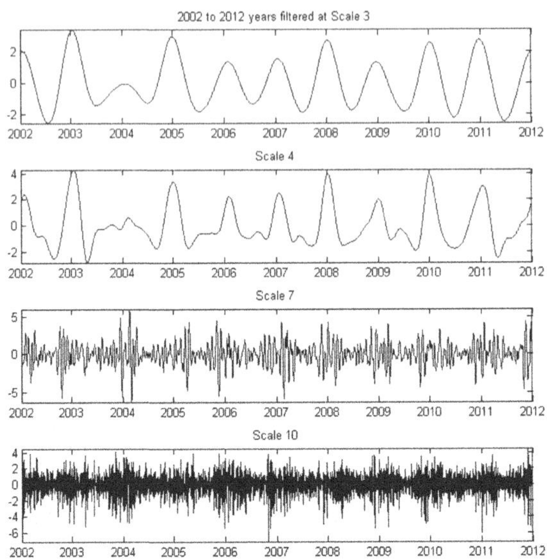

Fig. 4. Multiscale decomposition of P_{esc} at low and high scales

4 Classifier Design

The classification stage tries to discriminate if a certain situation corresponds to a rainfall event or not. The selected classifier was a Multilayer Perceptron (MLP), for its well known classification capabilities.

In the following points there are explained the whole classifier design steps.

4.1 Labelling

The first step is create a features vector to use in the classifier. Actually, this is probably the most important step in the classifier design. In this case, the input data are presented as time series from the initial study (scaled pressure waves, geostropic winds and related variables). As the rainfall events are presented in clusters and usually those clusters are enclosed in the pressure valleys, the feature extraction begins obtaining the time series extremes and performs a set of measurements between one maximum and the following one. The data obtained in a valley without rain, shall be labelled as "Dry" and the data found in a pressure valley with rain shall be labelled as "Rain". This method allows to perform an automatic labelling of the data that simplifies the process (see Shasha and Zhu 2004). Situated in each maximum of P_{esc}, there are obtained different parameters. The meaning of these measurements is different for each magnitude but all significative in the rainfall process. All the feature values were normalized to avoid training problems in the following stages. Processed the time series the obtained dataset had 24 features, each of them a training candidate for the classifier.

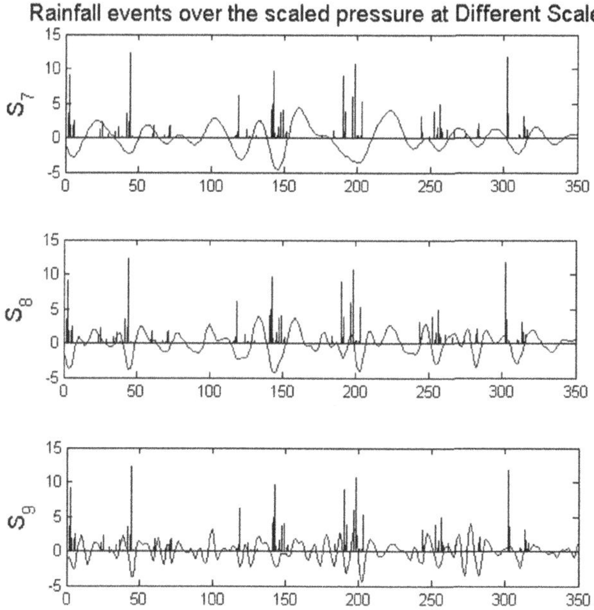

Fig. 5. Multiscale decomposition of P_{esc} at intermediate scales

4.2 Feature Extraction

To perform the feature extraction, a sequential forward selection (SFS) algorithm was applied, as it looks for the best training set. It was used a Multilayer Perceptron as selector, Duda (2000). The SFS process tried to classify 100 samples with the combinations of 24-features vector. The training results are shown in Fig. 6. The best training set was: $[p_{wind}$, min P_{ESC}, ΔZ_{500}, $\Delta H_{esc}]$. The error rises when additional features added, so the process was stopped there.

As a trade off between performance and complexity, the first two features were included in the training vector, since these features need to be forecasted. The other two variables will be included later when the system start to work.

4.3 Test Vectors Preparation

With the selected features, the data needs to be introduced in the Multi Layer Perceptron. The matrix with the input variables is usually called P_{matrix}, and the target vector T_{vector}. P_{matrix} holds $[p_{WIND}$, min $P_{ESC}]$ sample and T_{vector} 1 or 0, indicating if the P_{data} corresponds to "Rain" and 0 to "Dry". The dataset is divided into three subsets: Training dataset, for perform the training of the MLP – (185 vectors). Verification dataset: (185 vectors). Test dataset: Data to test the final classification (300 vectors) (Fig. 6).

The first two datasets are used to setup and train the classifier and the last one is used to test the classifier performance.

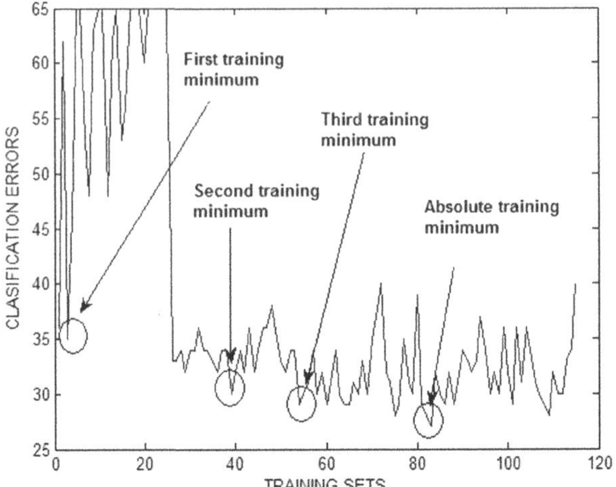

Fig. 6. SFS process

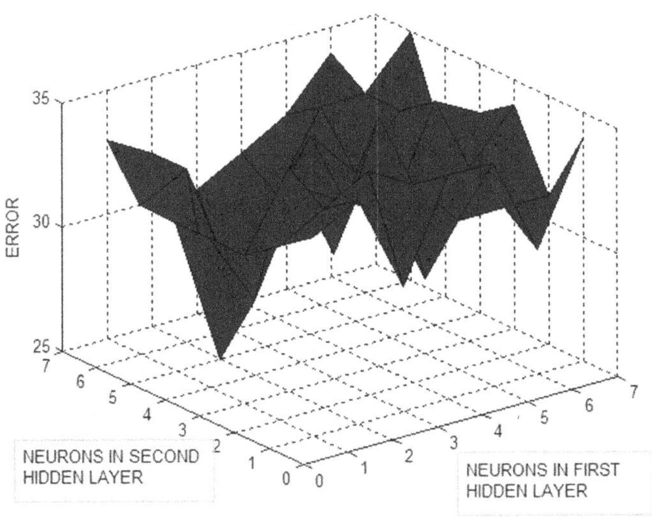

Fig. 7. MLP hidden layers selection

4.4 Classifier Setup and Training

It was selected a multilayer perceptron (MLP) with two hidden layers, as can generate arbitrarily complex boundaries to classify vectors into classes consisting of any union of polyhedral regions (Bishop 1996). There is no rule to select the optimal number of neurons for a MLP, some guidelines can be found in Duda (2000), etc. It was tested every configuration of a two-hidden layer network, from 1×1 neurons to 7×7 neurons, selecting the one with minimum mean squared error (MSE) (Fig. 7).

The best performance was achieved with two neurons in the first hidden layer and five in the second, with a classification performance of 87% (25 classification failures in the 185 verification samples). The training was repeated with the network until the number of errors was below 10% of MSE, at the end the network achieved 19 failures in the 185 verification samples, that means a 90% of a priori performance. This value needed to be finally confirmed with the test dataset. 4.5 Classifier performance assessment The network was tested with the test dataset, with vectors not previously used neither to train nor verify the classifier. It appeared 36 failures in 300 samples, that is a 88% of performance. In Table 1 all these data are summarized.

Table 1. Classification performance summary

	Verification dataset	Test dataset
Number of samples	185	300
Number of failures	19	36
Classification performance	90%	88%

5 Conclusions

This paper presents a complementary method to current forecasts provided by ensembles, as the rainfall is predicted using artificial neural networks and time series. It has been presented the study of the meteorological variables for the local rainfall study, explaining the filtering and classification stages. At the moment, it has been obtained 88% of classification performance that is quite successful. Currently, it is being developed the time series forecast, with promissory results. The accuracy and prediction range shall determine the overall system performance. The work continues the presented one in Buendia et al. (2008).

References

Addison, P.S.: The Illustrated Wavelet Transform Handbook, Introductory Theory and Applications in Science, Engineering, Medicine and Finance, 1st edn., 368 p. Taylor & Francis, Abingdon (2002)

Bishop, C.: Neural Networks for Pattern Recognition, 1st edn., 504 p. Oxford University Press, Oxford (1996)

Buendia, F.-S., Tarquis, A.M., Buenda, G., Andina, D.: Feature extraction via multiresolution MODWT analysis in a rainfall forecast system. In: World Multiconference on Systemics, Cybernetics and Informatics 2008 Proceedings, pp. 69–73 (2008)

Burton, A., Kilsby, C.G., Fowler, H.J., Cowpertwait, P.S.P., OConnell, P.E.: RainSim: a spatial temporal stochastic rainfall modelling system. Environ. Model Softw. **23**, 1356–1369 (2008)

Cowpertwait, P.S.P., OConnell, P.E., Metcalfe, A.V., Mawdsley, J.A.: Stochastic point process modelling of rainfall, I. Single site fitting and validation. J. Hydrol. **175**, 17–46 (1996)
Dubey, A.D.: Artificial neural network models for rainfall prediction in Pondicherry. Int. J. Comput. Appl. (0975 – 8887) **120**(3), 30–35 (2015)
Duda, R.O., Hart, P.E., Stork, D.G.: Pattern Classification, 2nd edn., 680 p. Wiley, New York (2000)
Holton, J.R.: An Introduction To Dynamic Meteorology, 4th edn., 534 p. Academic Press, Cambridge (2004)
Hu, M.J.-C.: Application of the adaline system to weather forecasting. Dissertation Department of Electrical Engineering, Stanford University (1964)
Lorenz, E.N.: The predictability of hydrodynamic flow. Trans. N. Y. Acad. Sci. Ser. II **25**(4), 409–432 (1963)
Lorenz, E.N.: Predictability, a problem partially solved. In: Palmer, T., Hagedorn, R. (eds.) Predictability of Weather and Climate, pp. 40–58. Cambridge University Press, Cambridge (2006)
Lovejoy, S., Mandelbrot, B.: Fractal properties of rain, and a fractal model. Tellus A **37A**, 209–232 (1985)
Lynch, P.: Chaos, predictability and ensemble forecasting. In: The Emergence of Numerical Weather Prediction: Richardson's Dream, pp. 229–234. Cambridge University Press (2006)
Mallat, S.: A Wavelet Tour of Signal Processing, 2nd edn., 620 p. Academic Press, Elsevier, Cambridge (1999)
Percibal, D.B., Walden, A.: Wavelet Methods for Time Series Analysis, 6220 p. Cambridge University Press, Cambridge (2002)
Rodriguez, M.A.: Predicción Meteorológica y Caos en Espacio-Tiempo (Spanish). Revista Española de Física **22**, 66–69 (2008)
Shasha, D., Zhu, Y.: High Performance Discovery in Time Series, Techniques and Case Studies. Monographs in Computer Science. Springer, Heidelberg (2004)
World Meteorological Organization: Guidelines on Ensemble Prediction Systems and Forecasting. WMO No-1091 (2012)

Dynamic Sign Language Recognition Using Gaussian Process Dynamical Models

Juan P. Velasquez[1], Hernán F. García[1,2(✉)], and Jorge I. Marín[1]

[1] GDSPROC Research Group, Universidad del Quinío, Armenia, Colombia
jorgemarin@uniquindio.edu.co
[2] Grupo de Investigación en Automática, Universidad Tecnológica de Pereira, La Julita, Pereira, USA
hernan.garcia@utp.edu.co

Abstract. This paper proposes the temporal modeling of the dynamic behavior of the Colombian sign language by using a dynamic latent space captured by a Gaussian process latent variable models. The database is built from the recording of 5 signs, which are recorded 40 times each, implying a total of 200 repetitions per class. Each recording consists of a movement composed of 120 frames, where each frame is the skeleton of the subject involved. To ensure system adaptability to different test subjects, the 200 instances are performed by 4 different subjects. The time series generated for each point in the skeleton produces a large amount of information that hinder the proper classification of the signs. For this reason, a Gaussian Process Dynamical Models (GPDM) is used to model the dynamics of the sign language. Furthermore, GPDM generates points associated with a latent space for a specific behavior according to the dynamics of the sign. Within the latent space, we use three different machines for pattern classification: support vector machine (SVM), artificial neural network (ANN), and least squares for classification (LSC). Finally, some static features from the time series are extracted and classified to compare with the dynamic features. The experimental results show that by modeling the temporal behavior of the sign signals, we can recognize accurately a given sign language.

1 Introduction

In modern society, technology is a lifestyle because in a single device, multiple services may converge, i.e., by just a click away you can enjoy activities such as entertainment, work or social interaction. In Colombia, the 93.08% of the population has no hearing impairment, so they can enjoy the aforementioned benefits. However, there is a remaining 1.03% of the population with a hearing impairment [4], who every day must face the technological world with limited access to the information due to their condition. A person with limited hearing at different levels suffers minor or major consequences due to this restriction. Consequences of this restriction are their cognitive development, sensory and motor functions, affective partner, among others [5]. It is important to remark that these consequences are acquired since infancy, implying that these people

J.M. Ferrández Vicente et al. (Eds.): IWINAC 2017, Part II, LNCS 10338, pp. 491–500, 2017.
DOI: 10.1007/978-3-319-59773-7_50

cannot develop in the same degree as the people with no hearing impairment. For this reason, it is necessary to implement a system capable of recognize the Colombian sign language. In this paper, we use a methodology based on GPDM to interpret dynamic signs from the Colombian sign language. Our methodology differs from the trend of using artificial neural networks (ANN) or hidden Markov models (HMM) to model the time series for a dynamic sign [3]. In addition, the modeling of signs can be used to develop devices that allow fluid communication between people with disabilities and no disabilities without using an alternate language.

Since the analysis of dynamic signs involves the processing a huge amount of information concerning to a stream of images, we adopted in this paper a framework based on the analysis of a sequence of skeletons provided by a Kinect sensor. The skeleton stream is preprocessed by using a dimensionality reduction. The purpose of dimensionality reduction is to discover multiple low-dimensionalities in a high-dimensional space. Dimensionality reduction is accomplished by implementing different transformations in the samples at a high-dimensional space [8]. One of the major difficulties to model time series is that the model is unable to determine the non-linearities present in it. Although there are tools capable of modeling this kind of problems, they require a lot of basis to train and to generate accurate models [7]. The kernel PCA is used as a non-linear kernel technique in the observation space, where the dimensionality reduction is implemented on the kernel space. Although the kernel PCA generates a non-linear latent space representation, this representation is unable to make a projection into the observation space [6–8].

Gaussian process latent variable-model (GP-LVM) was proposed by [6], providing a way to make projections from the latent space to the observation space. This method has been identified as an effective dimensionality reducer, being a dual representation of kernel PCA [6–8]. The GPDM comprises a mapping from a latent space to the information space, and a dynamic model on the latent space. These mappings are typically non-linear. Thus, the GPDM is obtained by marginalizing the parameters of two mappings and by optimization of the latent coordinates in the information training. In other words, GPDM generates a latent space with GP-LVM. More precisely, the idea behind GPDM is to model a probability density of states with a sequence of discrete time samples and information in the data space. Latent variables are denoted by noise and parametrized non-linear mappings [7].

2 Proposed Method

2.1 Gaussian Process Latent Variable Model (GP-LVM)

Let $Y = [y_1, \ldots, y_n]^T$ be a matrix representing the training data, and $X = [x1, \ldots, xn]^T$ denotes the matrix whose rows represent the corresponding position in the latent space. The GP-LVM generates a mapping to a latent space of low dimensionality, X, from a database of high dimensionality, Y. Given a covariance function for the Gaussian process $k(x, x')$, the likelihood for the given information can be seen in (1). Where the kernel matrix elements k are defined by the covariance function $K_{i,j} = k(x_i, y_j)$ [2].

$$p(Y|X,\Phi) = \frac{1}{\sqrt{(2\pi)^{ND}|K_y|^D}} exp\left(-\frac{1}{2}tr(K_y^{-1}YY^T)\right) \tag{1}$$

2.2 Gaussian Process Dynamical Model(GPDM)

In [7], it is proposed an extension for GP-LVM to find a latent space that reflects the order of the observed data. This extension is performed by specifying a prediction function on the sequence in the latent space.

$$x_t = h(x_{t-1}) + \epsilon_{dyn} \tag{2}$$

where ϵ_{dyn} $N(0, \beta^{-1}I)$. This mapping is marginalized on the latent distribution points generating a new objective function.

$$X, \phi_Y, \phi_{dyn} = argmax_{X,\phi_Y,\phi_{dyn}} P(Y|X, \phi_Y)P(X|\phi_{dyn}) \tag{3}$$

where $phiY$ are the hyper-parameter covariance function and phi_{dyn} is the sequence in the latent space [2–7].

2.3 Artificial Neural Network (ANN)

In this section, the explanation of a neural network is presented for a neural network with a hidden layer and one output since the operation of a complex neural-network topology is similar to a simple one. [1]. Let the output of the neural network, y, be:

$$y = v_0 + \sum_{i=1}^{c} v_i f(w_{i0} + \sum_{j=1}^{n} w_{ij}x_j) \tag{4}$$

From Eq. (4), c is the number of neurons in the hidden layer, n is the number of entries, v and w are the weights of the neural network, and f is the activation function of perceptrons comprising neurons in the hidden layer.

Since the Neural Network is an iterative solution, weights v and w are modified according to an error. Thus:

$$V_{t+1} = V_t + \alpha \begin{bmatrix} 1 \\ Z \end{bmatrix} e \tag{5}$$

From (5), V_t are the weights of the hidden layer in the current instant, V_{t+1} are the weights of the hidden layer in the next instant; Z are the values of r pasts by the activation function f, where r are the inputs multiplied by the W weights, e is the error, and α is the coefficient of learning of the Neuronal Network.

$$W_t + \alpha \begin{bmatrix} v_1 f'(r_1) \\ v_2 f'(r_2) \\ \cdots \\ v_c f'(r_c) \end{bmatrix} \left(\begin{bmatrix} 1 \\ x \end{bmatrix}\right)^T e \tag{6}$$

From (6), W_t are the weights of the input layer in the current instant, W_{t+1} are the weights of the input layer in the next instant, and x are the inputs.

2.4 Support Vector Machine (SVM)

Non-linearly Separable Case. In a SVM, the non-linearly separable case allows that some data are on the wrong side of margin limit, but with a penalty that increases with the distance from that limit [1].

Let $\xi_n = 0$ be the points that are within the limit of the correct margin, and $\xi_n = |t_n - y(\mathbf{x_n})|$ be the other points.

Thus, a point on the surface of decision, $y(\mathbf{x}) = 0$, is classified as $\xi_n = 1$, and points with $\xi_n \geq 1$ are classified incorrectly.

In particular, we want to minimize

$$\frac{1}{2}\|\mathbf{w}\|^2 + C\sum_{n=1}^{N}\xi_n \tag{7}$$

where $C > 0$, and subject to the restrictions $t_n y(\mathbf{x_n}) \geq 1 - \xi_n$, with $\xi_n \geq 0$

The aim is to maximize the margin, while the points that are on the wrong side of the margin are penalized.

The predictions are given by:

$$y(\mathbf{x}) = \sum_{n=1}^{N} a_n t_n k(\mathbf{x}, \mathbf{x_n}) + w_0 \tag{8}$$

The sign $y(\mathbf{x})$ indicates the class.

The value of w_0 can be obtained by

$$w_0 = \frac{1}{N_M}\sum_{n \epsilon M}(t_n - \sum_{m \epsilon S} a_m t_m k(\mathbf{x_n}, \mathbf{x_m})) \tag{9}$$

where S denotes the set of indices of support vectors. M denotes the set of data indices that has $0 < a_n < C$, and N_M is the cardinality of M.

3 Procedure

Using the Microsoft Kinect sensor is possible to take a snapshot of the skeleton of a person who is positioned in front of it. This skeleton provides information for 20 different joints of the human body. We recorded 120 frames for each realization, and 40 recordings for each sign. After performing the skeleton capture, we selected the most representative joints. These joints are the head, shoulders, elbows, wrists and hands. In total, we selected 9 joints. With these joints in a three-dimensional space of 120 frames, we performed a conversion to a two-dimensional latent space. With the points in this reduced space is possible to generate a training matrix to classify the sign. This training matrix is composed by 200 instances for 240 features corresponding to the two-dimensional latent space. Finally, with the dynamic-features model provided by the latent model, we trained three different classifiers: a radial basis SVM, a neural network classifier and least squares classifier. The flow chart of Fig. 1 shows the steps in the proposed method, and some real images for the skeleton and the latent space.

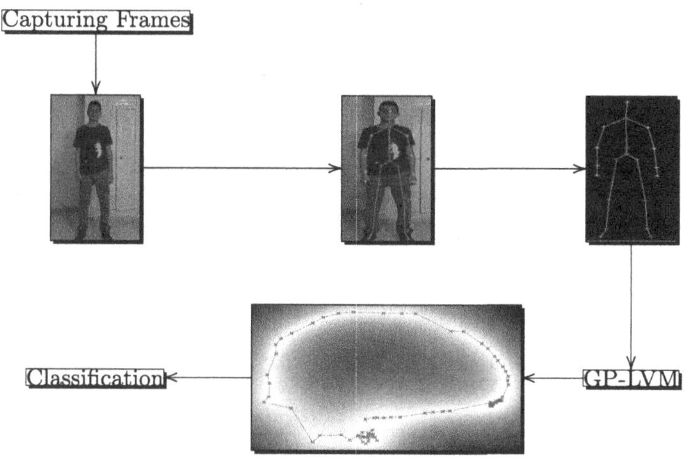

Fig. 1. Flow chart of the proposed method

Figure 2 shows some frames taken from the original 120 frames for a given sign. In the figures, the body joints are in blue, and the points selected for classification are in green.

Figure 3 shows five (5) latent spaces for each sign captured by the Kinect sensor. In this paper, the features obtained from the latent space are named dynamic features.

For comparison purposes, the results obtained with the dynamic features are compared by the results obtained with static features for the same classifier. The static features are obtained by measuring the power, minimum value, maximum value, mean and standard deviation for each selected skeleton-joint across the 120 frames.

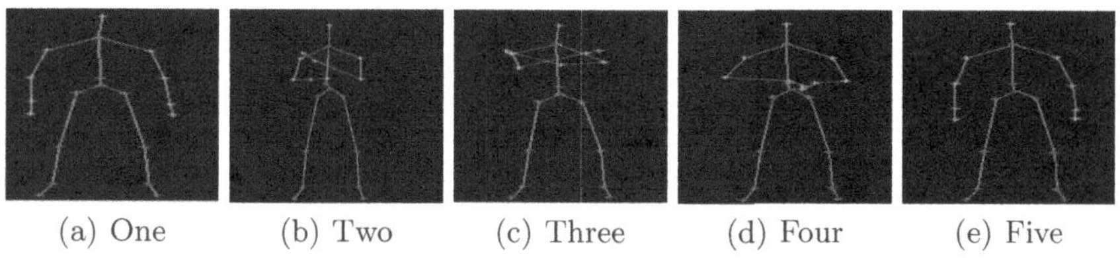

(a) One (b) Two (c) Three (d) Four (e) Five

Fig. 2. Dynamic behavior of the observed features. (Color figure online)

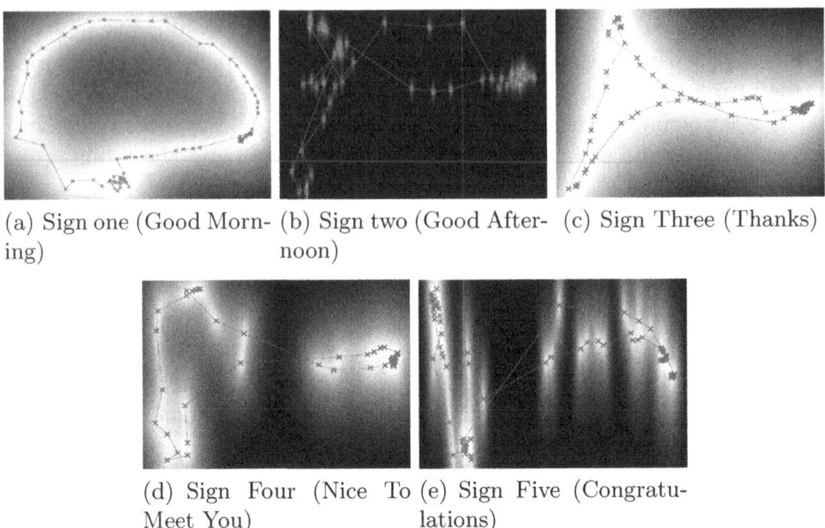

(a) Sign one (Good Morning)

(b) Sign two (Good Afternoon)

(c) Sign Three (Thanks)

(d) Sign Four (Nice To Meet You)

(e) Sign Five (Congratulations)

Fig. 3. Dynamic latent space features for a given sign realization.

To validate the system behavior, the classification accuracy is calculated using a k-fold validation of 5 partitions and 5 repetitions for each partition.

4 Results

4.1 Dynamic Features

Support Vector Machine (SVM). Figure 4 shows the accuracy of the system using the dynamic features obtained from the latent space. For the training

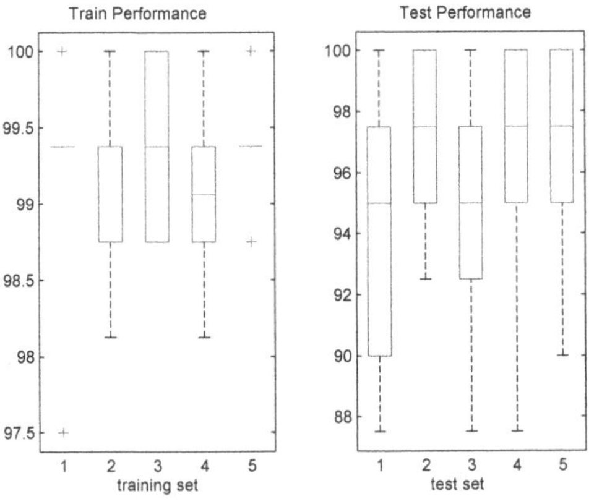

Fig. 4. System accuracy for training and validation in a latent SVM

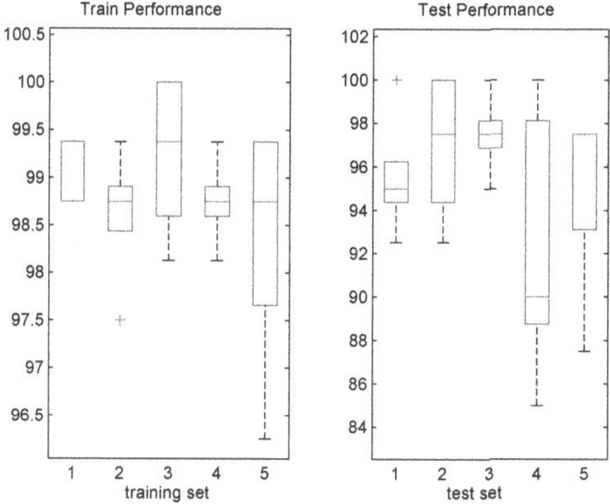

Fig. 5. System accuracy for training and validation in a latent Neural Network.

set, we obtained an accuracy above 90%. However, with the validation set, the system performance is reduced to an accuracy up to 88%, maintaining high performances.

Neural Network. Figure 5 shows that a neural network in contrast to SVM, using the dynamic features, reduces is accuracy for both train and test scenarios. However, the dynamic features proves to be an accurate descriptor of these sign languages.

Least Squares for Classification (LSC). Figure 3 shows the performance of the dynamic features for LSC classifier. The results show that for the test set, the performance decrease below of 80%, but these results are expected due to the lack of generalizability of the classifier.

4.2 Static Features

Support Vector Machine (SVM). Figure 7, shows that the performance of the SVM using static features decrease considerably, due to the lack of information that the static features brings to the classifier (below 70% for the test-set).

Neural Network. In the case of a neural network, Fig. 8, shows that the results are similar to those in a SVM. Again, the performance inaccurate for both training and validation sets.

Least Squares for Classification (LSC). In the case of least squares, Fig. 9 shows an the lowest performance, in which the static features proves that the static information captured for the entire temporal signals are not informative enough for a given recognition problem.

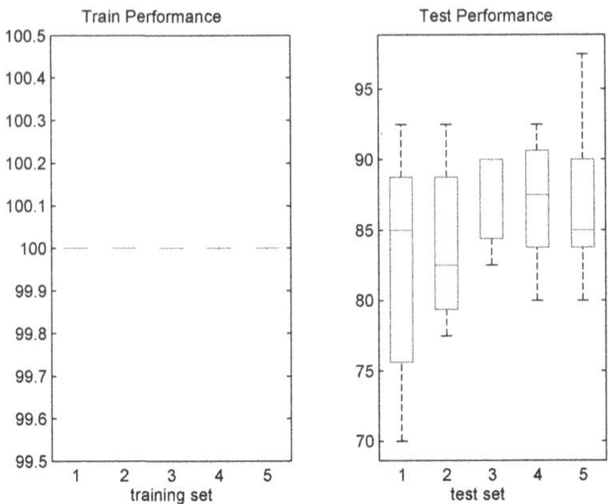

Fig. 6. System accuracy for training and validation in a latent LSC.

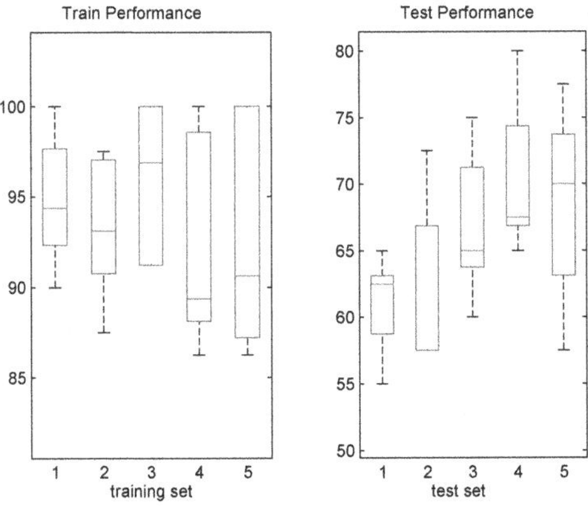

Fig. 7. System accuracy for training and validation in a static SVM.

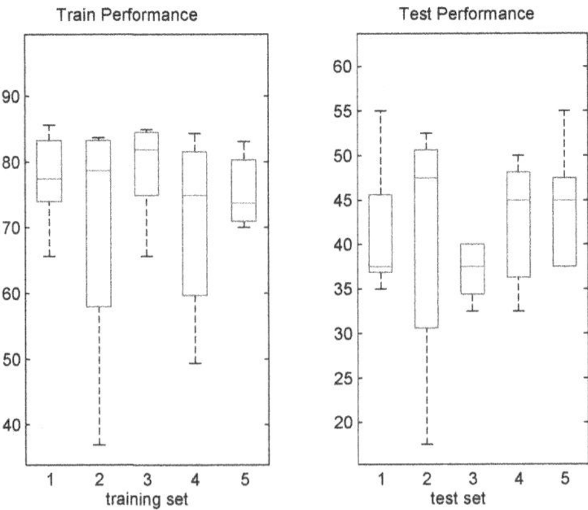

Fig. 8. System accuracy for training and validation in a static neural network.

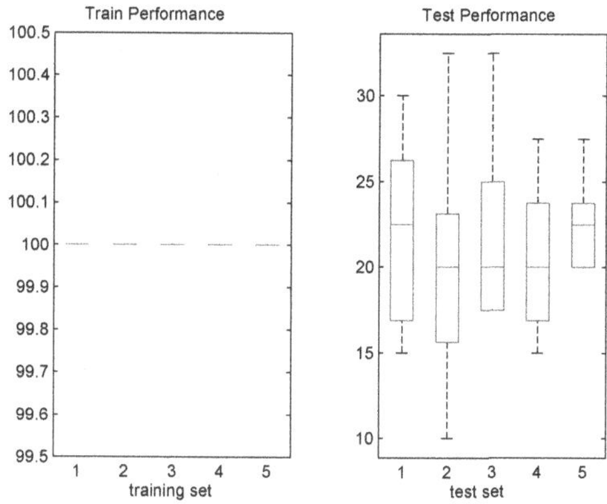

Fig. 9. System accuracy for training and validation in a static LSC.

5 Conclusions

In this paper we proposed a dynamic latent space framework for sign language modeling. The results show that the dynamic features proves to be very informative in a given sign language recognition problem. Besides, the experimental results show that both SVM and ANN classifiers, shows high performances compared against the static framework in which the recognition problem becomes inaccurate. The main reason of these results is that static features are unable to model the temporal behavior that the sign language exhibits in all of their signals. That is why the LSC classifier shows the lowest performance in the experiments. As future works, we plan to build a multi-output framework that captures the shared dynamical information for each joint of the sign language.

References

1. Bishop, C.M.: Pattern Recognition and Machine Learning (Informacion Science and Statistics). Springer-Verlag New York Inc., Secaucus (2006)
2. García, H.F., Álvarez, M.A., Orozco, Á.: Gaussian Process Dynamical Models For Emotion Recognition. Grupo de Investigación en Automática, Universidad Tecnológica de Pereira, La Julita, Pereira, Colombia
3. Gamage, N., Kuang, Y.C., Akmeliawati, R., Demidenko, S.: Gaussian process dynamical models for hand gesture interpretation in sign language (2011)
4. Instituto Nacional para Sordos (s.f.), Insor. Obtenido de Participación porcentual de la población sorda: http://www.insor.gov.co/observatorio/participacion-porcentual-de-la-poblacion-sorda/
5. Ceesordosjerez (s.f.), Obtenido de Consecuencias e implicaciones de la deficiencia auditiva: http://www.ceesordosjerez.es/form_profesorado/consecuencias%20e%20implicaciones%20de%20la%20da.pdf

6. Lawrence, N.D.: Gaussian Process Latent Variable Models for Visualisation of High Dimensional Data. Department of Computer Science, University of Sheffield (2004)
7. Wang, J.M., Fleet, D.J., Hertzmann, A.: Gaussian Process Dynamical Models. Department of Computer Science, University of Toronto, Toronto (2006)
8. Gao, X., Wang, X., Tao, D., Li, X.: Model supervised Gaussian process latent variable for dimensionality reduction. IEEE Trans. Syst. Man Cybern.-Part B: Cybern. **41**(2), 425–434 (2011)

Relevant Kinematic Feature Selection to Support Human Action Recognition in MoCap Data

J.D. Pulgarin-Giraldo[1(✉)], A.A. Ruales-Torres[1], A.M. Alvarez-Meza[2], and G. Castellanos-Dominguez[1]

[1] Signal Processing and Recognition Group, Universidad Nacional de Colombia, Manizales, Colombia
jdpulgaring@unal.edu.co

[2] Faculty of Engineering, Universidad Tecnológica de Pereira, Pereira, Colombia

Abstract. This paper presents a feature selection comparison oriented to human action recognition only with the kinematic features of skeleton representation. For this purpose, three relevance methods are used to rank the contribution of kinematic features for classifying an action is employed. Particularly, the method with the best results includes the supervised information regarding the action to find out a relevant set of features, encoding the most discriminative information. Experimental results are obtained on a well-known public data (MSR Action3D). Results are encouraging to use kernel theory methods to get better kinematic feature selection for each action with a good generalization indistinct to the subject.

Keywords: Center kernel alignment · Feature selection · Human motion · Kinematics · Motion capture data · Principal Component Analysis · Relevance · ReliefF

1 Introduction

Action recognition in human motion analysis of video data are as one of the most important areas in computer vision [1–5]. To date, a significant number of methods are available using a mathematical representation of human motion and developing methods for recognizing different activities under this description. The most frequent method to represent human motion is to use an approximate human skeleton configuration. Nonetheless, extracting accurate skeletal configurations is the field of work, yielding to group the action recognition methods depending on the data source: the skeletal configurations extracted from monocular videos and the ones extracted from 3D capturing systems. The first one is widely used in video surveillance and other actions recognitions tasks, since it allows extracting spatio-temporal interesting points and estimation of their statistics [6,7]. However, fast and reliable detection and tracking of body joints

J.M. Ferrández Vicente et al. (Eds.): IWINAC 2017, Part II, LNCS 10338, pp. 501–509, 2017.
DOI: 10.1007/978-3-319-59773-7_51

from traditional 2D videos is not a trivial task [6]. The second data source is extracted from 3D capturing systems, often called Motion Capture (MoCap).

MoCap is employed for applications of natural human-computer interaction, gesture recognition, and animation, thus showing the importance of reliable skeleton-based action representations. In this representation, feature extraction is not frequently discussed because algorithms are oriented to reply the dynamic process of the motion in the best way, as HMM with its hidden states and GP with lattice variables [8,9]. Most of the methods are oriented to predict/classify the action with a high accuracy, but the feature extraction generally is computed with non-parametric methods [10]. Even though many kinematic features may be extracted from MoCap data, their main restriction is how to extract relevant features. Most methods assign higher weights to the body segments that involve more information about the posture and gait as the lower limbs. However, the actions that include smaller body segments such as the upper limbs are dismissed [11,12]. Moreover, most of the human actions require to engage different joints of the skeleton at different levels and various times, this is, each movement has its fundamental mechanical structure, making necessary features that describe these dynamics. These features are the kinematic variables widely used in MoCap data thanks to its low cost and easy interpretation [11,12]. Namely, for this work, joints and their combinations, linear variables, angular variables, short-time linear and angular variables and norm estimations from the whole skeleton.

Here, three methodologies for feature relevance analysis are compared to enhance the interpretation of action recognition in human motion 3D capture. The first, Centered Kernel Alignment (CKA) strategy is employed to estimate a linear combination of relevant features taking advantage of both supervised information and the nonlinear mapping induced by the kernel. The second, Principal Component Analysis (PCA), a popular unsupervised learning method, projects features into a new feature space by maximizing the variance matrix. And the third, relief finds the proper feature subset which has the maximum score of classification. The relevance analysis allows ranking the input feature set to highlight the most relevant information that helps to recognize different actions, including smooth and cyclical with lower limbs, quickly actions with the upper limbs and combined actions with pelvis and trunk too. Experiments are carried out on MSR Action3D database [7,13,14], a well-known public MoCap data. Attained results show that CKA finds the most relevant kinetics variable with the lowest variance between actions.

2 Materials and Methods

2.1 Kinematic Variables

Let $\mathcal{X} = \{\boldsymbol{X}_i \in \mathbb{R}^{J \times D} : i \in [1, \ldots, N]\}$ be a multi-channel input sequence that holds N matrix samples. Each $\boldsymbol{X}_i = \{\boldsymbol{x}_{ij} \in \mathbb{R}^D : j \in [1, \ldots, J]\}$ gathers the skeletal posture at the i-th frame with J D-dimensional joints. As Fig. 1 illustrates, the normalization of each posture $\boldsymbol{X}_i$, with respect to the hips joint

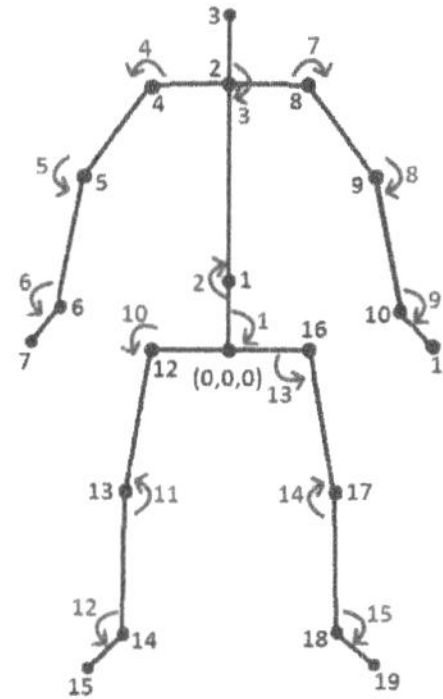

Fig. 1. Structure of the skeleton used in MSR Action3D dataset with a set of 20 joints (blue) and 15 angles (red) computed from it. Note that hips joint finally has not label because the structure is always centered over it (Color figure online)

coordinates, overcomes the bias effect due to the subject translation along the three-dimensional space ($D = 3$) when performing a human activity.

Then, the kinematic information is extracted by the following set of frame-wise features:

Joint Features. This set aims at characterizing the action information not only from the whole skeletal posture, but also from the interrelation of correlated joints in each frame. Thereby, posture features $\boldsymbol{G}_{i,i} \in \mathbb{R}^{J(J-1)/2 \times D}$, motion features $\boldsymbol{G}_{i,i-1} \in \mathbb{R}^{J(J-1)/2 \times D}$, and offset features $\boldsymbol{G}_{i,0} \in \mathbb{R}^{J(J-1)/2 \times D}$ at each frame i are computed from pair-wise skeletal differences [14]:

$$\boldsymbol{G}_{i,i} = \{\boldsymbol{x}_{ij} - \boldsymbol{x}_{ij'} : j, j' \in [1, \ldots, J]; j \neq j'\}, \tag{1}$$

$$\boldsymbol{G}_{i,i-1} = \left\{\boldsymbol{x}_{ij} - \boldsymbol{x}_{(i-1)j'} : \boldsymbol{x}_{ij} \in \boldsymbol{X}_i; \boldsymbol{x}_{(i-1)j'} \in \boldsymbol{X}_{i-1}\right\}, \tag{2}$$

$$\boldsymbol{G}_{i,0} = \{\boldsymbol{x}_{ij} - \boldsymbol{x}_{i0} : \boldsymbol{x}_{ij} \in \boldsymbol{X}_i; \boldsymbol{x}_{i0} \in \boldsymbol{X}_0\}, \tag{3}$$

Therefore, the vector of joint features holds the above three skeletal differences $\boldsymbol{y}_i^J = [\text{vec}(\boldsymbol{G}_{i,i}), \text{vec}(\boldsymbol{G}_{i,i-1}), \text{vec}(\boldsymbol{G}_{i,0})]$.

Linear Features. This set is widely used in evaluating the sports performance since they describe the quality of an action execution [11]. These features describe the Cartesian positions of the skeletal joints along with the end sites for hands, feet, and head. Besides, linear velocity and acceleration are also included as the first and second approximate derivatives $\boldsymbol{X'}_i = \boldsymbol{X}_i - \boldsymbol{X}_{i-1}$ and $\boldsymbol{X''}_i = \boldsymbol{X'}_i - \boldsymbol{X'}_{i-1}$, resulting in the feature vector $\boldsymbol{y}_i^L = [\text{vec}(\boldsymbol{X}_i), \text{vec}(\boldsymbol{X'}_i), \text{vec}(\boldsymbol{X''}_i)]$.

Angular Features. This group is also widely used to evaluate an action execution [2]. These kinematic features, termed $\boldsymbol{A}_i \in \mathbb{R}^A$, consist of the joint angle values for the skeletal representation, being A the amount of angles to compute (see Fig. 1). Also, the angular velocities $\boldsymbol{A}'_i \in \mathbb{R}^A$ and accelerations $\boldsymbol{A}''_i \in \mathbb{R}^A$ are straightforward estimated using approximate derivatives, so that the resulting feature vector is assembled as $\boldsymbol{y}_i^A = [\text{vec}(\boldsymbol{A}_i), \text{vec}(\boldsymbol{A}'_i), \text{vec}(\boldsymbol{A}''_i)]$.

Short-Time Features describe the temporal evolution of the joints and the angles along the action [15]. These features are computed as the maximum of each linear and angular feature within a frame window:

$$\boldsymbol{S}_i^L = \max_{i' \in [N_a, N_b]} \{\boldsymbol{X}_{i'}\} \qquad \forall i \in [N_m^s, N_m^e], \tag{4}$$

$$\boldsymbol{S}_i^A = \max_{i' \in [N_a, N_b]} \{\boldsymbol{A}_{i'}\} \qquad \forall i \in [N_m^s, N_m^e], \tag{5}$$

with $m \in [1, N_S]$, N_S as the total number of non-overlapped windows, N_m^s the start of the m-th window, and N_m^e its end. In addition, short time evolution of velocities ($\boldsymbol{S}_i^{'L}$, $\boldsymbol{S}_i^{'A}$) and acceleration ($\boldsymbol{S}_i^{''L}$, $\boldsymbol{S}_i^{''A}$) are included in the resulting vector $\boldsymbol{y}_i^S = [\text{vec}(\boldsymbol{S}_i^L), \text{vec}(\boldsymbol{S}_i^{'L}), \text{vec}(\boldsymbol{S}_i^{'L}), \text{vec}(\boldsymbol{S}_i^A), \text{vec}(\boldsymbol{S}_i^{'A}), \text{vec}(\boldsymbol{S}_i^{'A})]$.

Norm Features account for the total movement in the coordinate space [2]. Such a features are computed as the euclidean norm of the linear and angular velocities and accelerations, defined as $\boldsymbol{y}_i^F = [\|\boldsymbol{X}_i'\|_2, \|\boldsymbol{X}_i''\|_2, \|\boldsymbol{A}_i'\|_2, \|\boldsymbol{A}_i''\|_2]$.

Finally, we obtain the feature representation matrix $\boldsymbol{Y} \in \mathbb{R}^{N \times P}$, where $P = 3577$ is determined by concatenating all the computed features, summarized in Table 1, using $J = 20$ joints and $A = 15$ angles.

Table 1. Kinematic features extracted from skeletan structure in Fig. 1. Note that hips joint normalization reduces some features (eigenjoints and linears).

Parameter	Joints	Linear	Angular	Short-time linear	Short-time angular	Norm-2
Features	$\boldsymbol{G}_{i,i}(\boldsymbol{X}_i)$	$\boldsymbol{X}_i$	$\boldsymbol{A}_i(\boldsymbol{X}_i)$	$\boldsymbol{S}_i^L(\boldsymbol{X}, N_s)$	$\boldsymbol{S}_i^A(\boldsymbol{A}, N_s)$	$\|\boldsymbol{X}_i'\|_2$
	$\boldsymbol{G}_{i,i-1}(\boldsymbol{X}_i)$	$\boldsymbol{X}_i'$	$\boldsymbol{A}_i'(\boldsymbol{X}_i)$	$\boldsymbol{S}_i^{'L}(\boldsymbol{X}', N_s)$	$\boldsymbol{S}_i^{'A}(\boldsymbol{A}', N_s)$	$\|\boldsymbol{X}_i''\|_2$
	$\boldsymbol{G}_{i,0}(\boldsymbol{X}_i)$	$\boldsymbol{X}_i''$	$\boldsymbol{A}_i''(\boldsymbol{X}_i)$	$\boldsymbol{S}_i^{''L}(\boldsymbol{X}', N_s)$	$\boldsymbol{S}_i^{''A}(\boldsymbol{A}'', N_s)$	$\|\boldsymbol{A}_i'\|_2$
						$\|\boldsymbol{A}_i''\|_2$
Features per frame	189 × 3	19 × 3	15 × 3	19 × 3	15 × 3	1
	399 × 3	19 × 3	15 × 3	19 × 3	15 × 3	1
	399 × 3	19 × 3	15 × 3	19 × 3	15 × 3	1
						1
Total features per frame: 3577						

2.2 Feature Relevance Analysis

Principal Component Analysis. (PCA), often used as a feature extraction method, is a statistical eigendecomposition looking for directions with the highest variance to project the data [16]. The linear projection of PCA allows to select a relevant subset of features that better represents the variability of a dataset. Let the set $\boldsymbol{Y} = \{\boldsymbol{y}^p : p \in [1, \ldots, P]\}$, where $\boldsymbol{y}^p$ is the p-th feature of the set. The relevance of each feature is determined from the eigendecomposition by computing the vector $\boldsymbol{\rho}^{PCA} = \{\rho_p : p \in [1, \ldots, P]\}$, defined as follows:

$$\rho_p^{PCA} = \boldsymbol{\mathcal{E}}\{|\lambda_p \boldsymbol{\mu}_p|\} \qquad \forall p \in [1, \ldots, P], \tag{6}$$

where $\mathcal{E}\{\cdot\}$ stands for the average operator, $\{\lambda_p \in \mathbb{R}\}$ is the set of eigenvalues is descending order, and $\boldsymbol{\mu}_p \in \mathbb{R}^Q$ the projection coefficients from the p-th feature to the first Q principal components. Both, the eigenvalues and eigenvectors, are estimated from the data covariance matrix $\boldsymbol{\Sigma} = \boldsymbol{Y}^T\boldsymbol{Y} \in \mathbb{R}^{P\times P}$. The main assumption is that the largest values of ρ_p point out to the best features, since they exhibit higher overall correlations with the principal components.

Kernel-Based Feature Relevance. In order to get the most relevant feature vectors from $\boldsymbol{Y}$ regarding activity discrimination, we compute the pair-wise sample relationships through the introduced similarity kernel $\boldsymbol{K} \in \mathbb{R}^{N\times N}$ with elements:

$$k_{ij} = \kappa\left(\mathrm{d}_\Gamma\left(\boldsymbol{y}_i, \boldsymbol{y}_j\right)\right), \forall i, j \in [1, N] \tag{7}$$

where $\mathrm{d}_\Gamma : \mathbb{R}^P \times \mathbb{R}^P \to \mathbb{R}$ is a distance operator related to the positive definite kernel function $\kappa(\cdot) \in \mathbb{R}^+$. Here, a Mahalanobis distance is defined on the input P-dimensional space with inverse covariance matrix $\boldsymbol{\Gamma}\boldsymbol{\Gamma}^\top$ as $\mathrm{d}^2_\Gamma(\boldsymbol{y}_i, \boldsymbol{y}_j) = (\boldsymbol{y}_i - \boldsymbol{y}_j)$ $\boldsymbol{\Gamma}\boldsymbol{\Gamma}^\top (\boldsymbol{y}_i - \boldsymbol{y}_j)^\top$, with the matrix $\boldsymbol{\Gamma} \in \mathbb{R}^{P\times Q}$ linearly projecting $\boldsymbol{z}_i = \boldsymbol{y}_i\boldsymbol{\Gamma} \in \mathbb{R}^Q$, $Q \leq P$. Matrix $\boldsymbol{\Gamma}$ is trained by adding prior knowledge about the activity at each frame (e.g., jogging, forward punch, etc.) enclosed in the matrix $\boldsymbol{\Theta} \in \mathbb{R}^{N\times N}$. Namely, the elements of $\boldsymbol{\Theta}$ are computed as $\theta_{ij} = \delta\left(l_i - l_j\right)$. Moreover, the correlation between the matrices $\boldsymbol{K}$ and $\boldsymbol{\Theta}$ is assessed by the following Centered Kernel Alignment (CKA) function [17]:

$$\varrho\left(\boldsymbol{K}, \boldsymbol{\Theta}; \boldsymbol{\Gamma}\right) = \frac{\langle \boldsymbol{HKH}, \boldsymbol{H\Theta H}\rangle_F}{\|\boldsymbol{HKH}\|_F \|\boldsymbol{H\Theta H}\|_F}, \varrho \in [0, 1] \tag{8}$$

where $\boldsymbol{H} = \boldsymbol{I} - N^{-1}\mathbf{1}\mathbf{1}^\top$ is a centering matrix, $\boldsymbol{I} \in \mathbb{R}^{N\times N}$ is the identity matrix, $\mathbf{1} \in \mathbb{R}^N$ is an all-ones vector, and notations $\langle\cdot,\cdot\rangle_F$ and $\|\cdot,\cdot\|_F$ stand for the Frobenius inner product and norm, respectively. To learn a discriminative projection, we take maximize the CKA cost function described in (8) with respect to $\boldsymbol{\Gamma}$.

The matrix $\boldsymbol{\Gamma}$ that parameterizes the Mahalanobis encodes the discriminative properties of the input feature set. Therefore, the CKA-based feature relevance vector $\boldsymbol{\rho}^{CKA} \in \mathbb{R}^P$ is estimated by analyzing the contribution of each input feature for building the projection matrix $\boldsymbol{\Gamma}$ as:

$$\rho_p^{CKA} = \sum_{q=1}^{Q} |\gamma_{pq}|; \forall q \in [1, \ldots, Q], \tag{9}$$

with $\gamma_{pq} \in \boldsymbol{\Gamma}$. The main assumption behind the introduced relevance index is that the largest values of ρ_p should point out to a better discrimination since they exhibit higher overall dependencies to the estimated embedding.

ReliefF is a multivariate algorithm that selects the features that are the most distinguishable among the different activities. The algorithm iteratively randomly selects a sample and, based on its neighbors, weights the most the features that improve the discrimination of the sample from the neighbors of a different class. As a result, there is always concurrence between the weight and the class separability. Given the training set $\boldsymbol{Y} = \{y_i^p\}$, where the i-th sample of the training set is labeled as l_i, matrices $\boldsymbol{Y}_i \in \mathbb{R}^{K \times P}$ and $\overline{\boldsymbol{Y}_i} \in \mathbb{R}^{K \times P}$ indicate the K nearest neighbors of $\boldsymbol{y}_i$ labeled as l_i and the K nearest neighbors of the same sample with a different label, respectively. The similarity measure the sample $\boldsymbol{y}_i$ and its neighbors in the p-th feature is defined by [18]:

$$d_p(\boldsymbol{y}_i, \boldsymbol{Y}_i) = \mathcal{E}\{\frac{y_i^p - y_j^p}{\max(y_j^p) - \min(y_j^p)} : \boldsymbol{y}_j \in \boldsymbol{Y}_i\}. \tag{10}$$

Then, the relevance of each feature is given by:

$$\rho_p^R = \mathcal{E}\{d_p(\boldsymbol{y}_i, \overline{\boldsymbol{Y}}_i) - d_p(\boldsymbol{y}_i, \boldsymbol{Y}_i) : i \in [1, \ldots, N]\}. \tag{11}$$

3 Experiments Setup and Results

In order to assess the relevance of features in $\mathcal{X}$, three different sets of human activities are considered. Thereby, we aim at highlighting kinematic features that favor further discrimination stages. Our experiments are carried out on the well-known MSR Action3D human activity public dataset [14]. The actions selected in this dataset reasonably capture a wide variety of motions: smooth and cyclical involving the movement of lower limbs, quick and fast involving smaller body segments, and comprising combinations of arms, legs, trunk, and pelvis. For the sake of a fair comparison, we split the actions the same three subsets as in [14] and listed in Table 2. Given that the aim of the work is to assess the discriminative properties of each feature, the Naive-Bayes Nearest-Neighbor (NBNN), mainly led by the data distribution, is considered for activity classification. Classification performance and relevance measures are computed using a leave-one-subject-out (LOSO) validation scheme.

Table 2. Action sets that involves lower limbs, upper limbs and combination of trunk, pelvis and limbs.

Action Set 1 (AS1)	Action Set 2 (AS2)	Action Set 3 (AS3)
Bend	Draw	Forward kick
Forward punch	Draw circle	Golf swing
Hammer	Draw tick	High throw
Hand clap	Forward kick	Jogging
High throw	Hand catch	Pickup throw
Horizontal wave	Hands wave	Side kick
Pickup throw	High wave	Tennis serve
Tennis serve	Side boxing	Tennis swing

Relevance approaches depend on a value Q, that we estimate as the trade-off between the classification normalized accuracy $c \in \mathbb{R}$ and the percentage

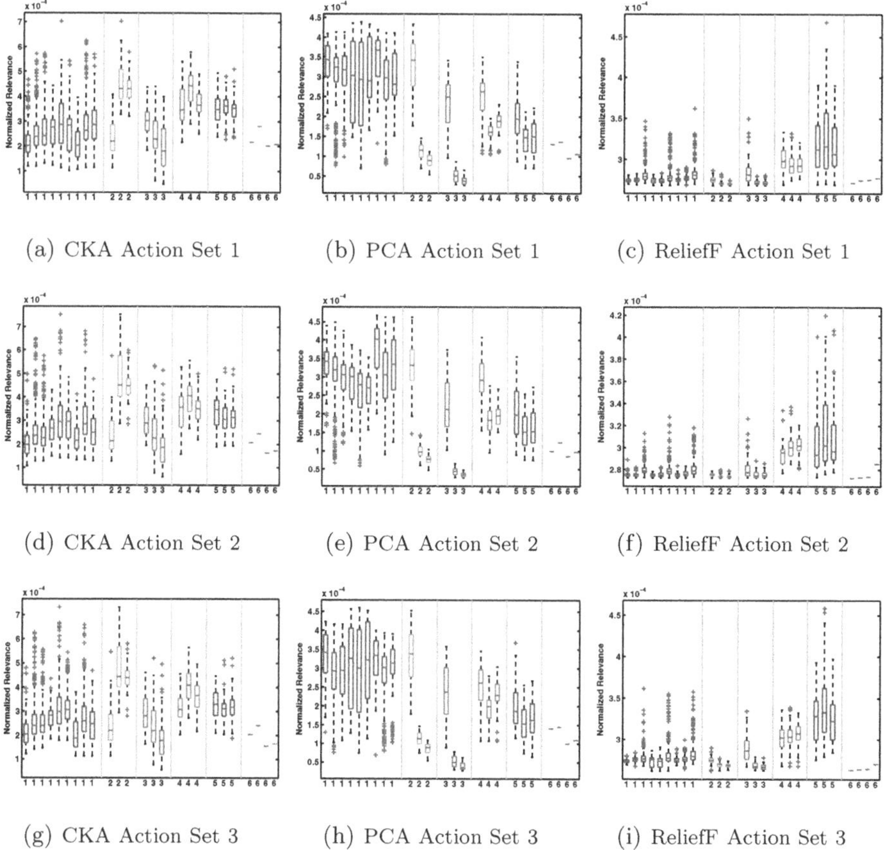

(a) CKA Action Set 1 (b) PCA Action Set 1 (c) ReliefF Action Set 1

(d) CKA Action Set 2 (e) PCA Action Set 2 (f) ReliefF Action Set 2

(g) CKA Action Set 3 (h) PCA Action Set 3 (i) ReliefF Action Set 3

Fig. 2. Relevance analysis for six feature groups. Joints 1□. Linear 2□. Angular 3□. Short-time linear 4□. Short-time angular 5□. Norm 6□ (Color figure online)

of features $p' = q/P$ in order to get the lowest dimension possible by $Q = \text{argmax}_q\, |p'^2 + c^2|^{1/2}$. Then, the calculated relevance vectors $\boldsymbol{\varrho}$ from Sect. 2.2 are employed to rank the original features.

Figure 2 groups the attained ρ values into boxplots depending on the kind of feature for each activity set and relevance approach. Particularly, PCA highlights the joint positions and their combinations, whereas CKA describes the actions with linear velocity and acceleration, and their short-time features. In the case of ReliefF, despite being the most relevant, the short-time angle kinematics widely vary along the observations implying a high dependence between the activity and the training set.

3.1 Discussion and Concluding Remarks

Carried out relevance analysis with the three approaches presents the same feature contribution for all activity sets. Even though the variability is significant in most of the feature groups, the intersubject variability is dismissed because of the exhaustive leave-one-subject-out validation scheme. This situation allows focusing the analysis in the variability of the actions, where the methods present a similar performance over the three actions subsets. Moreover, PCA (second column in Fig. 2) favors the joint position information, while ReliefF (third column in Fig. 2) highlights the evolution of angular kinematics. Nonetheless, the variability of both, PCA and ReliefF, is larger that the one obtained by CKA in the first column of Fig. 2. So the features determined by CKA show us that linear velocities and acceleration, and its evolution over time, describe large combinations of actions with the lowest variability between actions.

This framework should be expanded to analyze the channel relevance in the acquisition process. Human motion action involves an interaction between all body segments: every action has a biomechanical chain that produces it, so human action recognition must be given information about the most relevant body segments involved over the time. The results encourage us to use CKA through continue studying kinematic variables extracted from skeleton configuration.

As future work, it would be interesting to prune the obtain relevant features aiming to support larger action datasets, as well as to work with limited structures from other 3D capturing systems, e.g., inertial sensing for assessment motor disorders.

Acknowledgments. This work is supported by the project number 36075 funded by Universidad Nacional de Colombia sede Manizales, by program "Doctorados Nacionales 2014" number 647 funded by COLCIENCIAS, as well as partial Ph.D. financial support from Universidad Autonoma de Occidente.

References

1. Kale, G.V., Patil, V.H.: A study of vision based human motion recognition and analysis. IJACI **7**(2), 75–92 (2016)
2. Mandery, C., Plappert, M., Sol, J.B., Asfour, T.: Dimensionality reduction for whole-body human motion recognition. In: 19th International Conference on Information Fusion, FUSION, Heidelberg, Germany, 5–8 July 2016, pp. 355–362 (2016)
3. Althloothi, S., Mahoor, M.H., Zhang, X., Voyles, R.M.: Human activity recognition using multi-features and multiple kernel learning. Pattern Recogn. **47**(5), 1800–1812 (2014)
4. Li, M., Leung, H., Liu, Z., Zhou, L.: 3D human motion retrieval using graph kernels based on adaptive graph construction. Comput. Graph. Pergamon **54**, 104–112 (2016)
5. Wang, L., Zhao, G., Cheng, L., Pietikainen, M.: Machine Learning for Vision-Based Motion Analysis, 1st edn. Springer, Heidelberg (2011)
6. Wei, X.K., Chai, J.: Modeling 3D human poses from uncalibrated monocular images. In: IEEE 12th International Conference on Computer Vision, ICCV, Kyoto, Japan, 27 September–4 October 2009, pp. 1873–1880 (2009)
7. Li, W., Zhang, Z., Liu, Z.: Action recognition based on a bag of 3D points. In: IEEE Conference on Computer Vision and Pattern Recognition, CVPR Workshopps 2010, San Francisco, CA, USA, 13–18 June 2010, pp. 9–14 (2010)

8. Ravet, T., Tilmanne, J., d'Alessandro, N.: Hidden Markov model based real-time motion recognition and following. In: Proceedings of the 2014 International Workshop on Movement, Computing, MOCO 2014, pp. 82–87. ACM, New York (2014)
9. Jiang, Y., Saxena, A.: Modeling high-dimensional humans for activity anticipation using Gaussian process latent CRFs. In: Robotics: Science and Systems X, University of California, Berkeley, USA, 12–16 July 2014 (2014)
10. García-Vega, S., Álvarez-Meza, A.M., Castellanos-Domínguez, C.G.: MoCap data segmentation and classification using kernel based multi-channel analysis. In: Ruiz-Shulcloper, J., Sanniti di Baja, G. (eds.) CIARP 2013. LNCS, vol. 8259, pp. 495–502. Springer, Heidelberg (2013). doi:10.1007/978-3-642-41827-3_62
11. Pulgarin-Giraldo, J.D., Alvarez-Meza, A.M., Melo-Betancourt, L.G., Ramos-Bermudez, S., Castellanos-Dominguez, G.: A similarity indicator for differentiating kinematic performance between qualified tennis players. In: Beltrán-Castañón, C., Nyström, I., Famili, F. (eds.) CIARP 2016. LNCS, vol. 10125, pp. 309–317. Springer, Cham (2017). doi:10.1007/978-3-319-52277-7_38
12. Diaz-Martinez, N.F., Pulgarin-Giraldo, J.D., Vinasco-Isaza, L.E., Agredo, W.: Analysis of the alignment angles and flexion angle in women with patellofemoral pain syndrome. In: Torres, I., Bustamante, J., Sierra, D. (eds.) CLAIB 2016. IFMBE Proceedings. Springer, Singapore (2016)
13. Yang, X., Tian, Y.: Effective 3D action recognition using eigenjoints. J. Vis. Commun. Image Represent. **25**(1), 2–11 (2014)
14. Yang, X., Tian, Y.: Eigenjoints-based action recognition using Naïve-Bayes-Nearest-Neighbor. In: CVPR Workshops, pp. 14–19. IEEE Computer Society (2012)
15. Ofli, F., Chaudhry, R., Kurillo, G., Vidal, R., Bajcsy, R.: Sequence of the most informative joints (SMIJ): a new representation for human skeletal action recognition. J. Vis. Commun. Image Represent. **25**(1), 24–38 (2014)
16. Alvarez-Meza, A.M., Velasquez-Martinez, L.F., Castellanos-Dominguez, G.: Time-series discrimination using feature relevance analysis in motor imagery classification. Neurocomputing **151**(Part 1), 122–129 (2015)
17. Brockmeier, A.J., Choi, J.S., Kriminger, E.G., Francis, J.T., Principe, J.C.: Neural decoding with kernel-based metric learning. Neural Comput. **26**(6), 1080–1107 (2014)
18. Zeng, X., Wang, Q., Zhang, C., Cai, H.: Feature selection based on reliefF and PCA for underwater sound classification. In: Proceedings of 3rd International Conference on Computer Science and Network Technology, pp. 442–445 (2013)

Ensembles of Decision Trees for Recommending Touristic Items

Ameed Almomani, Paula Saavedra, and Eduardo Sánchez(✉)

Grupo de Sistemas Inteligentes (GSI),
Centro Singular de Investigación en Tecnologías de la Información (CITIUS),
Universidad de Santiago de Compostela,
15782 Santiago de Compostela, Spain
{ameed.almomani,paula.saavedra,eduardo.sanchez.vila}@usc.es

Abstract. This article analyzes the performance of ensembles of decision trees when applied to the task of recommending tourist items. The motivation comes from the fact that there is an increasing need to explain why a website is recommending some items and not others. The combination of decision trees and ensemble learning is therefore a good way to provide both interpretability and accuracy performance. The results demonstrate the superior performance of ensembles when compared to single decision tree approaches. However, basic colaborative filtering methods seem to perform better than ensembles in our dataset. The study suggests that the number of available features is a key aspect in order to get the true potential of this type of ensembles.

Keywords: Ensembles · Decision trees · Recomendations · Tourism

1 Introduction

Recommender systems are personalization tools aimed at suggesting relevant products and items to end users. Mainstream companies like Google, Microsoft, Netflix, and Amazon, do apply these systems in a daily basis to continuously learn preferences, tastes and human behaviours. The generated profiles are then used to boost search engines, shopping baskets and the catalogue of available products. Machine learning has played a big role in the development of the algorithms that work at the backend of these systems. Traditional content-based and user-based approaches rely on the popular k-Nearest Neighbours clustering technique to predict the utility/rating of an item. Nowadays, since the impact of the Netflix prize, ensemble models and learning-to-rank algorithms are the dominant concepts in the field.

Ensemble learning is a paradigm that aggregates instances of simple learner to obtain a more accurate prediction when compared with the outcome of a single learner [5,9]. Ensembles are widely used to assist the decision-making processes in many areas such as tourism, marketing, medical. Different methods have been proposed to come up with an efficient aggregation of learner predictions. The most popular ones are: bagging, boosting, and random forest [5,9].

J.M. Ferrández Vicente et al. (Eds.): IWINAC 2017, Part II, LNCS 10338, pp. 510–519, 2017.
DOI: 10.1007/978-3-319-59773-7_52

In the field of recommender systems, empirical evaluation of ensembles of popular collaborative-filtering learners shows a prediction improvement compared to all base CF algorithms [2]. In spite of their current success, ensemble algorithms might show important limitations in order to satisfy the new demands of users. People are becoming reluctant to explicit recommendations as they feel it as another instrument of the advertising industry. As a result, there is an increasing need to explain why a website is recommending some items and not others. In this context, decision trees provide a solution to the interpretability problem [1,10]. First, trees do not require a numeric rating like collaborative filtering (CF), and are also suitable to handle the cold start problem [7]. Second, in some tasks, the tree-based methods can outperform other classification models, and tree-based ensembles provide better accuracy than single tree learners [4]. However, their prediction accuracy can be determined by the size of the available data [2,6], and the number of the features [8]. Finally, tree-based methods have been proved useful to build recommender systems on different areas, and outperform other simple approaches [12].

In this work we explore the potential of ensembles of decision-trees in the field of gastronomic tourism. The following sections describe the hypothesis underlying the research work, the experiment carried out to gather the data, the evaluation of different ensemble models, and a final comparison with collaborative-filtering algorithms.

2 Hypothesis

The literature on ensemble learning is full of examples demonstrating their superior performance when compared with single learners. The first hypothesis therefore is that ensembles of decision-trees should also provide superior outcomes when working with our touristic dataset. We also expect ensembles performing better than traditional collaborative-filtering algorithms. A comparison was made to test this second hypothesis.

3 Methods

3.1 Experiment

In the context of the RECTUR project, an experiment was carried out with real users in Santiago(é)Tapas, a gastronomic contest that takes place every year in Santiago de Compostela. In 2011 the fourth edition was held with a total of 56 participating restaurants proposing and elaborating up to three tapas that were sold at a price of 2 euros. The experiment was designed to gather relevant data while preserving the spirit of the contest. Participants were local users as well as Spanish and international tourists. After consuming a tapa, participants were asked to evaluate their experience (Fig. 1). Users had to provide two ratings ranging from 0 to 5: (i) a rating of the tapa, and (ii) a rating of the overall experience (service, place atmosphere, etc.).

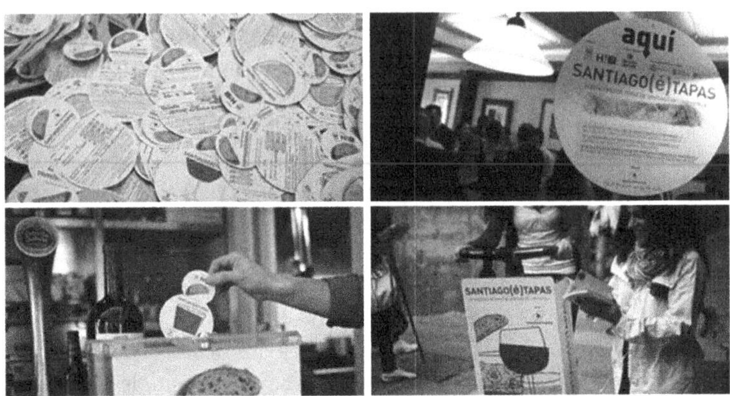

Fig. 1. The RECTUR contest.

Table 1. Tapa attributes and their corresponding values.

Attribute	Values
TapaKind	Cheese, egg, fish, meat, vegetable, shellfish and other
TapaCharacter	Traditional or daring
TapaRating	0–5

3.2 RECTUR Dataset

The data gathered in the experiment was collected in the RECTUR dataset. It is assumed that the choice of a tapa depends on the user preferences about the levels of tapa attributes, which will in turn depend on the user attributes and context elements. The consumption of a tapa determines a choice and will elicit a satisfaction response quantified as a user rating. For each tapa, we gathered the following attributes (Table 1): kind, character, and rating. Traditional tapas are those that follow popular well-known recipes, while daring tapas are creative and provide innovative recipes.

3.3 Ensemble Models

We first describe the core concept of *Tree-based methods*. The idea consists on splitting the features into a set of nodes or regions, and then fit the data on each node to make the prediction. A popular tree-based model is called *Classification and Regression Tree* (CART for short) [3].

The *Regression tree* version of CART is constructed through binary recursive partitioning, which is an iteration process that split the features into branches. The process continues by splitting each partition into a minimum number of nodes. In order to find the recursive binary splitting, both the splitting variable X_i and a split point z are considered such that the splitting at the split point is:

$$R_1(i,z) = \{X|X_i \geq z\} \ and \ R_2(i,z) = \{X|X_i < z\} \tag{1}$$

Thus a tree is formally described as:

$$T(X, \Theta) = \sum_{j=1}^{J} \gamma_j I(X \in R_j) \tag{2}$$

where γ_j constant assign to each terminal node, and $\Theta = \{R_j, \gamma_j\}$. The prediction will be the mean of the response variable in the region or terminal node.

The *classification tree* is similar to the regression tree, except it uses classes to predict the categorical response. A majority vote scheme in the terminal node is finally applied to estimate the prediction.

Now, we explain the notion of *Ensemble learning*. Ensembles are aggregations of simple learners, like CART, and the final prediction is estimated by combining the outcomes. In what follows, the three ensemble methods used in this study are described:

- ***Boosting*** builds a tree in a sequential fashion. This means each tree depends on the prior trees. Boosting can be implemented in regression as well as classification methods. The boosted tree is:

$$f_m(x) = \sum_{m=1}^{M} T(X, \theta_m) \tag{3}$$

  where M is the number of trees.
- ***Bagging*** builds different trees on M different bootstrapped training dataset. All trees are fully grown, and at each node, in the tree one searches over all features to find the feature that best splits the data at that node, and gets the prediction $\hat{f}^{*b}(x)$, and computes the average of prediction in regression:

$$\hat{f}_{bag}(x) = \frac{1}{M} \sum_{m=1}^{M} \hat{f}^{*b}(x) \tag{4}$$

- ***Random Forests*** is a particular case of Bagging. The main difference is that at each candidate split in the learning process, a random sample of the predictors or features is chosen among all the predictors or features. The goal is to build a large collection of decorrelated trees. The prediction in a regression problem is estimated as follows:

$$\hat{f}_{rf}(x) = \frac{1}{M} \sum_{m=1}^{M} \hat{f}^{*b}(x) \tag{5}$$

In a classification problem, the prediction in Bagging and Random Forests is made by means of the *majority vote* for the classes.

3.4 Classification and Regression Problems

In order to preserve individual preferences, we decided to build a tree for each single user. As a minimum number of observations is required to learn the model,

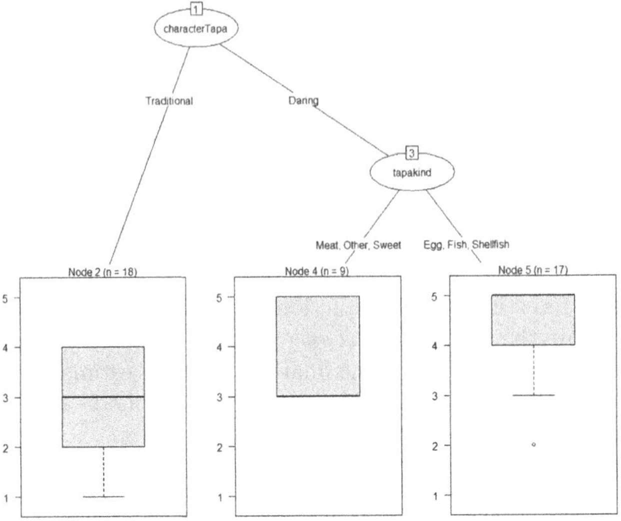

Fig. 2. The regression tree for the user number 1377.

we run experiments with three different thresholds: 26, 30, and 40. They determined the number of total users available on each experiment: 19, 10, and 7 users, respectively.

Two types of prediction problems were considered: regression and classification. In the regression problem the tapa rating is a numeric value and the rating prediction consists on calculating the average of the values on each region of each single learner. Figure 2 shows an instance of the regression problem for user number 1377 (u1377) who experienced 54 tapas. The tree consist of a series of splits, the first one made on the character of tapa, the second one on its kind. The tree segments the data into three regions: $R_1 = \{X|CharecterTapa = Tradition\}$, $R_2 = \{X|CharecterTapa = Daring, Tapakind = \{Meat\ or\ Sweet\ or\ other\}\}$, $R_3 = \{X|CharecterTapa = Daring, Tapakind = \{egg\ or\ Fish\ or\ Shellfish\}\}$. The rating predicted each region is 3, 4, and 4.5, respectively. In the classification problem, the tapa rating is converted into a categorical variable in the following way:

$$RatingClass = \begin{cases} H, & \text{if tapaRating=5} \\ M, & \text{if } 3 \leq tapaRating \leq 4 \\ L, & \text{if } tapaRating < 3 \end{cases} \quad (6)$$

As in the regression problem, the tree segments the data into three regions R_1, R_2, and R_3. The majority vote is used afterwards to estimate the prediction. Figure 3 pictures the classification tree for user number 1377 as well as the histograms showing the frequency of each class within each region. In this case the prediction is H, M, and M, for each of the three regions.

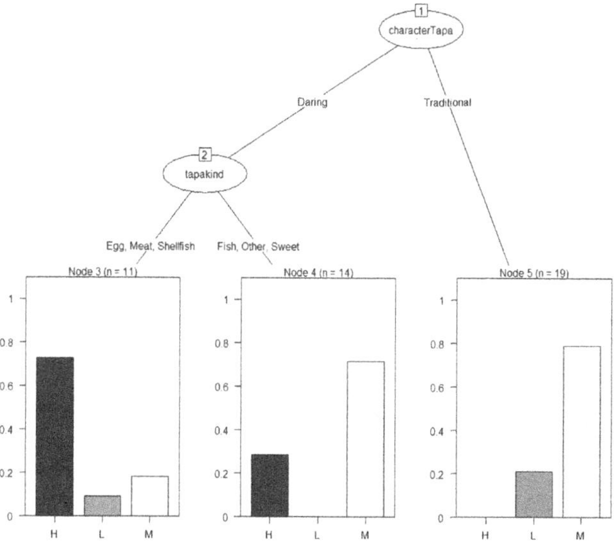

Fig. 3. The classification tree for the user number 1377.

3.5 Evaluation

For the classification problem we used the *Accuracy* metrics to measure the model performance. Accuracy is just the ratio between the correct and all generated predictions:

$$Accuracy = \frac{T_{correctPrediction}}{T_{allPrediction}} \tag{7}$$

As for the regression problem, the Root Mean Squared Error (*RMSE*) was used. RMSE is defined as the standard deviation of the difference between the actual and the predicted rating.

$$RMSE = \sqrt{\frac{\sum_{i=1}^{n}(\hat{r}_i - r_i)^2}{n}} \tag{8}$$

where $\hat{r}_i$ being the predicted rating, and r_i the actual one.

4 Results

4.1 Classification Problem

To explore the performance of the analyzed methods, we first provide some results on individual users. Table 2 shows the accuracy for three randomly chosen users satisfying the threshold values that were set in Sect. 3.4. It can be observed that Random Forest (RF) ranks the highest in all three cases. Afterwards, three clusters were created, each cluster made up with those users satisfying the following threshold values: 26, 30, and 40 consumed tapas. The accuracy average on each cluster for each method is shown in Fig. 4. The numbers confirm that RF outperforms the others in terms of Accuracy in all the clusters.

Table 2. Performance in classification problem: single users. Accuracy results for CART, Treebag, GBM, RF.

Users	Number of a tapas consumed	Methods	Accuracy
U1025	27	CART	0.4
		Treebag	0.22
		GBM	0.4
		RF	0.8
U1377	54	CART	0.6
		Treebag	0.0.58
		GBM	0.5
		RF	0.9
U204	35	CART	0.67
		Treebag	0.41
		GBM	0.33
		RF	1

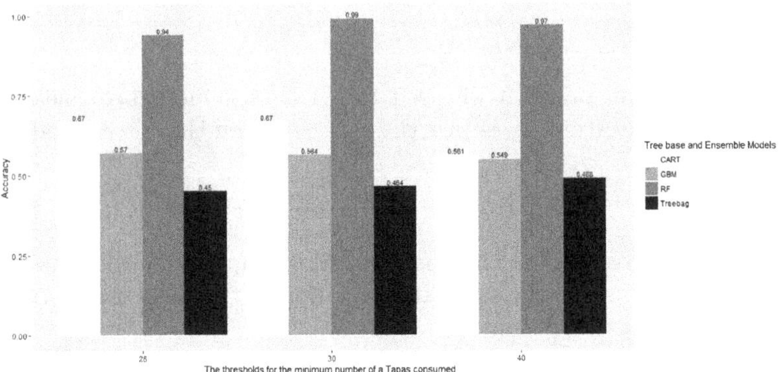

Fig. 4. Performance in classification problem: clusters. Accuracy average for CART, Treebag, GBM, and RF. Results are presented for three cluster of users, each cluster made up with those users satisfying the following threshold values: 26, 30, and 40 consumed tapas.

4.2 Regression Problem

Table 3 shows the RMSE for three randomly chosen users satisfying the threshold values that were set in Sect. 3.4. For this problem, the CART method ranks the highest (lowest RMSE) in all three cases. Figure 5 presents the results obtained for the clusters. The plots position GBM, an ensemble method, in the first place of the rank in two of the three clusters (30 and 40), with CART preserving the first place only in cluster with threshold 26.

Table 3. Performance in regression problem: single users. RMSE results for CART, Treebag, GBM, RF.

Users	Number of a tapas consumed	Methods	RMSE
U1025	27	CART	0.979
		Treebag	1.562
		GBM	1.248
		RF	1.176
U1377	54	CART	0.964
		Treebag	1.036
		GBM	1.012
		RF	1.292
U204	35	CART	0.935
		Treebag	0.989
		GBM	1.114
		RF	1.033

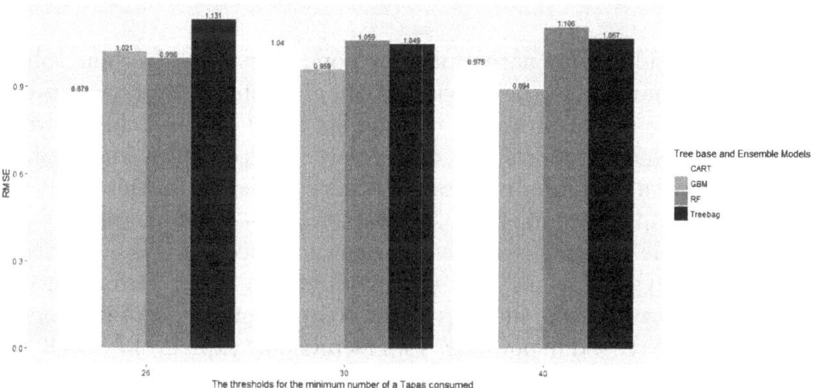

Fig. 5. Performance in regression problem: clusters. RMSE average for CART, Treebag, GBM, and RF. Results are presented for three cluster of users, each cluster made up with those users satisfying the following threshold values: 26, 30, and 40 consumed tapas.

4.3 Comparison with CF Approaches

The comparison was made for the regression problem only as the chosen CF approaches (user-based and matrix factorization) work with numeric values rather than classes or categories. Figure 6 illustrates the results in terms of RMSE for the three clusters already described. The plot shows the superior performance of UBCF, with GBM (clusters 30 and 40) and CART (cluster 26) in the second place. Surprisingly, matrix factorization offers the worse performance of all methods.

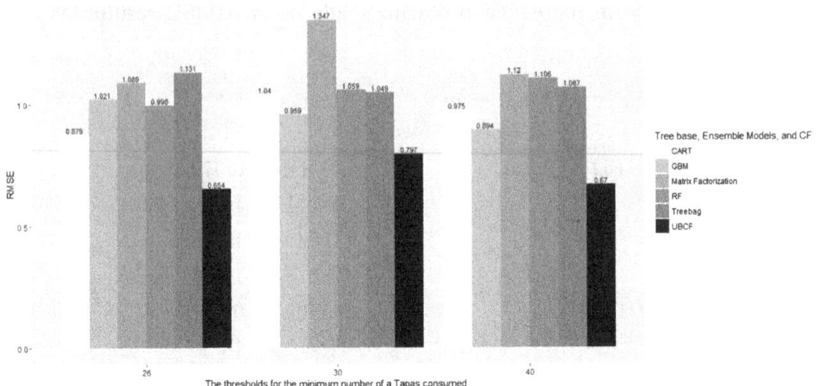

Fig. 6. Performance comparison. RMSE average for CART, Treebag, GBM, RF, UBCF and matrix factorization. Results are presented for three cluster of users, each cluster made up with those users satisfying the following threshold values: 26, 30, and 40 consumed tapas.

5 Discussion

The complexity and opaque nature of some popular machine-learning solutions make it hard to understand the reason why an algorithm delivers a certain recommendation. In quest of providing transparency and interpretability, we have developed choice-based models [11] that resort on decision-making principles to guide the recommendation process. The work presented in this paper takes another direction in that line of thinking exploring the combination of decision trees and ensemble learning. The results shown in Sects. 4.1 and 4.2 seem to confirm our first hypothesis, i.e. that ensembles yield a better performance than single learners. However, the findings of the comparison carried out in Sect. 4.3 is at odds with the second hypothesis. Two factors may explain this result. First, the comparison was made in terms of the regression problem, in which ensembles, and concretely the Random Forest method, are not as efficient as expected on the basis of its performance in the classification problem. Second, and most important, the number of tapa attributes in our dataset is small. It just handles two attributes per tapa, which is probably a very few number to take advantage of tree-based methods. Additional experiments carried out in our lab with other datasets (not shown) suggest that the efficiency of tree-based methods depends heavily on the number of available features. Nevertheless, the findings of this work suggest that ensembles of decision trees could be an interesting pathway to build novel algorithms offering both interpretability and performance.

Acknowledgments. This work has received financial support from the Ministry of Science and Innovation of Spain under grant TIN2014-56633-C3-1-R as well as from the Consellería de Cultura, Educación e Ordenación Universitaria (accreditation 2016–2019, ED431G/08) and the European Regional Development Fund (ERDF).

References

1. Ali, S., Tirumala, S.S., Sarrafzadeh, A.: Ensemble learning methods for decision making: status and future prospects. In: International Conference on Machine Learning and Cybernetics (ICMLC), vol. 1, pp. 211–216. IEEE (2015)
2. Bar, A., Rokach, L., Shani, G., Shapira, B., Schclar, A.: Improving simple collaborative filtering models using ensemble methods. In: Zhou, Z.-H., Roli, F., Kittler, J. (eds.) MCS 2013. LNCS, vol. 7872, pp. 1–12. Springer, Heidelberg (2013). doi:10.1007/978-3-642-38067-9_1
3. Breiman, L., Friedman, J.H., Olshen, R.A., Stone, C.J.: Classification and Regression Trees. Wadsworth and Brooks, Monterey (1984)
4. Erdal, H.I., Karakurt, O.: Advancing monthly streamflow prediction accuracy of CART models using ensemble learning paradigms. J. Hydrol. **477**, 119–128 (2013). Elsevier
5. Friedman, J., Hastie, T., Tibshirani, R.: The Elements of Statistical Learning: Data Mining, Inference, and Prediction. Springer Series in Statistics. Springer-Verlag New York, New York (2009)
6. Ghimire, B., Rogan, J., Galiano, V.R., Panday, P., Neeti, N.: An evaluation of bagging, boosting, and random forests for land-cover classification in Cape Cod, Massachusetts, USA. GIScience Remote Sens. **49**(5), 623–643 (2012). Taylor & Francis
7. Golbandi, N., Koren, Y., Lempel, R.: Adaptive bootstrapping of recommender systems using decision trees. In: Proceedings of the Fourth ACM International Conference on Web Search and Data Mining, pp. 595–604. ACM (2011)
8. Lavanya, D., Rani, K.U.: Ensemble decision making system for breast cancer data. Int. J. Comput. Appl. **51**(17) (2012). Foundation of Computer Science
9. Polikar, R.: Ensemble based systems in decision making. IEEE Circuits Syst. Mag. **6**(3), 21–45 (2006). IEEE
10. Quinlan, J.R.: Induction of decision trees. Mach. Learn. **1**(1), 81–106 (1986)
11. Saavedra, P., Barreiro, P., Durán, R., Crujeiras, R., Loureiro, M., Sánchez, V.E.: Choice-based recommender systems. In: Proceedings of RecSys 2016, Boston (2016)
12. Utku, A., Hacer, K., Yildiz, O., Akcayol, M.A.: Implementation of a new recommendation system based on decision tree using implicit relevance feedback. JSW **10**(12), 1367–1374 (2015)

Relating Facial Myoelectric Activity to Speech Formants

Pedro Gómez-Vilda[1](✉), D. Palacios-Alonso[1], A. Gómez-Rodellar[1], José Manuel Ferrández-Vicente[2], A. Álvarez-Marquina[1], R. Martínez-Olalla[1], and V. Nieto-Lluis[1]

[1] Neuromorphic Speech Processing Lab, Center for Biomedical Technology, Universidad Politécnica de Madrid, Campus de Montegancedo, 28223 Pozuelo de Alarcón, Madrid, Spain
pedro@fi.upm.es

[2] Universidad Politécnica de Cartagena, Campus Universitario Muralla del Mar, Pza. Hospital 1, 30202 Cartagena, Spain

Abstract. Speech articulation is conditioned by the movements produced by well determined groups of muscles in the larynx, pharynx, mouth and face. The resulting speech shows acoustic features which are directly related with muscle neuromotor actions. Formants are some of the observable correlates most related to certain muscle actions, such as the ones activating jaw and tongue. As the recording of speech is simple and ubiquitous, the use of speech as a vehicular tool for neuromotor action monitoring would open a wide set of applications in the study of functional grading of neurodegenerative diseases. A relevant question is how far speech correlates and neuromotor action are related. This question is answered by the present study using electromyographic recordings on the masseter and the acoustic kinematics related with the first formant. Correlation measurements help in establishing a clear relation between the time derivative of the first formant and the masseter myoelectric activity. Monitoring disease progress by acoustic kinematics in one case of Amyotrophic Lateral Sclerosis ALS is described.

Keywords: Speech neuromotor activity · Facial myoelectric activity · Dysfluency · Dysarthria · Amyotrophic Lateral Sclerosis

1 Introduction

Speech is the result of different cognitive processes planned in the brain cognitive cortex, interpreted as specific neuromotor actions in midbrain, transformed into agonist-antagonist actions in muscles, and transferred to air as sounds. Speech production is planned and instantiated in the linguistic neuromotor cortex (Broadmann's areas 4, 6, 8, and 44–47 [1]). The neuromotor speech sequence activates the muscles of the pharynx, tongue, larynx, chest and diaphragm through sub-thalamic secondary pathways. The source-filter model of speech production, hypothesizes that an excitation source is generated either

J.M. Ferrández Vicente et al. (Eds.): IWINAC 2017, Part II, LNCS 10338, pp. 520–530, 2017.
DOI: 10.1007/978-3-319-59773-7_53

by the joint action of chest and larynx muscles (phonation) or by turbulent airflow induced by air exhalation in different parts of the oro-naso-pharyngeal tract (ONPT). The excitation source, in its propagation through the ONPT is acoustically filtered, resulting in the enhancement or reduction of certain spectral bands. These can comprise either message codes in a specific language, personal biometric features, or reveal emotional, physiological and psychological state conditions. Among these, possible alterations of the speaker's neurological conditions are also encoded. Certain diseases affect mainly to neuromotor units in the basal ganglia, brain stem and cerebelar structures (from motor neuron connection to muscle spindle activation, or even motor fibre degeneration), and are known as neuromotor diseases. Speech alterations produced by neurological diseases may affect different levels of speech production, these being mainly the phonation and articulation levels in neuromotor diseases, or fluency levels in cognitive diseases. Failures in neurotransmission, or in improper speech planning will produce perturbations in the respiration, phonation and articulation giving place to specific dysphonias and dysarthrias, poor prosody (monotonous speech), poor VOT (especially when switching nasal to oral sounds), and deficient fluency (low syllable rate, longer inter-syllable pauses, etc.) [2]. The aim of the present work is to establish a clear connection between acoustic correlates and neuromotor muscular activity, therefore, fluency correlates of cognitive etiology will not be considered. The working hypothesis assumes that on the one hand the acoustic-phonetic correlates observed on the first two formants derived from the speech signal, and the myoelectric surface signal [3] measured on the masseter have to present common features corresponding to a close relationship based on the neuromotor actions governing the muscle contractions modulating the open/close (O/C) features of vowels and dyphthongs. For such, Sect. 2 is devoted to the description of the articulation biomechanical model involved, in Sect. 3 the procedures and methods for signal collecting and processing will be shown. Results are given in Sect. 4, and a discussion follows on their significance and relevance. Section 5 is devoted to conclusions.

2 Neuromotor Articulation Model

Regarding articulation activity, the muscular structures implied are those modifying the ONPT, basically at the level of the naso-pharyngeal switch, and the jaw, tongue and lip gestures, which condition the properties of the equivalent acoustic filter. These properties will affect mainly to resonances of the tract, modifying both their static (vowel) and dynamic (consonantal) patterns. Vowels are well defined from their resonances, associated to the concept of formants, which are frequency bands especially enhanced by the ONPT resonances. The relation between the first two formant positions and the nature of the resulting vowel is well established in literature [4]. The relation between resonances and the articulation gestures (velum, tongue, jaws and lips) is less straight forward, but in general it can be said that certain gestures are clearly related to static vowel properties as defined by their first two formants. In general, it will be observed that a relation exists between the vowel space and the two main articulation gestures, which are the jaw and tongue positions [4]. The specific relation between the jaw position and the first formant (F) is given in Fig. 1. The lower jaw position is mainly fixed by two muscles which act as agonist and antagonist, these being the masseter and the geinohyoid, respectively. The action of gravity is to be added as a third force (f_g) to the forces produced by these muscles (f_m, f_h). The jaw and tongue act solidly as a dynamic structure in some way, therefore it is difficult to separate their independent movements.

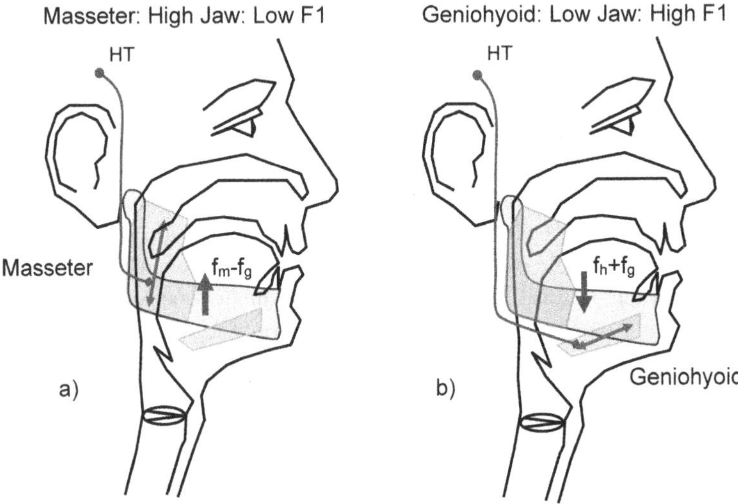

Fig. 1. Agonist-antagonist neuromotor actions regulating jaw position and the vowel feature open/close. (a) The neuromotor action promoted from hypothalamus neurons (HT) activate the corresponding trigeminal branch of the masseter. The result is a force (f_m) acting against gravity (f_g) moving the jaw upwards. (b) The neuromotor action activating the geniohyoid muscle produces a force (f_h) in the sense of gravity (f_g) pulling the jaw downwards.

For such, a certain jaw-tongue dynamic reference point (JTDRP) in the biomechanical system will be considered (equivalent center of actions), which could be related to formant positions. When its coordinates (x_A, y_A) experience a change, a corresponding change in the first two formants (F_1, F_2) can be expected. Lowering the JTDRP will result in an elevation of F_1, and vice-versa. Similarly, advancing the JTDRP will result in an elevation of F_2, and vice-versa. The back-front (B/F) and open-close (O/C) features may be justified on this basis. This relationship can be established as:

$$\begin{bmatrix} F_1(t) \\ F_2(t) \end{bmatrix} = \begin{bmatrix} a_{11} & a_{12} \\ a_{21} & a_{22} \end{bmatrix} \begin{bmatrix} x_A(t) \\ y_A(t) \end{bmatrix}; \quad \mathbf{A} = \begin{bmatrix} a_{11} & a_{12} \\ a_{21} & a_{22} \end{bmatrix} \tag{1}$$

where a_{ij} are the transformation weights explaining the position-to-formant associations, and t is the time. This relationship is known to be one-to-many, i.e. the same pair of formants $\{F_1, F_2\}$ may be associated to more than a single articulation position. This inconvenience may be handled by modelling the joint probability of all possible articulation positions associated to a given formant pair [4]. The first time derivative of (1) allows associating formant dynamics with the JTDRP kinematics as:

$$\begin{bmatrix} \frac{dF_1(t)}{dt} \\ \frac{dF_2(t)}{dt} \end{bmatrix} = \mathbf{A} \begin{bmatrix} \hat{v}_x(t) \\ \hat{v}_y(t) \end{bmatrix} \tag{2}$$

where it has been assumed that the system given by matrix $\mathbf{A}$ is linear and time-invariant, and $\hat{v}_x$ and $\hat{v}_y$ are the B/F and O/C velocity estimates of the JTDRP. Extending the biomechanical chain one step more, the derivatives of the velocity estimates will allow evaluating the accelerations experienced at the JTDRP:

$$\begin{bmatrix} \frac{d^2F_1(t)}{dt^2} \\ \frac{d^2F_2(t)}{dt^2} \end{bmatrix} = \begin{bmatrix} a_{11} & a_{12} \\ a_{21} & a_{22} \end{bmatrix} \begin{bmatrix} \frac{d\hat{v}_x(t)}{dt} \\ \frac{d\hat{v}_y(t)}{dt} \end{bmatrix} = \mathbf{A} \begin{bmatrix} \hat{a}_x(t) \\ \hat{a}_y(t) \end{bmatrix} \tag{3}$$

In what follows it will be assumed that the contribution to the first formant kinematics is mainly the result of vertical dynamics, as expressed by the following relation:

$$\frac{dF_1(t)}{dt} \cong a_{12}\hat{v}_y(t) \tag{4}$$

The time derivative of F_1 can be evaluated from Linear Predictive Spectral Estimation [5], whereas the jaw movement can be obtained from accelerometers [6]. In the present work, a different approach will be followed, where biomechanical dynamic variables are to be inferred from the surface myoelectric activity recorded on skin covering the facial surface over masseter [7], as illustrated in the next section.

3 Materials and Methods

The present study has a marked exploratory nature, as very few publications address the issue of using the myoelectric facial surface signals on the masseter to estimate neuromotor decay in neurological disease evaluation [7]. The main assumption is that the myoelectric signal recorded at the surface of the skin over the facial position of the masseter, will represent the joint action of many individual muscle fibre contractions under the neuromotor commands travelling the corresponding branch of the trigeminal nerve. The masseter is one of the most powerful body muscles, therefore it is a good candidate for this kind of measurements.

An experiment was designed to validate the working hypothesis on the relationship between the first formant dynamics and the electromyographic signal recorded on the masseter. The speaker was asked to produce the sequence /*ayayayayay*.../ (phonetically [*ajajajajaj*...]) during four sequences, because it

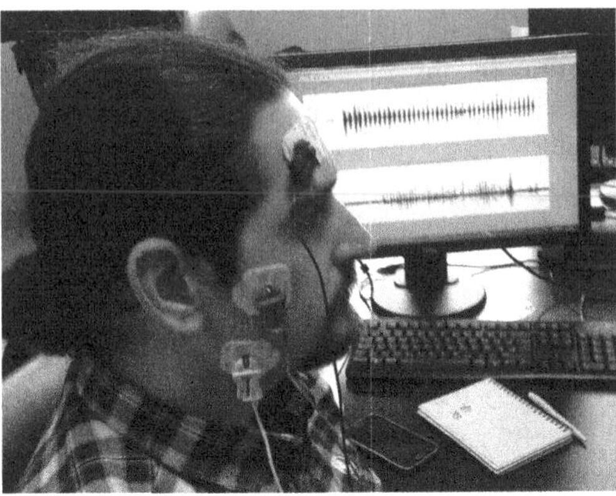

Fig. 2. Recording the myoelectric surface signal produced by the contraction of the masseter.

implies an intensive masseter activity. The acoustic signal was recorded with a Sennheiser microphone at 44100 Hz and 16 bits. The electromyographic signal was recorded with the equipment Biopac MP150 EMG100 at 2000 Hz and 16 bits. The fixture to record surface myoelectric signals from the masseter is shown in Fig. 2. Typically, two surface contact electrodes are fixed on the skin at the masseter attachment to the mandible, and at the mid-superior part of the muscular bundle attachment to the cheekbone, and a third reference electrode is placed in the forefront over the ipsilateral eyebrow. This fixture showed high signal and low noise levels. A 10-order Butterworth low-pass filter at 20 Hz cut-off frequency was applied on the resulting myoelectric signal for de-noising and artefact removing.

The recording protocol and signal processing methodology is completed in the following steps:

- Myoelectric surface signals are recorded simultaneously with voice signals. Synchronization is not a strict requirement, although the subject is asked to produce a sharp click with the tongue, which is recorded both as a myoelectric and an acoustic event (see the star mark on plots (a) and (d) in Fig. 3).
- The voice recordings are undersampled to 8 KHz.
- A ten-cycle segment of voice for the diphthong $[aj]$ signalled by the vertical arrows in Fig. 3b is selected for formant kinematic estimation.
- The ONPT transfer function of the voice segment is evaluated by an 8-pole adaptive inverse LP filter [5] with a low-memory adaptive step to grasp fine time variations.
- The first two formants are estimated by evaluating the roots of the associated inverse polynomials of the LP predictor each 2 ms with a frequency resolution of 2 Hz. The derivative of the first formant is given in Fig. 3c.
- The myoelectric signal is low-pass filtered with a 10-order Butterworth at a cut-off. Frequency of 20 Hz, producing as a result the signal given in Fig. 3d.

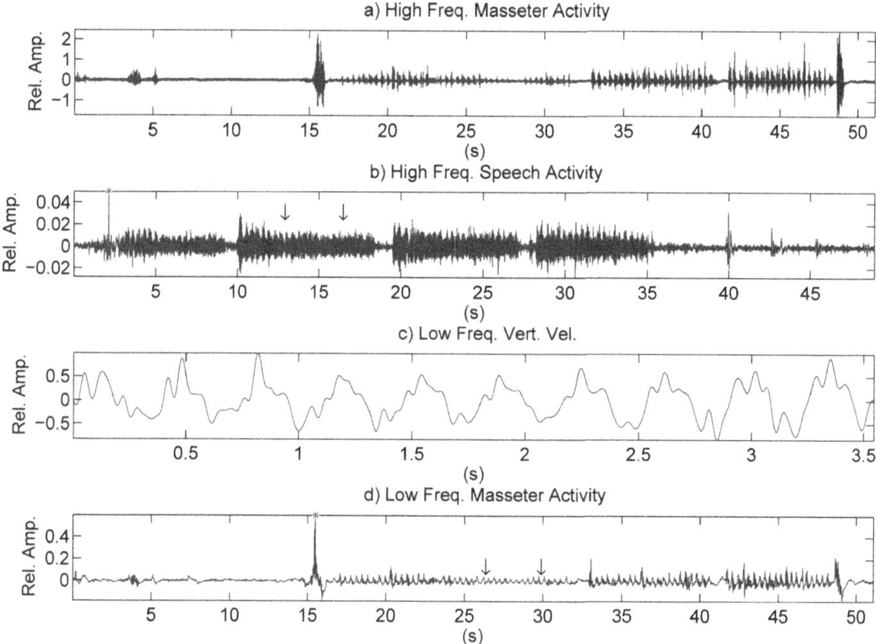

Fig. 3. Signals recorded for the study: (a) myoelectric surface signal; (b) acoustic signal showing the ten-cycle segment used in the estimation of the kinematic acoustic signal (vertical arrows); (c) ten-cycle segment of the first formant time derivative (kinematic acoustic signal); (d) low-pass filtered myoelectric surface signal, showing the segment that correlates best to the kinematic acoustic signal (vertical arrows). The stars in (b) and (d) show the alignment events.

- The derivative of the first formant as given in Fig. 3c is correlated along the low-pass filtered myoelectric signal given in Fig. 3d, producing a best match for the segment signalled by vertical arrows in (b) and (d).

The signal segments which best match under a correlation criterior are shown in Fig. 4. Each correspond to a ten [*aj*]-cycle segment. The upper template (a) shows the low-pass filtered time derivative of F_1, whereas the mid-template (b) shows the low-pass filtered surface myoelectric signal. They match almost exactly as far as their pseudo-periods are concerned. It may be seen that the myoelectric signal (b) has more contents of higher harmonics than (a). There are several possible explanations for this fact, the possible influence of a further low-pass effect contributed by the jaw-tongue biomechanical system being among them.

The bottom template (c) is the result of estimating the least-square error between (a) and (b). It may be seen that this error concentrates most of the high-frequency components of (b). The details of the correlation and best match process are given in the next section.

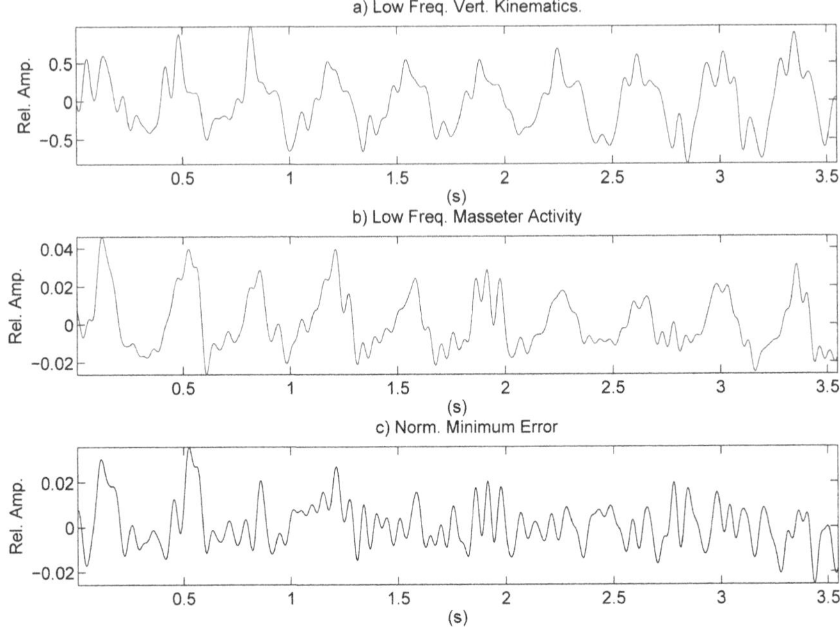

Fig. 4. Segments selected for correlation: (a) first formant time derivative (kinematic acoustic signal); (b) low-pass filtered myoelectric surface signal (best fit); (c) normalized minimum error between the acoustic kinematic and the myoelectric signals.

4 Results and Discussion

The correlation process consisted in sliding the time derivative of the first formant (kinematic acoustic signal shown in Fig. 3c), aligning it over the low-pass filtered surface myoelectric signal (Fig. 3d), and for each alignment step the correlation coefficients of Pearson and Spearman were evaluated. The alignment producing the largest Spearman's coefficient was marked as the best fit, and the corresponding segment of the myoelectric signal was selected:

$$t_{align} = \arg\max_{\zeta \in W} \left\{ \rho_S \left[s_m(t+\zeta), \frac{dF_1(t)}{dt} \right] \right\} \tag{5}$$

where W is the recording window, $s_m(t)$ is the low-pass filtered surface electromyogram on the masseter facial skin, and $\rho_S[s_1, s_2]$ is the function evaluating Spearsman's correlation coefficient between two time series $s_1(t)$ and $s_2(t)$. The best-fit segments are plotted in Fig. 4a and b. The linear and nonlinear regression measurements are given in the next section (Fig. 5).

The linear regression corresponds to a Pearson's coefficient of 0.735, with an estimation confidence given by an almost null p-value (p-v: 0.000). The nonlinear regression corresponds to a Spearman's rank-coefficient of 0.776, with an estimation confidence almost null (p-v: 0.000). At this point it would be interesting

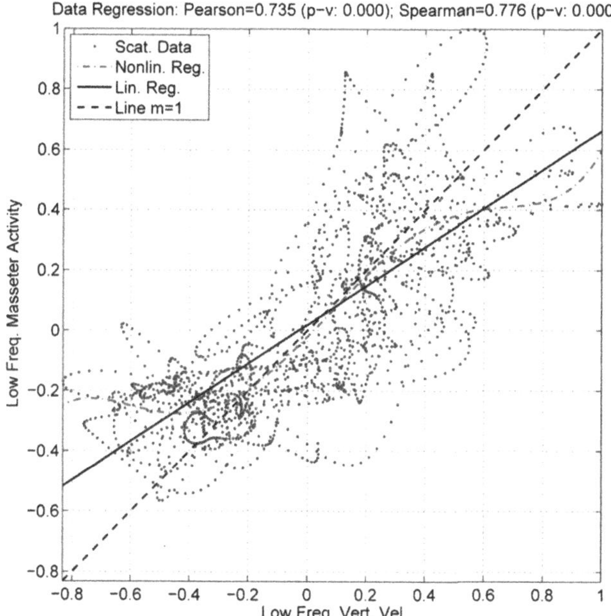

Fig. 5. Regressions between the acoustic kinematic and the myoelectric signals. The scatter plot of the dataset is given in blue dots. The full straight line gives the linear regression fit. The dash-dot red line shows a 5-th order polynomial nonlinear fit. The dash line slope is the unity. (Color figure online)

to analyze other alternatives, for instance, it should be reasonable to consider that being the myoelectric signal related with neuromotor actions, perhaps a better fit could be obtained on the second time derivative of the first formant (related to accelerations, and thus to forces). When this signal is used for the alignment with the same acoustic kinematic segment, the results are less relevant (Pearson's and Spearman's coefficients of 0.464, respectively). Therefore, it can be concluded, as far as the present experiment is concerned, that the logical association of the surface myoelectrical signal is more correlated with the acoustic kinematic signal than with its time derivative. This conclusion is of large relevance for the diagnose and monitoring of neurodegenerative diseases from the analysis of voice and speech. As the time derivatives of the formants can be associated with the kinematics of the JTDRP as given by (2), a possible correlate to neuromotor disease grade could be defined by the absolute velocity of the system, given as:

$$|v_{JTDRP}(t)| = \sqrt{\left(w_{21}\frac{dF_1(t)}{dt}\right)^2 + \left(w_{12}\frac{dF_2(t)}{dt}\right)^2} \tag{6}$$

where w_{12} and w_{21} are the coefficients of the inverse of matrix $\boldsymbol{A}$, assuming that invertibility conditions fulfill, and that vertical kinematics is expressed only in

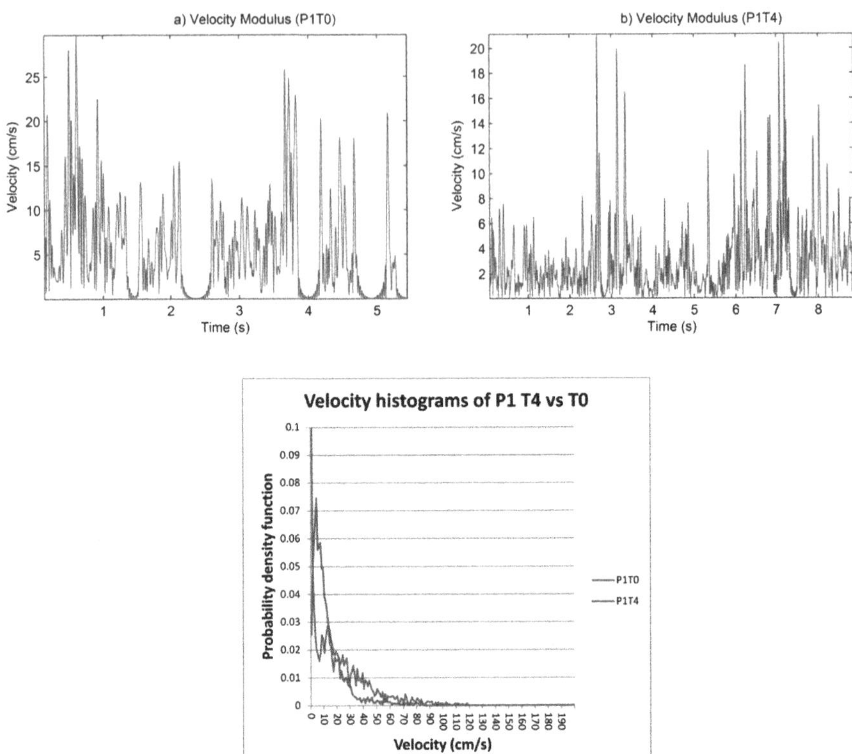

Fig. 6. Absolute velocity of the JTDRP for two recordings from an ALS patient: (a) First recording at month 0; (b) Last recording at month 12; (c) Comparison of the two probability density functions (blue-P1T0: month 0; red-P1-T4: month 12). (Color figure online)

F_1, and horizontal kinematics only in F_2. No matter how strong these conditions may seem, there are indications that this can be a plausible hypothesis, to be tested in a future study. The absolute velocity of the JTDRP given in (6) is a relevant correlate to articulation dysarthria and dysfluency, and can be used in comparing speech features from different utterances. In what follows the results of evaluating the degradation of the speaking performance of a 64-year old female patient suffering from Amyotrophic Lateral Sclerosis (ALS) [8] will be shown. The patient was recorded five times with a 3-month interval separation, uttering a pre-established sentence. The absolute velocity from each utterance was estimated and a probability density function was evaluated by Kolmogorov-Smirnov histogram fitting [9]. The velocity profiles for the first and last recording sessions, and the comparison of the relative probability density functions are given in Fig. 6. It may be seen that in the first recording (Fig. 6a) the speaker spent 5.3 s, whereas in the last one (Fig. 6b) the same sentence was uttered in almost 9 s. Besides, pauses between phonated segments can be appreciated in the first recording, whereas in the last one, such pauses were not found. The velocity activity is better organized in the first recording and it is distributed in a wider range of speed values (in cm/s), whereas the last recording shows smaller speed values. This can also be appreciated in the probability density functions given in Fig. 6c, where the first recording velocity distribution shows a gentle decay, whereas the last one shows a reduction in large velocities, which is transferred to low velocities (sharper decay). Based on these probability density functions, the Kullback-Leibler Divergence [10] was used to estimate the distance from these distributions with respect to a control subject. The results are given in Table 1.

Table 1. KLD for the first and last recordings relative to a female control subject.

Recording	KLD to control
P1T0	0.42657477
P1T4	0.93337742

It may be seen that the divergence between the first recording and the last recording is almost as large as the divergence from the first recording to the control subject, thus showing the degradation of the patient's condition regarding speech production.

5 Conclusions

Speech articulation is conditioned by the movements produced by well determined groups of muscles in the larynx, pharynx, mouth and face. As the recording of speech is simple and ubiquitous, the use of speech as a vehicular tool for neuromotor action monitoring would open a wide set of applications in the study of functional grading of neurodegenerative diseases. A relevant question is how far speech correlates and neuromotor action are related. This question was to be answered by the present study using electromyographic recordings on the masseter and the acoustic kinematics related with the first formant. Although the study presented is limited to one case and one sequence, there are interesting findings to be reported, among them the following:

- A clear association between the electromyographic signal and the acoustic kinematic one may be established. Correlation measures based in second order statistics satisfy the necessary conditions for this relation to be confirmed.
- The variable to which the electromyogram fits better is the time derivative of the first formant, which may be associated to the velocity of the JTDRP.
- The main difference between both the electromyographic signal and the acoustic kinematic one seems to be due to a larger contents of harmonics present in the electromyogram. This could indicate that the jaw-tongue biomechanical system is acting as a low-pass electromechanical filter.

- The absolute velocity associated to the JTDRP estimated as the time derivatives of the first and second formants seems to be a good index to disfluency and disarthria of neuromotor origin.
- These conclusions are to be validated on a wider database of speakers, including gender dependence.

Acknowledgments. This work is being funded by grants TEC2012-38630-C04-01, TEC2012-38630-C04-04 and TEC2016-77791-C4-4-R from the Ministry of Economic Affairs and Competitiveness of Spain.

References

1. Demonet, J.F., Thierry, G., Cardebat, D.: Renewal of the neurophysiology of language: functional neuroimaging. Physiol. Rev. **85**, 49–95 (2005)
2. Yunusova, Y., Weismer, G., Westbury, J.R., Lindstrom, M.J.: Articulatory movements during vowels in speakers with dysarthria and healthy controls. J. Speech Lang. Hear. Res. **51**(3), 596–611 (2008)
3. Phinyomark, A., Quaine, F., Charbonnier, S., Serviere, C., Tarpin-Bernard, F., Laurillau, Y.: EMG feature evaluation for improving myoelectric pattern recognition robustness. Expert Syst. Appl. **40**, 4832–4840 (2013)
4. Dromey, C., Jang, G.O., Hollis, K.: Assessing correlations between lingual movements and formants. Speech Commun. **55**(2), 315–328 (2013)
5. Deller, J.R., Proakis, J.G., Hansen, J.H.L.: Discrete-Time Processing of Speech Signals. Macmillan, NewYork (1993)
6. Green, J.R.: Mouth matters: scientific and clinical applications of speech movement analysis. Perspect. Speech Sci. Orofacial Disord. **25**, 6–16 (2015)
7. Wu, P., Gonzalez, I., Patsis, G., Jiang, D., Sahli, H., Kerckhofs, E., Vandekerckhove, M.: Objectifying facial expressivity assessment of Parkinson's patients: preliminary study. Comput. Math. Methods Med. **2014** (2014). Article no. 427826. http://dx.doi.org/10.1155/2014/427826
8. Gómez-Vilda, P., Londral, A.R.M., Rodellar-Biarge, V., Ferrández-Vicente, J.M., de Carvalho, M.: Monitoring amyotrophic lateral sclerosis by biomechanical modeling of speech production. Neurocomputing **151**, 130–138 (2015)
9. Webb, A.R.: Statistical Pattern Recognition. Wiley, Chichester (2002)
10. Salicrú, M., Morales, D., Menéndez, M.L., Pardo, L.: On the applications of divergence type measures in testing statistical hypotheses. J. Multivar. Anal. **51**, 372–391 (1994)

Low Dimensionality or Same Subsets as a Result of Feature Selection: An In-Depth Roadmap

Antonio J. Tallón-Ballesteros[(✉)] and José C. Riquelme

Department of Languages and Computer Systems,
University of Seville, Seville, Spain
atallon@us.es

Abstract. This paper addresses the situation that may happen after the application of feature subset selection in terms of a reduced number of selected features or even same solutions obtained by different algorithms. The data mining community has been working for a long time with the assumption that meaningful attributes are either highly correlated with the class or represent a consistent subset, that is, with no inconsistencies. We have analysed around a hundred data sets very varied with a number of attributes below one hundred, a number of instances not greater than fifty thousand and a number of classes below fifty. Basically, in the first round we applied two different feature subset selection methods to pick up the figures in terms of reduced dimensionality. After that, we divided them into different groups according to the number of selected attributes. Next, we deepened the analysis in every category and we added a new feature selection procedure. Finally, we assessed the performance of the original problem and the reduced subsets with four classifiers providing some prospective directions.

Keywords: Classification · Feature subset selection · Correlation · Consistency · Feature ranking

1 Introduction

Predictive data analytics [8] encompasses the business and data processes and computational models that enable a business to make data-driven decisions. The key idea is to move from data to insights to decisions. Machine learning algorithms work by searching through a set of possible prediction models for the model that best captures the relationship between the descriptive features and the target feature [22]. An obvious search criteria to drive this search is to look for models that are consistent with the data. The classifier training could achieve to three types of models: an under-fitted one, an over-fitted one and a just right one. Thus, it is true that there is a trade-off between the current data and the generalisation ability with unseen data. Data pre-processing (DP) is one of the crucial and time-consuming activities within Knowledge Discovery in Databases (KDD) [4]. Likely, feature selection [12] is said to be one of the most widespread

J.M. Ferrández Vicente et al. (Eds.): IWINAC 2017, Part II, LNCS 10338, pp. 531–539, 2017.
DOI: 10.1007/978-3-319-59773-7_54

approaches within DP. It pursues to pick up the most important features in order to simplify the model and predict more accurately.

This paper aims at analysing the situation obtained when CFS and CNS pick up only a very reduced number of attributes and to propose a strategy to deal with this drawback. The rest of this article is organized as follows: Sect. 2 describes some concepts about feature selection; Sect. 3 introduces our proposal; Sect. 4 shows the experimental results; finally, Sect. 5 states the concluding remarks.

2 Feature Selection

Feature selection (FS) is one of the possible approaches to reduce the dimensionality. It picks up among the original variables those that are better suited for the problem at hand [7]. There are different kinds of methods to contend with feature selection [11]. Filter methods are independent of the classifier, whereas wrapper methods use the inductive algorithm as the evaluation function. FS involves two phases: (a) to get a list of attributes according to an attribute evaluator and (b) to carry out a search on the initial list. All candidate lists would be evaluated using a measure evaluation and the best one will be returned. Correlation-based Feature Selection (CFS) [6] and Consistency-based search in feature selection (CNS) [3] are two powerful methods to deal with this problem. Both operate together with a search method such as Greedy Search or typically Best First. There are some desirable properties to be exhibited in the reduced feature space: (a) low dimensionality, (b) retention of sufficient information, (c) enhancement of separability in feature space for examples in different classes by removing effects du to noise attributes, and (d) comparability of features among examples in the same category [14]. A goal of feature selection is to avoid selecting too many or too few features than is necessary [16]. If too few features are selected, there is a good chance that information content in this set of features is low. On the other hand, if too many (irrelevant) features are selected, the effects due to noise present in (most real-world) data may overshadow the information present. Hence, this is a trade-off which must be addressed by any feature selection method.

3 Proposal

The current paper sheds light on how to deal with problems where feature subset selection procedures choose a small number of attributes or even those cases when the solution reached for both procedures is exactly the same. As representative feature subset selectors we have singled out CFS and CNS. CFS is continually used from the developing time by Mark A. Hall up to now and currently have more than two thousands of citations and around fifty from the current year. To give some examples, one of the most recent work has been produced in the context of activity monitoring [13]. CNS is a popular, but not so much as the aforesaid, feature subset selector falling also into filter category with around seven hundred citations. CNS has been claimed that sometimes chooses a small number of features that may not be enough to provide the classifier an appropriate performance [20].

The first step is to collect the number of selected attributes for the aforementioned two methods for problems with a number of features less or equal than one hundred and a number of instances not higher than fifty thousand. As usually in data analytics field, the data preparation techniques operate on the training set and the test set remains unchanged and is evaluated by the first time after the classifier training. We have experimented with problems from the UCI (University of California at Irvine) repository [2] as well as some classical problems from the literature on Machine Learning [17] or Artificial Intelligence [15]. We have analysed around a hundred of problems. We have divided the problems into four outstanding scenarios as follows: (a) Only one selected attribute, (b) Only two attributes are singled out by CFS, (c) Only two picked attributes by CNS and (d) Same solution is achieved by CFS and CNS. As a second step, we also evaluated the classification performance with a previous data preparation from the original data with a feature ranking method such as ReliefF [9] which is a very strong method; later, it was extended to a very detailed work in [10] and by coincidence is now marking the twentieth birthday. ReliefF requires a threshold that may not be appropriately tuned according to the no free-lunch Theorem [23]. We go further and we propose Leave-k-out ReliefF or ReliefF($-k$), to shorten, which is the application of ReliefF with the dropping of k attributes. The value of k is set depending on the number of original attributes. In this study, for problems with lower than 10 attributes we have experimented with values of 1,2,3 for k. Next, for data sets with a number of attributes in the range (10,20] k takes the values 2,3,4. And finally, for problems containing more attributes, that is between 21 and 30, k is configured with the values 3,4,5. We have not defined more sets of values for k because we did not come across with any problem not fulfilling the condition in the four scenarios explained earlier.

4 Experimental Results

Table 1 describes the data sets utilised. Some of them are classical from Supervised Machine Learning and the remaining ones are publicly available in the UCI (University of California at Irvine) repository [2]. They come from real-world applications of different fields such as Medicine, Public Health, Botanic or Biology. The problems have been sorted by the number of attributes selected by CFS and CNS in ascending order. The size of the problems meeting the conditions of the four described scenarios ranges from around twenty to more than three thousand. The number of features varies between four and twenty nine, whereas the number of classes is between two and more than twenty. The missing values have been replaced in the case of nominal variables by the mode or, when concerning continuous variables, by the mean, bearing in mind the full data set.

We have evaluated the original and the reduced data sets with four classifiers such as C4.5 [18], 1NN [1], PART [5] and SVM [21]. We have used the implementations provided by WEKA tool [22] with default parameters that are those

Table 1. Summary of the data sets used and selected features for each feature subset selector

Data set	Instances			Classes	Features		
	Total	Train	Test		Original	CFS	CNS
Liver	345	259	86	2	6	1	–
Post-op	90	67	23	3	20	1	1
Lenses	24	18	6	3	6	1	2
Golf	28	20	8	2	4	2	2
Iris	150	111	39	3	4	2	2
Hypo	3772	2829	943	4	29	2	6
Breast	286	215	71	2	15	4	2
Smoking	2855	2141	714	3	13	5	2
Primary-tumor	339	251	88	21	23	5	5
Ecoli	336	251	85	8	7	6	6
Yeast	1484	1112	372	10	8	7	7
Average	882.6	661.3	221.4	5.5	12.3	3.3	3.5
Max	3772	2829	943	21	29	7	7

suggested by the own authors of the algorithms. We have chosen CFS and CNS as representative feature subset selection methods, because they are based on different kind of measures, have few parameters and have provided a good performance inside the supervised machine learning area. Often, BestFirst search is the preferable option by the researchers for both FSS algorithms. CFS is likely the most used FSS in data mining. CNS is also powerful, however the quantity of published works is more reduced [19].

4.1 Scenario I

This subsection copes with problems where only one attribute is obtained after the CFS. Table 2 shows the results of the experiments in this first scenario. According to the results, it seems that CFS is not able to capture the outstanding relationships between the variables and the class label. It is especially dramatic in the case of 1NN. CNS picks up from 0 through 2 attributes depending on the problem at hand. With two features the situation has been relieved a bit but in the remaining cases the performance is not very promising in general terms and sometimes very poor. Particularly, in Post-op the number of attributes selected by CFS and CNS is only a 5% of the original set which is extremely reduced and only C4.5 classifier is able to get a better performance. Generally speaking, ReliefF(–k) get more stable results keeping at least a half of the features in data sets with less than ten attributes or up to a 80% of the characteristic space for a problem with twenty features. As a general idea, 1NN does not operate very well with only one selected feature.

Table 2. Scenario I: Accuracy test results

Data set	Classifier	FULL	CFS	CNS	ReliefF (–1)	ReliefF (–2)	ReliefF (–3)	ReliefF (–4)
Liver	*C*4.5	68.60	58.14		59.46	68.60	66.28	
	1*NN*	61.63	39.53		58.30	54.65	56.98	
	PART	61.63	58.14		59.46	68.60	66.28	
	SVM	58.14	58.14		57.92	58.14	58.14	
Ind. average		62.50	53.49		58.78	62.50	61.92	
Post – op	*C*4.5	52.17	56.52	56.52		52.17	52.17	52.17
	1*NN*	56.52	4.35	4.35		56.52	56.52	56.52
	PART	65.22	56.52	56.52		56.52	56.52	56.52
	SVM	56.52	56.52	56.52		56.52	56.52	56.52
Ind. average		57.61	43.48	43.48		55.43	55.43	55.43
Lenses	*C*4.5	66.67	50.00	66.67	66.67	66.67	66.67	
	1*NN*	16.67	50.00	66.67	50.00	83.33	66.67	
	PART	66.67	50.00	66.67	66.67	66.67	66.67	
	SVM	66.67	50.00	66.67	66.67	83.33	66.67	
Ind. average		54.17	50.00	66.67	62.50	75.00	66.67	
Global averages	*C*4.5	62.48	54.89			62.48	61.71	
	1*NN*	44.94	31.29			64.83	60.06	
	PART	64.50	54.89			63.93	63.16	
	SVM	60.44	54.89			66.00	60.44	
Partial averages	*C*4.5			61.59	63.06			52.17
	1*NN*			35.51	54.15			56.52
	PART			61.59	63.06			56.52
	SVM			61.59	62.29			56.52
ReliefF(−2) is a reasonable alternative to CFS and CNS								

The value of k affects clearly to the performance but a trade-off value may be two, thus ReliefF(–2) is a quite reasonable solution to the problem showed by CFS and CNS. PART decreased the accuracy with Post-op after feature selection from any of the two poles, that is when only one attribute is selected or even almost all the features are retained. ReliefF(–k) shows a very flat behaviour in Post-op because the results remained constant.

4.2 Scenario II

We move on to the outlook where CFS only singles out two attributes which results are shown in Table 3. CNS picks from two to six attributes. Iris is a classical problem in the literature; according to the results at least two out of four attributes are required to generalised with a high accuracy. Golf is a data set rooted from the first studies in the field of Artificial Intelligence and the removal of one attribute with ReliefF(–1) keeps the original results. If more

Table 3. Scenario II: Accuracy test results

Data set	Classifier	FULL	CFS	CNS	ReliefF (–1)	ReliefF (–2)	ReliefF (–3)	ReliefF (–4)	ReliefF (–5)
Golf	*C4.5*	62.50	62.50	62.50	62.50	62.50	62.50		
	1NN	75.00	50.00	50.00	75.00	50.00	37.50		
	PART	62.50	62.50	62.50	62.50	37.50	62.50		
	SVM	37.50	37.50	37.50	37.50	50.00	25.00		
Ind. average		59.38	53.13	53.13	59.38	50.00	46.88		
Iris	*C4.5*	94.87	94.87	94.87	94.87	94.87	94.87		
	1NN	94.87	94.87	94.87	94.87	94.87	89.74		
	PART	94.87	94.87	94.87	94.87	94.87	94.87		
	SVM	94.87	94.87	94.87	94.87	94.87	94.87		
Ind. average		94.87	94.87	94.87	94.87	94.87	93.59		
Hypo	*C4.5*	99.15	96.92	98.94			99.26	99.26	98.94
	1NN	90.99	96.50	94.27			90.88	90.99	90.88
	PART	98.83	96.92	98.94			98.83	98.83	98.73
	SVM	93.85	93.32	93.43			93.85	93.85	93.85
Ind. average		95.70	95.92	96.39			95.71	95.73	95.60
Global averages	*C4.5*	85.51	84.77	85.44			85.54		
	1NN	86.95	80.46	79.72			72.71		
	PART	85.40	84.77	85.44			85.40		
	SVM	75.41	75.23	75.27			71.24		
Partial averages	*C4.5*			85.44	78.69	78.69		99.26	
	1NN			79.72	84.94	72.44		90.99	
	PART			85.44	78.69	66.19		98.83	
	SVM			75.27	66.19	72.44		93.85	
ReliefF(−2) or ReliefF(−1) are suitable for low − dimensionality problems									
ReliefF(−k) with k = 3, 4, 5 is a good way for Hypo (initially 29 features)									

than one attribute is discarded, the situation could be acceptable for k = 2 in general terms, but for k = 3 only in PART happens improvements compared with k = 2. Hypo is a problem which original results are better than those with the reduced sets. Although, the situation is appropriate with CNS. ReliefF(–k) is a good approach and the original results are even overcome. The conclusion is very simple and could us to assert that two attributes or three are at least necessary for small problems. Hypo is a problem which exhibits a strong classifier dependency but ReliefF(–4) is a good way.

4.3 Scenario III

This subsection depicts in Table 4 the results of those problems where only two attributes where retained by CNS. The situation achieved is very limited because with only two attributes out of more than twelve is not very easy to get good results for a classifier in general terms. CFS picked up from four through five attributes. Roughly speaking, the classification performance is very pretty with the exception of 1NN in Smoking data set. The removal of around a 20% of attributes let to recover more or less similar results that the full feature space.

Table 4. Scenario III: Accuracy test results

Data set	Classifier	FULL	CFS	CNS	ReliefF (–2)	ReliefF (–3)	ReliefF (–4)
Breast	*C4.5*	70.42	69.01	69.01	70.42	70.42	70.42
	1NN	64.79	70.42	70.42	67.61	69.01	69.01
	PART	69.01	71.83	69.01	64.79	63.38	67.61
	SVM	64.79	66.20	64.79	66.20	66.20	64.79
Ind. average		67.25	69.37	68.31	67.25	67.25	67.96
Smoking	*C4.5*	68.63	69.47	69.47	67.65	69.47	69.47
	1NN	54.76	38.52	5.60	56.86	50.28	50.14
	PART	61.48	67.36	68.77	62.75	61.76	66.11
	SVM	69.47	69.47	69.47	69.47	69.47	69.47
Ind. average		63.59	61.20	53.33	64.18	62.75	63.80
Global averages	*C4.5*	69.53	69.24	69.24	69.03	69.95	69.95
	1NN	59.78	54.47	38.01	62.23	59.65	59.58
	PART	65.25	69.60	68.89	63.77	62.57	66.86
	SVM	67.13	67.83	67.13	67.83	67.83	67.13
$ReliefF(-k)$ *with* k *near to* 3 *exhibits a good performance*							

Table 5. Scenario IV: Accuracy test results

Data set	Classifier	FULL	CFS/CNS	ReliefF (–1)	ReliefF (–2)	ReliefF (–3)	ReliefF (–4)	ReliefF (–5)
Ecoli	*C4.5*	82.35	82.35	82.35	80.00	77.65		
	1NN	82.35	82.35	82.35	83.53	72.94		
	PART	80.00	80.00	80.00	78.82	76.47		
	SVM	83.53	83.53	83.53	83.53	77.65		
Ind. average		82.06	82.06	82.06	81.47	76.18		
$Primary - tumor$	*C4.5*	45.46	42.05			40.91	40.91	43.18
	1NN	36.36	30.68			36.36	37.50	37.50
	PART	43.18	42.05			40.91	39.77	38.64
	SVM	47.72	42.05			48.86	48.86	47.73
Ind. average		43.18	39.20			41.76	41.76	41.76
Yeast	*C4.5*	54.84	54.03	54.57	52.68	53.49		
	1NN	48.39	49.46	49.46	49.46	48.92		
	PART	56.72	54.30	55.65	55.91	54.30		
	SVM	55.91	54.84	54.57	54.30	53.76		
		53.97	53.16	53.56	53.09	52.62		
Global averages	*C4.5*	60.88	59.48			57.35		
	1NN	55.70	54.17			52.74		
	PART	59.97	58.78			57.23		
	SVM	62.39	60.14			60.09		
Partial averages	*C4.5*			68.46	66.34		40.91	43.18
	1NN			65.91	66.50		37.50	37.50
	PART			67.82	67.37		39.77	38.64
	SVM			69.05	68.92		48.86	47.73
$ReliefF(-2)$ *is convenient for* $low - dimensionality$ *data sets*								
$ReliefF(-k)$ *with* $k = 3, 4, 5$ *is a good way for* $Primary - tumor$ (23 *classes*)								

4.4 Scenario IV

Table 5 represents an overview where CFS and CNS pick up exactly the same features. The problems are now very handicapped because the number of classes is between eight and ten and the number of attributes is very close to the possible class labels. The situation is very delimited because the margin to discard attributes is not big because CFS and CNS have removed a single attribute for low-dimensionality problems and these are data sets are very complex especially to high number of classes. In the aforesaid scenario two attributes may be removed with ReliefF(–k) keeping a good performance. Contrarily, in Primary-tumor only five features are selected with CFS. Interestingly, ReliefF(–k) could discard safely at least three attributes that is at least a reduction close to a 15%.

5 Conclusions

A new feature ranking method called Leave-k-out ReliefF, also named ReliefF($-k$), was introduced. It was proposed as the alternative methodology when CFS or CNS only pick a very reduced number of attributes that could be 1 or 2 for any of these methods or even the same attributes are singled out by both methods. The recommendations depend on the number of original attributes and according to the test-bed are as follows. For problems with fewer than 10 attributes 1 or two attributes could be discarded safely. Finally, for problems with more features around 3 attributes could be removed from the input space.

Acknowledgments. This work has been partially subsidized by TIN2014-55894-C2-R project of the Spanish Inter-Ministerial Commission of Science and Technology (MICYT), FEDER funds and the P11-TIC-7528 project of the "Junta de Andalucía" (Spain).

References

1. Aha, D.W., Kibler, D., Albert, M.K.: Instance-based learning algorithms. Mach. Learn. **6**(1), 37–66 (1991)
2. Bache, K., Lichman, M.: UCI machine learning repository (2013)
3. Dash, M., Liu, H.: Consistency-based search in feature selection. Artif. Intell. **151**(1), 155–176 (2003)
4. Fayyad, U., Piatetsky-Shapiro, G., Smyth, P.: From data mining to knowledge discovery in databases. AI Mag. **17**(3), 37 (1996)
5. Frank, E., Witten, I.H.: Generating accurate rule sets without global optimization (1998)
6. Hall, M.A.: Correlation-based feature selection for machine learning. Ph.D. thesis, The University of Waikato (1999)
7. Han, J., Pei, J., Kamber, M.: Data Mining: Concepts and Techniques. Elsevier, Amsterdam (2011)
8. Kelleher, J.D., Mac Namee, B., D'Arcy, A.: Fundamentals of Machine Learning for Predictive Data Analytics: Algorithms, Worked Examples, and Case Studies. MIT Press, Cambridge (2015)

9. Kononenko, I.: Estimating attributes: analysis and extensions of RELIEF. In: Bergadano, F., Raedt, L. (eds.) ECML 1994. LNCS, vol. 784, pp. 171–182. Springer, Heidelberg (1994). doi:10.1007/3-540-57868-4_57
10. Kononenko, I., Šimec, E., Robnik-Šikonja, M.: Overcoming the myopia of inductive learning algorithms with RELIEFF. Appl. Intell. **7**(1), 39–55 (1997)
11. Langley, P.: Selection of Relevant Features in Machine Learning. Defense Technical Information Center, Fort Belvoir (1994)
12. Liu, H., Motoda, H.: Computational Methods of Feature Selection. CRC Press, Boca Raton (2007)
13. Martinez-Mozos, O., Sandulescu, V., Andrews, S., Ellis, D., Bellotto, N., Dobrescu, R., Ferrandez, J.M.: Stress detection using wearable physiological and sociometric sensors. Int. J. Neural Syst. **27**(02), 1650041 (2017)
14. Meisel, W.S.: Computer-oriented approaches to pattern recognition. Technical report. DTIC Document (1972)
15. Michalski, R.S., Carbonell, J.G., Mitchell, T.M.: Machine Learning: An Artificial Intelligence Approach. Springer Science & Business Media, Berlin (2013)
16. Piramuthu, S.: Evaluating feature selection methods for learning in data mining applications. Eur. J. Oper. Res. **156**(2), 483–494 (2004)
17. Quinlan, J.R.: Induction of decision trees. Mach. Learn. **1**(1), 81–106 (1986)
18. Quinlan, J.R.: C4. 5: Programming for Machine Learning. Morgan Kauffmann, Burlington (1993)
19. Tallón-Ballesteros, A.J., Hervás-Martínez, C., Riquelme, J.C., Ruiz, R.: Improving the accuracy of a two-stage algorithm in evolutionary product unit neural networks for classification by means of feature selection. In: Ferrández, J.M., Álvarez Sánchez, J.R., Paz, F., Toledo, F.J. (eds.) IWINAC 2011. LNCS, vol. 6687, pp. 381–390. Springer, Heidelberg (2011). doi:10.1007/978-3-642-21326-7_41
20. Tallón-Ballesteros, A.J., Riquelme, J.C., Ruiz, R.: Merging subsets of attributes to improve a hybrid consistency-based filter: a case of study in product unit neural networks. Connect. Sci. **28**(3), 242–257 (2016)
21. Vapnik, V.N.: The nature of Statistical Learning Theory. Springer, New York (1995)
22. Witten, I.H., Frank, E., Hall, M.A., Pal, C.J., Mining, D.: Practical Machine Learning Tools and Techniques. Morgan Kaufmann, Burlington (2016)
23. Wolpert, D.H.: The supervised learning no-free-lunch theorems. In: Roy, R., Köppen, M., Ovaska, S., Furuhashi, T., Hoffmann, F. (eds.) Soft Computing and Industry, pp. 25–42. Springer, London (2002)

Segmentation of Circular Contours from Laser Beams Measurements

J.M. Cuadra-Troncoso(✉), M.A. Muñoz-Bañón, F. de la Paz-López, and J.R. Álvarez-Sánchez(✉)

Dpto. de Inteligencia Artificial, UNED, Madrid, Spain
{jmcuadra,jras}@dia.uned.es

Abstract. The method for range scan segmentation described in a previous paper titled "Improving area center robot navigation using a novel range scan segmentation method", by some authors of present paper in 2011, uses an extended Kalman filter (EKF) for estimating straight segments equations in polar coordinates. That method, equivalent to a non-linear weighted least squares method, is extended in present work for estimating circle segments equations in polar coordinates, but only to the first stages of the full method, including acquisition of initial estimation of circles centers and radii to be used as initial values for EKF an the sequential iterative estimation of circle equations using EKF. The new problem of variance matrices being almost ill-conditioned for circle equations is addressed with a Tikhonov regularization, or ridge regression. Also a correction of initial values for estimations is proposed to solve the added problems found in circle equations estimation.

Keywords: Kalman segmentation · Circular contour · Circle extraction · Robot localization · Tikhonov regularization

1 Introduction

Some environments suitable for mobile robots include cylindrical objects, like round columns, as obstacles in addition to the usual straight walls. In order to improve SLAM (simultaneous localization and mapping) in such environments, the method for extracting straight segments from a range scan described by Cuadra et al. [1] can be extended to extract also circular segments.

The original method for extracting straight segments from a range scan entails several stages: segments clustering, initial values estimation, EKF (extended Kalman filter) sequential estimation of segments and merging of similar segments. It has been applied successfully [2,3] for on-line SLAM.

The clustering stage groups adjacent laser measurements into segments separated by corners or significant jumps between two adjacent measurements. Clustering is made using scale-space theory [4] to provide a multi-scale representation of the scan signal formed by smoothed versions of that signal. The interval tree procedure [5] is used in order to select the natural (most significant) scales to represent the world detected by the laser.

J.M. Ferrández Vicente et al. (Eds.): IWINAC 2017, Part II, LNCS 10338, pp. 540–550, 2017.
DOI: 10.1007/978-3-319-59773-7_55

The seeds for EKF initial values estimation are extracted from sets of consecutive measures of each segment core. The method do not use the whole segments because they could have fuzzy ends. For straight segments, the initial estimation is obtained using the repeated median filter [6]. This method is applicable only for linear models but this is not the case with circles.

EKF sequential estimation of segments, as a Gauss-Newton method, is executed using polar coordinates. In the case of linear models this estimate is equivalent to a linear regression [7], so the whole set of regression tools are available for use. One of these tools is specially useful for detecting segments ends: the outliers detection t-test [8].

Merging similar segments is done using the Chow test [8], in which adjacent segments with similar equations are merged together.

To include circular segments, as a first approach, we will consider only the convex part of the circles from the point of view of an observer located outside the circular object. With respect to the scan segmentation stages commented above, this paper deals with the three first stages but without the detection of segments ends. The ends detection of segments and their merging, plus the consideration of circle concave parts, will be addressed in future research.

The rest of his paper is structured as follow: Sect. 2 contains a summarized review on circle segmentation, Sect. 3 explains the clustering procedure, the EKF initialization is commented in Sect. 4, the circle equations estimation using EKF are described in Sect. 5, and the experiments result are commented in Sect. 6.

2 Circle Segmentation Summarized Review

Circle detection is of great interest in robot navigation and mapping applications. In a 2D laser scan, circles can represent: poles, round columns, trees, people, large coil reels, etc.

The methods for circles detection and segmentation use a variety of techniques. In the paper by Premevida and Nunes [9], a comparison between several methods using point-distance based segmentation (PDBS) and Kalman filtering based segmentation can be found. Recently, Zhou et al. [10] used PDBS enhanced with polynomial fitting and support vector machine (SVM) for final classification. The circle Hough transform (CHT) has been widely used. Press and Austin [11] compared several approaches using CHT for poles detection. Ascho and Spiecker [12] employ CHT followed by a circle parameters search and Huang et al. [13] use CHT and random sample consensus (RANSAC). Adaptive boosting (AdaBoost) classifier has been used by Arras et al. [14]. Xavier et al. [15] employ the recursive line fitting method named inscribed angle variance. Maximum likelihood estimation for finding circle parameters is used by Inoue et al. [16]. Least squares estimation using Levenberg-Marquardt algorithm is used by Teixidó et al. [17] and by Wasik et al. [18]. Curvature-based method is employed by Vázquez-Martín et al. [19].

3 Clustering

Scale-space theory provides a multi-scale representation of a signal formed by smoothed versions of the signal. Smoothing is performed convolving the signal with Gaussian kernels with different variance (scale parameter) values. Features are normally discovered as extrema or inflexion points of the signal, thus they are represented as zero-crossing level curves in the scale-space representation. Witkin's interval tree procedure associates a rectangle to each curve and defines a stability criterion for rectangles. Most stable rectangles define the natural scales.

In previous work [1] this procedure was applied to worlds composed of straight segments. In the present work the same procedure has been applied to worlds composed of straight and circular segments, see Fig. 1(a) and (b). Segments edges are extrema and inflexion points of the curve, so first and second derivative can be used to find them. Zero-crossing level curves for first and second derivative of the scale-space surface are shown in Fig. 1(c) and (d). Specially for the second derivative, noise yields a lot of curves. This curves could magnify low level environmental features yielding a too fragmented world representation. An adequate selection of scale levels, specially the lowest level could remove eventually the majority of the small curves. Noise is removed by applying the same filtering procedure, that can adapt itself to the mean amount of environmental noise, used in the previous work [1].

After filtering, the interval tree procedure is performed in order to find the most stable environmental features. Results are shown in Fig. 1(e) and (f). Features locations discovered using both derivatives have to be merged. Nearby features are mixed in one and groups of missing measurements are taking in account using their ends as features. Isolated missing values are interpolated and groups are replaced with convenient noiseless values. Finally, the discovered features are considered as fuzzy ends of segments, then sets of consecutive measures are extracted from each segment core to obtain the seeds for EKF initial values estimation.

In some cases no discovered segments could appear, as commented by Cuadra et al. [1], that situation will produce a group of not EKF estimated points, a hole. In this case a new segment will be estimated per each hole. This condition has not been tested yet in worlds with circles. It will be addressed in future research.

The use of polar coordinates instead rectangular ones has several advantages. In polar coordinates (φ, r) for each angle φ there is at most one r corresponding value, thus the world description $r = f(\varphi)$ is a function in the strict mathematical sense of the term. In rectangular coordinates (x, y) for each x there can be more than one value of y, or vice versa, thus the description $y = g(x)$ could not be a function in the strict mathematical sense of the term. This implies that in polar coordinates a complete ordination of points can be performed and hence the description $r = f(\varphi)$ is 1D while $y = g(x)$ is not strictly 1D. In this way, the computational complexity in polar representation is smaller than in rectangular representation. Also, in scale-space context there exists very desirable properties for 1D signals which are not always fulfilled in higher dimensions [4].

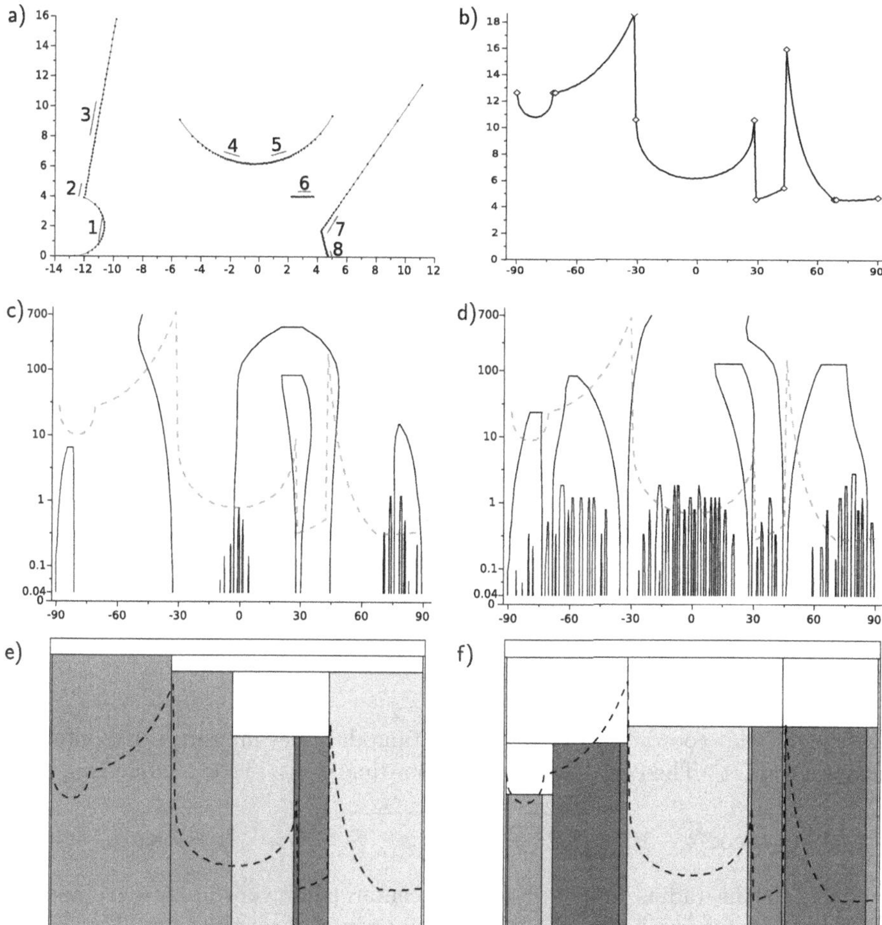

Fig. 1. Scan in rectangular coordinates (a), and in polar coordinates (b). Level curves first derivatives (c), and second ones (d). Stable features, colored rectangles, discovered from level curves after filtering for the first derivatives (e) and second ones (f). Scan in polar coordinates has been superimposed in (c), (d), (e), and (f). In (a), the areas numbered and marked in red are the resulting seeds for EKF initialization. No features generated by noise were discovered. The central circle and the left most straight line have two seeds, but this issue would be resolved in the merging stage. (Color figure online)

4 EKF Initialization

For straight segments, EKF initialization is made using the repeated median procedure, but this procedure is only suitable for linear models. For circles, we have developed a simple procedure slightly inspired by the repeated median procedure.

First, we compute, using rectangular coordinates, the center and radius for the circle passing through the first, central and last points in groups of consecutive points from a moving window, going over all the points in the seed. This process is repeated for successive odd number of points in the moving window starting from a size of three until reaching the whole seed set. Then, weighted medians of center coordinates and radii are computed, weights are set as the integer quotient of the points group size divided by two. Values corresponding to centers outside the circle, or to radius extremely big, are discarded before median computation. Once the process is finished, the center coordinates are converted to polar coordinates (ρ_0, θ_0) and together with the estimated radius R_0 they are used for EKF initial values $\beta_0 = (\rho_0, \theta_0, R_0)^{\mathsf{T}}$. The initial Jacobian H_0, see Sect. 5, is computed using β_0 and all the seed points angles, then the initial covariance matrix is computed as $P_0 = \left(H_0^{\mathsf{T}} H_0 + \lambda I_k\right)^{-1}$, we apply Tikhonov regularization: the λI_k addend, being $k = 3$, the model parameters number. See Sect. 5 for details.

This procedure is not as robust as the repeated median procedure for straight segments, and the initial estimation accuracy depends on the angle formed by the seed seen from circle center. The higher the angle, the greater the accuracy, see Table 1.

5 EKF Estimation

The use of polar coordinates instead of rectangular ones in regression context is advantageous [1]. The equation in polar coordinates (φ, r) for a circle is:

$$r = \rho \cos(\varphi - \theta) \pm \sqrt{R^2 - \rho^2 \sin^2(\varphi - \theta)} \qquad \alpha_1 < \varphi - \theta < \alpha_2$$

Being R the radius and ρ and θ the center polar coordinates, α_1 and α_2 are the angles formed by the circle tangents passing through origin. The $\pm$ sign yields the convex, $-$, and the concave, $+$, parts of the circle, see Fig. 2, in this work we are interested in the convex part. If circle contains origin of coordinates, then $\alpha_1 = -\pi$, $\alpha_2 = \pi$ and both signs in $\pm$ describe the same curve.

Following the formulation given by Peña [7] for a linear model: Kalman filter states are model parameters $\beta = (\rho, \theta, R)^{\mathsf{T}}$, there are not control actions u, measurement equation represents the linear model for the n-th observation for independent and dependent variables. Thus the EKF equations [20] can be written for our non linear model in this way:

$$s_n = g(u_n, s_{n-1}) + \delta_n \Longrightarrow \beta_n = \beta_{n-1}$$

$$y_n = h(s_n) + \varepsilon_n \Longrightarrow r_n = \rho_n \cos(\varphi_n - \theta_n) - \sqrt{R_n^2 - \rho_n^2 \sin^2(\varphi_n - \theta_n)} + \varepsilon_n$$

where $\delta_n \sim N(0, S_n)$ y $\varepsilon_n \sim N(0, Q_n)$ are Gaussian disturbances. In our case $\delta_n = 0$ and thus $S_n = 0$ and for regression models $\varepsilon_n \sim N\left(0, \sigma^2\right)$, being σ^2 the unknown measurement noise variance. Under the formulation conditions given above, the state distribution conditioned by the measurement is $N(\beta_n, P_n)$. Redefining P_n as $\frac{P_n}{\sigma^2}$, from now on P_n, algorithm equations are independent of σ^2

Table 1. Errors in initialization and after EKF iterations. "C1" and "C6" prefixes correspond to center at 1.4 m and 6.4 m. "N0" suffix, corresponds to initialization and iterations without Tikhonov regurarization. "NR" suffix is for Tikhonov regularization only on initialization. "TR" suffix is used when Tikhonov regularization is applied on both initialization and iterations. θ is measured in degrees, ρ and R in meters.

Errors		Mean	Median	Std. dev.	Min.	Perc. 95	Max.
C1-Init	$\Delta\theta_0$	1.06134	0.99516	0.58392	0.00064	2.83641	3.34063
	$\Delta\rho_0$	0.99610	0.99626	0.01640	0.92813	1.03466	1.03930
	ΔR	0.96495	0.96791	0.01222	0.89552	0.98257	0.98386
C1-N0	$\Delta\theta_0^k$	0.43340	0.30684	1.24088	0.00014	1.71379	26.6360
	$\Delta\rho_0^k$	0.16870	0.16473	0.11334	0.00063	0.36257	0.84788
	ΔR^k	0.15469	0.14953	0.10931	0.00035	0.34223	0.90484
C1-NR	$\Delta\theta_0^k$	0.02580	0.00664	0.06871	0.00002	0.32697	0.61353
	$\Delta\rho_0^k$	0.05884	0.04031	0.05918	0.00018	0.25374	0.26839
	ΔR^k	0.05050	0.03198	0.05444	0.00004	0.23355	0.25004
C1-TR	$\Delta\theta_0^k$	0.02916	0.00619	0.08146	0.00001	0.37294	0.77115
	$\Delta\rho_0^k$	0.06353	0.04244	0.06179	0.00022	0.25477	0.26890
	ΔR^k	0.05442	0.0353	0.05644	0.00003	0.23634	0.25701
C6-Init	$\Delta\theta_0$	0.10671	0.08946	0.08527	0.00032	0.35933	0.52414
	$\Delta\rho_0$	0.07335	0.06497	0.05092	0.00021	0.22546	0.28153
	ΔR	0.06906	0.06140	0.04907	0.00034	0.22971	0.27388
C6-N0	$\Delta\theta_0^k$	0.01528	0.01200	0.01631	0.00003	0.09115	0.13766
	$\Delta\rho_0^k$	0.01463	0.00587	0.03771	1.6e-06	0.27556	0.28875
	ΔR^k	0.01128	0.00482	0.02832	0.00005	0.20658	0.21516
C6-NR	$\Delta\theta_0^k$	0.01224	0.01066	0.00895	0.00002	0.03615	0.04112
	$\Delta\rho_0^k$	0.01589	0.01174	0.01549	0.00002	0.07450	0.09789
	ΔR^k	0.01143	0.00846	0.01064	8.9e-06	0.04870	0.06424
C6-TR	$\Delta\theta_0^k$	0.01218	0.10724	0.03543	0.00007	0.00968	0.01052
	$\Delta\rho_0^k$	0.02252	0.01460	0.02440	0.00017	0.12696	0.14992
	ΔR^k	0.01621	0.01056	0.01676	0.00002	0.08268	0.11023

and $Q_n = 1$. EKF linearizes functions $g(\rho, \theta, R) = I_3 \begin{pmatrix} \rho \\ \theta \\ R \end{pmatrix}$ and $h(r)$ using their Jacobian matrices $G_n = \left(\frac{\partial g(u_n, s_{n-1})}{\partial s_{n-1}}\right)$ y $H_n = \left(\frac{\partial h(s_n)}{\partial s_n}\right)$. In our case $G_n = I_3$ and

$$H_n = \begin{pmatrix} \frac{\partial r}{\partial \rho} \\ \frac{\partial r}{\partial \theta} \\ \frac{\partial r}{\partial R} \end{pmatrix}_{\beta_{n-1}} = \begin{pmatrix} \cos(\varphi_n - \theta_{n-1}) + \dfrac{\rho_{n-1}\sin^2(\varphi_n - \theta_{n-1})}{\sqrt{R_{n-1}^2 - \rho_{n-1}^2 \sin^2(\varphi_n - \theta_{n-1})}} \\ -\rho_{n-1}\sin(\varphi_n - \theta_{n-1}) - \dfrac{\rho_{n-1}\sin(\varphi_n - \theta_{n-1})\cos(\varphi_n - \theta_{n-1})}{\sqrt{R_{n-1}^2 - \rho_{n-1}^2 \sin^2(\varphi_n - \theta_{n-1})}} \\ -\dfrac{R_{n-1}}{\sqrt{R_{n-1}^2 - \rho_{n-1}^2 \sin^2(\varphi_n - \theta_{n-1})}} \end{pmatrix}$$

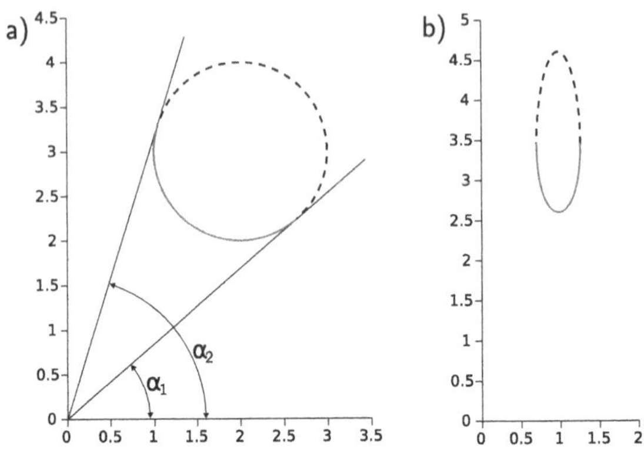

Fig. 2. Circle not containing the coordinates origin in rectangular coordinates (a), and in polar coordinates (b). The convex part, red continuous line, is the part seen by the robot. (Color figure online)

Algorithm 1. Non linear regression using Kalman filtering.

1: **procedure** EKF_NLR(r_n, φ_n; β_{n-1}, P_{n-1}, RSS_{n-1}) ▷ Add point (r_n, φ_n)
2: compute H_n with φ_n and β_{n-1} values
3: $H_n \leftarrow real(H_n)$ ▷ Take real part only if necessary
4: $a_n \leftarrow 1 + H_n^\top P_{n-1} H_n$
5: $K_n \leftarrow P_{n-1} H_n a_n^{-1}$
6: $e_n \leftarrow r_n - real\left(h\left(\varphi_n; \beta_{n-1}\right)\right)$ ▷ Take real part only if necessary
7: $\beta_n \leftarrow \beta_{n-1} + K_n e_n$
8: $P_n \leftarrow \left(P_{n-1}^{-1} + H_n^\top H_n + \lambda I_k\right)^{-1}$ ▷ Tikhonov regularization
9: $RSS_n \leftarrow RSS_{n-1} + \frac{(e_n)^2}{a_n}$
10: **return** β_n, P_n, RSS_n
11: **end procedure**

The EKF algorithm for non linear regression is applied to a group extracted in the clustering phase by inserting each point with the procedure shown in Algorithm 1. The initial values β_0 and P_0 are computed as explained in Sect. 4. The algorithm also computes the residual sum of squares, RSS, in a sequential way $O(n)$, see Algorithm 1 line 9, with an initial value $RSS_0 = 0$. RSS is used to compute the determination coefficient, it is used also in Chow test and it allows σ^2 estimation $\hat{\sigma}_n^2 = \frac{RSS_n}{n-k}$, being k the model parameters number, used in outliers detection t-test. It is interesting to mention that, due to non linear nature of the regression model, hypothesis contrasts have an asymptotic character.

We have observed P_n matrices close to being ill-conditioned in several experiments, this situation produces an increase in large errors of the estimates, see Sect. 6 for details. In order to resolve this situation we have applied the Tikhonov regularization [21], also known as ridge regression [8]. For P_o regularization we have tried some values for λ between 0.1 and 100, obtaining better results with

$\lambda = 10$. For P_n regularization we have also tried values for λ between 0.1 and 100, observing better results employing $\lambda = 1/n$.

Jacobian matrix computation entails two issues. First, the presence of square roots could produce complex numbers. In this case we use only the real part of Jacobian matrices. We have tested using complex modules, but they produce worse results. Second, the difference $\varphi_n - \theta_{n-1}$ has to be computed, to avoid wrong angles determination in Jacobian matrices, following the direction of the shortest spin that carries one value over the other:

$$\varphi_n - \theta_{n-1} = \begin{cases} \varphi_n - \theta_{n-1} + \pi & \text{if} \quad \varphi_n - \theta_{n-1} \leq -\frac{\pi}{2} \\ \varphi_n - \theta_{n-1} - \pi & \text{if} \quad \varphi_n - \theta_{n-1} \geq \frac{\pi}{2} \end{cases}$$

The EKF algorithm is iteratively executed to improve estimation. Specially, if the angle formed by the seed as seen from circle center is small, we correct large inaccuracies on estimations by doing the following estimation correction. Let $(\rho_0^k, \theta_0^k, R_0^k)$ be the initial values of estimations for iteration k, obtained from last estimation in iteration $k-1$, then the correction formulas are (see Fig. 3): $\hat{R_0}^k = \frac{d_1 + d_2}{2}$ $\hat{\rho}_0^k = \rho_0^k - R_0^k + \hat{R_0}^k$, and $\hat{\theta}_0^k = \theta_0^k + \arcsin \frac{d_2 - d_1}{2\rho_0^k}$, being d_1 and d_2 the distances from (ρ_0^k, θ_0^k) to the real segment ends. When inaccuracies are small, these corrections tend to worsen the EKF estimation, so it is best not to apply them. To that end, we compare RSS_k at the end of iteration k, with RSS_{k-1}, and if $RSS_{k-1} < RSS_k$, then original $(\rho_0^k, \theta_0^k, R_0^k)$ are used to repeat iteration k. From this moment the correction is never applied again. Iterations are performed until they reach a predetermined number or $RSS_{k-1} < RSS_k$ for some k.

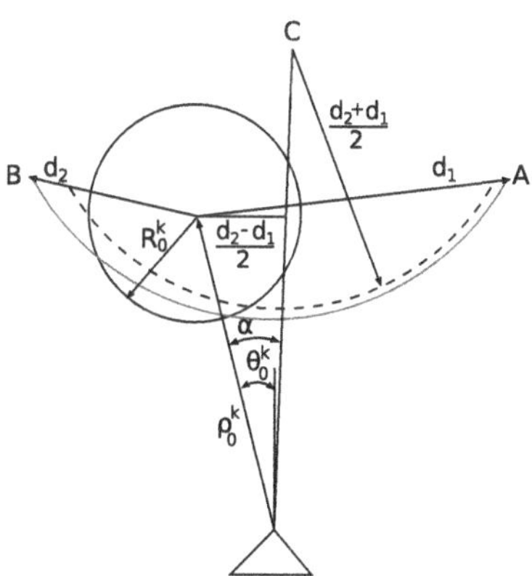

Fig. 3. Estimation correction: A and B are the extrema of the arc real points used in iterations. The small circle is the inaccurately estimated circle after iteration $k-1$. C is the corrected center with coordinates $\left(\hat{\rho}_0^k, \hat{\theta}_0^k\right)$ $\hat{\theta}_0^k = \theta_0^k + \alpha$, being $\alpha = \arcsin \frac{d_2 - d_1}{2\rho_0^k} < 0$, and $\hat{\rho}_0^k = \rho_0^k - R_0^k + \hat{R_0}^k$, and being $\hat{R_0}^k = \frac{d_1 + d_2}{2}$ the new radius of the corrected circle shown in dashed line.

6 Experimental Results

In this section we are going to describe and comment the experiments performed for algorithm validation. Circles simulating a laser scan with equally spaced angles were generated for the experiments. In addition, a noise component was added, to introduce uncertainty into the measurements, with $\sigma = 0.02\,\text{m}$, which is the usual noise in laser sensors commonly used in robotics. The experiments were done for a circle of radius $R = 1\,\text{m}$, situated in two different positions ($\theta = 0°$, $\rho = 1.4\,\text{m}$) and ($\theta = 0°$, $\rho = 6.4\,\text{m}$). In each of these cases the Kalman filter was initialized using seeds of size 9.

In order to test how affects to results the application of Tikhonov regularization in the updating of the Kalman filter covariance matrix, all experiments were performed in three ways: without applying the regularization in the initialization onP_0 nor in iterations on P_n, applying regularization in initialization but not in iteration, and applying it in both cases. This three cases are referred in Table 1 with suffixes "N0", "NR" and "TR" respectively. Results in initialization are named with "Init" suffix. 500 samples were generated in every experiment using the same random seeds for better comparison. EKF iterations maximum number has been set to 20.

In the experiments performed for the near circle (C1), it can be seen that the initializations of the filter are not favorable. When the circle is too close, the points chosen as seeds can resemble a rectilinear segment. In the experiments performed in the far circle case (C6), the results in the initialization are better, because in this case the arc of the circle seen is larger with respect to its center distance than in the previous case, and this is favorable for initial values computation. So, in general, the global results obtained in the far circle case are substantially better than in near circle case.

Applying Tikhonov regularization on initialization in the near circle case (C1) makes a significant improvement, but differences between NR and TR cases are not really significant, although NR seems to exhibit smaller errors. In the far circle case (C6), by applying the Tikhonov regularization in initialization, the maximum error is improved. Applying the Tikhonov regularization in iterations slightly increases errors in length parameters, but reduces maximum errors in angle parameter. In all cases the designed procedure gets good estimates of circle parameters.

7 Conclusions and Future Work

In this paper a procedure based on Gauss-Newton method implemented as a EKF has been used successfully for the estimation of the parameters of a circle from the points detected by a scan laser measurement including the usual noise. The procedure extends a previous work for straight segments estimation. Being a procedure based on the theory of regression models, all the tools from this theory can be used, although in the initial paper the regression theory tools were not tested.

A correction procedure of initial values for estimations was applied to solve the added problems found in circle equations when seeds used are in a small arc that cannot be distinguished from a straight segment. Also, the problem of variance matrices being almost ill-conditioned for circle equations is addressed with a Tikhonov regularization, or ridge regression.

Errors obtained in simulated experiments are small enough to ensure the viability of the procedure.

As future work, a deeper research on how to apply specific Tikhonov regularization should be done, as the methods for regularization commented by Li et al. [22]. Other research line could be to study the application of the tools from theory of regression commented in Sect. 1: outliers t-test for ends segments detection and Chow test for similar segments merging.

References

1. Cuadra Troncoso, J.M., Álvarez-Sánchez, J.R., de la Paz López, F., Fernández-Caballero, A.: Improving area center robot navigation using a novel range scan segmentation method. In: Ferrández, J.M., Álvarez Sánchez, J.R., Paz, F., Toledo, F.J. (eds.) IWINAC 2011. LNCS, vol. 6686, pp. 233–245. Springer, Heidelberg (2011). doi:10.1007/978-3-642-21344-1_25
2. Navarro Santosjuanes, I., Cuadra-Troncoso, J.M., de la Paz López, F., Arnau Prieto, R.: Improved polar scan-matching using an advanced line segmentation algorithm. In: Ferrández Vicente, J.M., Álvarez Sánchez, J.R., Paz López, F., Toledo Moreo, F.J. (eds.) IWINAC 2013. LNCS, vol. 7931, pp. 32–44. Springer, Heidelberg (2013). doi:10.1007/978-3-642-38622-0_4
3. Cuadra Troncoso, J.M., Álvarez-Sánchez, J.R., Navarro Santosjuanes, I., de la Paz López, F., Arnau Prieto, R.: Consistent robot localization using Polar Scan Matching based on Kalman segmentation. Robot. Auton. Syst. **63**, 219–225 (2015). Part 2, Cognition-Oriented Advanced Robotic Systems
4. Lindeberg, T.: Scale-space for discrete signals. IEEE Trans. Pattern Anal. Mach. Intell. **12**, 234–254 (1990)
5. Witkin, A.: Scale-space filtering: a new approach to multi-scale description. In: IEEE International Conference on Acoustics, Speech, and Signal Processing, ICASSP 1984, vol. 9, pp. 150–153, March 1984
6. Siegel, A.F.: Robust regression using repeated medians. Biometrika **69**(1), 242–244 (1982)
7. Peña, D.: On internal robustification of Plackett-Kalman algorithm for recursive estimation of regression linear models. Trabajos de Estadística y de Investigación Operativa **36**(1), 93–106 (1985). (in Spanish)
8. Johnston, J.: Econometric Methods, 3rd edn. McGraw Hill, New York City (1984)
9. Premebida, C., Nunes, U.: Segmentation and geometric primitives extraction from 2D laser range data for mobile robot applications. In: Actas do Encontro Científico Robótica 2005, pp. 17–25, April 2005
10. Zhou, X., Wang, Y., Zhu, Q., Miao, Z.: Circular object detection in polar coordinates for 2D LIDAR data. In: Tan, T., Li, X., Chen, X., Zhou, J., Yang, J., Cheng, H. (eds.) CCPR 2016. CCIS, vol. 662, pp. 65–78. Springer, Singapore (2016). doi:10.1007/978-981-10-3002-4_6

11. Press, S., Austin, D.: Approaches to pole detection using ranged laser data. In: Australasian Conference on Robotics and Automation. Australian Robotics and Automation Association, December 2004
12. Aschoff, T., Spiecker, H.: Algorithms for the automatic detection of trees in laser scanner data. In: Laser-Scanners for Forest and Landscape Assessment, vol. 26, pp. 71–75, October 2004
13. Huang, X., Sasaki, T., Hashimoto, H., Inoue, F.: Circle detection and fitting using laser range finder for positioning system. In: ICCAS 2010 - International Conference on Control, Automation and Systems, pp. 1366–1370. IEEE, October 2010
14. Arras, K.O., Mozos, Ó.M., Burgard, W.: Using boosted features for the detection of people in 2D range data. In: ICRA (2007)
15. Xavier, J., Pacheco, M., Castro, D., Ruano, A., Nunes, U.: Fast line, arc/circle and leg detection from laser scan data in a player driver. In: Proceedings of the 2005 IEEE International Conference on Robotics and Automation, pp. 3930–3935, April 2005
16. Inoue, F., Sasaki, T., Huang, X., Hashimoto, H.: Development of position measurement system for construction pile using laser range finder. In: Proceedings of the 28th International Symposium on Automation and Robotics in Construction, ISARC 2011, pp. 574–580 (2011)
17. Teixidó, M., Pallejà, T., Font, D., Tresanchez, M., Moreno, J., Palacín, J.: Two-dimensional radial laser scanning for circular marker detection and external mobile robot tracking. Sens. (Basel, Switz.) **12**(12), 16482–16497 (2012)
18. Wąsik, A., Ventura, R., Pereira, J.N., Lima, P.U., Martinoli, A.: Lidar-based relative position estimation and tracking for multi-robot systems. In: Reis, L., Moreira, A., Lima, P., Montano, L., Muñoz-Martinez, V. (eds.) Robot 2015. AISC, vol. 417, pp. 3–16. Springer, Cham (2016). doi:10.1007/978-3-319-27146-0_1
19. Vázquez-Martín, R., Núñez, P., Bandera, A., Sandoval, F.: Curvature-based environment description for robot navigation using laser range sensors. Sensors **9**(8), 5894–5918 (2009)
20. Thrun, S., Burgard, W., Fox, D.: Probabilistic Robotics. MIT Press, Cambridge (2005)
21. Tikhonov, A.N., Leonov, A.S., Yagola, A.G.: Nonlinear Ill-Posed Problems. Chapman & Hall, London (1998)
22. Li, Y., Gui, Q., Yongwei, G., Han, S., Kai, D.: Ridge-type Kalman filter and its algorithm. WSEAS Trans. Math. **13**, 852–862 (2014)

Visual Tools to Lecture Data Analytics and Engineering

Sung-Bae Cho[1] and Antonio J. Tallón-Ballesteros[2](✉)

[1] Department of Computer Science, Yonsei University, Seoul, Korea
sbcho@yonsei.ac.kr
[2] Department of Languages and Computer Systems, University of Seville, Seville, Spain
atallon@us.es

Abstract. This paper analyses some tools that could be appropriate as teaching resources for undergraduate or postgraduate levels. A comparison is performed between two machine learning tools such as Weka and RapidMiner on one side, and with Minitab, on the other side, that is a more statistical tool and also covers some parts of the Cross Industry Standard Process for Data Mining. We describe the functionalities of those frameworks and also the installation and running procedure. A road-map is carried out in order to state the main tasks that are available in these tools and to encourage other researchers or lecturers to introduce them in laboratory classes.

Keywords: Visual tools · Lecture · Data analytics · Machine learning · Data engineering

1 Introduction

Data Engineering [11] includes lot of tasks and one of the most relevant, depending on the decade could be named as Knowledge Discovery in Databases (KDD) [3] or CRISP-DM (CRoss Industry Standard Process for Data Mining) [14], in the end of the twenty century or in the beginning of the twenty-one century, respectively. KDD is a multidisciplinary paradigm of computer science comprising challenging tasks to transform a problem into useful models for prediction such as dealing with raw data, analysing the problem, data preparation [16] and data mining [8]. CRISP-DM is a process model which provides a framework for carrying out data mining projects which is independent of both the industry sector and the technology used. It aims to make large data mining projects, less costly, more reliable, more repeatable, more manageable, and faster. There is a great deal of data mining tools. Some applications like R, Weka [4], RapidMiner [2], Orange and ExcelMiner are undoubtedly the most popular software packages to analyse data and to discover knowledge in the raw data. There are another applications not so frequent such as Minitab [10] or XLSTAT [1]. All of them are suitable for Data Analytics [7] approaches or for Intelligent Data Engineering

J.M. Ferrández Vicente et al. (Eds.): IWINAC 2017, Part II, LNCS 10338, pp. 551–558, 2017.
DOI: 10.1007/978-3-319-59773-7_56

[15]. This research describes some visual tools such as Weka, RapidMiner and Minitab. The two first tools require a Java Virtual Machine (JVM) whereas the latter should installed on the host operating system through the installer. Visual frameworks to lecture are a key point of the digital society that we are living from a long time ago. On such a way, the undergraduate students from any level could be able to start with the tools and later to master them or even swapping to textual applications. Weka is a very extended and well-known platform that has been developed under the Java programming language. Nowadays, the usage of RapidMiner is making progress. One key point is that their interface is very similar to the graphical design products and the user could create a sheet that will populated with drag and drop actions. Their programming language is also Java. On the other hand, Minitab does not provide an Application Programming Interface (API) but for the beginners could an important push to jump to other tool or even to use both.

This article goals to introduce some visual tools that could be extremely handy to lecture subjects related with Data Analytics or Intelligent Data Engineering in the umbrella of undergraduate or postgraduate degrees. The rest of this paper is organized as follows: Sect. 2 describes Weka; Sect. 3 introduces RapidMiner; Sect. 4 goes into Minitab; finally, Sect. 5 states the concluding remarks.

2 Weka

Weka [4] is a framework that cover some parts of KDD. The installation of Weka is straighforward. We can use the installer or even we can download the .jar file and we can directly run weka.jar if we have one JVM installed. It is recommendable to run it under JDK 1.7 or 1.8 to be able to use the latest versions of Weka that incorporate new functionalities. Figure 1 represents all that is going to appear on the screen once we have started up the application. The top menu offers four options and among them Visualisation and Tools are related, respectively, with graphs (visualizers or plots) and viewers to see the data in plain arff or SQL format. Arff is the native format for Weka problems. The frame application depicts the main modules of Weka.

Explorer is likely the most executed part all over the world and is also the suitable place for new users to start the "learning" and to deepen into the software. Figure 2 depicts the Explorer and we could get an outlook about the options that we have at hand. Explorer is a visual environment that offers a Graphical User Interface (GUI) to access to all the packages. It is very outstanding to mention that only the option that could be run at every moment are available to the user. There are six tabs. The first tab called Preprocess and is ready to load a problem in different formats such as .arff, .csv, .bsi or .xrff. After the data loading, the remaining uppers tabs will be enabled and also the Filter frame of the current tab is able to be executed whose main purpose is to transform the data at the instance of feature level. The second tab named Classify is designed to execute a classifier with using the loaded file (automatically will be created the training

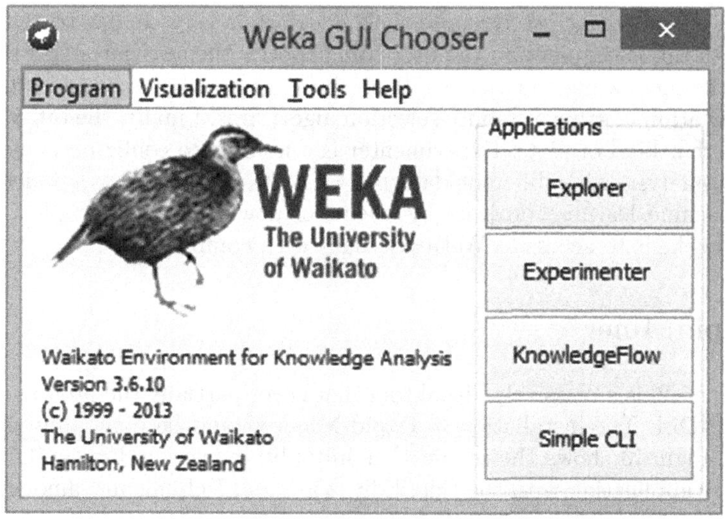

Fig. 1. Starting Weka

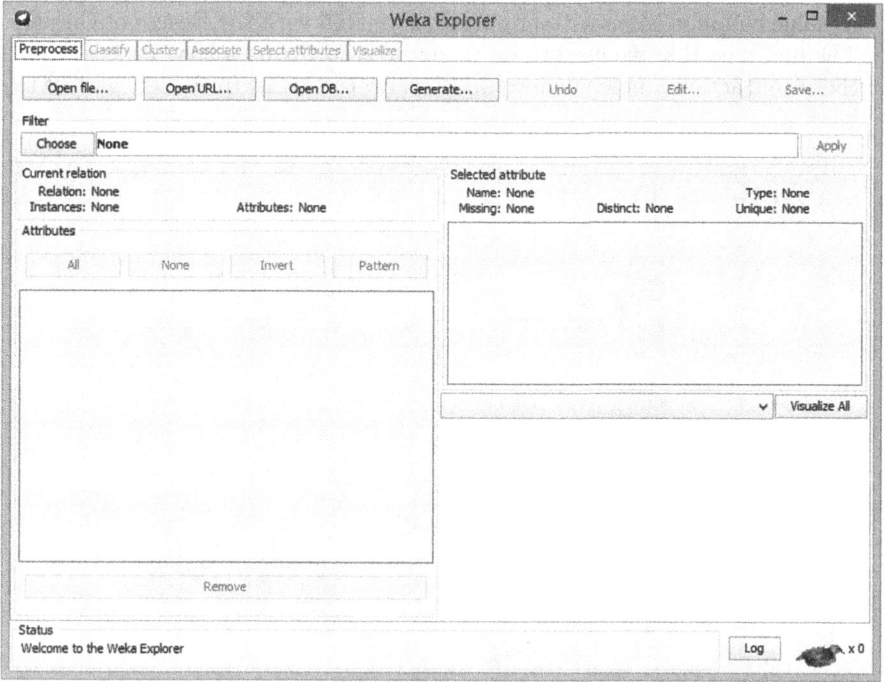

Fig. 2. Weka Explorer

and test sets) or even providing an additional file that could be the test set. The third tab offers some clusterers and their interface is very similar to "Classify". The fourth tab is simpler and the user could specify the associator and the start it or in the meanwhile top stop it. The tab Select attributes provides different implementation of some attribute selection algorithms. Finally, the tab Visualize offer different kind of plots. Experimenter is a module to configure experiments and data analysis with different data files. KnowledgeFlow is an application to create machine learning projects by means of flow diagrams. Simple CLI is a text-mode client to access to Weka packages with commands.

3 RapidMiner

RapidMiner [2] is a massively visual tool that cover partially the process of KDD or CRISP-DM. The installation of Rapid Miner should be done only using the installer. Figure 3 shows the screen that initially appears and is similar to any office suite application with the File, Edit, View and Help menus, among others. A process is the basic element is Rapid Miner and is similar to a sheet where the user should define their design using the Operators (objects) that are available and will be connected through lines, also named Wires. The definition is done by means of lots of Drag and Drop actions. Technically speaking, a process is the worksheet to create our design. Then, it needs to be simulated. In other words, it has some common ideas with applications related with the Design of Circuits.

The first step that we need to do therefore is to Create a New Process. Once we chose this action a new windows will receive the focus. In the left part of the

Fig. 3. Starting RapidMiner

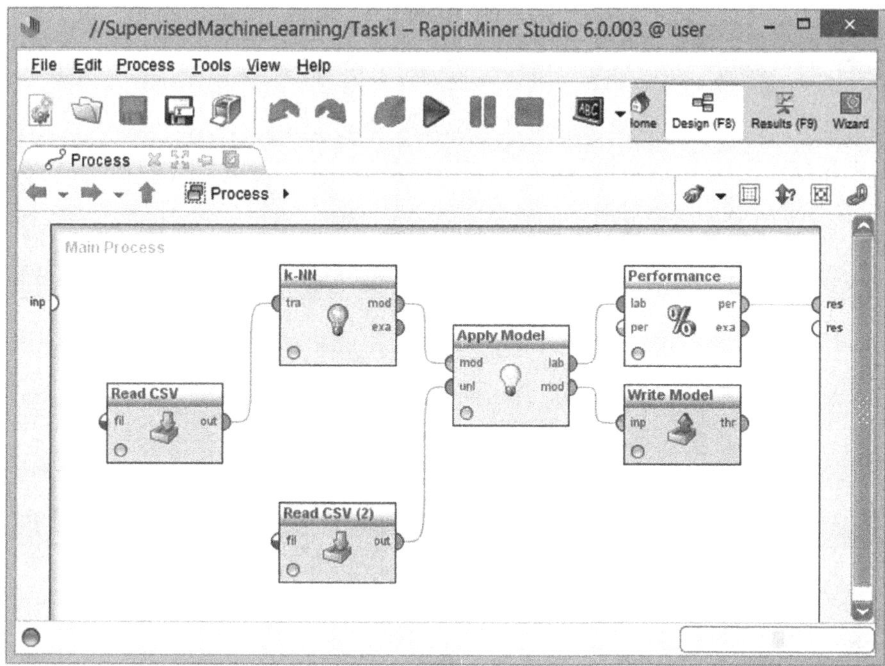

Fig. 4. A supervised machine learning task in RapidMiner

aforesaid window we have the view called Operators. In the mid of the windows there will be a sheet named Main Process which is the place to Drag and Drop the desired Operators and to connect them. The right part provides the current values of the parameters and also the compatibility level. The folders on the right are all the packages that could be deployed in order to use a concrete operator. We can use the Repository Access to select the operator Retrieve in order to load a data set or even the Import folder to load an external data set. Data Transformation is similar to the Preprocess tab of Weka. The folder Modeling contains all the typical tasks of Data Mining such as Classification and Regression (inside is include also Rule Induction related with Subgroup Discovery), Attribute Weighting, Clustering and Association. To conclude this section, Fig. 4 outlines an example of a design ready to run about a classification task with K-nn classifier using a training and a test set.

4 Minitab

It is a multi-language tool encompassing lot of treatments from a statistical point of view and also from unsupervised machine learning or supervised machine learning with continuous values for the outputs. During the installation you could customise the language that you prefer. It is a key point especially for those students which are not very ready to use learning tools in other languages that

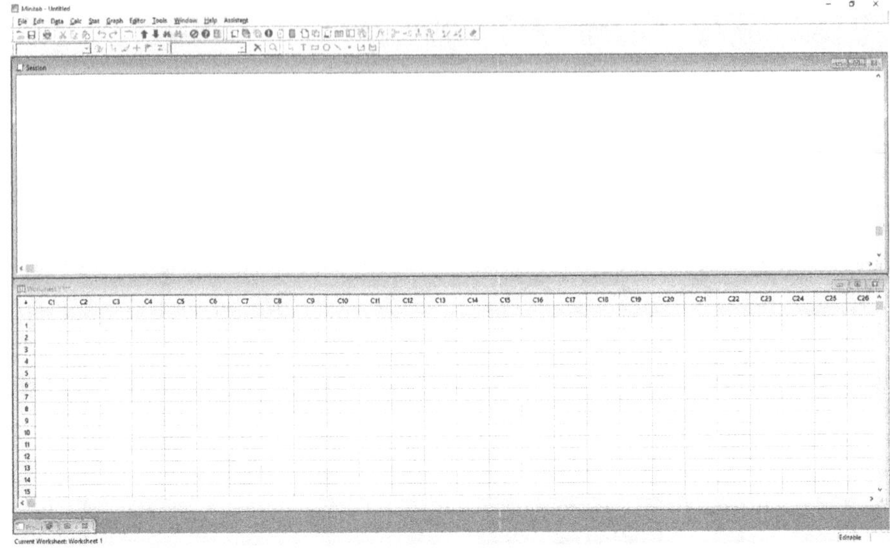

Fig. 5. Starting Minitab

their tongue. The number of different languages is around ten. It is a important difference with the other two tools that are described in this paper. The main purpose of this tool is to offer a wide range of options for statistical tasks such as getting different statistics of a sample such as central, dispersion or shape measures. In the context of KDD the Regression could be done in-depth with lot of options as well as Clustering. The options to apply data preparation are related with the correlation analysis [13].

Figure 5 depicts the aspect of the initial screen after the starting. This is the classical appearance of any program related with any Office Suite or more concretely with other Statistical tools such as SPSS [12]. We see the data sheet and also some menus with the name File, Edit, Graph and Calc to mention some of them. The first stage to work with this tool is to manually create the data set or loading from a MTW file which is the native format of Minitab and stands for MiniTab Worksheet. It is also valid to load CSV or Excel files. The tasks that are more related with KDD are included in the Stat menu. There you can click on Regression and some methods like mainly Nonlinear and Logistic Regression [5] will appear. Again, keeping in the aforementioned menu and going in Regression we can find the option Fit Regression Models or even Best Subsets. Figure 6 shows the Fitted Line Plot related with a Regression for Vitamin A taking into account the Calories.

Finally, inside the Stat menu, there is an item called Multivariate that concerns the Clustering approaches such as Principal Components Analysis (PCA) [6], Factor analysis, K-Means algorithm [9] or Discriminant Analysis.

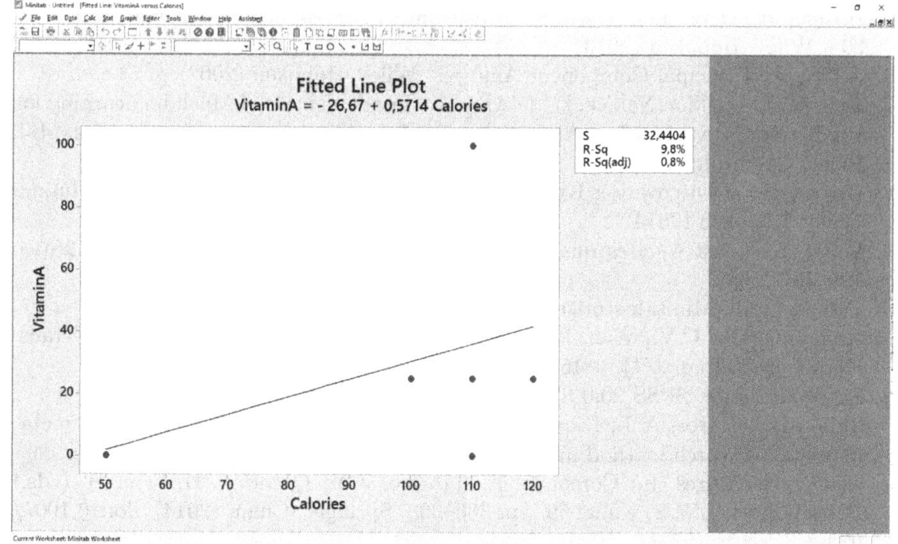

Fig. 6. The visual result of a regression task in Minitab

5 Conclusions

The described tools offer a great deal of possibilities to carry out any kind of data mining tool. Learning about Weka may be easier because the user does not need to design the workflow and only the available option could be chosen and the different kind of machine learning actions are separated in different tabs. On the other hand, Rapid Miner is a visual tool where the user may find difficulties at the beginning because the operators may not be very simple to master or even to find which is the name of the operator because the number of them may be around four thousands. The appearance of Rapid Miner is similar to other kind of computer science tools such and Integrated Development Environments for languages like C, C++, Java or web languages. Minitab is outstandingly ease to use because we only need to load the data and deploy the different menus to find the desired action.

References

1. Addinsoft. Xlstat v. 2015.1. 01: Data analysis and statistics software for Microsoft Excel (2015)
2. Akthar, F., Hahne, C.: Rapidminer 5 operator reference. Rapid-I GmbH (2012)
3. Fayyad, U., Piatetsky-Shapiro, G., Smyth, P.: From data mining to knowledge discovery in databases. AI Mag. **17**(3), 37 (1996)
4. Hall, M., Frank, E., Holmes, G., Pfahringer, B., Reutemann, P., Witten, I.H.: The weka data mining software: an update. ACM SIGKDD Explor. Newslett. **11**(1), 10–18 (2009)

5. Hosmer Jr., D.W., Lemeshow, S., Sturdivant, R.X.: Applied logistic regression, vol. 398. Wiley, Hoboken (2013)
6. Jolliffe, I.: Principal Component Analysis. Wiley, Hoboken (2002)
7. Kelleher, J.D., Mac Namee, B., D'Arcy, A.: Fundamentals of Machine Learning for Predictive Data Analytics: Algorithms, Worked Examples, and Case Studies. MIT Press, Cambridge (2015)
8. Larose, D.T.: Discovering Knowledge in Data: An Introduction to Data Mining. Wiley, Hoboken (2014)
9. Lloyd, S.: Least squares quantization in PCM. IEEE Trans. Inf. Theory **28**(2), 129–137 (1982)
10. INC Minitab. Minitab statistical software. Minitab Release **13** (2000)
11. Ramamoorthy, C.V., Wah, B.W.: Knowledge and data engineering. IEEE Trans. Knowl. Data Eng. **1**(1), 9–16 (1989)
12. SPSS Statistics. SPSS 20.0 SPSS Inc., Chicago, IL (2011)
13. Tallón-Ballesteros, A.J., Riquelme, J.C.: Tackling ant colony optimization meta-heuristic as search method in feature subset selection based on correlation or consistency measures. In: Corchado, E., Lozano, J.A., Quintián, H., Yin, H. (eds.) IDEAL 2014. LNCS, vol. 8669, pp. 386–393. Springer, Cham (2014). doi:10.1007/978-3-319-10840-7_47
14. Wirth, R., Hipp, J.: CRISP-DM: towards a standard process model for data mining. In: Proceedings of the 4th International Conference on the Practical Applications of Knowledge Discovery and Data Mining, pp. 29–39. Citeseer (2000)
15. Yin, H., Gao, Y., Li, B., Zhang, D., Yang, M., Li, Y., Klawonn, F., Tallón-Ballesteros, A.J. (eds.): IDEAL 2016. LNCS, vol. 9937. Springer, Cham (2016). doi:10.1007/978-3-319-46257-8
16. Zhang, S., Zhang, C., Yang, Q.: Data preparation for data mining. Appl. Artif. Intell. **17**(5–6), 375–381 (2003)

Author Index

Printed in the United States
By Bookmasters